Programme for International Student Assessment

PISA 2003 Data Analysis Manual

SAS® Users

OECD
ORGANISATION FOR ECONOMIC CO-OPERATION AND DEVELOPMENT

ORGANISATION FOR ECONOMIC CO-OPERATION AND DEVELOPMENT

The OECD is a unique forum where the governments of 30 democracies work together to address the economic, social and environmental challenges of globalisation. The OECD is also at the forefront of efforts to understand and to help governments respond to new developments and concerns, such as corporate governance, the information economy and the challenges of an ageing population. The Organisation provides a setting where governments can compare policy experiences, seek answers to common problems, identify good practice and work to co-ordinate domestic and international policies.

The OECD member countries are: Australia, Austria, Belgium, Canada, the Czech Republic, Denmark, Finland, France, Germany, Greece, Hungary, Iceland, Ireland, Italy, Japan, Korea, Luxembourg, Mexico, the Netherlands, New Zealand, Norway, Poland, Portugal, the Slovak Republic, Spain, Sweden, Switzerland, Turkey, the United Kingdom and the United States. The Commission of the European Communities takes part in the work of the OECD.

OECD Publishing disseminates widely the results of the Organisation's statistics gathering and research on economic, social and environmental issues, as well as the conventions, guidelines and standards agreed by its members.

Foreword

The OECD's Programme for International Student Assessment (PISA) surveys, which take place every three years, have been designed to collect information about 15-year-old students in participating countries. PISA examines how well students are prepared to meet the challenges of the future, rather than how well they master particular curricula. The data collected during each PISA cycle are an extremely valuable source of information for researchers, policy makers, educators, parents and students. It is now recognised that the future economic and social well-being of countries is closely linked to the knowledge and skills of their populations. The internationally comparable information provided by PISA allows countries to assess how well their 15-year-old students are prepared for life in a larger context and to compare their relative strengths and weaknesses.

The PISA 2003 database, on which this manual is focused, contains information on over a quarter of a million students from 41 countries. It includes not only information on their performance in the four main areas of assessment – reading, mathematics, science and problem solving – but also their responses to the Student Questionnaire that they complete as part of the assessment. Data from the school principals are also included.

The PISA 2003 Data Analysis Manual has evolved from the analytical workshops held in Sydney, Vienna, Paris and Bratislava, which exposed participants to the various techniques needed to correctly analyse the complex databases. It allows analysts to confidently replicate procedures used for the production of the PISA 2003 initial reports, *Learning for Tomorrow's World – First Results from PISA 2003* (OECD, 2004a) and *Problem Solving for Tomorrow's World – First Measures of Cross-Curricular Competencies from PISA 2003* (OECD, 2004b), and to accurately undertake new analyses in areas of special interest. In addition to the inclusion of the necessary techniques, the manual also includes a detailed account of the variables constructed from the student and school questionnaires. This information was previously published in the *Manual for the PISA 2000 Database* (OECD, 2002a).

The PISA 2003 Data Analysis Manual is in four parts – the first two sections give a detailed theoretical background and instructions for analysing the data; the third section lists the program codes (syntaxes and the macros), which are needed to carry out the analyses; and the fourth section contains a detailed description of the database.

PISA is a collaborative effort by the participating countries, and guided by their governments on the basis of shared policy-driven interests. Representatives of each country form the PISA Governing Board which decides on the assessment and reporting of results in PISA.

There are two versions of this manual – one for SPSS® users and one for SAS® users. The OECD recognises the creative work of Christian Monseur in preparing the text for both versions of the manual in collaboration with Sheila Krawchuk and Keith Rust, as well as his preparation of the program coding for the SAS® users' manual. The coding for the SPSS® users' manual was prepared by Wolfram Schulz and Eveline Gebhardt. The main editorial work was completed at the OECD Secretariat by Miyako Ikeda, Sophie Vayssettes, John Cresswell, Claire Shewbridge and Kate Lancaster. The PISA assessments and the data underlying the manuals were prepared by the PISA Consortium under the direction of Raymond Adams.

Table of Contents

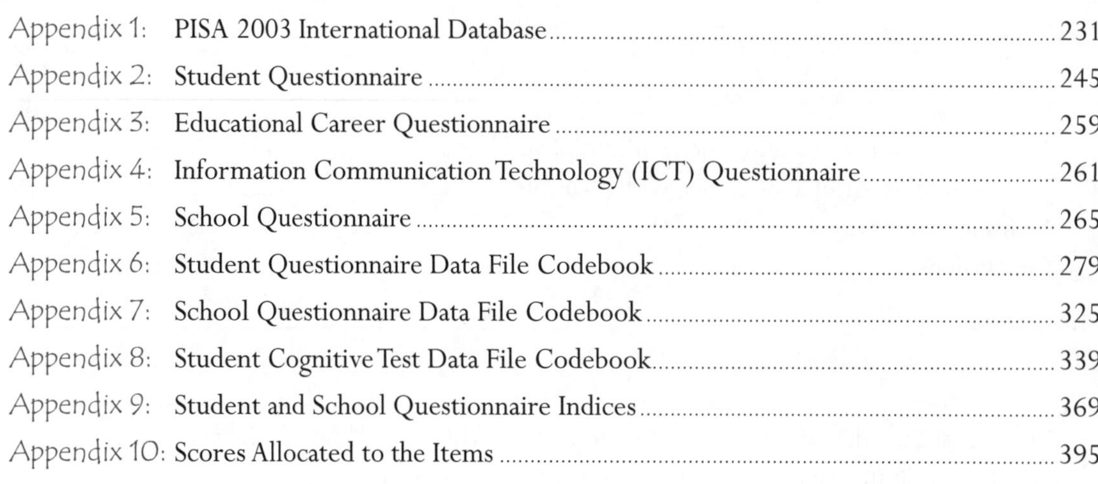

USERS' GUIDE

Preparation of data files

All data files (in text format) and the SAS® control files are available on the PISA Web site (*www.pisa.oecd.org*).

SAS® users

By running the SAS® control files, the PISA 2003 SAS® student data file and the PISA 2003 SAS® school data file are created. Please keep the both files in the same folder and run commands for assigning the folder as a SAS® library before starting analysis.

For example, if the student and school SAS® data files are saved in the folder of "c:\pisa2003\data\", the following commands need to be run to create a SAS® library:

```
libname PISA2003 "c:\pisa2003\data\";
run;
```

The ten SAS® macros presented in Chapter 15 need to be saved under "c:\pisa2003\prg".

SAS® syntax and macros

All syntaxes and macros used in this manual can be copied from the PISA Web site (*www.pisa.oecd.org*). Each chapter of the manual contains a complete set of syntaxes, which must be done sequentially, for all of them to run correctly, within the chapter.

Rounding of figures

In the tables and formulas, figures were rounded to a convenient number of decimal places, although calculations were always made with the full number of decimal places.

Country abbreviations used in this manual

AUS	Australia	FRA	France	KOR	Korea	PRT	Portugal
AUT	Austria	GBR	United Kingdom	LIE	Liechtenstein	RUS	Russian Federation
BEL	Belgium	GRC	Greece	LUX	Luxembourg	SVK	Slovakia
BRA	Brazil	HKG	Hong Kong-China	LVA	Latvia	SWE	Sweden
CAN	Canada	HUN	Hungary	MAC	Macao-China	THA	Thailand
CHE	Switzerland	IDN	Indonesia	MEX	Mexico	TUN	Tunisia
CZE	Czech Republic	IRL	Ireland	NLD	Netherlands	TUR	Turkey
DEU	Germany	ISL	Iceland	NOR	Norway	URY	Uruguay
DNK	Denmark	ITA	Italy	NZL	New Zealand	USA	United States
ESP	Spain	JPN	Japan	POL	Poland	YUG	Serbia
FIN	Finland						

Socio-economic status

The highest occupational status of parents (HISEI) is referred to as the socio-economic status of the students throughout this manual. It should be noted that occupational status is only one aspect of socio-economic status, which can also include education and wealth. The PISA 2003 database also includes a broader socio-economic measure called the index of Economic, Social and Cultural Status (ESCS), which is derived from the highest occupational status of parents, the highest educational level and an estimate related to household possessions.

Further documentation

For further information on the PISA 2003 results, see the PISA 2003 initial reports: *Learning for Tomorrow's World – First Results from PISA 2003* (OECD, 2004a) and *Problem Solving for Tomorrow's World – First Measures of Cross-Curricular Competencies from PISA 2003* (OECD, 2004b). For further information on the PISA assessment instruments and the method used in PISA, see the *PISA 2003 Technical Report* (OECD, forthcoming) and the PISA Web site (*www.pisa.oecd.org*).

The OECD's Programme for International Student Assessment

AN OVERVIEW OF PISA

The OECD's Programme for International Student Assessment (PISA) is a collaborative effort, involving all OECD countries and a significant number of partner countries, to measure how well 15-year-old students are prepared to meet the challenges of today's knowledge societies. The assessment looks to the future, focusing on young people's ability to use their knowledge and skills to meet real-life challenges, rather than on the mastery of specific school curricula. This orientation reflects a change in the goals and objectives of curricula themselves, which are increasingly concerned with knowledge application rather than merely knowledge acquisition. The age of 15 is used because in most OECD countries it is the age at which students are approaching the end of compulsory schooling.

PISA is the most comprehensive and rigorous international effort to date to assess student performance and to collect data about the student, as well as about the family and institutional factors potentially affecting performance. Decisions about the scope and nature of the assessment and the background information to be collected were made by leading experts in participating countries and steered jointly by their governments on the basis of shared, policy-driven interests. Substantial efforts and resources were devoted to achieving wide cultural and linguistic coverage in the assessment materials. Stringent quality assurance mechanisms were applied in translation, sampling and data collection. As a consequence, the results of PISA have a high degree of validity and reliability, and they can significantly improve understanding of the outcomes of education in a large number of the world's countries.

PISA is based on a dynamic model of lifelong learning in which new knowledge and skills necessary for successful adaptation to a changing world are continuously acquired throughout life. PISA focuses on skills that 15-year-olds will need in the future and seeks to assess their ability to perform them. PISA does assess students' knowledge, but it also examines their potential to reflect on their knowledge and experiences, and to apply that knowledge and those experiences to real-world issues. For example,

Table 1.1 ■ **Participating countries in PISA 2000 and in PISA 2003**

	PISA 2000	PISA 2003
OECD countries	Australia, Austria, Belgium, Canada, Czech Republic, Denmark, Finland, France, Germany, Greece, Hungary, Iceland, Ireland, Italy, Japan, Korea, Luxembourg, Mexico, Netherlands,[a] New Zealand, Norway, Poland, Portugal, Spain, Sweden, Switzerland, United Kingdom, United States.	Australia, Austria, Belgium, Canada, Czech Republic, Denmark, Finland, France, Germany, Greece, Hungary, Iceland, Ireland, Italy, Japan, Korea, Luxembourg, Mexico, Netherlands, New Zealand, Norway, Poland, Portugal, Slovak Republic, Spain, Sweden, Switzerland, Turkey, United Kingdom,[b] United States.
Partner countries	Albania, Argentina, Brazil, Bulgaria, Chile, Hong Kong-China, Indonesia, Israel, Latvia, Liechtenstein, Macedonia, Peru, Romania, Russian Federation, Thailand	Brazil, Hong Kong-China, Indonesia, Liechtenstein, Latvia, Macao-China, Russian Federation, Thailand, Tunisia, Uruguay, Serbia.[c]

a. Response rate is too low to ensure comparability. See Annex 3 in *Literacy Skills for the World of Tomorrow – Further Results From PISA 2000* (OECD, 2003a).

b. Response rate is too low to ensure comparability. See Annex 3 in *Learning for Tomorrow's World – First Results from PISA 2003* (OECD, 2004a).

c. For the country Serbia and Montenegro, data for Montenegro are not available in PISA 2003. The latter accounts for 7.9 per cent of the national population. The name "Serbia" is used as a shorthand for the Serbian part of Serbia and Montenegro.

in order to understand and evaluate scientific advice on food safety, an adult would not only need to know some basic facts about the composition of nutrients, but should also be able to apply that information. The term "literacy" is used to encapsulate this broader concept of knowledge and skills.

PISA is an ongoing survey with a data collection every three years. The first PISA survey was conducted in 2000 in 32 countries, using written tasks answered in schools under independently supervised test conditions following consistently applied standards. Another 11 countries participated in the same survey in late 2001 or early 2002. The second survey was conducted in 2003 in 41 countries. Table 1.1 gives the list of participating countries for PISA 2000 and PISA 2003.

PISA mainly assesses reading, mathematical and scientific literacy. For each data collection, one of these three domains is chosen as the major domain, while the others are considered as minor domains. PISA 2000 focused on reading, while the major domain for PISA 2003 was mathematical literacy. About 70 per cent of the testing time is devoted to the major domain and the remainder is shared by the minor domains.

Table 1.2 ■ **Assessment domains covered per data collection**

	Major domain	Minor domains
PISA 2000	Reading literacy	Mathematical literacy, scientific literacy
PISA 2003	Mathematical literacy	Reading literacy Scientific literacy Problem solving
PISA 2006	Scientific literacy	Mathematical literacy Reading literacy

In 2009, the major domain will again be reading literacy.

WHAT MAKES PISA UNIQUE?

PISA is not the first international comparative survey of student achievement. Others have been conducted over the past 40 years, primarily developed by the International Association for the Evaluation of Educational Achievement (IEA) and by the Education Testing Service's International Assessment of Educational Progress (IAEP).

These surveys have concentrated on outcomes linked directly to those parts of the curriculum that are essentially common across the participating countries. Aspects of the curriculum unique to one country or a smaller number of countries have usually not been taken into account in the assessments, regardless of how significant those parts of the curriculum are for the countries involved.

Key features associated with PISA include:

- Its policy orientation, with design and reporting methods determined by the need of governments to draw policy lessons;
- Its innovative "literacy" concept, which is concerned with the capacity of students to apply knowledge and skills in key subject areas and to analyse, reason and communicate effectively as they pose, solve and interpret problems in a variety of situations;
- Its relevance to lifelong learning, which does not limit PISA to assessing students' curricular and cross-curricular competencies but also asks them to report on their own motivation to learn, beliefs about themselves and learning strategies;

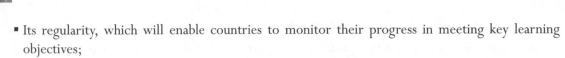

- Its regularity, which will enable countries to monitor their progress in meeting key learning objectives;
- Its breadth of geographical coverage and collaborative nature, with the 47 countries that have participated in a PISA assessment so far and the 13 additional countries that join the PISA 2006 assessment representing a total of one-third of the world population and almost nine-tenths of the world's gross domestic product (GDP);[1] and
- Its aged-based coverage of young people near the end of their compulsory schooling, which will enable countries to assess the performance of education systems. While most young people in OECD countries continue their initial education beyond the age of 15, this is normally close to the end of the initial period of basic schooling in which all young people follow a broadly common curriculum. It is useful to determine, at that stage, the extent to which they have acquired knowledge and skills that will help them in the future, including the individualized paths of further learning they may follow.

This emphasis on testing in terms of mastery and broad concepts is particularly significant in light of the concern among nations to develop human capital, which the OECD defines as the knowledge, skills, competencies and other attributes embodied in individuals that are relevant to personal, social and economic well-being.

Estimates of human capital have tended, at best, to be derived using proxies, such as level of education completed. When the interest in human capital is extended to include attributes that permit full social and democratic participation in adult life and that equip people to become lifelong learners, the inadequacy of these proxies becomes even clearer.

By directly testing for knowledge and skills close to the end of basic schooling, PISA examines the degree of preparedness of young people for adult life and, to some extent, the effectiveness of education systems. Its aim is to assess achievement in relation to the underlying objectives (as defined by society) of education systems, not in relation to the teaching and learning of a body of knowledge. This view of educational outcomes is needed if schools and education systems are encouraged to focus on modern challenges.

PISA defines the assessment domains as follows:

- *Mathematical literacy* An individual's capacity to identify and understand the role that mathematics plays in the world, to make well-founded judgements and to use and engage with mathematics in ways that meet the needs of that individual's life as a constructive, concerned and reflective citizen.
- *Reading literacy* An individual's capacity to understand, use and reflect on written texts, in order to achieve one's goals, to develop one's knowledge and potential and to participate in society.
- *Scientific literacy* The capacity to use scientific knowledge, to identify questions and to draw evidence-based conclusions in order to understand and help make decisions about the natural world and the changes made to it through human activity.
- *Problem-solving skills* An individual's capacity to use cognitive processes to confront and resolve real, cross-disciplinary situations where the solution path is not immediately obvious and where the literacy domains or curricular areas that might be applicable are not within a single domain of mathematics, science or reading.

More information on the assessment domains can be found in these PISA publications:

- *Measuring Student Knowledge and Skills – A New Framework for Assessment* (OECD, 1999a);
- *Sample Tasks from the PISA 2000 Assessment – Reading, Mathematical and Scientific Literacy* (OECD, 2002b);
- *Literacy Skills for the World of Tomorrow – Further Results from PISA 2000* (OECD, 2003a);
- *The PISA 2003 Assessment Framework – Mathematics, Reading, Science and Problem Solving Knowledge and Skills* (OECD, 2003b);
- *Learning for Tomorrow's World – First Results from PISA 2003* (OECD, 2004a); and
- *Problem Solving for Tomorrow's World – First Measures of Cross-Curricular Competencies* (OECD, 2004b).

HOW THE ASSESSMENT TAKES PLACE

The assessment of student performance

The PISA 2000 and the PISA 2003 assessments consisted of paper-and-pencil tests. The question format in the assessment is varied. Some questions require students to select or produce simple responses that can be directly compared with a single correct answer, such as multiple choice or closed constructed response items. Others are more constructive, requiring students to develop their own responses designed to measure broader constructs than those captured by more traditional surveys, allowing for a wider range of acceptable responses and more complex marking that can include partially correct responses.

Literacy in PISA is assessed through units consisting of a stimulus (*e.g.* text, table, chart, figure, etc.), followed by a number of tasks associated with this common stimulus. This is an important feature, allowing questions to go into greater depth than they could if each question introduced an entirely new context. It allows time for the student to assimilate material that can then be used to assess multiple aspects of performance.

Examples of items of the PISA 2000 assessment are available in *Sample Tasks from the PISA 2000 Assessment – Reading, Mathematical and Scientific Literacy* (OECD, 2002b).

Examples of items of the PISA 2003 assessment are available in *The PISA 2003 Assessment Framework – Mathematics, Reading, Science and Problem Solving Knowledge and Skills* (OECD, 2003b).

The context questionnaires and their use

To gather contextual information, PISA asks students and the principals of the participating schools to respond to background questionnaires of around 20 to 30 minutes in length. These questionnaires are central to the analysis of the results because they provide information about a range of student and school characteristics.

The questionnaires seek information about:

- The students and their family backgrounds, including the economic, social, and cultural capital of the students and their families;
- Aspects of students' lives, such as their attitudes to learning, their habits and life inside school and their family environment;

- Aspects of schools, such as the quality of the school's human and material resources, public and private funding, decision-making processes and staffing practices;
- The context of instruction, including instructional structures and types, class size and the level of parental involvement;
- Strategies of self-regulated learning, motivational preferences and goal orientations, self-regulated cognition mechanisms, action control strategies, preferences for different types of learning situations, learning styles and social skills required for cooperative learning (these aspects were part of an international option in the PISA 2000 assessment, but were included in the compulsory student questionnaire in PISA 2003); and
- Aspects of learning and instruction, including students' motivation, engagement and confidence in relation to the major domain of assessment, and the impact of learning strategies on achievement in this domain.

In PISA 2003 as well as in PISA 2000, an information and communication technology (ICT) questionnaire was offered as an international option. It focused on: *i)* availability and use of information technologies (IT), including the location where IT is mostly used as well as the type of use; *ii)* IT confidence and attitudes, including self-efficacy and attitudes towards computers; and *iii)* learning background of IT, focusing on where students learned to use computers and the Internet.

In PISA 2003, an educational career questionnaire was also offered as an international option. It collected data on aspects of the students' educational career in three areas: *i)* students' past education including grade repetition, interruptions of schooling, changes of schools and changes of study programme; *ii)* students' current education on aspects involving mathematics, focusing on the type of mathematics classes and their current level of achievement; and *iii)* students' future and occupation, focusing on expected education level and expected occupation at the age of 30.

The PISA 2003 questionnaires are available in Appendices 2 to 5 of this volume, as well as on the PISA Web site (*www.pisa.oecd.org*).

Several indices at the student level and at the school level were derived from the questionnaire data. These indices combine several answers provided by students or principals to build a broader concept that is not directly observable. For instance, one cannot directly observe the student's reading engagement, but it is possible to ask several questions like "I like talking about books with other people" that reflect the student's level of reading engagement.

More information on how these indices were constructed and their psychometric properties can be found in Appendix 9 as well as in *PISA 2003 Technical Report* (OECD, forthcoming).

ABOUT THIS MANUAL

PISA implemented complex methodological procedures to ensure reliable population estimates and their respective standard errors. More precisely, PISA 2000 and PISA 2003 used plausible values for reporting population achievement estimates and replicate weights for the computation of their respective standard errors.

In addition to these two methodological complexities, PISA collects data on a regular basis, in a particular context, and with standardised procedures.

This manual is designed to explain these complex methodologies through examples using the PISA data. The manual does not detail every aspect of the methodologies, but nevertheless, they are described to ensure that all potential PISA database users can understand them and use the PISA data in an appropriate way.

Analysing the PISA data is a process that has been simplified by using programming procedures within statistical software packages, such as SAS® and SPSS®. Consequently, this manual also contains examples of these procedures. There are, in fact, two versions of the manual – one for users of SAS® and one for users of SPSS®. Each version of the manual consists of four parts.

The first part, Chapter 1 to Chapter 5, is identical in both versions of the manual. It presents concepts and theories which are used in PISA. These chapters are:

1. The OECD's Programme for International Student Assessment
2. Sample Weights
3. Replicate Weights
4. The Rasch Model
5. Plausible Values

The second part, Chapter 6 to Chapter 14, is different in each manual. In each, they describe how to correctly analyse the PISA data and contain the necessary coding – either SAS® or SPSS®. These chapters are:

6. Computation of Standard Errors
7. Analyses with Plausible Values
8. Use of Proficiency Levels
9. Analyses with School-Level Variables
10. Standard Error on a Difference
11. OECD Average and OECD Total
12. Trends
13. Multilevel Analyses
14. Other Statistical Issues

The third part is also different in each manual: it consists of Chapter 15, which presents either the SAS® or the SPSS® macros that facilitate the computation of the estimates and standard errors.

The fourth part is identical in both versions of the manual. It consists of appendices that describe the details of the PISA 2003 data files.[2]

While chapters are organized by type of analyses, the manual progressively builds upon the statistical knowledge and the SAS® or SPSS® syntax knowledge previously presented. It is therefore advised to read the chapters in order, starting with Chapter 1.

There also exist specialised software packages that are configured to deal with complex samples and plausible values. These include WesVar®, from Westat Inc. (*www.westat.com/wesvar*); AM, from the American Institutes for Research (*www.am.air.org*); and SUDAAN, from the Research Triangle Institute (*www.rti.org/sudaan*).

In addition, the OECD has developed an interactive website that automatically performs simple statistical analyses – mainly computation of means and percentages – using the plausible value methodologies and the replicate weights (*http://pisaweb.acer.edu.au/oecd_2003/oecd_pisa_data.html*). This site also contains the complete PISA 2003 databases in ASCII format.

Notes

1. The combined population of all countries (excluding Chinese Taipei) that have or will have participated in the PISA 2000, 2003 and 2006 assessments amounts to 32 per cent of the 2002 world population. The GDP of these countries amounts to 87 per cent of the 2002 world GDP. The data on GDP and population sizes were derived from the U.N. World Development Indicators database.
2. The description of the PISA 2000 data files is covered in *Manual for the PISA 2000 Database* (OECD, 2002a).

Sample Weights

INTRODUCTION

National or international surveys usually collect data from a sample. Dealing with a sample rather than the whole population is preferable for several reasons.

First, for a census, all members of the population need to be identified. This identification process presents no major difficulty for human populations in some countries, where national databases with the name and address of all or nearly all citizens may be available. However, in other countries, it is not possible for the researcher to identify all members or sampling units of the target population, mainly because it would be too time consuming or because of the nature of the target population.

Second, even if all members of a population are easily identifiable, researchers may still draw a sample, because dealing with the whole population:

- Might require unreasonable budgets;
- Is time consuming and thus incompatible with publication deadlines; and
- Does not necessarily help with obtaining additional and/or required information.

Drawing a sample can be done in several ways depending on the population characteristics and the survey research questions. All sample designs aim to avoid bias in the selection procedure and achieve the maximum precision in view of the available resources. Nevertheless, biases in the selection can arise:

- If the sampling is done by a non-random method, which generally means that the selection is consciously or unconsciously influenced by human choices. The importance of randomness in the selection procedure should not be underestimated; and
- If the sampling frame (list, index or other population record) that serves as the basis for selection does not cover the population adequately, completely or accurately.

Biases can also arise if some sections of the population are impossible to find or refuse to co-operate. In educational surveys, schools might refuse to participate and within participating schools, some students might refuse to participate or simply be absent on the day of the assessment. The size of the bias introduced by the school or student non-response is proportional to the correlation between the school, or the student, propensity to participate and the survey measures. For instance, it may be that low achievers are more likely to be absent on the day of the assessment than high achievers. This is the reason why international education surveys require a minimal student participation rate. For PISA, this minimum is 80 per cent.

Finally, if the sampling units do not have the same chances to be selected and if the population parameters are estimated without taking into account these varying probabilities, then results might also be biased. To compensate for these varying probabilities, data need to be weighted. Weighting consists of acknowledging that some units in the sample are more important than others and have to contribute more than others for any population estimates. A sampling unit with a very small probability of selection will be considered as more important than a sampling unit with a high probability of selection. Weights are therefore inversely proportional to the probability of selection.

Nevertheless, a sample is only useful to the extent that it allows the estimation of some characteristics of the whole population. This means that the statistical indices computed on the sample, like a mean, a standard deviation, a correlation, a regression coefficient, and so on, can be generalized to the population. This generalization is more reliable if the sampling requirements have been met.

Depending on the sampling design, selection probabilities and procedures to compute the weights will vary. These variations are discussed in the next sections.

WEIGHTS FOR SIMPLE RANDOM SAMPLES

Selecting members of a population by simple random sampling is the most straightforward procedure. There are several ways to draw such a sample, for example:

- The *N* members[1] of a population are numbered and *n* of them are selected by random numbers without replacement;
- *N* numbered discs are placed in a container, mixed well, and *n* of them are selected at random;
- The *N* population members are arranged in a random order, and every $\frac{N}{n}^{\text{th}}$ member is then selected; or
- The *N* population members are each assigned a random number. The random numbers are sorted from lowest to highest or highest to lowest. The first *n* members make up one random sample.

The simple random sample gives an equal probability of selection to each member of the population. If *n* members are selected from a population of *N* members according to a simple random procedure, then the probability of each member, *i,* to be part of the sample is equal to:

$$p_i = \frac{n}{N}$$

For example, if 40 students are randomly selected from a population of 400 students, the probability of each student, *i,* to be part of the sample is equal to:

$$p_i = \frac{n}{N} = \frac{40}{400} = 0.1$$

In other words, each student has one chance out of ten to be selected.

As mentioned previously, weights are usually defined as the inverse of the probability of selection. In the case of a simple random sample, the weight will be equal to:

$$w_i = \frac{1}{p_i} = \frac{N}{n}$$

The weight of each of the 40 students selected from a population of 400 students will therefore be equal to:

$$w_i = \frac{1}{p_i} = \frac{N}{n} = \frac{400}{40} = 10$$

This means that each student in the sample represents himself or herself, as well as nine other students. Since each unit has the same selection probability in a simple random sample, the weight attached to each selected unit will also be identical. Therefore, the sum of the weights of the selected units will be equal to the population size, *i.e. N:*

$$\sum_{i=1}^{n} w_i = \sum_{i=1}^{n} \frac{N}{n} = N$$

In the example,

$$\sum_{i=1}^{40} 10 = 400$$

Furthermore, since all sampled units have the same weight, the estimation of any population parameter will not be affected by the weights. For instance, consider the mean of some characteristic, *X*. The weighted mean is equivalent to the sum of the product of the weight and *X* divided by the sum of the weights.

$$\hat{\mu}_{(X)} = \frac{\sum_{i=1}^{n} w_i x_i}{\sum_{i=1}^{n} w_i}$$

Since w_i is a constant, the weighted mean and the unweighted mean will be equal.

$$\hat{\mu}_{(X)} = \frac{\sum_{i=1}^{n} w_i x_i}{\sum_{i=1}^{n} w_i} = \frac{w_i \sum_{i=1}^{n} x_i}{w_i \sum_{i=1}^{n} 1} = \frac{\sum_{i=1}^{n} x_i}{n}$$

SAMPLING DESIGNS FOR EDUCATION SURVEYS

Simple random sampling is very rarely used in education surveys because:

- It is too expensive. Indeed, depending on the school population size, it is quite possible that selected students would attend many different schools. This would require the training of a large number of test administrators, the reimbursement of a large amount of travel expenses and so on;
- It is not practical. One would have to contact too many schools; and
- It would be impossible to link, from a statistical point of view, student variables and school, class, or teacher variables. Educational surveys usually try to understand the statistical variability of the student's outcome measure by school or class level variables. With just one or only a few students per school, this statistical relationship would have no stability.

Therefore, surveys in education usually draw a student sample in two steps. First, a sample of schools is selected from a complete list of schools containing the student population of interest. Then, a simple random sample of students or classes is drawn from within the selected schools. In PISA, usually 35 students from the population of 15-year-olds are randomly selected within the selected schools. If less than 35 15-year-olds attend a selected school, then all of the students will be invited to participate.

This two-stage sampling procedure will have an impact on the calculation of the weights and, similarly, the school selection procedure will affect the characteristics and properties of the student sample.

Suppose that the population of 400 students is distributed in ten schools, each school containing 40 students. Four schools are selected randomly and within schools, ten students are selected according to a similar procedure. Each school, denoted *i,* has a selection probability equal to:

$$p_{1\_i} = \frac{n_{sc}}{N_{sc}} = \frac{4}{10} = 0.4$$

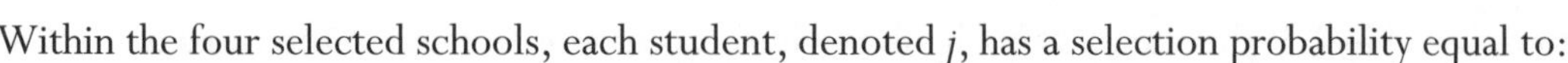

Within the four selected schools, each student, denoted j, has a selection probability equal to:

$$p_{2\_ij} = \frac{n_i}{N_i} = \frac{10}{40} = 0.25$$

with N_i being the number of students in school i and n_i the number of students sampled in school i. It means that within each selected school, each student has a chance of one in four to be sampled.

The final selection probability for student j attending school i is equal to the product of the school selection probability by the student selection probability within the school, *i.e.*:

$$p_{ij} = p_{1\_i} p_{2\_ij} = \frac{n_{sc} n_i}{N_{sc} N_i}$$

In the example, the final student probability is equal to:

$$p_{ij} = p_{1\_i} p_{2\_ij} = \frac{n_{sc} n_i}{N_{sc} N_i} = \frac{4*10}{10*40} = 0.4*0.25 = 0.10$$

The school weight, denoted w_{1_i}, the within-school weight, denoted w_{2_ij}, and the final school weight, denoted w_{ij}, are respectively equal to:

$$w_{1\_i} = \frac{1}{p_{1\_i}} = \frac{1}{0.4} = 2.5$$

$$w_{2\_ij} = \frac{1}{p_{2\_ij}} = \frac{1}{0.25} = 4$$

$$w_{ij} = \frac{1}{p_{ij}} = \frac{1}{0.1} = 10$$

Table 2.1 presents the selection probability at the school level, at the within-school level, and the final probability of selection for the selected students as well as the weight for these different levels where schools 2, 5, 7 and 10 have been selected.

Table 2.1 ■ **School, within-school, and final probability of selection and corresponding weights for a two-stage simple random sample with the first stage units being schools of equal size**

School label	School size N_i	School prob. p_{1_i}	School weight w_{1_i}	Within-school prob. p_{2_ij}	Within-school weight w_{2_ij}	Final student prob. p_{ij}	Final student weight w_{ij}	Sum of final weights $n_i w_{ij}$
1	40							
2	40	0.4	2.5	0.25	4	0.1	10	100
3	40							
4	40							
5	40	0.4	2.5	0.25	4	0.1	10	100
6	40							
7	40	0.4	2.5	0.25	4	0.1	10	100
8	40							
9	40							
10	40	0.4	2.5	0.25	4	0.1	10	100
Total			**10**					**400**

As shown by Table 2.1, the sum of the school weights corresponds to the number of schools in the population, *i.e.* 10, and the sum of the final weights corresponds to the number of students in the population, *i.e.* 400.

In practice, of course, schools differ in size. School enrolment numbers tend to be larger in urban areas as compared to rural areas. If schools are selected by simple random sampling, the school probability will not change, but within the selected schools, the student selection probability will vary according to the school size. In a small school, this probability will be large, while in a very large school, this probability will be small. Table 2.2 shows an example of the results obtained from schools of different sizes.

Table 2.2 ■ **School, within-school, and final probability of selection and corresponding weights for a two-stage simple random sample with the first stage units being schools of unequal size**

School label	School size	School prob.	School weight	Within-school prob.	Within-school weight	Final student prob.	Final student weight	Sum of final weights
1	10							
2	15	0.4	2.5	0.66	1.5	0.27	3.75	37.5
3	20							
4	25							
5	30	0.4	2.5	0.33	3	0.13	7.5	75
6	35							
7	40	0.4	2.5	0.25	4	0.1	10	100
8	45							
9	80							
10	100	0.4	2.5	0.1	10	0.04	25	250
Total	**400**		**10**					**462.5**

With a simple random sample of schools of unequal size, all schools will have the same selection probability and, as before, the sum of school weights will be equal to the number of schools in the population. Unfortunately, the sum of final student weights will not necessarily be equal to the number of students in the population. Further, the student final weight will differ among schools depending on the size of each school. This variability will reduce the reliability of all population parameter estimates.

Table 2.3 and Table 2.4 present the different probabilities and weights if the four smallest schools or the four largest schools are selected. As shown in these two tables, the sums of final student weights vary substantially from the expected value of 400. The sum of school weights, however, will always be equal to the number of schools in the population.

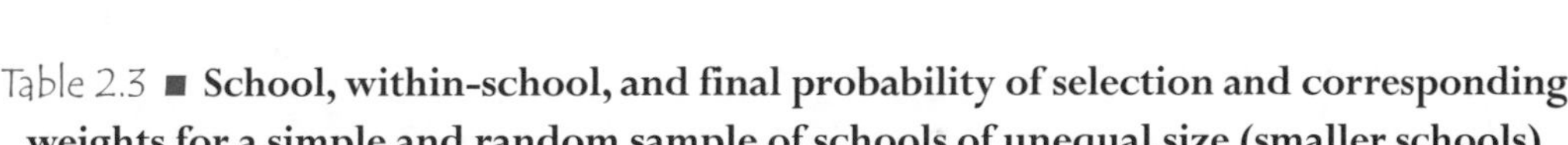

Table 2.3 ■ **School, within-school, and final probability of selection and corresponding weights for a simple and random sample of schools of unequal size (smaller schools)**

School label	School size	School prob.	School weight	Within-school prob.	Within-school weight	Final student prob.	Final student weight	Sum of final weight
1	10	0.4	2.5	1	1	0.4	4	40
2	15	0.4	2.5	0.66	1.5	0.27	3.75	37.5
3	20	0.4	2.5	0.5	2	0.2	5	50
4	25	0.4	2.5	0.4	2.5	0.16	6.25	62.5
Total			**10**					**190**

Table 2.4 ■ **School, within-school, and final probability of selection and corresponding weights for a simple and random sample of schools of unequal size (larger schools)**

School label	School size	School prob.	School weight	Within-school prob.	Within-school weight	Final student prob.	Final student weight	Sum of final weight
7	40	0.4	2.5	0.250	4	0.10	10.00	100.0
8	45	0.4	2.5	0.222	4.5	0.88	11.25	112.5
9	80	0.4	2.5	0.125	8	0.05	20.00	200.0
10	100	0.4	2.5	0.100	10	0.04	25.00	250.0
Total			**10**					**662.5**

The focus of international education surveys such as PISA is more on the student sample than on the school sample. Many authors even consider that such studies do not draw a school sample *per se*. They just consider the school sample as an operational stage to draw the student sample. Therefore, a sampling design that consists of a simple random sample of schools is inappropriate as it would underestimate or overestimate the student population size. It would also result in an important variability of final weights and consequently increase the sampling variance.

In order to avoid these disadvantages, schools are selected with probabilities proportional to their size (PPS). Larger schools will therefore have a higher probability of selection than smaller schools, but students in larger schools have a smaller within-school probability of being selected than students in small schools. With such procedures, the probability of a school to be selected is equal to the ratio of the school size multiplied by the number of schools to be sampled and divided by the total number of students in the population:

$$p_{1\_i} = \frac{N_i * n_{sc}}{N}$$

The formulae for computing the within-school probabilities and weights remain unchanged. The final probability and weight are still the product of the school and within-school probabilities or weights. For instance, the school probability for school 9 is equal to:

$$p_{1\_9} = \frac{N_9 * n_{sc}}{N} = \frac{80 * 4}{400} = \frac{4}{5} = 0.8$$

The student within-school probability for school 9 is equal to:

$$p_{2\_9j} = \frac{n_9}{N_9} = \frac{10}{80} = 0.125$$

The final probability is equal to:

$$p_{9j} = 0.8 * 0.125 = 0.1$$

Table 2.5 ■ **School, within-school, and final probability of selection and corresponding weights for a PPS sample of schools of unequal size**

School label	School size	School prob.	School weight	Within-school prob.	Within-school weight	Final student prob.	Final student weight	Sum of final weight
1	10							
2	15							
3	20	0.2	5.00	0.500	2.0	0.1	10	100
4	25							
5	30							
6	35							
7	40	0.4	2.50	0.250	4.0	0.1	10	100
8	45							
9	80	0.8	1.25	0.125	8.0	0.1	10	100
10	100	1	1.00	0.100	10.0	0.1	10	100
Total	**400**		**9.75**					**400**

As shown in Table 2.5, the school and within-school weights differ among schools, but final student weights do not vary. The weights will therefore not increase sampling variability. Further, the sum of final weights corresponds to the total number of students in the population. However, the sum of school weight differs from the expected value of 10, but this does not present a major problem as such educational surveys are mainly interested in the student sample.

With a PPS sample of schools, and an equal number of students selected in each selected school, the sum of the final student weights will always be equal to the total number of students in the population (non-response being ignored at this stage). This will be the case even if the smallest or the largest schools get selected. The sum of the school weights however will not be equal to the number of schools in the population. If the four smallest schools get selected, the sum of school weights will be equal to 25.666. If the four largest schools get selected, the sum of school weights will be equal to 6.97.

In order to keep the difference between the number of schools in the population and the sum of the school weights in the sample minimal, schools are selected according to a systematic procedure. The procedure consists of first sorting the schools according to their size. A sampling interval is computed as the ratio between the total number of students in the population and the number of schools in the sample, *i.e.:*

$$Int = \frac{N}{n_{sc}} = \frac{400}{4} = 100$$

Table 2.6 ■ **Selection of schools according to a PPS and systematic procedure**

School label	School size	From student number	To student number	Part of the sample
1	10	1	10	No
2	15	11	25	No
3	20	26	45	No
4	25	46	70	No
5	30	71	100	Yes
6	35	101	135	No
7	40	136	175	No
8	45	176	220	Yes
9	80	221	300	Yes
10	100	301	400	Yes

A random number from a uniform distribution [0.1] is drawn. Let us say 0.752. This random number is then multiplied by the sampling interval, *i.e.* 0.752 by 100 = 75.2. The school which contains the first student number greater than 75.2 is selected. Then the sampling interval is added to the value 75.2. The school which contains the student having the first student number greater than 175.2 will be selected. This systematic procedure is applied until the number of schools needed in the sample has been reached. In the example, the four selection numbers will be the following: 75.2, 175.2, 275.2 and 375.2.

Sorting the school sampling frame by the measure of size and then using a systematic selection procedure prevents obtaining a sample of only small schools or (more likely) a sample with only large schools. This therefore reduces the sampling variance on the sum of the school weights which is an estimate of the school population size.

WHY DO THE PISA WEIGHTS VARY?

As demonstrated in the previous section, a two-stage sample design with a PPS sample of schools should guarantee that all students will have the same probability of selection and therefore the same weight. However, the PISA data still needs to be weighted.

Table 2.7 clearly shows that PISA 2003 final weights present some variability. This variability is quite small for countries, such as Iceland, Luxembourg and Tunisia, but appears to be greater in countries such as Canada, Italy and the United Kingdom.

Table 2.8 presents the weighted and unweighted means per country on the mathematics scale for PISA 2003. The differences between the weighted and unweighted means are small for countries with small weight variability, such as Iceland, Luxembourg and Tunisia. On the contrary, the effect of the weights on the mean might be substantial for countries that present a large variability in weight. For instance, not using the weights would overestimate the mathematics performance of the Italian students by about 30 points on the PISA mathematics scale and underestimate the average performance of the Canadian students by nearly 11 score points.

Table 2.7 ■ **The 10th, 25th, 50th, 75th and 90th percentiles of PISA 2003 final weights**

	Percentile 10	Percentile 25	Percentile 50	Percentile 75	Percentile 90
AUS	4.70	11.86	19.44	25.06	29.55
AUT	13.00	14.92	17.24	20.33	25.53
BEL	4.09	10.48	12.96	15.32	19.22
BRA	222.44	309.68	407.59	502.14	627.49
CAN	1.16	2.18	5.09	13.17	36.28
CHE	1.35	2.88	6.70	15.55	21.76
CZE	5.19	12.55	17.77	23.77	27.33
DEU	140.10	160.05	180.05	208.72	243.21
DNK	8.86	10.07	11.73	13.29	16.22
ESP	3.97	4.38	15.50	48.73	83.84
FIN	2.80	9.94	11.60	12.24	13.29
FRA	142.51	148.21	159.98	177.56	213.43
GBR	7.73	10.71	23.12	136.69	180.64
GRC	15.07	17.18	21.71	27.56	30.90
HKG	13.31	14.26	15.15	16.60	19.36
HUN	16.13	19.27	22.25	25.37	29.41
IDN	21.82	42.47	106.18	272.23	435.96
IRL	11.33	12.01	13.51	15.31	17.99
ISL	1.06	1.12	1.16	1.20	1.36
ITA	2.56	14.93	20.65	66.11	108.66
JPN	217.14	248.47	258.13	281.97	314.52
KOR	80.82	89.60	96.72	107.86	117.81
LIE	1.00	1.00	1.01	1.03	1.06
LUX	1.00	1.01	1.03	1.06	1.09
LVA	4.26	5.17	6.47	7.40	8.92
MAC	1.14	3.12	4.80	6.60	8.09
MEX	3.09	6.36	13.00	27.49	67.09
NLD	24.84	35.41	43.80	52.42	65.60
NOR	11.11	11.59	12.47	13.53	14.76
NZL	7.41	8.99	10.77	12.34	13.98
POL	103.73	110.45	118.72	130.28	144.73
PRT	13.90	16.33	18.70	22.66	28.82
RUS	172.98	245.92	326.11	426.26	596.07
SVK	4.39	6.98	8.64	11.02	16.79
SWE	17.95	19.54	22.03	24.47	28.81
THA	74.96	101.57	119.35	130.48	154.26
TUN	31.27	31.41	32.19	33.32	34.62
TUR	22.06	50.49	109.69	135.98	152.65
URY	1.81	2.79	4.43	8.06	11.66
USA	296.10	418.79	554.25	704.78	885.84
YUG	8.68	12.83	16.62	18.20	19.73

Table 2.8 ■ **Weighted and unweighted country means on the PISA 2003 mathematics scale**

	Weighted mean	Unweighted mean	Difference
AUS	524.27	522.33	1.94
AUT	505.61	511.86	-6.25
BEL	529.29	533.19	-3.90
BRA	356.02	360.41	-4.40
CAN	532.49	521.40	11.09
CHE	526.55	518.24	8.31
CZE	516.46	534.95	-18.50
DEU	502.99	508.41	-5.43
DNK	514.29	513.69	0.60
ESP	485.11	494.78	-9.67
FIN	544.29	542.81	1.48
FRA	510.80	514.73	-3.93
GBR	508.26	514.44	-6.18
GRC	444.91	440.88	4.04
HKG	550.38	555.86	-5.48
HUN	490.01	488.59	1.42
IDN	360.16	361.51	-1.35
IRL	502.84	504.68	-1.84
ISL	515.11	515.05	0.05
ITA	465.66	496.00	-30.34
JPN	534.14	533.51	0.62
KOR	542.23	540.60	1.62
LIE	535.80	536.46	-0.67
LUX	493.21	493.48	-0.27
LVA	483.37	486.17	-2.80
MAC	527.27	522.79	4.48
MEX	385.22	405.40	-20.18
NLD	537.82	542.12	-4.29
NOR	495.19	495.64	-0.46
NZL	523.49	525.62	-2.13
POL	490.24	489.00	1.24
PRT	466.02	465.23	0.79
RUS	468.41	472.44	-4.03
SVK	498.18	504.12	-5.94
SWE	509.05	507.95	1.09
THA	416.98	422.73	-5.75
TUN	358.73	359.34	-0.61
TUR	423.42	426.72	-3.30
URY	422.20	412.99	9.21
USA	482.88	481.47	1.41
YUG	436.87	436.36	0.51

Different factors contribute to the variability of weights:

- *Oversampling or undersampling of some strata of the population*: usually, the school population is divided into different subgroups, called strata. For instance, a country might decide for convenience to separate the urban schools from the rural schools in the list of schools. In most cases, the number of students selected in the rural stratum and in the urban stratum will be proportional to what these two strata represent in the whole population. This stratification process guarantees for instance that a predefined number of schools within each stratum will be selected. Without the stratification, this number might vary. Nevertheless, for national reporting purposes, a country might decide to sample more students than what would have been sampled based on a proportional allocation in some part of the student population. Suppose that 90 per cent of the student population in a country attends academic tracks and 10 per cent of the students attend vocational tracks. If the national centre staff wants to compare the performance of the students by track, then it will be necessary to sample more vocational students than what would be sampled based on a proportional allocation.
- *Lack of accuracy or no updated size measure for schools on the school sampling frame*: when schools are selected with a probability proportional to their size, a measure of size needs to be included in the school list. In PISA, this measure of size is the number of 15-year-olds in each school in the population, but national statistics per school and per date of birth are not always available. Therefore, the measure of size can be the number of students in the modal grade for 15-year-olds, or the total number of students in the school divided by the number of grades. Further, even if national statistics per school and per date of birth are available, these data might be one or two years old. Therefore, inconsistencies between the number of 15-year-olds at the testing time and the measure of size used in the school sample frame generate some variability in the final weights. Let us suppose that school 9 in Table 5 has 100 15-year-old students at the time of testing. When schools were selected from the list of schools, the measure of size was set at 80. The school weight was set at 1.25. The within-school weight will be equal to 100 divided by 10, *i.e.* 10 rather than 8. Therefore, the final weight will be equal to 12.5 instead of the expected 10.
- *School and within-school weight adjustment for school and student non-response*: some schools, and within the selected and participating schools, some students, might refuse to participate. To compensate for this non-response, a weight adjustment is applied at each level where non-response occurs. For instance, if only 25 students out of the 35 selected students from a participating school are present on the day of the assessment, then the weight of the participating students will be multiplied by a ratio of 35 by 25.[2] The student participation rate will vary from one school to another, and therefore the final weights will vary. A similar procedure is also applied to compensate for the school non-response. More information about these adjustment factors is available in the *PISA 2003 Technical report* (OECD, forthcoming).

CONCLUSIONS

This chapter has briefly described: *i)* what a weight is and how to compute it; *ii)* what the PISA sampling design is and why such a design is considered as the most appropriate; *iii)* why the PISA weights show some variability; and *iv)* the impact of the weights on population estimates.

All statistical analyses or procedures on the PISA data should be weighted. Unweighted analyses will provide biased population parameter estimates.

Notes

1. *N* usually represents the size of the population and *n* the size of the sample.
2. In PISA 2003, the student weight adjustment for student non response might also differ in a particular school.

Replicate Weights

INTRODUCTION

In most cases, as mentioned in Chapter 2, national or international surveys collect data from a sample instead of conducting a full a census. However, for a particular population, there are thousands, even millions of possible samples, and each of them does not necessarily yield the same estimates of population statistics. Every generalisation made from a sample, *i.e.* every estimate of a population statistic, has an associated uncertainty or risk of error. The sampling variance corresponds to the measure of this uncertainty due to sampling.

This chapter explains the statistical procedures used for computing the sampling variance and its square root, the standard error. More specifically, this chapter discusses how to estimate sampling variances for population estimates derived from a complex sample design using replicate weights. First, the concept of sampling variance will be examined through a fictitious example for simple random sampling. Second, the computation of the standard error will be investigated for two-stage sampling. Third, replication methods for estimating sampling variances will be introduced for simple random samples and for two-stage samples respectively.

SAMPLING VARIANCE FOR SIMPLE RANDOM SAMPLING

Suppose that a teacher decides to implement the mastery learning approach in his or her classroom. This methodology requires that each lesson be followed by a student assessment. In the example given, the teacher's class has 36 students. The teacher quickly realises that it would be too time consuming to grade all assessments and therefore decides to select a sample of quizzes to find out whether the material taught has been assimilated (Bloom, 1979).

However, the random sampling of a few quizzes can result in the selection of high achievers or low achievers only, which would introduce an important error in the class mean performance estimate. These situations are extreme examples, but drawing a random sample will always generate some uncertainty.

In the same example, before selecting some quizzes, the teacher grades all of them and analyzes the results for the first lesson. Figure 3.1 presents the distribution of the 36 students' results. One student gets a grade 5, two students get a grade 6, and so on.

Figure 3.1 ■ **Distribution of the results of the 36 students**

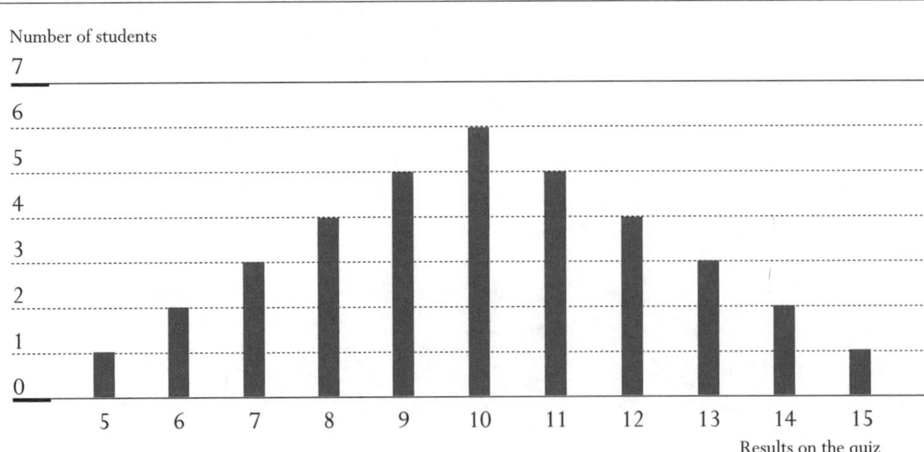

The distribution of the student grades corresponds to a normal distribution. The population mean and the population variance are respectively equal to:

$$\mu = \frac{1}{N}\sum_{i=1}^{N} x_i = \frac{(5+6+6+7+...+14+14+15)}{36} = \frac{360}{36} = 10$$

$$\sigma^2 = \frac{1}{N}\sum_{i=1}^{N}(x_i - \mu)^2 = \frac{\left[(5-10)^2 + (6-10)^2 + ... + (14-10)^2 + (15-10)^2\right]}{36} = \frac{240}{36} = 5.8333$$

The standard deviation is therefore equal to:

$$\sigma = \sqrt{\sigma^2} = \sqrt{5.833} = 2.415$$

The teacher then decides to randomly select a sample of two students after the next lesson to save on grading time. The number of possible samples of 2 students out of a population of 36 students is equal to:

$$C_{36}^{2} = \frac{36!}{(36-2)!2!} = 630$$

There are 630 possible samples of 2 students out of a population of 36 students. Table 3.1 describes these 630 possible samples. For instance, there are two possible samples which provide a mean estimate of 5.5 for student performance. These two samples are: *i)* the student with a grade 5 and the first student with a grade 6; and *ii)* the student with a 5 and the second student with a 6. Similarly, there are two ways of selecting a sample that would produce a mean grade of 6: *i)* the two sampled students both receive a grade 6; or *ii)* one student receives a 5 and the second student receives a 7. As only two students obtained a grade 6 (Figure 3.1), there is only one possible sample with two grades 6. Since Figure 3.1 shows that there is only one student who received a grade 5 and three students who received a grade 7, there are three possible samples of two students with a grade 5 and a grade 7.

Table 3.1 ■ **Description of the 630 possible samples of 2 students selected from 36 according to their mean**

Sample mean	Results of the two sampled students	Number of combinations of the two results	Number of samples
5.5	5 and 6	2	2
6	6 and 6 5 and 7	1 3	4
6.5	5 and 8 6 and 7	4 6	10
7	7 and 7 5 and 9 6 and 8	3 5 8	16
7.5	5 and 10 6 and 9 7 and 8	6 10 12	28
8	8 and 8 5 and 11 6 and 10 7 and 9	6 5 12 15	38

...

Table 3.1 (continued) ▪ **Description of the 630 possible samples of 2 students selected from 36 according to their mean**

Sample mean	Results of the two sampled students	Number of combinations of the two results	Number of samples
8.5	5 and 12	4	52
	6 and 11	10	
	7 and 10	18	
	8 and 9	20	
9	9 and 9	10	60
	5 and 13	3	
	6 and 12	8	
	7 and 11	15	
	8 and 10	24	
9.5	5 and 14	2	70
	6 and 13	6	
	7 and 12	12	
	8 and 11	20	
	9 and 10	30	
10	10 and 10	15	70
	5 and 15	1	
	6 and 14	4	
	7 and 13	9	
	8 and 12	16	
	9 and 11	25	
10.5	6 and 15	2	70
	7 and 14	6	
	8 and 13	12	
	9 and 12	20	
	10 and 11	30	
11	7 and 15	3	60
	8 and 14	8	
	9 and 13	15	
	10 and 12	24	
	11 and 11	10	
11.5	8 and 15	4	52
	9 and 14	10	
	10 and 13	18	
	11 and 12	20	
12	9 and 15	5	38
	10 and 14	12	
	11 and 13	15	
	12 and 12	6	
12.5	10 and 15	6	28
	11 and 14	10	
	12 and 13	12	
13	11 and 15	5	16
	12 and 14	8	
	13 and 13	2	
13.5	12 and 15	4	10
	13 and 14	6	
14	13 and 15	3	4
	14 and 14	1	
14.5	14 and 15	2	2
			630

As shown in Table 3.1, there are two possible samples with a mean of 5.5, four possible samples with a mean of 6, ten possible samples with a mean of 6.5, sixteen possible samples with a mean of 7, and so on.

Figure 3.2 is a chart of the frequency of samples by their mean estimates for all possible samples of 2 students from 36.

Figure 3.2 ■ **Sampling variance distribution of the mean**

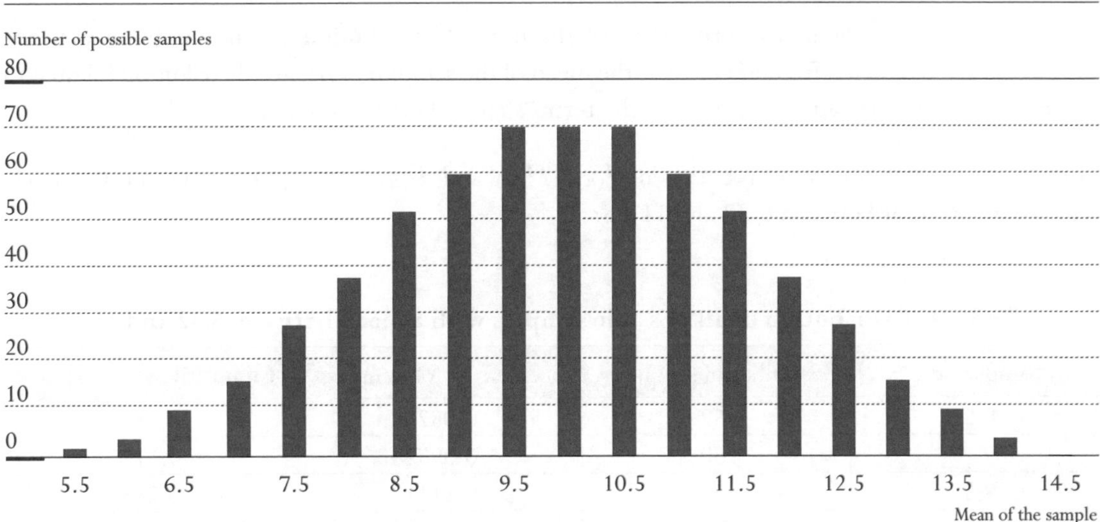

As for all distributions, this distribution of the means of all possible samples can be summarized by central tendency indices and dispersion indices, such as the mean and the variance (or its square root, *i.e.* the standard deviation).

$$\mu_{(\hat{\mu})} = [(2x5.5) + (4x6) + (10x6.5) + (16x7) + (28x7.5) + (38x8) + ... + (2x14.5)]/630 = 10$$

The mean of all possible sample means is equal to the student population mean, *i.e.* 10. This result is not a coincidence, but a fundamental property of the mean of a simple random sample, *i.e.* the mean of the means of all possible samples is equal to the population mean. In more formal language, the sample mean is an unbiased estimate of the population mean. Stated differently, the expected value of the sample mean is equal to the population mean.

However, it should be noted that there is an important variation around this expectation. In the example considered, sample means range from 5.5 to 14.5. The variance of this distribution, usually denoted as the sampling variance of the mean, can be computed as:

$$\sigma^2_{(\hat{\mu})} = [(5.5-10)^2 + (5.5-10)^2 + (6-10)^2 + ... + (14.5-10)^2 + (14.5-10)^2]/630 = 2.833$$

Its square root, denoted as the standard error, is equal to:

$$\sigma_{(\hat{\mu})} = \sqrt{\sigma^2_{(\hat{\mu})}} = \sqrt{2.833} = 1.68$$

However, what information does the standard error of the mean give, or more specifically, what does the value 1.68 tell us? The distribution of the means of all possible samples follows approximately a normal distribution. Therefore, based on the mathematical properties of the normal distribution, it can be said that:

- 68.2% of all possible sample means fall between -1 standard error and +1 standard error around the mean; and
- 95.4% of all possible sample means fall between -2 standard errors and +2 standard errors.

Let us check the mathematical properties of the normal distribution on the sampling variance distribution of the mean. Remember that, the mean of the sampling variance distribution is equal to 10 and its standard deviation, denoted by the term "standard error", is equal to 1.68.

How many samples have a mean between $\mu_{(\hat{\mu})} - \sigma_{(\hat{\mu})}$ and $\mu_{(\hat{\mu})} + \sigma_{(\hat{\mu})}$, *i.e.* between (10 – 1.68) and (10 + 1.68), or between 8.32 and 11.68?

Table 3.2 ■ **Distribution of all possible samples with a mean between 8.32 and 11.68**

Sample mean	Number of samples	Percentage of samples	Cumulative % of sample
8.5	52	0.0825	0.0825
9	60	0.0952	0.1777
9.5	70	0.1111	0.2888
10	70	0.1111	0.4
10.5	70	0.1111	0.5111
11	60	0.0952	0.6063
11.5	52	0.0825	0.6888
	434		

Table 3.2 shows that there are 434 samples out of 630 with a mean comprised between 8.32 and 11.68; these represent 68.8% of all samples. It can also be demonstrated that the percentage of samples with means between $\mu_{(\hat{\mu})} - 2\sigma_{(\hat{\mu})}$ and $\mu_{(\hat{\mu})} + 2\sigma_{(\hat{\mu})}$, *i.e.* between 6.64 and 13.36 is equal to 94.9.

To estimate the standard error of the mean, the mean of all possible samples has been computed. In reality though, only the mean of one sample is known. This, as will be shown, is enough to calculate an estimate of the sampling variance. It is therefore important to identify the factors responsible for the sampling variance from the one sample chosen.

The first determining factor is the size of the sample. If the teacher, in our example, decides to select four quizzes instead of two, then the sampling distribution of the mean will range from 6 (the four lowest results being 5, 6, 6 and 7) to 14 (the four highest results being 13, 14, 14 and 15). Remember that the sampling distribution ranged from 5.5 to 14.5 with samples of two units. Increasing the sample size reduces the variance of the distribution.

There are 58 905 possible samples of 4 students out of a population of 36 students. Table 3.3 gives the distribution of all possible samples of four students for a population of 36 students.

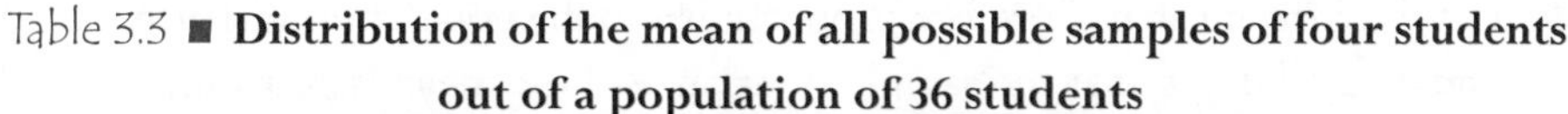

Table 3.3 ■ **Distribution of the mean of all possible samples of four students out of a population of 36 students**

Sample mean	Number of possible samples
6.00	3
6.25	10
6.50	33
6.75	74
7	159
7.25	292
7.50	510
7.75	804
8	1213
8.25	1700
8.50	2288
8.75	2896
9	3531
9.25	4082
9.50	4553
9.75	4830
10	4949
10.25	4830
10.50	4553
10.75	4082
11	3531
11.25	2896
11.50	2288
11.75	1700
12	1213
12.25	804
12.50	510
12.75	292
13	159
13.25	74
13.50	33
13.75	10
14	3

It can be easily shown that this distribution has a mean of 10 and a standard deviation, denoted standard error, of 1.155.

This proves that the size of the sample does not affect the expected value of the sample mean, but it does reduce the variance of the distribution of the sample means: the bigger the sample size, the lower the sampling variance of the mean.

The second factor that contributes to the sampling variance is the variance of the population itself. For example, if the results are reported out of a total score of 40 instead of 20, (*i.e.* the student results are all multiplied by two), then the mean of the student results will be 20, the variance will be 23.333 (*i.e.* four times 5.8333) and the standard deviation will be equal to 4.83 (*i.e.* two times 2.415).

It can be shown that the sampling variance from a sample of two students will be equal to 11.333 and that the standard error of the mean will be equal to 3.3665 (*i.e.* two times 1.68).

The standard error of the mean is therefore proportional to the population variance. Based on these examples, it can be established that the sampling variance of the mean is equal to:

$$\sigma^2_{(\hat{\mu})} = \frac{\sigma^2}{n}\left(\frac{N-n}{N-1}\right)$$

and the standard error of the sample mean is equal to:

$$\sigma_{(\hat{\mu})} = \sqrt{\sigma^2_{(\hat{\mu})}} = \frac{\sigma}{\sqrt{n}}\sqrt{\frac{N-n}{N-1}}$$

Where:

σ^2 = variance of the population;

σ = standard deviation of the population;

n = sample size; and

N = population size.

This formula can be checked with the example:

$$\sigma^2_{(\hat{\mu})} = \frac{\sigma^2}{n}\left(\frac{N-n}{N-1}\right) = \frac{5.833}{2}\left(\frac{36-2}{36-1}\right) = 2.8333$$

As the size of the population increases, the ratio $\left(\frac{N-n}{N-1}\right)$ tends toward 1. In such cases, a close approximation of the sampling variance of the mean is given by:

$$\sigma^2_{(\hat{\mu})} = \frac{\sigma^2}{n}$$

However, in practice, the population variance is unknown and is estimated from a sample. The sampling variance estimate on the mean, just as a mean estimate, can vary depending on the sample. Therefore, being based on a sample, only an estimate of the sampling variance on the mean (or any other estimate) can be computed.

In the remainder of this manual, the concepts of sampling variance and estimations of the sampling variance will be confounded to simplify the text and the mathematical notations. That is, symbols depicting the estimates of sampling variance will not have a hat (^) to differentiate them from true values, but the fact that they are estimates is to be understood.

SAMPLING VARIANCE FOR TWO-STAGE SAMPLING

Education surveys and more particularly international surveys rarely sample students by simply selecting a random sample of students. Schools get selected first and, within each selected school, classes or students are randomly sampled.

One of the differences between simple random sampling and two-stage sampling is that for the latter, selected students attending the same school cannot be considered as independent observations. This is because students within a school will usually have more common characteristics than students

from different educational institutions. For instance, they are offered the same school resources, may have the same teachers, and therefore are taught a common curriculum, and so on. Differences between students from different schools are also greater if different educational programs are not available in all schools. For instance, one would expect to observe more differences between students from a vocational school and students from an academic school, than those that would be observed between students from two vocational schools.

Further, it is well known that within a country, within sub-national entities, and within cities, people tend to live in areas according to their financial resources. As children usually attend schools close to their homes, it is likely that students attending the same school come from similar social and economic backgrounds.

A simple random sample of 4 000 students is thus likely to cover the diversity of the population better than a sample of 100 schools with 40 students observed within each school. It follows that the uncertainty associated with any population parameter estimate (*i.e.* standard error) will be greater for a two-stage sample than for a simple random sample of the same size.

The increase of the uncertainty due to the two-stage sample is directly proportional to the differences between the first stage units, known as primary sampling units (PSUs), *i.e.* schools for education surveys. The consequences of this uncertainty for two extreme and fictitious situations are given below:

- All students in the population are randomly assigned to schools. Therefore, there should not be any differences between schools. Randomly selecting 100 schools and then within the selected schools randomly drawing 40 students would be similar from a statistical point of view to directly selecting randomly 4 000 students as there are no differences between schools. The uncertainty associated with any population parameter estimate would be equal to the uncertainty obtained from a simple random sample of 4 000 students.

- All schools are different but within schools, all students are perfectly identical. Since within a particular school, all students are identical: observing only one student, or 40, would provide the same amount of information. Therefore, if 100 schools are selected and 40 students are observed per selected school, the effective sample size of this sample would be equal to 100. Therefore, the uncertainty associated with any population parameter estimate would be equal to the uncertainty obtained from a simple random sample of 100 students.

Of course, there is no educational system in the world that can be identified with either of these extreme and fictitious situations. Nevertheless, in some educational systems, school differences, at least regarding the survey's measure, for example, the academic performance, appear to be very small, while in some other educational systems, school differences can be quite substantial.

The academic performance of each student can be represented by a test score, or by the difference between his or her score and the country average score. In education research, it is common to split the difference between the student's score and the country average score into three parts: *i)* the distance between the student's performance and the corresponding class mean; *ii)* the distance between this class mean and the corresponding school mean; *iii)* the distance between this school mean and the country mean. The first difference relates to the within-class variance

(or the residual variance in terms of variance analysis). It indicates how much student scores can vary within a particular class. The second difference – the distance between the class mean and the school mean – is related to the between-classes-within-school variance. This difference reflects the range of differences between classes within schools. This between-classes-within-school variance might be substantial in educational institutions that offer both academic and vocational education. The third distance – the difference between the school average and the country average – is called the between-school variance. This difference indicates how much student performance varies among schools.

To obtain an estimate of these three components of the variance, it would be necessary to sample several schools, at least two classes per school and several students per class. PISA randomly selects 15-year-olds directly from student lists within the participating schools. Therefore, generally speaking, it is impossible to distinguish the between- and within-classes variances. PISA can only provide estimates of the between- and the within-school variances.

Table 3.4 provides the between-school and within-school variances on the mathematics scale for PISA 2003. In northern European countries, the between-school variances are very small compared to their within-school variance estimates. In these countries, the student variance mainly lies at the within-school level. In terms of student achievement then, schools in such countries do not vary greatly. However, in Austria, Belgium, Germany, Hungary and Turkey, for instance, more than 50 per cent of the student differences in performance are accounted for at the school level. This means that the student performance differs substantially among schools. Therefore, the uncertainty associated with any population parameters will be larger for these countries when compared to the uncertainty for northern European countries, given a comparable sample size of schools and students.

As Kish (1987) noted:

> Standard methods for statistical analysis have been developed on assumptions of simple random sampling. Assuming independence for individual elements (or observations) greatly facilitates the mathematics used for distribution theories of formulas for complex statistics. … However, independent selection of elements is seldom realised in practice, because much research is actually and necessarily accomplished with complex sample designs. It is economical to select clusters that are natural grouping of elements, and these tend to be somewhat homogeneous for most characteristics. The assumptions may fail mildly or badly; hence standard statistical analysis tends to result in mild or bad underestimates in length of reported probability intervals. Overestimates are possible, but rare and mild.

Kish established a state of the art knowledge of the sampling variance according to the type of estimator and the sampling design. The sampling variance distributions are well known for univariate and multivariate estimators for simple random samples. The use of stratification variables with a simple random sample still allows the mathematical computation of the sampling variances, but with a substantial increase of complexity. As shown in Table 3.5, the computation of sampling variances for two-stage samples is available for some designs, but it becomes quite difficult to compute for multivariate indices.

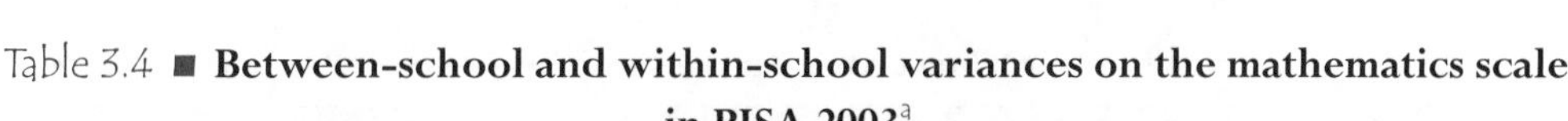

Table 3.4 ■ **Between-school and within-school variances on the mathematics scale in PISA 2003**[a]

	Between-school variance	Within-school variance
AUS	1919.11	7169.09
AUT	5296.65	4299.71
BEL	7328.47	5738.33
BRA	4128.49	5173.60
CAN	1261.58	6250.12
CHE	3092.60	6198.65
CZE	4972.45	4557.50
DEU	6206.92	4498.70
DNK	1109.45	7357.14
ESP	1476.85	6081.74
FIN	336.24	6664.98
FRA	3822.62	4536.22
GBR	1881.09	6338.25
GRC	3387.52	5991.75
HKG	4675.30	5298.26
HUN	5688.56	4034.66
IDN	2769.48	3343.87
IRL	1246.70	6110.71
ISL	337.56	7849.99
ITA	4922.84	4426.67
JPN	5387.17	4668.82
KOR	3531.75	5011.56
LIE	3385.41	5154.08
LUX	2596.36	5806.97
LVA	1750.22	6156.52
MAC	1416.99	6449.96
MEX	2476.01	3916.46
NLD	5528.99	3326.09
NOR	599.49	7986.58
NZL	1740.61	7969.97
POL	1033.90	7151.46
PRT	2647.70	5151.93
RUS	2656.62	6021.44
SVK	3734.56	4873.69
SWE	986.03	8199.46
THA	2609.38	4387.08
TUN	2821.00	3825.36
TUR	6188.40	4891.13
URY	4457.08	5858.42
USA	2395.38	6731.45
YUG	2646.00	4661.59

a. The results are based on the first plausible value for the mathematics scale, denoted PV1MATH in the PISA 2003 database (*www.pisa.oecd.org*).

Table 3.5 ■ **Current status of sampling errors**

Selection methods	Means and total of entire samples	Subclass means and differences	Complex analytical statistics, *e.g.* coefficients in regression
Simple random selection of elements	Known	Known	Known
Stratified selection of elements	Known	Available	Conjectured
Complex cluster sampling	Known for some sampling design	Available	Difficult

Note: Row 1 refers to standard statistical theory (Kish and Frankel, 1974).

Authors of sampling manuals usually distinguish two types of two-stage sampling:

- Two-stage sampling with first-stage units of equal sizes; and
- Two-stage sampling with first-stage units of unequal sizes.

Beyond this distinction, different characteristics of the population and of the sampling design need to be taken into account in the computation of the sampling variance, because they affect the sampling variance. Some of the factors to be considered are:

- Is the population finite or infinite?
- Was size a determining criterion in the selection of the first-stage units?
- Was a systematic procedure used for selecting first-stage or second-stage units?
- Does the sampling design include stratification variables?

The simplest two-stage sample design occurs with infinite populations of stage one and stage two units. As both stage units are infinite populations, PSUs are considered to be of equal sizes. If a simple random sample of PSUs is selected and if, within each selected PSU, a simple random sample of stage two units is selected then the sampling variance of the mean will be equal to:

$$\sigma^2_{(\hat{\mu})} = \frac{\sigma^2_{between\_PSU}}{n_{PSU}} + \frac{\sigma^2_{within\_PSU}}{n_{PSU}n_{within}}$$

Let us apply this formula to an education survey and let us consider the population of schools as infinite and the population of students within each school as infinite. The computation of the sampling variance of the mean is therefore equal to:

$$\sigma^2_{(\hat{\mu})} = \frac{\sigma^2_{between\_school}}{n_{school}} + \frac{\sigma^2_{within\_school}}{n_{students}}$$

Table 3.6 ■ **Between-school and within-school variances, number of participating students and schools in Denmark and Germany in PISA 2003**

	Denmark	Germany
Between-school variance	1 109.45	6 206.92
Within-school variance	7 357.14	4 498.70
Number of participating schools	206	216
Number of participating students	4218	4660

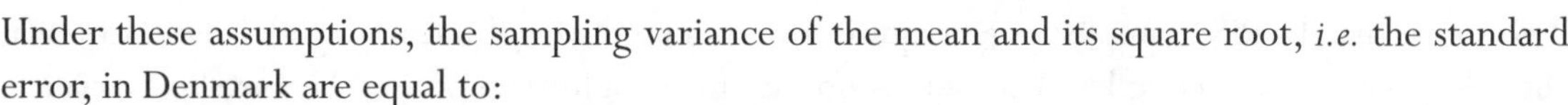

Under these assumptions, the sampling variance of the mean and its square root, *i.e.* the standard error, in Denmark are equal to:

$$\sigma^2_{(\hat{\mu})} = \frac{1109.45}{206} + \frac{7357.14}{4218} = 5.39 + 1.74 = 7.13$$

$$\sigma_{(\hat{\mu})} = \sqrt{7.13} = 2.67$$

The sampling variance of the mean and its square root, *i.e.* the standard error, in Germany are equal to:

$$\sigma^2_{(\hat{\mu})} = \frac{6206.92}{216} + \frac{4498.70}{4660} = 28.74 + 0.97 = 29.71$$

$$\sigma_{(\hat{\mu})} = \sqrt{29.71} = 5.45$$

If both samples were considered as simple random samples, then the standard error of the mean for Denmark and Germany would be respectively equal to 1.42 and 1.51.

Based on these results, we can make the following observations:

- The standard error of the mean is larger for two-stage sampling than for simple random sampling. For example, in the case of Germany, the standard errors for simple random sampling and for two-stage sampling are 1.51 and 5.45 respectively. Considering a two-stage sample as a simple random sample will therefore substantially underestimate standard errors and consequently confidence intervals will be too narrow. The confidence interval on the mathematic scale average, *i.e.* 503, would be equal to: [503 – (1.96*1.51);503 + (1.96*1.51)] = [500.05;505.96] in the case of a simple random sample, but equal to [484 – (1.96*5.45);484 + (1.96*5.45)] = [492.32;513.68] in the case of a two-stage sample. This indicates that any estimated mean value between 492.32 and 500.05 and between 505.96 and 513.68 may or may not be considered as statistically different from the German average, depending on the standard error used.
- The sampling variance of the mean for two-stage samples is mainly dependent on the between-school variance and the number of participating schools. Indeed, the between-school variance accounts for 76 percent of the total sampling variance in Denmark, *i.e.* 5.39/7.13 = 0.76. For Germany, the between-school variance accounts for 97 per cent of the total sampling variance (28.74/29.71 = 0.97). Therefore, one should expect larger sampling variance in countries with larger between-school variance, such as Germany and Austria for example.

However, the PISA population cannot be considered as an infinite population of schools with an infinite population of students. Further,

- Schools have unequal sizes;
- The PISA sample is a sample without replacement, *i.e.* a school cannot be selected twice;
- Schools are selected proportionally to their sizes and according to a systematic procedure; and
- Stratification variables are included in the sample design.

These characteristics of the sampling design will influence the sampling variance, so that the formula used above is also inappropriate. Indeed, *Learning for Tomorrow's World – First Results from PISA 2003* (OECD, 2004a) indicates that the standard errors on the mathematics scale mean for Denmark and Germany are 2.7 and 3.3, respectively.

This shows that the PISA sample design is quite efficient in reducing the sampling variance. However, the design becomes so complex that there is no easy formula for computing the sampling variance, or even estimators, such as means.

Since the IEA 1990 reading literacy study, replication or resampling methods have been used to compute estimates of the sampling variance for international education surveys. Even though these methods were known since the late 50s, they were not often used as they require numerous computations. With the availability of powerful personal computers in the 1990s and the increased use of international databases by non-mathematicians, international coordinating centres were encouraged to use resampling methods for estimating sampling variances from complex sample designs.

According to Rust and Rao (1996):

> The common principle that these methods have is to use computational intensity to overcome difficulties and inconveniences in utilizing an analytic solution to the problem at hand. Briefly, the replication approach consists of estimating the variance of a population parameter of interest by using a large number of somewhat different subsamples (or somewhat different sampling weights) to calculate the parameter of interest. The variability among the resulting estimates is used to estimate the true sampling error of the initial or full-sample estimate.

These methods will first be described for simple random samples and for two-stage samples. The PISA replication method will be presented subsequently.

REPLICATION METHODS FOR SIMPLE RANDOM SAMPLES

There are two main types of replication methods for simple random samples. These are known as the Jackknife and the Bootstrap. One of the most important differences between the Jackknife and the Bootstrap is related to the procedure used to produce the repeated subsamples or replicate samples. From a sample of *n* units, the Jackknife generates in a systematic way *n* replicate samples of *n*-1 units. The Bootstrap randomly generates a large number of repetitions of *n* units selected with replacement, with each unit having more than one chance of selection.

Since PISA does not use a Bootstrap replication method adapted to multi-stage sample designs, this section will only present the Jackknife method.

Suppose that a sample of ten students has been selected by simple random sampling. The Jackknife method will then generate ten subsamples, or replicate samples, each of nine students, as follows:

Table 3.7 ■ **Jackknife replicate samples and their means**

Student	1	2	3	4	5	6	7	8	9	10	Mean
Value	10	11	12	13	14	15	16	17	18	19	14.50
Replication 1	0	1	1	1	1	1	1	1	1	1	15.00
Replication 2	1	0	1	1	1	1	1	1	1	1	14.88
Replication 3	1	1	0	1	1	1	1	1	1	1	14.77
Replication 4	1	1	1	0	1	1	1	1	1	1	14.66
Replication 5	1	1	1	1	0	1	1	1	1	1	14.55
Replication 6	1	1	1	1	1	0	1	1	1	1	14.44
Replication 7	1	1	1	1	1	1	0	1	1	1	14.33
Replication 8	1	1	1	1	1	1	1	0	1	1	14.22
Replication 9	1	1	1	1	1	1	1	1	0	1	14.11
Replication 10	1	1	1	1	1	1	1	1	1	0	14.00

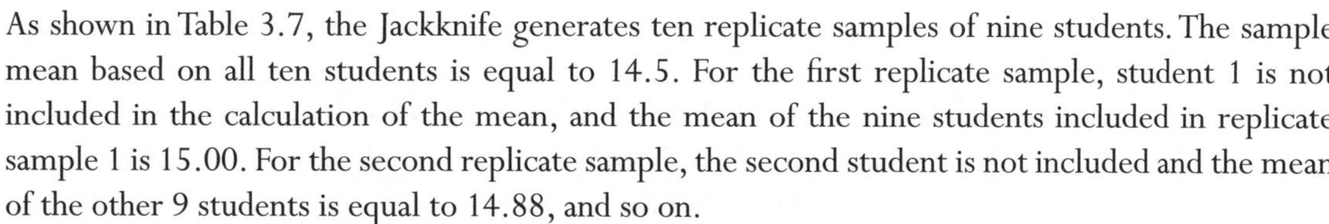

As shown in Table 3.7, the Jackknife generates ten replicate samples of nine students. The sample mean based on all ten students is equal to 14.5. For the first replicate sample, student 1 is not included in the calculation of the mean, and the mean of the nine students included in replicate sample 1 is 15.00. For the second replicate sample, the second student is not included and the mean of the other 9 students is equal to 14.88, and so on.

The Jackknife estimate of sampling variance of the mean is equal to:

$$\sigma^2_{jack} = \frac{n-1}{n}\sum_{i=1}^{n}(\hat{\theta}_{(i)} - \hat{\theta})^2 \text{ with}$$

$\hat{\theta}_{(i)}$ representing the statistic estimate for replicate sample i, and $\hat{\theta}$ representing the statistic estimate based on the whole sample.

Based on the data from Table 3.7, the Jackknife sampling variance of the mean is equal to:

$$\sigma^2_{(\hat{\mu})} = \frac{9}{10}\left[(15.00-14.50)^2 + (14.88-14.50)^2 + ... + (15.11-14.50)^2 + (14.00-14.50)^2\right]$$

$$\sigma^2_{(\hat{\mu})} = \frac{9}{10}(1.018519) = 0.9167$$

The usual population variance estimator is equal to:

$$\sigma^2 = \frac{1}{n-1}\sum_{i=1}^{n}(x_i - \hat{\mu})^2 = \frac{1}{9}\left[(10-14.5)^2 + (11-14.5)^2 + ... + (18-14.5)^2 + (19-14.5)^2\right] = 9.17$$

Therefore, the sampling variance of the mean, estimated by the mathematical formula, is equal to:

$$\sigma^2_{(\hat{\mu})} = \frac{\sigma^2}{n} = \frac{9.17}{10} = 0.917$$

As shown in this example, the Jackknife method and the mathematical formula provide identical estimation of the sampling variance. Rust (1996) mathematically demonstrates this equality.

$$\hat{\mu}_{(i)} - \hat{\mu} = \frac{\left[\left(\sum_{i=1}^{n} x_i\right) - x_i\right]}{n-1} - \frac{\left[\sum_{i=1}^{n} x_i\right]}{n} = -\frac{x_i}{n-1} + \left[\sum_{i=1}^{n} x_i\right]\left[\frac{1}{n-1} - \frac{1}{n}\right]$$

$$= -\frac{1}{(n-1)}\left[x_i - \left(\sum_{i=1}^{n} x_i\right)\left(1 - \frac{(n-1)}{n}\right)\right] = -\frac{1}{(n-1)}\left[x_i - \hat{\mu}(n-(n-1)\right] = -\frac{1}{(n-1)}(x_i - \hat{\mu})$$

Therefore,

$$\left(\hat{\mu}_{(i)} - \hat{\mu}\right)^2 = \frac{1}{(n-1)^2}(x_i - \hat{\mu})^2$$

$$\Rightarrow \sum_{i=1}^{n}(\hat{\mu}_{(i)} - \hat{\mu})^2 = \frac{1}{(n-1)^2}\sum_{i=1}^{n}(x_i - \hat{\mu})^2 = \frac{1}{(n-1)}\frac{\sum_{i=1}^{n}(x_i - \hat{\mu})^2}{(n-1)} = \frac{1}{(n-1)}\hat{\sigma}^2$$

$$\Rightarrow \sigma^2_{jack} = \frac{n-1}{n}\sum_{i=1}^{n}(\hat{\mu}_{(i)} - \hat{\mu})^2 = \frac{(n-1)}{n}\frac{1}{(n-1)}\hat{\sigma}^2 = \frac{\hat{\sigma}^2}{n}$$

The Jackknife method can also be applied to compute the sampling variance for other statistics, such as regression coefficients. In this particular example, the procedure will consist of the computation of 11 regression coefficients: one based on the whole sample and ten others with each being based on one replicate sample. The comparison between the whole sample regression coefficient and each of the ten replicate regression coefficients will provide an estimate of the sampling variance of that statistic.

Table 3.8 ■ **Values on variables X and Y for a sample of 10 students**

Student	1	2	3	4	5	6	7	8	9	10
Value Y	10	11	12	13	14	15	16	17	18	19
Value X	10	13	14	19	11	12	16	17	18	15

The regression coefficient for the whole sample is equal to 0.53.

Table 3.9 ■ **Regression coefficients for each replicate sample**

	Regression coefficient
Replicate 1	0.35
Replicate 2	0.55
Replicate 3	0.56
Replicate 4	0.64
Replicate 5	0.51
Replicate 6	0.55
Replicate 7	0.51
Replicate 8	0.48
Replicate 9	0.43
Replicate 10	0.68

The Jackknife formula, *i.e.* $\sigma^2_{jack} = \frac{n-1}{n}\sum_{i=1}^{n}(\hat{\theta}_{(i)} - \hat{\theta})^2$, can be applied to compute the sampling variance of the regression coefficient.

$$\sigma^2_{jack} = \frac{n-1}{n}\sum_{i=1}^{n}(\hat{\theta}_{(i)} - \hat{\theta})^2 = \frac{9}{10}\left[(0.35-0.53)^2 + (0.55-0.53)^2 + \ldots(0.68-0.53)^2\right] = 0.07$$

This result is identical to the result that the usual sampling variance formula for a regression coefficient would render.

RESAMPLING METHODS FOR TWO-STAGE SAMPLES

There are three types of replication methods for two-stage samples:

- The Jackknife, with two variants: one for unstratified samples and another one for stratified samples;
- The Balanced Repeated Replication (BRR) and its variant, Fay's modification;
- The Bootstrap.

PISA uses BRR with Fay's modification.[1]

THE JACKKNIFE FOR UNSTRATIFIED TWO-STAGE SAMPLE DESIGNS

If a simple random sample of PSUs is drawn without the use of any stratification variables, then it can be shown that the sampling variance of the mean obtained using the Jackknife method is mathematically equal to the formula provided in section 2 of this chapter, *i.e.*:

$$\sigma^2_{(\hat{\mu})} = \frac{\sigma^2_{between\_PSU}}{n_{PSU}} + \frac{\sigma^2_{within\_PSU}}{n_{PSU}\, n_{within}}$$

Consider a sample of ten schools and within selected schools, a simple random sample of students. The Jackknife method for an unstratified two-stage sample consists of generating ten replicates of nine schools. Each school is removed only once, in a systematic way.

Table 3.10 ■ **The Jackknife replicate samples for unstratified two-stage sample**

Replicate	R1	R2	R3	R4	R5	R6	R7	R8	R9	R10
School 1	0.00	1.11	1.11	1.11	1.11	1.11	1.11	1.11	1.11	1.11
School 2	1.11	0.00	1.11	1.11	1.11	1.11	1.11	1.11	1.11	1.11
School 3	1.11	1.11	0.00	1.11	1.11	1.11	1.11	1.11	1.11	1.11
School 4	1.11	1.11	1.11	0.00	1.11	1.11	1.11	1.11	1.11	1.11
School 5	1.11	1.11	1.11	1.11	0.00	1.11	1.11	1.11	1.11	1.11
School 6	1.11	1.11	1.11	1.11	1.11	0.00	1.11	1.11	1.11	1.11
School 7	1.11	1.11	1.11	1.11	1.11	1.11	0.00	1.11	1.11	1.11
School 8	1.11	1.11	1.11	1.11	1.11	1.11	1.11	0.00	1.11	1.11
School 9	1.11	1.11	1.11	1.11	1.11	1.11	1.11	1.11	0.00	1.11
School 10	1.11	1.11	1.11	1.11	1.11	1.11	1.11	1.11	1.11	0.00

For the first replicate, denoted R1, school 1 has been removed. The weights of the other schools in the first replicate are adjusted by a factor of 1.11, *i.e.* $\frac{10}{9}$ or, as a general rule, by a factor of $\frac{G}{G-1}$, with G being the number of PSUs in the sample. This adjustment factor is then applied when school replicate weights and within school replicate weights are combined to give the student replicate weights. For the second replicate, school 2 is removed and the weights in the remaining schools are adjusted by the same factor, and so on.

The statistic of interest is computed for the whole sample, and then again for each replicate. The replicate estimates are then compared to the whole sample estimate to obtain the sampling variance, as follows:

$$\sigma^2_{(\hat{\theta})} = \frac{(G-1)}{G} \sum_{i=1}^{G} (\hat{\theta}_{(i)} - \hat{\theta})^2$$

This formula is identical to the one used for a simple random sample, except that instead of using n replicates, n being the number of units in the sample, this formula uses G replicates, with G being the number of PSUs.

THE JACKKNIFE FOR STRATIFIED TWO-STAGE SAMPLE DESIGNS

As mentioned at the beginning of Chapter 2, two major principles underlie all sample designs. The first is the concern to avoid bias in the selection procedure, the second to achieve the maximum precision in view of the available financial resources.

To reduce the uncertainty, or to minimize the sampling variance without modifying the sample size, international and national education surveys usually implement the following procedures in the sampling design:

- PSUs are selected proportionally to their size and according to a systematic procedure. This procedure leads to an efficient student sampling procedure. Equal-sized samples of students can be selected from each school. At the same time, the overall selection probabilities (combining the school and student sampling components) do not vary much.
- National centres are encouraged to identify stratification variables that are statistically associated with the student performance. Characteristics, such as rural versus urban, academic versus vocational, private versus public, are associated with the student performance. The sampling variance reduction will be proportional to the explanatory power of these stratification variables on student performance.

The Jackknife for stratified two-stage samples allows the reduction of the sampling variance by taking both of these aspects into consideration. Failing to do so, would lead to a systematic overestimation of sampling variances.

Suppose that the list of schools in the population is divided into two parts called strata: rural schools and urban schools. Further, within these two strata, schools are sorted by size. Within each stratum, ten schools are selected systematically and proportionally to their size.

The Jackknife method for stratified two-stage sample designs consists of systematically pairing sampled schools within each stratum in the order in which they were selected. Therefore, schools will be paired with other similar schools.

Table 3.11 ■ **The Jackknife replicates for stratified two-stage sample designs**

Pseudo-stratum	School	R1	R2	R3	R4	R5	R6	R7	R8	R9	R10
1	1	2	1	1	1	1	1	1	1	1	1
1	2	0	1	1	1	1	1	1	1	1	1
2	3	1	0	1	1	1	1	1	1	1	1
2	4	1	2	1	1	1	1	1	1	1	1
3	5	1	1	2	1	1	1	1	1	1	1
3	6	1	1	0	1	1	1	1	1	1	1
4	7	1	1	1	0	1	1	1	1	1	1
4	8	1	1	1	2	1	1	1	1	1	1
5	9	1	1	1	1	2	1	1	1	1	1
5	10	1	1	1	1	0	1	1	1	1	1
6	11	1	1	1	1	1	2	1	1	1	1
6	12	1	1	1	1	1	0	1	1	1	1
7	13	1	1	1	1	1	1	0	1	1	1
7	14	1	1	1	1	1	1	2	1	1	1
8	15	1	1	1	1	1	1	1	0	1	1
8	16	1	1	1	1	1	1	1	2	1	1
9	17	1	1	1	1	1	1	1	1	0	1
9	18	1	1	1	1	1	1	1	1	2	1
10	19	1	1	1	1	1	1	1	1	1	2
10	20	1	1	1	1	1	1	1	1	1	0

Table 3.11 describes how replicates are generated for this method. Schools 1 to 10 are rural, and schools 11 to 20 are urban. Within each stratum, there are therefore five school pairs, or pseudo-strata (also called variance strata).

The Jackknife for stratified two-stage samples will generate as many replicates as there are pairs or pseudo strata. In this example, ten replicates will therefore be generated. For each replicate sample, one school is randomly removed within a particular pseudo-stratum and the weight of the remaining school in the pseudo-stratum is doubled. For replicate 1, denoted R1, school 2 is removed and the weight of school 1 is doubled in pseudo-stratum 1. For replicate 2, school 3 is removed and the weight of school 4 is doubled in pseudo-stratum 2, and so on.

As previously mentioned, the statistic of interest is computed based on the whole sample and then again based on each replicate sample. The replicate estimates are then compared to the whole sample estimate to obtain the sampling variance, as follows:

$$\sigma^2_{(\hat{\theta})} = \sum_{i=1}^{G} (\hat{\theta}_{(i)} - \hat{\theta})^2$$

This replication method is now generally used in IEA studies.

THE BALANCED REPEATED REPLICATION METHOD

While the Jackknife method consists of removing only one school for each replicate sample, the Balanced Repeated Replication (BRR) method proceeds by selecting at random one school within each pseudo-stratum to have its weight set to 0, and by doubling the weights of the remaining schools.

As this method results in a large set of possible replicates, a balanced set of replicate samples is generated according to Hadamard matrices in order to avoid lengthy computations. The number of replicates is the smallest multiple of four, greater than or equal to the number of pseudo-strata. In this example, as there are ten pseudo-strata, 12 replicates will be generated.

Table 3.12 ■ **The BRR replicates**

Pseudo-stratum	School	R1	R2	R3	R4	R5	R6	R7	R8	R9	R 10	R 11	R 12
1	1	2	0	0	2	0	0	0	2	2	2	0	2
1	2	0	2	2	0	2	2	2	0	0	0	2	0
2	3	2	2	0	0	2	0	0	0	2	2	2	0
2	4	0	0	2	2	0	2	2	2	0	0	0	2
3	5	2	0	2	0	0	2	0	0	0	2	2	2
3	6	0	2	0	2	2	0	2	2	2	0	0	0
4	7	2	2	0	2	0	0	2	0	0	0	2	2
4	8	0	0	2	0	2	2	0	2	2	2	0	0
5	9	2	2	2	0	2	0	0	2	0	0	0	2
5	10	0	0	0	2	0	2	2	0	2	2	2	0
6	11	2	2	2	2	0	2	0	0	2	0	0	0
6	12	0	0	0	0	2	0	2	2	0	2	2	2
7	13	2	0	2	2	2	0	2	0	0	2	0	0
7	14	0	2	0	0	0	2	0	2	2	0	2	2
8	15	2	0	0	2	2	2	0	2	0	0	2	0
8	16	0	2	2	0	0	0	2	0	2	2	0	2
9	17	2	0	0	0	2	2	2	0	2	0	0	2
9	18	0	2	2	2	0	0	0	2	0	2	2	0
10	19	2	2	0	0	0	2	2	2	0	2	0	0
10	20	0	0	2	2	2	0	0	0	2	0	2	2

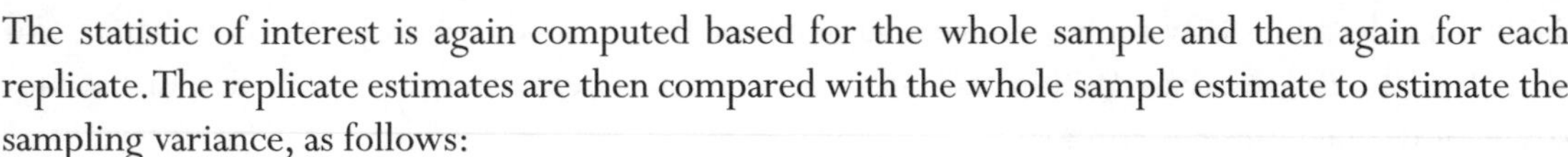

The statistic of interest is again computed based for the whole sample and then again for each replicate. The replicate estimates are then compared with the whole sample estimate to estimate the sampling variance, as follows:

$$\sigma^2_{(\hat{\theta})} = \frac{1}{G}\sum_{i=1}^{G}(\hat{\theta}_{(i)} - \hat{\theta})^2$$

With this replication method, each replicate sample only uses half of the available observations. This large reduction in sample might therefore become problematic for the estimation of a statistic on a rare subpopulation. Indeed, the number of remaining observations might be so small, even equal to 0, that the estimation of the population parameter for a particular replicate sample is impossible. To overcome this disadvantage, Fay developed a variant to the BRR method. Instead of multiplying the school weights by a factor of 0 or 2, Fay suggested multiplying the weights by a deflating factor *k* between 0 and 1, with the second inflating factor being equal to 2 minus *k*. For instance, if the deflating weight factor, denoted *k,* is equal to 0.6, then the inflating weight factor will be equal to 2- *k*, *i.e.* 1-0.6=1.4 (Judkins, 1990).

PISA uses the Fay method with a factor of 0.5. Table 3.13 describes how the replicate samples and weights are generated for this method.

Table 3.13 ■ **The Fay replicates**

Pseudo-stratum	School	R1	R2	R3	R4	R5	R6	R7	R8	R9	R 10	R 11	R 12
1	1	1.5	0.5	0.5	1.5	0.5	0.5	0.5	1.5	1.5	1.5	0.5	1.5
1	2	0.5	1.5	1.5	0.5	1.5	1.5	1.5	0.5	0.5	0.5	1.5	0.5
2	3	1.5	1.5	0.5	0.5	1.5	0.5	0.5	0.5	1.5	1.5	1.5	0.5
2	4	0.5	0.5	1.5	1.5	0.5	1.5	1.5	1.5	0.5	0.5	0.5	1.5
3	5	1.5	0.5	1.5	0.5	0.5	1.5	0.5	0.5	0.5	1.5	1.5	1.5
3	6	0.5	1.5	0.5	1.5	1.5	0.5	1.5	1.5	1.5	0.5	0.5	0.5
4	7	1.5	1.5	0.5	1.5	0.5	0.5	1.5	0.5	0.5	0.5	1.5	1.5
4	8	0.5	0.5	1.5	0.5	1.5	1.5	0.5	1.5	1.5	1.5	0.5	0.5
5	9	1.5	1.5	1.5	0.5	1.5	0.5	0.5	1.5	0.5	0.5	0.5	1.5
5	10	0.5	0.5	0.5	1.5	0.5	1.5	1.5	0.5	1.5	1.5	1.5	0.5
6	11	1.5	1.5	1.5	1.5	0.5	1.5	0.5	0.5	1.5	0.5	0.5	0.5
6	12	0.5	0.5	0.5	0.5	1.5	0.5	1.5	1.5	0.5	1.5	1.5	1.5
7	13	1.5	0.5	1.5	1.5	1.5	0.5	1.5	0.5	0.5	1.5	0.5	0.5
7	14	0.5	1.5	0.5	0.5	0.5	1.5	0.5	1.5	1.5	0.5	1.5	1.5
8	15	1.5	0.5	0.5	1.5	1.5	1.5	0.5	1.5	0.5	0.5	1.5	0.5
8	16	0.5	1.5	1.5	0.5	0.5	0.5	1.5	0.5	1.5	1.5	0.5	1.5
9	17	1.5	0.5	0.5	0.5	1.5	1.5	1.5	0.5	1.5	0.5	0.5	1.5
9	18	0.5	1.5	1.5	1.5	0.5	0.5	0.5	1.5	0.5	1.5	1.5	0.5
10	19	1.5	1.5	0.5	0.5	0.5	1.5	1.5	1.5	0.5	1.5	0.5	0.5
10	20	0.5	0.5	1.5	1.5	1.5	0.5	0.5	0.5	1.5	0.5	1.5	1.5

As with all replication methods, the statistic of interest is computed on the whole sample and then again on each replicate. The replicate estimates are then compared to the whole sample estimate to get the sampling variance, as follows:

$$\sigma^2_{(\hat{\theta})} = \frac{1}{G(1-k)^2}\sum_{i=1}^{G}(\hat{\theta}_{(i)} - \hat{\theta})^2$$

In PISA, it was decided to generate 80 replicate samples and therefore 80 replicate weights. Therefore, the formula becomes:

$$\sigma^2_{(\hat{\theta})} = \frac{1}{G(1-k)^2}\sum_{i=1}^{G}(\hat{\theta}_{(i)} - \hat{\theta})^2 = \frac{1}{80(1-0.5)^2}\sum_{i=1}^{80}(\hat{\theta}_{(i)} - \hat{\theta})^2 = \frac{1}{20}\sum_{i=1}^{80}(\hat{\theta}_{(i)} - \hat{\theta})^2$$

OTHER PROCEDURES FOR ACCOUNTING FOR CLUSTERED SAMPLES

For the past two decades, multi-level models and software packages have been introduced in the education research field. There is no doubt that these models allowed a break through in the unraveling of education phenomena. Indeed, multi-level regression models offer the possibility of taking into account the fact that students are nested within classes and schools: each contributing factor can be evaluated when establishing the outcome measure.

Multi-level regression software packages, such as MLWin or HLM, just like any professional statistical package, provide an estimate of the standard error for each of the estimated population parameters. While SAS® and SPSS® consider the sample as a simple random sample of population elements, MLWin and HLM recognize the hierarchical structure of the data, but consider that the school sample is a simple random one. They therefore do not take into account the complementary sample design information used in PISA to reduce the sampling variance. Consequently, in PISA, the sampling variances estimated with multi-level models will always be greater than the sampling variances estimated with Fay replicate samples.

As these multi-level model packages do not incorporate the additional sample design information, their standard error estimates are similar to the Jackknife method for unstratified samples. For instance, the German PISA 2003 data were analyzed using the multi-level model proposed by SAS® and called PROC MIXED. The standard errors of the mean of the five plausible values[2] for the combined reading literacy scale were respectively 5.4565, 5.3900, 5.3911, 5.4692, and 5.3461. The average of these five standard errors is equal to 5.41. Recall that the use of the formula in section 2 of this chapter produces an estimate of the sampling variance equal to 5.45.

With multi-level software packages, using replicates cannot be avoided if unbiased estimates of the standard errors for the estimates want to be obtained.

CONCLUSIONS

Since international education surveys use a two-stage sample design most of the time, it would be inappropriate to apply the sampling distribution formulas developed for simple random sampling. Doing so would lead to an underestimation of the sampling variances.

Sampling designs in education surveys can be very intricate. As a result, sampling distributions might not be available or too complex even for simple estimators, such as means. Since the 1990 IEA reading literacy study, sampling variances have been estimated through replication methods. These methods function by generating several subsamples, or replicate samples, from the whole sample. The statistic of interest is then estimated for each of these replicate samples and then compared to the whole sample estimate to provide an estimate of the sampling variance.

A replicate sample is formed simply through a transformation of the full sample weights according to an algorithm specific to the replication method. These methods therefore can be applied to any

estimators[3] – means, medians, percentiles, correlations, regression coefficients, etc. – which can be easily computed thanks to advanced computing resources. Further, using these replicate weights does not require an extensive knowledge in statistics, since these procedures can be applied regardless of the statistic of interest.

Notes

1. See reasons for this decision in the *PISA 2000 Technical Report* (OECD, 2002c).

2. See Chapter 4 for a description of plausible values.

3. Several empirical or theoretical studies have compared the different resampling methods for complex sampling design. As Rust and Krawchuk noted: "A benefit of both BRR and modified BRR over the Jackknife is that they have a sound theoretical basis for use with nonsmooth statistics, such as quantiles like the median. It has long been known that the Jackknife is inconsistent for estimating the variances of quantiles. That is, as the sample size increases for a given sample design, the estimation of the variances of quantiles does not necessarily become more precise when using the Jackknife." (Rust and Krawchuk, 2002).

The Rasch Model

INTRODUCTION

International surveys in education such as PISA are designed to estimate the performance in particular subject areas of various subgroups of students, at specific age or grade levels.

For the surveys to be considered valid, many items need to be developed and included in the final tests. The OECD publications related to the assessment frameworks indicate the breadth and depth of the PISA domains, showing that many items are needed to assess a domain as broadly defined as, for example, mathematical literacy.[1]

At the same time, it is unreasonable and perhaps undesirable to assess each sampled student with the whole item battery because:

- After extended testing time, students' results start to be affected by fatigue and this would therefore bias the outcomes of the surveys; and
- School principals would refuse to free their students for the very long testing period that would be required. This would reduce the school participation rate, which in turn might substantially bias the outcomes of the results.

To overcome the conflicting demands of limited student-level testing time and broad coverage of the assessment domain, students are assigned a subset of the item pool. The result of this is that only certain sub-samples of students respond to each item.

If the survey purpose is to estimate performance by reporting the percentage of correct answers for each item, it would not be necessary to report the performance of individual students. However, typically there is a need to summarise detailed item level information for communicating the outcomes of the survey to the research community, to the public and also to policy makers. In addition, educational surveys aim to explain the difference in results between countries, between schools and between students. For instance, a researcher might be interested in the difference in performance between boys and girls.

HOW CAN THE INFORMATION BE SUMMARISED?

At the country level, the most straightforward procedure for summarizing the item-level information would be to compute the average percentage of correct answers. This has been largely used in previous national or international surveys and is still used in some current international surveys, even when more complex models are implemented. These surveys may report the overall percentage of correct answers in mathematics and in science, as well as by content areas (for example, biology, physics, chemistry, earth sciences and so on). For instance, in mathematics, the overall percentage of correct answers for one country might be 54 per cent and for another, 65 per cent.

The great advantage of this type of reporting is that it can be understood by everyone. Everybody can imagine a mathematics test and can envision what is represented by 54 per cent and 65 per cent of correct answers. These two numbers also give a sense of the difference between the two countries.

Nevertheless, there are some weaknesses in this approach because the percentage of correct answers depends on the difficulty of the test. The actual size of the difference in results between two countries depends on the difficulty of the test and this may lead to misinterpretation.

International surveys do not aim to just report an overall level of performance. Over the past few decades, policy makers have also largely been interested in equity indicators. They may also be interested in the amount of dispersion of results in their country. In some countries the results may be clustered around the mean and in other countries there may be large numbers of students scoring very high results and very low results.

It would be impossible to compute dispersion indices with only the difficulty indices, based on percentage of correct answers of all the items. To do so, the information collected through the test needs also to be summarised at the student level.

To compare the results of two students assessed by two different tests, the tests must have exactly the same average difficulty. For PISA, as all items included in the main study are usually field trialled, test developers have some idea of the item difficulties and therefore can allocate the items to the different tests in such a way that the items in each test have more or less the same average difficulty. However, the two tests will never have exactly the same difficulty.

The distribution of the item difficulties will affect the distribution of the students' performance expressed as a raw score. For instance, a test with only items of medium difficulty will generate a different student score distribution to a test that consists of a large range of item difficulties.

This is also complicated to a further degree in PISA as it assesses three or even four domains per cycle. This multiple assessment reduces the number of items available for each domain per test and it is easier to guarantee the comparability of two tests of 60 items than it is with, for example, 15 items.

If the different tests are randomly assigned to students, then the equality of the sub-populations in terms of mean score and variance of the student's performance can be assumed. In other words,

- The mean of the raw score should be identical for the different tests; and
- The variance of the student raw scores should be identical for the different tests.

If this is not the case, then it would mean that the different tests do not have exactly the same psychometric properties. To overcome this problem of comparability of the student performance between tests, the student's raw scores can be standardised per test. As the equality of the sub-populations can be assumed, differences in the results are due to differences in the test characteristics. The standardisation would then neutralise the effect of test differences on student's performance.

However, usually, only a sample of students from the different sub-populations is tested. As explained in the two previous chapters, this sampling process generates an uncertainty around any population estimates. Therefore, even if different tests present exactly the same psychometric properties and are randomly assigned, the mean and standard deviation of the students' performance between the different tests can slightly differ. As the test characteristics and the sampling variability are confounded, the assumption cannot be made that the student raw scores obtained with different tests are fully comparable.

Other psychometric arguments can also be invoked against the use of raw scores based on the percentage of correct answers to assess student performance. Raw scores are on a ratio scale in so far as the interpretation of the results is limited to the number of correct answers. A student who

gets a 0 on this scale did not provide any correct answers, but could not be considered as having no competencies, while a student who gets 10 has twice the number of correct answers as a student who gets 5, but does not necessarily, have twice the competencies. Similarly, a student with a perfect score could not be considered as having all competencies (Wright and Stone, 1979).

THE RASCH MODEL FOR DICHOTOMOUS ITEMS

Introduction

Let us suppose that someone wants to estimate the competence of a high jumper. It might be measured or expressed as his or her:

- Individual record;
- Individual record during an official and international event;
- Mean performance during a particular period of time; or
- Most frequent performance during a particular period of time.

Figure 4.1 presents the proportion of success of two high jumpers per height for the last year of competition.

Figure 4.1 ■ **Proportion of success per height of the jump**

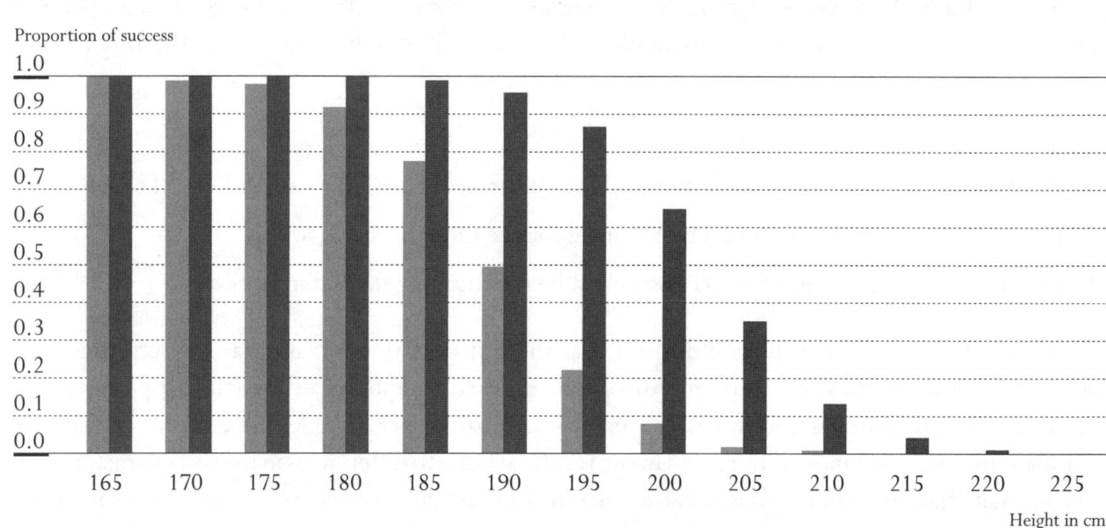

The two high jumpers always succeeded at 165 centimetres. Then the proportion of success progressively decreases to reach 0 for both at 225 centimetres. While it starts to decrease at 170 for the first high jumper, however, it starts to decrease at 185 for the second.

These data can be depicted by a logistic regression model. This statistical analysis consists of explaining a dichotomous variable by a continuous variable. In this example, the continuous variable will explain the success or the failure of a particular jumper by the height of the jump. The outcome of this analysis will allow the estimation of the probability of success, given any height. Figure 4.2 presents the probability of success for the two high jumpers.

Figure 4.2 ■ **Probability of success per height of the jump for the two high jumpers**

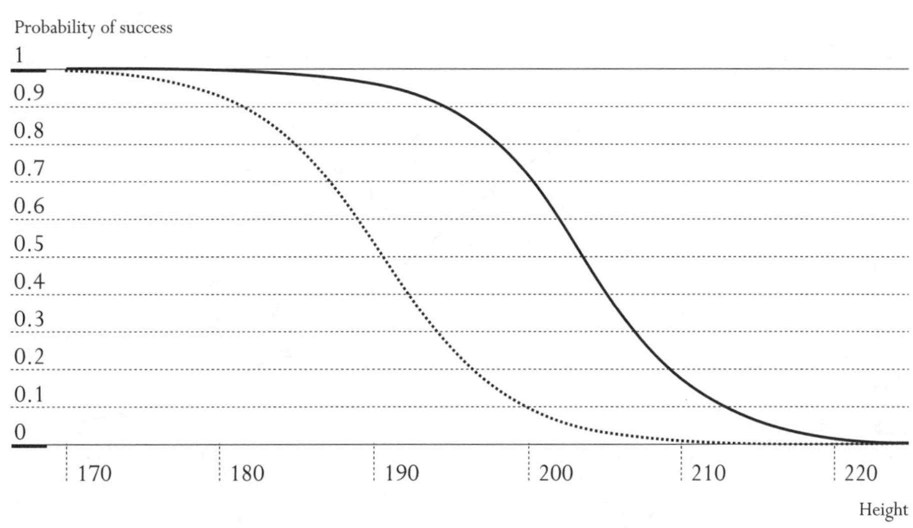

These two functions model the probability of success for the two high jumpers. The dotted curve represents the probability of success for the first high jumper and the solid curve, the probability of success for the second high jumper.

By convention,[2] the performance level would be defined as the height where the probability of success is equal to 0.50. This makes sense as below that level, the probability of success is lower than the probability of failure and beyond that level, this is the inverse.

In this particular example, the performance of the two high jumpers is respectively 190 and 202.5. Note that from Figure 4.1, the performance of the first jumper is directly observable whereas for jumper 2, it is not and needs to be estimated from the model. A key property of this kind of approach is that the level (*i.e.* the height) of the crossbar and the performance of the high jumpers are expressed on the same metric or scale.

Scaling cognitive data according to the Rasch model follows the same principle. The difficulty of the items is analogous to the difficulty of the jump based on the height of the crossbar. Further, just as a particular jump has two possible outcomes, *i.e.* success or failure, the answer of a student to a particular question is either correct or incorrect. Finally, just as each jumper's performance was defined at the point where the probability of success was 0.5, the student's performance/ability is likewise measured where the probability of success on an item equals 0.5.

A feature of the Rasch model is that it will create a continuum on which both student performance and item difficulty will be located and a probabilistic function links these two components. Low ability students and easy items will be located on the left side of the continuum or scale while high ability students and difficult items will be located on the right side of the continuum. Figure 4.3 represents the probability of success (dotted curve) and the probability of failure (solid curve) for an item of difficulty zero.

Figure 4.3 ■ **Probability of success to an item of difficulty zero as a function of student ability**

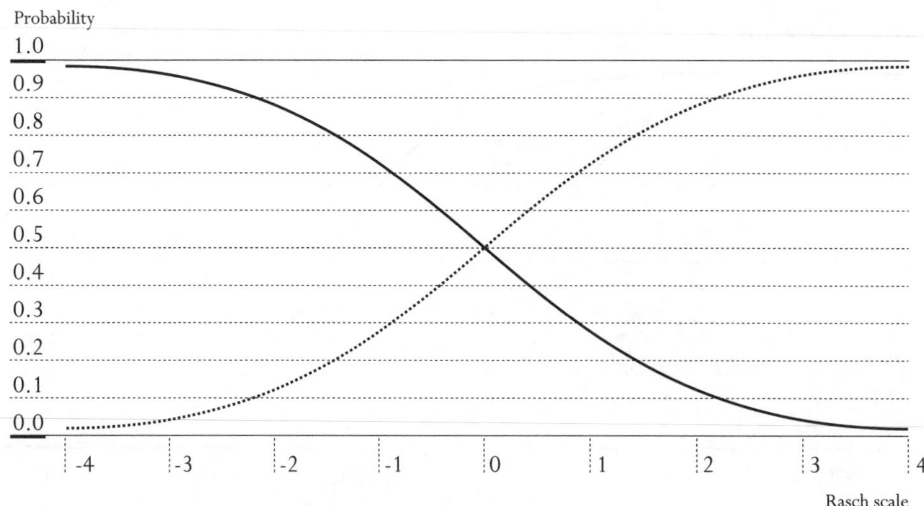

As shown by Figure 4.3, a student with an ability of zero has a probability of 0.5 of success on an item of difficulty zero and a probability of 0.5 of failure. A student with an ability of -2 has a probability of a bit more than 0.10 of success and a probability of a bit less than 0.90 of failure on the same item of difficulty zero. But this student will have a probability of 0.5 of succeeding on an item of difficulty -2.

From a mathematical point of view, the probability that a student i, with an ability denoted β_i, provides a correct answer to item j of difficulty δ_j is equal to:

$$P(X_{ij} = 1 \mid \beta_i, \delta_j) = \frac{\exp(\beta_i - \delta_j)}{1 + \exp(\beta_i - \delta_j)}$$

Similarly, the probability of failure is equal to:

$$P(X_{ij} = 0 \mid \beta_i, \delta_j) = \frac{1}{1 + \exp(\beta_i - \delta_j)}$$

It can be easily shown that:

$$P(X_{ij} = 1 \mid \beta_i, \delta_j) + P(X_{ij} = 0 \mid \beta_i, \delta_j) = 1$$

In other words, the probability of success and the probability of failure always sum to one. Table 4.1 to Table 4.5 present the probability of success for different student abilities and different item difficulties.

Table 4.1 ■ **Probability of success when student ability equals item difficulty**

Student ability	Item difficulty	Probability of success
-2	-2	0.50
-1	-1	0.50
0	0	0.50
1	1	0.50
2	2	0.50

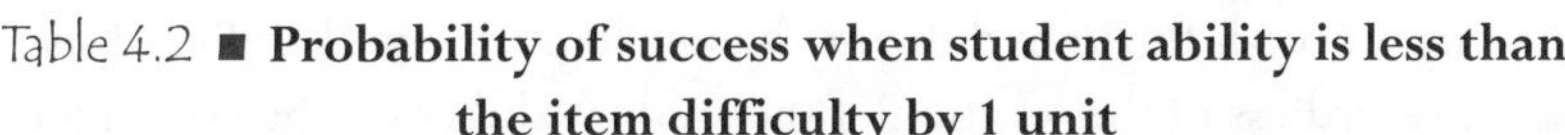

Table 4.2 ■ **Probability of success when student ability is less than the item difficulty by 1 unit**

Student ability	Item difficulty	Probability of success
-2	-1	0.27
-1	0	0.27
0	1	0.27
1	2	0.27
2	3	0.27

Table 4.3 ■ **Probability of success when student ability is greater than the item difficulty by 1 unit**

Student ability	Item difficulty	Probability of success
-2	-3	0.73
-1	-2	0.73
0	-1	0.73
1	0	0.73
2	3	0.73

Table 4.4 ■ **Probability of success when student ability is less than the item difficulty by 2 units**

Student ability	Item difficulty	Probability of success
-2	0	0.12
-1	1	0.12
0	2	0.12
1	3	0.12
2	4	0.12

Table 4.5 ■ **Probability of success when student ability is greater than the item difficulty by 2 units**

Student ability	Item difficulty	Probability of success
-2	-4	0.88
-1	-3	0.88
0	-2	0.88
1	-1	0.88
2	0	0.88

It should be noted that:

- When the student ability is equal to the item difficulty, the probability of success will always be equal to 0.50, regardless of the student ability and item difficulty locations on the continuum.
- If the item difficulty exceeds the student ability by one Rasch unit, denoted as a logit, then the probability of success will always be equal to 0.27, regardless of the location of the student ability on the continuum.

- If the student ability exceeds the item difficulty by one logit, the probability of success will always be equal to 0.73, regardless of the location of the student ability on the continuum.
- If two units separate the student ability and the item difficulty, the probabilities of success will be 0.12 and 0.88 respectively.

From these observations, it is evident that the only factor that influences the probability of success is the distance on the Rasch continuum between the student ability and the item difficulty.

These examples also illustrate the symmetry of the scale. If the student ability is lower than the item difficulty by one logit, then the probability of success will be 0.27 which is 0.23 lower than the probability of success when ability and difficulty are equal. If the student ability is higher than the item difficulty by one logit, the probability of success will be 0.73, which is 0.23 higher than the probability of success when ability and difficulty are equal. Similarly, a difference of two logits generates a change of 0.38.

Item calibration

Of course, in real settings a student's answer will either be correct or incorrect, so what then is the meaning of a probability of 0.5 of success in terms of correct or incorrect answers? In simple terms the following interpretations can be made:

- If 100 students each having an ability of 0 have to answer a item of difficulty 0, then the model will predict 50 correct answers and 50 incorrect answers;
- If a student with an ability of 0 has to answer 100 items, all of difficulty 0, then the model will predict 50 correct answers and 50 incorrect answers.

As described, the Rasch model, through a probabilistic function, builds a relative continuum on which the item's difficulty and the student's ability are located. With the example of high jumpers, the continuum already exists, *i.e.* this is the physical continuum of the meter height. With cognitive data, the continuum has to be built. By analogy, this consists of building a continuum on which the unknown height of the crossbars, *i.e.* the difficulty of the items, will be located. Three major principles underlie the construction of the Rasch continuum.

- The relative difficulty of an item results from the comparison of that item with all other items. Let us suppose that a test consists of only two items. Intuitively, the response pattern (0, 0) and (1, 1) (1 denotes a success and 0 denotes a failure), where the ordered pairs refer to the responses to items 1 and 2, respectively, is uninformative for comparing the two items. The responses in these patterns are identical. On the other hand, responses (1, 0) and (0, 1) are different and are informative on just that comparison. If 50 students have the (0, 1) response pattern and only 10 students have the (1, 0) response pattern, then the second item is substantially easier than the first item. Indeed, 50 students succeeded on the second item while failing the first one and only 10 students succeeded on the first item while failing the second. This means that if one person succeeds on one of these two items, the probability of succeeding on the second item is five times higher than the probability of succeeding on first item. It is, therefore, easier to succeed on the second than it is to succeed on the first. Note that the relative difficulty of the two items is independent of the student abilities.

- As difficulties are determined through comparison of items, this creates a relative scale, and therefore there is an infinite number of scale points. Broadly speaking, the process of overcoming this issue is comparable to the need to create anchor points on the temperature scales. For example, Celsius fixed two reference points: the temperature at which the water freezes and the temperature at which water boils. He labelled the first reference point as 0 and the second reference point at 100 and consequently defined the measurement unit as one-hundredth of the distance between the two reference points. In the case of the Rasch model, the measurement unit is defined by the probabilistic function involving the item difficulty and student ability parameters. Therefore, only one reference point has to be defined. The most common reference point consists of centring the item difficulties on zero. However, other arbitrary reference points can be used, like centring the student's abilities on zero.
- This continuum allows the computation of the relative difficulty of items partly submitted to different sub-populations. Let us suppose that the first, item was administered to all students and the second item was only administered to the low ability students. The comparison of items will only be performed on the subpopulation who was administered both items, *i.e.* the low ability student population. The relative difficulty of the two items will be based on this common subset of students.

Once the item difficulties have been placed on the Rasch continuum, the student scores can be computed. The line in Figure 4.4 represents a Rasch continuum. The item difficulties are located above that line and the item numbers are located below the line. For instance, item 7 represents a difficult item and item 17, an easy item. This test includes a few easy items, a large number of medium difficulty items and a few difficult items. The *x* symbols above the line represent the distribution of the student scores.

Figure 4.4 ■ **Student score and item difficulty distributions on a Rasch continuum**

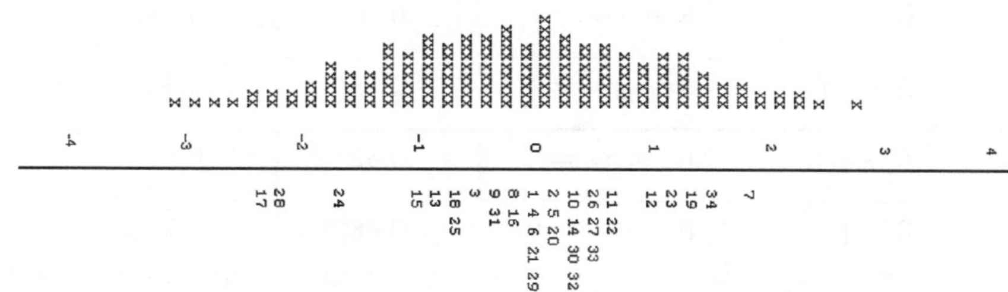

Computation of a student's score

Once the item difficulties have been located on the Rasch scale, student scores can be computed. In a previous section, it was mentioned that the probability that a student i, with an ability denoted β_i , provides a correct answer to item j of difficulty δ_j is equal to:

$$P(X_{ij} = 1 \mid \beta_i, \delta_j) = \frac{\exp(\beta_i - \delta_j)}{1 + \exp(\beta_i - \delta_j)}$$

Similarly, the probability of failure is equal to:

$$P(X_{ij} = 0 \mid \beta_i, \delta_j) = \frac{1}{1 + \exp(\beta_i - \delta_j)}$$

The Rasch model assumes the independence of the items, *i.e.* the probability of a correct answer does not depend on the responses given to the other items. Consequently, the probability of succeeding on two items is equal to the product of the two individual probabilities of success.

Let us consider a test of four items with the following items difficulties: -1, -0.5, 0.5 and 1. There are 16 possible responses patterns. These 16 patterns are presented in Table 4.6.

Table 4.6 ■ **Possible response patterns for a test of four items**

Raw score	Response patterns
0	(0,0,0,0)
1	(1,0,0,0), (0,1,0,0), (0,0,1,0), (0,0,0,1)
2	(1,1,0,0), (1,0,1,0), (1,0,0,1), (0,1,1,0), (0,1,0,1), (0,0,1,1)
3	(1,1,1,0),(1,1,0,1), (1,0,1,1), (0,1,1,1)
4	(1,1,1,1)

For any student ability denoted β_i, it is possible to compute the probability of any response pattern. Let us compute the probability of the response pattern (1,1,0,0) for three students with an ability of -1, 0, and 1.

Table 4.7 ■ **Probability for the response pattern (1,1,0,0) for three student abilities**

			$\beta_i = -1$	$\beta_i = 0$	$\beta_i = 1$
Item 1	$\delta_1 = -1$	Response = 1	0.50	0.73	0.88
Item 2	$\delta_2 = -0.5$	Response = 1	0.38	0.62	0.82
Item 3	$\delta_3 = 0.5$	Response = 0	0.82	0.62	0.38
Item 4	$\delta_4 = 1$	Response = 0	0.88	0.73	0.50
Probability of obtaining response pattern			0.14	0.21	0.14

The probability of success for the first student on the first item is equal to:

$$P(X_{ij} = 1 \mid \beta_i, \delta_j) = P(X_{1,1} = 1 \mid -1, -1) \frac{\exp(-1-(-1))}{1+\exp(-1-(-1))} = 0.5$$

The probability of success for the first student on the second item is equal to:

$$P(X_{ij} = 1 \mid \beta_i, \delta_j) = P(X_{1,2} = 1 \mid -1, -0.5) \frac{\exp(-1-(0.5))}{1+\exp(-1-(-0.5))} = 0.38$$

The probability of failure for the first student on the third item is equal to:

$$P(X_{ij}=0\mid\beta_i,\delta_j)=P(X_{1,3}=0\mid -1,0.5)\frac{1}{1+\exp(-1-0.5)}=0.82$$

The probability of failure for the first student on the fourth item is equal to:

$$P(X_{ij}=0\mid\beta_i,\delta_j)=P(X_{1,4}=0\mid -1,1)\frac{1}{1+\exp(-1-1)}=0.88$$

As these four items are considered as independent, the probability of the response pattern (1,1,0,0) for a student with an ability $\beta_i = -1$ is equal to:

0.50 X 0.38 X 0.82 X 0.88 = 0.14.

Given the item difficulties, a student with an ability $\beta_i = -1$ has 14 chances out of 100 to provide a correct answer to items 1 and 2 and to provide an incorrect answer to items 3 and 4. Similarly, a student with an ability of $\beta_i = 0$ has a probability of 0.21 to provide the same response pattern and a student with an ability of $\beta_i = 1$ has a probability of 0.14.

Figure 4.5 ■ **Response pattern probabilities for the response pattern (1,1,0,0)**

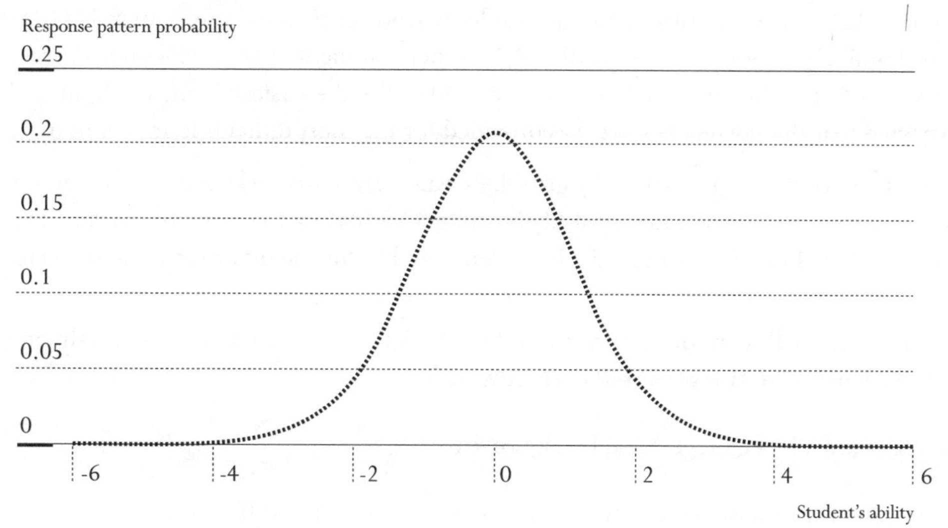

This process can be applied for a large range of student abilities and for all possible response patterns. Figure 4.5 presents the probability of observing the response pattern (1,1,0,0) for all students' abilities between –6 and +6. As shown, the most likely value corresponds to a student ability of 0. Therefore, the Rasch model will estimate the ability of any students with a response pattern (1,1,0,0) to 0.

Figure 4.6 presents the distribution of the probabilities for all response patterns with only one correct item. As shown in Table 4.6, there are four responses patterns with only one correct item, *i.e.* (1,0,0,0), (0,1,0,0), (0,0,1,0), (0,0,0,1).

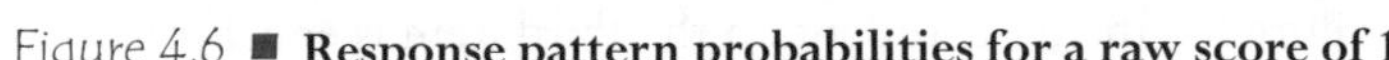

Figure 4.6 ■ **Response pattern probabilities for a raw score of 1**

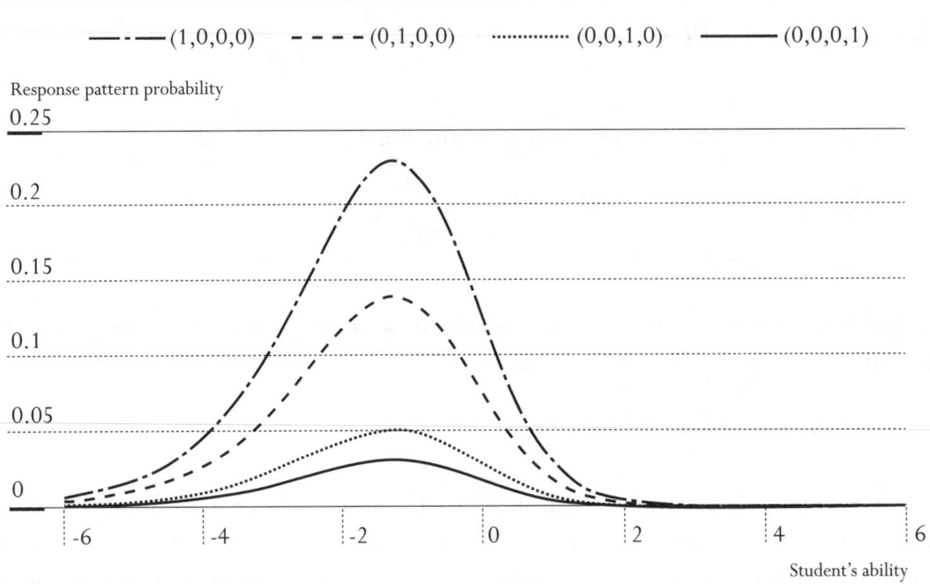

Figure 4.6 clearly shows that:

- The most likely response pattern for any students who succeed on only 1 item is (1,0,0,0) and the most unlikely response pattern is (0,0,0,1). When a student only provides one correct answer, it is expected that the correct answer was provided for the easiest item, *i.e.* item 1. It is also unexpected that this correct answer was provided for the most difficult item, *i.e.* item 4.
- Whatever the response pattern, the most likely value always corresponds to the same value for student ability. For instance, the most likely student ability for the response pattern (1,0,0,0) is around -1.25. This is also the most likely student's ability for the other response patterns.

The Rasch model will therefore return the value -1.25 for any students who get only one correct answer, whichever item was answered correctly.

Similarly, as shown by Figure 4.7 and by Figure 4.8:

- The most likely response pattern with two correct items is (1,1,0,0);
- The most likely student's ability is always the same for any response pattern that includes two correct answers (0 in this case);
- The most likely response pattern with three correct items is (1,1,1,0);
- The most likely student's ability is always the same for any response pattern that includes three correct answers (+1.25 in this case).

This type of Rasch ability estimate is usually denoted the Maximum Likelihood Estimate. As shown by these figures, per raw score, *i.e.* 0 correct answer, one correct answers, two correct answers, and so on, the Rasch model will return only one Maximum Likelihood Estimate.

Figure 4.7 ■ **Response pattern probabilities for a raw score of 2**[a]

(1,1,0,0) (1,0,1,0) (1,0,0,1)
(0,1,1,0) (0,1,0,1) (0,0,1,1)

Response pattern probability
0.25
0.2
0.15
0.1
0.05
0
-6 -4 -2 0 2 4 6
Student's ability

a. In this example, since the likelihood function for the response pattern (1,0,0,1) is perfectly similar to that for response pattern (0,1,1,0), these two lines are overlapped in the figure.

Figure 4.8 ■ **Response pattern probabilities for a raw score of 3**

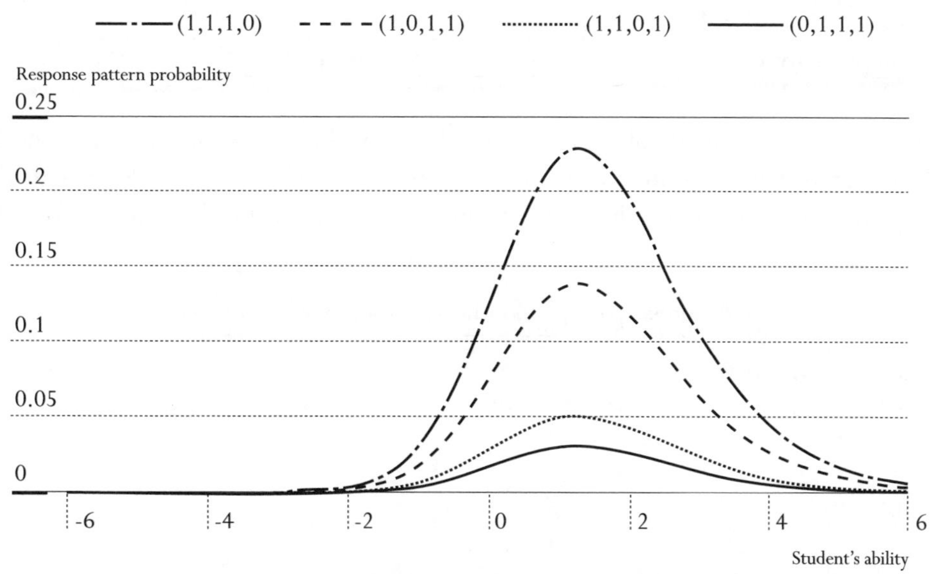

It has been shown that this Maximum Likelihood Estimate (or MLE) is biased and proposed to weight the contribution of each item by the information this item can provide (Warm, 1989). For instance, a difficult item does not provide much information for a low ability student. On the other hand, this item can provide more information for a high ability student. Therefore, for a low ability student, easy items will contribute more than difficult items and similarly, for a high ability student, difficult item will contribute more than easy items. So Warm estimates and MLEs are similar types of student individual ability estimates.

As the Warm estimate corrects the small bias in the MLE, it is usually preferred as the estimate of an individual's ability. Therefore, in the PISA, Weighted Likelihood Estimates (WLEs) are calculated by applying weights to MLE in order to account for the bias inherent in MLE as Warm proposed.

Computation of a student's score for incomplete designs

As stated previously, PISA uses a rotated booklet design for overcoming the conflicting demands of limited student level testing time and the broad coverage of the assessment domain. A testing design where students are assigned a subset of items is denoted as an incomplete design. The principles for computing the student's individual ability estimate described in the previous section are still applicable for incomplete designs.

Let us suppose that two students with abilities of -1 and 1 have to answer two out of the four items presented in Table 4.8. The student with $\beta_i = -1$ has to answer the first two items, *i.e.* the two easiest items and the student with $\beta_i = 1$ has to answer the last two items, *i.e.* the two most difficult items. Both students succeed on their first item and fail on their second item.

Table 4.8 ■ **Probability for the response pattern (1,0) for two students of different ability in an incomplete test design**

			$\beta_i = -1$	$\beta_i = 1$
Item 1	$\delta_1 = -1$	Response = 1	0.50	
Item 2	$\delta_2 = -0.5$	Response = 0	0.62	
Item 3	$\delta_3 = 0.5$	Response = 1		0.62
Item 4	$\delta_4 = 1$	Response = 0		0.50
Response pattern			0.31	0.31

Both patterns have a probability of 0.31 respectively for an ability of -1 and 1. As previously, these probabilities can be computed for a large range of student's abilities. Figure 4.9 presents the (1,0) response pattern probabilities for the easy test (dotted line) and for the difficult test (solid line).

Figure 4.9 ■ **Response pattern likelihood for an easy test and a difficult test**

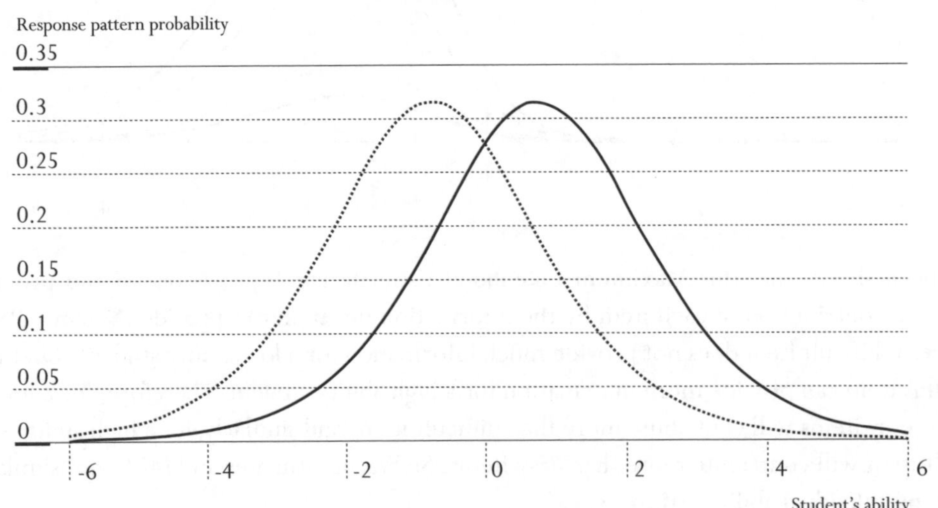

Based on Figure 4.9, we can state that for any student that succeeded on one item of the easy test, the model will estimate the student ability at -0.75 and that for any student that succeed one item of the difficult test, the model will estimate the student ability at 0.75. If raw scores were used as estimates of student ability, in both cases, we would get 1 out of 2, or 0.5.

In summary, the raw score does not take into account the difficulty of the item for the estimation of the raw score and therefore, the interpretation of the raw score depends on the item difficulties. On the other hand, the Rasch model uses the number of correct answers and the difficulties of the items administered to a particular student for his or her ability estimate. Therefore, a Rasch score can be interpreted independently of the item difficulties. As far as all items can be located on the same continuum, the Rasch model can return fully comparable student's ability estimates, even if students were assessed with different subset of items. Note, however, that valid ascertainment of the student's Rasch score depends upon having an accurate knowledge of the item difficulties.

Optimal conditions for linking items

Some conditions have to be satisfied when different tests are used. First of all, the data collected through these tests must be linked. Without any links, the data collected through two different tests cannot be reported on a single scale. Usually, tests are linked by having different students doing common items or having the same students assessed with the different tests.

Let us suppose that a researcher wants to estimate the growth in reading performance between a population of grade 2 students and a population of grade 4 students. Two tests will be developed and both will be targeted at the expected proficiency level of both populations. To ensure that both tests can be scaled on the same continuum, a few difficult items from the grade 2 test will be included in the grade 4 test, let us say items 7, 34, 19, 23 and 12.

Figure 4.10 ■ **Rasch item anchoring**

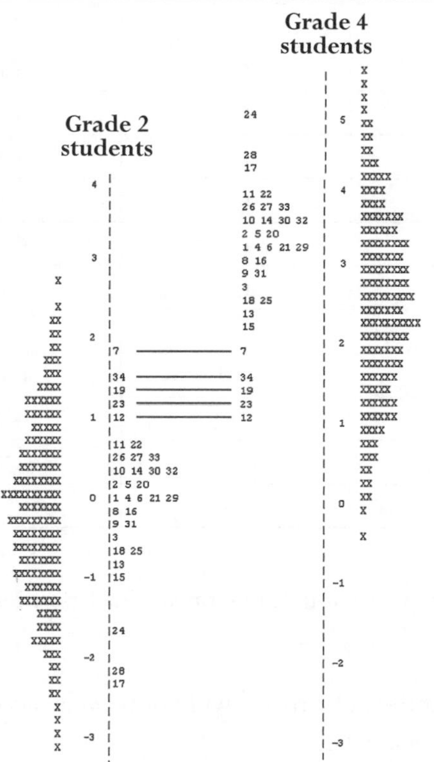

Figure 4.10 represents this item anchoring process. The left part of Figure 4.10 presents the outputs of the scaling of the grade 2 test with items centred on zero. For the scaling of grade 4 data, the reference point will be the grade 2 difficulty of the anchoring items. Then the difficulty of the other grade 4 items will be fixed according to this reference point, as shown on the right side of Figure 4.10.

With this anchoring process grade 2 and grade 4 item difficulties will be located on a single continuum. Therefore, the grade 2 and grade 4 students' ability estimates will also be located on the same continuum.

To accurately estimate the increase between grades 2 and 4, the researcher will ensure that the location of the anchor items is similar in both tests.

From a theoretical point of view, only one item is needed to link two different tests. However, this situation is far from being optimal. A balanced incomplete design presents the best guarantee for reporting the data of different tests on a single scale. This was adopted by PISA 2003 where the item pool was divided into 13 clusters of items. The item allocation to clusters takes into account the expected difficulty of the items and the expected time needed to answer the items. Table 4.9 presents the PISA 2003 test design. Thirteen clusters of items were denoted as C1 to C13 respectively. Thirteen booklets were developed and each of them has four parts, denoted as block 1 to block 4. Each booklet consists of four clusters. For instance, booklet 1 consists of cluster 1, cluster 2, cluster 4 and cluster 10.

Table 4.9 ■ **PISA 2003 test design**

	Block 1	*Block 2*	*Block 3*	*Block 4*
Booklet 1	C1	C2	C4	C10
Booklet 2	C2	C3	C5	C11
Booklet 3	C3	C4	C6	C12
Booklet 4	C4	C5	C7	C13
Booklet 5	C5	C6	C8	C1
Booklet 6	C6	C7	C9	C2
Booklet 7	C7	C8	C10	C3
Booklet 8	C8	C9	C11	C4
Booklet 9	C9	C10	C12	C5
Booklet 10	C10	C11	C13	C6
Booklet 11	C11	C12	C1	C7
Booklet 12	C12	C13	C2	C8
Booklet 13	C13	C1	C3	C9

With such design, each cluster appears four times, once in each position. Further, each pair of clusters appears once and only once.

This design should ensure that the link process will not be influenced by the respective location of the link items in the different booklets.

Extension of the Rasch model

Wright and Masters have generalised the original Rasch model to polytomous items, usually denoted as the partial credit model (Wright and Masters, 1982). With this model, items can be scored as incorrect, partially correct and correct. The PISA cognitive items were calibrated according to this model.

This polytomous items model can also be applied on Likert scale data. There is of course no correct or incorrect answer for such scales but the basic principles are the same: the possible answers can be ordered. PISA questionnaire data are scaled with the one-parameter logistic model for polytomous items.

OTHER ITEM RESPONSE THEORY MODELS

A classical distinction between Item Response Theory models concerns the number of parameters used to describe items. The Rasch model is designated as a one-parameter model because item characteristic curves only depend on the item difficulty. In the three-parameter logistic model, the item characteristic curves depend on: *i)* the item difficulty parameter; *ii)* the item discrimination parameter; and *iii)* what can be termed the "guessing" parameter. This last parameter accounts for the fact that, on a multiple choice test, all students have some chance of answering the item correctly, no matter how difficult the item is.

CONCLUSIONS

The Rasch model was designed to build a symmetric continuum on which both item difficulty and student ability are located. The item difficulty and the student ability are linked by a logistic function. With this function, it is possible to compute the probability that a student succeeds on an item.

Further, due to this probabilistic link, it is not a requirement to administer the whole item battery to every student. If some link items are guaranteed, the Rasch model will be able to create a scale on which every item and every student will be located. This last feature of the Rasch model constitutes one of the major reasons why this model has become fundamental in educational surveys.

Notes

1. See *Measuring Student Knowledge and Skills – A New Framework for Assessment* (OECD, 1999a) and *The PISA 2003 Assessment Framework – Mathematics, Reading, Science and Problem Solving Knowledge and Skills* (OECD, 2003b).

2. The probability of 0.5 was firstly used by psychophysics theories (Guilford, 1954).

Plausible Values

INDIVIDUAL ESTIMATES VERSUS POPULATION ESTIMATES

Education tests can have two major purposes:

- To measure the knowledge and skills of particular students. The performance of each student usually will have an impact on his or her future (school career, admission to post-secondary education, and so on). It is therefore particularly important to minimize the measurement error associated with each individual's estimate.
- To assess the knowledge or skills of a population. The performance of individuals will have no impact on their school career or professional life. In such a case, the goal of reducing error in making inferences about the target population is more important than the goal of reducing error at the individual level.

National or international education surveys belong to the second category.

International surveys such as PISA report student performance through plausible values (PVs).[1] The remainder of this chapter will explain the conceptual meaning of plausible values and the advantage of reporting with them. Individual estimators (such as the WLE defined in Chapter 4) will be compared with PVs for the purposes of estimating a range of population statistics.

THE MEANING OF PLAUSIBLE VALUES

An example taken from the physical sciences, measurement area can help illustrate this complex concept. Suppose that a city board decides to levy a new building tax to increase the city's revenue. This new tax will be proportional to the length of the family house living room. Inspectors visit all city houses to measure the length of the living rooms. They are given a measuring tape and are instructed to record the length in term of integers only, *i.e.* 1 metre, 2 metres, 3 metres, 4 metres and so on.

The results of this measure are shown in Figure 5.1. About 3 per cent of the living rooms have a reported length of 4 metres; slightly over 16 per cent of the living rooms have a reported length of 9 metres and so on.

Figure 5.1 ■ **Living room length expressed in integers**

Of course, the reality is quite different as length is a continuous variable. With a continuous variable, observations can take any value between the minimum and the maximum. On the other hand, with a discontinuous variable, observations can only take a predefined number of values. Figure 5.2 gives the length distribution of the living rooms per reported length.

Figure 5.2 ■ **Real length per reported length**

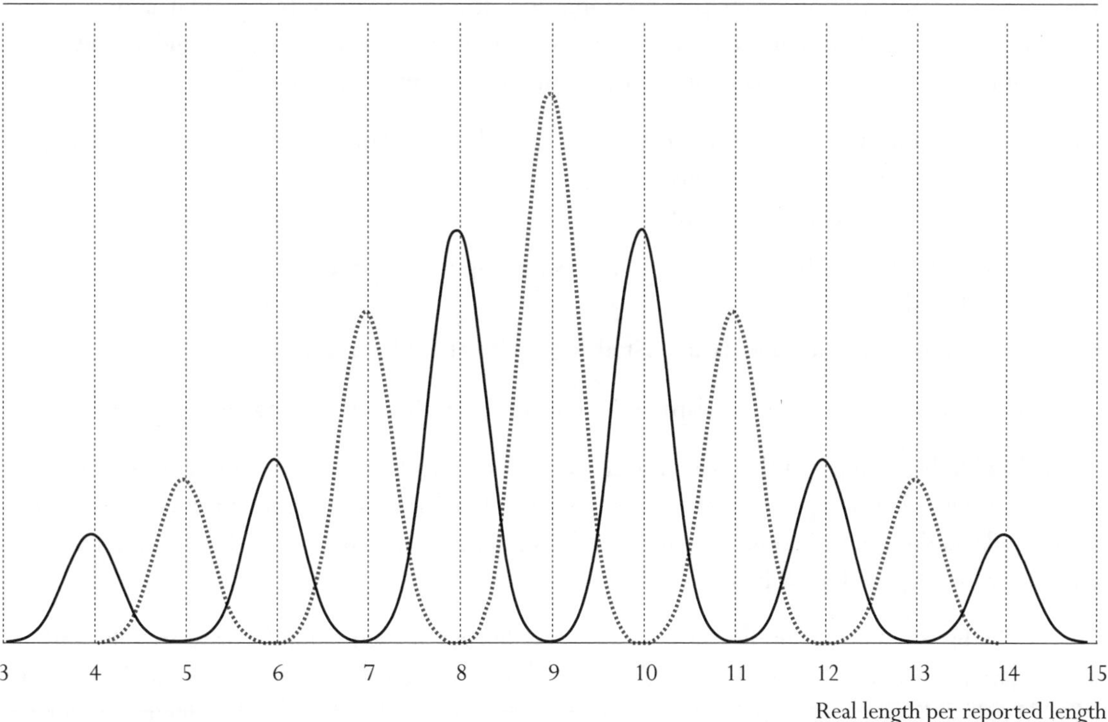

All living rooms with a reported length of 5 metres are not exactly 5 metres long. On average, they are 5 metres long, but their length varies around the mean. The difference between reported length and real length is due to the rounding process and measurement error. An inspector might incorrectly report 5 metres for a particular living room, when it really measures 4.15 metres. If the rounding process were the only source of error, then the reported length should be 4 metres. The second source of error, the error in measuring, explains the overlapping of the distribution.

In this particular example, the lengths of the living rooms are normally distributed around the mean, which is also the reported length. If the difference between the length and the closest integer is small, then the probability of not reporting this length with the closest integer is very small. For instance, it is unlikely that a length of 4.15 will be be reported as 5 metres or 3 metres. However, as the distance between the real length and the closest integer increases, the probability of not reporting this length with the closest integer will also increase. For instance, it is likely that a length of 4.95 will be reported as 5 metres, whereas a length of 4.50 will be reported equally as many times as 4 metres as it is 5 metres.

The methodology of PVs consists of:

- Mathematically computing distributions (denoted as posterior distributions) around the reported values and the reported length in the example; and
- Assigning to each observation a set of random values drawn from the posterior distributions.

PVs can therefore be defined as random values from the posterior distributions. In the example, a living room of 7.154 metres that was reported as 7 metres might be assigned any value from the normal distribution around the reported length of 7. It might be 7.45 as well as 6.55 or 6.95. Therefore, plausible values should not be used for individual estimation.

This fictitious example from the physical sciences can be translated successfully to the social sciences. For example, with a test of 6 dichotomous items, a continuous variable (*i.e.* mental ability) can be transformed into a discontinuous variable. The discontinuous variable will be the student raw score or the number of correct answers. The only possible scores are: 0, 1, 2, 3, 4, 5 and 6.

Contrary to most measures in the physical sciences, psychological or education measures encompass substantial measurement errors because:

- The concept to be measured is broader;
- They might be affected by the mental and physical dispositions of the students on the day of the assessment; and
- The conditions in which students are tested might also affect the results.

This means that there are large overlaps in the posterior distributions, as shown in Figure 5.3.

Further, with the example of the living room, the measurement error of the posterior distributions can be considered as independent of the living room.[2] In education, the measurement error is not always independent of the proficiency level of the students. It may be smaller for average students, and larger for low and high achievers.

Further, in this particular example, the posterior distributions for score 0 and score 6 are substantially skewed, as the posterior distributions of the living rooms with a reported length of 4 and 14 metres would be, if all living rooms smaller than 4 metres were reported as 4 and if all living rooms longer than 14 metres were reported as 14. This means that the posterior distributions are not normally distributed, as shown in Figure 5.3.

Figure 5.3 ■ **A posterior distribution on a test of 6 items**

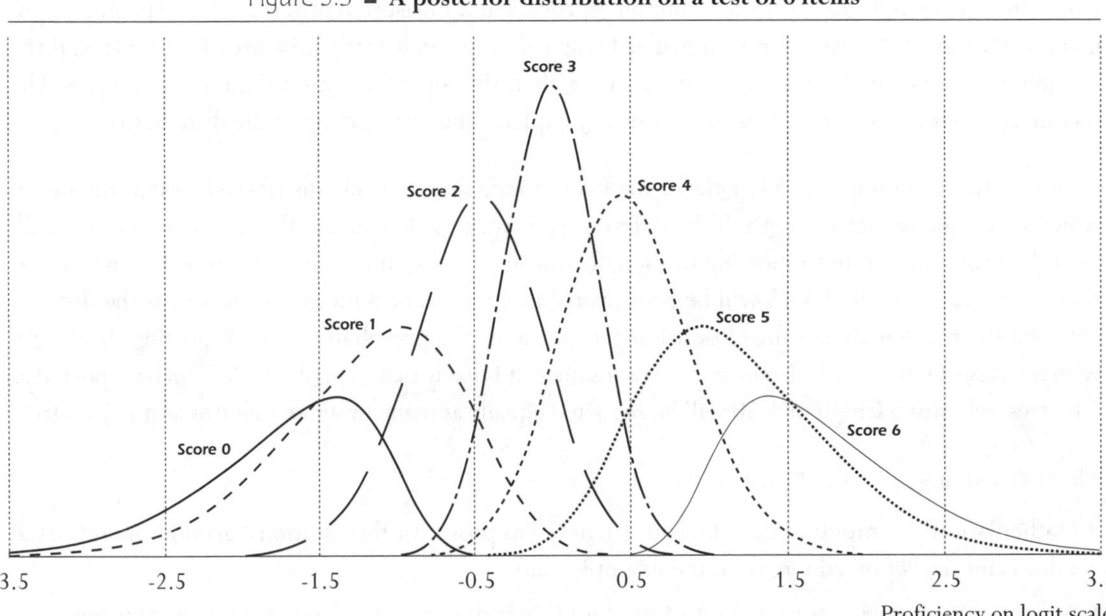

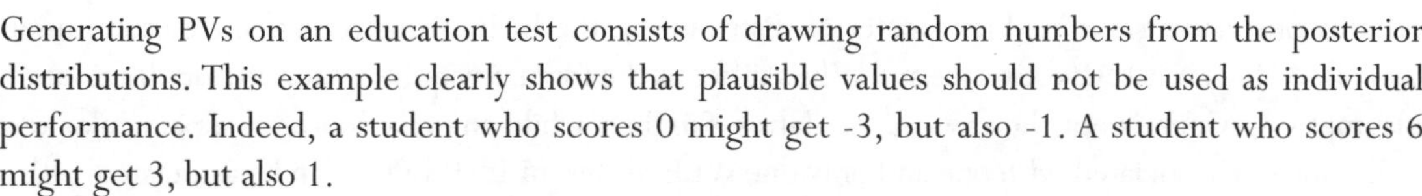

Generating PVs on an education test consists of drawing random numbers from the posterior distributions. This example clearly shows that plausible values should not be used as individual performance. Indeed, a student who scores 0 might get -3, but also -1. A student who scores 6 might get 3, but also 1.

It has been noted that

> The simplest way to describe plausible values is to say that plausible values are a representation of the range of abilities that a student might reasonably have. … Instead of directly estimating a student's ability θ, a probability distribution for a student's θ, is estimated. That is, instead of obtaining a point estimate for θ, (like a WLE), a range of possible values for a student's θ, with an associated probability for each of these values is estimated. Plausible values are random draws from this (estimated) distribution for a student's θ (Wu and Adams, 2002).[3]

All this methodology aims at building a continuum from a collection of discontinuous variables (*i.e.* the test score). It is meant to prevent biased inferences occurring as a result of measuring an unobservable underlying ability through a test using a relatively small number of items.

Finally, an individual estimate of student ability can also be derived from the posterior distributions. This derived individual estimate is called the Expected A Posteriori estimator (EAP). Instead of assigning a set of random values from the posterior distributions, the mean of the posterior distributions is assigned. Therefore, the EAP can be considered as the mean of an infinite set of plausible values for a particular student.

Figure 5.4 ■ **EAP estimators**

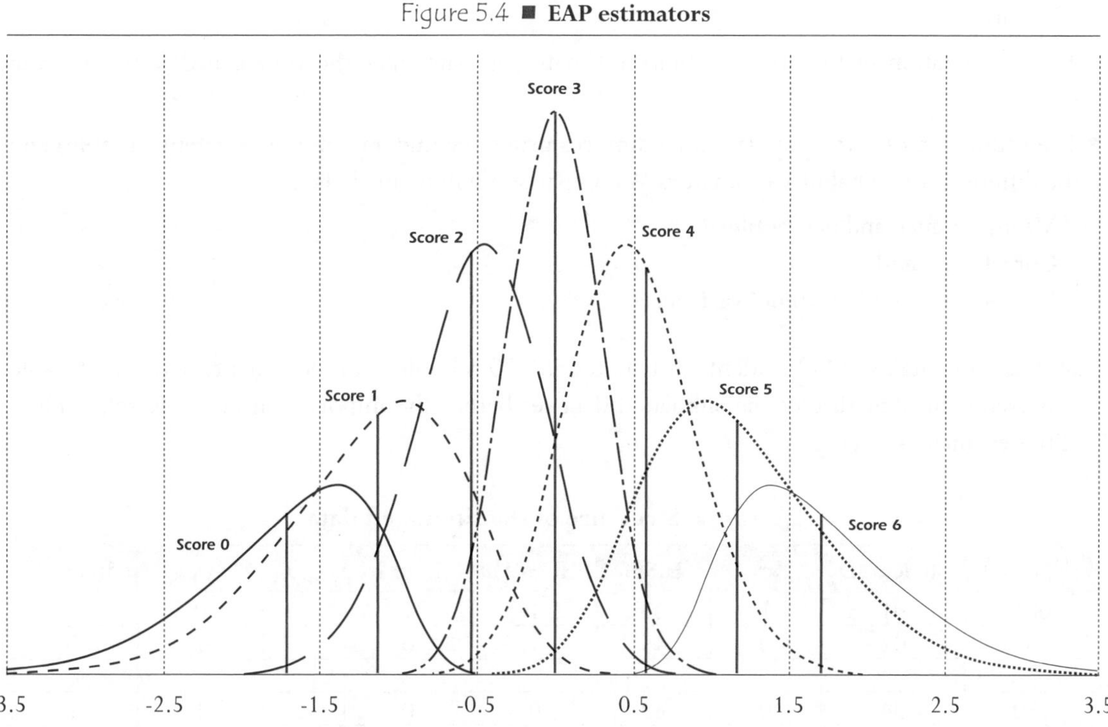

As only one value is assigned per posterior distribution, the EAP estimator is also a discontinuous variable.[4] However, EAP estimates and WLEs differ as the former requires a population distribution assumption, which is not the case for the latter. Further, while any raw score for a particular test will always be associated with one and only one WLE, different EAP values can be associated with a particular raw score, depending on the regressors used as conditioning variables.

Researchers not used to working with plausible values might consider this apparent randomization as a source of imprecision. The comparison of the different types of Rasch ability estimators (WLE, EAP and PVs) through the estimation of population statistics will overcome this perception. Although the PISA 2003 database only includes PVs ,[5] the comparison will incorporate EAP estimates to show biases that occur when data analysts average the plausible values at the student levels to obtain one score value per student.

COMPARISON OF THE EFFICIENCY OF WARM LIKELIHOOD ESTIMATES, EXPECTED A POSTERIORI ESTIMATES AND PVS FOR THE ESTIMATION OF SOME POPULATION STATISTICS[6]

A comparison between different student ability estimators can be performed on real data. Such a comparison will outline differences, but it will not identify the best estimators for a particular population statistic. A simulation can be used to illustrate this:

The simulation consists of three major steps:

- The generation of a data set including a continuous variable that represents the student abilities (*i.e.* denoted as the latent variable), some background variables (including the gender and an index of social background), denoted HISEI, and a pattern of item responses coded 0 for incorrect answer and 1 for a correct answer. The results presented hereafter are based on a fictitious test of 15 items.[7]
- The computation of the student ability estimator, in particular the WLEs, EAP estimates and PVs.[8]
- The estimation of some population parametres using the student ability (*i.e.* latent variable) and the different student ability estimators. A comparison will be made for:
  - Mean, variance and percentiles;
  - Correlation; and
  - Between- and within-school variance.

The data set contains 5 250 students distributed in 150 schools with 35 students per school. Table 5.1 presents the structure of the simulated data set before the importation of the Rasch student abilities estimators.

Table 5.1 ■ **Structure of the simulated data**

School ID	Student ID	Sex	HISEI	Item 1	Item 2	…	Item 14	Item 15
001	01	1	32	1	1		0	0
001	02	0	45	1	0		1	0
…	…							
150	34	0	62	0	0		1	1
150	35	1	50	0	1		1	1

Table 5.2 presents the mean and the variance of the latent variable, the WLEs, the five PVs and the EAP estimates. The average of the five PVs mean is also included.

Table 5.2 ■ **Means and variances for the latent variable and the different student ability estimators**

	Mean	Variance
Latent variable	0.00	1.00
WLE	0.00	1.40
EAP	0.00	0.75
PV1	0.01	0.99
PV2	0.00	0.99
PV3	0.00	1.01
PV4	0.00	1.01
PV5	-0.01	0.00
Average of the 5 PV statistics	0.00	1.00

Table 5.2 shows that a good estimate of the population's mean (*i.e.* the latent variable estimate) is obtained regardless of the type of the latent variable used (WLEs, EAP estimates or PVs). It can be empirically demonstrated that none of the estimates significantly differ from the expected mean, *i.e.* 0.00 in this particular case (Wu and Adams, 2002). Additionally, it can also be shown that the mean of the WLEs will not be biased if the test is well targeted, *i.e.* if the average of the item difficulties is around 0 on the Rasch scale (Wu and Adams, 2002). That is, on a well targeted test, students will obtain a raw score of about 50 per cent correct answers. If the test is too easy then the mean of the WLEs will be underestimated (this is called the ceiling effect), while if it is too difficult then the mean of the WLEs will be overestimated (this is called the floor effect).

These last results explain why the mean of the WLEs provided in the PISA 2000 data base differs from the mean of the plausible values, especially for non OECD countries. For the reading reflecting scale, the means obtained for Canada using WLEs and PVs are respectively 538.4 and 542.5 (*i.e.* very close). In contrast, the means obtained for Peru, using WLEs and PVs are respectively 352.2 and 322.7, which is a difference of about 0.3 standard deviations. There is bias when WLEs are used to estimate the mean, if the test is not well targeted. This comparison cannot be performed on the PISA 2003 database as it only reports student performance with plausible values.

For the population variance, Table 5.2 shows that PVs give estimates closest to the expected value, while WLEs overestimate it and the EAP underestimates it. These results are consistent with other simulation studies.

Table 5.3 presents some percentiles computed on the different ability estimators. For example, because the variance computed using plausible values is not biased, the percentiles based on PVs are also unbiased. However, because the EAP estimates and WLEs variances are biased, the percentiles and in particular extreme percentiles will also be biased. These results are consistent with other simulation studies previously cited.

Table 5.4 presents the correlation between the social background index (HISEI), gender and the latent variables and the different estimators of students' abilities. The correlation coefficients with the WLEs are both underestimated, while the correlation coefficients with the EAP estimates are overestimated. Only the correlation coefficients with the plausible values are unbiased.[9]

Table 5.3 ■ **Percentiles for the latent variable and the different student ability estimators**

	P5	P10	P25	P50	P75	P90	P95
Latent variable	-1.61	-1.26	-0.66	0.01	0.65	1.26	1.59
WLE	-2.15	-1.65	-0.82	-0.1	0.61	1.38	1.81
EAP	-1.48	-1.14	-0.62	-0.02	0.55	1.08	1.37
PV1	-1.68	-1.29	-0.71	-0.03	0.64	1.22	1.59
PV2	-1.67	-1.31	-0.69	-0.03	0.62	1.22	1.58
PV3	-1.67	-1.32	-0.70	-0.02	0.64	1.21	1.56
PV4	-1.69	-1.32	-0.69	-0.03	0.63	1.23	1.55
PV5	-1.65	-1.3	-0.71	-0.02	0.62	1.2	1.55
Average of the 5 PV statistics	-1.67	-1.31	-0.70	-0.03	0.63	1.22	1.57

Table 5.4 ■ **Correlation between HISEI, GENDER and the latent variable, the different student ability estimators**

	HISEI	GENDER
Latent variable	0.40	0.16
WLE	0.33	0.13
EAP	0.46	0.17
PV1	0.41	0.15
PV2	0.42	0.15
PV3	0.42	0.13
PV4	0.40	0.15
PV5	0.40	0.14
Average of the 5 PV statistics	0.41	0.14

It should be noted that the regression coefficients are all unbiased for the different types of estimators. Nevertheless, as variances are biased for some estimators, residual variances will also be biased. Therefore, the standard error on the regression coefficients will be biased in the case of the WLEs and the EAP estimates.

Finally, Table 5.5 presents the between- and within-school variances. Between-school variances for the different estimators do not differ from the expected value of 0.33. However, WLEs overestimate the within school variance, while the EAP estimates underestimate it. These results are consistent with other simulation studies (Monseur and Adams, 2002).

As this example shows, PVs provide unbiased estimates.

HOW TO PERFORM ANALYSES WITH PLAUSIBLE VALUES

As stated in the previous section, a set of PVs, usually five, are drawn for each student for each scale or subscale. Population statistics should be estimated using each plausible value separately. The reported population statistic is then the average of each plausible value statistic. For instance, if

Table 5.5 ■ **Between- and within-school variances**

	Between-school variance	Within-school variance
Latent variable	0.33	0.62
WLE	0.34	1.02
EAP	0.35	0.38
PV1	0.35	0.61
PV2	0.36	0.60
PV3	0.36	0.61
PV4	0.35	0.61
PV5	0.35	0.61
Average of the 5 PV statistics	0.35	0.61

one is interested in the correlation coefficient between the social index and the reading performance in PISA, then five correlation coefficients should be computed and then averaged.

Data analysts should never average the plausible values at the student level, *i.e.* computing in the data set the mean of the five plausible values at the student level and then computing the statistic of interest once using that average PV value. Doing so would be equivalent to an EAP estimate, with a bias as described in the previous section.

Mathematically, secondary analyses with plausible values can be described as follows. If θ is the population statistic and θ_i is the statistic of interest computed on one plausible value, then:

$\theta = \frac{1}{M}\sum_{i=1}^{M}\theta_i$, with M being the number of plausible values.

The plausible values also allow computing the uncertainty in the estimate of θ due to the lack of precision of the measurement test. If a perfect test could be developed, then the measurement error would be equal to zero and the five statistics from the plausible values would be exactly identical. Unfortunately, perfect tests do not exist and never will. This measurement variance, usually denoted imputation variance, is equal to:

$$B_M = \frac{1}{M-1}\sum_{i=1}^{M}(\theta_i - \theta)^2$$

It corresponds to the variance of the five plausible value statistics of interest. The final stage is to combine the sampling variance and the imputation variance as follows:

$V = U + \left(1 + \frac{1}{M}\right)B_M$, with U being the sampling variance.

In the following chapters, we will show how to compute sampling variances and imputation variances and how to combine them, using the PISA 2003 database.

CONCLUSIONS

This chapter was devoted to the meaning of the plausible values and the steps that are required when analysing data with PVs. A comparison between PVs and alternate individual ability estimates was presented to convince PISA data users of the superiority of this methodology for reporting population estimates.

Notes

1. The methodology of PVs was first implemented in NAEP studies (see Beaton, 1987).
2. The measurement error will be independent of the length of the living rooms if the inspectors are using a measuring instrument that is at least 15 metres long (such as a measuring tape). If they are using a standard metre, then the overall measurement error will be proportional to the length of the living room.
3. The probability distribution for a student's θ can be based on the cognitive data only, *i.e.* the item response pattern, but can also include additional information, such as student gender, social background, and so on. The probability distribution becomes therefore conditioned by this additional information. A mathematical explanation of the model used for the scaling of the PISA 2000 scaling can be found in the *PISA 2000 Technical Report* (OECD, 2002c).
4. If several regressors are used as conditioning variables, then the EAP estimator tends to a continuous variable.
5. PISA 2000 data files include both WLEs and PVs.
6. PVs and EAP estimators can be computed with or without regressors. As the PISA 2000 PVs were generated based on all variables collected through the student questionnaires, this comparison will only include PVs and EAP estimators with the use of regressors.
7. The data generation starts with a factorial analysis on a 3 by 3 squared correlation matrix. The correlation between the latent variable and gender was set at 0.20, the correlation between the latent variable and the social background indicator was set at 0.40 and the correlation between gender and the social background indicator was set at 0.00. Three random variables are drawn from normal distributions and combined according to the factorial regression coefficients to create the three variables of interest, *i.e.* reading, gender and social background. Based on the student score on the latent variable and a predefined set of 20 item difficulties; probabilities of success are computed according to the Rasch model. These probabilities are then compared to uniform distribution and recoded into 0 and 1. Finally, gender is recoded into a dichotomous variable.
8. The estimators were computed with the Conquest Software developed by M.L. Wu, R.J Adams and M.R. Wilson.
9. The results on the EAP and PV correlation coefficients are observed when the probability distributions are generated with conditioning variables. Without the conditioning, the correlation with the plausible values would be underestimated.

Computation of Standard Errors

INTRODUCTION

As shown in Chapter 3, replicates have to be used for the computation of the standard error for any population estimate. This chapter will give examples of such computations.

For PISA 2000 and PISA 2003, the Fay's variant of the Balanced Repeated Replication is used. The general formula for computing the sampling variance with this method is:

$$\sigma^2_{(\hat{\theta})} = \frac{1}{G(1-k)^2}\sum_{i=1}^{G}(\hat{\theta}_{(i)} - \hat{\theta})^2$$

Since the PISA databases include 80 replicates and since the Fay coefficient was set to 0.5 for both data collections, the above formula can be simplified as follows:

$$\sigma^2_{(\hat{\theta})} = \frac{1}{G(1-k)^2}\sum_{i=1}^{G}(\hat{\theta}_{(i)} - \hat{\theta})^2 = \frac{1}{80(1-0.5)^2}\sum_{i=1}^{80}(\hat{\theta}_{(i)} - \hat{\theta})^2 = \frac{1}{20}\sum_{i=1}^{80}(\hat{\theta}_{(i)} - \hat{\theta})^2$$

THE STANDARD ERROR ON UNIVARIATE STATISTICS FOR NUMERICAL VARIABLES

To compute the mean and its respective standard error, it is necessary to first compute this statistic by weighting the data with the student final weight, *i.e.* W_FSTUWT, and then to compute 80 other means, each of them by weighting the data with one of the 80 replicates, *i.e.* W_FSTR1 to W_FSTR80.

Box 6.1 presents the SAS® syntax for computing these 81 means based on the social background index (denoted HISEI for the PISA 2003 data for Germany) and Table 6.1 presents the HISEI final estimates as well as the 80 replicate estimates.

Box 6.1 ■ **SAS® syntax for the computation of 81 means**

```
libname PISA2003  "c:\pisa2003\data\";
options nofmterr notes;
run;

DATA temp;
        set pisa2003.stud;
        if (cnt="DEU");
        keep cnt schoolid stidstd w_fstuwt w_fstr1-w_fstr80 hisei;
RUN;
PROC MEANS DATA=temp VARDEF=WGT;
        VAR hisei;
        WEIGHT w_fstuwt;
RUN;
PROC MEANS DATA=temp VARDEF=WGT;
        VAR hisei;
        WEIGHT w_fstr1;
RUN;
PROC MEANS DATA=temp VARDEF=WGT;
        VAR hisei;
        WEIGHT w_fstr2;
RUN;
:
PROC MEANS DATA=temp VARDEF=WGT;
        VAR hisei;
        WEIGHT w_fstr79;
RUN;
PROC MEANS DATA=temp VARDEF=WGT;
        VAR hisei;
        WEIGHT w_fstr80;
RUN;
```


Table 6.1 ■ **HISEI mean estimates**

Weight	Mean estimate	Weight	Mean estimate
Final weight	**49.33**		
Replicate 1	49.44	Replicate 41	49.17
Replicate 2	49.18	Replicate 42	49.66
Replicate 3	49.12	Replicate 43	49.18
Replicate 4	49.46	Replicate 44	49.04
Replicate 5	49.24	Replicate 45	49.42
Replicate 6	49.34	Replicate 46	49.72
Replicate 7	49.13	Replicate 47	49.48
Replicate 8	49.08	Replicate 48	49.14
Replicate 9	49.54	Replicate 49	49.57
Replicate 10	49.20	Replicate 50	49.36
Replicate 11	49.22	Replicate 51	48.78
Replicate 12	49.12	Replicate 52	49.53
Replicate 13	49.33	Replicate 53	49.27
Replicate 14	49.47	Replicate 54	49.23
Replicate 15	49.40	Replicate 55	49.62
Replicate 16	49.30	Replicate 56	48.96
Replicate 17	49.24	Replicate 57	49.54
Replicate 18	48.85	Replicate 58	49.14
Replicate 19	49.41	Replicate 59	49.27
Replicate 20	48.82	Replicate 60	49.42
Replicate 21	49.46	Replicate 61	49.56
Replicate 22	49.37	Replicate 62	49.75
Replicate 23	49.39	Replicate 63	48.98
Replicate 24	49.23	Replicate 64	49.00
Replicate 25	49.47	Replicate 65	49.35
Replicate 26	49.51	Replicate 66	49.27
Replicate 27	49.35	Replicate 67	49.44
Replicate 28	48.89	Replicate 68	49.08
Replicate 29	49.44	Replicate 69	49.09
Replicate 30	49.34	Replicate 70	49.15
Replicate 31	49.41	Replicate 71	49.29
Replicate 32	49.18	Replicate 72	49.29
Replicate 33	49.50	Replicate 73	49.08
Replicate 34	49.12	Replicate 74	49.25
Replicate 35	49.05	Replicate 75	48.93
Replicate 36	49.40	Replicate 76	49.45
Replicate 37	49.20	Replicate 77	49.13
Replicate 38	49.54	Replicate 78	49.45
Replicate 39	49.32	Replicate 79	49.14
Replicate 40	49.35	Replicate 80	49.27

The mean that will be reported is equal to 49.33, *i.e.* the estimate obtained with the student final weight W_FSTUWT. The 80 replicate estimates are just used to compute the standard error on the mean of 49.33.

There are three major steps for the computation of the standard error:

1. Each replicate estimate will be compared with the final estimate 49.33 and the difference will be squared. Mathematically, it corresponds to $(\hat{\theta}_{(i)} - \hat{\theta})^2$ or in this particular case, $(\hat{\mu}_i - \hat{\mu})^2$. For the first replicate, it will be equal to: $(49.44 - 49.33)^2 = 0.0140$. For the second replicate, it corresponds to: $(49.18 - 49.33)^2 = 0.0228$. Table 6.2 presents the squared differences.

2. The sum of the squared differences is computed, and then divided by 20. Mathematically, it

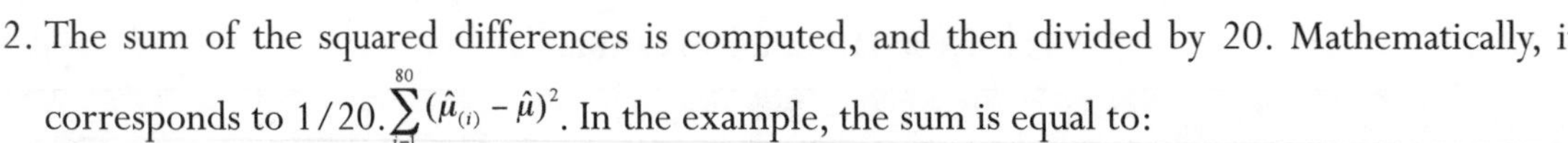

corresponds to $1/20.\sum_{i=1}^{80}(\hat{\mu}_{(i)}-\hat{\mu})^2$. In the example, the sum is equal to:

(0.0140 + 0.0228 + … + 0.0354 + 0.0031) = 3.5195

The sum divided by 20 is therefore equal to 3.5159/20 = 0.1760. This value represents the sampling variance on the mean estimate for HISEI.

3. The standard error is equal to the square root of the sampling variance, *i.e.* :

$$\sigma_{(\hat{\mu})} = \sqrt{\sigma^2_{(\hat{\mu})}} = \sqrt{0.1760} = 0.4195$$

This means that the sampling distribution on the HISEI mean for Germany has a standard deviation of 0.4195. This value also allows building a confidence interval around this mean. With a risk of type I error equal to 0.05, usually denoted α, the confidence interval will be equal to:

[49.33 – (1.96*0.4195);49.33 + (1.96*0.4195)]

[48.51;50.15]

Table 6.2 ■ **Squared differences between replicate estimates and the final estimate**

Weight	Squared difference	Weight	Squared difference
Replicate 1	0.0140	Replicate 41	0.0239
Replicate 2	0.0228	Replicate 42	0.1090
Replicate 3	0.0421	Replicate 43	0.0203
Replicate 4	0.0189	Replicate 44	0.0818
Replicate 5	0.0075	Replicate 45	0.0082
Replicate 6	0.0002	Replicate 46	0.1514
Replicate 7	0.0387	Replicate 47	0.0231
Replicate 8	0.0583	Replicate 48	0.0349
Replicate 9	0.0472	Replicate 49	0.0590
Replicate 10	0.0167	Replicate 50	0.0014
Replicate 11	0.0124	Replicate 51	0.3003
Replicate 12	0.0441	Replicate 52	0.0431
Replicate 13	0.0000	Replicate 53	0.0032
Replicate 14	0.0205	Replicate 54	0.0086
Replicate 15	0.0048	Replicate 55	0.0868
Replicate 16	0.0009	Replicate 56	0.1317
Replicate 17	0.0074	Replicate 57	0.0438
Replicate 18	0.2264	Replicate 58	0.0354
Replicate 19	0.0077	Replicate 59	0.0034
Replicate 20	0.2604	Replicate 60	0.0081
Replicate 21	0.0182	Replicate 61	0.0563
Replicate 22	0.0016	Replicate 62	0.1761
Replicate 23	0.0041	Replicate 63	0.1173
Replicate 24	0.0093	Replicate 64	0.1035
Replicate 25	0.0199	Replicate 65	0.0008
Replicate 26	0.0344	Replicate 66	0.0030
Replicate 27	0.0007	Replicate 67	0.0139
Replicate 28	0.1919	Replicate 68	0.0618
Replicate 29	0.0139	Replicate 69	0.0557
Replicate 30	0.0001	Replicate 70	0.0324
Replicate 31	0.0071	Replicate 71	0.0016
Replicate 32	0.0215	Replicate 72	0.0011
Replicate 33	0.0302	Replicate 73	0.0603
Replicate 34	0.0411	Replicate 74	0.0052
Replicate 35	0.0778	Replicate 75	0.1575
Replicate 36	0.0052	Replicate 76	0.0157
Replicate 37	0.0150	Replicate 77	0.0378
Replicate 38	0.0445	Replicate 78	0.0155
Replicate 39	0.0000	Replicate 79	0.0354
Replicate 40	0.0004	Replicate 80	0.0031
		Sum of squared differences	3.5195

In other words, there are 5 chances out of 100 that an interval formed in this way will fail to capture the population mean. It also means that the German population mean for HISEI is significantly different from, for example, a value of 51, as this number is not included in the confidence interval.

Chapter 9 will show how this standard error can be used for comparisons either between two or several countries, or between sub-populations within a particular country.

THE SAS® MACRO FOR COMPUTING THE STANDARD ERROR ON A MEAN

Writing all the SAS® syntax to compute these 81 means and then transferring them into an Microsoft® Excel® spreadsheet to finally obtain the standard error would be very time consuming. Fortunately, SAS® macros simplify iterative computations. The software package will execute N times the commands included between the beginning command (DO I=1 TO N) and the ending command (END). Further, it also saves the results in a temporary file that can be used subsequently for the computation of the standard error.

About 10 SAS® macros have been written to simplify the main PISA computations. These macros have been saved in different files (with the extension .sas). Box 6.2 shows a SAS® syntax where a macro is called for computing the mean and standard error of the variable HISEI.

Box 6.2 ■ **SAS® syntax for the computation of the mean of HISEI and its respective standard error**

```
libname PISA2003  "c:\pisa2003\data\";
options nofmterr notes;
run;

%include "c:\pisa2003\prg\macro_procmeans_nopv.sas";

data temp;
     set pisa2003.stud;
     if (cnt="DEU") ;
     w_fstr0=w_fstuwt;
     keep  cnt schoolid stidstd hisei bsmj st01q01 st03q01
                w_fstr0-w_fstr80 ;
run;

%BRR_PROCMEAN(INFILE=temp,
          REPLI_ROOT=w_fstr,
          BYVAR=cnt,
          VAR=hisei,
          STAT=mean,
          OUTFILE=exerciseA);
run;

proc print data=exerciseA;
     var cnt stat sestat;
run;
```

After the definition of the SAS® library and a few options, the command (`%include "c:\pisa2003\prg\macro_procmeans_nopv.sas";`) will create and save a new procedure for later use.

The "`data`" statement will create a temporary file by selecting from the PISA 2000 student database, the data for Germany (`if (cnt="DEU")`). To facilitate the iterative process, the final weight, W_FSTUWT, is recoded with the same replicate root, *i.e.* W_FSTR. The number 0 is added after this root to avoid any possible confusion with the 80 replicates.

As these iterative computations might be CPU consuming, it is advised to reduce the size of the input database by selecting the variables requested to perform a set of analyses. This can be easily done by the KEEP statement. In the example:

- The three international identification variables are kept, *i.e.*
  - CNT for the alphanumerical country code;
  - SCHOOLID for the alphanumerical school code; and
  - STIDSTD for the alphanumerical student code.
- The socio-economic index, denoted HISEI;
- The 81 final and replicate weights; and
- A few other variables that will be used later in this chapter.

The next six lines call the macro. Six pieces of information need to be provided:

- The input data file (`INFILE=temp`);
- The root of the final and replicate weights (`REPLI_ROOT=w_fstr`);
- One or several breakdown variables (`BYVAR=cnt`);
- The variable on which an estimate and its respective standard error will be computed (`VAR=hisei`);
- The requested statistic (`STAT=mean`); and
- The output data file in which the estimates and their respective standard errors will be stored (`OUTFILE=exerciseA`).

From the temporary input data file denoted '*temp*', this macro will compute per country the mean of HISEI and its standard error by using the 81 final and replicate weights denoted W_FSTR0 to W_FSTR80. The results will be stored in a file that will be labeled '*exercise1*'. This macro will return exactly the same values for the mean estimate and its respective standard error as the ones obtained through Table 6.1 and Table 6.2.

The structure of the output data file is presented in Table 6.3.

Table 6.3 ■ **Structure of the output data file *exerciseA***

CNT	STAT	SESTAT
DEU	49.33	0.42

If the data set had not been reduced to the data for Germany, then the number of rows in the output data file would be equal to the number of countries in the database.

There are a few restrictions as well as a few options with this macro:

- Only one input data file can be specified;
- The final and the replicate weights need to have the same root. The final weight will be assigned the number 0 while the 80 replicates, as already defined in the data set will range from 1 to 80;
- Several breakdown variables can be specified. For instance, if results per gender are needed, then the breakdown variables will be CNT and ST03Q01 (`BYVAR=cnt st03q01`);
- Only one numerical variable can be specified in the VAR statement;

- Only one statistic can be specified. The available statistics are presented in Table 6.4; and
- Only one output data file can be specified.

Table 6.4 ■ **Available statistics with the PROCMEANS_NOPV macro**[a]

Statistics available	Meaning
SUMWGT	Sum of the weight
MEAN	Mean
VAR	Variance
STD	Standard deviation
CV	Coefficient of variation
MEDIAN	Median
Q1	First quartile
Q3	Third quartile
QRANGE	Range between Q1 and Q3
Px	Percentile, with x between 1 and 99

a. Some other statistics are also available through the Proc Means procedure in SAS®, such as the minimum, the maximum, the range, the number of observations, and so on. Nevertheless, they are not included in the table, either because it does not make sense to apply these statistics on the PISA data, or because Fay's method cannot be applied on these statistics. For instance, as no weights are set to 0 in any replicates, the minimum or maximum value for a particular variable will always be the same. Therefore, the macro will return the value of 0, which is meaningless.

Box 6.3 presents the syntax for the computation of the standard deviation per gender and Table 6.5 the structure of the output data base.

Box 6.3 ■ **SAS® syntax for the computation of the standard deviation of HISEI and its respective standard error per gender**

```
/*Selecting only non missing data is optional*/
data temp;
     set temp;
     if (not missing (st03Q01));
run;
%BRR_PROCMEAN(INFILE=temp,
              REPLI_ROOT=w_fstr,
              BYVAR=cnt ST03Q01,
              VAR=hisei,
              STAT=std,
              OUTFILE=exerciseB);
run;
```

Table 6.5 ■ **Structure of the output data file *exerciseB***

CNT	ST03Q01	STAT	SESTAT
DEU	1	16.12	0.29
DEU	2	16.34	0.23

THE STANDARD ERROR ON PERCENTAGES

For variables such as gender, the statistic of interest is usually the percentage per category. The procedure for estimating the standard error is identical to the procedure used for the estimation of the standard error on a mean or a standard deviation, *i.e.* per category of the variable, 81 percentages have to be computed.

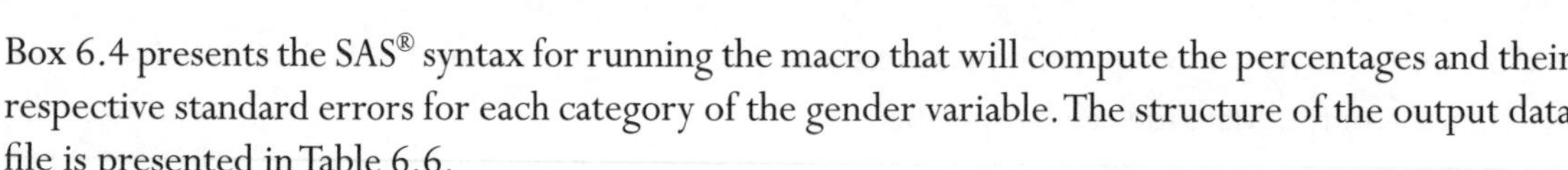

Box 6.4 presents the SAS® syntax for running the macro that will compute the percentages and their respective standard errors for each category of the gender variable. The structure of the output data file is presented in Table 6.6.

Box 6.4 ■ **SAS® syntax for the computation of percentages and their respective standard error for gender**

```
%include "c:\pisa2003\prg\macro_freq_nopv.sas";

%BRR_FREQ(INFILE=temp,
          REPLI_ROOT=w_fstr,
          BYVAR=cnt,
          VAR=ST03Q01,
          OUTFILE=exerciseC);
run;
```

Table 6.6 ■ **Structure of the output data file *exerciseC***

CNT	ST03Q01	STAT	SESTAT
DEU	1	49.66	1.04
DEU	2	50.34	1.04

Table 6.7 presents the estimates of the percentage of girls for the 81 weights and the squared differences. The percentage of girls that will be reported is equal to 49.66, *i.e.* the percentage obtained with the final student weight.

As previously, there are three major steps for the computation of the standard error:

1. Each replicate estimate will be compared with the final estimate 49.66 and the difference will be squared. Mathematically, it corresponds to $(\hat{\pi}_{(i)} - \hat{\pi})^2$. For the first replicate, it will be equal to: $(49.82 - 49.66)^2 = 0.0256$.

2. The sum of the squared differences is computed, and then divided by 20. Mathematically, it corresponds to $1/20.\sum_{i=1}^{80}(\hat{\pi}_{(i)} - \hat{\pi})^2$. In the example, the sum is equal to:

   $(0.0252 + 0.1044 + \ldots + 0.3610 + 0.1313) = 21.4412$

   The sum divided by 20 is therefore equal to $\frac{21.4412}{20} = 1.07206$. This value represents the sampling variance on the percentage estimate of girls.

3. The standard error is equal to the square root of the sampling variance, *i.e.*

$$\sigma_{(\hat{\pi})} = \sqrt{\sigma^2_{(\hat{\pi})}} = \sqrt{1.07206} = 1.035$$

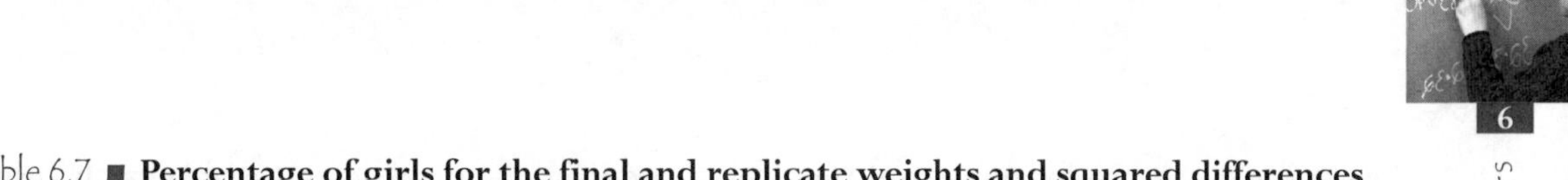

Table 6.7 ■ **Percentage of girls for the final and replicate weights and squared differences**

Weight	% Estimate	Squared difference	Weight	% Estimate	Squared difference
Final weight	**49.66**				
Replicate 1	49.82	0.03	Replicate 41	50.00	0.11
Replicate 2	49.98	0.10	Replicate 42	49.95	0.09
Replicate 3	49.44	0.05	Replicate 43	49.70	0.00
Replicate 4	49.32	0.11	Replicate 44	50.59	0.87
Replicate 5	49.39	0.07	Replicate 45	49.07	0.35
Replicate 6	49.06	0.36	Replicate 46	48.82	0.71
Replicate 7	48.59	1.14	Replicate 47	49.88	0.05
Replicate 8	48.85	0.66	Replicate 48	49.14	0.27
Replicate 9	49.06	0.36	Replicate 49	49.53	0.02
Replicate 10	49.72	0.00	Replicate 50	49.81	0.02
Replicate 11	50.05	0.15	Replicate 51	49.87	0.04
Replicate 12	49.31	0.13	Replicate 52	49.82	0.02
Replicate 13	49.29	0.13	Replicate 53	49.42	0.06
Replicate 14	49.47	0.04	Replicate 54	48.99	0.45
Replicate 15	49.90	0.06	Replicate 55	50.07	0.17
Replicate 16	50.82	1.35	Replicate 56	50.68	1.04
Replicate 17	49.11	0.30	Replicate 57	50.34	0.46
Replicate 18	49.51	0.02	Replicate 58	49.54	0.02
Replicate 19	49.79	0.02	Replicate 59	48.75	0.83
Replicate 20	50.75	1.18	Replicate 60	50.14	0.23
Replicate 21	50.24	0.33	Replicate 61	49.45	0.05
Replicate 22	49.79	0.02	Replicate 62	49.46	0.04
Replicate 23	49.87	0.04	Replicate 63	50.11	0.20
Replicate 24	49.37	0.08	Replicate 64	49.64	0.00
Replicate 25	49.50	0.02	Replicate 65	49.72	0.00
Replicate 26	49.82	0.02	Replicate 66	50.79	1.27
Replicate 27	49.92	0.07	Replicate 67	49.73	0.00
Replicate 28	49.55	0.01	Replicate 68	49.96	0.09
Replicate 29	50.22	0.31	Replicate 69	50.31	0.42
Replicate 30	49.16	0.25	Replicate 70	49.17	0.24
Replicate 31	50.51	0.73	Replicate 71	50.10	0.19
Replicate 32	49.98	0.10	Replicate 72	49.93	0.07
Replicate 33	50.67	1.02	Replicate 73	49.55	0.01
Replicate 34	49.29	0.13	Replicate 74	49.42	0.06
Replicate 35	48.96	0.49	Replicate 75	49.60	0.00
Replicate 36	49.98	0.10	Replicate 76	49.45	0.05
Replicate 37	50.23	0.33	Replicate 77	49.80	0.02
Replicate 38	48.25	1.99	Replicate 78	49.91	0.07
Replicate 39	49.56	0.01	Replicate 79	49.06	0.36
Replicate 40	49.66	0.00	Replicate 80	50.02	0.13
			Sum of squared differences		21.44

The same process can be used for the percentage of boys. It should be noted that the standard error for boys is equal to the one for girls. Indeed, it can be mathematically shown that the standard error on π is equal to the standard error on $1-\pi$, *i.e.* $\sigma_{(p)} = \sigma_{(1-p)}$. Nevertheless, if missing data for gender are kept in the data file, the standard error on the percentage of boys can slightly differ from the standard error on the percentage of girls.

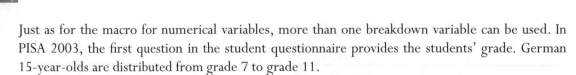

Just as for the macro for numerical variables, more than one breakdown variable can be used. In PISA 2003, the first question in the student questionnaire provides the students' grade. German 15-year-olds are distributed from grade 7 to grade 11.

Box 6.5 presents the SAS® syntax and Table 6.8 presents the distribution of students per grade and per gender. The percentages within the 'VAR' group variable add up to 100 per cent. In this example, the percentages of pupils in grades 7 to 11 within gender and country add up to 100 per cent. If 'BYVAR=CNT' and 'VAR=ST03Q01 ST01Q01' the sum of the percentages of all ten groups within the country will be 100 per cent.

Box 6.5 ■ **SAS® syntax for the computation of percentages of grade per gender**

```
/*Selecting only non missing data is optional*/
data temp1;
     set temp;
     if (not missing (st01Q01));
run;

%BRR_FREQ(INFILE=temp1,
              REPLI_ROOT=w_fstr,
              BYVAR=cnt st03q01,
              VAR= st01q01,
              OUTFILE=exerciseD);
run;
```

Table 6.8 ■ **Structure of the output data file *exerciseD***

CNT	ST03Q01	ST01Q01	STAT	SESTAT
DEU	1	7	1.15	0.26
DEU	1	8	13.09	0.83
DEU	1	9	59.33	1.00
DEU	1	10	26.28	1.08
DEU	1	11	0.17	0.08
DEU	2	7	2.28	0.45
DEU	2	8	16.92	1.04
DEU	2	9	60.32	1.06
DEU	2	10	20.41	0.79
DEU	2	11	0.08	0.05

As shown in Table 6.8, more boys tend to be in lower grades than girls and more girls tend to be in upper grades in Germany.

THE STANDARD ERROR ON REGRESSION COEFFICIENTS

For any requested statistic, the computation of the estimate and its standard error will follow exactly the same procedure as the ones described for the mean of HISEI and for the percentage of girls. The remainder of this chapter will explain the use of two other SAS® macros developed for analyzing PISA data.

The first macro is for simple linear regression analyses. Besides the four arguments common to all SAS® macros described in this manual, *i.e.* (i) INFILE=, (ii) REPLI_ROOT=, (iii) BYVAR=, (iv) OUTFILE=, two arguments need to be specified: the dependent variable and the independent variables. Only one dependent variable can be specified, whereas several independent variables can be specified.

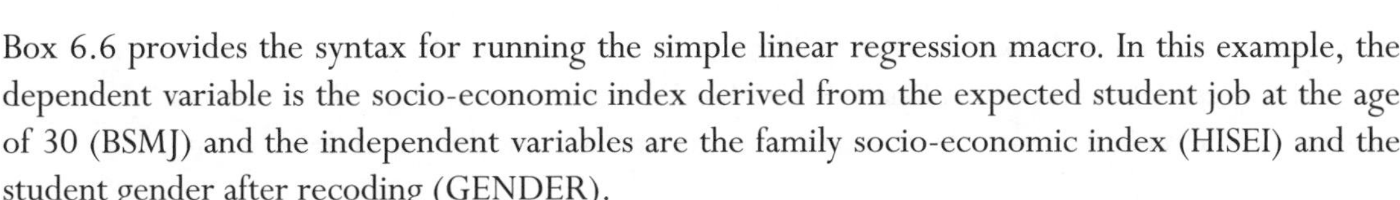

Box 6.6 provides the syntax for running the simple linear regression macro. In this example, the dependent variable is the socio-economic index derived from the expected student job at the age of 30 (BSMJ) and the independent variables are the family socio-economic index (HISEI) and the student gender after recoding (GENDER).

Box 6.6 ■ **SAS® syntax for the regression analyses (1)**

```
data temp;
     set temp;
     if (st03q01=1) then gender=1;
     if (st03q01=2) then gender=0;
run;

%include "c:\pisa2003\prg\macro_reg_nopv.sas";

%BRR_REG(    INFILE=temp,
             REPLI_ROOT=w_fstr,
             VARDEP=bsmj,
             EXPLICA=hisei gender,
             BYVAR=cnt,
             OUTFILE=exerciseE);
run;
```

After a recoding of the gender variable into a dichotomous 0-1 variable, the macro is defined by the "`%include`" statement.

Table 6.9 presents the structure of the output data file of the regression analysis.

Table 6.9 ■ **Structure of the output data file *exerciseE***

CNT	CLASS	STAT	SESTAT
DEU	Intercept	32.90	1.29
DEU	Hisei	0.37	0.03
DEU	gender	2.07	0.62

There are two ways to determine whether the regression coefficients are significantly different from 0. The first method consists of building a confidence interval around the estimated regression coefficient. The confidence interval for the GENDER regression coefficient on BSMJ can be computed for a value of α equal to 0.05 as:

$$[2.07 - (1.96*0.62);2.07 + (1.96*0.62)] = [0.85;3.29]$$

As the value 0 is not included in this confidence interval, the regression coefficient is significantly different from 0. As the value 0 was assigned to the boys and the value 1 to the girls, it means that on average, girls have significantly higher job expectations.

Another way to test the null hypothesis of the regression coefficient consists of dividing the regression coefficient by its standard error. This procedure will standardize the regression coefficient. It also means that the sampling distribution of the standardized regression coefficient, under the null hypothesis, has an expected mean of 0 and a standard deviation of 1. Therefore, if the ratio of the regression coefficient to its standard error is lower than -1.96 or higher than 1.96, it will be considered as significantly different from 0.

It should be mentioned that *exerciseF* will provide different results from *exerciseE*. In *exerciseE*, GENDER is considered as an explanatory variable. With *exerciseF*, GENDER is used as a breakdown variable. In the second model, there is only one explanatory variable, *i.e.* HISEI.

Box 6.7 ■ **SAS® syntax for the regression analyses (2)**

```
%BRR_REG(INFILE=temp,
        REPLI_ROOT=w_fstr,
        VARDEP=bsmj,
          EXPLICA=hisei,
        BYVAR=cnt gender,
        OUTFILE=exerciseF);
run;
```

Table 6.10 presents the structure of the output data file for the second model.

Table 6.10 ■ **Structure of the output data file *exerciseF***

CNT	GENDER	CLASS	STAT	SESTAT
DEU	0	Intercept	32.54	1.44
DEU	0	Hisei	0.37	0.03
DEU	1	Intercept	35.33	1.66
DEU	1	Hisei	0.36	0.03

THE STANDARD ERROR ON CORRELATION COEFFICIENTS

Box 6.8 and Table 6.11 present, respectively, the SAS® syntax and the structure of the output data file for the macro devoted to the computation of a correlation between two and only two variables.

Box 6.8 ■ **SAS® syntax for the correlation macro**

```
%include "c:\pisa2003\prg\macro_corr_nopv.sas";

%BRR_CORR(INFILE=temp,
            REPLI_ROOT=w_fstr,
            BYVAR=cnt,
            VAR1=hisei,
            VAR2=bsmj,
            OUTFILE=exerciseG);
Run;
```

Table 6.11 ■ **Structure of the output data file *exerciseG***

CNT	STAT	SESTAT
DEU	0.34	0.02

CONCLUSIONS

This chapter described the computation of the standard error by using the 80 replicates. For any given statistic, the procedure is the same.

Further, by using examples, the SAS® syntax for running the SAS® macros, developed to facilitate the computation of the standard errors, has been provided.

However, none of the macros described in this chapter can be used if plausible values are included in the analyses. Chapter 7 will describe how to proceed with such variables.

Analyses with Plausible Values

INTRODUCTION

Mathematics was the major domain in PISA 2003, while reading, science and problem solving were minor domains. One scale was created for each minor domain, while five scales were generated for the mathematics assessment: a mathematics scale and four subscales (space and shape, change and relationships, quantity and uncertainty).

As described in Chapter 5, these cognitive data were scaled with the Rasch model and the performance of students was denoted with plausible values. For each scale and subscale, five plausible values per student were included in the international data bases. This chapter describes how to perform analyses with plausible values (PVs).

Since PVs were mainly used for reporting student performance on the cognitive test, this chapter is only useful when conducting analyses on achievement data and their relationships with student or school characteristics.

UNIVARIATE STATISTICS ON PLAUSIBLE VALUES

The computation of a statistic with plausible values will always consist of six steps, regardless of the required statistic:

1. The required statistic and its respective standard error have to be computed for each plausible value. In Chapter 6, it was mentioned that 81 estimates were necessary to get the final estimate and its standard error. Therefore, any analysis that involves five plausible values will require 405 estimates. If a mean needs to be estimated, then 405 means will be calculated. The means estimated with the final weight are denoted $\hat{\mu}_1, \hat{\mu}_2, \hat{\mu}_3, \hat{\mu}_4$ and $\hat{\mu}_5$. From the 80 replicates applied on each of the five plausible values, five sampling variances are estimated, denoted respectively $\sigma^2_{(\hat{\mu}_1)}$, $\sigma^2_{(\hat{\mu}_2)}$, $\sigma^2_{(\hat{\mu}_3)}$, $\sigma^2_{(\hat{\mu}_4)}$ and $\sigma^2_{(\hat{\mu}_5)}$. These five mean estimates and their respective sampling variances are given in Table 7.1.

2. The final mean estimate is equal to the average of the five mean estimates, *i.e.*

$$\hat{\mu} = \frac{1}{5}(\hat{\mu}_1 + \hat{\mu}_2 + \hat{\mu}_3 + \hat{\mu}_4 + \hat{\mu}_5)$$

3. The final sampling variance is equal to the average of the five sampling variances, *i.e.*

$$\sigma^2_{(\hat{\mu})} = \frac{1}{5}(\sigma^2_{(\hat{\mu}_1)} + \sigma^2_{(\hat{\mu}_2)} + \sigma^2_{(\hat{\mu}_3)} + \sigma^2_{(\hat{\mu}_4)} + \sigma^2_{(\hat{\mu}_5)})$$

4. The imputation variance, also denoted measurement error variance, is computed as $\sigma^2_{(test)} = \frac{1}{4}\sum_{i=1}^{5}(\hat{\mu}_i - \hat{\mu})^2$. Indeed, as PISA returns five plausible values per scale, then $\sigma^2_{(test)} = \frac{1}{M-1}\sum_{i=1}^{M}(\hat{\mu}_i - \hat{\mu})^2 = \frac{1}{4}\sum_{i=1}^{5}(\hat{\mu}_i - \hat{\mu})^2$. This formula is similar to the one used for the estimation of a population variance, except that in this particular case, observations are not compared with the population mean, but each PV mean is compared with the final mean estimate.

5. The sampling variance and the imputation variance are combined to obtain the final error variance as $\sigma^2_{(error)} = \sigma^2_{(\hat{\mu})} + (1.2\sigma^2_{(test)})$.

   Indeed, $\sigma^2_{(error)} = \sigma^2_{(\hat{\mu})} + \left(\left(1 + \frac{1}{M}\right)\sigma^2_{(test)}\right) = \sigma^2_{(\hat{\mu})} + \left(\left(1 + \frac{1}{5}\right)\sigma^2_{(test)}\right) = \sigma^2_{(\hat{\mu})} + ((1.2)\,\sigma^2_{(test)})$

6. The standard error is equal to the square root of the error variance.

Table 7.1 ■ **The 405 mean estimates**

Weight	PV1	PV2	PV3	PV4	PV5
Final	$\hat{\mu}_{1}$	$\hat{\mu}_{2}$	$\hat{\mu}_{3}$	$\hat{\mu}_{4}$	$\hat{\mu}_{5}$
Replicate 1	$\hat{\mu}_{1\_1}$	$\hat{\mu}_{2\_1}$	$\hat{\mu}_{3\_1}$	$\hat{\mu}_{4\_1}$	$\hat{\mu}_{5\_1}$
Replicate 2	$\hat{\mu}_{1\_2}$	$\hat{\mu}_{2\_2}$	$\hat{\mu}_{3\_2}$	$\hat{\mu}_{4\_2}$	$\hat{\mu}_{5\_2}$
Replicate 3	$\hat{\mu}_{1\_3}$	$\hat{\mu}_{2\_3}$	$\hat{\mu}_{3\_3}$	$\hat{\mu}_{4\_3}$	$\hat{\mu}_{5\_3}$
....	....	....	....	....	....
....	....	....	....	....	....
Replicate 80	$\hat{\mu}_{1\_80}$	$\hat{\mu}_{2\_80}$	$\hat{\mu}_{3\_80}$	$\hat{\mu}_{4\_80}$	$\hat{\mu}_{5\_80}$
Sampling variance	$\sigma^2_{(\hat{\mu}_1)}$	$\sigma^2_{(\hat{\mu}_2)}$	$\sigma^2_{(\hat{\mu}_3)}$	$\sigma^2_{(\hat{\mu}_4)}$	$\sigma^2_{(\hat{\mu}_5)}$

The mean estimate on the mathematics scale and its respective standard error for the PISA 2003 German data can be computed. The macro described in Chapter 6 and labeled PROCMEANS_NOPV can be sequentially used five times and the results can be combined in an Microsoft® Excel® spreadsheet. Table 7.2 presents the different PV means and their respective sampling variances, as well as the mean estimates on the first and last replicates.

Table 7.2 ■ **Mean estimates and their respective sampling variances on the mathematics scale for Germany**

Weight	PV1	PV2	PV3	PV4	PV5
Final	503.08	503.10	502.72	503.03	503.00
Replicate 1	503.58	504.16	503.43	503.96	503.94
....	....	....	....	....	....
Replicate 80	503.18	503.62	503.46	503.30	503.83
Sampling variance	$(3.34)^2$	$(3.27)^2$	$(3.36)^2$	$(3.28)^2$	$(3.32)^2$

Box 7.1 presents the SAS® syntax for running sequentially the PROCMEANS_NOPV macro described in Chapter 6.

The final mean estimate for Germany on the combined reading scale is equal to:

$$\hat{\mu} = \frac{1}{5}\left(\hat{\mu}_1 + \hat{\mu}_2 + \hat{\mu}_3 + \hat{\mu}_4 + \hat{\mu}_5\right), \text{ i.e.}$$

$$\hat{\mu} = \frac{(503.08 + 503.10 + 502.72 + 503.03 + 503.00)}{5} = 502.99$$

The final sampling variance on the mean estimate for the combined reading literacy scale is equal to:

$$\sigma^2_{(\hat{\mu})} = \frac{1}{5}(\sigma^2_{(\hat{\mu}_1)} + \sigma^2_{(\hat{\mu}_2)} + \sigma^2_{(\hat{\mu}_3)} + \sigma^2_{(\hat{\mu}_4)} + \sigma^2_{(\hat{\mu}_5)}) \text{ , i.e.}$$

$$\sigma^2_{(\hat{\mu})} = \frac{(3.34)^2 + (3.27)^2 + (3.36)^2 + (3.28)^2 + (3.32)^2}{5} = 10.98$$

The imputation variance is equal to:

$$\sigma^2_{(test)} = \frac{1}{4}\sum_{i=1}^{5}(\hat{\mu}_i - \hat{\mu})^2 \text{, i.e.}$$

$$\sigma^2_{(test)} = \frac{\left[(503.08 - 502.99)^2 + (503.10 - 502.99)^2 + ... + (503.00 - 502.99)^2\right]}{4} = \frac{0.09}{4} = 0.02$$

The final error variance is equal to:

$$\sigma^2_{(error)} = \sigma^2_{(\hat{\mu})} + \left(1.2\sigma^2_{(test)}\right) \text{ ,i.e.}$$

$$\sigma^2_{(error)} = 10.98 + (1.2 * 0.02) = 11.00$$

The final standard error is therefore equal to:

$$SE = \sqrt{\sigma^2_{(error)}} = \sqrt{11.00} = 3.32$$

Box 7.1 ■ **SAS® syntax for computing the mean on the mathematics scale**

```
libname PISA2003  "c:\pisa2003\data\";
options nofmterr notes;
run;

data temp;
     set pisa2003.stud;
     if (cnt="DEU") ;
     w_fstr0=w_fstuwt;
     if (st03q01=1) then gender=1;
     if (st03q01=2) then gender=0;
     keep cnt schoolid stidstd w_fstr0-w_fstr80
          pv1math pv2math pv3math pv4math pv5math
          st03q01 gender hisei bsmj;
run;

%include "c:\pisa2003\prg\macro_procmeans_nopv.sas";

%BRR_PROCMEAN(INFILE=temp,
             REPLI_ROOT=w_fstr,
             BYVAR=cnt,
             VAR=pv1math,
             STAT=mean,
             OUTFILE=exercise1);
run;
%BRR_PROCMEAN(INFILE=temp,
             REPLI_ROOT=w_fstr,
             BYVAR=cnt,
             VAR=pv2math,
             STAT=mean,
             OUTFILE=exercise2);
                                                  ...
```

```
run;
%BRR_PROCMEAN(INFILE=temp,
              REPLI_ROOT=w_fstr,
              BYVAR=cnt,
              VAR=pv3math,
              STAT=mean,
              OUTFILE=exercise3);
run;
%BRR_PROCMEAN(INFILE=temp,
              REPLI_ROOT=w_fstr,
              BYVAR=cnt,
              VAR=pv4math,
              STAT=mean,
              OUTFILE=exercise4);
run;
%BRR_PROCMEAN(INFILE=temp,
              REPLI_ROOT=w_fstr,
              BYVAR=cnt,
              VAR=pv5math,
              STAT=mean,
              OUTFILE=exercise5);
run;
```

Running sequentially the PROCMEANS_NOPV macro five times and combining the results can be avoided: a SAS® macro has been developed for dealing with PVs. This macro also computes:

- The five mean estimates;
- The five sampling variances;
- The imputation variance; and
- The final standard error by combining the final sampling variance and the imputation variance.

Box 7.2 ■ **SAS® syntax for computing the mean and its standard error on plausible values**

```
data temp1;
     set pisa2003.stud;
     if (cnt="DEU") ;
     w_fstr0=w_fstuwt;
     mcomb1=pv1math;
     mcomb2=pv2math;
     mcomb3=pv3math;
     mcomb4=pv4math;
     mcomb5=pv5math;
     if (st03q01=1) then gender=1;
     if (st03q01=2) then gender=0;
     keep cnt schoolid stidstd w_fstr0-w_fstr80
          mcomb1-mcomb5
          st03q01 gender hisei bsmj;
run;

%include "c:\pisa2003\prg\macro_procmeans.sas";
%BRR_PROCMEAN_PV(INFILE=temp1,
                 REPLI_ROOT=w_fstr,
                 BYVAR=cnt,
                 PV_ROOT=mcomb,
                 STAT=mean,
                 OUTFILE=exercise6);
run;
```

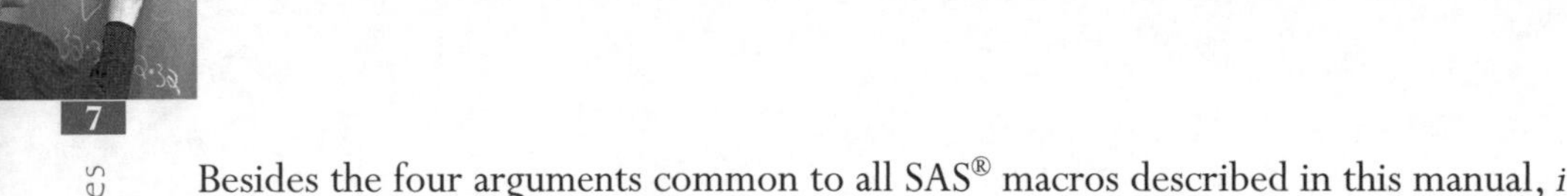

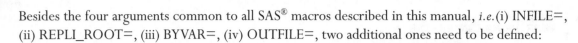

Besides the four arguments common to all SAS® macros described in this manual, *i.e.*(i) INFILE=, (ii) REPLI_ROOT=, (iii) BYVAR=, (iv) OUTFILE=, two additional ones need to be defined:

- The root of the variable names for the five plausible values. In the PISA database, PV names are usually PV1READ, PV2READ,…, PV1MATH, PV2MATH,… These variable names cannot be used directly by the macro, as it will automatically add the numbers 1 to 5 at the end of the root variable name. Therefore, in the "data" statement, new variables are created to fit the macro requirements. When calling the macro, the argument PV_ROOT will be equal to MCOMB.
- The STAT argument to specify the requested statistics. Available statistics have been described in Chapter 6.

The structure of the output data file *exercise6* is presented in Table 7.3.

Table 7.3 ■ **Structure of the output data file *exercise6***

CNT	STAT	SESTAT
DEU	502.99	3.32

Similar to the SAS® macros described in the previous chapter, more than one breakdown variable can be used. For instance, if one wants to determine whether the dispersion of the mathematics performance is larger for girls than for the boys, the macro PROCMEANS can be used as follows:

Box 7.3 ■ **SAS® syntax for computing the standard deviation and its standard error on plausible values per gender**

```
/*Selecting only non missing data is optional*/
data temp2;
     set temp1;
     if (not missing (st03Q01));
run;
%BRR_PROCMEAN_PV(INFILE=temp2,
                 REPLI_ROOT=w_fstr,
                 BYVAR=cnt st03q01,
                 PV_ROOT=mcomb,
                 STAT=std,
                 OUTFILE=exercise7);
run;
```

The structure of the output data file is presented in Table 7.4.

Table 7.4 ■ **Structure of the output data file *exercise7***

CNT	ST03Q01	STAT	SESTAT
DEU	1	99.29	2.05
DEU	2	105.05	2.54

According to Table 7.4, the standard deviation ('STAT') is not larger for boys than for girls. Unfortunately, as will be explained in Chapter 10, these two standard errors ('SESTAT') cannot be used to test the equality of the two standard deviation coefficients, since the standard deviation estimates for boys and girls may be correlated.

THE STANDARD ERROR ON PERCENTAGES WITH PLAUSIBLE VALUES

The second macro, first presented in Chapter 6, was developed for the computation of percentages and their respective standard errors. Chapter 8 will deal with the applying of this macro to plausible values: an entire chapter needs to be devoted to this type of analyses because of the issues involved.

THE STANDARD ERROR ON REGRESSION COEFFICIENTS WITH PLAUSIBLE VALUES

Suppose that the statistical effect of gender and student socio-economic background on the performance in mathematics needs to be estimated. Just like estimating a mean, this question can be solved by sequentially applying five times the macro REG_NOPV described in Chapter 6.

Box 7.4 presents the SAS® syntax for such an approach.

Box 7.4 ■ **SAS® syntax for computing regression coefficients and their standard errors on plausible values**

```
%BRR_REG(INFILE=temp,
       REPLI_ROOT=w_fstr,
       VARDEP=pv1math,
        EXPLICA=hisei gender,
       BYVAR=cnt,
       OUTFILE=exercise8);
run;
%BRR_REG(INFILE=temp,
       REPLI_ROOT=w_fstr,
       VARDEP=pv2math,
        EXPLICA=hisei gender,
       BYVAR=cnt,
       OUTFILE=exercise9);
run;
%BRR_REG(INFILE=temp,
       REPLI_ROOT=w_fstr,
       VARDEP=pv3math,
        EXPLICA=hisei gender,
       BYVAR=cnt,
       OUTFILE=exercise10);
run;
%BRR_REG(INFILE=temp,
       REPLI_ROOT=w_fstr,
       VARDEP=pv4math,
        EXPLICA=hisei gender,
       BYVAR=cnt,
       OUTFILE=exercise11);
run;
%BRR_REG(INFILE=temp,
       REPLI_ROOT=w_fstr,
       VARDEP=pv5math,
        EXPLICA=hisei gender,
       BYVAR=cnt,
       OUTFILE=exercise12);
run;
```

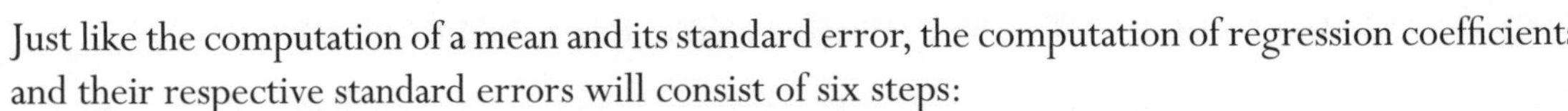

Just like the computation of a mean and its standard error, the computation of regression coefficients and their respective standard errors will consist of six steps:

1. For each plausible value and for each explanatory variable, computation of regression coefficients with the final and the 80 replicate weights. 405 regression coefficients per explanatory variable will be computed. The SAS® macro REG_NOPV applied sequentially five times will return, per explanatory variable, five estimates, denoted $\hat{\beta}_1, \ldots, \hat{\beta}_5$ and five standard errors, denoted $\sigma_{(\hat{\beta}_1)}, \ldots, \sigma_{(\hat{\beta}_5)}$. Table 7.5 gives the mathematical expression for these 405 estimates and Table 7.6 gives some of the values for the 405 regression coefficients obtained on the German data for the HISEI variable.

2. The final regression coefficient estimate is equal to $\hat{\beta} = \frac{\hat{\beta}_1 + \hat{\beta}_2 + \hat{\beta}_3 + \hat{\beta}_4 + \hat{\beta}_5}{5}$, *i.e.* for HISEI

$$\hat{\beta} = \frac{2.30 + 2.27 + 2.26 + 2.31 + 2.34}{5} = 2.30$$

3. The final sampling variance estimate is equal to:

$$\sigma^2_{(\hat{\beta})} = \frac{1}{5}\left(\sigma^2_{(\hat{\beta}_1)} + \sigma^2_{(\hat{\beta}_2)} + \sigma^2_{(\hat{\beta}_3)} + \sigma^2_{(\hat{\beta}_4)} + \sigma^2_{(\hat{\beta}_5)}\right), \text{ i.e. for HISEI}$$

$$\sigma^2_{(\hat{\beta})} = \frac{(0.11)^2 + (0.11)^2 + (0.11)^2 + (0.11)^2 + (0.11)^2}{5} = 0.012$$

4. The imputation variance is equal to $\sigma^2_{(test)} = \frac{1}{4}\sum_{i=1}^{5}(\hat{\beta}_i - \hat{\beta})^2$, *i.e.* for HISEI

$$\sigma^2_{(test)} = \frac{(2.30 - 2.30)^2 + (2.27 - 2.30)^2 + \ldots + (2.34 - 2.30)^2}{4} = \frac{0.0041}{4} = 0.001$$

5. The final error variance is equal to $\sigma^2_{(error)} = \sigma^2_{(\hat{\beta})} + (1.2\sigma^2_{(test)})$, *i.e.* for HISEI

$$\sigma^2_{(error)} = 0.01248 + (1.2 * 0.001) = 0.01368$$

6. The final standard error is equal to $SE = \sqrt{\sigma^2_{(error)}} = \sqrt{0.01368} = 0.117$

As 2.30 divided by 0.117 is about 19.66, the regression coefficient for HISEI is significantly different from 0.

Table 7.5 ■ **The 405 regression coefficient estimates**

Weight	PV1	PV2	PV3	PV4	PV5
Final	$\hat{\beta}_1$	$\hat{\beta}_2$	$\hat{\beta}_3$	$\hat{\beta}_4$	$\hat{\beta}_5$
Replicate 1	$\hat{\beta}_{1\_1}$	$\hat{\beta}_{2\_1}$	$\hat{\beta}_{3\_1}$	$\hat{\beta}_{4\_1}$	$\hat{\beta}_{5\_1}$
Replicate 2	$\hat{\beta}_{1\_2}$	$\hat{\beta}_{2\_2}$	$\hat{\beta}_{3\_2}$	$\hat{\beta}_{4\_2}$	$\hat{\beta}_{5\_2}$
Replicate 3	$\hat{\beta}_{1\_3}$	$\hat{\beta}_{2\_3}$	$\hat{\beta}_{3\_3}$	$\hat{\beta}_{4\_3}$	$\hat{\beta}_{5\_3}$
....	....	....	....	....	....
....	....	....	....	....	....
Replicate 80	$\hat{\beta}_{1\_80}$	$\hat{\beta}_{2\_80}$	$\hat{\beta}_{3\_80}$	$\hat{\beta}_{4\_80}$	$\hat{\beta}_{5\_80}$
Sampling variance	$\sigma^2_{(\hat{\beta}_1)}$	$\sigma^2_{(\hat{\beta}_2)}$	$\sigma^2_{(\hat{\beta}_3)}$	$\sigma^2_{(\hat{\beta}_4)}$	$\sigma^2_{(\hat{\beta}_5)}$

Table 7.6 ■ **HISEI regression coefficient estimates and their respective sampling variance on the mathematics scale for Germany after controlling for gender**

Weight	PV1	PV2	PV3	PV4	PV5
Final	2.30	2.27	2.26	2.31	2.34
Replicate 1	2.31	2.30	2.31	2.33	2.35
....	....	....	....	....	....
Replicate 80	2.24	2.21	2.21	2.23	2.27
Sampling variance	$(0.11)^2$	$(0.11)^2$	$(0.11)^2$	$(0.11)^2$	$(0.11)^2$

A SAS® macro has also been developed for regression analyses with plausible values as dependent variables. The SAS® syntax is presented in Box 7.5.

Box 7.5 ■ **SAS® syntax for running the simple linear regression macro with PVs**

```
%include "c:\pisa2003\prg\macro_reg.sas";

%BRR_REG_PV(INFILE=temp1,
            REPLI_ROOT=w_fstr,
            BYVAR=cnt,
            PV_ROOT=mcomb,
            EXPLICA=hisei gender,
            OUTFILE=exercise13);
run;
```

Besides the four arguments common to all macros, the root of the plausible value variable names has to be specified as well as the list of independent variables. The structure of the output data file is presented in Table 7.7.

Table 7.7 ■ **Structure of the output data file** ***exercise13***

CNT	CLASS	STAT	SESTAT
DEU	Intercept	409.20	7.22
DEU	Hisei	2.30	0.117
DEU	gender	-13.83	3.56

A quick overview of these results shows that all regression parameters are significantly different from 0.

THE STANDARD ERROR ON CORRELATION COEFFICIENTS WITH PLAUSIBLE VALUES

A SAS® macro has also been developed for computing the correlation between a set of plausible values and another variable. The SAS® syntax for running this macro is presented in Box 7.6 and the structure of the output data file is presented in Table 7.8.

Box 7.6 ■ **SAS® syntax for running the correlation macro with PVs**

```
%include "c:\pisa2003\prg\macro_corr.sas";

%BRR_CORR_PV(INFILE=temp1,
             REPLI_ROOT=w_fstr,
             BYVAR=cnt,
             EXPLICA=hisei,
             PV_ROOT=mcomb,
             OUTFILE=exercise14);
run;
```

Table 7.8 ■ **Structure of the output data file *exercise14***

CNT	STAT	SESTAT
DEU	0.39	0.02

CORRELATION BETWEEN TWO SETS OF PLAUSIBLE VALUES

Some researchers may be interested in the correlation between the different PISA domains and sub-domains. For instance, some might want to compute the correlation between the reading sub-domains or between the mathematics sub-domains, or between reading and mathematics using the PISA 2000 and PISA 2003 databases.

As described in the *PISA 2003 Technical Report* (OECD, forthcoming), the PISA assessment used incomplete assessment designs, *i.e.* students have to answer a subset of the item battery. Further, while all students were assessed in the major domain, only a subset of students was assessed in minor domains.

PISA 2000 only included PVs for students for a minor domain if they answered questions for that minor domain. Therefore, using the PISA 2000 database to compute the correlation between reading and mathematics, for example, would require working on a subset of students.[1]

To facilitate secondary analyses, PISA 2003 returned PVs for all domains and for all students, regardless of whether they were actually assessed or not. Ignoring the assessment status is possible, because the cognitive data in PISA are scaled according to multi dimensional models.

Since this is easier to illustrate graphically, suppose that only two domains were assessed, more specifically mathematics/quantity and mathematics/space and shape. If the mathematics/quantity and mathematics/space and shape materials were scaled independently, the correlation between the two sub-domains would be largely underestimated. In order to avoid this problem, both materials are scaled together. The model will build a two-dimensional posterior distribution, instead of two one-dimensional posterior distributions as described in Chapter 5. Figure 7.1 graphically presents a two-dimensional normal distribution.

To correctly describe such distributions, two means, two variances, and one correlation are needed. If the correlation is equal to 0, then the two axes will be orthogonal. As the absolute value of the correlation starts to increase, the angle formed by the two axes becomes less than 90 degrees.[2]

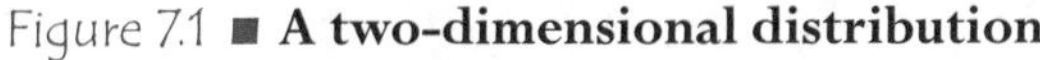

Figure 7.1 ■ **A two-dimensional distribution**

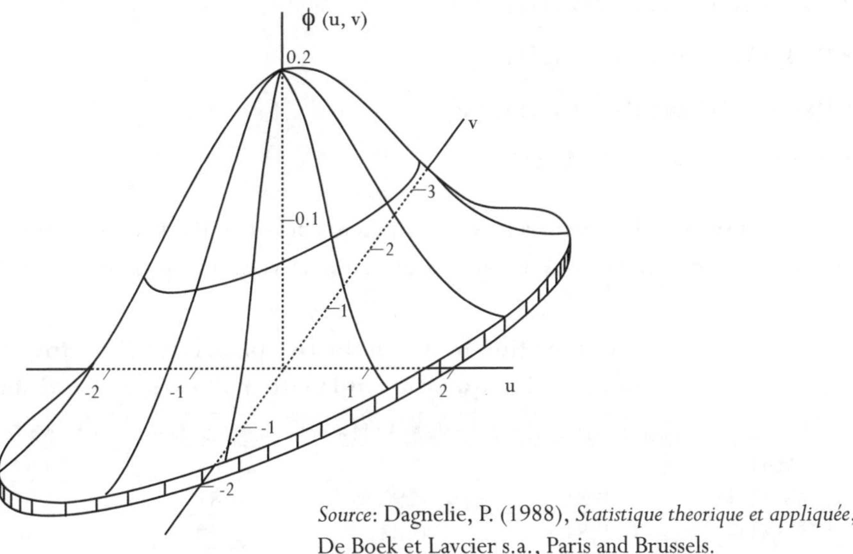

Source: Dagnelie, P. (1988), *Statistique theorique et appliquée*, De Boek et Lavcier s.a., Paris and Brussels.

Two axes perfectly overlapping would represent a correlation of 1.0 (or -1.0). These different cases are illustrated in Figure 7.2.

Figure 7.2 ■ **Axes for two-dimensional normal distributions**

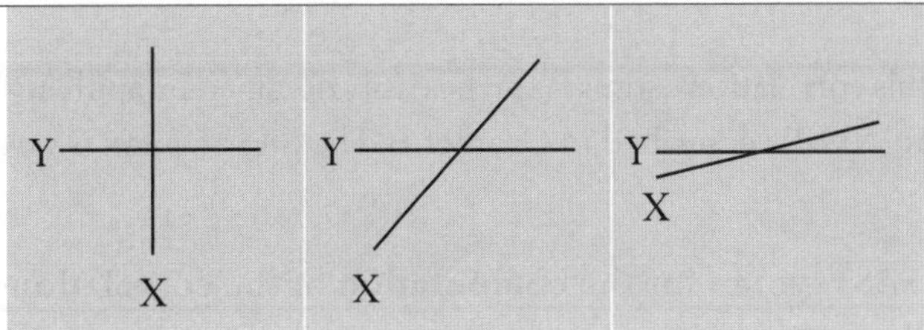

With a two-dimensional model, the first plausible value for mathematics/quantity will be drawn at the same time as the first plausible value for mathematics/space and shape. Per student, this will consist of randomly drawing one dot in the scatter plot. The values of the two plausible values will be the coordinates of the dot on the two axes. The same procedure is applied for the second, third, fourth and fifth PVs.

As the PISA domains and sub-domains highly correlate, as shown by the graph on the far right in Figure 7.2, it is very unlikely for a student to get a high score for the first plausible value in mathematics/quantity (PV1MATH4) and a low score for the first plausible value in mathematics/space and shape (PV1MATH1). If plausible values were drawn independently for these two mathematics sub-domains, such a case would be possible and therefore the correlation would be underestimated.

Since each draw is independent, to calculate the correlation between the two domains, the correlation between each set of plausible values below needs to be computed:

- PV1MATH1 and PV1MATH4;
- PV2MATH1 and PV2MATH4;
- PV3MATH1 and PV3MATH4;
- PV4MATH1 and PV4MATH4; and
- PV5MATH1 and PV5 MATH4.

Table 7.9 presents the 25 correlation coefficients between the five plausible values in mathematics/quantity and mathematics/space and shape, respectively, for Germany in PISA 2003.

Table 7.9 ■ **Correlation between the five plausible values for each domain, mathematics/quantity and mathematics/space and shape**

	PV1MATH1	PV2MATH1	PV3MATH1	PV4MATH1	PV5MATH1
PV1MATH4	0.90	0.83	0.84	0.84	0.83
PV2MATH4	0.83	0.90	0.84	0.84	0.83
PV3MATH4	0.84	0.83	0.90	0.84	0.83
PV4MATH4	0.83	0.83	0.84	0.90	0.83
PV5MATH4	0.83	0.83	0.84	0.84	0.90

As shown in Table 7.9, the correlation coefficients on the diagonal of the square matrix are substantially higher than the other correlation coefficients. Therefore, the final correlation estimate between these two mathematics sub-domains will be the average of the five correlation coefficients on the diagonal.

The standard error on this correlation estimate can be easily obtained by applying five times sequentially the SAS® macro CORR_NOPV described in Chapter 6. The SAS® syntax is given in Box 7.7.

Box 7.7 ■ **SAS® syntax for the computation of the correlation between mathematics/quantity and mathematics/space and shape**

```
data temp;
     set pisa2003.stud;
     if (cnt="DEU") ;
     w_fstr0=w_fstuwt;
     keep  cnt schoolid stidstd w_fstr0-w_fstr80
                 pv1math1 pv2math1 pv3math1 pv4math1 pv5math1
                 pv1math4 pv2math4 pv3math4 pv4math4 pv5math4;
run;
%include "c:\pisa2003\prg\macro_corr_nopv.sas";


%BRR_CORR(INFILE=temp,
          REPLI_ROOT=w_fstr,
          BYVAR=cnt,
          VAR1=pv1math1,
          VAR2=pv1math4,
          OUTFILE=exercise15);
run;
                                                                ...
```

```
%BRR_CORR(INFILE=temp,
          REPLI_ROOT=w_fstr,
          BYVAR=cnt,
          VAR1=pv2math1,
          VAR2=pv2math4,
          OUTFILE=exercise16);
run;
%BRR_CORR(INFILE=temp,
          REPLI_ROOT=w_fstr,
          BYVAR=cnt,
          VAR1=pv3math1,
          VAR2=pv3math4,
          OUTFILE=exercise17);
run;
%BRR_CORR(INFILE=temp,
          REPLI_ROOT=w_fstr,
          BYVAR=cnt,
          VAR1=pv4math1,
          VAR2=pv4math4,
          OUTFILE=exercise18);
run;
%BRR_CORR(INFILE=temp,
          REPLI_ROOT=w_fstr,
          BYVAR=cnt,
          VAR1=pv5math1,
          VAR2=pv5math4,
          OUTFILE=exercise19);
run;
```

Table 7.10 ■ **The five correlation estimates between mathematics/quantity and mathematics/space and shape and their respective sampling variances**

	PV1	PV2	PV3	PV4	PV5
Correlation	0.8953	0.8964	0.8996	0.8978	0.8958
Sampling variance	$(0.0040)^2$	$(0.0033)^2$	$(0.0034)^2$	$(0.0037)^2$	$(0.0038)^2$

The final correlation estimate is equal to:

$$\hat{\rho} = \frac{\hat{\rho}_1 + \hat{\rho}_2 + \hat{\rho}_3 + \hat{\rho}_4 + \hat{\rho}_5}{5}, \text{ i.e.}$$

$$\hat{\rho} = \frac{0.8953 + 0.8964 + ... + 0.8958}{5} = 0.8970$$

The final sampling variance is equal to:

$$\sigma^2_{(\hat{\rho})} = \frac{\sum_{i=1}^{5} \sigma^2_{(\hat{\rho}_i)}}{5}, \text{ i.e.}$$

$$\sigma^2_{(\hat{\rho})} = \frac{(0.0040)^2 + (0.0033)^2 + ... + (0.0038)^2}{5} = 0.000013$$

The measurement variance can be estimated as:

$$\sigma^2_{(test)} = \frac{1}{4}\sum_{i=1}^{5}(\hat{\rho}_i - \hat{\rho})^2 = 0.000003$$

The final variance is equal to:

$$\sigma^2_{(error)} = \sigma^2_{(\hat{\rho})} + \left(1.2\sigma^2_{(test)}\right) = 0.000017$$

The final standard error is equal to:

$$SE = \sqrt{\sigma^2_{(error)}} = \sqrt{0.000017} = 0.0041$$

The computation of the correlation between two domains or between a sub-domain and a domain might be problematic in some cases in the PISA data bases. PISA 2000 used two scaling models:

- A three-dimensional model with mathematics, reading and science; and
- A five-dimensional model with mathematics, reading (retrieving information, interpreting, and reflecting) and science.

PISA 2003 also used two scaling models:

- A four-dimensional model with mathematics, problem solving, reading and science; and
- A seven-dimensional model with mathematics/space and shape, mathematics/change and relationships, mathematics/uncertainty, mathematics/quantity, problem solving, reading and science.

The PISA databases should contain two sets of plausible values for each of the minor domains. As this would be too confusing, only one set was provided. Therefore, the correlation coefficients are underestimated.

This can be confirmed by examining the data. In the case of a minor domain and a subscale of the major domain, the correlation coefficients on the diagonal do not differ from the other correlations, since these two sets of plausible values were generated by two different models.

In PISA 2003, as well as in PISA 2000, the plausible values for the minor domains included in the databases were generated with the major domain as a combined scale. This means that:

- The correlation between a minor domain and the combined scale of the major domain can be computed;
- The correlation between two minor domains can be computed;
- The correlation between the sub-domains can be computed; and
- It is not possible to compute the correlation between minor domains and one of the subscales of the major domain.

A FATAL ERROR SHORTCUT

A common fatal error when analysing with plausible values involves computing the the mean of the five plausible values, before further analysis.

In Chapter 5, the EAP student performance estimator was described. As a reminder, the EAP estimator is equal to the mean of the posterior distribution. Therefore, computing at the student level the mean of the five plausible values is more or less equal to the EAP estimate.

In Chapter 5, the efficiency of the EAP estimator was also compared with the WLE and the PVs for some statistics estimations. It was indicated that the EAP estimator:

- Underestimates the standard deviation;
- Overestimates the correlation between the student performance and some background variables; and
- Underestimates the within-school variance.

Therefore, computing the mean of the five PVs and then computing statistics on this new score would bias the results just as the EAP does. Table 7.11 provides, per country, the standard deviation of the combined literacy scale using the correct method as described in this chapter and also the incorrect method of averaging the five PVs at the student level and then computing the standard deviation on this new score. The result of the latter is denoted as pseudo-EAP.

As shown by Table 7.11, the pseudo-EAP underestimates the standard deviation.

Table 7.11 ■ **Standard deviations for mathematics scale using the correct method (plausible values) and by averaging the plausible values at the student level (pseudo-EAP)**

	Plausible values	Pseudo EAP		Plausible values	Pseudo EAP
AUS	95.42	91.90	KOR	92.38	89.07
AUT	93.09	89.91	LIE	99.06	95.42
BEL	109.88	106.65	LUX	91.86	88.28
BRA	99.72	94.79	LVA	87.90	83.92
CAN	87.11	83.37	MAC	86.95	82.72
CHE	98.38	94.97	MEX	85.44	80.52
CZE	95.94	92.50	NLD	92.52	89.89
DEU	102.59	99.54	NOR	92.04	88.31
DNK	91.32	87.52	NZL	98.29	95.07
ESP	88.47	84.52	POL	90.24	86.49
FIN	83.68	79.77	PRT	87.63	83.91
FRA	91.70	88.07	RUS	92.25	87.81
GBR	92.26	89.18	SVK	93.31	89.86
GRC	93.83	89.49	SWE	94.75	91.07
HKG	100.19	96.99	THA	81.95	77.15
HUN	93.51	89.71	TUN	81.97	76.86
IDN	80.51	74.86	TUR	104.74	100.79
IRL	85.26	82.03	URY	99.68	95.21
ISL	90.36	86.55	USA	95.25	92.12
ITA	95.69	92.00	YUG	84.65	80.43
JPN	100.54	96.96			

AN UNBIASED SHORTCUT

Table 7.1 and Table 7.5 respectively give the 405 mean and regression coefficient estimates needed for the computation of a mean or regression coefficient final estimate and the respective standard errors.

On average, analyzing one PV instead of five PVs provides unbiased population estimates as well as unbiased sampling variances on these estimates. It will not be possible to estimate the imputation variance using this method, however.

Therefore, an unbiased shortcut could consist of:

- Computing, using one of the five PVs, the statistical estimate and its sampling variance by using the final student weight as well as the 80 replicate weights;
- Computing the statistical estimate by using the final student weight on the four other PVs;
- Computing the final statistical estimate by averaging the plausible value statistical estimates;
- Computing the imputation variance, as previously described; and
- Combining the imputation variance and the sampling variance, as previously described.

This unbiased shortcut is presented in Table 7.12 for the estimation of a mean and its standard error. This shortcut only requires the computation of 85 estimates instead of 405. The final estimate of this shortcut will be equal to the one obtained with the long procedure, but the standard error might differ slightly.

Table 7.12 ■ **Unbiased shortcut for a population estimate and its standard error**

Weight	PV1	PV2	PV3	PV4	PV5
Final	$\hat{\mu}_1$	$\hat{\mu}_2$	$\hat{\mu}_3$	$\hat{\mu}_4$	$\hat{\mu}_5$
Replicate 1	$\hat{\mu}_{1\_1}$				
Replicate 2	$\hat{\mu}_{1\_2}$				
Replicate 3	$\hat{\mu}_{1\_3}$				
....	....				
....	....				
Replicate 80	$\hat{\mu}_{1\_80}$				
Sampling variance	$\sigma^2_{(\hat{\mu}_1)}$				

CONCLUSIONS

This chapter describes the different steps for analyzing data with plausible values. It also provides some SAS® macros to facilitate the computations.

Attention was also drawn to a common error that consists of computing the average of the plausible values at the student level and adding this value to the database to be used as the student score in analyses. Unlike that method, the correct method involves the averaging process always occurring at the latest stage, that is on the statistic that will be reported.

The particular issue of analyzing two sets of plausible values was also presented in the case of a correlation. The procedure that was applied can also be extended to a linear regression analysis.

Finally, an unbiased shortcut was described which is useful for time consuming procedures, such as multilevel procedures.

Notes

1. For more information, see the *Manual for the PISA 2000 Database* (OECD, 2002b).
2. A correlation coefficient can be expressed by the cosines of the angle formed by the two variables.

Use of Proficiency Levels

INTRODUCTION

The values for student performance in reading, mathematics and science literacy are usually considered as continuous latent variables. In order to facilitate the interpretation of the scores assigned to students, the combined reading literacy scale and the mathematics and science scales were designed to have an average score of 500 points and a standard deviation of 100 across OECD countries in PISA 2000. This means that about two-thirds of the OECD students perform between 400 and 600 points.

In PISA 2003, five mathematics scales, namely, the mathematics scale, the mathematics/space and shape scale, the mathematics/change and relationships scale, the mathematics/quantity scale and the mathematics/uncertainty scale, were constructed for the first time, in order to have an average score among OECD countries of 500 points. However, unlike the mathematics scale, the PISA 2003 reading and science scales were anchored to the results from PISA 2000.

In order to improve the accessibility of the results to policy makers and educators, described proficiency scales were developed for the assessment domains. Since these scales are divided according to levels of difficulty and performance, a ranking of the student performance can be obtained, as well as a description of the skill associated with that proficiency level. Each successive level is associated with tasks of increased difficulty.

In PISA 2000, five levels of reading proficiency were defined and reported in the PISA 2000 initial report *Knowledge and Skills for Life: First Results from PISA 2000* (OECD, 2001). In PISA 2003, six levels of mathematics proficiency levels were also defined and reported in the PISA 2003 initial report *Learning for Tomorrow's World – First Results from PISA 2003* (OECD, 2004a).

This chapter will show how to derive the proficiency levels from the PISA databases and how to use them.

GENERATION OF THE PROFICIENCY LEVELS

Proficiency levels are not included in the PISA databases, but they can be derived from the plausible values.

In PISA 2003, the cutpoints that frame the proficiency levels in mathematics are precisely 357.77, 420.07, 482.38, 544.68, 606.99 and 669.3.[1] While some researchers might understand that different possible scores can be assigned to each student, understanding that different levels can be assigned to a single student is more difficult. Therefore, they might be tempted to compute the average of the five plausible values and then assign to each student a proficiency level based on this average.

As discussed in Chapter 5 and Chapter 7, such procedure is similar to assigning to each student an EAP score, and the biases of such estimators are now well known. Since using EAP scores underestimates the standard deviation, the estimation of the percentages of students at each level of proficiency will consequently underestimate the percentages at the lowest and highest levels, and overestimate the percentages at the central levels.

As already stated, international education surveys do not intend to precisely estimate the performance of particular students; they aim to describe population characteristics. Therefore, particular students can be allocated different proficiency levels for different plausible values. Thus, five plausible proficiency levels will be assigned to each student respectively according to their five plausible values. The SAS® syntax for the generation of the plausible proficiency levels in mathematics is provided in Box 8.1.

PISA 2000 provided cutpoints for proficiency levels in reading only. Therefore, proficiency levels can only be generated on the combined reading literacy scale and on the three subscales from the PISA 2000 database.

PISA 2003 provided cutpoints for proficiency levels in mathematics. Therefore, proficiency levels can be generated on the mathematics scale and on the four mathematics subscales as well as on the combined reading literacy scale.

Box 8.1 ■ **SAS® syntax for the generation of the proficiency levels**

```
libname PISA2003  "c:\pisa2003\data\";
options nofmterr notes;
run;

data temp;
    set pisa2003.stud;
    if (cnt="DEU");
    array math (25)
          pv1math pv2math pv3math pv4math pv5math
          pv1math1 pv2math1 pv3math1 pv4math1 pv5math1
          pv1math2 pv2math2 pv3math2 pv4math2 pv5math2
          pv1math3 pv2math3 pv3math3 pv4math3 pv5math3
          pv1math4 pv2math4 pv3math4 pv4math4 pv5math4;
    array levelmat (25)
          mlev1-mlev5
          m1lev1-m1lev5
          m2lev1-m2lev5
          m3lev1-m3lev5
          m4lev1-m4lev5;
    do i=1 to 25;
          if (math(i)<=357.77) then levelmat(i)=0;
          if (math(i)>357.77 and math(i)<=420.07) then levelmat(i)=1;
          if (math(i)>420.07 and math(i)<=482.38) then levelmat(i)=2;
          if (math(i)>482.38 and math(i)<=544.68) then levelmat(i)=3;
          if (math(i)>544.68 and math(i)<=606.99) then levelmat(i)=4;
          if (math(i)>606.99 and math(i)<=669.30) then levelmat(i)=5;
          if (math(i)>669.30) then levelmat(i)=6;
    end;
    w_fstr0=w_fstuwt;
    keep   cnt schoolid stidstd
                w_fstr0-w_fstr80
                mlev1-mlev5
                m1lev1-m1lev5
                m2lev1-m2lev5
                m3lev1-m3lev5
                m4lev1-m4lev5
                st03q01 matheff;
run;
```

The statement "`array`" allows the definition of a variable vector. In Box 8.1, two vectors are defined. The first, labelled MATH, includes the five plausible values for the mathematics scales and the four mathematics subscales. The second, labelled LEVELMAT, will create 25 new variables, labelled MLEV1 to MLEV5 for the mathematics scales, M1LEV1 to M1LEV5 to the mathematic/space and shape subscale, M2LEV1 to M2LEV5 for the mathematics/change and relationship subscale, M3LEV1 to M3LEV5 for the mathematics/uncertainty subscale and M4LEV1 to M4LEV5 for the mathematics/quantity subscale.

The iterative process will recode each plausible value variable into a new with seven categories labeled 0 to 6 for mathematics.

The computation of the percentage of students at each proficiency level and its respective standard error is exactly similar to the computation of a mean estimate and its standard error as described in Chapter 7, *i.e.:*

- For each plausible value, the percentage of students at each proficiency level and its respective standard error have to be computed. Per proficiency level, 5 percentage estimates denoted $\hat{\pi}_1$, $\hat{\pi}_2$, $\hat{\pi}_3$, $\hat{\pi}_4$ and $\hat{\pi}_5$ will be obtained. Out of the 80 replicates applied on each of the 5 proficiency level variables, per level of proficiency, 5 sampling variances will be estimated, denoted respectively $\sigma^2_{(\hat{\pi}_1)}$, $\sigma^2_{(\hat{\pi}_2)}$, $\sigma^2_{(\hat{\pi}_3)}$, $\sigma^2_{(\hat{\pi}_4)}$ and $\sigma^2_{(\hat{\pi}_5)}$. These five percentage estimates and their respective sampling variances are given in Table 8.1.

- The final mean estimate is equal to the average of the 5 mean estimates, *i.e.:*

$$\hat{\pi} = \frac{1}{5}\left(\hat{\pi}_1 + \hat{\pi}_2 + \hat{\pi}_3 + \hat{\pi}_4 + \hat{\pi}_5\right)$$

- The final sampling variance is equal to the average of the 5 sampling variances, *i.e.:*

$$\sigma^2_{(\hat{\pi})} = \frac{1}{5}(\sigma^2_{(\hat{\pi}_1)} + \sigma^2_{(\hat{\pi}_2)} + \sigma^2_{(\hat{\pi}_3)} + \sigma^2_{(\hat{\pi}_4)} + \sigma^2_{(\hat{\pi}_5)})$$

- The imputation variance, also denoted measurement error variance is computed as:[2]

$$\sigma^2_{(test)} = \frac{1}{4}\sum_{i=1}^{5}(\hat{\pi}_i - \hat{\pi})^2$$

- The sampling variance and the imputation variance are combined to obtain the final error variance as

$$\sigma^2_{(error)} = \sigma^2_{(\hat{\pi})} + \left(1.2\sigma^2_{(test)}\right)$$

- The standard error is equal to the square root of the error variance.

This process is repeated for each proficiency level.

In this way 405 percentages will be estimated per proficiency level. As there are seven levels in mathematics, 2 835 percentages will be estimated.

Table 8.1 ■ **405 percentage estimates for a particular proficiency level**

Weight	PV1	PV2	PV3	PV4	PV5
Final	$\hat{\pi}_1$	$\hat{\pi}_2$	$\hat{\pi}_3$	$\hat{\pi}_4$	$\hat{\pi}_5$
Replicate 1	$\hat{\pi}_{1\_1}$	$\hat{\pi}_{2\_1}$	$\hat{\pi}_{3\_1}$	$\hat{\pi}_{4\_1}$	$\hat{\pi}_{5\_1}$
Replicate 2	$\hat{\pi}_{1\_2}$	$\hat{\pi}_{2\_2}$	$\hat{\pi}_{3\_2}$	$\hat{\pi}_{4\_2}$	$\hat{\pi}_{5\_2}$
Replicate 3	$\hat{\pi}_{1\_3}$	$\hat{\pi}_{2\_3}$	$\hat{\pi}_{3\_3}$	$\hat{\pi}_{4\_3}$	$\hat{\pi}_{5\_3}$
....	....	....	....	....	....
....	....	....	....	....	....
Replicate 80	$\hat{\pi}_{1\_80}$	$\hat{\pi}_{2\_80}$	$\hat{\pi}_{3\_80}$	$\hat{\pi}_{4\_80}$	$\hat{\pi}_{5\_80}$
Sampling variance	$\sigma^2_{(\hat{\pi}_1)}$	$\sigma^2_{(\hat{\pi}_2)}$	$\sigma^2_{(\hat{\pi}_3)}$	$\sigma^2_{(\hat{\pi}_4)}$	$\sigma^2_{(\hat{\pi}_5)}$

The seven proficiency levels in mathematics are:

- Below Level 1;
- Level 1;
- Level 2;
- Level 3;
- Level 4;
- Level 5; and
- Level 6.

Applying sequentially five times the FREQ_NOPV macro described in Chapter 5 will return, per proficiency level, five percentage estimates and five standard error estimates that can be combined to get the final estimate and its standard error.

Box 8.2 presents the SAS® syntax for running sequentially five times the FREQ_NOPV macro. Table 8.2 presents per proficiency level, the five estimates and their respective sampling variances.

To combine the results:

- Per proficiency level, the five percentage estimates are averaged;
- Per proficiency level, the five sampling variances are averaged;
- By comparing the final estimate and the five PV estimates, the imputation variance is computed;
- The final sampling variance and the imputation variance are combined as usual to get the final error variance; and
- The standard error is obtained by taking the square root of the error variance.

Box 8.2 ■ **SAS® syntax for computing the percentages of students per proficiency level in mathematics**

```
%include "c:\pisa2003\prg\macro_freq_nopv.sas";

%BRR_FREQ(INFILE=temp,
              REPLI_ROOT=w_fstr,
              BYVAR=cnt,
              VAR=mlev1,
              OUTFILE=exercise20);
run;
%BRR_FREQ(INFILE=temp,
              REPLI_ROOT=w_fstr,
              BYVAR=cnt,
              VAR=mlev2,
              OUTFILE=exercise21);
run;
%BRR_FREQ(INFILE=temp,
              REPLI_ROOT=w_fstr,
              BYVAR=cnt,
              VAR=mlev3,
              OUTFILE=exercise22);
run;
%BRR_FREQ(INFILE=temp,
              REPLI_ROOT=w_fstr,
              BYVAR=cnt,
              VAR=mlev4,
              OUTFILE=exercise23);
run;
%BRR_FREQ(INFILE=temp,
              REPLI_ROOT=w_fstr,
              BYVAR=cnt,
              VAR=mlev5,
              OUTFILE=exercise24);
run;
```

Table 8.2 ■ **Estimates and sampling variances per proficiency level in mathematics for Germany**

Level		PV1	PV2	PV3	PV4	PV5
Below Level 1	$\hat{\pi}_i$	9.69	9.02	9.12	9.36	8.75
	$\sigma^2_{(\hat{\pi}_i)}$	$(0.79)^2$	$(0.73)^2$	$(0.75)^2$	$(0.74)^2$	$(0.71)^2$
Level 1	$\hat{\pi}_i$	11.87	12.68	12.67	12.33	12.52
	$\sigma^2_{(\hat{\pi}_i)}$	$(0.74)^2$	$(0.74)^2$	$(0.72)^2$	$(0.71)^2$	$(0.72)^2$
Level 2	$\hat{\pi}_i$	18.20	18.83	19.53	18.87	19.56
	$\sigma^2_{(\hat{\pi}_i)}$	$(0.80)^2$	$(0.80)^2$	$(0.86)^2$	$(0.89)^2$	$(0.88)^2$
Level 3	$\hat{\pi}_i$	23.11	22.69	22.14	22.23	22.66
	$\sigma^2_{(\hat{\pi}_i)}$	$(0.72)^2$	$(0.67)^2$	$(0.68)^2$	$(0.62)^2$	$(0.81)^2$
Level 4	$\hat{\pi}_i$	21.05	20.95	20.30	20.85	19.91
	$\sigma^2_{(\hat{\pi}_i)}$	$(0.89)^2$	$(0.93)^2$	$(0.85)^2$	$(0.82)^2$	$(0.85)^2$
Level 5	$\hat{\pi}_i$	11.65	11.74	12.50	12.13	12.82
	$\sigma^2_{(\hat{\pi}_i)}$	$(0.65)^2$	$(0.66)^2$	$(0.70)^2$	$(0.65)^2$	$(0.73)^2$
Level 6	$\hat{\pi}_i$	4.42	4.09	3.74	4.23	3.78
	$\sigma^2_{(\hat{\pi}_i)}$	$(0.35)^2$	$(0.38)^2$	$(0.33)^2$	$(0.37)^2$	$(0.36)^2$

The final results are presented in Table 8.3.

Table 8.3 ■ **Final estimates of the percentage of students per proficiency level in mathematics and their respective standard errors for Germany**

Proficiency level	%	SE
Below Level 1	9.19	0.84
Level 1	12.42	0.81
Level 2	19.00	1.05
Level 3	22.57	0.82
Level 4	20.61	1.02
Level 5	12.17	0.87
Level 6	4.05	0.48

A SAS® macro has been developed for computing the percentage of students at each proficiency level as well as its respective standard error in one run. Box 8.3 presents the SAS® syntax for running the macro and Table 8.4 presents the structure of the output data file.

Box 8.3 ■ **SAS® syntax for computing the percentage of students per proficiency level**

```
%include "c:\pisa2003\prg\macro_freq.sas";

%BRR_FREQ_PV(INFILE=temp,
           REPLI_ROOT=w_fstr,
           BYVAR=cnt,
           PV_ROOT=mlev,
           OUTFILE=exercise25);
run;
```

This macro has five arguments. Besides the four usual arguments, the root of the proficiency level variable names has to be specified. For the mathematics scale, as specified in the data statement of Box 8.1, this will be set as MLEV.

Table 8.4 ■ **Structure of the output data file *exercise25***

CNT	MLEV	STAT	SESTAT
DEU	0	9.19	0.84
DEU	1	12.42	0.81
DEU	2	19.00	1.05
DEU	3	22.57	0.82
DEU	4	20.61	1.02
DEU	5	12.17	0.87
DEU	6	4.05	0.48

As before, several breakdown variables can be used. For instance, the distribution of students across proficiency levels per gender can be obtained as in Box 8.4.

Box 8.4 ■ **SAS® syntax for computing the percentage of students per proficiency level and per gender**

```
/*Selecting only non missing data is optional*/
data temp1;
     set temp;
     if (not missing (st03Q01));
run;
%include "c:\pisa2003\prg\macro_freq.sas";
%BRR_FREQ_PV(INFILE=temp1,
               REPLI_ROOT=w_fstr,
               BYVAR=cnt st03q01,
               PV_ROOT=mlev,
               OUTFILE=exercise26);
run;
```

In this case, the sum of the percentages will be equal to 100 per country and per gender, as shown by Table 8.5.

Table 8.5 ■ **Output data file for *exercise26***

CNT	ST03Q01	MLEV	STAT	SESTAT
DEU	1	0	9.24	1.05
DEU	1	1	12.15	1.02
DEU	1	2	19.92	1.42
DEU	1	3	23.92	1.37
DEU	1	4	20.65	1.18
DEU	1	5	11.25	0.97
DEU	1	6	2.87	0.57
DEU	2	0	8.88	1.04
DEU	2	1	12.53	0.99
DEU	2	2	18.14	1.21
DEU	2	3	21.43	0.98
DEU	2	4	20.72	1.32
DEU	2	5	13.03	1.14
DEU	2	6	5.27	0.65

As shown by Table 8.5, the percentage of boys at Level 6 is higher than the percentage of girls at Level 6.

The statistical significance of these differences cannot be evaluated with this procedure. More details on this issue will be provided in Chapter 10.

OTHER ANALYSES WITH PROFICIENCY LEVELS

One of the indices constructed in PISA 2003 is an index of mathematics self-efficacy, denoted MATHEFF.

For PISA 2003, analysing the relationship between proficiency levels and mathematics self-efficacy is relevant, as there is probably a reciprocal relationship between these two concepts. A better self-perception in mathematics is thought to increase the student's proficiency in mathematics, but an increase in the latter might in return affect the former.

Suppose that the statistic of interest is the average self-efficacy per proficiency level. In statistical terms, mathematics self-efficacy is considered as the dependent variable and the level of proficiency, the independent variable. There is no macro that can directly compute the mean of a continuous variable per proficiency level. On the other hand, the PROCMEANS_NOPV macro described in Chapter 6 can be applied sequentially five times and the results could be combined in an Microsoft® Excel® spreadsheet, for instance. This will be the case whenever proficiency levels are used as independent or as classification variables.

Box 8.5 presents the SAS® syntax for computing the mean of student self-efficacy per proficiency level. The mean estimates and their respective standard errors are presented in Table 8.6.

Box 8.5 ■ **SAS® macro for computing the mean of self-efficacy in mathematics per proficiency level**

```
%include "c:\pisa2003\prg\macro_procmeans_nopv.sas";

%BRR_PROCMEAN(INFILE=temp,
                  REPLI_ROOT=w_fstr,
                  BYVAR=cnt mlev1,
                  VAR=matheff,
                  STAT=mean,
                  OUTFILE=exercise27);
run;
%BRR_PROCMEAN(INFILE=temp,
                  REPLI_ROOT=w_fstr,
                  BYVAR=cnt mlev2,
                  VAR=matheff,
                  STAT=mean,
                  OUTFILE=exercise28);
run;
%BRR_PROCMEAN(INFILE=temp,
                  REPLI_ROOT=w_fstr,
                  BYVAR=cnt mlev3,
                  VAR=matheff,
                  STAT=mean,
                  OUTFILE=exercise29);
run;
%BRR_PROCMEAN(INFILE=temp,
                  REPLI_ROOT=w_fstr,
                  BYVAR=cnt mlev4,
                  VAR=matheff,
                  STAT=mean,
                  OUTFILE=exercise30);
run;
%BRR_PROCMEAN(INFILE=temp,
                  REPLI_ROOT=w_fstr,
                  BYVAR=cnt mlev5,
                  VAR=matheff,
                  STAT=mean,
                  OUTFILE=exercise31);
run;
```

Table 8.6 ■ **Mean estimates and standard errors for self-efficacy in mathematics per proficiency level**

Level		PV1	PV2	PV3	PV4	PV5
Below Level 1	$\hat{\mu}_i$	-0.68	-0.70	-0.74	-0.72	-0.77
	$\sigma^2_{(\hat{\mu}_i)}$	$(0.06)^2$	$(0.06)^2$	$(0.06)^2$	$(0.05)^2$	$(0.06)^2$
Level 1	$\hat{\mu}_i$	-0.44	-0.45	-0.42	-0.43	-0.40
	$\sigma^2_{(\hat{\mu}_i)}$	$(0.06)^2$	$(0.05)^2$	$(0.06)^2$	$(0.04)^2$	$(0.05)^2$
Level 2	$\hat{\mu}_i$	-0.18	-0.16	-0.17	-0.18	-0.18
	$\sigma^2_{(\hat{\mu}_i)}$	$(0.03)^2$	$(0.03)^2$	$(0.03)^2$	$(0.03)^2$	$(0.03)^2$
Level 3	$\hat{\mu}_i$	0.09	0.09	0.12	0.11	0.10
	$\sigma^2_{(\hat{\mu}_i)}$	$(0.03)^2$	$(0.03)^2$	$(0.03)^2$	$(0.03)^2$	$(0.03)^2$
Level 4	$\hat{\mu}_i$	0.43	0.45	0.41	0.45	0.44
	$\sigma^2_{(\hat{\mu}_i)}$	$(0.03)^2$	$(0.03)^2$	$(0.03)^2$	$(0.03)^2$	$(0.03)^2$
Level 5	$\hat{\mu}_i$	0.85	0.84	0.86	0.79	0.82
	$\sigma^2_{(\hat{\mu}_i)}$	$(0.04)^2$	$(0.04)^2$	$(0.03)^2$	$(0.04)^2$	$(0.04)^2$
Level 6	$\hat{\mu}_i$	1.22	1.23	1.27	1.28	1.29
	$\sigma^2_{(\hat{\mu}_i)}$	$(0.05)^2$	$(0.05)^2$	$(0.06)^2$	$(0.05)^2$	$(0.07)^2$

SAS syntax also allows embedding macros within macros. The SAS® macro presented in Box 8.6 will perform exactly the same computations as the SAS® syntax presented in Box 8.5.

Box 8.6 ■ **SAS® macro for computing the mean of self-efficacy in mathematics per proficiency level**

```
%include "c:\pisa2003\prg\macro_procmeans_nopv.sas";

%MACRO repeat5();
%do m=1 %to 5;
     %BRR_PROCMEAN(INFILE=temp,
                   REPLI_ROOT=w_fstr,
                   BYVAR=cnt mlev&m,
                   VAR=matheff,
                   STAT=mean,
                   OUTFILE=ex&m);
     run;
%end;
%mend repeat5;
%repeat5;
run;
```

To combine the results:

- Per proficiency level, the five mean estimates are averaged;
- Per proficiency level, the five sampling variances are averaged;
- By comparing the final estimate and the five PV estimates, the imputation variance is computed;

- The final sampling variance and the imputation variance are combined as usual to get the final error variance; and
- The standard error is obtained by taking the square root of the error variance.

Final results are presented in Table 8.7.

The definition of a new SAS® macro always starts with the statement "%MACRO" followed by the name given to the macro and ends with the statement "%mend" followed by the name of the macro.

The iteration process starts with the statement "%do i=1 %to 5" and ends with "%end". In the example, the iteration process will repeat 5 times the commands included between the start and the end commands. It will therefore run the PROCMEAN macro five times.

Between each of the five runs, two elements will change:

- The second breakdown variable. The first run will use MLEV1, the second MLEV2, and so on. This change is implemented by adding the i value to the root of the variable name MLEV; and
- The output data file. For the first run, results will be stored in the output data file *ex1*; for the second run, it will be stored in *ex2* and so on.

This new macro can also be improved by adding the syntax that will combine the results from the 5 runs to get the final estimate and its standard error, as in Box 8.7.

Box 8.7 ■ **SAS® macro for computing the mean of self-efficacy in mathematics per proficiency level**

```
%MACRO repeat5();
%do m=1 %to 5;
     %BRR_PROCMEAN(INFILE=temp,
                   REPLI_ROOT=w_fstr,
                   BYVAR=cnt mlev&m,
                   VAR=matheff,
                   STAT=mean,
                   OUTFILE=ex&m);
     run;
     data ex&m;
            set ex&m;
            stat&m=stat;
            sestat&m=sestat;
            mlev=mlev&m;
            keep cnt mlev stat&m sestat&m;
     run;
%end;
data exercise32;
     merge ex1 ex2 ex3 ex4 ex5;
     by cnt mlev;
     stat=(stat1+stat2+stat3+stat4+stat5)/5;
     samp=((sestat1**2)+(sestat2**2)+(sestat3**2)+(sestat4**2)+(sestat5**
2))/5;
     mesvar=(((stat1-stat)**2)+((stat2-stat)**2)+((stat3-stat)**2)+
((stat4-stat)**2)+((stat5-stat)**2))/5;
     sestat=(samp+(1.2*mesvar))**0.5;
     keep cnt mlev stat sestat;
run;
%mend repeat5;
%repeat5;
run;
```

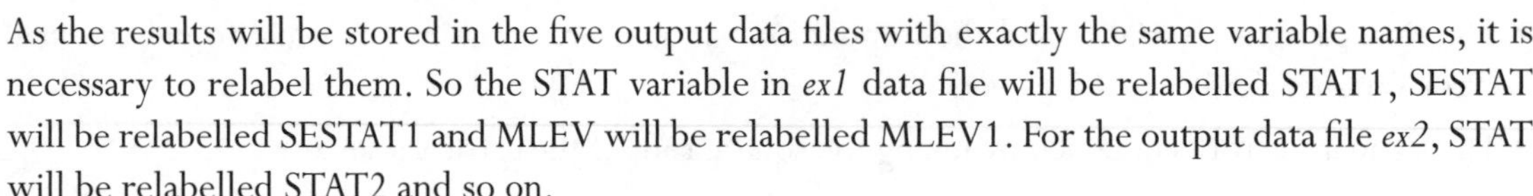

As the results will be stored in the five output data files with exactly the same variable names, it is necessary to relabel them. So the STAT variable in *ex1* data file will be relabelled STAT1, SESTAT will be relabelled SESTAT1 and MLEV will be relabelled MLEV1. For the output data file *ex2*, STAT will be relabelled STAT2 and so on.

Once the iteration process is completed, the output data files are merged according to the breakdown variables (in this particular case, by CNT) and by proficiency levels (MLEV).

Then,

- The final estimate is computed by averaging the five estimates;
- The final sampling variance is computed by averaging the five sampling variances;
- The imputation variance is computed; and
- The standard error is computed by combining the sampling variance and the imputation variance and taking the square root.

The structure of the output data file *exercise32* is presented in Table 8.7.

Table 8.7 ■ **Structure of the output data file *exercise32***

CNT	MLEV	STAT	SESTAT
DEU	0	-0.72	0.07
DEU	1	-0.43	0.06
DEU	2	-0.17	0.03
DEU	3	0.10	0.03
DEU	4	0.44	0.03
DEU	5	0.83	0.05
DEU	6	1.26	0.07

Table 8.7 shows that high self-efficacy in mathematics (STAT) is associated with higher proficiency level (MLEV).

CONCLUSIONS

This chapter shows how to compute the percentage of students per proficiency level. As shown, the algorithm is similar to the one used for other statistics.

The difficulty of conducting analyses using proficiency levels as the explanatory (independent) variables was also discussed.

Notes

1. In PISA 2000, the cutpoints that frame the proficiency levels in reading are precisely: 334.7526, 407.4667, 480.1807, 552.8948 and 625.6088.

2. This formula is a simplification of the general formula provided in Chapter 4. M, denoting the number of plausible values, has been replaced by 5.

Analyses with School Level Variables

INTRODUCTION

The target population in PISA is 15-year-old students. This population was chosen because, at this age in most OECD countries, students are nearing the end of their compulsory schooling, so PISA should be able to give an indication of the cumulative effect of the education for the student over the years. There is a two-stage sampling procedure used in PISA. After the population is defined, school samples are selected with a probability proportional to size. Subsequently, 35 students are randomly selected from each school. As the target population is based on age, it is therefore possible that the students will come from a variety of grades.

Table 9.1 presents the distribution of 15-year-olds per country and per grade in PISA 2003.

Table 9.1 ■ **Estimates of student percentage per grade and per country in PISA 2003**[a]

	7	8	9	10	11	12
AUS	0.01	0.14	8.34	72.26	19.21	0.05
AUT	0.30	5.07	43.18	51.45		
BEL	0.33	3.69	29.64	65.49	0.85	
BRA	13.70	24.82	42.89	18.08	0.51	
CAN	0.57	2.47	13.74	82.04	1.17	0.00
CHE	0.75	16.90	62.77	19.40	0.18	
CZE	0.15	2.82	44.67	52.36		
DEU	1.70	14.99	59.94	23.25	0.12	
DNK	0.07	9.10	86.96	3.83	0.05	
ESP	0.03	3.18	27.03	69.73	0.02	
FIN	0.26	12.43	87.31			
FRA	0.20	5.37	34.86	57.29	2.23	0.05
GBR			0.02	33.81	63.56	2.61
GRC	0.22	2.09	6.55	76.13	15.01	
HKG	5.12	10.75	25.70	58.36	0.08	
HUN	1.08	5.00	65.13	28.76	0.02	
IDN	2.40	12.68	48.78	34.51	1.57	0.07
IRL	0.02	2.78	60.87	16.68	19.65	
ISL				100.00		
ITA	0.18	1.38	14.20	79.95	4.28	
JPN				100.00		
KOR			1.57	98.33	0.10	
LIE	0.61	20.37	71.26	7.75		
LUX		14.85	55.79	29.25	0.10	
LVA	1.09	16.76	75.96	6.08	0.13	
MAC	12.30	25.88	36.82	24.66	0.34	
MEX	3.62	10.95	40.76	43.69	0.93	0.04
NLD	0.14	4.44	45.61	49.32	0.47	0.02
NOR			0.62	98.68	0.69	
NZL		0.06	6.79	89.38	3.74	0.02
POL	0.72	3.07	95.70	0.51		
PRT	4.25	10.58	20.26	64.32	0.58	
RUS	0.35	2.58	28.74	67.23	1.10	
SVK	0.58	0.92	37.10	60.93	0.46	
SWE	0.03	2.36	93.00	4.61		
THA	0.18	1.09	44.06	53.26	1.41	
TUN	15.39	21.99	25.15	34.52	2.94	
TUR	0.84	4.39	3.20	52.12	39.19	0.25
URY	5.67	9.67	18.22	59.36	7.09	
USA	0.28	2.40	29.71	60.63	6.98	
YUG			97.60	2.40		

a. The results are based on the information provided in the student tracking forms. These results are therefore not biased due to a differential grade participation rate.

In a few countries, most of the 15-year-old population tend to be in a modal grade, whereas in others, the 15-year-old population is spread across several grades.

The PISA target population can spread over several grades for different reasons:

- If the student does not pass a particular grade examination, he or she has to repeat the grade. For example in some countries there may be up to about 35 per cent of students who have already repeated at least one grade.
- Even if grade retention is not used, the 15-year-old population might be separated at the testing time into two grades. For logistical reasons, PISA testing takes place in a single calendar year. As the recommended testing window is around April (in the northern hemisphere), the PISA target population is defined as all students between 15 years and 3 months old and 16 years and 2 months old at the beginning of the testing period. If the entrance rules for compulsory education are defined in terms of complete calendar years, then the PISA target population will attend just one grade.

As the 15-year-old population attends different grades in most OECD countries, the within-school samples can only consist of a random sample of students. Consequently, the PISA participating students are attending several grades and within a particular grade, are in several classes, depending on the school size. Largely because the PISA sample is not class based, PISA 2000 and PISA 2003 did not collect data at the teacher level. However, PISA collects data at the school level. This chapter describes how and why school level data should be analysed.

Since the PISA target population attends several grades in most countries, it would be interesting to compute the average performance growth between two adjacent grades, so that performance differences between countries could be translated into school year effect. However, this would certainly lead to an overestimation of the performance growth: 15-year-olds attending lower grades are either lower achievers or younger students, and 15-year-olds attending higher grades are either high achievers or older students. Therefore, comparisons of different grade sub-populations cannot be made with confidence. Equalizing these sub-populations by controlling the student performance by a set of background characteristics can be attempted, but things are really never equal.

LIMITS OF THE PISA SCHOOL SAMPLES

As mentioned earlier, the following statement is valid for both PISA and IEA studies:

> Although the student's samples were drawn from within a sample of schools, the school sample was designed to optimize the resulting sample of students, rather than to give an optimal sample of schools. For this reason, it is always preferable to analyse the school-level variables as attributes of students, rather than as elements in their own right (Gonzalez and Kennedy, 2003).

This advice is particularly important in PISA as the target population is not defined as a grade, but as all students of a particular age.

In some countries, lower secondary and upper secondary education are provided by the same school, whereas in others, this is not the case because lower and upper secondary education are provided by different schools. In these countries, usually, the transition between lower and upper secondary education occurs around the age of 15, *i.e.* in most cases, at the end of compulsory education. As PISA focuses on the 15-year-old population, it means that one part of the target population is attending upper secondary education, while the other is attending lower secondary education. Consequently, in some countries, 15-year-olds can be in different educational institutions.

As discussed in Chapter 2, schools are selected from the school sample frame by the PPS sampling method, *i.e.* proportionally to the number of 15-year-olds attending the school. This might mean, for example that upper secondary schools only attended by students over the PISA age of 15 should not be included in the school sample frame. Similarly, lower secondary schools without any 15-year-olds should not be included in the school sample frame.

Thus, neither the lower secondary school population, nor the upper secondary school population represents the 15-year-old school population. In other words, the PISA school target population does not necessarily match the school population(s) within a particular country.

This lack of a perfect match between the usual school population(s) and the PISA school population affects the way school data should be analysed. To avoid biases for the population estimates, school data have to be imported into the student data files and have to be analysed with the student final weight. This means, for example, that one will not estimate the percentage of public schools versus private schools, but will estimate the percentage of 15-year-olds attending private schools versus public schools. From a pedagogical and or policy point of views, what is really important is not the percentage of schools that present such characteristics, but the percentage of students who are affected by these characteristics, *i.e.* the percentage of students attending a school with such characteristics.

MERGING THE SCHOOL AND STUDENT DATA FILES

Box 9.1 provides the SAS® syntax for merging the student data file and the school data file. Both files need first to be sorted by the identification variables, *i.e.* CNT, SCHOOLID and STIDSTD in the student data file and CNT and SCHOOLID in the school data file. Afterwards, the two sorted data files can be merged according to the common identification variables, *i.e.* CNT and SCHOOLID.

Box 9.1 ■ **SAS® syntax for merging the student data file and the school data file**

```
libname PISA2003  "c:\pisa2003\data\";
options nofmterr notes;
run;

data temp1;
     set pisa2003.stud;
run;
proc sort data=temp1;
     by cnt schoolid stidstd;
run;
data temp2;
     set pisa2003.schi;
run;
proc sort data = temp2;
     by cnt schoolid;
run;
data pisa2003.alldata;
     merge temp1 temp2;
     by cnt schoolid;
run;
```

ANALYSES OF THE SCHOOL VARIABLES

After merging the student data file and the school data file, school data can be analyzed like any student level variables as school variables are now considered as attributes of students. However, in this case, it is even more critical to use the replicate weights to compute sampling errors. Failure to do so would give a completely misleading inference.

The remainder of this chapter explains the methods for computing the percentages of students by school location and their respective standard errors as well as the student average performance on the mathematics scale per school location.

Box 9.2 presents the question about school location in the school questionnaire.

Box 9.2 ■ **School question on school location in PISA 2003**

Q 1 Which of the following best describes the community in which your school is located?

(Please <tick> only one box.)

A <village, hamlet or rural area> (fewer than 3 000 people) ❑ 1
A <small town> (3 000 to about 15 000 people) ❑ 2
A <town> (15 000 to about 100 000 people) ❑ 3
A <city> (100 000 to about 1 000 000 people) ❑ 4
A large <city> with over 1 000 000 people ❑ 5

Box 9.3 provides the SAS® syntax. As previously indicated, the SAS® macro might be CPU-consuming and thus it is advised to keep only the variables indispensable for the analyses.

Box 9.3 ■ **SAS® syntax for computing the percentage of students and the average mathematics performance per school location**

```
data temp;
      set pisa2003.alldata;
      if (cnt="DEU");
      w_fstr0=w_fstuwt;
      mcomb1=pv1math;
      mcomb2=pv2math;
      mcomb3=pv3math;
      mcomb4=pv4math;
      mcomb5=pv5math;
      keep cnt schoolid stidstd
           w_fstr0-w_fstr80
           mcomb1-mcomb5
           sc01q01;
run;
%include "c:\pisa2003\prg\macro_freq_nopv.sas";
%BRR_FREQ(INFILE=temp,
          REPLI_ROOT=w_fstr,
          BYVAR=cnt,
          VAR=sc01q01,
          OUTFILE=exercise33);
run;
%include "c:\pisa2003\prg\macro_procmeans.sas";
%BRR_PROCMEAN_PV(INFILE=temp,
             REPLI_ROOT=w_fstr,
             BYVAR=cnt sc01q01,
             PV_ROOT=mcomb,
             STAT=mean,
             OUTFILE=exercise34);
run;
```

Table 9.2 and Table 9.3 present the structure of the output data files *exercise33* and *exercise34*.

Table 9.2 ■ **Structure of the output data file *exercise33***

CNT	SC01Q01	STAT	SESTAT
DEU	1	5.04	1.37
DEU	2	24.61	2.70
DEU	3	38.76	3.75
DEU	4	19.53	2.77
DEU	5	12.06	1.98

Table 9.3 ■ **Structure of the output data file *exercise34***

CNT	SC01Q01	STAT	SESTAT
DEU	1	489.65	14.81
DEU	2	507.46	6.19
DEU	3	496.74	8.92
DEU	4	510.24	13.19
DEU	5	507.07	14.13

As a reminder, the school data was analysed at the student level and weighted by the student final weight. Therefore, results should be interpreted as: 5.04 per cent of the 15-year-olds are attending a school located in a village with less than 3 000 people. Twenty-five per cent of the students are attending a school located in a small town (from 3 000 to 15 000 people) and so on. The students attending a school located in a small village on average perform at 489.65 and so on.

As the percentages for some categories might be small, the standard error will be large for the mean estimates.

All the SAS® macros described in the previous chapters can be used on the school variables once they have been imported in the student data file.

CONCLUSIONS

For statistical and pedagogical reasons, the data collected through the school questionnaire, as well as the variables derived from that instrument, have to be analysed at the student level.

All the SAS® macros developed can be used without any modifications. The interpretation of the results should clearly state the analysis level, *i.e.* for instance the percentage of students attending a school located in a small village and not the percentage of schools located in a small village.

Standard Error on a Difference

INTRODUCTION

Suppose that X represents the student score for a mathematics test and Y the student score for a science test for the same sample of students. To summarize the score distribution for both tests, one can compute:

- $\mu_{(X)}, \mu_{(Y)}$, representing respectively the mean of X and the mean of Y,
- $\sigma^2_{(X)}, \sigma^2_{(Y)}$, representing respectively the variance of X and the variance of Y

It can be shown that:

$$\mu_{(X+Y)} = \mu_{(X)} + \mu_{(Y)} \text{ and}$$

$$\sigma^2_{(X+Y)} = \sigma^2_{(X)} + \sigma^2_{(Y)} + 2\operatorname{cov}(X,Y)$$

If a total score is computed by just adding the mathematics and science scores, then according to these two formulae, the mean of this total score will be the sum of the two initial means and the variance of the total score will be equal to the sum of the variance of the two initial variables X and Y plus two times the covariance between X and Y. This covariance represents the relationship between X and Y. Usually, high achievers in mathematics are also high achievers in science and thus one should expect in this particular example a positive and high covariance.

Similarly,

$$\mu_{(X-Y)} = \mu_{(X)} - \mu_{(Y)} \text{ and}$$

$$\sigma^2_{(X-Y)} = \sigma^2_{(X)} + \sigma^2_{(Y)} - 2\operatorname{cov}(X,Y)$$

In other words, the variance of a difference is equal to the sum of the variances of the two initial variables minus two times the covariance between the two initial variables.

As described in Chapter 3, a sampling distribution has the same characteristics as any distribution, except that units consist of sample estimates and not observations. Therefore,

$$\sigma^2_{(\hat{\mu}_X - \hat{\mu}_Y)} = \sigma^2_{(\hat{\mu}_X)} + \sigma^2_{(\hat{\mu}_Y)} - 2\operatorname{cov}(\hat{\mu}_X, \hat{\mu}_Y)$$

The sampling variance of a difference is equal to the sum of the two initial sampling variances minus two times the covariance between the two sampling distributions on the estimates.

Suppose that one wants to determine whether the girls' performance is on average higher than the boys' performance. As for all statistical analyses, the null hypothesis has to be tested. In this particular example, it will consist of computing the difference between the boys' performance mean and the girls' performance mean or the inverse. The null hypothesis will be:

$$H_0 : \hat{\mu}_{(boys)} - \hat{\mu}_{(girls)} = 0$$

To test this null hypothesis, the standard error on this difference has to be computed and then compared to the observed difference. The respective standard errors on the mean estimate for boys and for girls ($\sigma_{(\hat{\mu}_{boys})}, \sigma_{(\hat{\mu}_{girls})}$) can be easily computed.

What does the covariance between the two variables, *i.e.* $\hat{\mu}_{(boys)}, \hat{\mu}_{(girls)}$, tell us? A positive covariance means that if $\hat{\mu}_{(boys)}$ increases, then $\hat{\mu}_{(girls)}$ will also increase. A covariance equal or close to 0 means that $\hat{\mu}_{(boys)}$ can increase or decrease with $\hat{\mu}_{(girls)}$ remaining unchanged. Finally, a negative covariance means that if $\hat{\mu}_{(boys)}$ increases, then $\hat{\mu}_{(girls)}$ will decrease, and inversely.

How are $\hat{\mu}_{(boys)}$ and $\hat{\mu}_{(girls)}$ correlated? Suppose that in the school sample, a coeducational school attended by low achievers is replaced by a coeducational school attended by high achievers. The country mean will increase slightly, as well as the boys' and the girls' means. If the replacement process is continued, $\hat{\mu}_{(boys)}$ and $\hat{\mu}_{(girls)}$ will likely increase in a similar pattern. Indeed, a coeducational school attended by high achieving boys is usually also attended by high achieving girls. Therefore, the covariance between $\hat{\mu}_{(boys)}$ and $\hat{\mu}_{(girls)}$ will be positive.

Let us now suppose that all schools are single gender. A boys' school can replace a girls' school in the sample and therefore $\hat{\mu}_{(boys)}$ and $\hat{\mu}_{(girls)}$ will change. If gender is used as a stratification variable, *i.e.* all girls' schools are allocated to an explicit stratum and all boys schools are allocated to another explicit stratum, then a girls' school can only be replaced by another girls school. In this case, only $\hat{\mu}_{(girls)}$ will change. As might change without affecting $\hat{\mu}_{(boys)}$, the expected value of the covariance between $\hat{\mu}_{(boys)}$ and $\hat{\mu}_{(girls)}$ is 0.

Finally, a negative covariance means that if a school is attended by high achieving boys, then that school is also attended by low achieving girls or the inverse. This situation is not so likely.

In summary, the expected value of the covariance will be equal to 0 if the two sub-samples are independent. If the two sub-samples are not independent, then the expected value of the covariance might differ from 0.

In PISA, as well as in IEA studies, country samples are independent. Therefore, for any comparison between two countries, the expected value of the covariance will be equal to 0, and thus the standard error on the estimate is:

$$\sigma_{(\hat{\theta}_i - \hat{\theta}_j)} = \sqrt{\sigma^2_{(\hat{\theta}_i)} + \sigma^2_{(\hat{\theta}_j)}}, \text{ with } \theta \text{ being any statistic.}$$

For instance, on the mathematics scale in PISA 2003, the German mean is equal to 503 with a standard error of 3.3, and the Belgian mean is equal to 529 with a standard error of 2.3. Therefore, the difference between Belgium and Germany will be 529-503=26 and the standard error on this difference is:

$$\sigma_{(\hat{\theta}_i - \hat{\theta}_j)} = \sqrt{\sigma^2_{(\hat{\theta}_i)} + \sigma^2_{(\hat{\theta}_j)}} = \sqrt{(3.3)^2 + (2.3)^2} = \sqrt{10.89 + 5.29} = \sqrt{16.18} = 4.02$$

The difference divided by its standard error, *i.e.* 26/4.02 = 6.46, is greater than 1.96, which is significant. This means that Belgian's performance is greater than Germany's.

Similarly, the percentage of students below Level 1 is equal to 9.2 in Germany (with a standard error of 0.8) and to 7.2 in Belgium (with a standard error of 0.6). The difference is equal to 9.2-7.2=2 and the standard error on this difference is equal to:

$$\sigma_{(\hat{\theta}_i - \hat{\theta}_j)} = \sqrt{\sigma^2_{(\hat{\theta}_i)} + \sigma^2_{(\hat{\theta}_j)}} = \sqrt{(0.6)^2 + (0.8)^2} = \sqrt{0.36 + 0.64} = \sqrt{1} = 1$$

The standardised difference is equal to 2 (*i.e.* 2/1), which is significant. Thus the percentage of students below Level 1 is greater in Germany than in Belgium.

Within a particular country, any sub-samples will be considered as independent if the categorical variable used to define the sub-samples was used as an explicit stratification variable. For instance, since Canada used the provinces as an explicit stratification variable, then these sub-samples are independent and any comparison between two provinces does not require the estimation of the covariance between the sampling distributions.

As a general rule, any comparison between countries does not require the estimation of the covariance, but it is strongly advised to estimate the covariance between the sampling distributions for any within-country comparisons.

As described earlier in this section, the estimation of the covariance between, for instance, $\hat{\mu}_{(boys)}$ and $\hat{\mu}_{(girls)}$ would require the selection of several samples and then the analysis of the variation of $\hat{\mu}_{(boys)}$ in conjunction with $\hat{\mu}_{(girls)}$. Such procedure is of course unrealistic. Therefore, as for any computation of a standard error in PISA, replication methods using the supplied replicate weights will be used to estimate the standard error on a difference.

THE STANDARD ERROR OF A DIFFERENCE WITHOUT PLAUSIBLE VALUES

Let us suppose that a researcher wants to test whether girls in Germany have higher job expectations than boys.

As described in Chapter 6, the SAS® macro PROCMEANS_NOPV can be used to estimate the average job expectation for boys and girls respectively.

Box 10.1 presents the SAS® syntax for the computation of the mean for the job expectations at the age of 30 (BSMJ) per gender. Table 10.1 presents the structure of the output data file as well as the results per gender.

Box 10.1 ■ **SAS® syntax for computing the mean of job expectations per gender**

```
libname PISA2003  "c:\pisa2003\data\";
options nofmterr notes;
run;

data temp;
     set pisa2003.stud;
     if (cnt="DEU") ;
     if (not missing (st03Q01));
     w_fstr0=w_fstuwt;
     if (st03q01=1) then gender=1;
     if (st03q01=2) then gender=0;
     keep cnt schoolid stidstd w_fstr0-w_fstr80
          pv1math pv2math pv3math pv4math pv5math
          st03q01 gender hisei bsmj;
run;

%include "c:\pisa2003\prg\macro_procmeans_nopv.sas";

%BRR_PROCMEAN(INFILE=temp,
              REPLI_ROOT=w_fstr,
              BYVAR=cnt st03q01,
              VAR=bsmj,
              STAT=mean,
              OUTFILE=exercise35);
run;
```

Table 10.1 ■ **Structure of the output data file *exercise35***

CNT	ST03Q01	STAT	SESTAT
DEU	1	53.05	0.57
DEU	2	50.58	0.69

On average, the job expectation is 53.05 for girls and 50.58 for boys. As German schools are usually coeducational and as gender is not used as an explicit stratification variable, the expected value of the covariance might differ from 0.

To compute the standard error per gender, it is necessary to compute the mean estimate for each of the 80 replicate weights. Table 10.2 presents the mean estimate per weight and per gender.

The final difference estimate will be the difference between the two final estimates, *i.e.* 53.05 – 50.58 = 2.47.

The procedure to estimate the final standard error is quite straightforward. It is exactly similar to the procedure described in Chapter 6, except that θ is now a difference, and not a mean or a regression coefficient. The different steps are:

- The difference between the girls and the boys means is computed per replicate;
- Each of the 80 difference estimates is compared with the final difference estimate, then squared;
- The sum of the square is computed then divided by 20 to obtain the sampling variance on the difference; and
- The standard error is the square root of the sampling variance.

These different steps can be summarized as:

$$\sigma_{(\hat{\theta})} = \sqrt{\frac{1}{20}\sum_{i=1}^{80}(\hat{\theta}_{(i)} - \hat{\theta})^2} \text{ with } \theta \text{ being a difference.}$$

Concretely:

- For the first replicate, the difference between the girls mean estimate and the boys mean estimate is equal to (53.29-50.69)=2.60. For the second replicate, the difference estimate will be equal to (53.16-50.53)=2.63 and so on for the 80 replicates. All these difference estimates are presented in Table 10.3.
- Each of the 80 replicate difference estimates is compared with the final difference estimate and this difference is squared. For the first replicate, it will be $(2.60-2.47)^2 = 0.0164$. For the second replicates, it will be $(2.63-2.47)^2 = 0.0258$. These squared differences are also presented in Table 10.3.
- These squared differences are summed. This sum is equal to: (0.0164+0.0258+.....+0.0641) = 9.7360. The sampling variance on the difference is therefore equal to:

  $$\frac{9.7360}{20} = 0.4868.$$

- The standard error is equal to the square root of 0.4868, *i.e.* 0.6977.

As $\frac{2.47}{0.6977}$ is greater than 1.96, job expectations for girls are statistically greater than job expectations for boys in Germany.

If the researcher had considered the two German sub-samples as independent, then he or she would have obtained for the standard error on this difference:

$$\sigma_{(\hat{\theta}_i - \hat{\theta}_j)} = \sqrt{\sigma^2_{(\hat{\theta}_i)} + \sigma^2_{(\hat{\theta}_j)}} = \sqrt{(0.57)^2 + (0.69)^2} = 0.895$$

In this particular case, the difference between the unbiased estimate of the standard error (*i.e.* 0.698) and the biased estimate of the standard error (*i.e.* 0.895) is quite small. As it will be shown later in this chapter, the difference between the biased and unbiased estimates of the standard error can be substantial.

Table 10.2 ■ **Mean estimates for the final and 80 replicate weights per gender**

Weight	Mean estimate for girls	Mean estimate for boys	Weight	Mean estimate for girls	Mean estimate for boys
Final weight	**53.05**	**50.58**			
Replicate 1	53.29	50.69	Replicate 41	52.69	50.55
Replicate 2	53.16	50.53	Replicate 42	53.28	51.23
Replicate 3	53.16	50.45	Replicate 43	53.07	50.39
Replicate 4	53.30	50.70	Replicate 44	52.95	49.72
Replicate 5	52.79	50.28	Replicate 45	53.31	51.04
Replicate 6	53.14	50.76	Replicate 46	53.72	50.80
Replicate 7	53.04	50.36	Replicate 47	52.91	51.03
Replicate 8	52.97	50.11	Replicate 48	53.10	50.53
Replicate 9	53.28	51.37	Replicate 49	53.05	50.81
Replicate 10	53.01	50.55	Replicate 50	53.79	50.90
Replicate 11	53.26	50.70	Replicate 51	52.65	50.15
Replicate 12	53.16	49.86	Replicate 52	53.30	50.45
Replicate 13	52.81	50.94	Replicate 53	52.68	50.12
Replicate 14	53.21	50.71	Replicate 54	52.74	50.01
Replicate 15	53.39	50.23	Replicate 55	53.50	50.11
Replicate 16	53.06	50.46	Replicate 56	52.54	50.58
Replicate 17	53.34	50.48	Replicate 57	53.31	51.03
Replicate 18	52.71	50.42	Replicate 58	53.13	50.34
Replicate 19	53.18	50.87	Replicate 59	52.72	50.37
Replicate 20	52.82	50.44	Replicate 60	53.49	51.43
Replicate 21	53.36	50.74	Replicate 61	53.13	50.71
Replicate 22	53.15	50.72	Replicate 62	53.61	51.27
Replicate 23	53.24	50.65	Replicate 63	52.74	50.15
Replicate 24	52.68	50.51	Replicate 64	53.19	50.25
Replicate 25	52.76	50.44	Replicate 65	53.28	51.04
Replicate 26	52.79	50.43	Replicate 66	52.91	50.94
Replicate 27	53.01	50.58	Replicate 67	53.25	50.85
Replicate 28	53.24	50.12	Replicate 68	53.12	50.74
Replicate 29	52.86	50.68	Replicate 69	53.08	50.31
Replicate 30	52.85	50.02	Replicate 70	52.92	50.44
Replicate 31	52.90	50.85	Replicate 71	53.35	50.63
Replicate 32	53.25	50.60	Replicate 72	53.25	50.75
Replicate 33	53.32	50.54	Replicate 73	52.54	50.42
Replicate 34	52.42	50.55	Replicate 74	52.58	50.20
Replicate 35	52.91	50.72	Replicate 75	52.49	49.75
Replicate 36	53.06	50.36	Replicate 76	52.98	50.96
Replicate 37	52.67	50.73	Replicate 77	53.04	50.24
Replicate 38	53.36	50.16	Replicate 78	53.30	50.44
Replicate 39	52.57	50.36	Replicate 79	52.93	50.36
Replicate 40	53.07	50.58	Replicate 80	52.98	50.76

Table 10.3 ■ **Difference estimates for the final and 80 replicate weights**

Weight	Difference between boys and girls (G - B)	Squared difference between the replicate and the final estimates	Weight	Difference between boys and girls (G - B)	Squared difference between the replicate and the final estimates
Final weight	**2.47**				
Replicate 1	2.60	0.0164	Replicate 41	2.14	0.1079
Replicate 2	2.63	0.0258	Replicate 42	2.05	0.1789
Replicate 3	2.72	0.0599	Replicate 43	2.68	0.0440
Replicate 4	2.61	0.0180	Replicate 44	3.23	0.5727
Replicate 5	2.51	0.0011	Replicate 45	2.28	0.0373
Replicate 6	2.39	0.0067	Replicate 46	2.92	0.2038
Replicate 7	2.68	0.0450	Replicate 47	1.88	0.3488
Replicate 8	2.86	0.1483	Replicate 48	2.56	0.0084
Replicate 9	1.92	0.3085	Replicate 49	2.23	0.0567
Replicate 10	2.46	0.0002	Replicate 50	2.89	0.1768
Replicate 11	2.57	0.0089	Replicate 51	2.49	0.0004
Replicate 12	3.30	0.6832	Replicate 52	2.85	0.1440
Replicate 13	1.87	0.3620	Replicate 53	2.56	0.0072
Replicate 14	2.50	0.0009	Replicate 54	2.73	0.0667
Replicate 15	3.16	0.4756	Replicate 55	3.39	0.8520
Replicate 16	2.60	0.0173	Replicate 56	1.96	0.2631
Replicate 17	2.87	0.1577	Replicate 57	2.28	0.0351
Replicate 18	2.29	0.0327	Replicate 58	2.79	0.1017
Replicate 19	2.31	0.0269	Replicate 59	2.35	0.0158
Replicate 20	2.38	0.0078	Replicate 60	2.05	0.1749
Replicate 21	2.62	0.0221	Replicate 61	2.42	0.0027
Replicate 22	2.43	0.0014	Replicate 62	2.34	0.0164
Replicate 23	2.59	0.0142	Replicate 63	2.59	0.0137
Replicate 24	2.17	0.0901	Replicate 64	2.94	0.2230
Replicate 25	2.32	0.0227	Replicate 65	2.24	0.0539
Replicate 26	2.36	0.0132	Replicate 66	1.97	0.2524
Replicate 27	2.43	0.0015	Replicate 67	2.40	0.0050
Replicate 28	3.12	0.4225	Replicate 68	2.38	0.0089
Replicate 29	2.18	0.0844	Replicate 69	2.76	0.0848
Replicate 30	2.84	0.1333	Replicate 70	2.48	0.0002
Replicate 31	2.06	0.1709	Replicate 71	2.72	0.0609
Replicate 32	2.65	0.0312	Replicate 72	2.50	0.0006
Replicate 33	2.78	0.0970	Replicate 73	2.12	0.1217
Replicate 34	1.87	0.3611	Replicate 74	2.39	0.0073
Replicate 35	2.19	0.0809	Replicate 75	2.73	0.0693
Replicate 36	2.69	0.0490	Replicate 76	2.02	0.2031
Replicate 37	1.94	0.2825	Replicate 77	2.80	0.1058
Replicate 38	3.20	0.5355	Replicate 78	2.86	0.1519
Replicate 39	2.21	0.0683	Replicate 79	2.57	0.0091
Replicate 40	2.48	0.0001	Replicate 80	2.22	0.0641
			Sum of squared differences		9.7360

A SAS® macro has been developed for the computation of standard errors on differences. Box 10.2 resents the SAS® syntax for running this macro.

Box 10.2 ■ **SAS® macro for the computation of standard errors on differences**

```
%include "c:\pisa2003\prg\macro_procmeans_dif_nopv.sas";

%BRR_PROCMEAN_DIF(INFILE=temp,
                    REPLI_ROOT=w_fstr,
                    BYVAR=cnt ,
                    VAR=bsmj,
                    COMPARE=st03q01,
                    CATEGORY=1 2,
                    STAT=mean,
                    OUTFILE=exercise36);
run;
```

Beside the four arguments common to all SAS® macros, four other arguments have to be specified:

- The VAR argument informs the macro of the numerical variable on which a mean or a standard deviation will be computed per value of a categorical variable. In the example, VAR equals BSMJ.
- The COMPARE argument specifies the categorical variables on which the contrasts will be based.
- The CATEGORY argument specifies the values of the categorical variables for which contrasts are required. As gender has only two categories, denoted 1 and 2, the CATEGORY statement is set as "1 2". If a categorical variable has four categories and if these four categories are specified in the CATEGORY statement, then the macro will compute the standard error on the difference between:
  - Category 1 and category 2;
  - Category 1 and category 3;
  - Category 1 and category 4;
  - Category 2 and category 3;
  - Category 2 and category 4; and
  - Category 3 and category 4.

  If only categories 1 and 2 are specified, then only the contrast between 1 and 2 will be computed, regardless of the number of categories for this categorical variable.
- The STAT argument specifies the required statistic. See Chapter 5 for available statistics.

Table 10.4 ■ **Structure of the output data file *exercise36***

CNT	CONTRAST	STAT	SESTAT
DEU	1-2	2.47	0.6977

It is worth noting that for dichotomous variables, the standard error on the difference can also be computed by a regression model.

Box 10.3 ■ **An alternative SAS® macro for computing the standard error on a difference for dichotomous variable**

```
%include "c:\pisa2003\prg\macro_reg_nopv.sas";

%BRR_REG(INFILE=temp,
          REPLI_ROOT=w_fstr,
          VARDEP=bsmj,
          EXPLICA=gender,
          BYVAR=cnt,
          OUTFILE=exercise37);
run;
```

Table 10.5 ■ **Structure of the output data file *exercise37***

CNT	CLASS	STAT	SESTAT
DEU	intercept	50.58	0.686
DEU	gender	2.47	0.698

Except for the sign, the difference estimate and its respective standard error are equal to the regression coefficient estimate and its standard error. For polytomous categorical variables, the use of the regression macro would require the recoding of the categorical variables into *h*-1 dichotomous variables, with *h* being equal to the number of categories. Further, the regression macro will compare each category with the reference category, while the macro PROC_MEANS_DIF_NOPV will provide all contrasts.

THE STANDARD ERROR OF A DIFFERENCE WITH PLAUSIBLE VALUES

The procedure for computing the standard error on a difference that involves plausible values consists of:

- Using each plausible value and for the final and 80 replicate weights, the requested statistic, a mean for example, has to be computed per value of the categorical variable;
- Computing, per contrast, per plausible value and per replicate weight, the difference between the two categories. There will be 405 difference estimates: Table 10.6 presents the structure of these 405 differences;
- A final difference estimate equal to the average of the five difference estimates;
- Computing, per plausible value, the sampling variance by comparing the final difference estimate with the 80 replicate estimates;
- A final sampling variance equal to the average of the five sampling variances;
- Computing imputation variance, also denoted measurement error variance;
- Combining the sampling variance and the imputation variance to obtain the final error variance; and
- A standard error equal to the square root of the error variance.

Table 10.6 ■ **Gender difference estimates and their respective sampling variances on the mathematics scale**

Weight	PV1	PV2	PV3	PV4	PV5
Final	-8.94	-9.40	-8.96	-7.46	-10.12
Replicate 1	-9.64	-10.05	-10.29	-8.74	-11.45
....					
Replicate 80	-8.56	-8.52	-8.85	-7.70	-9.84
Sampling variance	$(4.11)^2$	$(4.36)^2$	$(4.10)^2$	$(4.31)^2$	$(4.28)^2$

A SAS® macro has been developed to compute standard errors on differences that involve plausible values. Box 10.4 provides the SAS® syntax. In this example, the standard error on the difference between the boys' and the girls' performance on the mathematics scale is computed.

Box 10.4 ■ **SAS® syntax to compute standard errors on differences that involve plausible values**

```
data temp1;
     set pisa2003.stud;
     if (cnt="DEU") ;
     if (not missing (st03Q01));
     w_fstr0=w_fstuwt;
     mcomb1=pv1math;
     mcomb2=pv2math;
     mcomb3=pv3math;
     mcomb4=pv4math;
     mcomb5=pv5math;
        keep cnt schoolid stidstd w_fstr0-w_fstr80
          mcomb1-mcomb5
          st03q01;
run;
%include "c:\pisa2003\prg\macro_procmeans_dif.sas";
%BRR_PROCMEAN_DIF_PV(INFILE=temp1,
                      REPLI_ROOT=w_fstr,
                      BYVAR=cnt,
                      PV_ROOT=mcomb,
                      COMPARE=st03q01,
                      CATEGORY=1 2,
                      STAT=mean,
                      OUTFILE=exercise38);
run;
```

In comparison with the previous SAS® macro, the VAR argument is replaced by the PV_ROOT argument.

Table 10.7 ■ **Structure of the output data file *exercise38***

CNT	CONTRAST	STAT	SESTAT
DEU	1-2	-8.98	4.37

As the absolute value of the ratio between the difference estimate and its respective standard error is greater than 1.96, the null hypothesis is rejected. Thus girls perform on average lower than boys in Germany. It is also worth noting that these results might also be obtained through the regression macro for plausible values.

Table 10.8 provides for all PISA 2003 countries the gender difference estimates on the mathematics scale, as well as the unbiased standard errors and the biased standard errors.

Table 10.8 ■ **Gender differences on the mathematics scale, unbiased standard errors and biased standard errors**

Country	Mean difference	Unbiased standard error	Biased standard error	Country	Mean difference	Unbiased standard error	Biased standard error
AUS	-5.34	3.75	4.04	KOR	-23.41	6.77	6.90
AUT	-7.57	4.40	5.59	LIE	-28.84	10.92	9.58
BEL	-7.51	4.81	4.69	LUX	-17.17	2.81	2.40
BRA	-16.26	4.06	7.49	LVA	-2.81	3.97	5.97
CAN	-11.17	2.13	2.78	MAC	-21.26	5.83	5.83
CHE	-16.63	4.87	5.98	MEX	-10.90	3.94	5.91
CZE	-14.97	5.08	6.11	NLD	-5.12	4.29	5.36
DEU	-8.98	4.37	5.59	NOR	-6.22	3.21	4.04
DNK	-16.58	3.20	4.50	NZL	-14.48	3.90	4.23
ESP	-8.86	2.98	4.02	POL	-5.59	3.14	4.18
FIN	-7.41	2.67	3.24	PRT	-12.25	3.31	5.41
FRA	-8.51	4.15	4.60	RUS	-10.12	4.36	6.75
GBR	-6.66	4.90	4.84	SVK	-18.66	3.65	5.30
GRC	-19.40	3.63	6.11	SWE	-6.53	3.27	4.30
HKG	-4.06	6.64	7.96	THA	4.02	4.24	5.22
HUN	-7.79	3.54	4.69	TUN	-12.17	2.51	4.01
IDN	-3.34	3.39	6.02	TUR	-15.13	6.16	10.33
IRL	-14.81	4.19	4.54	URY	-12.09	4.15	5.51
ISL	15.41	3.46	3.15	USA	-6.25	2.89	4.65
ITA	-17.83	5.89	5.96	YUG	-1.21	4.36	6.14
JPN	-8.42	5.89	7.04				

In nearly all countries, the unbiased standard error is smaller than the biased standard error, reflecting a positive covariance between the two sampling distributions. In a few countries, the difference between the two standard errors is small, but it is substantial for some other countries, such as Brazil, Greece, Indonesia and Turkey.

MULTIPLE COMPARISONS

In Chapter 3, it was noted that every statistical inference is associated with what is usually called a type I error. This error represents the risk of rejecting a null hypothesis that is true.

Let us suppose that at the population level, there is no difference in the mathematics between boys and girls. A sample is drawn and the gender difference in mathematics performance is computed. As this difference is based on a sample, a standard error on the difference has to be computed. If the standardised difference, *i.e.* the gender difference divided by its standard error, is less than -1.96 or greater than 1.96, that difference would be reported as significant. In fact, there are 5 chances out of 100 to observe a standardised difference lower than -1.96 or higher than 1.96 and still have the null hypothesis true. In other words, there are 5 chances out of 100 to reject the null hypothesis, when there is no true gender difference in the population.

If 100 countries are participating in the international survey and if the gender difference is computed for each of them, then it is statistically expected to report 5 of the 100 gender differences as significant, when there are no true differences at the population level.

For every country, the type I error is set at 0.05. For two countries, as countries are independent samples, the probability of not making a type I error, *i.e.* accepting both null hypotheses, is now equal to 0.9025 (0.95 times 0.95).

Table 10.9 ■ **The cross tabulation of the different probabilities**

		Country A	
		0.05	0.95
Country B	0.05	0.0025	0.0475
	0.95	0.0475	0.9025

This statistical issue is even more amplified for tables of multiple comparisons of achievement. Suppose that the means of three countries need to be compared. This will involve three tests: country A versus country B, country A versus country C, and country B versus country C. The probability of not making a type I error is therefore equal to:

$$(1-\alpha)(1-\alpha)(1-\alpha) = (1-\alpha)^3.$$

Broadly speaking, if X comparisons are tested, then the probability of not making a type I error is equal to:

$$(1-\alpha)^x$$

Dunn (1961) developed a general procedure that is appropriate for testing a set of *a priori* hypotheses, while controlling the probability of making a type I error. It consists of adjusting the value α. Precisely, the value α is divided by the number of comparisons and then its respective critical value is used.

In the case of three comparisons, the critical value for an $\alpha = 0.05$ will therefore be equal to 2.24 instead of 1.96. Indeed,

$$\frac{0.05}{3} = 0.01666$$

As the risk is shared by both tails of the sampling distribution, one has to find the z score that corresponds to the cumulative proportion of 0.008333. Consulting the cumulative function of the standardised normal distribution will return the value -2.24.

Nevertheless, the researcher still has to decide how many comparisons are involved. In PISA, it was decided that no correction of the critical value would be applied, except on multiple comparison tables. Indeed, in many cases, readers are primarily interested in finding out whether a given value in a particular country is different from a second value in the same or another country, *e.g.* whether females in a country perform better than males in the same country. Therefore, as only one test is performed at a time, then no adjustment is required.

On the other hand, with multiple comparison tables, the reader is interested in comparing the performance of one country with all other countries. For example, if one wants to compare the performance of country 1 with all other countries, we will have the following comparisons: country 1 versus country 2, country 1 versus country 3, and country 1 versus country L. Therefore, the adjustment will be based on L-1 comparisons.

In PISA 2003, as the results of 40 countries were published in the initial reports, the critical value will be based on 39 comparisons and will be equal to 3.2272. As more countries participated in PISA 2003, this critical value is slightly higher than the critical value for PISA 2000.[1]

CONCLUSIONS

This chapter was devoted to the computation of standard errors on differences. After a description of the statistical issues for such estimates, the different steps for computing such standard errors were presented. The SAS® macros to facilitate such computations were also described.

It was clearly stated that any comparison between countries does not require the estimation of the covariance. However, it is strongly advised that the covariance between the sampling distributions for any within-country comparisons should be estimated.

The two SAS® macros can however be used for between-country comparisons. As the expected value of the covariance is equal to 0, in a particular case, one might get a small positive or negative estimated covariance. Therefore, the standard error returned by the SAS® macro might be slightly different from the standard errors based only on the initial standard errors.

Finally, the correction of the critical value for multiple comparisons was discussed.

Note

1. The critical value in the multiple comparisons for PISA 2000 was 3.144.

OECD Average and OECD Total

INTRODUCTION

In all PISA initial and thematic reports, the OECD gives the results for each country, but also two additional aggregated estimates: the OECD average and the OECD total.

The OECD average, sometimes also referred to as the country average, is the mean of the data values for all OECD countries for which data are available or can be estimated. The OECD average can be used to see how a country compares on a given indicator with a typical OECD country. The OECD average does not take into account the absolute size of the population in each country, *i.e.* each country contributes equally to the average. The contribution of the smallest OECD country, *i.e.* Luxembourg, is equivalent to the one of the largest country, *i.e.* the United States.

The OECD total considers all the OECD countries as a single entity, to which each country contributes proportionally to the number of 15-year-olds enrolled in its schools. It illustrates how a country compares with the OECD as a whole.

In PISA 2003, all OECD countries as well as several partner countries participated. It is possible, however, that for a particular cycle, data for one or several OECD countries may not be available for specific indicators. Researchers should, therefore, keep in mind that the terms OECD average and OECD total refer to the OECD countries included in the respective comparisons for each cycle and for a particular comparison.

For simple statistics such as a mean or a percentage, the OECD average and the OECD total statistics and their respective standard errors can be mathematically computed. If C OECD countries participated, then the OECD average mean and its respective sampling variance are equal to:

$$\hat{\mu} = \frac{\sum_{h=1}^{C} \hat{\mu}_h}{C} \quad \text{and} \quad \sigma^2_{(\hat{\mu})} = \frac{\sum_{h=1}^{C} \sigma^2_{(\hat{\mu}_h)}}{C^2}$$

The OECD total mean and its respective sampling variance are equal to:

$$\hat{\mu} = \frac{\sum_{h=1}^{C} w_h \hat{\mu}_h}{\sum_{h=1}^{C} w_h} \quad \text{and} \quad \sigma^2_{(\hat{\mu})} = \frac{\sum_{h=1}^{C} w_h^2 \sigma^2_{(\hat{\mu}_h)}}{\left[\sum_{h=1}^{C} w_h\right]^2},$$

with w_h being the sum of the student final weights for a particular country.

While these formulae can be used for the computation of a mean or a percentage, they cannot be used for most other statistics. Such statistics can only be obtained directly from the data set.

RECODING OF THE DATABASE FOR THE ESTIMATION OF THE OECD TOTAL AND OECD AVERAGE

As stated in Chapter 3, the sum of the student final weights per country is an estimate of the 15-year-old population in that country. Therefore, the OECD total statistic can easily be obtained by deleting the partner country data. Then the statistic is computed, without using the country (CNT) breakdown variable. The standard error is obtained as usual by using the 80 replicates. Box 11.1 provides the SAS® syntax for the computation of the mathematics performance in PISA 2003 per gender for the OECD total and Table 11.1 provides the results of the procedure.

Box 11.1 ■ **SAS® syntax for the OECD total for the mathematics performance per gender**

```
libname PISA2003  "c:\pisa2003\data\";
options nofmterr notes;
run;

data temp;
     set pisa2003.stud;
     if (cnt in ('AUS','AUT','BEL','CAN','CZE','DNK','FIN','FRA',
                 'DEU','GBR','GRC','HUN','ISL','IRL','ITA','JPN','KOR',
                 'LUX','MEX','NLD','NZL','NOR','POL','PRT','SVK',
                  'ESP','SWE','CHE','TUR','USA'));
     if (not missing (st03Q01));
     pv1=pv1math;
     pv2=pv2math;
     pv3=pv3math;
     pv4=pv4math;
     pv5=pv5math;
     w_fstr0=w_fstuwt;
     keep  cnt schoolid stidstd
                 pv1-pv5
                 w_fstr0-w_fstr80
                 st03q01;
run;

%include "c:\pisa2003\prg\macro_procmeans.sas";

%BRR_PROCMEAN_PV( INFILE=temp,
                        REPLI_ROOT=w_fstr,
                        BYVAR=st03q01,
                        PV_ROOT=pv,
                        STAT=mean,
                        OUTFILE=exercise39);
run;
```

It should be noted that, even due to the low school response rate, the United Kingdom contribute to the OECD total and OECD average computations.

Table 11.1 ■ **Structure of the output data file *exercise39***

ST03Q01	STAT	SESTAT
1	483.93	1.25
2	494.04	1.32

The OECD average requires an additional step. The student final weights need to be recoded, so that the sum of the student final weights per country is equal to a constant, *e.g.* 1000. This can easily be implemented with the PROC UNIVARIATE procedure, as described in Box 11.2.[1] Table 11.2 presents the results of the procedure.

Box 11.2 ■ **SAS® syntax for the OECD average for the mathematics performance per gender**

```
data temp;
     set pisa2003.stud;
     if (cnt in ('AUS','AUT','BEL','CAN','CZE','DNK','FIN','FRA',
                 'DEU','GRC','GBR','HUN','ISL','IRL','ITA','JPN','KOR',
                 'LUX','MEX','NLD','NZL','NOR','POL','PRT','SVK',
                  'ESP','SWE','CHE','TUR','USA'));
     pv1=pv1math;
     pv2=pv2math;
     pv3=pv3math;
     pv4=pv4math;
     pv5=pv5math;
     w_fstr0=w_fstuwt;
     keep  cnt schoolid stidstd
                pv1-pv5
                w_fstr0-w_fstr80
                st03q01;
run;

proc sort data=temp;
     by cnt schoolid stidstd;
run;

proc univariate data=temp;
     var w_fstr0;
     by cnt;
     output out=cntwgt sum=sumwgt;
run;
data tempnew;
     merge temp cntwgt;
     by cnt;
     array wgt (81)
          w_fstr0-w_fstr80;
     do i=1 to 81;
          wgt(i)=(1000*wgt(i))/sumwgt;
     end;
run;
/*Selecting only non missing data is optional*/
data tempnew1;
     set tempnew;
     if (not missing (st03Q01));
run;
%BRR_PROCMEAN_PV(INFILE=tempnew1,
                 REPLI_ROOT=w_fstr,
                 BYVAR=st03q01,
                 PV_ROOT=pv,
                 STAT=mean,
                 OUTFILE=exercise40);
run;
```

Table 11.2 ■ **Structure of the output data file *exercise40***

ST03Q01	STAT	SESTAT
1	494.41	0.76
2	505.53	0.75

It is worth noting that the standard error is higher for the OECD total than it is for the OECD average. In the case of the OECD total, 40 per cent of the data come from just two countries (the United States and Japan), and these two countries do not have large sample sizes compared to the other OECD countries.

DUPLICATION OF THE DATA FOR AVOIDING THREE RUNS OF THE PROCEDURE

If a researcher is interested in the country estimates as well as the OECD total and the OECD average, then three runs of the procedure are needed: one for the country estimates, one for the OECD total estimate and one for the OECD average estimate.

In order to avoid such repetitions, it is possible to duplicate three times the data for the OECD countries in such a way that the procedure directly provides the estimates for each country, as well as the OECD total and the OECD average estimates.

Box 11.3 presents the SAS® syntax for the generation of such data sets. It consists of the following steps:

- A new categorical variable, denoted OECD and separating OECD and partner countries, is computed. A value of 1 for this variable designates OECD countries, whereas a value of 4 designates partner countries. A second alphanumerical variable, denoted COUNTRY and set as CNT, is created.
- After sorting TEMP1, OECD countries are selected and saved in TEMP2. The variable OECD is set as 2 and the COUNTRY variable is set as TOT.
- On TEMP2 file, the sum of the student final weights per country is computed through the PROC UNIVARIATE procedure and the results are saved in a temporary file named CNTWGT.
- The final weights are transformed in such a way that the sum per country is equal to 1 000. The same linear transformation is applied to the 80 replicates. The COUNTRY variable is set as AVE and the OECD variable is set as 3. These new data are saved into TEMP3.
- After sorting TEMP2 and TEMP3, the three temporary files are merged and saved in a final SAS® data file.

SAS macros presented in the previous chapters can be applied on this new data file. The breakdown variables are now OECD and COUNTRY instead of CNT. The output data file will consist of 43 rows. The first 30 rows will be the results of OECD countries. The next two rows will present the OECD total and the OECD average estimates. Finally, the 11 last rows will present the estimates for the partner countries.

COMPARISONS BETWEEN OECD AVERAGE OR OECD TOTAL ESTIMATES AND A COUNTRY ESTIMATE

As a reminder, only OECD countries that are fully adjudicated contribute to the OECD average and the OECD total estimates and their respective standard errors. Therefore, the expected value of the covariance between a country sampling variance and the OECD aggregate sampling variance will differ from 0 if the country's values are included in the OECD aggregate values, because the two are not independent. Indeed, if the sampling variance of one country increases, then the OECD aggregate sampling variance will also increase.

If a researcher wants to test the null hypothesis between an OECD country and the OECD aggregate estimate, then the covariance should be estimated, as explained in Chapter 10. Since the covariance is expected to be positive, then the correct standard error estimate should be smaller than the standard error obtained from the formulae.

Box 11.3 ■ **SAS® syntax for the creation of a larger data set that will allow in one run the computation of the OECD total and the OECD average**

```
data temp1;
     set pisa2003.stud;
     if (cnt in ('AUS','AUT','BEL','CAN','CZE','DNK','FIN','FRA',
                 'DEU','GRC','GBR','HUN','ISL','IRL','ITA','JPN','KOR',
                 'LUX','MEX','NLD','NZL','NOR','POL','PRT','SVK',
                'ESP','SWE','CHE','TUR','USA')) then oecd=1;
     if (cnt in ('BRA','HKG','IDN','LVA','LIE','MAC'
       ,'RUS','YUG','THA','TUN','URY')) then oecd=4;
     country=cnt;
run;
proc sort data=temp1;
     by oecd cnt schoolid stidstd;;
run;
data temp2;
     set temp1;
     if (oecd=1);
     country="TOT";
     oecd=2;
run;

proc univariate data=temp2 noprint;
     var w_fstuwt;
     by cnt;
     output out=cntwgt sum=sumwgt;
run;
data temp3;
     merge temp2 cntwgt;
     by cnt;
     array wgt (81)
            w_fstuwt w_fstr1-w_fstr80;
     do i=1 to 81;
            wgt(i)=(1000*wgt(i))/sumwgt;
     end;
     country="AVE";
     oecd=3;
run;
proc sort data=temp2;
     by oecd cnt schoolid stidstd;
run;
proc sort data=temp3;
     by oecd cnt schoolid stidstd;
run;
data pisa2003.student;
     merge temp1 temp2 temp3;
     by oecd cnt schoolid stidstd;
run;
```

Since partner countries do not contribute at all to the OECD aggregate estimates, estimating the covariance is not necessary. The standard error on the difference can be directly obtained from the country standard error and the aggregate standard error.

Table 11.3 provides:

- The country mean performance in mathematics as well as the OECD average and the OECD total;
- The standard error on these mean estimates;
- The difference between the country and the OECD total;
- The standard error on this difference, using the formula provided in Chapter 10, *i.e.* without an estimation of the covariance;
- The standard error on this difference, using the replicate, *i.e.* with an estimation of the covariance;
- The difference between the country and the OECD average;
- The standard error on this difference, using the formula provided in Chapter 10, *i.e.* without an estimation of the covariance; and
- The standard error on this difference, using the replicate, *i.e.* with an estimation of the covariance.

The correct standard error estimates are in bold. The differences between the biased and unbiased estimates for OECD countries are not very large.

The differences for partner countries are not very large either. As the expected covariance for partner countries are 0, both standard errors are on average unbiased. However, it is recommended to use the standard error directly obtained with the formula.

Table 11.3 ■ **Country mathematics performance means and their respective standard errors, country difference with OECD total and OECD average, their respective standard errors with or without estimation of the covariance**

	Country		OECD total			OECD average		
	Mean	*SE*	*DIF*	*SE without*	*SE with*	*DIF*	*SE without*	*SE with*
AUS	524.27	2.15	35.27	2.40	**2.12**	24.27	2.24	**2.03**
AUT	505.61	3.27	16.61	3.44	**3.49**	5.61	3.33	**3.27**
BEL	529.29	2.29	40.29	2.52	**2.42**	29.29	2.37	**2.23**
CAN	532.49	1.82	43.49	2.11	**2.08**	32.49	1.92	**1.96**
CHE	526.55	3.38	37.56	3.55	**3.48**	26.55	3.44	**3.38**
CZE	516.46	3.55	27.46	3.70	**3.90**	16.46	3.60	**3.51**
DEU	502.99	3.32	13.99	3.49	**3.42**	2.99	3.38	**3.30**
DNK	514.29	2.74	25.29	2.95	**2.99**	14.29	2.82	**2.67**
ESP	485.11	2.41	-3.89	2.64	**2.60**	-14.89	2.49	**2.47**
FIN	544.29	1.87	55.29	2.15	**2.07**	44.29	1.97	**1.91**
FRA	510.80	2.50	21.80	2.72	**2.45**	10.80	2.58	**2.46**
GBR	508.26	2.43	19.26	2.65	**2.41**	8.26	2.51	**2.39**
GRC	444.91	3.90	-44.09	4.05	**3.94**	-55.09	3.95	**3.81**
HUN	490.01	2.84	1.02	3.03	**3.20**	-9.99	2.91	**2.95**
IRL	502.84	2.45	13.84	2.67	**2.56**	2.84	2.53	**2.41**
ISL	515.11	1.42	26.11	1.78	**1.78**	15.11	1.56	**1.48**
ITA	465.66	3.08	-23.33	3.26	**3.11**	-34.34	3.14	**2.98**
JPN	534.14	4.02	45.14	4.16	**3.88**	34.14	4.06	**3.94**
KOR	542.23	3.24	53.23	3.41	**3.34**	42.23	3.30	**3.16**
LUX	493.21	0.97	4.21	1.45	**1.48**	-6.79	1.16	**1.20**
MEX	385.22	3.64	-103.78	3.80	**3.55**	-114.78	3.70	**3.64**

...

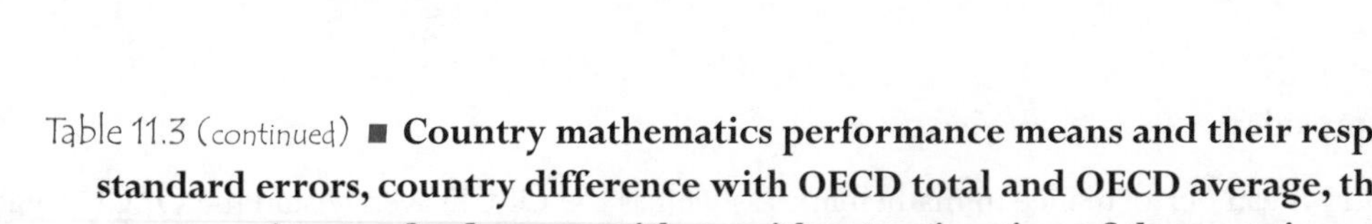

Table 11.3 (continued) ■ **Country mathematics performance means and their respective standard errors, country difference with OECD total and OECD average, their respective standard errors with or without estimation of the covariance**

	Country		OECD total			OECD average		
	Mean	*SE*	*DIF*	*SE without*	*SE with*	*DIF*	*SE without*	*SE with*
NLD	537.82	3.13	48.83	3.31	**3.19**	37.82	3.19	**3.10**
NOR	495.19	2.38	6.19	2.61	**2.69**	-4.81	2.46	**2.41**
NZL	523.49	2.26	34.49	2.50	**2.41**	23.49	2.34	**2.31**
POL	490.24	2.50	1.24	2.72	**2.82**	-9.76	2.58	**2.54**
PRT	466.02	3.40	-22.98	3.57	**3.30**	-33.98	3.46	**3.23**
SVK	498.18	3.35	9.19	3.51	**3.46**	-1.82	3.41	**3.31**
SWE	509.05	2.56	20.05	2.77	**2.48**	9.05	2.64	**2.40**
TUR	423.42	6.74	-65.58	6.82	**6.48**	-76.58	6.77	**6.46**
USA	482.88	2.95	-6.11	3.14	**2.38**	-17.12	3.02	**2.90**
TOT	489.00	1.07						
AVE	500.00	0.63						
BRA	356.02	4.83	-132.98	**4.95**	4.89	-143.98	**4.87**	4.77
HKG	550.38	4.54	61.39	**4.66**	4.80	50.38	**4.58**	4.68
IDN	360.16	3.91	-128.84	**4.05**	4.03	-139.84	**3.96**	3.88
LIE	535.80	4.12	46.80	**4.26**	4.16	35.80	**4.17**	4.13
LVA	483.37	3.69	-5.62	**3.84**	3.88	-16.62	**3.74**	3.76
MAC	527.27	2.89	38.27	**3.08**	3.13	27.27	**2.95**	2.85
RUS	468.41	4.20	-20.59	**4.33**	4.47	-31.59	**4.24**	4.33
THA	416.98	3.00	-72.02	**3.18**	3.38	-83.02	**3.06**	3.20
TUN	358.73	2.54	-130.26	**2.75**	2.55	-141.27	**2.61**	2.57
URY	422.20	3.29	-66.80	**3.46**	3.41	-77.80	**3.35**	3.30
YUG	436.87	3.75	-52.13	**3.90**	3.85	-63.13	**3.81**	3.78

CONCLUSIONS

This chapter was devoted to the concept of the OECD total and the OECD average. For simple statistics such as a mean or a percentage, these aggregated estimates and their respective standard errors can directly be obtained from the country individual estimates.

In most cases, nevertheless, the estimate and its standard error can only be computed from the database. SAS® syntax was provided.

In order to avoid three runs for obtaining individual country estimates as well as OECD aggregate estimates, the SAS® syntax for creating a larger data set was also provided.

Finally, following the issues raised in the previous chapter devoted to comparisons, any comparison that involves a particular country and an OECD aggregate estimate was discussed.

Note

1. As an alternative, a country weight, CNTFAC1, can be also used.

Trends

INTRODUCTION

Policy makers and researchers demand information on how indicators change over time. The longer the time period the more reliable the trend indicator. One example would be an analysis of the impact of reforms to the education system, where policy makers would seek to measure changes in the targeted area to gauge how effective their policies have been. In the early 1960s, for example, most of the OECD countries implemented education reforms to facilitate access to tertiary education, mainly through financial help. One indicator of the impact of these reforms would be to calculate the percentage of the population with a tertiary qualification for several different years to show how this has evolved. Computing this trend indicator is a straightforward statistical manipulation, since the measure (*i.e.* whether or not an individual has completed tertiary education) is quite objective and the information is in most cases available at the population level. Nevertheless, such measures can be slightly biased by, for example, differing levels of immigration over the time period, student exchange programmes, and so on.

Of course trends over time on one particular indicator need careful interpretation. Policy makers would also need to take into account changes to the economic context of the country, such as rising unemployment rates. For example, an increase in the percentage of tertiary graduates does not necessarily prove that the reform to the education system was effective. Further, when comparing trend indicators across countries it is import to consider how comparable the definition of the indicator is from country to country, for example tertiary education might mean something different in each country.

The PISA project offers a unique opportunity to extend the computation of trend indicators on educational outcomes by looking at student performance in reading, mathematical and scientific literacy.

For the trend measures to be reliable, the comparability of the target population, the data collection procedures, and the assessment framework need to be consistent over time. Being able to use the results from PISA as trend indicators is one of the major aims of the project.

PISA 2000 and PISA 2003 used the same assessment frameworks and the data collection procedures were essentially unchanged. In PISA 2000, the target population was defined as all 15-year-olds in grade 5 or higher grades. In PISA 2003, it was defined as all 15-year-olds in grade 7 or higher grades. In PISA 2000, only a very small percentage of 15-year-olds were attending grade 5 or grade 6 (Austria = 0.03%, Canada = 0.03%, Czech Republic = 0.06%, Germany = 0.02%, Hungary = 0.59%, Latvia = 0.27%, Portugal = 1.25% and Russia = 0.04%). Therefore, except for Portugal, the change in the target population should not significantly affect trend indicators.

Other issues that need to be included in the interpretation of trend indicators are student and school participation rates and coverage indices. A higher or a lower school participation rate might explain partly observed differences.

Behind these preliminary precautions, the computation of trend indicators in PISA raises two statistical issues:

- PISA collects data on a sample and therefore any statistic has to be associated with a sampling error. The next section will discuss how to compute such sampling error on a trend indicator.
- Between 20 and 30 items per domain from the 2000 assessments were included in the 2003 assessment to ensure a psychometric link. These anchor items were used to scale the PISA 2000 and the PISA 2003 assessments on a common scale. As one can easily imagine, selecting other

anchor items would have returned slightly different results on the trend performance indicators. It follows that any comparison between two PISA cycles in the student performance will require the addition of another error component, *i.e.* the item sampling error.

THE COMPUTATION OF THE STANDARD ERROR FOR TREND INDICATORS ON VARIABLES OTHER THAN PERFORMANCE

For any country, the PISA 2000 and the PISA 2003 samples are independent. Therefore, the standard error on any trend indicators not involving achievement variables can be computed as follows:

$$\sigma_{(\hat{\theta}_{2003}-\hat{\theta}_{2000})} = \sqrt{\sigma^2_{(\hat{\theta}_{2003})} + \sigma^2_{(\hat{\theta}_{2000})}}$$, with θ representing any statistic.

However, the computation of a difference between PISA 2000 and PISA 2003 and its standard error are relevant only if the two measures are identical. For instance, in the PISA 2000 and PISA 2003 databases, there are several indices derived from the student questionnaires with exactly the same variable names (for instance, HEDRES for home educational resources, BELONG for the student's sense of belonging to the school, and so on). The questions that were used to derive these indices have not changed, but as the scaling was done independently in 2000 and in 2003, there is no guarantee that the 2000 and the 2003 metrics are comparable. Further, these indices were standardised at the OECD level to get a mean of 0 and a standard deviation of 1. The 2000 standardisation differs from the 2003 one. It is therefore not recommended to compute trend indicators on questionnaire indices.

In the case of the PISA questionnaire indices, as the questions have not been modified, the underlying concepts are similar. Therefore, the correlation coefficients between these indices and the student performance can directly be compared. However, as the item parameters were estimated in 2003 without any link with the PISA 2000 data, the metric of the scales might be slightly different and an absolute increase in, for example, the sense of belonging might be simply a result of the scaling, or the standardisation, without any attitudinal change in the student. For the same reasons, regression coefficients for indices derived from student questionnaire data cannot be compared between 2000 and 2003.

The Highest International Social and Economic Index (denoted HISEI in the databases) satisfies all the conditions for the computation of trend indicators. Indeed, the questions were not changed and the transformation used on the ISCO categories in 2000 was implemented in 2003 without any modification.

Table 12.1 presents, per country, the mean estimate of HISEI and its standard error for PISA 2000 and PISA 2003, as well as the difference between the two estimates, the standard error of this difference and the standardised difference, *i.e.* the difference divided by its standard error.

For Germany (DEU), the means for HISEI in 2000 and in 2003 are respectively equal to 48.85 and 49.33. The difference between these two data collection is therefore equal to:

$$49.33 - 48.55 = 0.48.$$

The standard errors on these mean estimates are equal to 0.32 and 0.42. The standard error on the difference estimate is equal to:

$$\sigma_{(\hat{\theta}_{2003}-\hat{\theta}_{2000})} = \sqrt{\sigma^2_{(\hat{\theta}_{2003})} + \sigma^2_{(\hat{\theta}_{2000})}} = \sqrt{(0.32)^2 + (0.42)^2} = 0.53$$

The standardised difference, *i.e.* the difference estimate divided by its standard error, is equal to:

$$\frac{0.48}{0.53} = 0.91$$

As the standardised difference is included in the interval [-1.96;1.96], the difference on the mean estimate for HISEI between 2000 and 2003 is not statistically different from 0 with a type I error of 0.05.

Table 12.1 shows that the difference is statistically different from 0 in 13 countries: Austria, Belgium, Brazil, the Czech Republic, Indonesia, Iceland, Korea, Liechtenstein, Luxembourg, Mexico, Thailand, the United Kingdom and the United States.

It would be unrealistic to consider these differences as simply a reflection of social and economic changes in these 13 countries. In a period of three years, some changes can occur, but these cannot explain by themselves the size of the observed increases or decreases.

Table 12.1 ■ **Trend indicators between PISA 2000 and PISA 2003 for HISEI per country**

	PISA 2000		PISA 2003		Difference		
	Mean	SE	Mean	SE	Estimate	SE	STD difference
AUS	52.25	(0.50)	52.59	(0.30)	0.34	(0.58)	0.59
AUT	49.72	(0.29)	47.06	(0.52)	-2.66	(0.59)	-4.49
BEL	48.95	(0.39)	50.59	(0.38)	1.65	(0.54)	3.05
BRA	43.93	(0.59)	40.12	(0.64)	-3.81	(0.87)	-4.39
CAN	52.83	(0.22)	52.58	(0.27)	-0.25	(0.35)	-0.73
CHE	49.21	(0.53)	49.30	(0.43)	0.09	(0.68)	0.13
CZE	48.31	(0.27)	50.05	(0.34)	1.74	(0.44)	3.98
DEU	48.85	(0.32)	49.33	(0.42)	0.48	(0.53)	0.91
DNK	49.73	(0.43)	49.26	(0.45)	-0.47	(0.63)	-0.75
ESP	44.99	(0.62)	44.29	(0.58)	-0.70	(0.85)	-0.83
FIN	50.00	(0.40)	50.23	(0.36)	0.23	(0.54)	0.42
FRA	48.27	(0.44)	48.66	(0.47)	0.39	(0.64)	0.61
GBR	51.26	(0.35)	49.65	(0.39)	-1.61	(0.52)	-3.07
GRC	47.76	(0.60)	46.94	(0.72)	-0.83	(0.93)	-0.88
HUN	49.53	(0.47)	48.58	(0.33)	-0.95	(0.57)	-1.65
IDN	36.38	(0.77)	33.65	(0.61)	-2.73	(0.98)	-2.77
IRL	48.43	(0.48)	48.34	(0.49)	-0.09	(0.69)	-0.13
ISL	52.73	(0.28)	53.72	(0.26)	0.99	(0.38)	2.62
ITA	47.08	(0.31)	46.83	(0.38)	-0.24	(0.49)	-0.50
JPN	50.54	(0.62)	49.98	(0.31)	-0.56	(0.69)	-0.80
KOR	42.80	(0.42)	46.32	(0.36)	3.52	(0.55)	6.36
LIE	47.46	(0.94)	50.73	(0.75)	3.27	(1.21)	2.71
LUX	44.79	(0.27)	48.17	(0.22)	3.38	(0.35)	9.76
LVA	50.15	(0.54)	50.28	(0.52)	0.13	(0.75)	0.18
MEX	42.48	(0.68)	40.12	(0.68)	-2.37	(0.96)	-2.46
NLD	50.85	(0.47)	51.26	(0.38)	0.42	(0.61)	0.68
NOR	53.91	(0.38)	54.63	(0.39)	0.72	(0.54)	1.33
NZL	52.20	(0.37)	51.46	(0.36)	-0.74	(0.51)	-1.45
POL	46.03	(0.47)	44.96	(0.34)	-1.07	(0.58)	-1.85
PRT	43.85	(0.60)	43.10	(0.54)	-0.75	(0.81)	-0.92
RUS	49.38	(0.45)	49.86	(0.38)	0.49	(0.59)	0.82
SWE	50.57	(0.39)	50.64	(0.38)	0.07	(0.55)	0.12
THA	33.02	(0.57)	36.01	(0.43)	2.99	(0.72)	4.18
USA	52.40	(0.79)	54.55	(0.37)	2.15	(0.87)	2.47

It is also possible that the quality of the samples might explain some of the differences. As a student's propensity to participate positively correlate with his or her academic records and as on average low achievers come from lower social background variables than high achievers, an increase or a decrease in the student participation rates might affect the HISEI mean.

A change in the percentage of missing data for the HISEI variable would be another explanation that can be easily verified. On average, students who do not provide their parents' jobs are lower achievers. Therefore, one should expect low social background characteristics, so that an increase of missing data could be associated with an increase of the HISEI mean and inversely.

Table 12.2 provides the percentages of missing data for the HISEI variables in PISA 2000 and PISA 2003 databases. These results do not really confirm the hypothesis. For instance, in the United States, the percentages of missing data were respectively about 14 per cent in 2000 and about 6 per cent in 2003 and the means of HISEI were respectively 52.40 and 54.55. In 9 out of the 13 countries where the HISEI means significantly differ, either an increase of the HISEI mean is associated with a decrease of the percentage of missing data or the inverse. In the three other countries, *i.e.* Belgium, the Czech Republic and Mexico, the relationship is consistent with the hypothesis.

Table 12.2 ■ **Percentages of missing data for HISEI**

	PISA 2000		PISA 2003		Difference		
	%	SE	%	SE	Estimate	SE	STD difference
AUS	4.15	(0.38)	7.91	(1.56)	3.76	(1.61)	2.33
AUT	2.06	(0.20)	3.62	(0.32)	1.56	(0.38)	4.13
BEL	5.02	(0.45)	6.11	(0.48)	1.09	(0.66)	1.66
BRA	7.90	(0.62)	8.75	(1.03)	0.86	(1.20)	0.71
CAN	3.00	(0.18)	12.34	(0.76)	9.34	(0.78)	11.93
CHE	3.36	(0.32)	3.06	(0.26)	-0.30	(0.41)	-0.72
CZE	1.90	(0.42)	5.65	(1.19)	3.75	(1.26)	2.97
DEU	3.05	(0.34)	9.92	(0.63)	6.87	(0.72)	9.55
DNK	7.12	(0.85)	2.73	(0.37)	-4.40	(0.92)	-4.76
ESP	4.48	(0.49)	3.70	(0.37)	-0.78	(0.62)	-1.27
FIN	1.96	(0.22)	1.44	(0.16)	-0.52	(0.27)	-1.92
FRA	6.23	(0.51)	4.61	(0.45)	-1.61	(0.68)	-2.37
GBR	5.15	(0.44)	7.23	(1.17)	2.07	(1.25)	1.66
GRC	4.04	(0.57)	5.81	(0.41)	1.78	(0.70)	2.53
HUN	3.02	(0.36)	5.39	(0.42)	2.37	(0.55)	4.31
IDN	6.99	(0.64)	8.67	(0.53)	1.67	(0.83)	2.03
IRL	3.23	(0.34)	4.32	(0.57)	1.09	(0.66)	1.65
ISL	2.19	(0.24)	2.30	(0.25)	0.11	(0.35)	0.31
ITA	2.73	(0.46)	2.47	(0.28)	-0.26	(0.54)	-0.48
JPN	62.52	(3.47)	11.25	(0.81)	-51.27	(3.56)	-14.41
KOR	7.34	(0.49)	2.36	(0.21)	-4.97	(0.54)	-9.29
LIE	5.49	(1.41)	3.02	(0.85)	-2.47	(1.64)	-1.50
LUX	9.55	(0.50)	3.62	(0.29)	-5.92	(0.58)	-10.27
LVA	5.02	(0.52)	3.34	(0.39)	-1.68	(0.66)	-2.56
MEX	8.51	(0.59)	5.07	(0.44)	-3.43	(0.74)	-4.65

...

Table 12.2 (continued) ■ **Percentages of missing data for HISEI**

	PISA 2000		PISA 2003		Difference		
	%	SE	%	SE	Estimate	SE	STD difference
NLD	3.07	(0.65)	7.64	(1.34)	4.57	(1.49)	3.07
NOR	2.44	(0.31)	3.18	(0.39)	0.74	(0.50)	1.49
NZL	3.92	(0.39)	14.13	(0.43)	10.22	(0.58)	17.60
POL	6.90	(0.79)	2.33	(0.30)	-4.57	(0.85)	-5.39
PRT	3.72	(0.42)	2.76	(0.28)	-0.96	(0.50)	-1.90
RUS	3.16	(0.33)	2.14	(0.30)	-1.02	(0.45)	-2.27
SWE	2.48	(0.30)	2.63	(0.31)	0.15	(0.43)	0.35
THA	10.95	(1.38)	5.85	(0.64)	-5.09	(1.52)	-3.35
USA	14.58	(1.95)	5.88	(0.38)	-8.70	(1.99)	-4.38

This simple example shows that the interpretation of trend indicators is quite complex. The social and economic structure of a country should remain unchanged over a period of three years, so that no differences occur between two cycles. However, as shown, this difference appears significant in all 13 countries.

Changes in the school or student participation rates and in the distribution of missing data might sometimes explain these significant differences. It is therefore recommended to implement some verification before trying to interpret calculated differences as a real change in the population characteristics.

THE COMPUTATION OF THE STANDARD ERROR FOR TREND INDICATORS ON PERFORMANCE VARIABLES

Anchoring of the PISA 2000 and PISA 2003 performance scales

The PISA 2000 database contains five plausible values for each of the following domains or subdomains:

- Mathematics
- Reading
  - Reading/retrieving information
  - Reading/interpreting
  - Reading/reflecting
- Science

The PISA 2003 database also contains five plausible values for each of the following domains or subdomains:

- Mathematics
  - Mathematics/space and shape
  - Mathematics/change and relationship
  - Mathematics/uncertainty
  - Mathematics/quantity

- Problem solving
- Reading
- Science

The psychometric procedures used to link the PISA 2000 and PISA 2003 performance scales are different for mathematics than they are for reading and science.

Reading was the major domain in 2000 and 28 of the 140 items developed for the 2000 assessment were used for the 2003 assessment. The 2003 data were therefore reported on the 2000 reading scale. The science assessment data of 2003 are also reported on the 2000 science scale as 25 of the 30 items developed for the 2000 assessment were used for the 2003 assessment.

Mathematics, as the major domain, was the subject of major development work for PISA 2003. Further, the mathematics assessment in 2000 only covered two of the four content areas (*space and shape* and *change and relationships*). Twenty items out of the 85 items used in the 2003 assessment come from the 2000 assessment. Because of this broadening in the assessment, it was deemed inappropriate to report the PISA 2003 mathematics scores based on the scale for the PISA 2000 mathematics scores.

However, to provide countries with some trend indicators, the mathematics subscales space and shape and change and relationship of the PISA 2000 were reported on the PISA 2003 scales.[1]

The steps for anchoring the PISA 2003 reading and science data on the 2000 scales are:

1. Calibration of the 2003 reading and science data to get the PISA 2003 item parameters, *i.e.* the relative difficulty of the item on the Rasch scale.
2. Based on these item parameters, generation of the plausible values for reading and science on the PISA 2003 data.
3. Based on the item parameters of step 1, but only on the link items, generation of plausible values for reading and science on the PISA 2000 data. By this time, two sets for plausible values are available for PISA 2000: the original set of plausible values included in the PISA 2000 database and the set of plausible values based on the PISA 2003 item parameters. Unfortunately, the mean and the standard deviation of the new set of plausible values will slightly differ from the PISA 2000 original plausible values. These differences reflect the changes in the difficulty of the link items between 2000 and 2003. As a reminder, the mean and the standard deviation for the OECD average were set respectively at 500 and 100 in 2000. Let us suppose that the new set of plausible values return a mean of 505 and a standard deviation of 110. The new set of plausible values for the PISA 2000 data has to be transformed so that their mean and standard deviation is respectively equal to 500 and 100.
4. This step consists of the computation of the linear transformation that will guarantee that the mean and the standard deviation of the new set of plausible values on the PISA 2000 data has a mean of 500 and a standard deviation of 100. This linear transformation can be written as

$$PV_{cal\_2000} = \alpha + \beta * PV_{cal\_2003} \text{ with } \beta = \frac{\sigma_{cal\_2000}}{\sigma_{cal\_2003}} \text{ and } \alpha = (\mu_{cal\_2000} - \beta * (\mu_{cal\_2003})).$$

In the example, $\beta = 100 / 110 = 0.909$ and $\alpha = (500 - (0.909 * 505)) = 40.955$;[2] and

5. This linear transformation is applied on the PISA 2003 plausible values. This linear transformation applied on the reading or science PISA 2003 plausible values guarantees that the student performance in 2003 is comparable to the student performance in 2000.

As stated earlier, with another set of link items, the linear transformation would have been different. As a consequence, there is an uncertainty in the transformation due to sampling of the link items, referred as the linking error.

The steps for anchoring the two mathematics PISA 2000 subscales on the PISA 2003 subscales are:

1. Calibration of the 2003 mathematics data to get the PISA 2003 item parameters;
2. Based on these item parameters, generation of the PISA 2003 plausible values; and
3. Based on the 2003 item parameters, generation of plausible values for the mathematics PISA 2000 data.

Inclusion of the linking error in the computation of the standard error

For each link item, we have two item parameter estimates that are now on the same metric: the 2000 item parameter and the 2003 item parameter. Some of these link items show an increase of the relative difficulty, some show a decrease, but on average, the difference is equal to 0. This means that some items seem more difficult in 2003 than they were in 2000 or the inverse.

As the subset of link items can be considered as a simple random sample of an infinite population of link items, the linking error can be computed as:

$$\sigma_{(Linking\_error)} = \sqrt{\frac{\sigma^2}{n}} \text{ where:}$$

σ^2 represents the variance of the item parameter differences, and n denotes the number of link items used.

If the item parameters from the 2003 calibration perfectly match the item parameters from the 2000 calibration, then the relative difficulty of the link items would not have changed. All the differences between the relative difficulty in 2000 and in 2003 would be equal to 0 and therefore, the linking error would be equal to 0.

As the differences in the item parameters increase, the variance of these differences will increase and consequently the linking error will increase. It makes sense for the uncertainty around the trend to be proportional to the changes in the item parameters.

Also, the uncertainty around the trend indicators is inversely proportional to the number of link items. From a theoretical point of view, only one item is needed to measure a trend, but with only one item, the uncertainty will be very large. If the number of link items increases, the uncertainty will decrease.

Table 12.3 provides the centred item parameters (*i.e.* item difficulty differences) for the reading link items for PISA 2000 and PISA 2003, as well as the difference between the two sets of estimates.

Table 12.3 ■ **Item parameter estimates in 2000 and 2003 for the reading link items**

Item Name	Centered *Delta* in 2003	Centered *Delta* in 2000	Difference
R055Q01	-1.28	-1.347	-0.072
R055Q02	0.63	0.526	-0.101
R055Q03	0.27	0.097	-0.175
R055Q05	-0.69	-0.847	-0.154
R067Q01	-2.08	-1.696	0.388
R067Q04	0.25	0.546	0.292
R067Q05	-0.18	0.212	0.394
R102Q04A	1.53	1.236	-0.290
R102Q05	0.87	0.935	0.067
R102Q07	-1.42	-1.536	-0.116
R104Q01	-1.47	-1.205	0.268
R104Q02	1.44	1.135	-0.306
R104Q05	2.17	1.905	-0.267
R111Q01	-0.19	-0.023	0.164
R111Q02B	1.54	1.395	-0.147
R111Q06B	0.89	0.838	-0.051
R219Q01T	-0.59	-0.520	0.069
R219Q01E	0.10	0.308	0.210
R219Q02	-1.13	-0.887	0.243
R220Q01	0.86	0.815	-0.041
R220Q02B	-0.14	-0.114	0.027
R220Q04	-0.10	0.193	0.297
R220Q05	-1.39	-1.569	-0.184
R220Q06	-0.34	-0.142	0.196
R227Q01	0.40	0.226	-0.170
R227Q02T	0.16	0.075	-0.086
R227Q03	0.46	0.325	-0.132
R227Q06	-0.56	-0.886	-0.327

The variance of the difference is equal to 0.047486. The link error is therefore equal to:

$$\sigma_{(Linking\_error)} = \sqrt{\frac{\sigma^2}{n}} = \sqrt{\frac{0.047486}{28}} = 0.041.$$

On the PISA reading scale with a mean of 500 and a standard deviation of 100, it corresponds to 3.75.

The linking errors between PISA 2000 and PISA 2003 are:

- Reading.. 3.75
- Science.. 3.02
- Mathematics/space and shape.................... 6.01
- Mathematics/change and relationship...... 4.84

A common transformation has been estimated from the link items, and this transformation is applied to all participating countries. It follows that any uncertainty that is introduced through the linking is common to all students and all countries. Thus, for example, suppose that the linking error between PISA 2000 and PISA 2003 in reading resulted in an overestimation of student scores by two points on the PISA 2000 scale. It follows that every student's score would be overestimated by two score points. This overestimation will have effects on certain, but not all, summary statistics computed from the PISA 2003 data. For example, consider the following:

- Each country's mean would be overestimated by an amount equal to the link error, in our example this is two score points;
- The mean performance of any subgroup would be overestimated by an amount equal to the linking error, in our example this is two score points;
- The standard deviation of student scores would not be affected because the overestimation of each student by a common error does not change the standard deviation;
- The difference between the mean scores of two countries in PISA 2003 would not be influenced because the overestimation of each student by a common error would have distorted each country's mean by the same amount;
- The difference between the mean scores of two groups (*e.g.* males and females) in PISA 2003 would not be influenced, because the overestimation of each student by a common error would have distorted each group's mean by the same amount;
- The difference between the performance of a group of students (*e.g.* a country) between PISA 2000 and PISA 2003 would be influenced because each student's score in PISA 2003 would be influenced by the error; and
- A change in the difference between two groups from PISA 2000 to PISA 2003 would not be influenced. This is because neither of the components of this comparison, which are differences in scores in 2000 and 2003 respectively, is influenced by a common error that is added to all student scores in PISA 2003.

In general terms, the linking error need only be considered when comparisons are being made between PISA 2000 and PISA 2003 results, and then usually when group means are being compared.

The most obvious example of a situation where there is a need to use the linking error is in the comparison of the mean performance for a country between PISA 2000 and PISA 2003.

In PISA 2000, the mean in reading literacy for Germany is equal to 483.99 with a standard error of 2.47. In PISA 2003, the mean for Germany is equal to 491.36 and the standard error is equal to 3.39. The difference between 2000 and 2003 is therefore equal to 491.36-483.99= 7.37. The average performance of the German students has therefore increased by 7.37 scores on the PISA 2000 reading scale.

The standard error on this difference, as mentioned here above, is influenced by the linking error. The standard error is therefore equal to:

$$SE = \sqrt{\sigma^2_{(\hat{\mu}_{2000})} + \sigma^2_{(\hat{\mu}_{2003})} + \sigma^2_{(linking\_error)}}$$

$$SE = \sqrt{(2.47)^2 + (3.39)^2 + (3.75)^2} = 5.63$$

As the standardised difference between PISA 2000 and PISA 2003, *i.e.* (7.37/5.63) is included in the interval [-1.96; 1.96], the null hypothesis of no difference is not rejected. In other words, Germany's performance in reading has not changed between 2000 and 2003.

Table 12.4 provides the estimates of the reading performance in Germany per gender in 2000 and 2003, with their respective standard errors, as well as the difference estimates and their respective standard errors.

Table 12.4 ■ **Mean performance in reading per gender for Germany**

		Performance in reading	Standard error
2003	Girls	512.93	3.91
	Boys	470.80	4.23
	Difference	42.13	4.62
2000	Girls	502.20	3.87
	Boys	467.55	3.17
	Difference	34.65	5.21

As the comparison for a particular country between 2000 and 2003 is affected by the linking error, the comparison for a particular subgroup between 2000 and 2003 is also affected by the linking error. Therefore, the standard error has to include the linking error.

The trend indicators for German boys and for German girls are, respectively, equal to:

$$Trends_{Girls} = 512.93 - 502.20 = 10.73$$

$$SE_{Girls} = \sqrt{(3.91)^2 + (3.87)^2 + (3.75)^2} = 6.66$$

$$Trends_{Boys} = 470.80 - 467.55 = 3.25$$

$$SE_{Boys} = \sqrt{(4.23)^2 + (3.17)^2 + (3.75)^2} = 6.48$$

Both differences are not statistically different from 0.

On the other hand, the gender difference in 2003 is not affected by the linking error. Indeed, both subgroup estimates will be underestimated or overestimated by the same amount and therefore the computation of the difference will neutralize this difference. Consequently, the trend indicator on the gender difference and its standard error will be equal to:

$$Trends_{Gender\_dif} = 42.13 - 34.65 = 7.43$$

$$SE_{Gender\_dif} = \sqrt{(4.62)^2 + (5.21)^2} = 6.96$$

This means that the change in gender difference in Germany for reading between 2000 and 2003 was not statistically significant, even though it appears from Table 12.4 to have widened considerably.

In the PISA 2000 and PISA 2003 initial reports, student performance is also reported by proficiency levels (see Chapter 8). As the linking error affects the country mean estimate, the percentages of students at each level will also be affected. However, an overestimation or an underestimation of the PISA 2003 results of *X* points on the PISA scale will have a different impact on the percentages of students at each proficiency level for each country. If the percentage is small, then the impact will be small. If the percentage is large, then the impact will be larger. It would have been too complex to provide for each country and for each proficiency level a linking error. It was therefore decided not to take into account the linking error for the comparison of percentages of students at each proficiency level between PISA 2000 and PISA 2003. This means that the standard errors on the difference between 2000 and 2003 are underestimated.

CONCLUSIONS

This chapter was devoted to the computation of the standard error on trend indicators. The comparison of any variable other than performance variables is quite straightforward as the PISA 2000 and the PISA 2003 samples are independent. However, as stated previously, such comparisons are only relevant if the 2000 and the 2003 measures are comparable.

The comparison of performance mean estimates is more complex as it might require the inclusion of the linking error in the standard error depending on the statistic. For instance, Figure 2.6d in *Learning for Tomorrow's World – First Results from PISA 2003* (OECD, 2004a), presents the trends in mathematics/space and shape average performance between 2000 and 2003. The trend indicator has integrated the linking error in its standard error. Figure 2.6c in the same report presents the trends between 2000 and 2003 on the 5th, 10th, 25th, 75th, 90th and 95th percentiles and the linking error was not integrated into the standard error of the trends. Broadly speaking, the PISA 2003 initial report has integrated the linking error only in tables where the country mean performance is compared between 2000 and 2003.

Due to the growing interest in trend indicators and their political impacts, it is essential to interpret significant changes with caution. A significant change might simply be due to a difference in the school or student participation rate or in the pattern of missing data.

Notes

1. The PISA 2000 database has been updated to integrate this new set of plausible values.

2. Actually, the linear transformation was applied on the plausible values before their transformation on the PISA scale with a mean of 500 and a standard deviation of 100. Further, different transformations were applied by gender (*i.e.* girls, boys and missing gender). The linear transformations per gender are: (i) girls: 2000_PVs = 0.0970 + (0.8739 * 2003_PVs), (ii) boys: 2000_PVs = 0.0204 + (0.8823 * 2003_PVs), (iii) missing gender: 2000_PVs = 0.0552 + (0.8830 * 2003_PVs). In science, the linear transformation is: 2000_PVs = –0.01552 + (1.0063 * 2003_PVs).

Multilevel Analyses

INTRODUCTION

For the past two decades, education survey data have increasingly been analysed with multilevel models. Indeed, since linear regression models fail to take into account the potential effects that may arise from the way in which students are assigned to schools or to classes within schools, they may give an incomplete or misleading representation of the efficiency of the education systems. In some countries, for instance, the socio-economic background of a student may partly determine the type of school that he or she attends and there may be little variation in the socio-economic background of students within each school. In other countries or systems, schools may draw on students from a wide range of socio-economic backgrounds, but within the school, the socio-economic background of the student impacts the type of class he or she is allocated to and, as a result the within-school variance is also affected. A linear regression model that does not take into account the hierarchical structure of the data will not differentiate between these two systems.

The use of multilevel models (Goldstein, 1995), also called hierarchical linear models (Bryk and Raudenbush, 1992), acknowledges the fact that students are nested within classes and schools. The relative variation in the outcome measure – between students, within the same school and between schools – can therefore be evaluated.

SIMPLE LINEAR REGRESSION

A linear equation can always be represented by a straight line. An equation with two variables will be represented in a two dimension space, and an equation with three variables, in a three dimensional space, and so on.

The following equation is graphically represented in Figure 13.1.

$$Y = 5 + 4X$$

Since all linear equations are represented by a straight line, it is only necessary to identify two points that belong to the line to be able to graph it. If X is equal to 1, then Y will be equal to 9. If X is equal to 10, then Y will be equal to 45. The straight line with the points (1, 9) and (10, 45) corresponds to the equation.

Figure 13.1 ■ **Graphical representation of a linear equation**

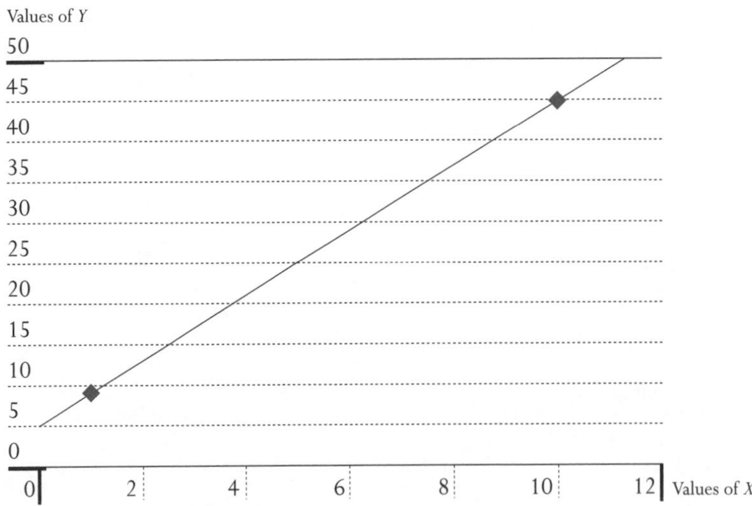

Figure 13.1 shows the graphical representation of the equation $Y = 5 + 4X$. As the figure shows, the line crosses the Y axis at 5. The point (0,5) is called the intercept. It gives the value of Y when X is equal to 0. The X factor, or regression coefficient in statistical terms, gives the slope of the straight line. It tells us about the Y increase for an additional unit on the X axis. In the example considered, if X increases by one unit, then Y increases by four units.

The general expression of a linear equation with two variables is:

$Y = a + bX$, with a the intercept and b the regression coefficient.

Although human processes can also be described with a similar approach, they are less deterministic. Let us graphically represent the relationship that might exist between the family socio-economic background (SES) of students and their academic performance at school.

Figure 13.2 ■ **Relationship between student socio-economic background and academic performance**

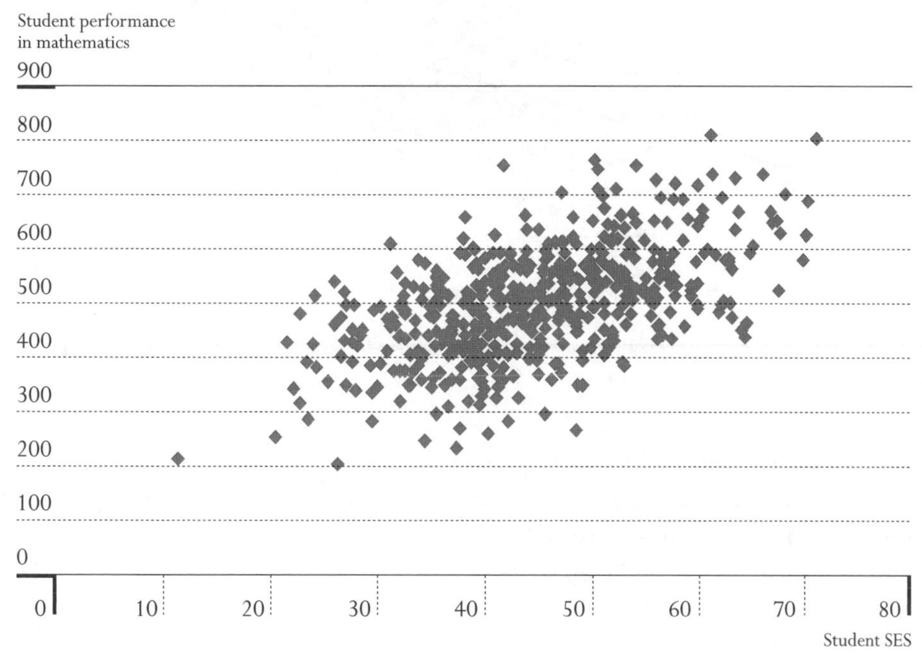

As Figure 13.2 shows, there is a positive relationship between a student's socio-economic background and academic performance. Students from higher socio-economic backgrounds tend to perform better at school. However, unlike a linear equation, not all points are located on a straight line, meaning that some students from a low socio-economic background may perform well academically, and that some students from a high socio-economic background may perform poorly.

Statisticians use a linear regression analysis to quantify such relationships. The process in this particular example is similar to a linear equation with two variables. It will consist of computing an equation $Y_i = \alpha + \beta X$, with Y_i being the academic performance of student i, and X_i being his or her family socio-economic background. This equation can also be represented by a straight line denoted regression line.

The regression line in Figure 13.3 corresponds to the regression equation, $Y_i = 250.5 + 5.5X_i$. One measure of socio-economic status used for PISA 2000 and for PISA 2003 (Ganzeboom *et al.*, 1992) is the index of highest occupational status of parents called HISEI. This index ranges from 15 to 90 with an average of about 50 and a standard deviation of 15. The performance in mathematics has an international mean of 500 and a standard deviation of 100. This equation shows that an increase of one unit on the HISEI scale is associated with an increase of 5.5 points on the PISA mathematics scale, on average.

Figure 13.3 ■ **Regression line of the socio-economic background on the student performance in mathematics**

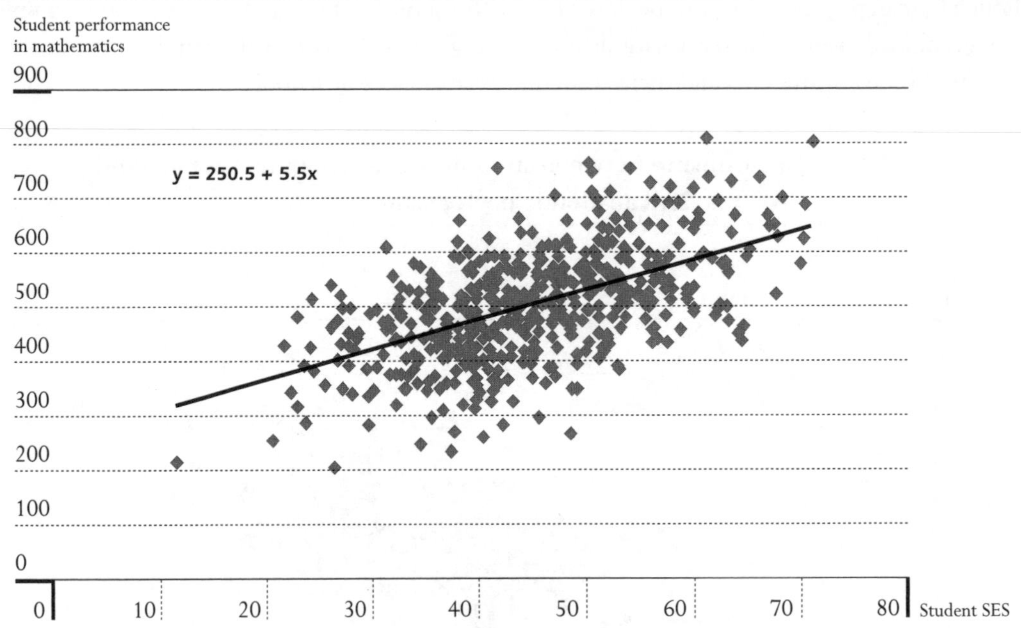

This regression equation can also be used to predict the mathematics performance of a student if the socio-economic background is known. For instance, this regression equation will predict, for each student with a HISEI value of 60, a score of 250.5 + (5.5 x 60) = 580.5. In other words, any student with a HISEI of 60 will have a predicted score of 580.5. However, as shown by Figure 13.3, some of these students have a performance very close to this predicted score, usually denoted $\hat{Y}_i$, but the others either perform better, or at a lower level.

Before the computation of the regression equation, each student in the sample could be characterised by HISEI, X_i, and by performance in mathematics, Y_i. Now, each student can also be characterised by his or her predicted score, $\hat{Y}_i$, and by the difference between the observed score and predicted score $(Y_i - \hat{Y}_i)$, usually denoted as the residual (or ε_i).

Table 13.1 ■ **HISEI, observed score, predicted score and residual**

Students	HISEI	Observed score	Predicted score	Residual
1	49	463	520	-57
2	53	384	542	-158
3	51	579	531	+48
4	42	404	481.5	-77.5
5	42	282	481.5	-199.5

The first student has an HISEI value of 49 and a mathematics performance of 463. Based on his or her socio-economic background, one would have predicted a score of 520. This student has, therefore, a lower performance than expected. The residual is equal to -57. On the other hand, the third student has a performance of 579 and an expected score of 531. This student performs better than expected.

Table 13.1 shows that the observed scores, the predicted scores and the residual scores present some variability on which variance coefficients can be computed. The regression equation and the regression line are constructed in a way that minimise the variance of the residual, denoted residual variance. This means that:

- The regression equation must include the point (μ_x, μ_y);
- The mean of the predicted score is equal to the mean of the observed score ($\mu_y = \mu_{\hat{y}}$); and
- The mean of the residual must be equal to 0.

Finally, a regression analysis can be extended to several explanatory variables. If *k* predictors are incorporated in the regression, then the equation will be written as:

$$Y_i = \alpha + \beta_1 X_{1i} + \beta_2 X_{2i} + ... + \beta_k X_{ki}$$

For instance, the mathematics performance on the PISA test can be explained by the student family background, gender, the time spent each week on homework, interest in mathematics and so on.

Box 13.1 ■ **Interpretation of a regression coefficient and an intercept**

A regression coefficient reflects the change of units on the Y axis (the dependent variable – in this particular case, the increase on the mathematics scale) per unit change of the X axis. The interpretation of a regression coefficient depends on the measurement unit of an independent variable. Therefore, the statistical effect of different independent variables can not be compared, unless these independent variables have the same measurement units.

To achieve this, independent variables can be standardised so that the measurement units become the standard deviation. If all variables have a standard deviation of 1, the regression coefficients of different variables can be directly compared. The regression coefficients will reflect the increase on the mathematic scale per standard deviation of the independent variables.

Suppose that two independent variables denoted X1 and X2 are used to explain the mathematical performance of students in two countries. The tables below provide the regression coefficients and the standard deviation of X1 and X2 before and after standardising the independent variables.

Before standardisation				
	X1		X2	
	β_1	$\sigma_{(x_1)}$	β_1	$\sigma_{(x_2)}$
Country A	10	2	15	3
Country B	5	1	7.5	1.5

After standardisation				
	X1		X2	
	β_1	$\sigma_{(x_1)}$	β_1	$\sigma_{(x_2)}$
Country A	5	1	5	1
Country B	5	1	5	1

...

The results are quite different. Based on the regression coefficients after standardisation, it seems that the two independent variables have the same statistical effect on the mathematic performance in both countries. Assume that X1 represents the time spent at home for the homework. In country A, the increase of one hour spent on homework is associated with an increase of 10 points on the mathematic scale while in country B, an additional hour is associated with the increase of 5 points on the mathematic scale. While the standardisation of the variables allows comparisons, the interpretation of a particular regression coefficient becomes more complex as it does not refer anymore to the original scale.

Thus, there is no single algorithm to solve this problem. It depends on the nature of the independent variable and the purpose of the analyses.

The interpretation of the intercept is even more complex as it depends on the standard deviation and the mean of the independent variables. Let us suppose that HISEI is standardised to a mean of zero and a standard deviation of one. The regression coefficient would reflect the increase in mathematics per standard deviation on the socio-economic status scale. The intercept would therefore represent the performance of a student with a transformed HISEI score of 0. In a model with only standardised variables, it would reflect the performance of a hypothetical student who has average scores for all independent variables.

SIMPLE LINEAR VERSUS MULTILEVEL REGRESSION ANALYSES

The previous simple linear regression showed the relationship between socio-economic background and mathematics performance at the population level, *i.e.* the 15-year-olds attending an educational institution.

A relationship between the socio-economic background of the student and performance in mathematics does not necessarily imply that richer countries will have a higher performance average than developing countries. Further, the relationship observed at the student level across schools does not necessary imply that the same phenomenon will be identified within each school.

Multilevel regression analyses recognize that sampled units are nested within larger units. Instead of computing one regression equation on the whole dataset, the multilevel regression analysis will compute a regression equation per larger unit. In all education surveys, students are nested within schools. Therefore, a multilevel regression analysis will compute a regression equation per school.

Figure 13.4 shows four graphs that highlight the distinction between a linear regression and a multilevel linear regression model. These four graphs represent the relationship between student socio-economic backgrounds and mathematics performance estimates in different countries.

The thick black line represents the regression line when the hierarchical structure of the data is not taken into account. The thin red lines represent the relationship between these two variables within particular schools. For each school, there is a regression line (a red line in this particular example). The larger black point on the linear regression lines (black) represents the point with the mean of X and Y as coordinates, (μ_x, μ_y), and the red point on the multilevel regression lines represents the point with the school mean of X and Y as coordinates, (μ_{xi}, μ_{yi}).

Figure 13.4 ■ **Linear regression analysis versus multilevel regression analysis**

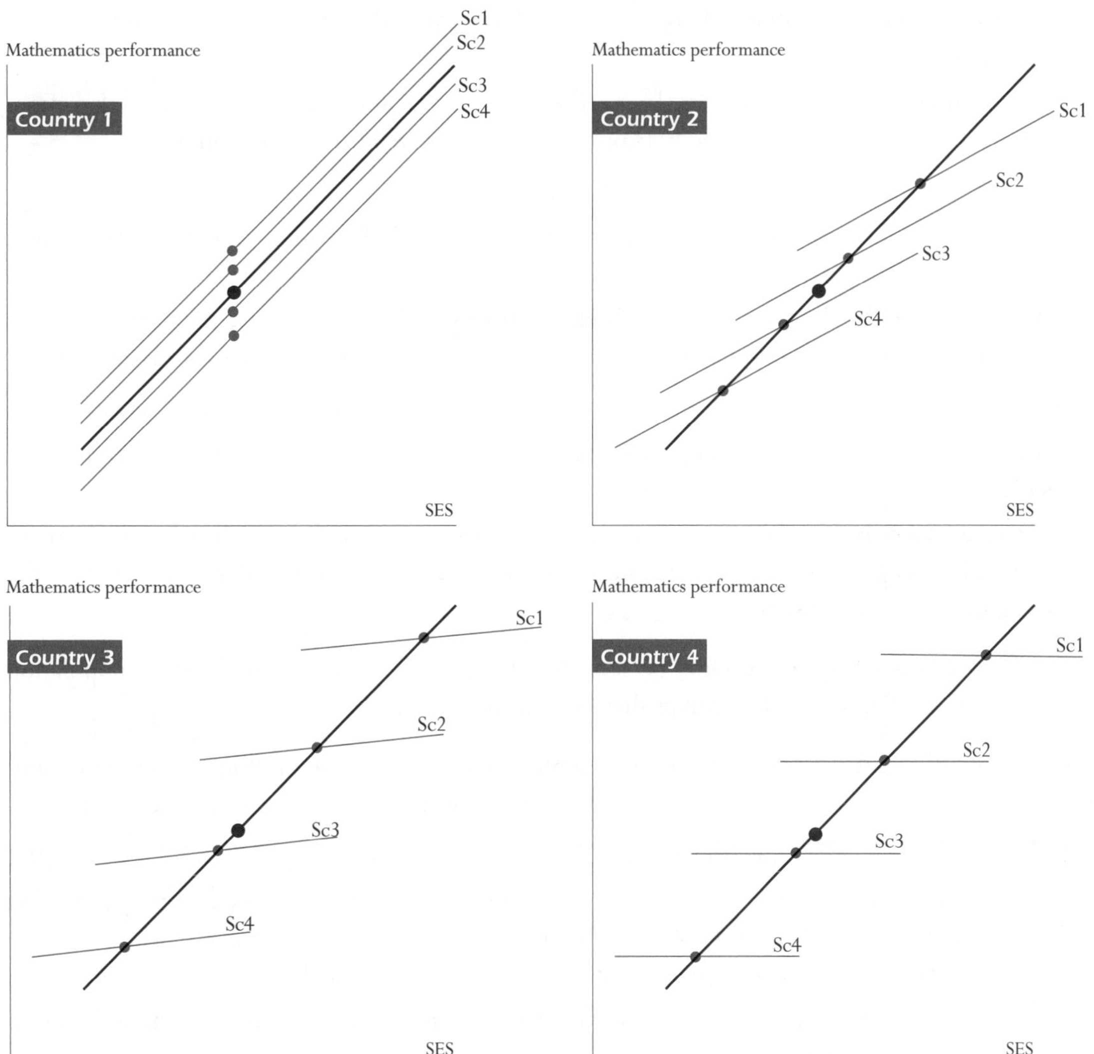

The simple linear regression analysis, graphically represented by the black lines, shows that the expected score of a student from a higher socio-economic background is considerably higher than the expected score of a student from a lower socio-economic background. The comparison between the four graphs shows the similarity of the relationship between the student's socio-economic background and the student performance at that level between countries. Based on simple linear regression analyses, one would conclude that the relationship between the socio-economic background and the student performance is identical in the different countries.

However, the multilevel regression analyses clearly distinguish the relationship between the two variables in the four countries.

In country 1, the multilevel regression lines are similar and close to the simple linear regression line. This means that:

- Regarding the socio-economic background of the student (*X* axis):
  - The different schools are all attended by students coming from a wide range of socio-economic backgrounds. All the within-school regression lines cover the whole range of values on the *X* axis; and
  - The schools have the same social intake, *i.e.* the mean of the student socio-economic background. Indeed, the projections of the red dots on the *X* axis are very close to each other.
- Regarding the student performance in mathematics (*Y* axis):
  - In each school, there are low, medium and high achievers. All the within-school regression lines cover the *Y* axis; and
  - On average, the schools have a similar level of performance. Indeed, the projections of the red dots on the *Y* axis are very close to each other. It also means that the between-school variance is quite small.
- Regarding the relationship between the socio-economic background and mathematics performance:
  - In each school, there is a strong relationship between the socio-economic background and achievement; and
  - Within all schools, low socio-economic background students perform well below high socio-economic background students. The slope of the within-school regression line indicates the strength of the relationship.

Each school in country 1 can therefore be considered as a simple random sample of the population and each school reflects the relationships that exist at the population level.

The opposite of country 1 is graphically represented by country 4. The multilevel regression lines differ considerably from the simple linear regression line. In that particular case, it means that:

- Regarding the socio-economic background of the student (*X* axis):
  - The schools do not cover the range of socio-economic backgrounds that exist at the population level. School 1 is mainly attended by high socio-economic background students while school 4 is mainly attended by low socio-economic background students; and
  - The schools have therefore different socio-economic intakes as the projections of the red dots on the *X* axis would show. In other words, there is a significant socio-economic segregation at the school level.
- Regarding the student performance in mathematics (*Y* axis):
  - The schools do not cover the range of the student performance that exists at the population level. School 1 is mainly attended by high achievers and school 4 is mainly attended by low achievers; and
  - Schools largely differ by their average performance level, as the projections of the red dots on the *Y* axis would show. In country 4, the school performance variance is therefore very important.
- Regarding the relationship between the socio-economic background and mathematics performance:
  - In each school, there is no relationship between socio-economic background and achievement; and
  - Within a particular school, the socio-economic background of the student does not matter. What does matter is not the socio-economic background of the student but the school he or she will attend. But the socio-economic background of the student will determine the school he or she will attend.

Countries 2 and 3 present intermediate situations between these two extreme examples.

FIXED EFFECT VERSUS RANDOM EFFECT

For the cases examined so far, the within-school regression lines were all parallel, but multilevel regression analyses also allow the regression slope to vary. In the former, the effect, *i.e.* the *X* effect, will be considered as fixed, while in the latter, the effect will be considered as random. Figure 13.5 represents a case with a random effect.

Figure 13.5 ■ **A random multilevel model**

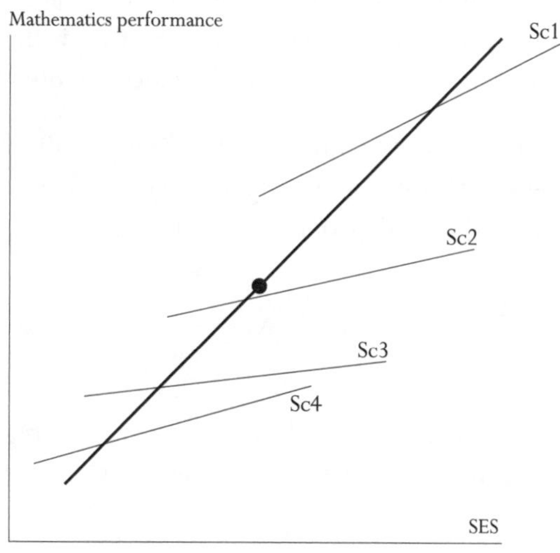

Mathematically, in the case of one explanatory variable, the two models can be differentiated as follows:

$$Y_{ij} = \alpha_j + \beta X_{ij} + \varepsilon_{ij} \text{ for a fixed effect}$$
$$\alpha_j = \gamma_{00} + U_{0j}$$

and

$$Y_{ij} = \alpha_j + \beta_j X_{ij} + \varepsilon_{ij} \text{ for a random effect}$$
$$\alpha_j = \gamma_{00} + U_{0j}$$
$$\beta_j = \gamma_{10} + U_{1j}$$

The subscript *i* in the equations refers to the student[1] (also denoted level 1 in the multilevel model literature), and the subscript *j* refers to the school (or level 2). In an equation, the presence of the subscript *j* for a regression coefficient means that it can vary from one school to another.

The term ε_{ij} denotes the residual of the equation, *i.e.* the difference between the observed score Y_{ij} and the predicted score $\hat{Y}_{ij}$. This residual is normally distributed with a mean of 0 and a constant level 1 (*i.e.* the student level) variance, usually denoted σ^2.

As shown by these two equations, the intercept α_j is always considered as a random effect. Considering the intercept as a fixed parameter would reduce the multilevel model to a linear regression analysis. The intercept α_j can further be divided into a fixed part, *i.e.* γ_{00} denotes the overall intercept and is equal to the average of the school intercepts α_j, and secondly into a random part, *i.e.* U_{0j}, denoting school departure from the overall intercept. This school departure U_{0j} is assumed to have a mean of 0 and a variance τ_0^2.

The β coefficient in the first equation has no subscript j, meaning that the effect X cannot vary from one school to the other. The regression lines are therefore parallel and thus the X effect is considered as fixed. On the other hand, the β coefficient in the second equation has a subscript j, meaning that it can vary from one school to another. The regression lines are no longer parallel and thus the X effect is now considered as random. As previously, this regression coefficient β_j can be divided into a fixed part and a random part. The fixed part γ_{10} is called overall regression coefficient and corresponds to the mean of the regression coefficients β_j. The random part U_{1j} is the school departure from the overall regression coefficient. It has a mean of 0 and a variance denoted τ_1^2.

Random effects and fixed effects can be combined in a single multilevel regression analysis. For instance, in the following equation, two student explanatory variables are introduced in the model, one is considered as fixed, X_1, and the other one as random, X_2.

$$Y_{ij} = \alpha_j + \beta_1 X_{1ij} + \beta_{2j} X_{2ij}$$

SOME EXAMPLES WITH SAS®

Usually, two types of indices are relevant in multilevel analyses: the regression coefficients and the decomposition of the variance into the different levels, *i.e.* the student level (or level 1) and school level (or level 2).

Multilevel regression analyses always report the residual variance at the different levels – the between-school variance and the within-school variance that are not explained by the predictors included in the model.

However, scientific reports usually show the explained variance. The conversion of the residual variance into percentages of explained variance just requires the comparison of the school and student variance coefficients with their respective residual variance coefficients.

Example 1

The decomposition of the total variance can be easily obtained with a multilevel regression model. Applying the following model

$$Y_{ij} = \alpha_j + \varepsilon_{ij}$$

$$\alpha_j = \gamma_{00} + U_{0j}$$

will provide unbiased estimates of the between-school variance and the within-school variance. As the regression model has no predictors, the school intercepts, *i.e.* α_j will therefore be equal or close to the school means. The variance of U_{0j} will be equal to the school variance. As each student will be assigned his or her school mean as predicted score, the variance of ε_{ij} will be equal to the within-school variance.

The SAS® PROC MIXED procedure allows for modeling multilevel regression. However, it requires the standardisation of the weights, *i.e.* the sum of the weights is equal to the number of students in the dataset. If the BY statement is used, then the standardisation will be done by category of the breakdown variable.

Box 13.2 provides the SAS® syntax for this standardisation, as well as a short checking procedure.[2]

Box 13.2 ■ **Standardisation of the PISA 2003 final weights**

```
libname PISA2003  "c:\pisa2003\data\";
options nofmterr notes;
run;

data temp1;
     set pisa2003.stud;
     keep cnt schoolid stidstd w_fstuwt pv1math ;
run;
proc sort data=temp1;
     by cnt;
run;
proc univariate data=temp1 noprint;
     var w_fstuwt;
     by cnt;
     output out=temp2 sum=wgt N=nbre;
run;
data temp3;
     merge temp1 temp2;
     by cnt;
     std_wgt=(w_fstuwt*nbre)/wgt;
run;
/* VERIFICATION */

proc means data=temp3 noprint;
     var std_wgt;
     by cnt;
     output out=cnt N=nbstud Sum=wgtsum;
run;
proc print data=cnt;
     var nbstud wgtsum;
run;
```

Box 13.3 provides the SAS® syntax for a multilevel regression model as well as the SAS® syntax for the computation of the intra-class correlation.

Box 13.3 ■ **SAS® syntax for a multilevel regression model – Example 1**

```
proc mixed data= temp3 method=ml;
     class schoolid;
     model pv1math = /solution;
     random intercept/subject=schoolid solution;
     weight std_wgt;
     by cnt;
     ods output covparms=decompvar solutionf=fixparm solutionr=ranparm;
run;
proc transpose data=decompvar out=rho;
     var estimate;
     by cnt;
     id covparm;
run;
data rho;
     set rho;
     rho=intercept/(intercept+residual);
     keep cnt intercept residual rho;
run;
proc print data=rho;
run;
```

The `class` statement defines the second level of the analyses. Like all linear models, the `model` statement specifies the dependent and independent variables. In this particular example, there is no predictor. Therefore the between-school and within-school residual variances will be equal to the school and within-school variance estimates. The `random` statement distinguishes between fixed and random predictors, as explained in the previous section. It should be noted that "`intercept`" always needs to be mentioned. The `weight` and the `by` statements are self-explanatory. Finally, the `ods` statement will save the results in three data files. The variance estimates will be saved in the file "*decompvar*", the fixed parameters will be saved in the file "*fixparm*" and the random parameters will be saved in the file "*randparm*".

Table 13.2 provides the between-school and within-school variance estimates and the intra-class correlation. These variance estimates were saved in the file "*decompvar* ". As shown in Box 13.3, the intra-class correlation[3] is equal to:

$$\rho = \frac{\sigma^2_{\text{between-}school}}{\sigma^2_{\text{between-}school} + \sigma^2_{within-school}} = \frac{\tau_0^2}{\tau_0^2 + \sigma^2}$$

with σ^2_{school} or τ_0^2 the between-school variance and $\sigma^2_{within-school}$ or σ^2 the within-school variance. In Australia, the between-school variance is equal to 1919.11 and the within-school variance is equal to 7169.09. The intra-class correlation is therefore the percentage of the total variance that is accounted for by the school. It reflects how schools differ in their student average performance. In Australia, the intra-class correlation is therefore equal to 1919.11/(1919.11+7169.09) = 0.21. The estimate of the intra-class correlation ranges from 0.04 in Iceland to 0.63 in the Netherlands.

Example 2

The following examples of the school parameter estimates are based on the data of Luxembourg, where there are 29 schools in the PISA database. In Example 2, the socio-economic background of the student, denoted HISEI, is introduced as a fixed factor.

Preparation of the data file

In the PISA databases, there are no missing data for the final weight and for the student performance estimate. However, there are missing values for variables that might be used as predictors in a multilevel regression model. These missing data generate two major issues:

- The sum of the weights will slightly differ from the number of cases that will be used by the regression models. Note that cases with missing values are automatically[4] dropped from any regression models.
- The school and student variances from different models cannot be compared as missing values are not always random. For instance, low socio-economic background students are usually less likely to provide answers about their mother's and/or father's occupations.

To avoid these two problems, it is recommended to delete any cases with missing data for the different predictors that will be used in the regression models before the weight standardisation. As the next multilevel regression model examples will use two student level variables, *i.e.* HISEI for the student socio-economic background, and ST03Q01 for the student gender and two school level variables, *i.e.* the percentage of girls in the school, PCGIRLS, and the type of schools, SCHLTYPE, cases with missing data for at least one of these four variables will be deleted before the weight standardisation.

Table 13.2 ■ **Between- and within-school variance estimates and intra-class correlation (rho)**

Country	Between-school variance	Within-school variance	rho
AUS	1919.11	7169.09	0.21
AUT	5296.65	4299.71	0.55
BEL	7328.47	5738.33	0.56
BRA	4128.49	5173.60	0.44
CAN	1261.58	6250.12	0.17
CHE	3092.60	6198.65	0.33
CZE	4972.45	4557.50	0.52
DEU	6206.92	4498.70	0.58
DNK	1109.45	7357.14	0.13
ESP	1476.85	6081.74	0.20
FIN	336.24	6664.98	0.05
FRA	3822.62	4536.22	0.46
GBR	1881.09	6338.25	0.23
GRC	3387.52	5991.75	0.36
HKG	4675.30	5298.26	0.47
HUN	5688.56	4034.66	0.59
IDN	2769.48	3343.87	0.45
IRL	1246.70	6110.71	0.17
ISL	337.56	7849.99	0.04
ITA	4922.84	4426.67	0.53
JPN	5387.17	4668.82	0.54
KOR	3531.75	5011.56	0.41
LIE	3385.41	5154.08	0.40
LUX	2596.36	5806.97	0.31
LVA	1750.22	6156.52	0.22
MAC	1416.99	6449.96	0.18
MEX	2476.01	3916.46	0.39
NLD	5528.99	3326.09	0.62
NOR	599.49	7986.58	0.07
NZL	1740.61	7969.97	0.18
POL	1033.90	7151.46	0.13
PRT	2647.70	5151.93	0.34
RUS	2656.62	6021.44	0.31
SVK	3734.56	4873.69	0.43
SWE	986.03	8199.46	0.11
THA	2609.38	4387.08	0.37
TUN	2821.00	3825.36	0.42
TUR	6188.40	4891.13	0.56
URY	4457.08	5858.42	0.43
USA	2395.38	6731.45	0.26
YUG	2646.00	4661.59	0.36

Box 13.4 presents the SAS® syntax. It consists of:

- Merging the student data file and the school data file with the variables of interest;
- Deleting the cases with at least one missing data for the predictor; and
- Standardising the weight.

Before deletion of cases with missing values, there are 3 923 records in the Luxembourg database. After deletion, 3 782 are left. About 3.5 per cent of the cases are deleted. If too many cases are deleted, for instance, more than 10 per cent, then either the variables with too many missing values should be dropped from the analyses, or imputation methods should be used.

Rerunning the empty multilevel model

After deletion, the empty multilevel model, *i.e.* a multilevel regression model without any predictor, is run to obtain the between-school and within-school variance estimates. The between-school and the within-school variance estimates, saved in the "*decompvar2*" file, are now respectively equal to 2 563.07 and 5 734.39 instead of 2 596.36 and 5 806.97.

Box 13.4 ■ **SAS® syntax for standardising PISA 2003 final weights with deletion of cases with missing values in Luxembourg**

```
data temp1;
     set pisa2003.stud;
     if (cnt="LUX");
     keep cnt schoolid stidstd w_fstuwt pv1math hisei st03q01;
run;
proc sort data=temp1;
     by cnt schoolid stidstd;
run;
data temp2;
     set pisa2003.schi;
     if (cnt="LUX");
     keep cnt schoolid schltype pcgirls;
run;
proc sort data=temp2;
     by cnt schoolid ;
run;
data temp3;
     merge temp1 temp2;
     by cnt schoolid;
     nbmiss=0;
     array miss (3)
            hisei st03q01 schltype;
     do i=1 to 3;
            if (miss(i) in (.,.M,.N,.I)) then nbmiss=nbmiss+1;
     end;
     if (nbmiss > 0) then delete;
run;
proc univariate data=temp3 noprint;
     var w_fstuwt;
     by cnt;
     output out=temp4 sum=wgt N=nbre;
run;
data temp5;
     merge temp3 temp4;
     by cnt;
     std_wgt=(w_fstuwt*nbre)/wgt;
run;
/* VERIFICATION */

proc means data=temp5 noprint;
     var std_wgt;
     by cnt;
     output out=cnt N=nbstud Sum=wgtsum;
run;
proc print data=cnt;
     var nbstud wgtsum;
run;

proc mixed data= temp5 method=ml;
     class schoolid;
     model pv1math = /solution;
     random intercept/subject=schoolid solution;
     weight std_wgt;
     by cnt;
     ods output covparms=decompvar2 solutionf=fixparm2
solutionr=ranparm2;
run;
```

The "*fixparm2*" file contains the fixed parameters. With an empty model, it will present only γ_{00}, *i.e.* 492.36 for the data of Luxembourg.

The "*ranparm2*" file lists the random parameters. With an empty model, only the school departure U_{0j} will be listed. Table 13.3 is a printout of the "*ranparm2*" file. It contains:

- The breakdown variables used in the model, *i.e.* CNT;
- The effect, *i.e.* the intercept or as it will be shown later, the random predictor, the estimate;
- The class variable, *i.e.* the SCHOOLID;
- The estimate;
- The standard error on the estimate;
- The number of degrees of freedom (the number of students minus the number of schools);
- The *t* statistic; and
- The probability that the estimates differ from 0.

Table 13.3 ■ **Printout of the random parameter file**

CNT	Effect	SCHOOLid	Estimate	StdErrPred	DF	tValue	Probt
LUX	Intercept	00001	0.71	13.00	3753	0.05	0.96
LUX	Intercept	00002	66.39	11.63	3753	5.71	0.00
LUX	Intercept	00003	-23.71	11.03	3753	-2.15	0.03
LUX	Intercept	00004	-44.68	12.18	3753	-3.67	0.00
LUX	Intercept	00005	-8.56	10.68	3753	-0.80	0.42
LUX	Intercept	00006	61.90	11.34	3753	5.46	0.00
LUX	Intercept	00007	-68.69	12.39	3753	-5.54	0.00
LUX	Intercept	00008	61.14	11.62	3753	5.26	0.00
LUX	Intercept	00009	81.64	11.10	3753	7.36	0.00
LUX	Intercept	00010	-62.00	11.37	3753	-5.45	0.00
LUX	Intercept	00011	33.19	25.14	3753	1.32	0.19
LUX	Intercept	00012	-11.35	12.54	3753	-0.91	0.37
LUX	Intercept	00013	15.56	10.47	3753	1.49	0.14
LUX	Intercept	00014	8.01	11.25	3753	0.71	0.48
LUX	Intercept	00015	37.55	12.36	3753	3.04	0.00
LUX	Intercept	00016	-46.59	10.95	3753	-4.26	0.00
LUX	Intercept	00017	-33.61	10.98	3753	-3.06	0.00
LUX	Intercept	00018	-76.02	12.54	3753	-6.06	0.00
LUX	Intercept	00019	-70.43	12.96	3753	-5.43	0.00
LUX	Intercept	00020	57.54	11.17	3753	5.15	0.00
LUX	Intercept	00021	8.04	11.01	3753	0.73	0.47
LUX	Intercept	00022	-0.67	25.14	3753	-0.03	0.98
LUX	Intercept	00023	84.27	10.90	3753	7.73	0.00
LUX	Intercept	00024	29.88	11.12	3753	2.69	0.01
LUX	Intercept	00025	63.74	11.69	3753	5.45	0.00
LUX	Intercept	00026	-33.65	11.15	3753	-3.02	0.00
LUX	Intercept	00027	-8.29	11.53	3753	-0.72	0.47
LUX	Intercept	00028	-36.89	13.84	3753	-2.66	0.01
LUX	Intercept	00029	-84.43	10.96	3753	-7.71	0.00

For instance, the departure of the school 00001 from the overall intercept 492.36 is only 0.71. This departure does not differ from 0, as shown by the *t* statistic and its associated probability value. In other words, the intercept of school 00001 is not significantly different from the overall intercept. On the other hand, the intercept of school 00002 is significantly higher than the overall intercept.

Shrinkage factor

In the case of an empty model, one might consider that the sum of the overall intercept γ_{00} and a particular school departure U_{0j} should be perfectly equal to the school performance mean.

Multilevel models shrink the school departures. To illustrate this shrinkage process, suppose we have an educational system with 100 schools. Assume that the school performance means are perfectly identical. In other words, the school variance is equal to 0. If 20 students are tested within each school, it is expected that school mean estimates will slightly differ from the school means. Indeed, within particular schools, predominantly high achievers or low achievers may be sampled so that the school mean is respectively overestimated or underestimated. As the number of sampled students within schools increases, the difference between the school mean and its estimate is likely to decrease. Therefore, the shrinkage factor is inversely proportional to the number of sampled students within schools.

The shrinkage factor[5] is equal to:

$$\frac{n_j \sigma^2_{\text{between-}school}}{n_j \sigma^2_{\text{between-}school} + \sigma^2_{within-school}},$$

with n_j being the number of students in school *j* in the sample (Goldstein, 1997).

Table 13.4 presents, for each school, the average performance in mathematics, the number of students used in the multilevel regression model, the departure from the overall intercept estimated by the empty multilevel regression model, as presented in Table 13.3 and the sum of the overall intercept γ_{00} and the school departure U_{0j}.

As shown, the difference between the school performance mean and the sum $\gamma_{00} + U_{0j}$ is:

- Proportional to the school departure, *i.e.* the shrinkage factor mainly affects low and high performing schools; and
- Inversely proportional to the number of observed students in the school.

Introduction of HISEI as a fixed effect

With the introduction of the student level variable HISEI as a fixed effect, the equation can be written as:

$$Y_{ij} = \alpha_j + \beta_1 (HISEI)_{ij} + \varepsilon_{ij}$$
$$\alpha_j = \gamma_{00} + U_{0j}$$

The SAS® syntax for this model is presented in Box 13.5 and parts of the SAS® output is presented in Box 13.6.

Table 13.4 ■ **School performance in mathematics, number of students per school and corrected mean**

School	School mean	Number of students	Departure U_{0j}	$\gamma_{00} + U_{0j}$
00001	493.1	67	0.7	493.1
00002	560.0	120	66.4	558.8
00003	468.3	179	-23.7	468.6
00004	446.6	94	-44.7	447.7
00005	483.7	233	-8.6	483.8
00006	555.2	146	61.9	554.3
00007	421.8	83	-68.7	423.7
00008	554.6	116	61.1	553.5
00009	575.1	167	81.6	574.0
00010	429.4	131	-62.0	430.4
00011	535.2	8	33.2	525.6
00012	480.7	78	-11.3	481.0
00013	508.0	289	15.6	507.9
00014	500.5	150	8.0	500.4
00015	530.9	87	37.6	529.9
00016	445.2	184	-46.6	445.8
00017	458.3	183	-33.6	458.8
00018	414.2	73	-76.0	416.3
00019	419.6	66	-70.4	421.9
00020	550.7	162	57.5	549.9
00021	500.5	174	8.0	500.4
00022	491.5	8	-0.7	491.7
00023	577.6	185	84.3	576.6
00024	522.7	169	29.9	522.2
00025	557.3	117	63.7	556.1
00026	458.2	151	-33.7	458.7
00027	483.9	126	-8.3	484.1
00028	453.9	53	-36.9	455.5
00029	406.9	183	-84.4	407.9

Box 13.5 ■ **SAS® syntax for a multilevel regression model – Example 2**

```
proc mixed data= temp5 method=ml;
     class schoolid;
     model pv1math = hisei /solution;
     random intercept/subject=schoolid solution;
     weight std_wgt;
     by cnt;
     ods output covparms=decompvar3 solutionf=fixparm3 solutionr=ranparm3;
run;
```

Box 13.6 ■ **SAS® output – Example 2**

```
                    Covariance Parameter Estimates

                Cov Parm      Subject        Estimate
                Intercept     SCHOOLid       1949.09
                Residual                      5551.53

                      Solution for Fixed Effects

                            Standard
Effect          Estimate    Error       DF       t Value       Pr > |t|

Intercept       446.76      9.2590      28       48.25         <.0001
HISEI           0.9479      0.08237     3752     11.51         <.0001
```

Only one change has been introduced in comparison with the syntax presented in Box 13.3. The name HISEI has been added to the `model` statement.

The overall intercept γ_{00} is now equal to 446.76 and the within-school regression coefficient β_1 is equal to 0.9479. This means that, within a particular school, an increase of 1 unit on the HISEI scale will be associated with an increase of 0.9479 on the mathematics scale. By comparison, the linear regression coefficient of HISEI on the mathematics performance is equal to 2.05. The Luxembourg education system seems to behave like country 2 or as country 3 in Figure 13.4.

The between-school and within-school residual variable estimates, respectively denoted τ_0^2 and σ^2, are equal to 1949.09 and 5551.53.

The percentage of variance explained by the HISEI variable can be computed as:

$$1-\frac{1949.09}{2563.07}=0.24 \text{ at the school level and}$$

$$1-\frac{5551.53}{5734.39}=0.03 \text{ at the student level.}$$

How can a student level variable explain about 25 per cent of the between-school variance and only 3 per cent of the within-school variance? This mainly reflects the school socio-economic background segregation. Some of the Luxembourg schools are mainly attended by high socio-economic background students while some other schools are mainly attended by students with low socio-economic backgrounds.

Figure 13.6 provides a graphical explanation of this phenomenon. The between-school variance in any case can be graphically represented by the variability of the school intercepts on the *Y* axis.

Note that the between-school variance can be obtained by an empty multilevel regression model. In that particular case, the intercept is close to the orthogonal projection of the school performance average on the *Y* axis, as shown by the black line in Figure 13.6. As explained in the previous section, the difference between the school mean and the intercept results from the application of the shrinkage factor.

The between-school residual variance can be obtained by the extension of the regression line on the *Y* axis, as shown by the red discontinuous line in Figure 13.6. As one can see, the range of the black intercepts is larger than the range of the red intercepts.

Broadly speaking, a student level variable will have an impact on the between-school variance if:

- Schools differ in the mean and the range of students in regard with that variable (see countries 2, 3 and 4) in Figure 13.4; and
- The within-school regression coefficient of that variable differs from 0. The case of country 4 in Figure 13.4 illustrates a case where using the HISEI variable at the student level in the model will not reduce the between-school variance. On the other hand, the introduction of the school social intake, *i.e.* the school HISEI mean, will have in country 4 a substantial impact on the between-school variance.

Figure 13.6 ■ **Graphical representation of the between-school variance reduction**

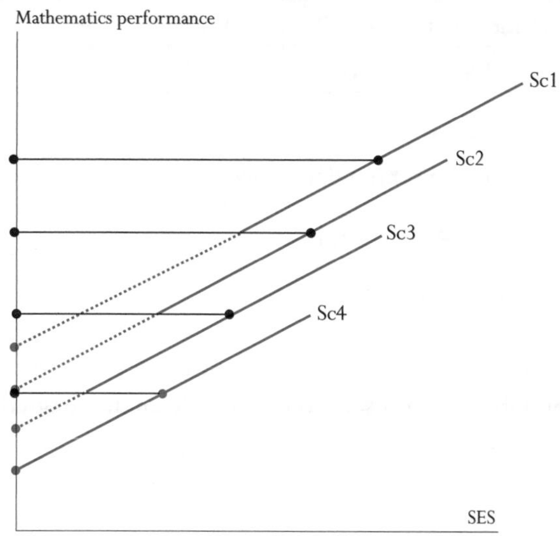

Example 3

Example 3 is similar to Example 2, except that HISEI is now considered as a random effect. The SAS® syntax is presented in Box 13.7. The equation can therefore be written as:

$$Y_{ij} = \alpha_j + \beta_{1j}(HISEI)_{ij} + \varepsilon_{ij}$$

$$\alpha_j = \gamma_{00} + U_{0j}$$

$$\beta_{1j} = \gamma_{10} + U_{1j}$$

Box 13.7 ■ **SAS® syntax for a multilevel regression model – Example 3**

```
proc mixed data= temp5 method=ml;
     class schoolid;
     model pv1math = hisei/solution;
     random intercept hisei/subject=schoolid solution;
     weight std_wgt;
     by cnt;
ods output covparms=decompvar4 solutionf=fixparm4 solutionr=ranparm4;
run;
```

The variable HISEI has been added to the `random` statement.

The fixed parameter file contains the overall intercept γ_{00} and HISEI overall regression coefficient γ_{10}. Like the school intercepts which are divided into two parts, an overall intercept and a school departure, the within-school regression coefficient is divided into two parts: an overall regression coefficient (the fixed part, denoted γ_{10}) and a school regression coefficient departure (the random part, denoted U_{1j}).

The overall intercept and regression coefficient are presented inTable 13.5. The overall intercept is equal to 449.59 and the overall HISEI regression coefficient is equal to 0.89. As shown by the *t* statistic and its associated probability, both parameters are significantly different from 0.

Table 13.5 ■ **Fixed parameter output - Example 3**

CNT	Effect	Estimate	StdErrPred	tValue	Probt
LUX	Intercept	449.59	9.69	46.39	0.00
LUX	HISEI	0.89	0.11	8.17	0.00

The random parameter file lists the school departures:

- U_{0j} from the intercept γ_{00}, *i.e.* 449.59 ; and
- U_{1j} from HISEI regression coefficient γ_{10}, *i.e.* 0.89.

As HISEI is now considered as a random effect, it is meaningless to interpret the school departure from the overall intercept.Table 13.6 presents the school departure from the overall HISEI regression coefficient for the first 13 schools.

Table 13.6 ■ **Random parameter output - Example 3**

CNT	Effect	SCHOOL	Estimate	StdErrPred	DF	tValue	Probt
LUX	HISEI	00001	0.22	0.31	3724	0.71	0.48
LUX	HISEI	00002	0.04	0.26	3724	0.15	0.88
LUX	HISEI	00003	0.29	0.26	3724	1.13	0.26
LUX	HISEI	00004	-0.51	0.29	3724	-1.75	0.08
LUX	HISEI	00005	-0.08	0.25	3724	-0.31	0.76
LUX	HISEI	00006	0.07	0.28	3724	0.26	0.79
LUX	HISEI	00007	-0.04	0.29	3724	-0.13	0.90
LUX	HISEI	00008	-0.13	0.27	3724	-0.49	0.62
LUX	HISEI	00009	-0.29	0.25	3724	-1.19	0.23
LUX	HISEI	00010	-0.17	0.26	3724	-0.65	0.52
LUX	HISEI	00011	0.07	0.34	3724	0.19	0.85
LUX	HISEI	00012	-0.04	0.28	3724	-0.14	0.89
LUX	HISEI	00013	0.82	0.22	3724	3.66	0.00

The HISEI regression coefficient for school 00001 is equal to 0.89+0.22=1.11, but it cannot be considered as significantly different from the overall intercept. Out of the 13 schools presented in Table 13.6, only school 00013 presents a regression coefficient that significantly differs from the overall coefficient, as shown by the *t* statistics of the probability. The HISEI regression coefficient is equal to 0.89+0.82=1.71 and as shown by the *t* statistic or the probability, this within-school regression coefficient is significantly different from the overall regression coefficient.

SAS® now provides three variance estimates:

- The between-school residual variance τ_0^2, *i.e.* 2 147.22;
- The within-school residual variance σ^2, *i.e.* 5 509.38; and
- The variance of HISEI regression coefficients τ_1^2, *i.e.* 0.1272. This is also the variability of the regression coefficient departure.

In comparison with Example 2, the between-school residual variance has slightly increased and the within-school residual variance has slightly decreased. The reduction of the within-school variance is not surprising as the random effect can only better fit the data.

Figure 13.7 helps to understand the increase of the between-school residual variance. The regression coefficient for school 00001 (Sc1) is slightly less steep so that the extension of the regression line will be higher than previously on the *Y* axis. Further, the regression coefficient is slightly steeper for school 00004 (Sc4), so that the extension of the regression line will be a bit lower on the *Y* axis.

Figure 13.7 ■ **Reduction of the between-school residual variance for a fixed and a random model**

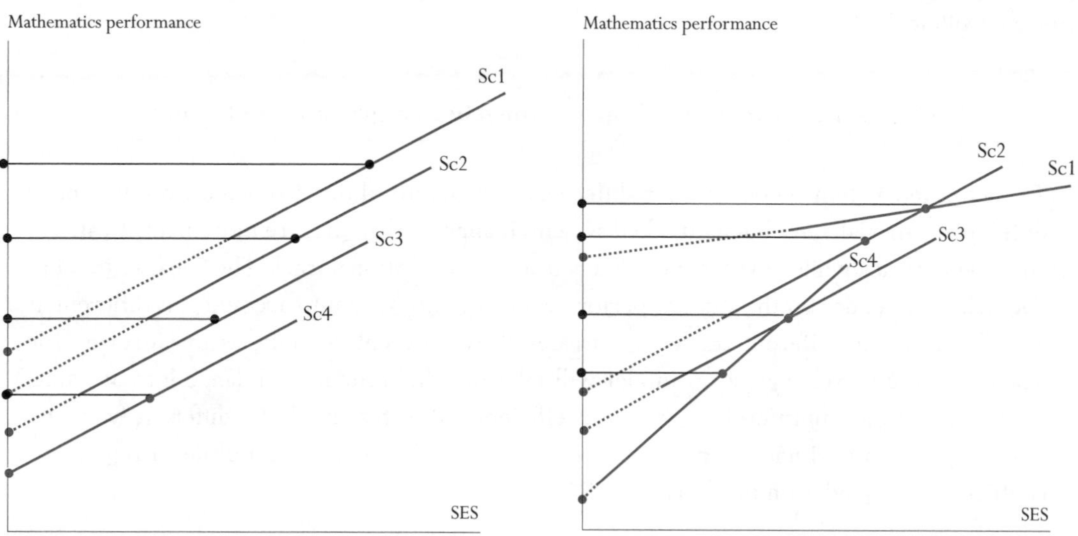

Example 4

In Example 4, the student gender, denoted ST03Q01 in the PISA database, is added as a fixed factor to the previous model. The equation can be written as:

$$Y_{ij} = \alpha_j + \beta_{1j}(HISEI)_{ij} + \beta_2(ST03Q01)_{ij}$$

$$\alpha_j = \gamma_{00} + U_{0j}$$

$$\beta_{1j} = \gamma_{10} + U_{1j}$$

Box 13.8 presents the SAS® syntax.

Box 13.8 ■ **SAS® syntax for a multilevel regression model - Example 4**

```
proc mixed data= temp5 method=ml;
     class schoolid;
     model pv1math = hisei st03q01 /solution;
     random intercept hisei /subject=schoolid solution;
     weight std_wgt;
     by cnt;
     ods output covparms=decompvar5 solutionf=fixparm5 solutionr=ranparm5;
run;
```

The fixed parameters are respectively equal to 419.68 for the overall intercept, 0.86 for the overall HISEI regression coefficient and 20.7927 for the overall gender coefficient.

The between-school residual variance τ_0^2 is equal to 2 167.41 and the within-school residual variance σ^2 is equal to 5 415.34. Finally, the variance of the school HISEI regression coefficient τ_1^2 is equal to 0.1313.

This model explains $1-\frac{2167.41}{2563.07}=15.3$ per cent of the between-school variance and $1-\frac{5415.34}{5734.39}=5.6$ per cent of the within-school variance.

The gender regression coefficient of 20.8 reflects the expected gender difference within any school, after controlling for HISEI.

Box 13.9 ■ **Interpretation of the within-school regression coefficient**

The expected within-school gender difference can greatly differ from the overall gender difference, especially in a highly tracked system. It appears that girls are more likely to attend an academic track while boys are more likely to attend a vocational track. The linear regression coefficient of gender on the student performance does not take into account this differential attendance. If the different tracks are organised by different schools, as in Germany for instance, a multilevel regression model will take this differential attendance into account, so that the gender multilevel regression coefficient will substantially be different from the linear regression coefficient. The table below provides the linear and multilevel regression coefficients for gender on the German PISA 2003 data.

At the population level, boys outperform girls by 8.9 in mathematics while girls outperform boys by 42.1 in reading. But within a particular school, the expected differences in mathematics and in reading are respectively equal to 30.7 and -19.3.

Gender differences in Germany

	Mathematics	Reading
Linear regression coefficient	8.9	-42.1
Multilevel regression coefficient	30.7	-19.3

Gender can also be considered as a random factor. The equation can therefore be written as:

$$Y_{ij} = \alpha_j + \beta_{1j}(HISEI)_{ij} + \beta_{2j}(ST03Q01)_{ij}$$
$$\alpha_j = \gamma_{00} + U_{0j}$$
$$\beta_{1j} = \gamma_{10} + U_{1j}$$
$$\beta_{2j} = \gamma_{20} + U_{2j}$$

Box 13.10 presents the variance estimate of the random parameters as well as the regression coefficient estimates of the fixed parts of the model.

Box 13.10 ■ **SAS® output – Example 4**

```
                 Covariance Parameter Estimates

         Cov Parm          Subject         Estimate

         Intercept         SCHOOLid         1904.81
         HISEI             SCHOOLid          0.1348
         ST03Q01           SCHOOLid         70.5088
         Residual                           5400.88

                 Solution for Fixed Effects

                               Standard
  Effect       Estimate         Error       DF      t Value     Pr > |t|

  Intercept      419.36       10.0173       28        41.86     <.0001
  HISEI          0.8607        0.1098       28         7.84     <.0001
  ST03Q01       21.0238        3.1526       25         6.67     <.0001
```

As shown by Box 13.10, the variability of U_{2j}, *i.e.* the school departure on the gender regression coefficient is quite large. This indicates that the gender differences vary from one school to another.

Example 5

The last equation in Example 4 was $Y_{ij} = \alpha_j + \beta_{1j} (HISEI)_{ij} + \beta_{2j} (ST03Q01)_{ij}$. This equation mainly models the student performance variability within-schools by introducing student level predictors. However, due to the segregation effect, these student level predictors can explain some of the between-school variance.

It is also possible to introduce a predictor school level variable. Suppose that one is interested in the effect of the school type on the school mean performance. The equation can be written as:

$$Y = \alpha_j + \beta_{1j}(HISEI)_{ij} + \beta_{2j}(ST03Q01)_{ij} + \varepsilon_{ij}$$
$$\alpha_j = \gamma_{00} + \gamma_{01}(SCHLTYPE)_j + U_{0j}$$
$$\beta_{1j} = \gamma_{10} + U_{1j}$$
$$\beta_{2j} = \gamma_{20} + U_{2j}$$

In other words, as the school type variable is identical for all students within a particular school, this variable will only have an effect on the school intercepts. Given the socio-economic background and the gender composition of the schools, does the school type explain why some schools perform better than expected and why some schools perform at a lower level than expected?

The SAS® syntax is presented in Box 13.11.

Box 13.11 ■ **SAS® syntax for a multilevel regression model - Example 5**

```
proc mixed data= temp5 method=ml;
     class schoolid;
     model pv1math = hisei st03q01 schltype/solution;
     random intercept hisei /subject=schoolid solution;
     weight std_wgt;
     by cnt;
     ods output covparms=decompvar6 solutionf=fixparm6 solutionr=ranparm6;
run;
```

Table 13.7 presents the results for the fixed parameters.

Table 13.7 ■ **Fixed parameters - Example 5**

CNT	Effect	Estimate	StdErrPred	DF	tValue	Probt
LUX	Intercept	320.47	66.69	27	4.81	0.00
LUX	HISEI	0.86	0.11	28	7.84	0.00
LUX	ST03Q01	20.69	2.59	3723	7.98	0.00
LUX	SCHLTYPE	35.14	23.36	3723	1.50	0.13

As shown by Table 13.7, the school type variable is not significant. In other words, it cannot be stated that government-dependent private schools differ from public schools once the student socio-economic background and the student gender is controlled.

Example 6

The model can finally be extended by trying to understand why the school HISEI and ST03Q01 regression coefficients vary. Two hypotheses to test are:

- The HISEI regression coefficients differ between public school and government-dependent private schools; and
- The ST03Q01 regression coefficients are related to the percentage of boys and girls in the school.

The equation can be written as:

$$Y_{ij} = \alpha_j + \beta_{1j}(HISEI)_{ij} + \beta_{2j}(ST03Q01)_{ij} + \varepsilon_{ij}$$
$$\alpha_j = \gamma_{00} + \gamma_{01}(SCHLTYPE)_j + U_{0j}$$
$$\beta_{1j} = \gamma_{10} + \gamma_{11}(SCHLTYPE)_j + U_{1j}$$
$$\beta_{2j} = \gamma_{20} + \gamma_{21}(PCGIRLS)_j + U_{2j}$$

Box 13.12 presents the SAS® syntax for running this model. Testing whether the HISEI regression coefficients differ according to the school type is similar to testing the interaction between the school type and the HISEI regression coefficients. Therefore, in SAS®, the term "`hisei*schltype`" has to be added in the `model` statement, as well as "`st03q01*pcgirls`".

Box 13.12 ■ **SAS® syntax for a multilevel regression model - Example 6**

```
proc mixed data= temp5 method=ml;
     class schoolid;
     model pv1math = hisei st03q01 schltype hisei*schltype
           st03q01*pcgirls /solution;
     random intercept hisei st03q01 /subject=schoolid solution;
     weight std_wgt;
     by cnt;
     ods output covparms=decompvar7 solutionf=fixparm7 solutionr=ranparm7;
run;
```

Box 13.13 ■ **SAS® output – Example 6**

```
                    Covariance Parameter Estimates

              Cov Parm        Subject         Estimate

              Intercept       SCHOOLid         1757.37
              HISEI           SCHOOLid          0.1427
              ST03Q01         SCHOOLid         71.0154
              Residual                         5397.46

                       Solution for Fixed Effects

                                    Standard
Effect               Estimate        Error       DF      t Value     Pr > |t|

Intercept              291.40      71.2226       27         4.09       0.0003
HISEI                  1.8608       0.9020       27         2.06       0.0489
ST03Q01               19.8837      11.7303       24         1.70       0.1030
SCHLTYPE              45.1278      24.8607     3698         1.82       0.0696
HISEI*SCHLTYPE        -0.3505       0.3138     3698        -1.12       0.2640
ST03Q01*PCGIRLS        2.6220      24.8656     3698         0.11       0.9160
```

Table 13.8 presents the fixed parameters in relation to the equation. As shown by the last row, the HISEI regression coefficient is not significantly associated with the type of school.

Table 13.8 ■ **Fixed parameter estimates - Example 6**

Effect	Coefficient estimate	Coefficient
Intercept	291.40	γ_{00}
HISEI	1.86	γ_{10}
ST03Q01	19.88	γ_{20}
SCHLTYPE	45.12	γ_{01}
HISEI*SCHLTYPE	-0.35	γ_{11}
ST03Q01*PCGIRLS	2.62	γ_{21}

Table 13.9 ■ **Random parameter variance estimates - Example 6**

Effect	Variance estimate	Coefficient
Intercept	1757.37	U_{0j}
HISEI	0.1427	U_{1j}
ST03Q01	71.0154	U_{2j}
Residual	5397.46	ε_{ij}

As shown by the reported probability, both null hypotheses have to be accepted, *i.e.* the school type is not associated with the HISEI slopes and the within-school gender difference is not associated with the percentage of girls in the school.

LIMITATIONS OF THE MULTILEVEL MODEL IN THE PISA CONTEXT

This section aims to alert potential PISA data users of the limitations or the dangers of such models in the PISA context.

Such models are designed to decompose the student variance into:

- The between-school variance;
- The within-school variance; and
- The within-class variance.

As PISA draws, per participating school, a random sample of an age population across grades and across classes, it allows the decomposition of the variance into two levels: a between-school variance and a within-school variance. Further, the overall variance is expected to be larger with an age sample than with a grade sample, unless the age population is attending a single grade, as in Iceland or Japan.

To allow meaningful international comparisons, these types of indicators require a common definition for a school and for a class. While there are no major issues on what a student is, there are from one country to another important differences between what a school is and what a class is.

International surveys in education are primarily interested in the student sample and therefore one might consider the school sample as a necessary step to draw an efficient sample of students that minimizes the cost of testing. In this context, the definition of what a school is or what a class is, does not present any major issues. However, the increasing importance and popularity of multilevel analyses calls for more attention on these definition issues.

PISA 2000 and PISA 2003 do not give a detailed definition of a school. The emphasis in the sampling procedures was on developing a list of units that would guarantee full coverage of the enrolled 15-year-old population and that would additionally give acceptable response rates. Once a school was

selected, it also had to be practical to sample 35 students or so from that school to assess them. Thus, the school frame was constructed with issues of student coverage and practical implementation of PISA administration in mind, rather than analytic considerations. Therefore, in the PISA databases, it is possible that the school identification represents different educational institutions that may not be comparable without any restriction. For instance, in some PISA countries, schools are defined as administrative units that may consist of several buildings not necessarily located close together. Other countries used the building as the school sampling unit and finally, a few countries defined a school as a track within a particular building. It is likely that the larger these aggregates are, the smaller the differences between these aggregates will be and the larger the differences within these aggregates will be. In this context, one would expect to observe high intra-class correlations in these countries and a non-significant within-school regression coefficient for the student socio-economic background (Kirsch *et al.*, 2002).

Besides this problem of an international definition of a school, data users have to be aware of the following issues:

- The choice of a school definition in a particular country may be dictated by the availability of the data. Indeed, the national centres have to include a measure of size of the 15-year-old population in the school sample frame (see Chapter 2). This information may be available at the administrative unit level, but not at the building level. In federal countries that count several educational systems, the available data might differ from one system to the other, so that the concept of a school might differ even within a particular country.
- For practical or operational reasons, the concept of schools might differ between two PISA data collections. For instance, some countries used the administrative units in the PISA 2000 school sample frame and the building units in the PISA 2003 school sample frame. Such changes were implemented to increase the school participation rate. These conceptual changes will influence the results of any variance decomposition and might also affect the outcomes of multilevel models. Moving from an administrative definition to a building definition will increase the intra-class correlation and should decrease the slope of the within-school regression coefficient. If such changes occur in a country, it is strongly advised not to compute any trends on variance decomposition or multilevel regressions.

As this example shows, multilevel analyses and variance decomposition analyses need to be interpreted in the light of:

- The structure of the educational systems; and
- The school definition used in the school sample frame.

Under the limitations provided in this section, multilevel regression analyses are certainly suitable and appropriate to describe how students are assigned to schools and what the major criteria are for such assignment. However, 10 or even 20 student and school variables will never be able to model the complexity of an educational system. Further, PISA is measuring a cumulative process of about ten years of schooling. What we are doing today can certainly not explain what we are today. Consequently, the pedagogical practices and the school environment in which 15-year-olds are currently learning is unable to fully explain how these students perform today. In this context, policy recommendations should be made and interpreted with caution.

CONCLUSIONS

This chapter firstly describes the concept of multilevel analyses and how to perform such models with SAS®. It starts with the simplest model, denoted the empty model, and then progressively adds complexity by adding variables. Finally, in the PISA context, important methodological issues that limit the international comparability of the results have been discussed

Notes

1. For consistency with the literature on multilevel regression, subscripts i and j have been inverted in comparison with Chapter 2.
2. Multiplying the full student weight W_FSTUWT with the variable CNTFAC2 produces the same weights (COMPUTE std_wgt = w_fstuwt*cntfac2) as the syntax in Box 13.2. But the resulting standardised weights should only be used for multi-level models based on variables without any missing values. When estimating multi-level models including variables with missing values different standardised weight should be computed after deleting all cases with missing values.
3. See also Table 13.4 in Chapter 4.
4. A correlation matrix computed with the pairwise deletion option can however be used as input for a linear regression analysis.
5. This shrinkage factor has to be associated to the expected school mean square in an ANOVA model. Indeed,

$$E(MS_{school}) = n_j\sigma^2_{\text{between-}school} + \sigma^2_{within-school}$$

Other Statistical Issues

INTRODUCTION

The PISA 2000 and the PISA 2003 initial reports included descriptions of the relationship between questionnaire indices and student performance by dividing the questionnaire indices into quarters and then reporting the mean achievement per quarter. The PISA reports also include the statistical concepts of relative risk and attributable risk. This chapter is devoted to these two specific issues.

ANALYSES BY QUARTERS

As described in Chapter 4, the indices derived from the questionnaire data were generated with the Rasch model and students' estimates were reported with the WLEs. As previously mentioned, a WLE individual's estimate is a discontinuous variable.

Table 14.1 presents the distribution of the questionnaire index *interest in and enjoyment of mathematics* from the German PISA 2003 data set. This table shows the discontinuous character of the variable.

To divide a questionnaire index into quarters, the 25th, 50th, and 75th percentiles have to be computed. These percentiles are respectively -0.6369, 0.029, and 0.973 for the *interest in and enjoyment of mathematics* index for Germany.

There are two possible recoding procedures: lower versus equal or greater and equal or lower versus greater.

The SAS® syntax is presented in Box 14.1.

Box 14.1 ■ **Two SAS® syntax procedures for the recoding into quarters**

```
libname PISA2003  "c:\pisa2003\data\";
options nofmterr notes;
run;

data temp;
     set pisa2003.stud;
     if (cnt="DEU");
     keep cnt schoolid stidstd w_fstuwt w_fstr1-w_fstr80 intmat;
run;

proc univariate data=temp vardef=wgt noprint;
     var intmat ;
     by cnt;
     weight w_fstuwt;
     output out=pct pctlpts=25 50 75 pctlpre=pe;
run;

     if (intmat < pe25) then q1=1;
     if (intmat >= pe25 and intmat < pe50) then q1=2;
     if (intmat >= pe50 and intmat < pe75) then q1=3;
     if (intmat >= pe75) then q1=4;
     if (intmat in (.,.M,.N,.I)) then q1=.;

     if (intmat <= pe25) then q2=1;
     if (intmat > pe25 and intmat <= pe50) then q2=2;
     if (intmat > pe50 and intmat <= pe75) then q2=3;
     if (intmat > pe75) then q2=4;
     if (intmat in (.,.M,.N,.I)) then q2=.;
run;
proc freq data=temp;
     table q1;
     weight w_fstuwt;
     by cnt;
run;
proc freq data=temp;
     table q2;
     weight w_fstuwt;
     by cnt;
run;
```

Depending on the procedure adopted, the percentages of students in the bottom quarter, second quarter, third quarter, and top quarter are respectively equal to 24.88, 21.39, 27.80 and 25.93 or 34.53, 21.60, 25.33 and 18.54.

Neither of these two procedures generate quarters that precisely include 25 per cent of the students. Since the percentages of students in each quarter can vary among countries, no international comparisons can be performed.

It was therefore necessary to distribute the students with a WLE equal to one of the 3 percentiles into the two respective adjacent quarters. For instance, 7.39 per cent of the students get a score

Table 14.1 ■ **Distribution of the questionnaire index interest in and enjoyment of mathematics for Germany**

WLE	Percentage	Cumulative percentage	WLE	Percentage	Cumulative percentage
-1.783	10.20	10.20	0.477	0.10	64.30
-1.733	0.02	10.23	0.643	0.10	64.40
-1.700	0.02	10.25	0.643	9.53	73.93
-1.469	0.02	10.27	0.869	0.03	73.96
-1.258	7.53	17.80	0.912	0.04	74.00
-1.179	0.02	17.82	0.925	0.05	74.05
-1.147	0.02	17.85	0.940	0.02	74.07
-1.077	0.03	17.88	0.973	7.39	81.46
-0.971	0.08	17.95	1.044	0.03	81.49
-0.929	6.77	24.73	1.146	0.03	81.52
-0.739	0.15	24.88	1.299	5.27	86.79
-0.637	9.66	34.53	1.338	0.02	86.81
-0.619	0.13	34.66	1.346	0.04	86.85
-0.370	0.02	34.68	1.464	0.02	86.87
-0.335	0.07	34.74	1.568	0.04	86.91
-0.319	11.37	46.11	1.587	4.58	91.49
-0.250	0.01	46.13	1.702	0.01	91.51
-0.160	0.10	46.22	1.761	0.02	91.53
-0.045	0.05	46.27	1.792	0.04	91.57
0.029	9.86	56.13	1.817	0.05	91.62
0.057	0.04	56.17	1.827	0.03	91.64
0.068	0.08	56.25	1.891	4.72	96.37
0.132	0.07	56.32	2.091	0.04	96.41
0.229	0.06	56.39	2.119	0.02	96.43
0.300	0.02	56.41	2.161	0.07	96.50
0.345	7.75	64.15	2.335	0.04	96.54
0.448	0.02	64.17	2.373	3.46	100.00
0.462	0.02	64.20			

equal to percentile 75. As 74.07 per cent of the students get a lower score, it is necessary to sample 0.93 per cent of the students with a score equal to percentile 75 and allocate them to the third quarter. The remaining 6.46 per cent will be allocated to the fourth quarter.

This random subsampling process is implemented by adding a small random variable to the questionnaire index. That random noise will generate more categories and therefore the three new percentiles will be able to divide the index variable into quarters that exactly include 25 per cent of the students. Box 14.2 presents the SAS® syntax for the addition of a random variable, as well as the computation of the percentiles and the recoding into quarters.

Box 14.2 ■ **SAS® syntax for the questionnaire indices recoding into quarters**

```
data temp;
     set temp;
     newindex=intmat+(0.01*normal(-12345));
run;
proc univariate data=temp vardef=wgt noprint;
     var newindex ;
     by cnt;
     weight w_fstuwt;
     output out=pct1 pctlpts=25 50 75 pctlpre=per;
run;
data temp;
     merge pct1 temp;
     by cnt;
     if (newindex < per25) then quart=1;
     if (newindex >= per25 and newindex < per50) then quart=2;
     if (newindex >= per50 and newindex < per75) then quart=3;
     if (newindex >= per75) then quart=4;
     if (newindex in (.,.M,.N,.I)) then quart=.;
run;
proc freq data=temp;
     table quart;
     weight w_fstuwt;
     by cnt;
run;
```

The outcomes of the PROC FREQ procedure will demonstrate that 25 per cent are allocated to each quarter.

This random allocation of some parts of the population to one of the four quarters adds an error component to the standard error. Indeed, in the example, the composition of the 0.93 per cent of the students allocated to the third quarter and the composition of the remaining 6.46 per cent allocated to the fourth quarter might differ between two runs of the procedure.

To account for this new error component, the statistical approach adopted for the analyses of plausible values can be implemented. It will therefore consist of:

- Computing for each student a set of five plausible quarters;
- Per plausible quarter, computing the required statistic and its respective sampling variance by using the final and 80 replicate weights;
- Averaging the five estimates and their respective sampling variances;
- Computing the imputation variance; and
- Combining the sampling variance and the imputation variance to obtain the final error variance.

If the dependent variable is a set of plausible values, the procedure described in Chapter 6 will be used, except that each plausible value will be analyzed with a different plausible quarter. Box 14.3 presents the SAS® syntax for the computation of the average mathematics performance per quarter of any questionnaire derived index.

Box 14.3 ■ **SAS® syntax for the computation of the average mathematics performance per quarter of a questionnaire derived index**

```
%MACRO quarter(independ);
data temp;
     set pisa2003.stud;
     mpv1=pv1math;
     mpv2=pv2math;
     mpv3=pv3math;
     mpv4=pv4math;
     mpv5=pv5math;
     w_fstr0=w_fstuwt;
     if (&independ in (.,.M,.N,.I)) then delete;
     new1=&independ+0.01*normal(-01);
     new2=&independ+0.01*normal(-23);
     new3=&independ+0.01*normal(-45);
     new4=&independ+0.01*normal(-67);
     new5=&independ+0.01*normal(-89);
     keep  country schoolid stidstd cnt
                mpv1-mpv5
                w_fstr0-w_fstr80
                &independ new1-new5;
run;

proc sort data=temp;
by cnt;
run;

proc summary data=temp;
     class cnt;
     var new1-new5;
     weight w_fstr0;
     output out=cutpoint p25=p25n1-p25n5
            p50=p50n1-p50n5 p75=p75n1-p75n5;
run;

data cutpoint;
     set cutpoint;
     if (_TYPE_ = 1);
run;

data temp;
     merge temp cutpoint;
     by cnt;
     array new(5)
            new1-new5;
     array p25(5)
            p25n1-p25n5;
     array p50(5)
            p50n1-p50n5;
     array p75(5)
            p75n1-p75n5;
     array cat(5)
            cat1-cat5;
     do i=1 to 5;
            if (new(i) <= p25(i)) then cat(i)=1;
            if (new(i) >  p25(i) and new(i) <= p50(i)) then cat(i)=2;
            if (new(i) >  p50(i) and new(i) <= p75(i)) then cat(i)=3;
            if (new(i) >  p75(i)) then cat(i)=4;
            if (new(i) eq .) then delete;
     end;
     drop _TYPE_ _FREQ_ p25n1-p25n5 p50n1-p50n5 p75n1-p75n5;
run;
```

...

```
%include "c:\pisa2003\prg\macro_procmeans_nopv.sas";

%do ij=1 %to 5;

%BRR_PROCMEAN(INFILE=temp,
                     REPLI_ROOT=w_fstr,
                     BYVAR=cnt cat&ij,
                     VAR=mpv&ij,
                     STAT=mean,
                     OUTFILE=ex&ij);
run;

data ex&ij;
     set ex&ij;
     stat&ij=stat;
     sestat&ij=sestat;
     cat=cat&ij;
     keep cnt cat stat&ij sestat&ij;
run;

%end;

data tp;
     merge ex1 ex2 ex3 ex4 ex5;
     by cnt cat;
     stat=(stat1+stat2+stat3+stat4+stat5)/5;
     varimp=(((stat1-stat)**2)+((stat2-stat)**2)+
((stat3-stat)**2)+((stat4-stat)**2)+((stat5-stat)**2))/4;
     varsamp=((sestat1**2)+(sestat2**2)+(sestat3**2)+(sestat4**2)+
(sestat5**2))/5;
     var=varsamp+(1.2*varimp);
     sestat=var**0.5;
run;

%mend quarter;

%quarter(intmat);
run;
```

The different steps of this procedure are:

1. From the initial questionnaire index, five new variables are created by adding a random number;
2. For each new variable, the 25th, 50th and 75th percentiles are computed and then imported in the temporary data file;
3. The five new variables are compared with their respective percentiles and the quarter allocations are saved in five categorical variables;
4. The PROCMEAN SAS® macro is run sequentially five times, each run with a particular plausible value and a particular plausible quarter; and
5. The results are combined to get the final estimate and the final standard error.

THE CONCEPTS OF RELATIVE RISK AND ATTRIBUTABLE RISK

Relative risk

The notion of relative risk is a measure of association between an antecedent factor and an outcome factor (Cornfield, 1951). The relative risk is simply the ratio of two risks, *i.e.* the risk of observing the outcome when the antecedent is present, and the risk of observing the outcome when the antecedent is not present. Table 14.2 presents the notation that will be used.

Table 14.2 ■ **Labels used in a two-way table**

		Outcome measure		
		Yes	No	Total
Antecedent measure	Yes	p_{11}	p_{12}	$p_{1.}$
	No	p_{21}	p_{22}	$p_{2.}$
	Total	$p_{.1}$	$p_{.2}$	$p_{..}$

$p_{..}$ is equal to $\frac{n_{..}}{n_{..}}$, with $n_{..}$ the total number of students and $p_{..}$ is therefore equal to 1, $p_{i.}$, $p_{.j}$ respectively represent the marginal probabilities for each row and for each column. The marginal probabilities are equal to the marginal frequencies divided by the total number of students. Finally, the p_{ij} values represent the probabilities for each cell and are equal to the number of observations in a particular cell divided by the total number of observations.

In this document, the conventions for the two-way table will be the following:

- The rows represent the antecedent factor with:
  - The first row for having the antecedent; and
  - The second row for not having the antecedent.
- The columns represent the outcome with:
  - The first column for having the outcome; and
  - The second column for not having the outcome.

In these conditions, the relative risk is equal to:

$$RR = \frac{(p_{11} / p_{1.})}{(p_{21} / p_{2.})}$$

Let us suppose that a psychologist wants to analyse the risk of a student repeating a grade if the parents recently divorced. The psychologist draws a simple random sample of students of grade 10. In this particular example, the outcome variable is present if the child is repeating grade 10 and the antecedent factor is considered present if the student's parents divorced in the past two years. The results he obtained are presented in Table 14.3 and in Table 14.4.

Table 14.3 ■ **Distribution of 100 students by marital status of the parents and grade repetition**

	Repeat the grade	Not repeat the grade	Total
Parents divorced	10	10	20
Parents not divorced	5	75	80
Total	15	85	100

Table 14.4 ■ **Probabilities by marital status of the parents and grade repetition**

	Repeat the grade	Not repeat the grade	Total
Parents divorced	0.10	0.10	0.20
Parents not divorced	0.05	0.75	0.80
Total	0.15	0.85	1.00

The relative risk is therefore equal to:

$$RR = \frac{(p_{11}/p_{1.})}{(p_{21}/p_{2.})} = \frac{(0.10/0.20)}{(0.05/0.80)} = \frac{0.5}{0.0625} = 8$$

This means that the probability of repeating grade 10 is eight times larger if the parents recently divorced than if they had not recently divorced.

Attributable risk

The attributable risk is equal to:

$$AR = \frac{(p_{11}p_{22}) - (p_{12}p_{21})}{(p_{.1}p_{2.})}$$

In the previous example, the attributable risk is equal to:

$$AR = \frac{(p_{11}p_{22}) - (p_{12}p_{21})}{(p_{.1}p_{2.})} = \frac{(0.10\text{x}0.75) - (0.10\text{x}0.05)}{(0.15\text{x}0.80)} = 0.583$$

The attributable risk is interpreted as follows. If the risk factor could be eliminated, then the rate of occurrence of the outcome characteristic in the population would be reduced by this coefficient. With the next version of the formula, the meaning of the attributable risk, *i.e.* a reduction of the outcome if the risk factor disappears, is more obvious.

$$AR = \frac{(p_{.1}) - (p_{21}/p_{2.})}{(p_{.1})}$$

The expression $p_{.1}$ represents the proportion of children in the whole sample with the outcome. The expression $(p_{21}/p_{2.})$ represents the proportion of children who are not at risk, but nevertheless suffer from the outcome. The difference of these two proportions provides the absolute reduction if the risk was eliminated. Dividing this difference by the first expression transforms this absolute reduction into a relative reduction or a reduction expressed as a percentage.

These two formulae give the same coefficient:

$$AR = \frac{(p_{.1}) - (p_{21} / p_{2.})}{(p_{.1})} = \frac{(0.15) - (0.05/0.80)}{(0.15)} = 0.583$$

To express this result as a percentage, the coefficient needs to be multiplied by 100.

INSTABILITY OF THE RELATIVE AND ATTRIBUTABLE RISKS

The relative risk and the attributable risk were developed for dichotomous variables. More and more often, these two coefficients are extended and are used with continuous variables. To apply the coefficients to continuous variables, a cutpoint for each variable needs to be set and the continuous variables need to be dichotomised.

It is important to recognise that when applied to dichotomised variables, the computed values of the relative risk and the attributable risk will depend on the value of the chosen cutpoint.

To demonstrate the influence of the cutpoint on the relative and attributable risks, two random variables were generated with a correlation of 0.30. These two variables were then transformed into dichotomous variables by using respectively the 10th, 15th, 20th, 25th and 30th percentiles as cutpoints. Table 14.5 presents the relative risk and the attributable risk for a range of choices for the cutpoints.

Table 14.5 ■ **Relative risk and attributable risk for different cutpoints**

Percentile	Relative risk	Attributable risk
10	2.64	0.13
15	2.32	0.16
20	1.90	0.15
25	1.73	0.15
30	1.63	0.15

Table 14.5 shows that the relative risk and, to a lesser extent, the attributable risk coefficients are dependent on the setting of the cutpoints, and therefore the interpretation of the value needs to be made in the light of this observation.

Such a comparison of the relative and attributable risks was computed for the PISA data to identify the changes depending on the cutpoint location. The antecedent factor was the mother's educational level and the outcome variable was reading achievement. Low reading achievement (having the outcome) was successively defined within countries as being below the 10th, 15th, 20th, 25th 30th and 35th percentiles.

The relative risks for these different cutpoints are respectively on average (across OECD countries) equal to 2.20, 1.92, 1.75, 1.62, 1.53, and 1.46. The attributable risks are equal to 0.25, 0.21, 0.19, 0.17, 0.15, and 0.14, respectively.

Nevertheless, the correlations between the different relative risks and attributable risks are rather high, as shown in Table 14.6

Table 14.6 ■ **Correlation between relative risks and attributable risks at the 10th percentile with the 15th, 20th, 25th 30th and 35th percentiles**

	RR	AR
P15	0.96	0.98
P20	0.93	0.97
P25	0.92	0.96
P30	0.90	0.94
P35	0.87	0.92

In PISA, it was decided to use the 25th percentile as the cutpoint for continuous variables when calculating relative and attributable risks.

COMPUTATION OF THE RELATIVE RISK AND ATTRIBUTABLE RISK

Depending on the variables involved in the computation of the relative risk and attributable risk, the procedure might differ. Indeed, these two statistical concepts require as input two dichotomous variables, such as gender (ST03Q01).

However, most of the variables in the PISA data bases are not dichotomous; they are categorical or continuous variables.

The recoding of a categorical into a dichotomous variable does not raise special issues. From a theoretical point of view, the purpose of the comparison needs to be decided upon, and the recoding will follow. For instance, in PISA 2003, the education levels of the parents are reported by using the ISCED classification (OECD, 1999b). If the contrast is on the distinction between tertiary versus non tertiary education, then the categorical variable can be recoded into a dichotomous variable. Students whose parents do not have a tertiary qualification will be considered at risk.

Numerical variables also have to be recoded into dichotomous variables. As stated earlier, the OECD has decided to divide numerical variables based on the 25th percentile.

In the PISA 2000 and PISA 2003 databases, all numerical variables, except the performance scales, are discontinuous variables. To ensure that the 25th percentile will divide the variables into two categories that will include, respectively, 25 and 75 per cent, a random variable has to be added to the initial variable, as described in the section devoted to the analyses per quarter. Five relative risk and/or five attributable risk estimates are computed and then combined.

Finally, if plausible values are involved as outcome measures, then five estimates will also be computed and then combined. However, it is not necessary to add a random variable to the initial variable as it constitutes a continuous variable.

CONCLUSIONS

This chapter was devoted to some statistical issues related to the way the OECD reported the PISA 2000 and PISA 2003 results in the initial reports, in particular questionnaire indices by quarters and the relative and attributable risks.

SAS® Macros

INTRODUCTION

This chapter presents the SAS® syntax of the ten macros used in the previous chapters. They are also included in the CD provided with the manual and summarized in Table 15.1. The file names are in red and the macro names as well as their arguments are in black. These ten macros have four common arguments:

- INFILE =
- REPLI_ROOT=
- BYVAR =
- OUTFILE =

Further, all macros that deal with plausible values have an additional common argument, *i.e.* PV_ROOT. The other arguments are specific to a particular macro: these specific arguments were largely explained in the previous chapters.

STRUCTURE OF THE SAS® MACROS

All SAS® macros have the same structure.

- The first step consists of:
  - Saving the INFILE data file into a temporary data file denoted BRRDATA and dropping all variables that are not necessary for the analysis; and
  - Sorting that file by all variables specified in the BYVAR argument.
- The second step is the iterative part of the macro:
  - The SAS® procedure (PROC MEANS, PROC FREQ, PROC REG, PROC CORR) is repeated 81 times or 405 times, depending on the procedure;
  - At each run, the results are stored in a temporary file, with the number of the replicate and the number of the plausible values if needed are then added to that file; and
  - That file is merged with another temporary file that keeps the results of all runs.
- The third step consists of data file transformations to allow the computation of the final estimate and its respective standard error. This step is quite specific to each SAS® macro.
- The final step is devoted to the computation of the final statistic and its respective standard error:
  - The final estimates and 80 replicates are separated, *i.e.* BRR_TEMP1 is divided into BRR_TEMP2 (final estimates) and BRR_TEMP3 (replicate estimates). In the case of the plausible values, the five estimates are averaged and the measurement error is computed;
  - The two files are then merged to create BRR_TEMP4 and the squared differences between the final estimate and the 80 replicates are computed;
  - Through a PROC UNIVARIATE procedure, the sum of the squared differences is computed and divided by 20. These results are saved in BRR_TEMP5; and
  - BRR_TEMP3 (finale estimates and, in the case of the plausible values, the measurement variance) and BRR_TEMP5 (the sampling variance estimates) are combined. The final estimates and their respective standard errors are saved in the OUTFILE datafile.

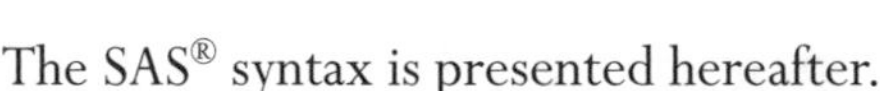

The SAS® syntax is presented hereafter.

Table 15.1 ■ **Synthesis of the ten SAS® macros**

Requested statistics	Without plausible values	With plausible values

Mean, STD, VAR, Quartiles, Median, Percentiles	**Macro_procmeans_nopv.sas**
	`BRR_PROCMEAN(`
	`INFILE =,`
	`REPLI_ROOT =,`
	`BYVAR = ,`
	`VAR =,`
	`STAT =,`
	`OUTFILE =);`
		Macro_procmeans.sas
		`BRR_PROCMEAN_PV(`
		`INFILE =,`
		`REPLI_ROOT =,`
		`BYVAR = ,`
		`PV_ROOT =,`
		`STAT =,`
		`OUTFILE =);`

Frequencies	**Macro_freq_nopv.sas**
	`BRR_FREQ(`
	`INFILE=,`
	`REPLI_ROOT=,`
	`BYVAR=,`
	`VAR=,`
	`OUTFILE=);`
		Macro_freq.sas
		`BRR_FREQ_PV(`
		`INFILE=,`
		`REPLI_ROOT=,`
		`BYVAR=,`
		`PV_ROOT=,`
		`OUTFILE=);`

Regression coefficients	**Macro_reg_nopv.sas**
	`BRR_REG(`
	`INFILE=,`
	`REPLI_ROOT=,`
	`VARDEP=,`
	`EXPLICA=,`
	`BYVAR=,`
	`OUTFILE=);`
		Macro_reg.sas
		`BRR_REG_PV(`
		`INFILE=,`
		`REPLI_ROOT=,`
		`EXPLICA=,`
		`BYVAR=,`
		`PV_ROOT=,`
		`OUTFILE=);`

Correlation coefficients	**Macro_corr_nopv.sas**
	`BRR_CORR(`
	`INFILE=,`
	`REPLI_ROOT=,`
	`BYVAR=,`
	`VAR1=,`
	`VAR2=,`
	`OUTFILE=);`
		Macro_corr.sas
		`BRR_CORR_PV(`
		`INFILE=,`
		`REPLI_ROOT=,`
		`BYVAR=,`
		`EXPLICA=,`
		`PV_ROOT=,`
		`OUTFILE=);`

Differences on mean, STD, VAR, Quartiles, Median, Percentiles	**Macro_procmeans_dif_nopv.sas**
	`BRR_PROCMEAN_DIF(`
	`INFILE =,`
	`REPLI_ROOT =,`
	`BYVAR =,`
	`VAR =,`
	`COMPARE =,`
	`CATEGORY =,`
	`STAT =,`
	`OUTFILE =);`
		Macro_procmeans_dif.sas
		`BRR_PROCMEAN_DIF_PV(`
		`INFILE =,`
		`REPLI_ROOT =,`
		`BYVAR =,`
		`PV_ROOT =,`
		`COMPARE =,`
		`CATEGORY =,`
		`STAT =,`
		`OUTFILE =);`

Box 15.1 ■ **SAS® syntax of BRR_PROCMEAN**

```
%MACRO BRR_PROCMEAN(INFILE =,
                    REPLI_ROOT =,
                    BYVAR = ,
                    VAR =,
                    STAT =,
                    OUTFILE =);

/*

MEANING OF THE MACRO ARGUMENTS

INFILE     =  INPUT DATA FILE.
REPLI_ROOT =  ROOT OF THE FINAL WEIGHT AND 80 REPLICATE weight VARIABLE NAMES.
              FINAL WEIGHT VARIABLE NAME MUST BE THE REPLICATION ROOT FOLLOWED BY 0.
BYVAR   =  BREAKDOWN VARIABLES
VAR        =  VARIABLE ON WHICH THE REQUESTED STATISTIC WILL BE COMPUTED
STAT    =  REQUESTED STATISTIC
              SUMWGT    =  SUM OF THE WEIGHTS
              MEAN      =  MEAN
              VAR       =  VARIANCE
              STD       =  STANDARD DEVIATION
              CV     =   COEFFICIENT OF VARIATION
              MEDIAN    =  MEDIAN
              Q1     =   FIRST QUARTILE
              Q3     =   THIRD QUARTILE
              QRANGE    =  RANGE BETWEEN Q1 AND Q3
              PX     =   PERCENTILE, WITH X BETWEEN 1 AND 99
OUTFILE    =  FILE WITH THE ESTIMATES AND THEIR STANDARD ERROR ESTIMATES

*/

OPTIONS NONOTES;

PROC DATASETS LIBRARY=WORK NOLIST;
     DELETE BRR_TEMP1;
RUN;
PROC SORT DATA=&INFILE OUT=BRRDATA (KEEP=&REPLI_ROOT.0-&REPLI_ROOT.80 &BYVAR
&VAR);
       BY &BYVAR;
RUN;
%DO I = 0 %TO 80;
     PROC MEANS DATA=BRRDATA VARDEF=WGT NOPRINT;
            VAR &VAR ;
            BY &BYVAR;
            WEIGHT &REPLI_ROOT&I;
            OUTPUT OUT=MEAN_TEMP &STAT=PV;
     RUN;
     DATA MEAN_TEMP;
            SET MEAN_TEMP;
            L=&I;
     RUN;
     PROC APPEND BASE = BRR_TEMP1 DATA=MEAN_TEMP;
     RUN;
%END;
```

Box 15.1 (continued) ■ **SAS® syntax of BRR_PROCMEAN**

```
DATA BRR_TEMP2(KEEP=&BYVAR PV)BRR_TEMP3(KEEP=&BYVAR STAT);
     SET BRR_TEMP1;
     IF L > 0 THEN OUTPUT BRR_TEMP2;
     ELSE DO;
            STAT =PV;
            OUTPUT BRR_TEMP3;
     END;
RUN;

PROC SORT DATA=BRR_TEMP2;
     BY &BYVAR;
RUN;

PROC SORT DATA=BRR_TEMP3;
     BY &BYVAR;
RUN;

DATA BRR_TEMP4;
     MERGE BRR_TEMP2 BRR_TEMP3;
     BY &BYVAR;
     VARI=((PV-STAT)**2)*(1/20);
RUN;

PROC UNIVARIATE DATA=BRR_TEMP4 NOPRINT;
     VAR VARI;
     BY &BYVAR;
     OUTPUT OUT=BRR_TEMP5 SUM=SS;
RUN;

OPTIONS NOTES;
     DATA &OUTFILE;
     MERGE BRR_TEMP3 BRR_TEMP5;
     BY &BYVAR;
     SESTAT=(SS)**0.5;
     KEEP &BYVAR STAT SESTAT;
RUN;

PROC DATASETS LIBRARY=WORK NOLIST;
     DELETE BRR_TEMP1 BRR_TEMP2 BRR_TEMP3 BRR_TEMP4 BRR_TEMP5 MEAN_TEMP BRRDATA;
RUN;

%MEND BRR_PROCMEAN;
```

Box 15.2 ■ **SAS® syntax of BRR_PROCMEAN_PV**

```
%MACRO BRR_PROCMEAN_PV(INFILE =,
                       REPLI_ROOT =,
                       BYVAR = ,
                       PV_ROOT =,
                       STAT =,
                       OUTFILE =);
/*
MEANING OF THE MACRO ARGUMENTS

INFILE     =    INPUT DATA FILE.
REPLI_ROOT =    ROOT OF THE FINAL WEIGHT AND 80 REPLICATES VARIABLE
NAMES.
                FINAL WEIGHT VARIABLE NAME MUST BE THE REPLICATION ROOT
FOLLOWED BY 0.
BYVAR           =    BREAKDOWN VARIABLES
PV_ROOT    =    ROOT OF THE 5 PLAUSIBLE VALUES VARIABLES NAMES
STAT       =    REQUESTED STATISTIQUE
                     SUMWGT=     SUM OF THE WEIGHT
                     MEAN        =    MEAN
                     VAR         =    VARIANCE
                     STD         =    STANDARD DEVIATION
                     CV          =    COEFFICIENT OF VARIATION
                     MEDIAN=     MEDIAN
                     Q1          =    FIRST QUARTILE
                     Q3          =    THIRD QUARTILE
                     QRANGE=     RANGE BETWEEN Q1 AND Q3
                     PX          =    PERCENTILE, WITH X BETWEEN 1
AND 99

OUTFILE    =    FILE WITH THE STATISTIC ESTIMATES AND THEIR STANDARD
ERROR ESTIMATE
*/

OPTIONS NONOTES;

PROC DATASETS LIBRARY=WORK NOLIST;
     DELETE BRR_TEMP1;
RUN;

PROC SORT DATA=&INFILE
     OUT=BRRDATA(KEEP=&REPLI_ROOT.0-&REPLI_ROOT.80 &BYVAR &PV_ROOT.1-&PV_
ROOT.5);
     BY &BYVAR;
RUN;

%DO I = 0 %TO 80;
     PROC MEANS DATA=BRRDATA VARDEF=WGT NOPRINT;
            VAR &PV_ROOT.1 - &PV_ROOT.5 ;
            BY &BYVAR;
            WEIGHT &REPLI_ROOT&I;
            OUTPUT OUT=MEAN_TEMP &STAT=PV1 - PV5;
     RUN;

     DATA MEAN_TEMP;
            SET MEAN_TEMP;
            L=&I;
     RUN;

     PROC APPEND BASE = BRR_TEMP1 DATA=MEAN_TEMP;
     RUN;

%END;
```

Box 15.2 (continued) ■ **SAS® syntax of BRR_PROCMEAN_PV**

```
DATA BRR_TEMP2(DROP=STAT FIN1-FIN5 MESVAR) BRR_TEMP3(KEEP=&BYVAR STAT
FIN1-FIN5 MESVAR);
     SET BRR_TEMP1;
     IF L > 0 THEN OUTPUT BRR_TEMP2;
     ELSE DO;
            STAT =(PV1+PV2+PV3+PV4+PV5)/5;
            FIN1=PV1;
            FIN2=PV2;
            FIN3=PV3;
            FIN4=PV4;
            FIN5=PV5;
            MESVAR=(((STAT-FIN1)**2)+((STAT-FIN2)**2)+((STAT-
FIN3)**2)+((STAT-FIN4)**2)+((STAT-FIN5)**2))/4;
            OUTPUT BRR_TEMP3;
     END;
RUN;

PROC SORT DATA=BRR_TEMP2;
     BY &BYVAR;
RUN;

PROC SORT DATA=BRR_TEMP3;
     BY &BYVAR;
RUN;

DATA BRR_TEMP4;
     MERGE BRR_TEMP2 BRR_TEMP3;
     BY &BYVAR;
     ARRAY A (5)
            PV1-PV5;
     ARRAY B (5)
            FIN1-FIN5;
     ARRAY C(5)
            VAR1-VAR5;
     DO I=1 TO 5;
     C(I)=(1/20)*((A(I)-B(I))**2);
     END;
RUN;

PROC UNIVARIATE DATA=BRR_TEMP4 NOPRINT;
     VAR VAR1 VAR2 VAR3 VAR4 VAR5;
     BY &BYVAR;
     OUTPUT OUT=BRR_TEMP5 SUM=SS1 SS2 SS3 SS4 SS5;
RUN;

OPTIONS NOTES;

DATA &OUTFILE;
     MERGE BRR_TEMP3 BRR_TEMP5;
     BY &BYVAR;
     SAMP=(SS1+SS2+SS3+SS4+SS5)/5;
     FINVAR=(SAMP+(1.2*MESVAR));
     SESTAT=(FINVAR)**0.5;
     KEEP &BYVAR STAT SESTAT;
RUN;

PROC DATASETS LIBRARY=WORK NOLIST;
     DELETE BRR_TEMP1 BRR_TEMP2 BRR_TEMP3 BRR_TEMP4 BRR_TEMP5 MEAN_TEMP
BRRDATA;
RUN;

%MEND BRR_PROCMEAN_PV;
```

Box 15.3 ■ **SAS® syntax of BRR_FREQ**

```
%MACRO BRR_FREQ( INFILE=,
                 REPLI_ROOT=,
                 BYVAR=,
                 VAR=,
                 OUTFILE=);

/*

MEANING OF THE MACRO ARGUMENTS

INFILE          =       INPUT DATA FILE.
REPLI_ROOT =      ROOT OF THE FINAL WEIGHT AND 80 REPLICATES VARIABLE
NAMES.
                        FINAL WEIGHT VARIABLE NAME MUST BE THE
REPLICATION ROOT FOLLOWED BY 0.
BYVAR           =       BREAKDOWN VARIABLES
VAR             =       VARIABLES ON WHICH PERCENTAGES WILL BE COMPUTED
OUTFILE         =       FILE WITH THE STATISTIC ESTIMATES AND THEIR
STANDARD ERROR ESTIMATE

*/

OPTIONS NONOTES;

PROC DATASETS LIBRARY=WORK NOLIST;
     DELETE BRR_TEMP0;
RUN;

PROC SORT DATA=&INFILE
     OUT=BRRDATA(KEEP=&REPLI_ROOT.0-&REPLI_ROOT.80 &BYVAR &VAR);
     BY &BYVAR &VAR;
RUN;

%DO I = 0 %TO 80;
     PROC FREQ DATA=BRRDATA NOPRINT;
            TABLE &VAR /OUT=FREQ_TEMP ;
            BY &BYVAR;
            WEIGHT &REPLI_ROOT&I;
     RUN;

     DATA FREQ_TEMP;
            SET FREQ_TEMP;
            L=&I;
            KEEP &BYVAR L &VAR PERCENT;
     RUN;

     PROC APPEND BASE = BRR_TEMP0 DATA=FREQ_TEMP;
     RUN;
%END;

PROC SORT DATA=BRR_TEMP0 OUT=BRR_TEMP1 (RENAME=(PERCENT=PV));
     BY &BYVAR L &VAR;
RUN;

DATA BRR_TEMP2(KEEP=&BYVAR &VAR PV)BRR_TEMP3(KEEP=&BYVAR &VAR STAT);
     SET BRR_TEMP1;
     IF L > 0 THEN OUTPUT BRR_TEMP2;
     ELSE DO;
            STAT =PV;
            OUTPUT BRR_TEMP3;
     END;
RUN;
```

Box 15.3 (continued) ■ **SAS® syntax of BRR_FREQ**

```
PROC SORT DATA=BRR_TEMP2;
     BY &BYVAR &VAR;
RUN;

PROC SORT DATA=BRR_TEMP3;
     BY &BYVAR &VAR;
RUN;

DATA BRR_TEMP4;
     MERGE BRR_TEMP2 BRR_TEMP3;
     BY &BYVAR &VAR;
     VARI=((PV-STAT)**2)*(1/20);
RUN;

PROC UNIVARIATE DATA=BRR_TEMP4 NOPRINT;
     VAR VARI;
     BY &BYVAR &VAR;
     OUTPUT OUT=BRR_TEMP5 SUM=SS;
RUN;

OPTIONS NOTES;

DATA &OUTFILE;
     MERGE BRR_TEMP3 BRR_TEMP5;
     BY &BYVAR &VAR;
     SESTAT=(SS)**0.5;
     KEEP &BYVAR &VAR STAT SESTAT;
RUN;

PROC DATASETS LIBRARY=WORK NOLIST;
     DELETE BRR_TEMP0 BRR_TEMP1 BRR_TEMP2 BRR_TEMP3 BRR_TEMP4 BRR_TEMP5
FREQ_TEMP BRRDATA;
RUN;

%MEND BRR_FREQ;
```

Box 15.4 ■ **SAS® syntax of BRR_FREQ_PV**

```
%MACRO BRR_FREQ_PV(      INFILE=,
                         REPLI_ROOT=,
                         BYVAR=,
                         PV_ROOT=,
                         OUTFILE=);

/*

MEANING OF THE MACRO ARGUMENTS

INFILE              =      INPUT DATA FILE.
REPLI_ROOT          =      ROOT OF THE FINAL WEIGHT AND 80 REPLICATES
VARIABLE NAMES.
                           FINAL WEIGHT VARIABLE NAME MUST BE THE
REPLICATION ROOT FOLLOWED BY 0.
BYVAR                             =      BREAKDOWN VARIABLES
PV_ROOT             =      ROOT OF THE 5 PROFICIENCY LEVEL VARIABLES NAMES
OUTFILE             =      FILE WITH THE STATISTIC ESTIMATES AND THEIR
STANDARD ERROR ESTIMATE

*/

OPTIONS NONOTES;

PROC DATASETS LIBRARY=WORK NOLIST;
     DELETE BRR_TEMP0;
RUN;

%DO I = 1 %TO 5;

     PROC SORT DATA=&INFILE
          OUT=BRRDATA(KEEP=&REPLI_ROOT.0-&REPLI_ROOT.80 &BYVAR &PV_
ROOT&I);
          BY &BYVAR &PV_ROOT&I;
     RUN;

     %DO J = 0 %TO 80;

          PROC FREQ DATA=BRRDATA NOPRINT;
               TABLE &PV_ROOT&I /OUT=FREQ_TEMP ;
               BY &BYVAR;
               WEIGHT &REPLI_ROOT&J;
          RUN;

          DATA FREQ_TEMP;
               SET FREQ_TEMP;
               K=&I;
               L=&J;
               &PV_ROOT=&PV_ROOT&I;
               KEEP &BYVAR K L PERCENT &PV_ROOT;
          RUN;

          PROC APPEND BASE = BRR_TEMP0 DATA=FREQ_TEMP;
          RUN;

     %END;

%END;
```

Box 15.4 (continued – 1) ■ **SAS® syntax of BRR_FREQ_PV**

```
PROC SORT DATA=BRR_TEMP0;
     BY &BYVAR L &PV_ROOT;
RUN;

PROC TRANSPOSE DATA=BRR_TEMP0 OUT=BRR_TEMP1 PREFIX=PV;
     BY &BYVAR L &PV_ROOT;
     VAR PERCENT;
RUN;

DATA BRR_TEMP1;
     SET BRR_TEMP1;
     DROP _NAME_ _LABEL_;
RUN;

DATA BRR_TEMP2(DROP=STAT FIN1-FIN5 MESVAR)BRR_TEMP3(KEEP=&BYVAR &PV_ROOT
STAT FIN1-FIN5 MESVAR);
     SET BRR_TEMP1;
     IF L > 0 THEN OUTPUT BRR_TEMP2;
     ELSE DO;
            STAT =(PV1+PV2+PV3+PV4+PV5)/5;
            FIN1=PV1;
            FIN2=PV2;
            FIN3=PV3;
            FIN4=PV4;
            FIN5=PV5;
            MESVAR=(((STAT-FIN1)**2)+((STAT-FIN2)**2)+((STAT-
FIN3)**2)+((STAT-FIN4)**2)+((STAT-FIN5)**2))/4;
            OUTPUT BRR_TEMP3;
     END;
RUN;

PROC SORT DATA=BRR_TEMP2;
     BY &BYVAR &PV_ROOT;
RUN;

PROC SORT DATA=BRR_TEMP3;
     BY &BYVAR &PV_ROOT;
RUN;
```

Box 15.4 (continued – 2) ■ **SAS® syntax of BRR_FREQ_PV**

```
DATA BRR_TEMP4;
     MERGE BRR_TEMP2 BRR_TEMP3;
     BY &BYVAR &PV_ROOT;
     ARRAY A (5)
            PV1-PV5;
     ARRAY B (5)
            FIN1-FIN5;
     ARRAY C (5)
            VAR1-VAR5;
     DO I=1 TO 5;
            C(I)=(1/20)*((A(I)-B(I))**2);
     END;
RUN;

PROC UNIVARIATE DATA=BRR_TEMP4 NOPRINT;
     VAR VAR1 VAR2 VAR3 VAR4 VAR5;
     BY &BYVAR &PV_ROOT;
     OUTPUT OUT=BRR_TEMP5 SUM=SS1 SS2 SS3 SS4 SS5;
RUN;

OPTIONS NOTES;

DATA &OUTFILE;
     MERGE BRR_TEMP3 BRR_TEMP5;
     BY &BYVAR &PV_ROOT;
     SAMP=(SS1+SS2+SS3+SS4+SS5)/5;
     FINVAR=(SAMP+(1.2*MESVAR));
     SESTAT=(FINVAR)**0.5;
     KEEP &BYVAR &PV_ROOT STAT SESTAT;
RUN;

PROC DATASETS LIBRARY=WORK NOLIST;
     DELETE BRR_TEMP0 BRR_TEMP1 BRR_TEMP2 BRR_TEMP3 BRR_TEMP4 BRR_TEMP5
MEAN_TEMP BRRDATA;
RUN;

%MEND BRR_FREQ_PV;
```

Box 15.5 ■ **SAS® syntax of BRR_REG**

```
%MACRO BRR_REG(   INFILE=,
                  REPLI_ROOT=,
                  VARDEP=,
                  EXPLICA=,
                  BYVAR=,
                  OUTFILE=);

/*

MEANING OF THE MACRO ARGUMENTS

INFILE      =     INPUT DATA FILE.
REPLI_ROOT  =     ROOT OF THE FINAL WEIGHT AND 80 REPLICATES VARIABLE
NAMES.
                  FINAL WEIGHT VARIABLE NAME MUST BE THE REPLICATION ROOT
FOLLOWED BY 0.
VARDEP      =     DEPENDENT VARIABLE
EXPLICA     =     LIST OF INDEPENDENT VARIABLES
BYVAR             =     BREAKDOWN VARIABLES
OUTFILE     =     FILE WITH THE STATISTIC ESTIMATES AND THEIR STANDARD
ERROR ESTIMATE.

*/

OPTIONS NONOTES;

PROC DATASETS LIBRARY=WORK NOLIST;
     DELETE BRR_TEMP1;
RUN;

PROC SORT DATA=&INFILE OUT=BRRDATA (KEEP=&REPLI_ROOT.0-&REPLI_ROOT.80
&BYVAR &VARDEP &EXPLICA);
     BY &BYVAR;
RUN;

%DO I = 0 %TO 80;

     PROC REG DATA=BRRDATA OUTEST=COEF_TEMP NOPRINT;
            MODEL &VARDEP=&EXPLICA;
            WEIGHT &REPLI_ROOT&I;
            BY &BYVAR;
     RUN;

     DATA COEF_TEMP;
            SET COEF_TEMP;
            L=&I;
     RUN;

     PROC APPEND BASE = BRR_TEMP1 DATA=COEF_TEMP;
     RUN;
%END;

PROC SORT DATA=BRR_TEMP1;
     BY &BYVAR L;
RUN;

PROC TRANSPOSE DATA=BRR_TEMP1 OUT=BRR_TEMP;
     BY &BYVAR L;
     VAR INTERCEPT &EXPLICA;
RUN;

DATA BRR_TEMP1 ;
     SET BRR_TEMP (RENAME=(_NAME_=CLASS COL1=COEF));
RUN;
```

Box 15.5 (continued) ■ **SAS® syntax of BRR_REG**

```
%LET I=1;
%DO %WHILE(%LENGTH(%SCAN(&EXPLICA,&I)));
     %LET I=%EVAL(&I+1);
%END;
%LET NB=%EVAL(&I-1);

%DO J=0 %to &NB;
     %IF &J=0 %THEN %DO;
            %LET INDEP=Intercept;
     %END;
     %IF &J>0 %THEN %DO;
            %LET INDEP=%SCAN(&EXPLICA,&J);
     %END;

     DATA BRR_TEMP1;
            SET BRR_TEMP1;
            IF (UPCASE(CLASS)=UPCASE("&INDEP")) THEN ORDRE=&J;
     RUN;
%END;

DATA BRR_TEMP2(KEEP=&BYVAR CLASS COEF) BRR_TEMP3(KEEP=&BYVAR CLASS ORDRE
STAT);
     SET BRR_TEMP1;
     IF L > 0 THEN OUTPUT BRR_TEMP2;
     ELSE DO;
            STAT =COEF;
            OUTPUT BRR_TEMP3;
     END;
RUN;

PROC SORT DATA=BRR_TEMP2;
     BY &BYVAR CLASS;
RUN;

PROC SORT DATA=BRR_TEMP3;
     BY &BYVAR CLASS;
RUN;

DATA BRR_TEMP4;
     MERGE BRR_TEMP2 BRR_TEMP3;
     BY &BYVAR CLASS;
     VARI=((COEF-STAT)**2)*(1/20);
RUN;

PROC UNIVARIATE DATA=BRR_TEMP4 NOPRINT;
     VAR VARI;
     BY &BYVAR CLASS;
     OUTPUT OUT=BRR_TEMP5 SUM=SS;
RUN;

DATA BRR_TEMP6;
     MERGE BRR_TEMP3 BRR_TEMP5;
     BY &BYVAR CLASS;
     SESTAT=(SS)**0.5;
     KEEP &BYVAR CLASS ORDRE STAT SESTAT;
RUN;

OPTIONS NOTES;

PROC SORT DATA=BRR_TEMP6 OUT=&OUTFILE (DROP=ORDRE);
     BY &BYVAR ORDRE;
RUN;
PROC DATASETS LIBRARY=WORK NOLIST;
     DELETE BRR_TEMP BRR_TEMP1 BRR_TEMP2 BRR_TEMP3 BRR_TEMP4 BRR_TEMP5
BRR_TEMP6 COEF_TEMP BRRDATA;
RUN;

%MEND BRR_REG;
```

Box 15.6 ■ **SAS® syntax of BRR_REG_PV**

```
%MACRO BRR_REG_PV(INFILE=,
                  REPLI_ROOT=,
                  EXPLICA=,
                  BYVAR=,
                  PV_ROOT=,
                  OUTFILE=);

/*

MEANING OF THE MACRO ARGUMENTS

INFILE      =      INPUT DATA FILE.
REPLI_ROOT =       ROOT OF THE FINAL WEIGHT AND 80 REPLICATES VARIABLE
NAMES.
                   FINAL WEIGHT VARIABLE NAME MUST BE THE REPLICATION ROOT
FOLLOWED BY 0.
EXPLICA     =      LIST OF INDEPENDENT VARIABLES
BYVAR              =      BREAKDOWN VARIABLES
PV_ROOT     =      ROOT OF THE 5 PLAUSIBLE VALUES VARIABLES NAMES
OUTFILE     =      FILE WITH THE STATISTIC ESTIMATES AND THEIR STANDARD
ERROR ESTIMATE
*/
OPTIONS NONOTES;

PROC DATASETS LIBRARY=WORK NOLIST;
     DELETE BRR_TEMP1;
RUN;

PROC SORT DATA=&INFILE OUT=BRRDATA (KEEP=&REPLI_ROOT.0-&REPLI_ROOT.80
&BYVAR &PV_ROOT.1-&PV_ROOT.5 &EXPLICA);
     BY &BYVAR;
RUN;

%DO I = 0 %TO 80;
     PROC REG DATA=BRRDATA OUTEST=COEF_TEMP NOPRINT;
            MODEL &PV_ROOT.1=&EXPLICA;
            MODEL &PV_ROOT.2=&EXPLICA;
            MODEL &PV_ROOT.3=&EXPLICA;
            MODEL &PV_ROOT.4=&EXPLICA;
            MODEL &PV_ROOT.5=&EXPLICA;
            WEIGHT &REPLI_ROOT&I;
            BY &BYVAR;
     RUN;

     DATA COEF_TEMP;
            SET COEF_TEMP;
            L=&I;
     RUN;

     PROC APPEND BASE = BRR_TEMP1 DATA=COEF_TEMP;
     RUN;

%END;

PROC SORT DATA=BRR_TEMP1;
     BY &BYVAR L;
RUN;

PROC TRANSPOSE DATA=BRR_TEMP1 OUT=BRR_TEMP PREFIX=PV;
     BY &BYVAR L;
     VAR INTERCEPT &EXPLICA;
RUN;

DATA BRR_TEMP1 ;
     SET BRR_TEMP (RENAME=(_NAME_=CLASS));
     DROP _LABEL_;
RUN;
```

Box 15.6 (continued – 1) ■ **SAS® syntax of BRR_REG_PV**

```
%LET I=1;
%DO %WHILE(%LENGTH(%SCAN(&EXPLICA,&I)));
     %LET I=%EVAL(&I+1);
%END;
%let NB=%EVAL(&I-1);

%DO J=0 %to &NB;
     %IF &J=0 %THEN %DO;
        %LET INDEP=Intercept;
     %END;
     %IF &J>0 %THEN %DO;
           %LET INDEP=%SCAN(&EXPLICA,&J);
     %END;

     DATA BRR_TEMP1;
                 SET BRR_TEMP1;
                 IF (UPCASE(CLASS)=UPCASE("&INDEP")) THEN ORDRE=&J;
     RUN;
%END;

DATA BRR_TEMP2(KEEP=&BYVAR CLASS ORDRE PV1-PV5)  BRR_TEMP3(KEEP=&BYVAR
CLASS ORDRE FIN1-FIN5 STAT MESVAR);
     SET BRR_TEMP1;
     IF L > 0 THEN OUTPUT BRR_TEMP2;
     ELSE DO;
           STAT =(PV1+PV2+PV3+PV4+PV5)/5;
           FIN1=PV1;
           FIN2=PV2;
           FIN3=PV3;
           FIN4=PV4;
           FIN5=PV5;
           MESVAR=(((STAT-FIN1)**2)+((STAT-FIN2)**2)+((STAT-
FIN3)**2)+((STAT-FIN4)**2)+((STAT-FIN5)**2))/4;
           OUTPUT BRR_TEMP3;
     END;
RUN;

PROC SORT DATA=BRR_TEMP2;
     BY &BYVAR CLASS;
RUN;

PROC SORT DATA=BRR_TEMP3;
     BY &BYVAR CLASS;
RUN;

DATA BRR_TEMP4;
     MERGE BRR_TEMP2 BRR_TEMP3;
     BY &BYVAR CLASS;
     ARRAY A (5)
           PV1-PV5;
     ARRAY B (5)
           FIN1-FIN5;
     ARRAY C(5)
           VAR1-VAR5;
     DO I=1 TO 5;
           C(I)=(1/20)*((A(I)-B(I))**2);
     END;
RUN;

PROC UNIVARIATE DATA=BRR_TEMP4 NOPRINT;
     VAR VAR1 VAR2 VAR3 VAR4 VAR5;
     BY &BYVAR CLASS;
     OUTPUT OUT=BRR_TEMP5 SUM=SS1 SS2 SS3 SS4 SS5;
RUN;
```

Box 15.6 (continued - 2) ■ **SAS® syntax of BRR_REG_PV**

```
DATA BRR_TEMP6;
     MERGE BRR_TEMP3 BRR_TEMP5;
     BY &BYVAR CLASS;
     SAMP=(SS1+SS2+SS3+SS4+SS5)/5;
     FINVAR=(SAMP+(1.2*MESVAR));
     SESTAT=(FINVAR)**0.5;
     KEEP &BYVAR CLASS ORDRE STAT SESTAT;
RUN;

OPTIONS NOTES;

PROC SORT DATA=BRR_TEMP6 OUT=&OUTFILE (DROP=ORDRE);
     BY &BYVAR ORDRE;
RUN;

PROC DATASETS LIBRARY=WORK NOLIST;
     DELETE BRR_TEMP BRR_TEMP1 BRR_TEMP2 BRR_TEMP3 BRR_TEMP4 BRR_TEMP5
BRR_TEMP6 COEF_TEMP BRRDATA;
RUN;

%MEND BRR_REG_PV;
```

Box 15.7 ■ **SAS® syntax of BRR_CORR**

```
%MACRO BRR_CORR( INFILE=,
                 REPLI_ROOT=,
                 BYVAR=,
                 VAR1=,
                 VAR2=,
                 OUTFILE=);

/*

MEANING OF THE MACRO ARGUMENTS

INFILE      =    INPUT DATA FILE.
REPLI_ROOT  =    ROOT OF THE FINAL WEIGHT AND 80 REPLICATES VARIABLE
NAMES.
                 FINAL WEIGHT VARIABLE NAME MUST BE THE REPLICATION ROOT
FOLLOWED BY 0.
BYVAR            =     BREAKDOWN VARIABLES
VAR1        =    FIRST NUMERIC VARIABLE
VAR2        =    SECOND NUMERIC VARIABLE
OUTFILE     =    FILE WITH THE STATISTIC ESTIMATES AND THEIR STANDARD
ERROR ESTIMATE

*/

OPTIONS NONOTES;

PROC DATASETS LIBRARY=WORK NOLIST;
     DELETE BRR_TEMP1;
RUN;

PROC SORT DATA=&INFILE OUT=BRRDATA (KEEP=&REPLI_ROOT.0-&REPLI_ROOT.80
&BYVAR &VAR1 &VAR2);
     BY &BYVAR;
RUN;
```

Box 15.7 (continued – 1) ■ **SAS® syntax of BRR_CORR**

```
%DO I = 0 %TO 80;

     PROC CORR DATA=BRRDATA VARDEF=WGT NOPRINT OUTP=CORR_TEMP;
            VAR &VAR1 ;
            WITH &VAR2;
            BY &BYVAR;
            WEIGHT &REPLI_ROOT&I;
     RUN;

     DATA CORR_TEMP;
            SET CORR_TEMP;
            L=&I;
     RUN;

     PROC APPEND BASE = BRR_TEMP1 DATA=CORR_TEMP;
     RUN;
%END;

DATA BRR_TEMP1;
     SET BRR_TEMP1;
     IF (_TYPE_ NE "CORR") THEN DELETE;
     PV=&VAR1;
     KEEP &BYVAR L PV;
RUN;

DATA BRR_TEMP2(KEEP=&BYVAR PV) BRR_TEMP3(KEEP=&BYVAR STAT);
     SET BRR_TEMP1;
     IF L > 0 THEN OUTPUT BRR_TEMP2;
     ELSE DO;
            STAT =PV;
            OUTPUT BRR_TEMP3;
     END;
RUN;
```

Box 15.7 (continued – 2) ■ **SAS® syntax of BRR_CORR**

```
PROC SORT DATA=BRR_TEMP2;
     BY &BYVAR;
RUN;

PROC SORT DATA=BRR_TEMP3;
     BY &BYVAR;
RUN;

DATA BRR_TEMP4;
     MERGE BRR_TEMP2 BRR_TEMP3;
     BY &BYVAR;
     VARI=((PV-STAT)**2)*(1/20);
RUN;

PROC UNIVARIATE DATA=BRR_TEMP4 NOPRINT;
     VAR VARI;
     BY &BYVAR;
     OUTPUT OUT=BRR_TEMP5 SUM=SS;
RUN;

OPTIONS NOTES;

DATA &OUTFILE;
     MERGE BRR_TEMP3 BRR_TEMP5;
     BY &BYVAR;
     SESTAT=(SS)**0.5;
     KEEP &BYVAR STAT SESTAT;
RUN;

PROC DATASETS LIBRARY=WORK NOLIST;
     DELETE BRR_TEMP1 BRR_TEMP2 BRR_TEMP3 BRR_TEMP4 BRR_TEMP5 CORR_TEMP
BRRDATA;
RUN;

%MEND BRR_CORR;
```

Box 15.8 ■ SAS® syntax of BRR_CORR_PV

```
%MACRO BRR_CORR_PV(INFILE=,
                          REPLI_ROOT=,
                          BYVAR=,
                          EXPLICA=,
                          PV_ROOT=,
                          OUTFILE=);

/*

MEANING OF THE MACRO ARGUMENTS

INFILE              =      INPUT DATA FILE.
REPLI_ROOT =       ROOT OF THE FINAL WEIGHT AND 80 REPLICATES VARIABLE
NAMES.
                           FINAL WEIGHT VARIABLE NAME MUST BE THE
REPLICATION ROOT FOLLOWED BY 0.
BYVAR               =      BREAKDOWN VARIABLES
EXPLICA             =      NUMERIC VARIABLE
PV_ROOT             =      ROOT OF THE 5 PLAUSIBLE VALUES VARIABLES NAMES
OUTFILE             =      FILE WITH THE STATISTIC ESTIMATES AND THEIR
STANDARD ERROR ESTIMATE

*/

OPTIONS NONOTES;

PROC DATASETS LIBRARY=WORK NOLIST;
     DELETE BRR_TEMP1;
RUN;

PROC SORT DATA=&INFILE OUT=BRRDATA(KEEP=&REPLI_ROOT.0-&REPLI_ROOT.80
&BYVAR &PV_ROOT.1-&PV_ROOT.5 &EXPLICA);
     BY &BYVAR;
RUN;

%DO I = 0 %TO 80;
     PROC CORR DATA=BRRDATA VARDEF=WGT NOPRINT OUTP=CORR_TEMP;
          VAR &PV_ROOT.1 - &PV_ROOT.5 ;
          WITH &EXPLICA;
     BY &BYVAR;
     WEIGHT &REPLI_ROOT&I;
 RUN;

     DATA CORR_TEMP;
          SET CORR_TEMP;
          L=&I;
     RUN;

     PROC APPEND BASE = BRR_TEMP1 DATA=CORR_TEMP;
     RUN;

%END;

 DATA BRR_TEMP1;
     SET BRR_TEMP1;
     IF (_TYPE_ NE "CORR") THEN DELETE;
     PV1=&PV_ROOT.1;
     PV2=&PV_ROOT.2;
     PV3=&PV_ROOT.3;
     PV4=&PV_ROOT.4;
     PV5=&PV_ROOT.5;
     KEEP &BYVAR L PV1-PV5;
RUN;
```

Box 15.8 (continued) ■ **SAS® syntax of BRR_CORR_PV**

```
DATA BRR_TEMP2(DROP=STAT FIN1-FIN5 MESVAR) BRR_TEMP3(KEEP=&BYVAR STAT
FIN1-FIN5 MESVAR);
     SET BRR_TEMP1;
     IF L > 0 THEN OUTPUT BRR_TEMP2;
     ELSE DO;
            STAT =(PV1+PV2+PV3+PV4+PV5)/5;
            FIN1=PV1;
            FIN2=PV2;
            FIN3=PV3;
            FIN4=PV4;
            FIN5=PV5;
            MESVAR=(((STAT-FIN1)**2)+((STAT-FIN2)**2)+((STAT-
FIN3)**2)+((STAT-FIN4)**2)+((STAT-FIN5)**2))/4;
            OUTPUT BRR_TEMP3;
     END;
RUN;

PROC SORT DATA=BRR_TEMP2;
     BY &BYVAR;
RUN;

PROC SORT DATA=BRR_TEMP3;
     BY &BYVAR;
RUN;

DATA BRR_TEMP4;
     MERGE BRR_TEMP2 BRR_TEMP3;
     BY &BYVAR;
     ARRAY A (5)
            PV1-PV5;
     ARRAY B (5)
            FIN1-FIN5;
     ARRAY C(5)
            VAR1-VAR5;
     DO I=1 TO 5;
            C(I)=(1/20)*((A(I)-B(I))**2);
     END;
RUN;

PROC UNIVARIATE DATA=BRR_TEMP4 NOPRINT;
     VAR VAR1 VAR2 VAR3 VAR4 VAR5;
     BY &BYVAR;
     OUTPUT OUT=BRR_TEMP5 SUM=SS1 SS2 SS3 SS4 SS5;
RUN;

OPTIONS NOTES;

DATA &OUTFILE;
     MERGE BRR_TEMP3 BRR_TEMP5;
     BY &BYVAR;
     SAMP=(SS1+SS2+SS3+SS4+SS5)/5;
     FINVAR=(SAMP+(1.2*MESVAR));
     SESTAT=(FINVAR)**0.5;
     KEEP &BYVAR STAT SESTAT;
RUN;

PROC DATASETS LIBRARY=WORK NOLIST;
     DELETE BRR_TEMP1 BRR_TEMP2 BRR_TEMP3 BRR_TEMP4 BRR_TEMP5 CORR_TEMP
BRRDATA;
RUN;

%MEND BRR_CORR_PV;
```

Box 15.9 ■ **SAS® syntax of BRR_PROCMEAN_DIF**

```
%MACRO BRR_PROCMEAN_DIF(INFILE =,
                        REPLI_ROOT =,
                        BYVAR =,
                        VAR =,
                        COMPARE =,
                        CATEGORY =,
                        STAT =,
                        OUTFILE =);
/*

MEANING OF THE MACRO ARGUMENTS

INFILE      =     INPUT DATA FILE.
REPLI_ROOT  =     ROOT OF THE FINAL WEIGHT AND 80 REPLICATES VARIABLE
NAMES.
                        FINAL WEIGHT VARIABLE NAME MUST BE THE
REPLICATION ROOT FOLLOWED BY 0.
BYVAR             =     BREAKDOWN VARIABLES
VAR         =     VARIABLES FOR WHIXH THE STATISTIC IS REQUESTED
COMPARE     =     BREAKDOWN VARIABLE NAME FOR WICH CATEGORY CONTRASTS
ARE REQUESTED
CATEGORY    =     LIST OF THE "COMPARE" VARIABLE CATEGORIES FOR WHICH A
CONTRAT IS REQUESTED
STAT        =     REQUESTED STATISTIQUE
                        SUMWGT      =     SUM OF THE WEIGHT
                        MEAN        =     MEAN
                        VAR               =     VARIANCE
                        STD               =     STANDARD DEVIATION
                        CV                =     COEFFICIENT OF
VARIATION
                        MEDIAN      =     MEDIAN
                        Q1                =     FIRST QUARTILE
                        Q3                =     THIRD QUARTILE
                        QRANGE      =     RANGE BETWEEN Q1 AND Q3
                        PX                =     PERCENTILE, WITH X
BETWEEN 1 AND 99
OUTFILE     =     FILE WITH THE STATISTIC ESTIMATES AND THEIR STANDARD
ERROR ESTIMATE
*/

OPTIONS NONOTES;

PROC DATASETS LIBRARY=WORK NOLIST;
     DELETE BRR_TEMP0 BRR_TEMP1 ;
RUN;

PROC SORT DATA=&INFILE OUT=BRRDATA(KEEP=&REPLI_ROOT.0-&REPLI_ROOT.80
&BYVAR &COMPARE &VAR);
     BY &BYVAR &COMPARE;
RUN;

%DO I = 0 %TO 80;

     PROC MEANS DATA=BRRDATA VARDEF=WGT NOPRINT;
          VAR &VAR ;
          BY &BYVAR &COMPARE;
          WEIGHT &REPLI_ROOT&I;
          OUTPUT OUT=MEAN_TEMP &STAT=PV;
     RUN;

     DATA MEAN_TEMP;
          SET MEAN_TEMP;
          L=&I;
     RUN;

     PROC APPEND BASE = BRR_TEMP0 DATA=MEAN_TEMP;
     RUN;
%END;
```

Box 15.9 (continued – 1) ■ **SAS® syntax of BRR_PROCMEAN_DIF**

```
%LET DEBUT=1;
%LET SUIVANT=2;
%LET COMPTE=1;

%LET I=1;

%DO %WHILE(%LENGTH(%SCAN(&CATEGORY,&I)));
     %LET I=%EVAL(&I+1);
%END;

%LET NBCAT=%EVAL(&I-1);
%LET NBDIF=%EVAL((&NBCAT*(&NBCAT-1))/2);
%LET ORDRE=1;

%DO J=1 %TO &NBDIF;

     %DO K=&DEBUT %TO &NBCAT-1;

           %LET CAT1=%SCAN(&CATEGORY,&DEBUT);
           %LET CAT2=%SCAN(&CATEGORY,&SUIVANT);

           DATA BRR_DIF1;
                  SET BRR_TEMP0 (RENAME=(PV=M1PV));
                  LENGTH CONTRAST $5;
                  CONTRAST="&CAT1.-&CAT2";
                  IF (&COMPARE=&CAT1);
                  KEEP &BYVAR L CONTRAST M1PV &compare;
           RUN;

           DATA BRR_DIF2 ;
                  SET BRR_TEMP0 (RENAME=(PV=M2PV));
                IF (&COMPARE=&CAT2);
                  KEEP &BYVAR L M2PV &compare;
           RUN;
           PROC SORT DATA=BRR_DIF1;
                 BY &BYVAR L;
           RUN;

           PROC SORT DATA=BRR_DIF2;
                 BY &BYVAR L;
           RUN;

           DATA BRR_TEMP_DIF;
                 MERGE BRR_DIF1 BRR_DIF2;
                 BY &BYVAR L;
                 IF (M1PV EQ . OR M2PV EQ .) THEN DELETE;
                 PV=M1PV-M2PV;
                 ORDRE=&ORDRE;
                 KEEP &BYVAR CONTRAST L PV ORDRE;
           RUN;
           PROC APPEND BASE = BRR_TEMP1 DATA=BRR_TEMP_DIF;
           RUN;

           %LET SUIVANT=%EVAL(&SUIVANT+1);
           %LET COMPTE=%EVAL(&COMPTE+1);
           %LET ORDRE=%EVAL(&ORDRE+1);

     %END;

     %LET DEBUT=%EVAL(&DEBUT+1);
     %LET SUIVANT=%EVAL(&DEBUT+1);

%END;
```

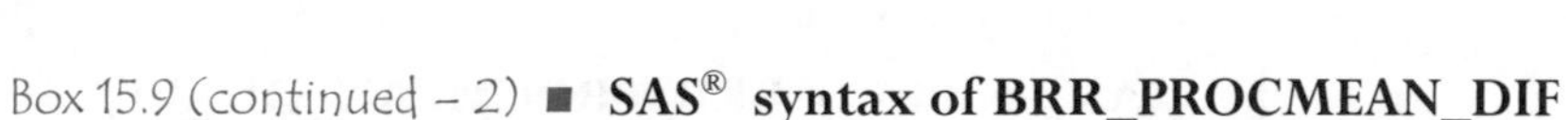

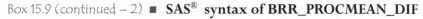

Box 15.9 (continued – 2) ■ **SAS® syntax of BRR_PROCMEAN_DIF**

```
DATA BRR_TEMP2(KEEP=&BYVAR CONTRAST PV) BRR_TEMP3(KEEP=&BYVAR CONTRAST
ORDRE STAT);
     SET BRR_TEMP1;
     IF L > 0 THEN OUTPUT BRR_TEMP2;
     ELSE DO;
            STAT =PV;
            OUTPUT BRR_TEMP3;
     END;
RUN;

PROC SORT DATA=BRR_TEMP2;
     BY &BYVAR CONTRAST;
RUN;

PROC SORT DATA=BRR_TEMP3;
     BY &BYVAR CONTRAST;
RUN;

DATA BRR_TEMP4;
     MERGE BRR_TEMP2 BRR_TEMP3;
     BY &BYVAR CONTRAST;
     VARI=((PV-STAT)**2)*(1/20);
RUN;

PROC UNIVARIATE DATA=BRR_TEMP4 NOPRINT;
     VAR VARI;
     BY &BYVAR CONTRAST;
     OUTPUT OUT=BRR_TEMP5 SUM=SS;
RUN;

DATA BRR_TEMP6;
     MERGE BRR_TEMP3 BRR_TEMP5;
     BY &BYVAR CONTRAST;
     SESTAT=(SS)**0.5;
     KEEP &BYVAR CONTRAST ORDRE STAT SESTAT;
RUN;

OPTIONS NOTES;

PROC SORT DATA=BRR_TEMP6 OUT=&OUTFILE (DROP=ORDRE);
     BY &BYVAR ORDRE;
RUN;

PROC DATASETS LIBRARY=WORK NOLIST;
     DELETE BRR_TEMP0 BRR_TEMP1 BRR_TEMP2 BRR_TEMP3 BRR_TEMP4 BRR_TEMP5
BRR_TEMP6
     MEAN_TEMP BRRDATA BRR_DIF1 BRR_DIF2 BRR_TEMP_DIF;
RUN;

%MEND BRR_PROCMEAN_DIF;
```

Box 15.10 ■ **SAS® syntax of BRR_PROCMEAN_DIF_PV**

```
%MACRO BRR_PROCMEAN_DIF_PV(INFILE =,
                           REPLI_ROOT =,
                           BYVAR =,
                           PV_ROOT =,
                           COMPARE =,
                            CATEGORY =,
                           STAT =,
                           OUTFILE =);
/*

MEANING OF THE MACRO ARGUMENTS

INFILE          =     INPUT DATA FILE.
REPLI_ROOT =     ROOT OF THE FINAL WEIGHT AND 80 REPLICATES VARIABLE
NAMES.
                      FINAL WEIGHT VARIABLE NAME MUST BE THE
REPLICATION ROOT FOLLOWED BY 0.
BYVAR           =     BREAKDOWN VARIABLES
PV_ROOT         =     ROOT OF THE 5 PLAUSIBLE VALUES VARIABLES NAMES
COMPARE         =     BREAKDOWN VARIABLE NAME FOR WICH CATEGORY
CONTRASTS ARE REQUESTED
CATEGORY   =     LIST OF THE "COMPARE" VARIABLE CATEGORIES FOR WHICH A
CONTRAT IS REQUESTED
STAT       =     REQUESTED STATISTIQUE
                      SUMWGT          =     SUM OF THE WEIGHT
                      MEAN      =     MEAN
                      VAR             =     VARIANCE
                      STD             =     STANDARD DEVIATION
                      CV        =     COEFFICIENT OF VARIATION
                      MEDIAN          =     MEDIAN
                      Q1        =     FIRST QUARTILE
                      Q3        =     THIRD QUARTILE
                      QRANGE          =     RANGE BETWEEN Q1 AND Q3
                      PX        =     PERCENTILE, WITH X BETWEEN 1 AND 99
OUTFILE         =     FILE WITH THE STATISTIC ESTIMATES AND THEIR
STANDARD ERROR ESTIMATE

*/

OPTIONS NONOTES;

PROC DATASETS LIBRARY=WORK NOLIST;
     DELETE BRR_TEMP0 BRR_TEMP1 ;
RUN;

PROC SORT DATA=&INFILE OUT=BRRDATA(KEEP=&REPLI_ROOT.0-&REPLI_ROOT.80
&BYVAR &COMPARE &PV_ROOT.1-&PV_ROOT.5);
     BY &BYVAR &COMPARE;
RUN;

%DO I = 0 %TO 80;

     PROC MEANS DATA=BRRDATA VARDEF=WGT NOPRINT;
            VAR &PV_ROOT.1 - &PV_ROOT.5 ;
            BY &BYVAR &COMPARE;
            WEIGHT &REPLI_ROOT&I;
            OUTPUT OUT=MEAN_TEMP &STAT=PV1 - PV5;
     RUN;

     DATA MEAN_TEMP;
            SET MEAN_TEMP;
            L=&I;
     RUN;

     PROC APPEND BASE = BRR_TEMP0 DATA=MEAN_TEMP;
     RUN;

%END;
```

Box 15.10 (continued – 1) ■ **SAS® syntax of BRR_PROCMEAN_DIF_PV**

```
%LET DEBUT=1;
%LET SUIVANT=2;
%LET COMPTE=1;
%LET I=1;

%DO %WHILE(%LENGTH(%SCAN(&CATEGORY,&I)));
     %LET I=%EVAL(&I+1);
%END;

%LET NBCAT=%EVAL(&I-1);
%LET NBDIF=%EVAL((&NBCAT*(&NBCAT-1))/2);
%LET ORDRE=1;

%DO J=1 %TO &NBDIF;
     %DO K=&DEBUT %TO &NBCAT-1;
            %LET CAT1=%SCAN(&CATEGORY,&DEBUT);
            %LET CAT2=%SCAN(&CATEGORY,&SUIVANT);

            DATA BRR_DIF1;
                   SET BRR_TEMP0 (RENAME=(PV1=M1PV1 PV2=M1PV2 PV3=M1PV3
PV4=M1PV4 PV5=M1PV5));
                   LENGTH CONTRAST $5;
                   CONTRAST="&CAT1.-&CAT2";
                   IF (&COMPARE=&CAT1);
                   KEEP &BYVAR L CONTRAST M1PV1-M1PV5 &compare;
            RUN;

            DATA BRR_DIF2 ;
                   SET BRR_TEMP0 (RENAME=(PV1=M2PV1 PV2=M2PV2 PV3=M2PV3
PV4=M2PV4 PV5=M2PV5));
                   IF (&COMPARE=&CAT2);
                   KEEP &BYVAR L M2PV1-M2PV5 &compare;
            RUN;

PROC SORT DATA=BRR_DIF1;
                   BY &BYVAR L;
            RUN;

            PROC SORT DATA=BRR_DIF2;
                   BY &BYVAR L;
            RUN;

            DATA BRR_TEMP_DIF;
                   MERGE BRR_DIF1 BRR_DIF2;
                   BY &BYVAR L;
                   IF (M1PV1 EQ . OR M2PV1 EQ .) THEN DELETE;
                   PV1=M1PV1-M2PV1;
                   PV2=M1PV2-M2PV2;
                   PV3=M1PV3-M2PV3;
                   PV4=M1PV4-M2PV4;
                   PV5=M1PV5-M2PV5;
                   ORDRE=&ORDRE;
                   KEEP &BYVAR CONTRAST L PV1-PV5 ORDRE;
            RUN;

            PROC APPEND BASE = BRR_TEMP1 DATA=BRR_TEMP_DIF;
            RUN;

            %LET SUIVANT=%EVAL(&SUIVANT+1);
            %LET COMPTE=%EVAL(&COMPTE+1);
            %LET ORDRE=%EVAL(&ORDRE+1);
     %END;

%LET DEBUT=%EVAL(&DEBUT+1);
%LET SUIVANT=%EVAL(&DEBUT+1);

%END;
```

Box 15.10 (continued – 2) ■ **SAS® syntax of BRR_PROCMEAN_DIF_PV**

```
DATA BRR_TEMP2(DROP=STAT FIN1-FIN5 MESVAR) BRR_TEMP3(KEEP=&BYVAR CONTRAST
ORDRE STAT FIN1-FIN5 MESVAR);
     SET BRR_TEMP1;
     IF L > 0 THEN OUTPUT BRR_TEMP2;
     ELSE DO;
            STAT =(PV1+PV2+PV3+PV4+PV5)/5;
            FIN1=PV1;
            FIN2=PV2;
            FIN3=PV3;
            FIN4=PV4;
            FIN5=PV5;
            MESVAR=(((STAT-FIN1)**2)+((STAT-FIN2)**2)+((STAT-
FIN3)**2)+((STAT-FIN4)**2)+((STAT-FIN5)**2))/4;
            OUTPUT BRR_TEMP3;
   END;
RUN;

PROC SORT DATA=BRR_TEMP2;
     BY &BYVAR CONTRAST;
RUN;

PROC SORT DATA=BRR_TEMP3;
     BY &BYVAR CONTRAST;
RUN;

DATA BRR_TEMP4;
     MERGE BRR_TEMP2 BRR_TEMP3;
     BY &BYVAR CONTRAST;
     ARRAY A (5)
            PV1-PV5;
     ARRAY B (5)
            FIN1-FIN5;
     ARRAY C(5)
            VAR1-VAR5;
     DO I=1 TO 5;
            C(I)=(1/20)*((A(I)-B(I))**2);
     END;
RUN;

PROC UNIVARIATE DATA=BRR_TEMP4 NOPRINT;
     VAR VAR1 VAR2 VAR3 VAR4 VAR5;
     BY &BYVAR CONTRAST;
     OUTPUT OUT=BRR_TEMP5 SUM=SS1 SS2 SS3 SS4 SS5;
RUN;

DATA BRR_TEMP6;
     MERGE BRR_TEMP3 BRR_TEMP5;
     BY &BYVAR CONTRAST;
     SAMP=(SS1+SS2+SS3+SS4+SS5)/5;
     FINVAR=(SAMP+(1.2*MESVAR));
     SESTAT=(FINVAR)**0.5;
     KEEP &BYVAR CONTRAST ORDRE STAT SESTAT;
RUN;

OPTIONS NOTES;

PROC SORT DATA=BRR_TEMP6 OUT=&OUTFILE (DROP=ORDRE);
     BY &BYVAR ORDRE;
RUN;

PROC DATASETS LIBRARY=WORK NOLIST;
     DELETE BRR_TEMP0 BRR_TEMP1 BRR_TEMP2 BRR_TEMP3 BRR_TEMP4 BRR_TEMP5
BRR_TEMP6
     MEAN_TEMP BRRDATA BRR_DIF1 BRR_DIF2 BRR_TEMP_DIF;
RUN;

%MEND BRR_PROCMEAN_DIF_PV;
```

Appendices

APPENDIX 1 ▪ PISA 2003 INTERNATIONAL DATABASE

WHAT IS THE GENERAL STRUCTURE OF THE PISA 2003 INTERNATIONAL DATABASE?

This document describes the international database of the OECD Programme for International Student Assessment (PISA) 2003. The database can be accessed through the PISA web page (*www.pisa.oecd.org*). The database comprises data collected in 2003 in 41 countries and processed in the second half of 2003 and in 2004. The first results were released in December 2004 (for the full set of results see OECD, 2004a).

The purpose of this document is to provide all of the necessary information to analyse the data in accordance with the methodologies used to collect and process the data. It does not provide detailed information regarding these methods.

The following sources can provide additional information about PISA:

- The PISA Web site (*www.pisa.oecd.org*) provides: *i)* descriptions about the programme, contact information, participating countries and results of PISA 2003 as well as PISA 2000; *ii)* the complete micro-level database, all questionnaires, publications and national reports of PISA 2003 and PISA 2000, in a downloadable format; and *iii)* an opportunity for users to generate their own tables or request specific ones.
- *Learning for Tomorrow's World – First Results from PISA 2003* (OECD, 2004a) includes the first results from PISA 2003. It presents evidence on student performance in reading, mathematical and scientific literacy and problem solving, reveals factors that influence the development of these skills at home and at school, and examines what the implications are for policy development.
- The *PISA 2003 Assessment Framework – Mathematics, Reading, Science and Problem Solving Knowledge and Skills* (OECD, 2003) describes the framework and instruments underlying the PISA 2003 assessment. It introduces the PISA approach to assessing mathematical, reading and scientific literary and problem solving with its three dimensions of processes, content and context. Further it presents tasks from the PISA 2003 assessment together with how these tasks were scored and how they relate to the conceptual framework underlying PISA.
- The *PISA 2003 Technical Report* (OECD, forthcoming) presents the methodology and procedures used in PISA.

The PISA database provides detailed information on all instruments used in PISA 2003 for:

- 30 OECD member countries: Australia, Austria, Belgium, Canada, the Czech Republic, Denmark, Finland, France, Germany, Greece, Hungary, Iceland, Ireland, Italy, Japan, Korea, Luxembourg, Mexico, the Netherlands, New Zealand, Norway, Poland, Portugal, the Slovak Republic, Spain, Sweden, Switzerland, Turkey, the United Kingdom and the United States.
- 11 OECD partner countries: Brazil, Hong Kong-China, Indonesia, Latvia, Liechtenstein, Macao-China, the Russian Federation, Serbia, Thailand, Tunisia and Uruguay.

WHICH INSTRUMENTS WERE INCLUDED IN PISA 2003?

Test design

In PISA 2003, a rotated test design was used to assess student performance in mathematical, reading and scientific literacy and problem solving (for the complete conceptual frameworks see OECD, 2003b). This type of test design ensures a wide coverage of content while at the same time keeping the testing burden on individual students low. Thirteen test booklets were distributed at random to students. These booklets included questions assessing reading literacy, mathematical literacy, scientific literacy and problem solving, but not all booklets assessed the same domains. Students were randomly assigned a testing booklet within each of the sampled schools.

- Booklets 1 and 2 contained reading and mathematics questions;
- Booklets 3 and 4 contained mathematics and problem solving questions;
- Booklets 5 and 6 contained mathematics and science questions;
- Booklets 7 and 8 contained reading, mathematics and science questions;
- Booklet 9 contained reading, mathematics, science and problem solving questions;
- Booklets 10 and 11 contained reading, mathematics and problem solving questions; and
- Booklets 12 and 13 contained mathematics, science and problem solving questions.

In addition to the thirteen two-hour booklets, a special one-hour booklet, referred to as the UH Booklet (or the *Une Heure* booklet) was prepared for use in schools catering exclusively to students with special needs. The UH booklet was shorter and contained items deemed most suitable for students with special educational needs. The UH booklet contained seven mathematics items, six reading items, eight science items and five problem solving items.

Questionnaires

Student questionnaires

A student questionnaire (see Appendix 2) was designed to collect information about the student's family, home environment, reading habits, school and everyday activities. This information was later analysed both independently and in relation to performance.

Additionally, the programme included two additional optional questionnaires for students. The first one was an educational career questionnaire (see Appendix 3) asking the students' past educational career, present educational settings and expected occupation. National centres were allowed to select any of the items included in this questionnaire for inclusion without having to administer all of the questions. The second one was an information communication technology (ICT) questionnaire (see Appendix 4), including questions regarding the students' use of, familiarity with and attitudes towards ICT. ICT was defined as the use of any equipment or software for processing or transmitting digital information that performs diverse general functions whose options can be specified or programmed by its user.

School questionnaire

The principals or head administrators of the participating schools responded to a school questionnaire (see Appendix 5) covering issues such as the demographics of the school, school staffing, the school environment, human and material educational resources in the school, selection and transfer policies, and educational and decision-making practices in the school.

Structure of the testing session

The student testing session consisted of:

- Two 60-minute sessions assessing reading, mathematical and scientific literacy and problem solving;
- 35 minutes for the student questionnaire;
- Two minutes for the international option of educational career questionnaire; and
- Five minutes for the international option of ICT familiarity questionnaire.

The school principal or head administrator answered a 20 minutes school questionnaire.

WHAT IS AVAILABLE FROM THE PISA 2003 INTERNATIONAL DATABASE?

What is available for downloading?

The downloadable files are classified into six categories. Some of them are quite small, while others (*e.g.* the micro-level data files) are quite large, taking a long time to download. The six categories of file are:

Questionnaires

The following questionnaires are available: student questionnaire, educational career questionnaire, ICT familiarity questionnaire and school questionnaire. Appendices 2 to 5 of this document show these questionnaires, with the variable name of each item in the left-hand margin. For example:

			<Female>	<Male>
ST03Q01	**Q 3**	Are you <female> or <male>?	❑ 1	❑ 2

Codebooks

The codebooks are useful in relating the actual items from the instruments (assessment tests or questionnaires) to the data available in the data files as they identify the variable name with all possible values which are valid for that variable. In addition to the name of the variable, they also show its label, all possible responses (code and label), type of variable (*e.g.* string or numeric) and the columns where the values are shown in the actual data file. Three codebooks are available: the codebook for student questionnaire (see Appendix 6), the codebook for cognitive test item (see Appendix 8) and the codebook for school questionnaire (see Appendix 7). For example, in the case of the previous item (ST03Q01), the codebook shows:

ST03Q01	Sex – Q3		F(1.0)	29-29
	1	Female		
	2	Male		
	7	N/A		
	8	M/R		
	9	Mis		

SAS® Control files

These files will read the raw text file, and convert it into a SAS® data file assigning label and values (valid and missing). The three SAS® control files will read and convert: the school questionnaire, the student questionnaire and the cognitive test item data files. These files have extension *.SAS.

SPSS® Control files

Similarly to the SAS® control files, these files will read the raw text file, and convert it into a SPSS® data file assigning labels and values (valid and missing). The three SPSS® control files will read and convert: the school questionnaire, the student questionnaire and the cognitive test item data files. The files have extension *.SPS.

Data files in text format

The item by item database is available in text format, which once read by the SAS® or SPSS® control files will be correctly formatted and labelled. As it is, it includes one row for each student with his or her responses to all items. These files have extension *.TXT and are in ASCII form.

Compendia

Compendia show the full item by country results for the three student questionnaires, the school questionnaire and the students' performance. The following three files are available: the test item compendium, the student questionnaire compendium and the school questionnaire compendium. There are two types of data for each item: percentages by categories and performances by categories. Standard errors are also reported for the percentages and for the means.

WHICH FILES ARE INCLUDED IN THE PISA 2003 INTERNATIONAL DATABASE?

The PISA international database consists of three data files. The files are in text (or ASCII) format and are accompanied by the corresponding SAS® and SPSS® control (syntax) files, which can be used to read the text into a SAS® or SPSS® database. Besides the data collected through the international questionnaire, some countries collected data through national options, which are not included in the international database. These files are quite large as they include one record for each student or school.

How are the files named?

The data files in the international database are named according to the following convention:

□□□ □□□□_□□□□

- The last four numbers are "2003" for the PISA 2003 data files. This indicates the cycle of PISA.
- The next four characters represent the instruments: "Stui" for the student questionnaire, "Schi" for the school questionnaire and "Cogn" for the tests.
- The first three characters of the files are always "Int". This indicates that the file refers to the international data.

Student questionnaire data file (filename: int_stui_2003.txt)

For each student who participated in the assessment, the following information is available:

- Identification variables for the country, adjudicated sub-national region, stratum, school and student;
- The student responses on the three questionnaires, *i.e.* the student questionnaire and the two international options: educational career questionnaire and ICT questionnaire;
- The student indices (see Appendix 9) derived from the original questions in the questionnaires;
- The students' performance scores in mathematics, reading, science and problem solving; and
- The student weights and the 80 reading Fay's replicates for the computation of the sampling variance estimates.

School questionnaire data file (filename: int_schi_2003.txt)

For each school that participated in the assessment, the following information is available:

- The identification variables for the country, adjudicated sub-national region, stratum and school;
- The school responses on the school questionnaire;
- The school indices (see Appendix 9) derived from the original questions in the school questionnaire; and
- The school weight.

Cognitive test item data file (filename: int_cogn_2003.txt)

For each student who participated in the assessment, the following information is available:

- Identification variables for the country, adjudicated sub-national region, booklet ID, school and student; and
- The students' responses for each item included in the test, expressed in a one-digit format.[1]

Which records are included in the international database?

Records included in the database

Student level

- All PISA students who attended one of the two test sessions; and
- PISA students who only attended the questionnaire session are included if they provided a response to the father's occupation questions or the mother's occupation questions on the student questionnaire (Questions 7 to 10).

School level

- All participating schools – that is, any school where at least 25 per cent of the sampled eligible students were assessed – have a record in the school level international database, regardless of whether the school returned the school questionnaire.

Records excluded from the database

Student level

- Additional data collected by some countries for a national or international option such as a grade sample;

- Sampled students who were reported as not eligible, students who were no longer at school, students who were excluded for physical, mental or linguistic reasons, and students who were absent on the testing day;
- Students who refused to participate in the assessment sessions; and
- Students from schools where less than 25 percent of the sampled and eligible students participated.

School level

- Schools where fewer than 25 per cent of the sampled eligible students participated in the testing sessions.

How are missing data represented?

The coding of the data distinguishes between four different types of missing data:

- Item level non-response: 9 for a one-digit variable, 99 for a two-digit variable, 999 for a three-digit variable, and so on. Missing codes are shown in the codebooks. This missing code is used if the student or school principal was expected to answer a question, but no response was actually provided;
- Multiple or invalid responses: 8 for a one-digit variable, 98 for a two-digit variable, 998 for a three-digit variable, and so on. This code is used for Multiple choice items in both test booklets and questionnaires where an invalid response was provided. This code is not used for open-ended questions;
- Not applicable: 7 for a one-digit variable, 97 for a two-digit variables, 997 for a three-digit variable, and so on for the student questionnaire data file and for the school data file. Code 'n' is used for a one-digit variable in the test booklet data file. This code is used when it was not possible for the student to answer the question. For instance, this code is used if a question was misprinted or if a question was deleted from the questionnaire by a national centre. The not-applicable codes and code 'n' are also used in the test booklet file for questions that were not included in the test booklet that the student received; and
- Not reached items: all consecutive missing values starting from the end of each test session were replaced by the non-reached code, 'r', except for the first value of the missing series, which is coded as missing.

How are students and schools identified?

The student identification from the student files consists of three variables, which together form a unique identifier for each student:

- The country identification variable labelled COUNTRY. The country codes used in PISA are the ISO 3166 country codes;
- The school identification variable labelled SCHOOLID. These are sequential numbers, which were randomly assigned for confidentiality reasons; and
- The student identification variable labelled STIDSTD. These are sequential numbers, which were randomly assigned for confidentiality reasons.

The variable labelled SUBNATIO has been included to differentiate adjudicated sub-national entities within countries. This variable is used for four countries as follows:

- Italy: the value '1' is assigned to the region Veneto-Nord-Est, '2' to the region Trento-Nord-Est, '3' to the region Toscana-Centro, '4' to the region Piemonte-Nord-Ovest, '5' to the region Lombardia-Nord Ovest, '6' to the region Bolzano and the value '7' to all other (non-adjudicated) Italian regions;
- Spain: the value '1' to the non-adjudicated regions in Spain, '2' to Castilia and Leon, '3' to Catalonia and '4' is assigned to Basque Country; and
- United Kingdom: the value '1' is assigned to England, Northern Ireland and Wales, and the value '2' is assigned to Scotland.

The variable labelled STRATUM contains information on the explicit strata used for sampling. Some of them were combined into larger units for policy or confidentiality reasons.

The school identification consists of two variables, which together form a unique identifier for each school:

- The country identification variable labelled COUNTRY. The country codes used in PISA are the ISO 3166 country codes; and
- The school identification variable labelled SCHOOLID.

THE STUDENT QUESTIONNAIRE FILE

The responses to the student questionnaires

The student files contain the original variables collected through the student context questionnaires, *i.e.* the compulsory student questionnaire and the two international options: the education career questionnaire and the ICT questionnaire.

The names that are used to represent these variables in the international database are directly related to the international version of the context questionnaires. Each variable name consists of seven characters.

□□ □□ □ □□

The sixth and seventh characters refer to the item number of the question. For instance, ST02Q01 is the day of birth, ST02Q02 is the month of birth and ST02Q03 is the year of birth.

The fifth character refers to the type of coding:
Q for items with original coding; and
R for recoded items.

The third and fourth characters refer to the question number as it appears in the international version of the questionnaire. For instance, ST02 refers to the second question in the student questionnaire relating to the date of birth.

The first two characters refer to the instrument:
ST for the student questionnaire;
EC for the education career questionnaire; and
IC for the ICT questionnaire.

The weights and replicates

The weights

The variable W_FSTUWT is the final student weight. The sum of the weights constitutes an estimate of the size of the target population. If an analysis performed on the international level weighted by W_FSTUWT, large countries would have a stronger contribution to the results than small countries. Two country adjustment factors are included in the file:

- CNTFAC1 can be used for the computation of equal country weights. The weight W_FSTUWT*CNTFAC1 will give an equal weight of 1000 cases to each country so that smaller and larger countries contribute equally to the analysis. In order to obtain weights with equally weighted OECD countries, one needs to add the variable OECD indicating country membership as an additional multiplier (W_FSTUWT*CNTFAC1*OECD); and
- CNTFAC2 allows the computation of normalised or standardised weights. The weight W_FSTUWT*CNTFAC2 will give countries weights according to their sample sizes so that the sum of weights in each country is equal to the number of students in the database.

When analyses are carried out across countries, the country adjustment factors should also be applied to the Fay's replicates. The detail explanation of calculating weights is in Chapter 2.

Fay's replicates

Eighty Fay's replicates (W_FSTR1 to W_FSTR80) are included in the data files because they are needed to compute unbiased standard error estimates associated with any population parameter estimates. The standard error provides an estimate of the degree to which a statistic such as a mean score may be expected to vary about the true population mean. A 95 per cent confidence interval for a mean may be constructed in such a way that, if the sampling procedure were repeated a large number of times, and the sample statistic re-computed each time, the confidence interval would be expected to contain the population estimate 95 per cent of the time. Fay's replicates take into account the complex two-stage stratified sample design. If this is not done, one underestimates the standard error, thereby running the risk of obtaining statistical significance when in fact there is none. More detail description and application of Fay's replicates are found in Chapter 3.

The student performance scores

Performance scores

For each domain, *i.e.* mathematics, reading, science and problem solving, and four mathematics scales (change and relationships, space and shape, quantity and uncertainty), a set of five plausible values transformed to the international PISA metric are provided:

- PV1MATH to PV5MATH for mathematics ability;
- PV1MATH1 to PV5MATH1 for mathematics/ space and shape ability;
- PV1MATH2 to PV5MATH2 for mathematics/ change and relationships ability;
- PV1MATH3 to PV5MATH3 for mathematics/ uncertainty ability;
- PV1MATH4 to PV5MATH4 for mathematics/ quantity ability;
- PV1READ to PV5READ for reading ability; and
- PV1SCIE to PV5SCIE for science ability.

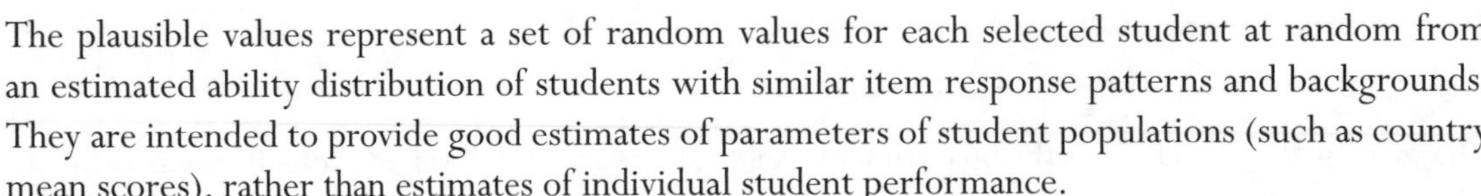

The plausible values represent a set of random values for each selected student at random from an estimated ability distribution of students with similar item response patterns and backgrounds. They are intended to provide good estimates of parameters of student populations (such as country mean scores), rather than estimates of individual student performance.

Mathematics and problem solving plausible values were transformed to PISA scale using the data for the OECD countries participating in PISA 2003. This linear transformation used weighted data, with an additional adjustment factor so that each country contributes equally in the computation of the standardisation parameters.

The weighted average of five means and five standard deviations of plausible values for each scale is 500 and 100, respectively for the OECD countries but the means and variances of the individual plausible values are not exactly 500 and 100, respectively. The same transformation as for mathematics was applied to the four mathematics sub-scales.

PISA 2003 reading and science plausible values were mapped to PISA 2000 scale and the PISA 2000 transformation, that gives OECD mean 500 and standard deviation of 100 to the reading and science scales in PISA 2000.

For a full description of plausible values can be found in Chapter 5 and the application of plausible values for analysis is in Chapter 7.

The student questionnaire indices

Several of PISA's measures reflect indices that summarise students' responses. Two types of indices are provided in the student questionnaire file. Simple indices are constructed through the arithmetical transformation or recoding of one or more items. Scale indices are constructed through the scaling of items. For description of PISA student indices, see Appendix 9. The details on the methods and the reliabilities of the indices see the *PISA 2003 Technical Report* (OECD, forthcoming).

Item deletions

In the student questionnaire, Question 2 concerning students' dates of birth and Question 18(a) to (e) concerning possessions at home were deleted from the student data file. Question 11(a) to (e) were recoded into ST11R01 and Question 13(a) to (e) were recoded into ST13R01. Question 35(a) was used in computation of minutes of mathematics per week (MMINS).

In the educational career questionnaire, Question 8 was used to create the PISA 2003 index of expected occupational status at the age of 30 (BSMJ).

THE SCHOOL FILE

The responses to the school questionnaire

The school files contain the original variables collected through the school context questionnaire.

The names which are used to represent these variables in the international database are directly related to the international version of the school questionnaire. Each variable name consists of seven characters.

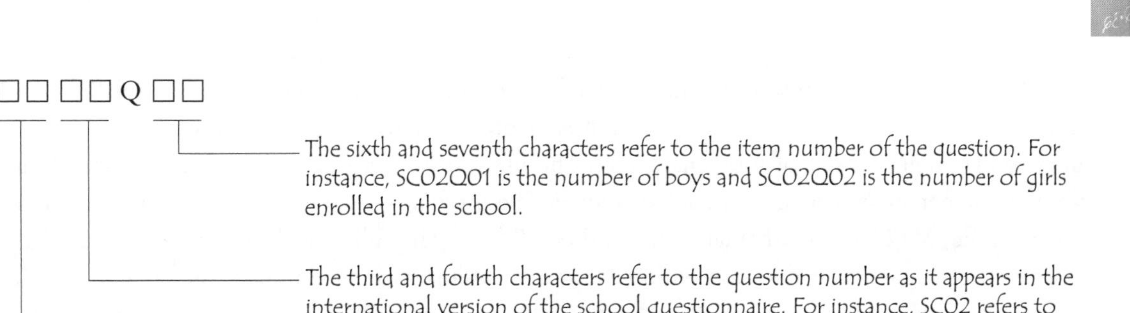

□□ □□Q □□
The sixth and seventh characters refer to the item number of the question. For instance, SC02Q01 is the number of boys and SC02Q02 is the number of girls enrolled in the school.
The third and fourth characters refer to the question number as it appears in the international version of the school questionnaire. For instance, SC02 refers to the second question in the school questionnaire relating to enrolment.

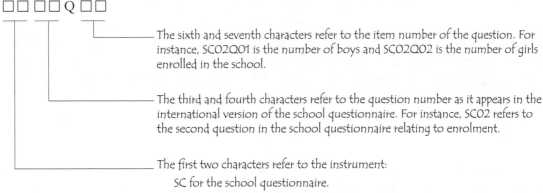

The first two characters refer to the instrument:
SC for the school questionnaire.

The school weight

The school base weight, SCWEIGHT, which has been adjusted for school non-response, is provided at the end of the school file. PISA uses an age-based sample instead of a grade-based sample. Additionally, the PISA sample of schools in some countries included primary schools, lower secondary schools, upper secondary schools, or even special education schools. For these two reasons, it is difficult to conceptually define the school population, except this it is the population of schools with at least one 15-year-old student. While in some countries, the population of schools with 15-year-olds is similar to the population of secondary schools, in other countries these two populations of schools are very different.

A recommendation is to analyse the school data at the student level. From a practical point of view, it means that the school data should be imported into the student data file. From a theoretical point of view, while it is possible to estimate the percentages of schools following a specific school characteristic, it is not meaningful. Instead, the recommendation is to estimate the percentages of students following the same school characteristic. For instance, the percentages of private schools versus public schools will not be estimated, but the percentages of students attending private school versus the percentage of students attending public schools will.

As school data will be imported in the student data file, the final weight and the 80 Fay's replicates will be used in a similar what to how they are used for the student data.

The school questionnaire indices

Several of PISA's measures reflect indices that summarise school principals' responses. Two types of indices are provided in the school questionnaire file. Simple indices are constructed through the arithmetical transformation or recoding of one or more items. Scale indices are constructed through the scaling of items. For a description of PISA indices, see Appendix 9. The details on the methods and the reliabilities of the indices see the *PISA 2003 Technical Report* (OECD, forthcoming).

THE FILE WITH THE STUDENT TEST DATA

The file with the test data contains individual students' responses to all items used for the international item calibration and in the generation of the plausible values. All item responses included in this file have a one-digit format, which contains the score for the student on that item.

The PISA items are organised into units. Each unit consists of a piece of text or related texts, followed by one or more questions. Each unit is identified by a short label and by a long label. The units' short labels consist of four characters. The first character is R, M, S or X respectively for reading, mathematics, science or problem solving. The three next characters indicate the unit name. For example, M124 is a mathematics unit called *Walking*. The full item label (usually seven-digit) represents each particular question within a unit. Thus items within a unit have the same initial four characters: all items in the unit *Walking* begin with 'M124', plus a question number: for example, the third question in the *Walking* unit is M124Q03.

Users may notice that the question numbers in some cases are not sequential, and in other cases, that question numbers are missing. The initial item numbering was done before the field trial, with some changes occurring after it (the field trial took place a year before the main assessment). For example, during the development of the main study instruments, some items were re-ordered within a unit, while others were deleted from the item pool.

In this file, the items are sorted by domain and alphabetically by short label within domain. This means that the mathematics items appear at the beginning of the file, followed by the reading items, the science items and then the problem solving items. Within domains, units with smaller numeric labels appear before those with larger label, and within each unit, the first question will precede the second, and so on.

For items omitted by students, embedded missing and non-reached missing items were differentiated. All consecutive missing values clustered at the end of each booklet were replaced by a non-reached code 'r', except for the first value of the missing series. Embedded and non-reached missing items were treated differently in the scaling. Non-reached items for students who were reported to have left the session earlier than expected were considered not applicable in all analyses.

Recoding of the assessment items

Some of the items needed to be recoded prior to the national and international scaling processes:

- Double-digit coded items (mathematics, science and problem solving only) were truncated by retaining only the first digit, which corresponds to the score initially assigned to the item. An exception is item M462Q01 where code 13 was recoded into 0;
- Other items were recoded and/or combined. These items have been re-labelled. The character 'T' was added to the end of the previous short label for such items;
- Numerical variables were recoded into scores, *i.e.* incorrect answer (0), correct answer (1), missing answer (9) or not applicable (7);
- Some questions consisted of several true/false or yes/no items. One question was also composed of several multiple-choice items (M833Q01). These items were combined into new variables. The new codes correspond to the number of correct answers on the subset of items; and
- Finally, four items, which comprised a subset of items (R219Q01, M192Q01, M520Q01 and M520Q03), were combined to form new variables. The combined codes correspond to the number of correct answers to each of the sub-items included in these four items.

Item deletions

Assessment data were initially scaled by country, and item parameter estimates were analysed across countries. During the item adjudication process, some items were flagged for particular countries and a consultation process took place to perform additional checks on these items. The consultations resulted in the deletion of a few items at the national level and two items at the international level. At the international level the two deleted items were S327Q02 and M434Q01T. The nationally deleted items are listed in Table A1.1. These deleted items at the national level, as well as two deleted items at the international level were recoded as not applicable and were not included in either the international scaling or the generation of plausible values.

Table A1.1 ■ **Items deleted at the national level**

Item	Country	Item	Country
M144Q03	Iceland (booklet 4 only)	R219Q01E	Tunisia
M155Q01	Korea	R219Q01T	Tunisia
M179Q01T	Italy (Italian version only)	R227Q01	Spain (Catalonian and Castilian versions),
M273Q01	Denmark (booklet 7 only)	S131Q02T	Russia
M402Q02	Hungary	S252Q02	Spain (Castilian, Galician, and Valencian versions)
M442Q02	Uruguay	S268Q02T	Norway
M603Q02	Canada	S326Q01	Portugal
M704Q01T	Switzerland (Italian version only)	X414Q01	Russia
M800Q01	Uruguay	X603Q02T	Italy (Italian version only)
R055Q03	Austria, Luxembourg (German version only), Germany, Switzerland (German version only), Belgium (German version only), Italy (German version only), Liechtenstein	X603Q03	Italy (Italian version only)
R102Q04a	Korea	R111Q6B	Tunisia

International scores assigned to the items

The final scores allocated to the different categories are presented in Appendix 10. The codes are grouped according o the scores they were assigned for the final international calibration.

ADDITIONAL TECHNICAL INFORMATION AND GLOSSARY

Codebook

A codebook is a document that identifies the variables and all possible values associated with them. In addition to the name of the variable, it also shows the variable label, all possible responses (*i.e.* in the case of multiple-choice items it shows the values for all alternatives and the full label of each alternative), type of variable (*e.g.* string or numeric) and the columns where the values are shown in the actual data file.

Compendia

Compendia include a set of tables showing statistics for every item included in the questionnaires, and the relationship with performance. The tables show the percentage of students per category of response and the performance for the group of students in each category of response.

Double-digit coding

Students' responses could give valuable information about their ideas and thinking, besides being correct or incorrect. The marking guides for mathematics and science included a system of two-digit coding for marking so that the frequency of various types of correct and incorrect responses could be recoded. The first digit is the actual score. The second digit is used to categorise the different kinds of responses on the basis of the strategies used by the student to answer the item. There are two main advantages of using double-digit codes. Firstly, more information can be collected about students' misconceptions, common errors, and different approaches to solving problems. Secondly, double-digit coding allows a more structured way of presenting the codes, clearly indicating the hierarchical levels of groups of codes. The assessment data files including the second digit were available to national centres.

ISO 3166

For International Standardization Organization (ISO) country codes, see *http://www.iso.org*.

SAS®

SAS® is a statistical package. For further information, see *http://www.sas.com*.

SPSS®

SPSS® is a statistical package. For further information, see *http://www.spss.com*.

WesVar®

WesVar® is a statistical package that computes estimates and their variance estimates from survey data using replication methods. The information generated can then be used to estimate sampling errors for different types of survey statistics. It can be used in conjunction with a wide range of complex sample designs, including multistage, stratified, and unequal probability samples. For further information, see *http://www.westat.com/wesvar*.

Note

1. The responses from open-ended items could give valuable information about students' ideas and thinking, which could be fed back into curriculum planning. For this reason, the marking guides for these items in mathematics and science were designed to include a two-digit marking so that the frequency of various types of correct and incorrect response could be recorded. The first digit was the actual score. The second digit was used to categorise the different kings of response on the basis of the strategies used by the student to answer the item. The international database includes only the first digit.

APPENDIX 2 ■ STUDENT QUESTIONNAIRE

Variable name

SECTION A: ABOUT YOU

Variable name			
ST01Q01	**Q1a**	**What <grade> are you in?**	
		______ *<grade>*	
ST01Q02	**Q1b**	**Which one of the following <programmes> are you in?**	
		(Please <tick> only one box.)	
		<Programme 1>	❑ 01
		<Programme 2>	❑ 02
		<Programme 3>	❑ 03
		<Programme 4>	❑ 04
		<Programme 5>	❑ 05
		<Programme 6>	❑ 06
ST02Q02 ST02Q03	**Q2**	**On what date were you born?**	
		(Please write the day, month and year you were born.)	
		<_____ ___________ *198* ___>	
		Day *Month* *Year*	
ST03Q01	**Q3**	**Are you <female> or <male>?**	
		Female	❑ 1
		Male	❑ 2

SECTION B: YOU AND YOUR FAMILY

Variable name			
	Q4	**Who usually lives at <home> with you?**	
		(Please <tick>as many boxes as apply.)	
ST04Q01	a)	Mother	❑ 1
ST04Q02	b)	Other female guardian (*e.g.* stepmother or foster mother)	❑ 1
ST04Q03	c)	Father	❑ 1
ST04Q04	d)	Other male guardian (*e.g.* stepfather or foster father)	❑ 1
ST04Q05	e)	Others (*e.g.* brother, sister, cousin, grandparents)	❑ 1

ST05Q01	**Q5**	**What is your mother currently doing?** *(Please <tick> only one box.)*
		a) Working full-time <for pay> ❑1
		b) Working part-time <for pay> ❑2
		c) Not working, but looking for a job ❑3
		d) Other (*e.g.* home duties, retired) ❑4
ST06Q01	**Q6**	**What is your father currently doing?** *(Please <tick> only one box.)*
		a) Working full-time <for pay> ❑1
		b) Working part-time <for pay> ❑2
		c) Not working, but looking for a job ❑3
		d) Other (*e.g.* home duties, retired) ❑4
ST07Q01	**Q7**	**What is your mother's main job?** (*e.g.* <school teacher, nurse, sales manager>)
		(If she is not working now, please tell us her last main job.)
		Please write in the <job title>________________________
	Q8	**What does your mother do in her main job?** (*e.g.* <teaches high school students, cares for patients, manages a sales team>)
		Please use a sentence to describe the kind of work she does or did in that job.
		____
ST09Q01	**Q9**	**What is your father's main job?** (*e.g.* <school teacher, carpenter, sales manager>)
		(If he is not working now, please tell us his last main job.)
		Please write in the <job title>________________________
	Q10	**What does your father do in his main job?** (*e.g.* <teaches high school students, builds houses, manages a sales team>)
		Please use a sentence to describe the kind of work he does or did in that job.
		____

ST11R01	**Q11**	**Which of the following did your mother complete at <school>?** *(Please <tick> as many boxes as apply.)*
		a) <ISCED level 3A> ☐1
		b) <ISCED level 3B, 3C> ☐1
		c) <ISCED level 2> ☐1
		d) <ISCED level 1> ☐1
		e) None of the above ☐1

	Q12	**Does your mother have any of the following qualifications?** *(Please <tick> as many boxes as apply.)*	*Yes*
ST12Q01		a) <ISCED 5A, 6>	☐1
ST12Q02		b) <ISCED 5B>	☐1
ST12Q03		c) <ISCED 4>	☐1

ST13R01	**Q13**	**Which of the following did your father complete at <school>?** *(Please <tick> as many boxes as apply.)*
		a) <ISCED level 3A> ☐1
		b) <ISCED level 3B, 3C> ☐1
		c) <ISCED level 2> ☐1
		d) <ISCED level 1> ☐1
		e) None of the above ☐1

	Q14	**Does your father have any of the following qualifications?** *(Please <tick> as many boxes as apply.)*	Yes
ST14Q01		a) <ISCED 5A, 6>	☐1
ST14Q02		b) <ISCED 5B>	☐1
ST14Q03		c) <ISCED 4>	☐1

	Q15a	**In what country were you and your parents born?** *(Please <tick> one answer per column.)*		
			<Country of test>	Other country
ST15Q01		You	☐1	☐2
ST15Q02		Mother	☐1	☐2
ST15Q03		Father	☐1	☐2

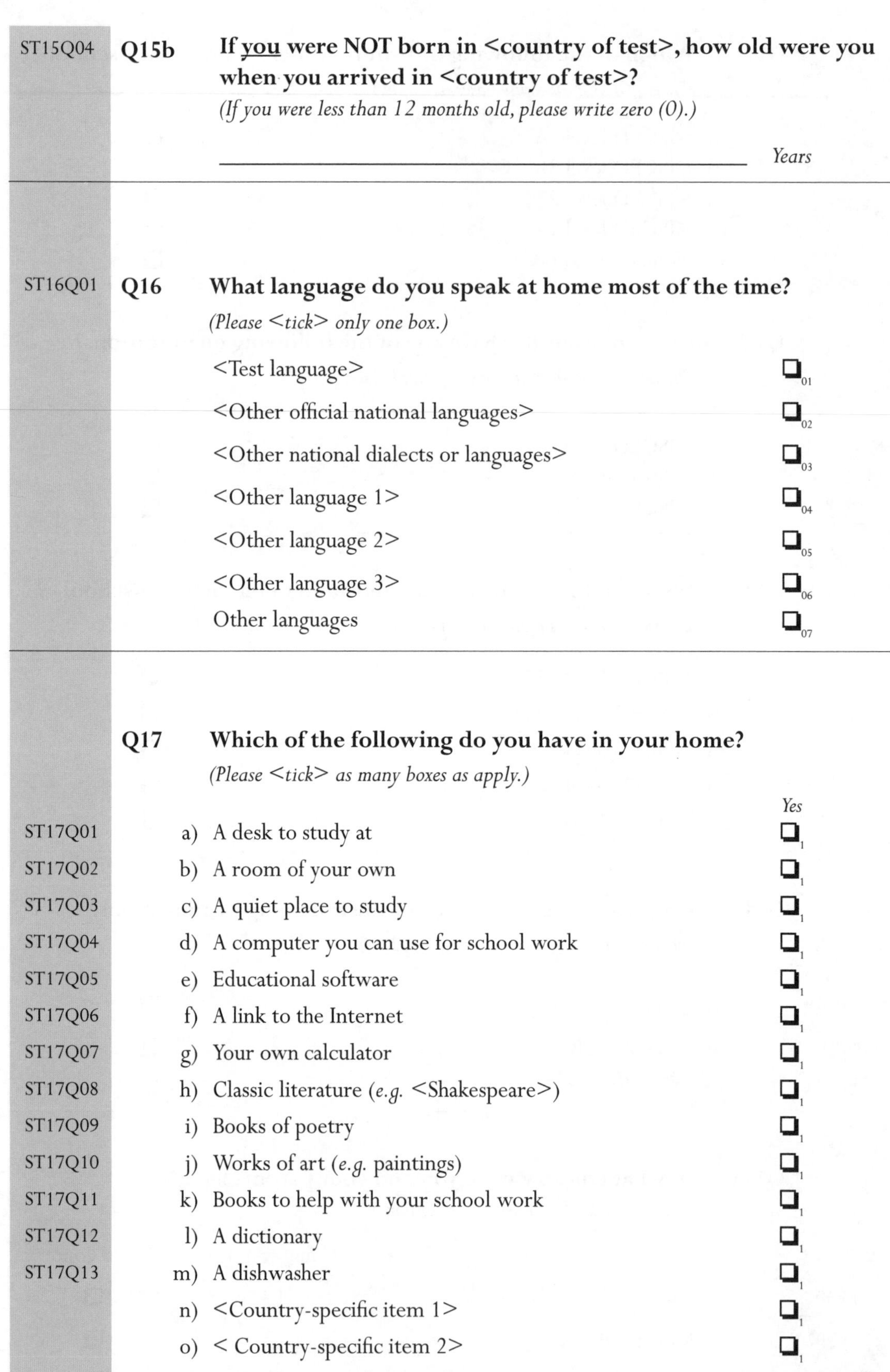

ST15Q04 **Q15b** **If <u>you</u> were NOT born in <country of test>, how old were you when you arrived in <country of test>?**

(If you were less than 12 months old, please write zero (0).)

____________________ *Years*

ST16Q01 **Q16** **What language do you speak at home most of the time?**

(Please <tick> only one box.)

<Test language>	☐ 01
<Other official national languages>	☐ 02
<Other national dialects or languages>	☐ 03
<Other language 1>	☐ 04
<Other language 2>	☐ 05
<Other language 3>	☐ 06
Other languages	☐ 07

Q17 **Which of the following do you have in your home?**

(Please <tick> as many boxes as apply.)

			Yes
ST17Q01	a)	A desk to study at	☐ 1
ST17Q02	b)	A room of your own	☐ 1
ST17Q03	c)	A quiet place to study	☐ 1
ST17Q04	d)	A computer you can use for school work	☐ 1
ST17Q05	e)	Educational software	☐ 1
ST17Q06	f)	A link to the Internet	☐ 1
ST17Q07	g)	Your own calculator	☐ 1
ST17Q08	h)	Classic literature (*e.g.* <Shakespeare>)	☐ 1
ST17Q09	i)	Books of poetry	☐ 1
ST17Q10	j)	Works of art (*e.g.* paintings)	☐ 1
ST17Q11	k)	Books to help with your school work	☐ 1
ST17Q12	l)	A dictionary	☐ 1
ST17Q13	m)	A dishwasher	☐ 1
	n)	<Country-specific item 1>	☐ 1
	o)	< Country-specific item 2>	☐ 1
	p)	< Country-specific item 3>	☐ 1

Q18 **How many of these do you have at your home?**
(Please <tick> only one box in each row.)

	None	One	Two	Three or more
a) <Cellular> phone	☐1	☐2	☐3	☐4
b) Television	☐1	☐2	☐3	☐4
c) Computer	☐1	☐2	☐3	☐4
d) Motor car	☐1	☐2	☐3	☐4
e) Bathroom	☐1	☐2	☐3	☐4

ST19Q01 **Q19** **How many books are there in your home?**
There are usually about <40 books per metre> of shelving. Do not include magazines, newspapers or your schoolbooks.

(Please <tick> only one box.)

0-10 books	☐1
11-25 books	☐2
26-100 books	☐3
101-200 books	☐4
201-500 books	☐5
More than 500 books	☐6

SECTION C: YOUR EDUCATION

ST20Q01 **Q20** **Did you attend <ISCED 0>?**

No	☐1
Yes, for one year or less	☐2
Yes, for more than one year	☐3

ST21Q01 **Q21** **How old were you when you started <ISCED 1>?**

_____________ Years

Q22 **Have you ever repeated a <grade>?**
(Please <tick> only one box on each row.)

		No, never	Yes, once	Yes, twice or more
ST22Q01	a) At <ISCED 1>	☐1	☐2	☐3
ST22Q02	b) At <ISCED 2>	☐1	☐2	☐3
ST22Q03	c) At <ISCED 3>	☐1	☐2	☐3

	Q23	Which of the following do you <u>expect</u> to complete? *(Please <tick> as many as apply.)*	
ST23Q01	a)	<ISCED level 2>	❑ 1
ST23Q02	b)	<ISCED level 3B or C>	❑ 1
ST23Q03	c)	<ISCED level 3A>	❑ 1
ST23Q04	d)	<ISCED level 4>	❑ 1
ST23Q05	e)	<ISCED level 5B>	❑ 1
ST23Q06	f)	<ISCED level 5A or 6>	❑ 1

Q24 *Thinking about what you have learned in school:*
To what extent do you agree with the following statements?
(Please <tick> only one box on each row.)

			Strongly agree	Agree	Disagree	Strongly disagree
ST24Q01	a)	School has done little to prepare me for adult life when I leave school.	❑ 1	❑ 2	❑ 3	❑ 4
ST24Q02	b)	School has been a waste of time.	❑ 1	❑ 2	❑ 3	❑ 4
ST24Q03	c)	School has helped give me confidence to make decisions.	❑ 1	❑ 2	❑ 3	❑ 4
ST24Q04	d)	School has taught me things which could be useful in a job.	❑ 1	❑ 2	❑ 3	❑ 4

SECTION D: YOUR SCHOOL

	Q25	Which of the following are reasons why you attend this school? *(Please <tick> as many as apply.)*	
ST25Q01	a)	This is the local school for students who live in this area.	❑ 1
ST25Q02	b)	This school is known to be a better school than others in the area.	❑ 1
ST25Q03	c)	This school offers specific study programmes.	❑ 1
ST25Q04	d)	This school has a particular religious philosophy.	❑ 1
ST25Q05	e)	Previously, family members attended this school.	❑ 1
ST25Q06	f)	Other reasons.	❑ 1

Q26 *Thinking about the teachers at your school:*

To what extent do you agree with the following statements?

(Please <tick> only one box in each row.)

		Strongly agree	Agree	Disagree	Strongly disagree
ST26Q01	a) Students get along well with most teachers.	☐1	☐2	☐3	☐4
ST26Q02	b) Most teachers are interested in students' well-being.	☐1	☐2	☐3	☐4
ST26Q03	c) Most of my teachers really listen to what I have to say.	☐1	☐2	☐3	☐4
ST26Q04	d) If I need extra help, I will receive it from my teachers.	☐1	☐2	☐3	☐4
ST26Q05	e) Most of my teachers treat me fairly.	☐1	☐2	☐3	☐4

Q27 **My school is a place where:**

(Please <tick> only one box in each row.)

		Strongly agree	Agree	Disagree	Strongly disagree
ST27Q01	a) I feel like an outsider (or left out of things).	☐1	☐2	☐3	☐4
ST27Q02	b) I make friends easily.	☐1	☐2	☐3	☐4
ST27Q03	c) I feel like I belong.	☐1	☐2	☐3	☐4
ST27Q04	d) I feel awkward and out of place.	☐1	☐2	☐3	☐4
ST27Q05	e) Other students seem to like me.	☐1	☐2	☐3	☐4
ST27Q06	f) I feel lonely.	☐1	☐2	☐3	☐4

ST28Q01 **Q28** **In the last two full weeks you were in school, how many times did you arrive late for school?**

(Please <tick> only one box)

None	☐1
One or two times	☐2
Three or four times	☐3
Five or more times	☐4

Q29 *The following question asks about the time you spend studying and doing different kinds of homework outside of your regular classes. This should include* ***all of your studying and homework****.*

On average, how many hours do you spend *each week* on the following?

When answering include time at the weekend too.

ST29Q01	a) Homework or other study set by your teachers	_____ hours per week
ST29Q02	b) <Remedial classes> at school	_____ hours per week
ST29Q03	c) <Enrichment classes> at school	_____ hours per week
ST29Q04	d) Work with a <tutor>	_____ hours per week
ST29Q05	e) Attending <out-of-school> classes	_____ hours per week
ST29Q06	f) Other study	_____ hours per week

SECTION E: LEARNING MATHEMATICS

Q30 *Thinking about your views on mathematics:*

To what extent do you agree with the following statements?

(Please <tick> only one box in each row.)

		Strongly agree	Agree	Disagree	Strongly disagree
ST30Q01	a) I enjoy reading about mathematics.	❑1	❑2	❑3	❑4
ST30Q02	b) Making an effort in mathematics is worth it because it will help me in the work that I want to do later on.	❑1	❑2	❑3	❑4
ST30Q03	c) I look forward to my mathematics lessons.	❑1	❑2	❑3	❑4
ST30Q04	d) I do mathematics because I enjoy it.	❑1	❑2	❑3	❑4
ST30Q05	e) Learning mathematics is worthwhile for me because it will improve my career <prospects, chances>.	❑1	❑2	❑3	❑4
ST30Q06	f) I am interested in the things I learn in mathematics.	❑1	❑2	❑3	❑4
ST30Q07	g) Mathematics is an important subject for me because I need it for what I want to study later on.	❑1	❑2	❑3	❑4
ST30Q08	h) I will learn many things in mathematics that will help me get a job.	❑1	❑2	❑3	❑4

Q31 How confident do you feel about having to do the following mathematics tasks?

(Please <tick> only one box in each row.)

		Very confident	Confident	Not very confident	Not at all confident
ST31Q01	a) Using a <train timetable> to work out how long it would take to get from one place to another.	❑1	❑2	❑3	❑4
ST31Q02	b) Calculating how much cheaper a TV would be after a 30% discount.	❑1	❑2	❑3	❑4
ST31Q03	c) Calculating how many square metres of tiles you need to cover a floor.	❑1	❑2	❑3	❑4
ST31Q04	d) Understanding graphs presented in newspapers.	❑1	❑2	❑3	❑4
ST31Q05	e) Solving an equation like 3x+5=17.	❑1	❑2	❑3	❑4
ST31Q06	f) Finding the actual distance between two places on a map with a 1:10 000 scale.	❑1	❑2	❑3	❑4
ST31Q07	g) Solving an equation like 2(x+3)=(x + 3)(x - 3).	❑1	❑2	❑3	❑4
ST31Q08	h) Calculating the petrol consumption rate of a car.	❑1	❑2	❑3	❑4

Q32 *Thinking about studying mathematics:*
To what extent do you agree with the following statements?

(Please <tick> only one box in each row.)

		Strongly agree	Agree	Disagree	Strongly disagree
ST32Q01	a) I often worry that it will be difficult for me in mathematics classes.	❑1	❑2	❑3	❑4
ST32Q02	b) I am just not good at mathematics.	❑1	❑2	❑3	❑4
ST32Q03	c) I get very tense when I have to do mathematics homework.	❑1	❑2	❑3	❑4
ST32Q04	d) I get good <marks> in mathematics.	❑1	❑2	❑3	❑4
ST32Q05	e) I get very nervous doing mathematics problems.	❑1	❑2	❑3	❑4
ST32Q06	f) I learn mathematics quickly.	❑1	❑2	❑3	❑4
ST32Q07	g) I have always believed that mathematics is one of my best subjects.	❑1	❑2	❑3	❑4
ST32Q08	h) I feel helpless when doing a mathematics problem.	❑1	❑2	❑3	❑4
ST32Q09	i) In my mathematics class, I understand even the most difficult work.	❑1	❑2	❑3	❑4
ST32Q10	j) I worry that I will get poor <marks> in mathematics.	❑1	❑2	❑3	❑4

Q33 *The following question asks about the time you spend studying and doing* ***mathematics*** *homework outside of your regular mathematics classes.*

On average, how much time do you spend *each week* on the following?

When answering include time at the weekend too.

ST33Q01	a) Homework or other study set by your mathematics teacher	______ *hours per week*
ST33Q02	b) <Remedial classes> in mathematics at school	______ *hours per week*
ST33Q03	c) <Enrichment classes> in mathematics at school	______ *hours per week*
ST33Q04	d) Work with a <mathematics tutor>	______ *hours per week*
ST33Q05	e) Attending <out-of-school> mathematics classes	______ *hours per week*
ST33Q06	f) Other mathematics activities (*e.g.* <mathematics competitions, mathematics club>)	______ *hours per week*

Q34 *There are different ways of studying mathematics.*

To what extent do you agree with the following statements?

(Please <tick> only one box in each row.)

		Strongly agree	Agree	Disagree	Strongly disagree
ST34Q01	a) When I study for a mathematics test, I try to work out what are the most important parts to learn.	❑1	❑2	❑3	❑4
ST34Q02	b) When I am solving mathematics problems, I often think of new ways to get the answer.	❑1	❑2	❑3	❑4
ST34Q03	c) When I study mathematics, I make myself check to see if I remember the work I have already done.	❑1	❑2	❑3	❑4
ST34Q04	d) When I study mathematics, I try to figure out which concepts I still have not understood properly.	❑1	❑2	❑3	❑4
ST34Q05	e) I think how the mathematics I have learnt can be used in everyday life.	❑1	❑2	❑3	❑4
ST34Q06	f) I go over some problems in mathematics so often that I feel as if I could solve them in my sleep.	❑1	❑2	❑3	❑4
ST34Q07	g) When I study for mathematics, I learn as much as I can off by heart.	❑1	❑2	❑3	❑4

		Strongly agree	Agree	Disagree	Strongly disagree
ST34Q08	h) I try to understand new concepts in mathematics by relating them to things I already know.	❑1	❑2	❑3	❑4
ST34Q09	i) In order to remember the method for solving a mathematics problem, I go through examples again and again.	❑1	❑2	❑3	❑4
ST34Q10	j) When I cannot understand something in mathematics, I always search for more information to clarify the problem.	❑1	❑2	❑3	❑4
ST34Q11	k) When I am solving a mathematics problem, I often think about how the solution might be applied to other interesting questions.	❑1	❑2	❑3	❑4
ST34Q12	l) When I study mathematics, I start by working out exactly what I need to learn.	❑1	❑2	❑3	❑4
ST34Q13	m) To learn mathematics, I try to remember every step in a procedure.	❑1	❑2	❑3	❑4
ST34Q14	n) When learning mathematics, I try to relate the work to things I have learnt in other subjects.	❑1	❑2	❑3	❑4

SECTION F: YOUR <MATHEMATICS> CLASSES

Q35a How many minutes, on average, are there in a <class period>?

Minutes in a *<class period>:* __________ *minutes*

ST35Q02 **Q35b In the last full week you were in school, how many <class periods> did you spend in <mathematics>?**

Number of **mathematics** *<class periods>:* __________ *<class periods>*

ST35Q03 **Q35c In the last full week you were in school, how many <class periods> did you have <in total>?**

Number of **ALL** *<class periods>*
(including your <mathematics> classes): __________ *<class periods>*

ST36Q01 **Q36 On average, about how many students attend your <mathematics> class?**

__________ *students*

Q37 *Thinking about your <mathematics> classes:* **To what extent do you agree with the following statements?**

(Please <tick> only one box in each row.)

		Strongly agree	Agree	Disagree	Strongly disagree
ST37Q01	a) I would like to be the best in my class in mathematics.	❑1	❑2	❑3	❑4
ST37Q02	b) In mathematics I enjoy working with other students in groups.	❑1	❑2	❑3	❑4
ST37Q03	c) I try very hard in mathematics because I want to do better in the exams than the others.	❑1	❑2	❑3	❑4
ST37Q04	d) When we work on a project in mathematics, I think that it is a good idea to combine the ideas of all the students in a group.	❑1	❑2	❑3	❑4
ST37Q05	e) I make a real effort in mathematics because I want to be one of the best.	❑1	❑2	❑3	❑4
ST37Q06	f) I do my best work in mathematics when I work with other students.	❑1	❑2	❑3	❑4
ST37Q07	g) In mathematics I always try to do better than the other students in my class.	❑1	❑2	❑3	❑4
ST37Q08	h) In mathematics, I enjoy helping others to work well in a group.	❑1	❑2	❑3	❑4
ST37Q09	i) In mathematics I learn most when I work with other students in my class.	❑1	❑2	❑3	❑4
ST37Q10	j) I do my best work in mathematics when I try to do better than others.	❑1	❑2	❑3	❑4

Q38 **How often do these things happen in your <mathematics> lessons?**

(Please <tick> only one box in each row.)

		Every lesson	Most lessons	Some lessons	Never or hardly ever
ST38Q01	a) The teacher shows an interest in every student's learning.	❑1	❑2	❑3	❑4
ST38Q02	b) Students don't listen to what the teacher says.	❑1	❑2	❑3	❑4
ST38Q03	c) The teacher gives extra help when students need it.	❑1	❑2	❑3	❑4

		Every lesson	Most lessons	Some lessons	Never or hardly ever
ST38Q04	d) Students work from books and other printed material.	❑1	❑2	❑3	❑4
ST38Q05	e) The teacher helps students with their learning.	❑1	❑2	❑3	❑4
ST38Q06	f) There is noise and disorder.	❑1	❑2	❑3	❑4
ST38Q07	g) The teacher continues teaching until the students understand.	❑1	❑2	❑3	❑4
ST38Q08	h) The teacher has to wait a long time for students to <quieten down>.	❑1	❑2	❑3	❑4
ST38Q09	i) Students cannot work well.	❑1	❑2	❑3	❑4
ST38Q10	j) The teacher gives students an opportunity to express opinions.	❑1	❑2	❑3	❑4
ST38Q11	k) Students don't start working for a long time after the lesson begins.	❑1	❑2	❑3	❑4

Variable name		
EC01Q01	**Q1**	**Did you ever miss two or more consecutive months of <ISCED 1>?** *(Please <tick> only one box.)* No, never ☐1 Yes, once ☐2 Yes, twice or more ☐3
EC02Q01	**Q2**	**Did you ever miss two or more consecutive months of <ISCED 2>** *(Please <tick> only one box.)* No, never ☐1 Yes, once ☐2 Yes, twice or more ☐3
EC03Q01	**Q3**	**Did you change schools when you were attending <ISCED 1>?** *(Please <tick> only one box.)* No, I attended all of <ISCED 1> at the same school. ☐1 Yes, I changed schools once. ☐2 Yes, I changed schools twice or more. ☐3
EC04Q01	**Q4**	**Did you change schools when you were attending <ISCED 2>?** *(Please <tick> only one box.)* No, I attended all of <ISCED 2> at the same school. ☐1 Yes, I changed schools once. ☐2 Yes, I changed schools twice or more. ☐3
EC05Q01	**Q5**	**Have you changed your <study programme> since you started <grade X>?** *(<example>)* Yes ☐1 No ☐2

EC06Q01 EC06Q02 **Q6 What type of <mathematics class> are you taking?**

(Please <tick> only one box.)

<high level>	❑1
<medium level>	❑2
<basic level>	❑3

EC07Q01 **<Q7 In your last school report, what was your mark in mathematics?**

________ >

An alternative form of the question – see below – may be used. If the first version is chosen, National Project Managers will be required to indicate the substantive meaning of the mark entered. For example, C = Pass, D = Fail, or 50 = Pass, or 6 = Pass.

EC07Q02 **<Q7 In your last school report, how did your <mark> in mathematics compare with the <pass mark>?**

(Please <tick> only one box.)

At or above the <pass mark>	❑1
Below the <pass mark>	❑2 >

EC08Q01 **Q8 What kind of job do you expect to have when you are about 30 years old?**

Write the job title. ________________________________

APPENDIX 4 ■ INFORMATION COMMUNICATION TECHNOLOGY (ICT) QUESTIONNAIRE

Variable name

The following questions ask about computers:
This does not include calculators or games consoles like a <Sony PlayStation™>.

Q1 Is there a computer available for you to use at any of these places?

(Please <tick> one box on each row.)

Variable name		Yes	No
IC01Q01	a) At home	❑1	❑2
IC01Q02	b) At school	❑1	❑2
IC01Q03	c) At other places	❑1	❑2

IC02Q01 **Q2 Have you ever used a computer?**

Yes	No
❑1	❑2

If you use a computer in any setting, please continue.
If you do not, please stop here. <Instructions>

IC03Q01 **Q3 How long have you been using computers?**

(Please tick only one box.)

Less than one year.	❑1
One to three years.	❑2
Three to five years.	❑3
More than five years.	❑4

Q4 How often do you use a computer at these places?

(Please <tick> one box on each row.)

Variable name		Almost every day	A few times each week	Between once a week and once a month	Less than once a month	Never
IC04Q01	a) At home	❑1	❑2	❑3	❑4	❑5
IC04Q02	b) At school	❑1	❑2	❑3	❑4	❑5
IC04Q03	c) At other places	❑1	❑2	❑3	❑4	❑5

Q5 **How often do you use:**

(Please <tick> one box on each row.)

		Almost every day	A few times each week	Between once a week and once a month	Less than once a month	Never
IC05Q02	a) The Internet to look up information about people, things, or ideas?	❑1	❑2	❑3	❑4	❑5
IC05Q03	b) Games on a computer?	❑1	❑2	❑3	❑4	❑5
IC05Q04	c) Word processing (*e.g.* <Microsoft® Word® or WordPerfect®>)?	❑1	❑2	❑3	❑4	❑5
IC05Q05	d) The Internet to collaborate with a group or team?	❑1	❑2	❑3	❑4	❑5
IC05Q06	e) Spreadsheets (*e.g.* <IBM® Lotus 1-2-3® or Microsoft® Excel®>)?	❑1	❑2	❑3	❑4	❑5
IC05Q07	f) The Internet to download software (including games)?	❑1	❑2	❑3	❑4	❑5
IC05Q08	g) Drawing, painting or graphics programs on a computer?	❑1	❑2	❑3	❑4	❑5
IC05Q09	h) Educational software such as mathematics programs?	❑1	❑2	❑3	❑4	❑5
IC05Q10	i) The computer to help you learn school material?	❑1	❑2	❑3	❑4	❑5
IC05Q11	j) The Internet to download music?	❑1	❑2	❑3	❑4	❑5
IC05Q12	k) The computer for programming?	❑1	❑2	❑3	❑4	❑5
	l) A computer for electronic communication (*e.g.* e-mail or "chat rooms")?	❑1	❑2	❑3	❑4	❑5

Q6 **How well can you do each of these tasks on a computer?**

(Please <tick> one box on each row.)

		I can do this very well by myself.	I can do this with help from someone.	I know what this means but I cannot do it.	I don't know what this means.
IC06Q01	a) Start a computer game.	❑1	❑2	❑3	❑4
IC06Q02	b) Use software to find and get rid of computer viruses.	❑1	❑2	❑3	❑4
IC06Q03	c) Open a file.	❑1	❑2	❑3	❑4
IC06Q04	d) Create/edit a document.	❑1	❑2	❑3	❑4

...

		I can do this very well by myself.	I can do this with help from someone.	I know what this means but I cannot do it.	I don't know what this means.
IC06Q05	e) Scroll a document up and down a screen.	☐1	☐2	☐3	☐4
IC06Q06	f) Use a database to produce a list of addresses.	☐1	☐2	☐3	☐4
IC06Q07	g) Copy a file from a floppy disk.	☐1	☐2	☐3	☐4
IC06Q08	h) Save a computer document or file.	☐1	☐2	☐3	☐4
IC06Q09	i) Print a computer document or file.	☐1	☐2	☐3	☐4
IC06Q10	j) Delete a computer document or file.	☐1	☐2	☐3	☐4
IC06Q11	k) Move files from one place to another on a computer.	☐1	☐2	☐3	☐4
IC06Q12	l) Get on to the Internet.	☐1	☐2	☐3	☐4
IC06Q13	m) Copy or download files from the Internet.	☐1	☐2	☐3	☐4
IC06Q14	n) Attach a file to an e-mail message.	☐1	☐2	☐3	☐4
IC06Q15	o) Create a computer program (*e.g.* in <Logo, Pascal, Basic>).	☐1	☐2	☐3	☐4
IC06Q16	p) Use a spreadsheet to plot a graph.	☐1	☐2	☐3	☐4
IC06Q17	q) Create a presentation (*e.g.* using <Microsoft® PowerPoint®>).	☐1	☐2	☐3	☐4
IC06Q18	r) Play computer games.	☐1	☐2	☐3	☐4
IC06Q19	s) Download music from the Internet.	☐1	☐2	☐3	☐4
IC06Q20	t) Create a multi-media presentation (with sound, pictures, video).	☐1	☐2	☐3	☐4
IC06Q21	u) Draw pictures using a mouse.	☐1	☐2	☐3	☐4
IC06Q22	v) Write and send e-mails.	☐1	☐2	☐3	☐4
IC06Q23	w) Construct a web page.	☐1	☐2	☐3	☐4

Q7 *Thinking about your experience with computers:* **To what extent do you agree with the following statements?**

(Please <tick> one box on each row.)

		Strongly agree	Agree	Disagree	Strongly disagree
IC07Q01	a) It is very important to me to work with a computer.	☐1	☐2	☐3	☐4
IC07Q02	b) I think playing or working with a computer is really fun.	☐1	☐2	☐3	☐4

...

		Strongly agree	Agree	Disagree	Strongly disagree
IC07Q03	c) I use a computer because I am very interested.	❑1	❑2	❑3	❑4
IC07Q04	d) I lose track of time when I am working with the computer.	❑1	❑2	❑3	❑4

IC08Q01 **Q8** **Who taught you most about how to use COMPUTERS?**

(Please <tick> only one box.)

My school.	❑1
My friends.	❑2
My family.	❑3
I taught myself.	❑4
Others.	❑5

IC09Q01 **Q9** **Who taught you most about how to use the INTERNET?**

(Please <tick> only one box.)

I don't know how to use the Internet.	❑1
My school.	❑2
My friends.	❑3
My family.	❑4
I taught myself.	❑5
Others.	❑6

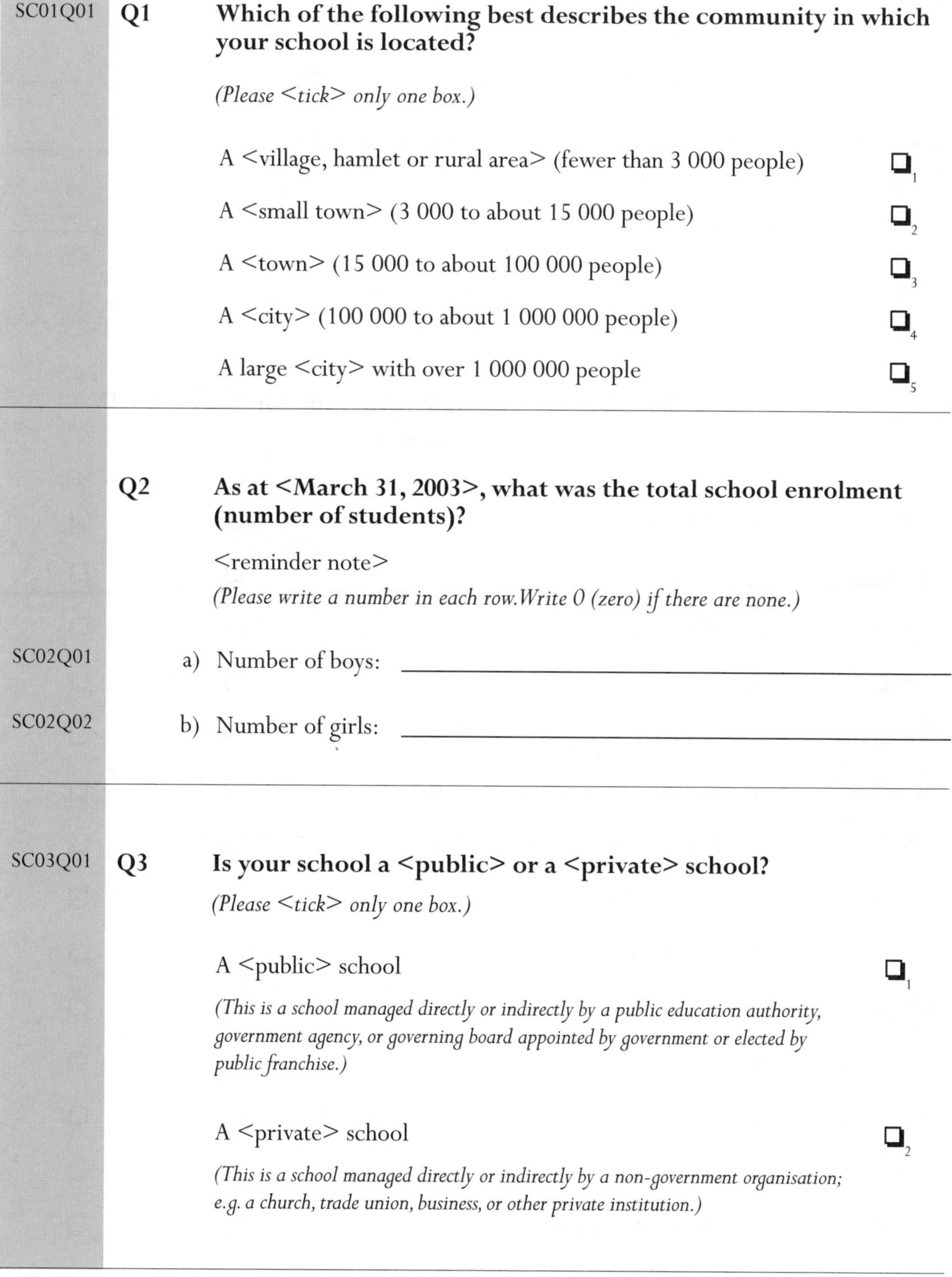

SC01Q01 **Q1** **Which of the following best describes the community in which your school is located?**

(Please <tick> only one box.)

A <village, hamlet or rural area> (fewer than 3 000 people)	☐ 1
A <small town> (3 000 to about 15 000 people)	☐ 2
A <town> (15 000 to about 100 000 people)	☐ 3
A <city> (100 000 to about 1 000 000 people)	☐ 4
A large <city> with over 1 000 000 people	☐ 5

Q2 **As at <March 31, 2003>, what was the total school enrolment (number of students)?**

<reminder note>

(Please write a number in each row. Write 0 (zero) if there are none.)

SC02Q01 a) Number of boys: ____________________

SC02Q02 b) Number of girls: ____________________

SC03Q01 **Q3** **Is your school a <public> or a <private> school?**

(Please <tick> only one box.)

A <public> school ☐ 1

(This is a school managed directly or indirectly by a public education authority, government agency, or governing board appointed by government or elected by public franchise.)

A <private> school ☐ 2

(This is a school managed directly or indirectly by a non-government organisation; e.g. a church, trade union, business, or other private institution.)

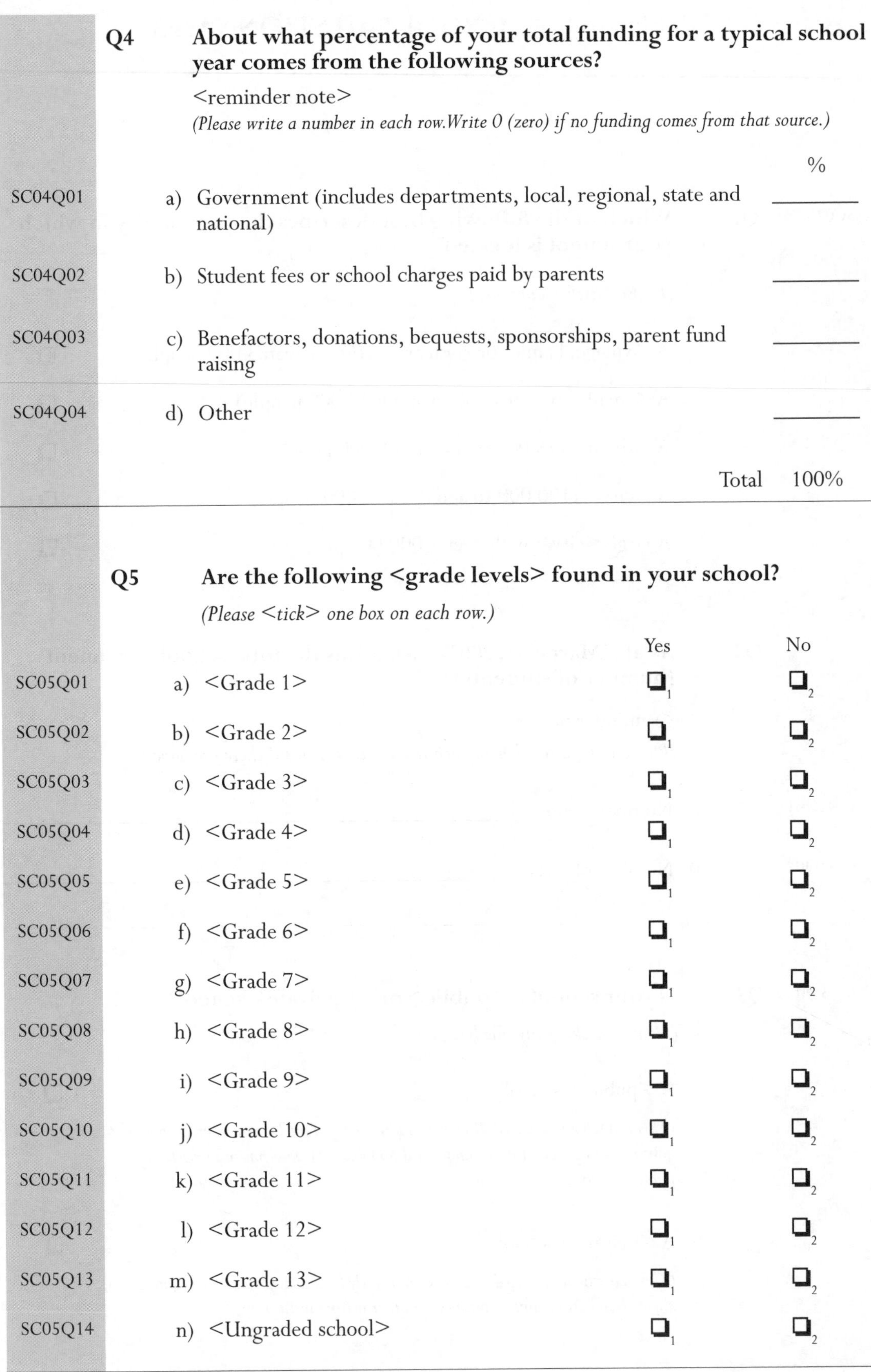

Q4 About what percentage of your total funding for a typical school year comes from the following sources?

<reminder note>

(Please write a number in each row. Write 0 (zero) if no funding comes from that source.)

		%
SC04Q01	a) Government (includes departments, local, regional, state and national)	______
SC04Q02	b) Student fees or school charges paid by parents	______
SC04Q03	c) Benefactors, donations, bequests, sponsorships, parent fund raising	______
SC04Q04	d) Other	______
	Total	100%

Q5 Are the following <grade levels> found in your school?

(Please <tick> one box on each row.)

		Yes	No
SC05Q01	a) <Grade 1>	☐1	☐2
SC05Q02	b) <Grade 2>	☐1	☐2
SC05Q03	c) <Grade 3>	☐1	☐2
SC05Q04	d) <Grade 4>	☐1	☐2
SC05Q05	e) <Grade 5>	☐1	☐2
SC05Q06	f) <Grade 6>	☐1	☐2
SC05Q07	g) <Grade 7>	☐1	☐2
SC05Q08	h) <Grade 8>	☐1	☐2
SC05Q09	i) <Grade 9>	☐1	☐2
SC05Q10	j) <Grade 10>	☐1	☐2
SC05Q11	k) <Grade 11>	☐1	☐2
SC05Q12	l) <Grade 12>	☐1	☐2
SC05Q13	m) <Grade 13>	☐1	☐2
SC05Q14	n) <Ungraded school>	☐1	☐2

Q6 **About what percentage of students in your school repeated a <grade>, at these <ISCED levels>, last <academic> year?**

(Please write a number in each row. Write 0 (zero) if nobody repeated a <grade>. <Tick> the not applicable box if the <ISCED level> does not appear in your school.)

		%	Not applicable
SC06Q01	The approximate percentage of students repeating a <grade> at <ISCEDC 2> in this school last year was:	______	❑997
SC06Q02	The approximate percentage of students repeating a <grade> at <ISCEDC 3> in this school last year was:	______	❑997

The following is a list of programmes that may be in your school and that are available to *15-year-old* *students.*

- <Programme 1>
- <Programme 2>
- <Programme 3>
- <Programme 4>

Q7 **For each of these programmes in your school:**

<reminder note>

(Please write a number in each row for each programme in your school.)

	<Prog 1>	<Prog 2>	<Prog 3>	<Prog 4>
a) How many <instructional> weeks are in the school year?	______	______	______	______
b) How many hours in total are there in the school week? (include lunch breaks, <study hall time>, and after school activities)	______	______	______	______
c) How many hours for <instruction> are there in the school week? (exclude lunch breaks and after school activities)	______	______	______	______

	Q8	Is your school's capacity to provide instruction hindered by a shortage or inadequacy of any of the following?				
		(Please <tick> one box in each row.)	Not at all	Very little	To some extent	A lot
SC08Q01	a)	Availability of qualified mathematics teachers	☐1	☐2	☐3	☐4
SC08Q02	b)	Availability of qualified science teachers	☐1	☐2	☐3	☐4
SC08Q03	c)	Availability of qualified <test language> teachers	☐1	☐2	☐3	☐4
SC08Q04	d)	Availability of qualified <other national language> teachers	☐1	☐2	☐3	☐4
SC08Q05	e)	Availability of qualified foreign language teachers	☐1	☐2	☐3	☐4
SC08Q06	f)	Availability of experienced teachers	☐1	☐2	☐3	☐4
SC08Q07	g)	Availability of <emergency/replacement> teachers	☐1	☐2	☐3	☐4
SC08Q08	h)	Availability of support personnel	☐1	☐2	☐3	☐4
SC08Q09	i)	Instructional materials (*e.g.* textbooks)	☐1	☐2	☐3	☐4
SC08Q10	j)	Budget for supplies (*e.g.* paper, pencils)	☐1	☐2	☐3	☐4
SC08Q11	k)	School buildings and grounds	☐1	☐2	☐3	☐4
SC08Q12	l)	Heating/cooling and lighting systems	☐1	☐2	☐3	☐4
SC08Q13	m)	Instructional space (*e.g.* classrooms)	☐1	☐2	☐3	☐4
SC08Q14	n)	Special equipment for disabled students	☐1	☐2	☐3	☐4
SC08Q15	o)	Computers for instruction	☐1	☐2	☐3	☐4
SC08Q16	p)	Computer software for instruction	☐1	☐2	☐3	☐4
SC08Q17	q)	Calculators for instruction	☐1	☐2	☐3	☐4
SC08Q18	r)	Library materials	☐1	☐2	☐3	☐4
SC08Q19	s)	Audio-visual resources	☐1	☐2	☐3	☐4
SC08Q20	t)	Science laboratory equipment and materials	☐1	☐2	☐3	☐4

Q9 **In your school, about how many computers are:**
<reminder note>

(Please write a number in each row. Write 0 (zero) if there are none.)

		Number
SC09Q01	a) In the school altogether?	_______
SC09Q02	b) Available to 15-year-old students?	_______
SC09Q03	c) Available only to teachers?	_______
SC09Q04	d) Available only to administrative staff?	_______
SC09Q05	e) Connected to the Internet/World Wide Web?	_______
SC09Q06	f) Connected to a local area network (LAN)?	_______

Q10 **How much consideration is given to the following factors when students are admitted to your school?**

(Please <tick> one box in each row.)

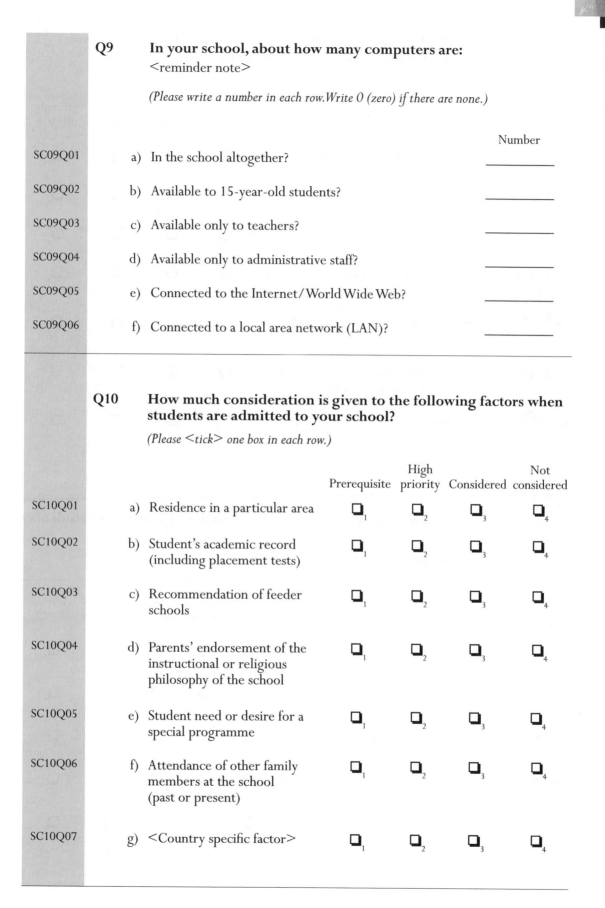

		Prerequisite	High priority	Considered	Not considered
SC10Q01	a) Residence in a particular area	❑1	❑2	❑3	❑4
SC10Q02	b) Student's academic record (including placement tests)	❑1	❑2	❑3	❑4
SC10Q03	c) Recommendation of feeder schools	❑1	❑2	❑3	❑4
SC10Q04	d) Parents' endorsement of the instructional or religious philosophy of the school	❑1	❑2	❑3	❑4
SC10Q05	e) Student need or desire for a special programme	❑1	❑2	❑3	❑4
SC10Q06	f) Attendance of other family members at the school (past or present)	❑1	❑2	❑3	❑4
SC10Q07	g) <Country specific factor>	❑1	❑2	❑3	❑4

Q11 Think about the students in your school. How much do you agree with the following statements?

(Please <tick> one box in each row.)

		Strongly agree	Agree	Disagree	Strongly disagree
SC11Q01	a) Students enjoy being in school.	❑1	❑2	❑3	❑4
SC11Q02	b) Students work with enthusiasm.	❑1	❑2	❑3	❑4
SC11Q03	c) Students take pride in this school.	❑1	❑2	❑3	❑4
SC11Q04	d) Students value academic achievement.	❑1	❑2	❑3	❑4
SC11Q05	e) Students are cooperative and respectful.	❑1	❑2	❑3	❑4
SC11Q06	f) Students value the education they can receive in this school.	❑1	❑2	❑3	❑4
SC11Q07	g) Students do their best to learn as much as possible.	❑1	❑2	❑3	❑4

Q12 Generally, in your school, how often are <15-year-old> students assessed using:

(Please <tick> only one box in each row.)

		Never	1 to 2 times a year	3 to 5 times a year	Monthly	More than once a month
SC12Q01	a) Standardised tests?	❑1	❑2	❑3	❑4	❑5
SC12Q02	b) Teacher-developed tests?	❑1	❑2	❑3	❑4	❑5
SC12Q03	c) Teachers' judgmental ratings?	❑1	❑2	❑3	❑4	❑5
SC12Q04	d) Student <portfolios>?	❑1	❑2	❑3	❑4	❑5
SC12Q05	e) Student assignments/ projects/homework?	❑1	❑2	❑3	❑4	❑5

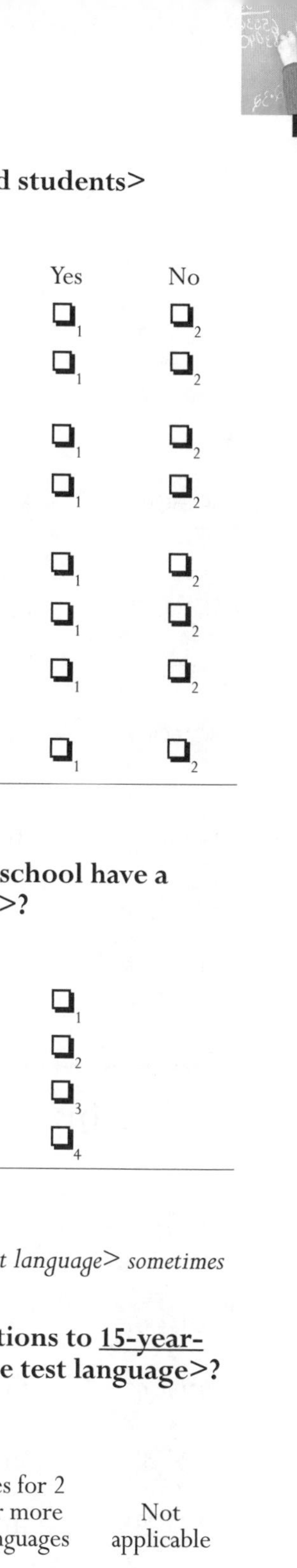

Q13 In your school, are assessments of <15-year-old students> used for any of the following purposes?

(Please <tick> only one box in each row.)

		Yes	No
SC13Q01	a) To inform parents about their child's progress.	❑1	❑2
SC13Q02	b) To make decisions about students' retention or promotion.	❑1	❑2
SC13Q03	c) To group students for instructional purposes.	❑1	❑2
SC13Q04	d) To compare the school to <district or national> performance.	❑1	❑2
SC13Q05	e) To monitor the school's progress from year to year.	❑1	❑2
SC13Q06	f) To make judgements about teachers' effectiveness.	❑1	❑2
SC13Q07	g) To identify aspects of instruction or the curriculum that could be improved.	❑1	❑2
SC13Q08	h) To compare the school with other schools.	❑1	❑2

Q14 About how many 15-year-old students in your school have a <first language> that is not <the test language>?

(Please <tick> only one box.)

SC14Q01	a) 40% or more	❑1
SC14Q02	b) 20% or more but less than 40%	❑2
SC14Q03	c) 10% or more but less than 20%	❑3
SC14Q04	d) Less than 10%	❑4

Q15 *Schools with students whose <first language> is not <the test language> sometimes offer specific language options to these students.*

Does your school offer any of the following options to <u>15-year-old</u> students whose <first language> is not <the test language>?

(Please <tick> one box in each row.)

		No, not for any languages	Yes for one language	Yes for 2 or more languages	Not applicable
SC15Q01	a) Instruction in their language is offered as a separate subject.	❑1	❑2	❑3	❑4
SC15Q02	b) Instruction in other parts of the curriculum is offered in their language.	❑1	❑2	❑3	❑4

Q16 *Schools sometimes organise instruction differently for students with different abilities and interests in mathematics.*

Which of the following options describe what your school does for 15-year-old students in mathematics classes?

(Please <tick> one box in each row.)

		For all classes	For some classes	Not for any classes
SC16Q01	a) Mathematics classes study similar content, but at different levels of difficulty.	❑1	❑2	❑3
SC16Q02	b) Different classes study different content or sets of mathematics topics that have different levels of difficulty.	❑1	❑2	❑3
SC16Q03	c) Students are grouped by ability within their mathematics classes.	❑1	❑2	❑3
SC16Q04	d) In mathematics classes, teachers use a pedagogy suitable for <students with heterogeneous abilities> (*i.e.* students are not grouped by ability).	❑1	❑2	❑3

Q17 **In your school, do any of the following activities to promote engagement with mathematics occur?**

(Please <tick> one box in each row)

		Yes	No
SC17Q01	a) <Enrichment mathematics>	❑1	❑2
SC17Q02	b) <Remedial mathematics>	❑1	❑2
SC17Q03	c) <Mathematics competitions>	❑1	❑2
SC17Q04	d) <Mathematics clubs>	❑1	❑2
SC17Q05	e) <Computer clubs> (specifically related to mathematics)	❑1	❑2

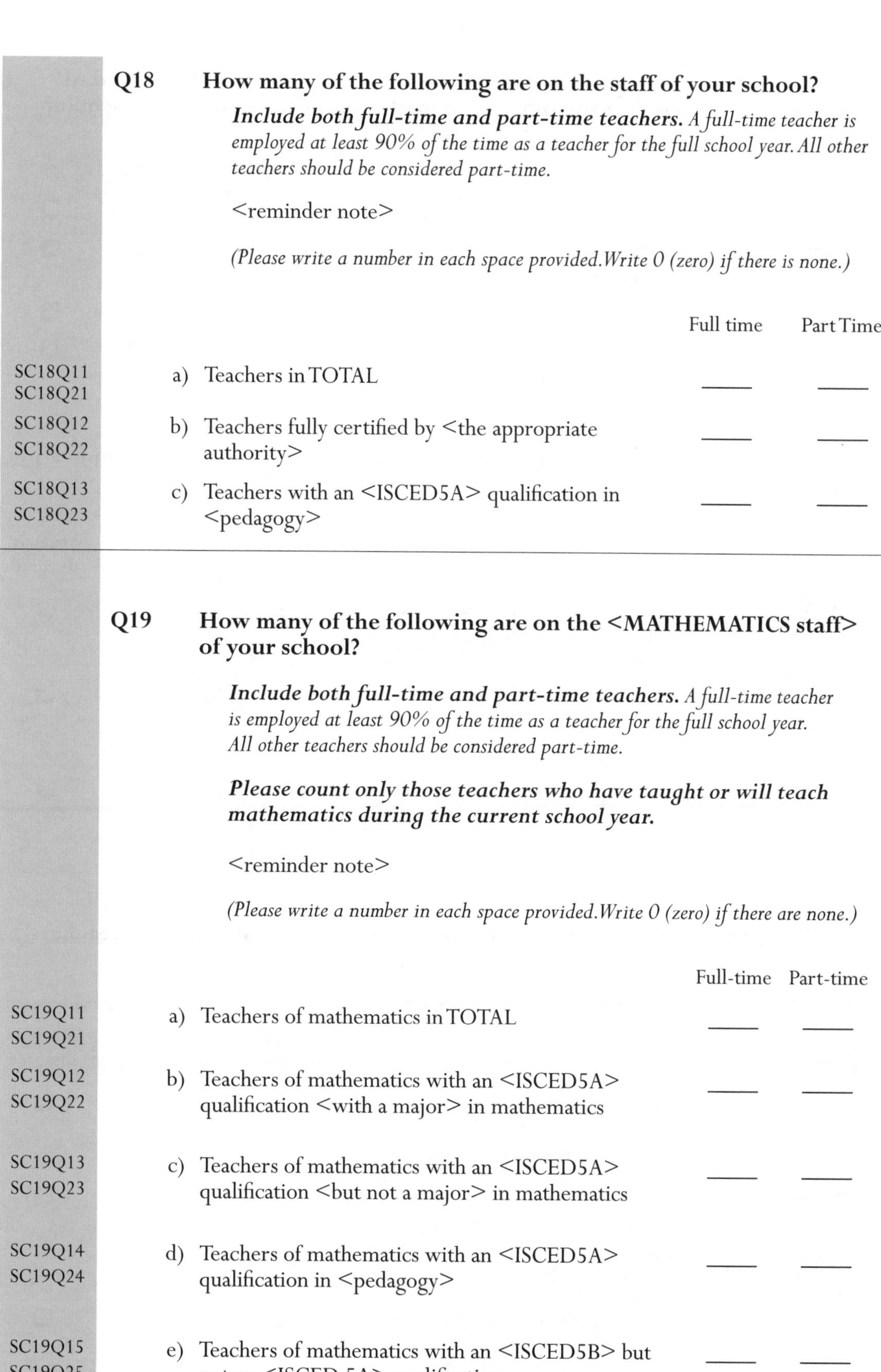

Q18 How many of the following are on the staff of your school?

Include both full-time and part-time teachers. *A full-time teacher is employed at least 90% of the time as a teacher for the full school year. All other teachers should be considered part-time.*

<reminder note>

(Please write a number in each space provided. Write 0 (zero) if there is none.)

		Full time	Part Time
SC18Q11 SC18Q21	a) Teachers in TOTAL	____	____
SC18Q12 SC18Q22	b) Teachers fully certified by <the appropriate authority>	____	____
SC18Q13 SC18Q23	c) Teachers with an <ISCED5A> qualification in <pedagogy>	____	____

Q19 How many of the following are on the <MATHEMATICS staff> of your school?

Include both full-time and part-time teachers. *A full-time teacher is employed at least 90% of the time as a teacher for the full school year. All other teachers should be considered part-time.*

Please count only those teachers who have taught or will teach mathematics during the current school year.

<reminder note>

(Please write a number in each space provided. Write 0 (zero) if there are none.)

		Full-time	Part-time
SC19Q11 SC19Q21	a) Teachers of mathematics in TOTAL	____	____
SC19Q12 SC19Q22	b) Teachers of mathematics with an <ISCED5A> qualification <with a major> in mathematics	____	____
SC19Q13 SC19Q23	c) Teachers of mathematics with an <ISCED5A> qualification <but not a major> in mathematics	____	____
SC19Q14 SC19Q24	d) Teachers of mathematics with an <ISCED5A> qualification in <pedagogy>	____	____
SC19Q15 SC19Q25	e) Teachers of mathematics with an <ISCED5B> but not an <ISCED 5A> qualification	____	____

	Q20	**During the last year, have any of the following been used to monitor the practice of mathematics teachers at your school?**		
		(Please <tick> one box in each row.)	Yes	No
SC20Q01	a)	Tests or assessments of student achievement	❑1	❑2
SC20Q02	b)	Teacher peer review (of lesson plans, assessment instruments, lessons)	❑1	❑2
SC20Q03	c)	Principal or senior staff observations of lessons	❑1	❑2
SC20Q04	d)	Observation of classes by inspectors or other persons external to the school	❑1	❑2

	Q21	**How much do you agree with these statements about <u>innovation</u> in your school?**				
		(Please <tick> one box in each row.)	Strongly agree	Agree	Disagree	Strongly disagree
SC21Q01	a)	Mathematics teachers are interested in trying new methods and teaching practices.	❑1	❑2	❑3	❑4
SC21Q02	b)	There is a preference among mathematics teachers to stay with well-known methods and practices.	❑1	❑2	❑3	❑4
SC21Q03	c)	There are frequent disagreements between "innovative" and "traditional" mathematics teachers.	❑1	❑2	❑3	❑4

	Q22	**How much do you agree with these statements about <u>teachers' expectations</u> in your school?**				
		(Please <tick> one box in each row.)	Strongly agree	Agree	Disagree	Strongly disagree
SC22Q01	a)	There is consensus among mathematics teachers that academic achievement must be kept as high as possible.	❑1	❑2	❑3	❑4
SC22Q02	b)	There is consensus among mathematics teachers that it is best to adapt academic standards to the students' level and needs.	❑1	❑2	❑3	❑4
SC22Q03	c)	There are frequent disagreements between mathematics teachers who consider each other to be "too demanding" or "too lax".	❑1	❑2	❑3	❑4

			Strongly agree	Agree	Disagree	Strongly disagree
	Q23	**How much do you agree with these statements about <u>teaching goals</u> in your school?** *(Please <tick> one box in each row.)*				
SC23Q01	a)	There is consensus among mathematics teachers that the social and emotional development of the student is as important as their acquisition of mathematical skills and knowledge in mathematics classes.	☐1	☐2	☐3	☐4
SC23Q02	b)	There is consensus among mathematics teachers that the development of mathematical skills and knowledge in students is the most important objective in mathematics classes.	☐1	☐2	☐3	☐4
SC23Q03	c)	There are frequent disagreements between mathematics teachers who consider each other as "too focused on skill acquisition" or "too focused on the affective development" of the student.	☐1	☐2	☐3	☐4

			Strongly agree	Agree	Disagree	Strongly disagree
	Q24	**Think about the teachers in your school. How much do you agree with the following statements?** *(Please <tick> one box in each row.)*				
SC24Q01	a)	The morale of teachers in this school is high.	☐1	☐2	☐3	☐4
SC24Q02	b)	Teachers work with enthusiasm.	☐1	☐2	☐3	☐4
SC24Q03	c)	Teachers take pride in this school.	☐1	☐2	☐3	☐4
SC24Q04	d)	Teachers value academic achievement.	☐1	☐2	☐3	☐4

Q25 In your school, to what extent is the learning of students hindered by:

(Please <tick> one box in each row.)

		Not at all	Very little	To some extent	A lot
SC25Q01	a) Teachers' low expectations of students?	❑1	❑2	❑3	❑4
SC25Q02	b) Student absenteeism?	❑1	❑2	❑3	❑4
SC25Q03	c) Poor student-teacher relations?	❑1	❑2	❑3	❑4
SC25Q04	d) Disruption of classes by students?	❑1	❑2	❑3	❑4
SC25Q05	e) Teachers not meeting individual students' needs?	❑1	❑2	❑3	❑4
SC25Q06	f) Teacher absenteeism?	❑1	❑2	❑3	❑4
SC25Q07	g) Students skipping classes?	❑1	❑2	❑3	❑4
SC25Q08	h) Students lacking respect for teachers?	❑1	❑2	❑3	❑4
SC25Q09	i) Staff resisting change?	❑1	❑2	❑3	❑4
SC25Q10	j) Student use of alcohol or illegal drugs?	❑1	❑2	❑3	❑4
SC25Q11	k) Teachers being too strict with students?	❑1	❑2	❑3	❑4
SC25Q12	l) Students intimidating or bullying other students?	❑1	❑2	❑3	❑4
SC25Q13	m) Students not being encouraged to achieve their full potential?	❑1	❑2	❑3	❑4

Q26 In your school, who has the main responsibility for:

(Please <tick> as many boxes as appropriate in each row.)

		Not a main responsibility of the school	School's <governing board>	Principal	<Department Head>	Teacher(s)
SC26Q01	a) Selecting teachers for hire?	❑1	❑1	❑1	❑1	❑1
SC26Q02	b) Firing teachers?	❑1	❑1	❑1	❑1	❑1
SC26Q03	c) Establishing teachers' starting salaries?	❑1	❑1	❑1	❑1	❑1
SC26Q04	d) Determining teachers' salary increases?	❑1	❑1	❑1	❑1	❑1
SC26Q05	e) Formulating the school budget?	❑1	❑1	❑1	❑1	❑1
SC26Q06	f) Deciding on budget allocations within the school?	❑1	❑1	❑1	❑1	❑1

...

		Not a main responsibility of the school	School's <governing board>	Principal	<Department Head>	Teacher(s)
SC26Q07	g) Establishing student disciplinary policies?	❑1	❑1	❑1	❑1	❑1
SC26Q08	h) Establishing student assessment policies?	❑1	❑1	❑1	❑1	❑1
SC26Q09	i) Approving students for admittance to the school?	❑1	❑1	❑1	❑1	❑1
SC26Q10	j) Choosing which textbooks are used?	❑1	❑1	❑1	❑1	❑1
SC26Q11	k) Determining course content?	❑1	❑1	❑1	❑1	❑1
SC26Q12	l) Deciding which courses are offered?	❑1	❑1	❑1	❑1	❑1

Q27 In your school, which of the following <bodies> exert a direct influence on decision making about staffing, budgeting, instructional content and assessment practises?

(Please <tick> as many boxes as apply.)

		Area of influence:			
		Staffing	Budgeting	Instructional content	Assessment practises
SC27Q01	a) Regional or national education authorities (*e.g.* inspectorates)	❑1	❑1	❑1	❑1
SC27Q02	b) The school's <governing board>	❑1	❑1	❑1	❑1
SC27Q03	c) Employers	❑1	❑1	❑1	❑1
SC27Q04	d) Parent groups	❑1	❑1	❑1	❑1
SC27Q05	e) Teacher groups (*e.g.* staff association, curriculum committees, trade union)	❑1	❑1	❑1	❑1
SC27Q06	f) Student groups (*e.g.* student association, youth organisation)	❑1	❑1	❑1	❑1
SC27Q07	g) External examination boards	❑1	❑1	❑1	❑1

COUNTRY (1) Country ID

Format: A3 Columns: 1-3

008	Albania
032	Argentina
036	Australia
040	Austria
056	Belgium
076	Brazil
100	Bulgaria
124	Canada
152	Chile
203	Czech Republic
208	Denmark
246	Finland
250	France
276	Germany
300	Greece
344	Hong Kong-China
348	Hungary
352	Iceland
360	Indonesia
372	Ireland
376	Israel
380	Italy
392	Japan
410	Korea
428	Latvia
438	Liechtenstein
442	Luxembourg
446	Macao-China
484	Mexico
528	Netherlands
554	New Zealand
578	Norway
604	Peru
616	Poland
620	Portugal
643	Russian Federation
703	Slovakia
724	Spain
752	Sweden
756	Switzerland
764	Thailand
788	Tunisia
792	Turkey
807	Macedonia
826	United Kingdom
840	United States
858	Uruguay
891	Serbia

CNT (2) Country Alphanumeric ISO Code

Format: A3 Columns: 4-6

SUBNATIO (3) Adjudicated sub-region

Format: A4 Columns: 7-10

0360	Australia
0400	Austria
0560	Belgium
0760	Brazil
1240	Canada
2030	Czech Republic
2080	Denmark
2460	Finland
2500	France
2760	Germany
3000	Greece
3440	Hong Kong-China
3480	Hungary
3520	Iceland
3600	Indonesia
3720	Ireland
3801	Italy: Veneto-Nord Est

3802	Italy: Trento-Nord-Est
3803	Italy: Toscana-Centro
3804	Italy: Piemonte-Nord-Ovest
3805	Italy: Lombardia-Nord Ovest
3806	Italy: Bolzano
3807	Italy: Other regions
3920	Japan
4100	Korea
4280	Latvia
4380	Liechtenstein
4420	Luxembourg
4460	Macao SAR
4840	Mexico
5280	Netherlands
5540	New Zealand
5780	Norway
6160	Poland
6200	Portugal
6430	Russian Federation
7030	Slovak Republic
7241	Spain: Other regions
7242	Spain: Castilia y Leon
7243	Spain: Catalonia
7244	Spain: Basque Country
7520	Sweden
7560	Switzerland
7640	Thailand
7880	Tunisia
7920	Turkey
8261	United Kingdom: England, Wales & Northern Ireland
8262	United Kingdom: Scotland
8400	United States
8580	Uruguay
8910	Serbia

SCHOOLID (4) School ID

Format: A5 Columns: 11-15

STIDSTD (5) Student ID

Format: A5 Columns: 16-20

ST01Q01 (6) Grade Q1a

Format: F2 Columns: 22-23

97 N/A
98 Invalid
99 Missing

ST02Q02 (7) Birth Month Q2

Format: F2 Columns: 24-25

97 N/A
98 Invalid
99 Missing

ST02Q03 (8) Birth Year Q2

Format: F2 Columns: 26-27

97 N/A
98 Invalid
99 Missing

ST03Q01 (9) Sex Q3

Format: F1 Columns: 28-28

1 Female
2 Male
7 N/A
8 Invalid
9 Missing

ST04Q01 (10) Live at home: mother Q4a

Format: F1 Columns: 29-29

1 Tick
2 No tick
7 N/A
8 Invalid
9 Missing

ST04Q02 (11) Live at home: female guard Q4b

Format: F1 Columns: 30-30

1 Tick
2 No tick
7 N/A
8 Invalid
9 Missing

ST04Q03 (12) Live at home: father Q4c

Format: F1 Columns: 31-31

1 Tick
2 No tick
7 N/A
8 Invalid
9 Missing

ST04Q04 (13) Live at home: male guard Q4d

Format: F1 Columns: 32-32

1 Tick
2 No tick
7 N/A
8 Invalid
9 Missing

ST04Q05 (14) Live at home: others Q4e

Format: F1 Columns: 33-33

Value	Label
1	Tick
2	No tick
7	N/A
8	Invalid
9	Missing

ST05Q01 (15) Mother currently doing Q5

Format: F1 Columns: 34-34

Value	Label
1	Working full-time
2	Working part-time
3	Looking for work
4	Other
7	N/A
8	Invalid
9	Missing

ST06Q01 (16) Father currently doing Q6

Format: F1 Columns: 35-35

Value	Label
1	Working full-time
2	Working part-time
3	Looking for work
4	Other
7	N/A
8	Invalid
9	Missing

ST07Q01 (17) Mother's main job Q7

Format: A4 Columns: 36-39

Value	Label
9997	N/A
9998	Invalid
9999	Missing

ST09Q01 (18) Father's main job Q9

Format: A4 Columns: 40-43

Value	Label
9997	N/A
9998	Invalid
9999	Missing

ST11R01 (19) Mother: highest level completed at school Q11

Format: F1 Columns: 44-44

Value	Label
1	None
2	ISCED 1
3	ISCED 2
4	ISCED 3B, C
5	ISCED 3A
9	Missing

ST12Q01 (20) Mother <ISCED5A or 6> Q12a

Format: F1 Columns: 45-45

Value	Label
1	Tick
2	No tick
7	N/A
8	Invalid
9	Missing

ST12Q02 (21) Mother <ISCED5B> Q12b

Format: F1 Columns: 46-46

Value	Label
1	Tick
2	No tick
7	N/A
8	Invalid
9	Missing

ST12Q03 (22) Mother <ISCED4> Q12c

Format: F1 Columns: 47-47

Value	Label
1	Tick
2	No tick
7	N/A
8	Invalid
9	Missing

ST13R01 (23) Father: highest level completed at school Q13

Format: F1 Columns: 48-48

Value	Label
1	None
2	ISCED 1
3	ISCED 2
4	ISCED 3B, C
5	ISCED 3A
9	Missing

ST14Q01 (24) Father <ISCED 5A or 6> Q14a

Format: F1 Columns: 49-49

Value	Label
1	Tick
2	No tick
7	N/A
8	Invalid
9	Missing

ST14Q02 (25) Father <ISCED 5B> Q14b

Format: F1 Columns: 50-50

Value	Label
1	Tick
2	No tick
7	N/A
8	Invalid
9	Missing

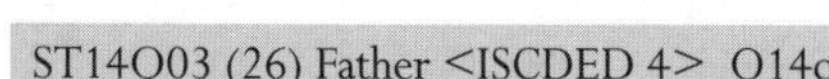

ST14Q03 (26) Father <ISCDED 4> Q14c

Format: F1 Columns: 51-51

1	Tick
2	No tick
7	N/A
8	Invalid
9	Missing

ST15Q01 (27) Country of birth: self Q15a_a

Format: F2 Columns: 52-53

1	<Test Country>
2	<Other Country>
97	N/A
98	Invalid
99	Missing

ST15Q02 (28) Country of birth: mother Q15a_b

Format: F2 Columns: 54-55

1	<Test Country>
2	<Other Country>
97	N/A
98	Invalid
99	Missing

ST15Q03 (29) Country of birth: father Q15a_c

Format: F2 Columns: 56-57

1	<Test Country>
2	<Other Country>
97	N/A
98	Invalid
99	Missing

ST15Q04 (30) Country of birth: age Q15b

Format: F8.3 Columns: 58-65

997.000	N/A
998.000	Invalid
999.000	Missing

ST16Q01 (31) Language at home Q16

Format: F2 Columns: 66-67

1	<Test language>
2	<Other national language>
3	<Other national dialects>
4	<Other languages>
97	N/A
98	Invalid
99	Missing

ST17Q01 (32) Possessions: desk Q17a

Format: F1 Columns: 68-68

1	Tick
2	No tick
7	N/A
8	Invalid
9	Missing

ST17Q02 (33) Possessions: own room Q17b

Format: F1 Columns: 69-69

1	Tick
2	No tick
7	N/A
8	Invalid
9	Missing

ST17Q03 (34) Possessions: study place Q17c

Format: F1 Columns: 70-70

1	Tick
2	No tick
7	N/A
8	Invalid

ST17Q04 (35) Possessions: computer Q17d

Format: F1 Columns: 71-71

1	Tick
2	No tick
7	N/A
8	Invalid
9	Missing

ST17Q05 (36) Possessions: software Q17e

Format: F1 Columns: 72-72

1	Tick
2	No tick
7	N/A
8	Invalid
9	Missing

ST17Q06 (37) Possessions: Internet Q17f

Format: F1 Columns: 73-73

1	Tick
2	No tick
7	N/A
8	Invalid
9	Missing

ST17Q07 (38) Possessions: calculator Q17g

Format: F1 Columns: 74-74

1	Tick
2	No tick
7	N/A
8	Invalid
9	Missing

ST17Q08 (39) Possessions: literature Q17h

Format: F1 Columns: 75-75

1	Tick
2	No tick
7	N/A
8	Invalid
9	Missing

ST17Q09 (40) Possessions: poetry Q17i

Format: F1 Columns: 76-76

1	Tick
2	No tick
7	N/A
8	Invalid
9	Missing

ST17Q10 (41) Possessions: art Q17j

Format: F1 Columns: 77-77

1	Tick
2	No tick
7	N/A
8	Invalid
9	Missing

ST17Q11 (42) Possessions: textbooks Q17k

Format: F1 Columns: 78-78

1	Tick
2	No tick
7	N/A
8	Invalid
9	Missing

ST17Q12 (43) Possessions: dictionary Q17l

Format: F1 Columns: 79-79

1	Tick
2	No tick
7	N/A
8	Invalid
9	Missing

ST17Q13 (44) Possessions: dishwasher Q17m

Format: F1 Columns: 80-80

1	Tick
2	No tick
7	N/A
8	Invalid
9	Missing

ST17Q14 (45) Possessions: <Cntry item 1> Q17n

Format: A5 Columns: 81-85

04001	Austria: DVD
04002	Austria: No DVD
05611	Belgium (Fl.): DVD
05612	Belgium (Fl.): No DVD
05621	Belgium (Fr.): DVD
05622	Belgium (Fr.): No DVD
20301	Czech Republic: Own mobile phone
20302	Czech Republic: No own mobile phone
27601	Germany: Own garden
27602	Germany: No own garden
30001	Greece: Video camera
30002	Greece: No Video camera
34401	Hong Kong: Encyclopaedia
34402	Hong Kong: No encyclopaedia
34801	Hungary: Video casette recorder
34802	Hungary: No video casette recorder
37201	Ireland: Games console
37202	Ireland: No games console
38001	Italy: Ancient furniture
38002	Italy: No ancient furniture
41001	Korea: DVD
41002	Korea: No DVD
44201	Luxembourg: Satellite dish
44202	Luxembourg: No satellite dish
44601	Macao: Encyclopaedia
44602	Macao: No encyclopaedia
55401	New Zealand: Clothes dryer
55402	New Zealand: No clothes dryer
57801	Norway: Swimming pool
57802	Norway: No swimming pool
61601	Poland: Satellite or cable TV (> 29 channels)
61602	Poland: No satellite or cable TV (> 29 channels)
72401	Spain: Video
72402	Spain: No video
75601	Switzerland: Musical instrument
75602	Switzerland: No musical instrument
78801	Tunisia: Telephone
78802	Tunisia: No telephone

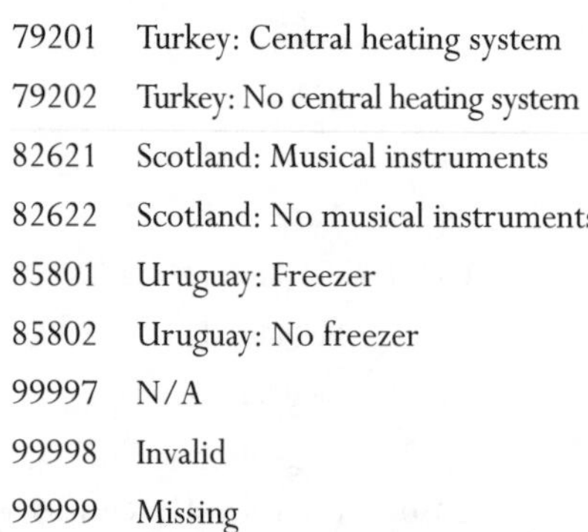

79201 Turkey: Central heating system
79202 Turkey: No central heating system
82621 Scotland: Musical instruments
82622 Scotland: No musical instruments
85801 Uruguay: Freezer
85802 Uruguay: No freezer
99997 N/A
99998 Invalid
99999 Missing

ST17Q15 (46) Possessions: <Cntry item 2> Q17o

Format: A5 Columns: 86-90

04001 Austria: MP3 player
04002 Austria: No MP3 player
05611 Belgium (Fl.): Swimming pool
05612 Belgium (Fl.): No swimming pool
20301 Czech Republic: Your own discman or mp3 player
20302 Czech Republic: No own discman or mp3 player
30001 Greece: HiFi equipment
30002 Greece: No HiFi equipment
34401 Hong Kong: Musical instrument (*e.g.*, piano, violin)
34402 Hong Kong: No musical instrument (*e.g.*, piano, violin)
34801 Hungary: CD player
34802 Hungary: No CD player
37201 Ireland: VCR or DVD
37202 Ireland: No VCR or DVD
38001 Italy: DVD player
38002 Italy: No DVD player
44201 Luxembourg: Own television set
44202 Luxembourg: No own television set
44601 Macao: Musical instrument (*e.g.*, piano, violin)
44602 Macao: No musical instrument (*e.g.*, piano, violin)
55401 New Zealand: DVD
55402 New Zealand: No DVD
57801 Norway: Housekeeper
57802 Norway: No housekeeper
61601 Poland: VCR or DVD
61602 Poland: No VCR or DVD
72401 Spain: DVD
72402 Spain: No DVD
78801 Tunisia: Electricity
78802 Tunisia: No electricity
79201 Turkey: Washing machine
79202 Turkey: No washing machine
82621 Scotland: Cable/satellite TV
82622 Scotland: No Cable/satellite TV
85801 Uruguay: DVD
85802 Uruguay: No DVD
99997 N/A
99998 Invalid
99999 Missing

ST17Q16 (47) Possessions: <Cntry item 3> Q17p

Format: A5 Columns:

04001 Austria: Digital camera
04002 Austria: No digital camera
05611 Belgium (Fl.): CDs with classical music
05612 Belgium (Fl.): No CDs with classical music
30001 Greece: Air conditioning
30002 Greece: No air conditioning
34801 Hungary: DVD
34802 Hungary: No DVD
38001 Italy: Musical instrument (except flute)
38002 Italy: No musical instrument (except flute)
44201 Luxembourg: Own mobile phone
44202 Luxembourg: No own mobile phone
72401 Spain: Video console (Playstation, X-Box, Nintendo, etc.)
72402 Spain: No video console (Playstation, X-Box, Nintendo, etc.)
78801 Tunisia: Running water
78802 Tunisia: No running water
79201 Turkey: Vacuum cleaner
79202 Turkey: No vacuum cleaner
82621 Scotland: Kitchen range (eg AGA, Rayburn)
82622 Scotland: No kitchen range (eg AGA, Rayburn)
85801 Uruguay: Water heater
85802 Uruguay: No water heater
99997 N/A
99998 Invalid
99999 Missing

ST19Q01 (48) How many books at home Q19

Format: F1 Columns: 96-96

1 0-10 books
2 11-25 books
3 26-100 books
4 101-200 books
5 201-500 books
6 More than 500 books
7 N/A
8 Invalid
9 Missing

ST20Q01 (49) Attend <ISCED 0> Q20

Format: F1 Columns: 97-97

1 No
2 Yes, one year or less
3 Yes, more than one year
7 N/A
8 Invalid
9 Missing

ST21Q01 (50) <ISCED 1>Years Q21

Format: F5.1 Columns: 98-102

997.0 N/A
998.0 Invalid
999.0 Missing

ST22Q01 (51) Repeat <ISCED 1> Q22a

Format: F1 Columns: 103-103

1 No, never
2 Yes, once
3 Yes, twice or more
7 N/A
8 Invalid
9 Missing

ST22Q02 (52) Repeat <ISCED 2> Q22b

Format: F1 Columns: 104-104

1 No, never
2 Yes, once
3 Yes, twice or more
7 N/A
8 Invalid
9 Missing

ST22Q03 (53) Repeat <ISCED 3> Q22c

Format: F1 Columns: 105-105

1 No, never
2 Yes, once
3 Yes, twice or more
7 N/A
8 Invalid
9 Missing

ST23Q01 (54) Expect <ISCED 2> Q23a

Format: F1 Columns: 106-106

1 Tick
2 No tick
7 N/A
8 Invalid
9 Missing

ST23Q02 (55) Expect <ISCED 3B or 3C> Q23b

Format: F1 Columns: 107-107

1 Tick
2 No tick
7 N/A
8 Invalid
9 Missing

ST23Q03 (56) Expect <ISCED 3A> Q23c

Format: F1 Columns: 108-108

1 Tick
2 No tick
7 N/A
8 Invalid
9 Missing

ST23Q04 (57) Expect <ISCED 4> Q23d

Format: F1 Columns: 109-109

1 Tick
2 No tick
7 N/A
8 Invalid
9 Missing

ST23Q05 (58) Expect <ISCED 5B> Q23e

Format: F1 Columns: 110-110

1 Tick
2 No tick
7 N/A
8 Invalid
9 Missing

ST23Q06 (59) Expect <ISCED 5A or 6> Q23f

Format: F1 Columns: 111-111

1 Tick
2 No tick
7 N/A
8 Invalid
9 Missing

ST24Q01 (60) School: done little Q24a

Format: F1 Columns: 112-112

1 Strongly agree
2 Agree
3 Disagree
4 Strongly disagree
7 N/A
8 Invalid
9 Missing

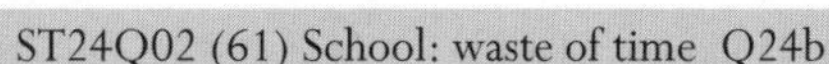

ST24Q02 (61) School: waste of time Q24b

Format: F1 Columns: 113-113
1 Strongly agree
2 Agree
3 Disagree
4 Strongly disagree
7 N/A
8 Invalid
9 Missing

ST24Q03 (62) School: give confidence Q24c

Format: F1 Columns: 114-114
1 Strongly agree
2 Agree
3 Disagree
4 Strongly disagree
7 N/A
8 Invalid
9 Missing

ST24Q04 (63) School: useful Q24d

Format: F1 Columns: 115-115
1 Strongly agree
2 Agree
3 Disagree
4 Strongly disagree
7 N/A
8 Invalid
9 Missing

ST25Q01 (64) Attend: local Q25a

Format: F1 Columns: 116-116
1 Tick
2 No tick
7 N/A
8 Invalid
9 Missing

ST25Q02 (65) Attend: better Q25b

Format: F1 Columns: 117-117
1 Tick
2 No tick
7 N/A
8 Invalid
9 Missing

ST25Q03 (66) Attend: specific program Q25c

Format: F1 Columns: 118-118
1 Tick
2 No tick
7 N/A
8 Invalid
9 Missing

ST25Q04 (67) Attend: religious Q25d

Format: F1 Columns: 119-119
1 Tick
2 No tick
7 N/A
8 Invalid
9 Missing

ST25Q05 (68) Attend: family Q25e

Format: F1 Columns: 120-120
1 Tick
2 No tick
7 N/A
8 Invalid
9 Missing

ST25Q06 (69) Attend: other Q25f

Format: F1 Columns: 121-121
1 Tick
2 No tick
7 N/A
8 Invalid
9 Missing

ST26Q01 (70) Well with students Q26a

Format: F1 Columns: 122-122
1 Strongly agree
2 Agree
3 Disagree
4 Strongly disagree
7 N/A
8 Invalid
9 Missing

ST26Q02 (71) Interested in students Q26b

Format: F1 Columns: 123-123
1 Strongly agree
2 Agree
3 Disagree
4 Strongly disagree
7 N/A
8 Invalid
9 Missing

ST26Q03 (72) Listen to me Q26c

Format: F1 Columns: 124-124
1 Strongly agree
2 Agree
3 Disagree
4 Strongly disagree
7 N/A
8 Invalid
9 Missing

ST26Q04 (73) Give extra help Q26d

Format: F1 Columns: 125-125

1 Strongly agree
2 Agree
3 Disagree
4 Strongly disagree
7 N/A
8 Invalid
9 Missing

ST26Q05 (74) Treat me fairly Q26e

Format: F1 Columns: 126-126

1 Strongly agree
2 Agree
3 Disagree
4 Strongly disagree
7 N/A
8 Invalid
9 Missing

ST27Q01 (75) Feel an outsider Q27a

Format: F1 Columns: 127-127

1 Strongly agree
2 Agree
3 Disagree
4 Strongly disagree
7 N/A
8 Invalid
9 Missing

ST27Q02 (76) Make friends Q27b

Format: F1 Columns: 128-128

1 Strongly agree
2 Agree
3 Disagree
4 Strongly disagree
7 N/A
8 Invalid
9 Missing

ST27Q03 (77) Feel I belong Q27c

Format: F1 Columns: 129-129

1 Strongly agree
2 Agree
3 Disagree
4 Strongly disagree
7 N/A
8 Invalid
9 Missing

ST27Q04 (78) Feel awkward Q27d

Format: F1 Columns: 130-130

1 Strongly agree
2 Agree
3 Disagree
4 Strongly disagree
7 N/A
8 Invalid
9 Missing

ST27Q05 (79) Think I'm liked Q27e

Format: F1 Columns: 131-131

1 Strongly agree
2 Agree
3 Disagree
4 Strongly disagree
7 N/A
8 Invalid
9 Missing

ST27Q06 (80) Feel lonely Q27f

Format: F1 Columns: 132-132

1 Strongly agree
2 Agree
3 Disagree
4 Strongly disagree
7 N/A
8 Invalid
9 Missing

ST28Q01 (81) Late for school Q28

Format: F1 Columns: 133-133

1 None
2 1 or 2 times
3 3 or 4 times
4 5 or more times
7 N/A
8 Invalid
9 Missing

ST29Q01 (82) Hours all: homework Q29a

Format: F3 Columns: 134-141

997 N/A
998 Invalid
999 Missing

ST29Q02 (83) Hours all: <Remedial> Q29b

Format: F3 Columns: 142-149

997 N/A
998 Invalid
999 Missing

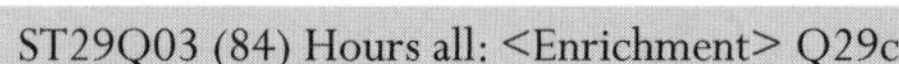

ST29Q03 (84) Hours all: <Enrichment> Q29c

Format: F3 Columns: 150-157

997 N/A
998 Invalid
999 Missing

ST29Q04 (85) Hours all: tutor Q29d

Format: F3 Columns: 158-165

997 N/A
998 Invalid
999 Missing

ST29Q05 (86) Hours all: <out-of-school> Q29e

Format: F3 Columns: 166-173

997 N/A
998 Invalid
999 Missing

ST29Q06 (87) Hours all: other study Q29f

Format: F3 Columns: 174-181

997 N/A
998 Invalid
999 Missing

ST30Q01 (88) Attitude: enjoy reading Q30a

Format: F1 Columns: 182-182

1 Strongly agree
2 Agree
3 Disagree
4 Strongly disagree
7 N/A
8 Invalid
9 Missing

ST30Q02 (89) Attitude: effort Q30b

Format: F1 Columns: 183-183

1 Strongly agree
2 Agree
3 Disagree
4 Strongly disagree
7 N/A
8 Invalid
9 Missing

ST30Q03 (90) Attitude: look forward Q30c

Format: F1 Columns: 184-184

1 Strongly agree
2 Agree
3 Disagree
4 Strongly disagree
7 N/A
8 Invalid
9 Missing

ST30Q04 (91) Attitude: enjoy Maths Q30d

Format: F1 Columns: 185-185

1 Strongly agree
2 Agree
3 Disagree
4 Strongly disagree
7 N/A
8 Invalid
9 Missing

ST30Q05 (92) Attitude: career Q30e

Format: F1 Columns: 186-186

1 Strongly agree
2 Agree
3 Disagree
4 Strongly disagree
7 N/A
8 Invalid
9 Missing

ST30Q06 (93) Attitude: interested Q30f

Format: F1 Columns: 187-187

1 Strongly agree
2 Agree
3 Disagree
4 Strongly disagree
7 N/A
8 Invalid
9 Missing

ST30Q07 (94) Attitude: further study Q30g

Format: F1 Columns: 188-188

1 Strongly agree
2 Agree
3 Disagree
4 Strongly disagree
7 N/A
8 Invalid
9 Missing

ST30Q08 (95) Attitude: job Q30h

Format: F1 Columns: 189-189

1 Strongly agree
2 Agree
3 Disagree
4 Strongly disagree
7 N/A
8 Invalid
9 Missing

ST31Q01 (96) Confident: timetable Q31a

Format: F1 Columns: 190-190

1	Very confident
2	Confident
3	Not very confident
4	Not at all confident
7	N/A
8	Invalid
9	Missing

ST31Q02 (97) Confident: discount Q31b

Format: F1 Columns: 191-191

1	Very confident
2	Confident
3	Not very confident
4	Not at all confident
7	N/A
8	Invalid
9	Missing

ST31Q03 (98) Confident: area Q31c

Format: F1 Columns: 192-192

1	Very confident
2	Confident
3	Not very confident
4	Not at all confident
7	N/A
8	Invalid
9	Missing

ST31Q04 (99) Confident: graphs Q31d

Format: F1 Columns: 193-193

1	Very confident
2	Confident
3	Not very confident
4	Not at all confident
7	N/A
8	Invalid
9	Missing

ST31Q05 (100) Confident: linear Q31e

Format: F1 Columns: 194-194

1	Very confident
2	Confident
3	Not very confident
4	Not at all confident
7	N/A
8	Invalid
9	Missing

ST31Q06 (101) Confident: distance Q31f

Format: F1 Columns: 195-195

1	Very confident
2	Confident
3	Not very confident
4	Not at all confident
7	N/A
8	Invalid
9	Missing

ST31Q07 (102) Confident: quadratics Q31g

Format: F1 Columns: 196-196

1	Very confident
2	Confident
3	Not very confident
4	Not at all confident
7	N/A
8	Invalid
9	Missing

ST31Q08 (103) Confident: rate Q31h

Format: F1 Columns: 197-197

1	Very confident
2	Confident
3	Not very confident
4	Not at all confident
7	N/A
8	Invalid
9	Missing

ST32Q01 (104) Feel study: worry Q32a

Format: F1 Columns: 198-198

1	Strongly agree
2	Agree
3	Disagree
4	Strongly disagree
7	N/A
8	Invalid
9	Missing

ST32Q02 (105) Feel study: not good Q32b

Format: F1 Columns: 199-199

1	Strongly agree
2	Agree
3	Disagree
4	Strongly disagree
7	N/A
8	Invalid
9	Missing

ST32Q03 (106) Feel study: tense Q32c

Format: F1 Columns: 200-200

1 Strongly agree
2 Agree
3 Disagree
4 Strongly disagree
7 N/A
8 Invalid
9 Missing

ST32Q04 (107) Feel study: good <marks> Q32d

Format: F1 Columns: 201-201

1 Strongly agree
2 Agree
3 Disagree
4 Strongly disagree
7 N/A
8 Invalid
9 Missing

ST32Q05 (108) Feel study: nervous Q32e

Format: F1 Columns: 202-202

1 Strongly agree
2 Agree
3 Disagree
4 Strongly disagree
7 N/A
8 Invalid
9 Missing

ST32Q06 (109) Feel study: quickly Q32f

Format: F1 Columns: 203-203

1 Strongly agree
2 Agree
3 Disagree
4 Strongly disagree
7 N/A
8 Invalid
9 Missing

ST32Q07 (110) Feel study: best subject Q32g

Format: F1 Columns: 204-204

1 Strongly agree
2 Agree
3 Disagree
4 Strongly disagree
7 N/A
8 Invalid
9 Missing

ST32Q08 (111) Feel study: helpless Q32h

Format: F1 Columns: 205-205

1 Strongly agree
2 Agree
3 Disagree
4 Strongly disagree
7 N/A
8 Invalid
9 Missing

ST32Q09 (112) Feel study: underst. diffc. Q32i

Format: F1 Columns: 206-206

1 Strongly agree
2 Agree
3 Disagree
4 Strongly disagree
7 N/A
8 Invalid
9 Missing

ST32Q10 (113) Feel study: poor <marks> Q32j

Format: F1 Columns: 207-207

1 Strongly agree
2 Agree
3 Disagree
4 Strongly disagree
7 N/A
8 Invalid
9 Missing

ST33Q01 (114) Hours maths: homework Q33a

Format: F3 Columns: 208-215

997 N/A
998 Invalid
999 Missing

ST33Q02 (115) Hours maths: <remedial> Q33b

Format: F3 Columns: 216-223

997 N/A
998 Invalid
999 Missing

ST33Q03 (116) Hours maths: <enrichment> Q33c

Format: F3 Columns: 224-231

997 N/A
998 Invalid
999 Missing

ST33Q04 (117) Hours maths: tutor Q33d

Format: F3 Columns: 232-239

997 N/A
998 Invalid
999 Missing

ST33Q05 (118) Hours maths: <out-of-school> Q33e

Format: F3 Columns: 240-247

997 N/A
998 Invalid
999 Missing

ST33Q06 (119) Hours maths: other Q33f

Format: F3 Columns: 248-255

997 N/A
998 Invalid
999 Missing

ST34Q01 (120) Learn: important parts Q34a

Format: F1 Columns: 256-256

1 Strongly agree
2 Agree
3 Disagree
4 Strongly disagree
7 N/A
8 Invalid
9 Missing

ST34Q02 (121) Learn: new ways Q34b

Format: F1 Columns: 257-257

1 Strongly agree
2 Agree
3 Disagree
4 Strongly disagree
7 N/A
8 Invalid
9 Missing

ST34Q03 (122) Learn: check myself Q34c

Format: F1 Columns: 258-258

1 Strongly agree
2 Agree
3 Disagree
4 Strongly disagree
7 N/A
8 Invalid
9 Missing

ST34Q04 (123) Learn: concepts Q34d

Format: F1 Columns: 259-259

1 Strongly agree
2 Agree
3 Disagree
4 Strongly disagree
7 N/A
8 Invalid
9 Missing

ST34Q05 (124) Learn: everyday life Q34e

Format: F1 Columns: 260-260

1 Strongly agree
2 Agree
3 Disagree
4 Strongly disagree
7 N/A
8 Invalid
9 Missing

ST34Q06 (125) Learn: solve when sleep Q34f

Format: F1 Columns: 261-261

1 Strongly agree
2 Agree
3 Disagree
4 Strongly disagree
7 N/A
8 Invalid
9 Missing

ST34Q07 (126) Learn: by heart Q34g

Format: F1 Columns: 262-262

1 Strongly agree
2 Agree
3 Disagree
4 Strongly disagree
7 N/A
8 Invalid
9 Missing

ST34Q08 (127) Learn: by relating Q34h

Format: F1 Columns: 263-263

1 Strongly agree
2 Agree
3 Disagree
4 Strongly disagree
7 N/A
8 Invalid
9 Missing

ST34Q09 (128) Learn: examples Q34i

Format: F1 Columns: 264-264

1 Strongly agree
2 Agree
3 Disagree
4 Strongly disagree
7 N/A
8 Invalid
9 Missing

ST34Q10 (129) Learn: clarify Q34j		
Format:	F1	Columns: 265-265
	1	Strongly agree
	2	Agree
	3	Disagree
	4	Strongly disagree
	7	N/A
	8	Invalid
	9	Missing

ST34Q11 (130) Learn: applied Q34k		
Format:	F1	Columns: 266-266
	1	Strongly agree
	2	Agree
	3	Disagree
	4	Strongly disagree
	7	N/A
	8	Invalid
	9	Missing

ST34Q12 (131) Learn: exactly Q34l		
Format:	F1	Columns: 267-267
	1	Strongly agree
	2	Agree
	3	Disagree
	4	Strongly disagree
	7	N/A
	8	Invalid
	9	Missing

ST34Q13 (132) Learn: procedure Q34m		
Format:	F1	Columns: 268-268
	1	Strongly agree
	2	Agree
	3	Disagree
	4	Strongly disagree
	7	N/A
	8	Invalid
	9	Missing

ST34Q14 (133) Learn: relate Q34n		
Format:	F1	Columns: 269-269
	1	Strongly agree
	2	Agree
	3	Disagree
	4	Strongly disagree
	7	N/A
	8	Invalid
	9	Missing

ST35Q02 (134) Maths <class periods> Q35b		
Format:	F3	Columns: 270-277
	997	N/A
	998	Invalid
	999	Missing

ST35Q03 (135) All <class periods> Q35c		
Format:	F3	Columns: 278-285
	997	N/A
	998	Invalid
	999	Missing

ST36Q01 (136) Students in maths Q36		
Format:	F3	Columns: 286-293
	997	N/A
	998	Invalid
	999	Missing

ST37Q01 (137) Attitudes: be the best Q37a		
Format:	F1	Columns: 294-294
	1	Strongly agree
	2	Agree
	3	Disagree
	4	Strongly disagree
	7	N/A
	8	Invalid
	9	Missing

ST37Q02 (138) Attitudes: group work Q37b		
Format:	F1	Columns: 295-295
	1	Strongly agree
	2	Agree
	3	Disagree
	4	Strongly disagree
	7	N/A
	8	Invalid
	9	Missing

ST37Q03 (139) Attitudes: exams Q37c		
Format:	F1	Columns: 296-296
	1	Strongly agree
	2	Agree
	3	Disagree
	4	Strongly disagree
	7	N/A
	8	Invalid
	9	Missing

ST37Q04 (140) Attitudes: project Q37d

Format: F1 Columns: 297-297

1 Strongly agree
2 Agree
3 Disagree
4 Strongly disagree
7 N/A
8 Invalid
9 Missing

ST37Q05 (141) Attitudes: effort Q37e

Format: F1 Columns: 298-298

1 Strongly agree
2 Agree
3 Disagree
4 Strongly disagree
7 N/A
8 Invalid
9 Missing

ST37Q06 (142) Attitudes: work with other Q37f

Format: F1 Columns: 299-299

1 Strongly agree
2 Agree
3 Disagree
4 Strongly disagree
7 N/A
8 Invalid
9 Missing

ST37Q07 (143) Attitudes: do better Q37g

Format: F1 Columns: 300-300

1 Strongly agree
2 Agree
3 Disagree
4 Strongly disagree
7 N/A
8 Invalid
9 Missing

ST37Q08 (144) Attitudes: helping Q37h

Format: F1 Columns: 301-301

1 Strongly agree
2 Agree
3 Disagree
4 Strongly disagree
7 N/A
8 Invalid
9 Missing

ST37Q09 (145) Attitudes: learn most Q37i

Format: F1 Columns: 302-302

1 Strongly agree
2 Agree
3 Disagree
4 Strongly disagree
7 N/A
8 Invalid
9 Missing

ST37Q10 (146) Attitudes: best work Q37j

Format: F1 Columns: 303-303

1 Strongly agree
2 Agree
3 Disagree
4 Strongly disagree
7 N/A
8 Invalid
9 Missing

ST38Q01 (147) Lesson: interested Q38a

Format: F1 Columns: 304-304

1 Every lesson
2 Most lessons
3 Some lessons
4 Never or hardly ever
7 N/A
8 Invalid
9 Missing

ST38Q02 (148) Lesson: don't listen Q38b

Format: F1 Columns: 305-305

1 Every lesson
2 Most lessons
3 Some lessons
4 Never or hardly ever
7 N/A
8 Invalid
9 Missing

ST38Q03 (149) Lesson: extra help Q38c

Format: F1 Columns: 306-306

1 Every lesson
2 Most lessons
3 Some lessons
4 Never or hardly ever
7 N/A
8 Invalid
9 Missing

ST38Q04 (150) Lesson: book work Q38d		
Format:	F1	Columns: 307-307
	1	Every lesson
	2	Most lessons
	3	Some lessons
	4	Never or hardly ever
	7	N/A
	8	Invalid
	9	Missing

ST38Q05 (151) Lesson: help learning Q38e		
Format:	F1	Columns: 308-308
	1	Every lesson
	2	Most lessons
	3	Some lessons
	4	Never or hardly ever
	7	N/A
	8	Invalid
	9	Missing

ST38Q06 (152) Lesson: noise Q38f		
Format:	F1	Columns: 309-309
	1	Every lesson
	2	Most lessons
	3	Some lessons
	4	Never or hardly ever
	7	N/A
	8	Invalid
	9	Missing

ST38Q07 (153) Lesson: understand Q38g		
Format:	F1	Columns: 310-310
	1	Every lesson
	2	Most lessons
	3	Some lessons
	4	Never or hardly ever
	7	N/A
	8	Invalid
	9	Missing

ST38Q08 (154) Lesson: <quieten down> Q38h		
Format:	F1	Columns: 311-311
	1	Every lesson
	2	Most lessons
	3	Some lessons
	4	Never or hardly ever
	7	N/A
	8	Invalid
	9	Missing

ST38Q09 (155) Lesson: can't work well Q38i		
Format:	F1	Columns: 312-312
	1	Every lesson
	2	Most lessons
	3	Some lessons
	4	Never or hardly ever
	7	N/A
	8	Invalid
	9	Missing

ST38Q10 (156) Lesson: opinions Q38j		
Format:	F1	Columns: 313-313
	1	Every lesson
	2	Most lessons
	3	Some lessons
	4	Never or hardly ever
	7	N/A
	8	Invalid
	9	Missing

ST38Q11 (157) Lesson: late start Q38k		
Format:	F1	Columns: 314-314
	1	Every lesson
	2	Most lessons
	3	Some lessons
	4	Never or hardly ever
	7	N/A
	8	Invalid
	9	Missing

EC01Q01 (158) Missing two months <ISCED 1> EC1		
Format:	F1	Columns: 315-315
	1	No, never
	2	Yes, once
	3	Yes, twice or more
	7	N/A
	8	Invalid
	9	Missing

EC02Q01 (159) Missing two months <ISCED 2> EC2		
Format:	F1	Columns: 316-316
	1	No, never
	2	Yes, once
	3	Yes, twice or more
	7	N/A
	8	Invalid
	9	Missing

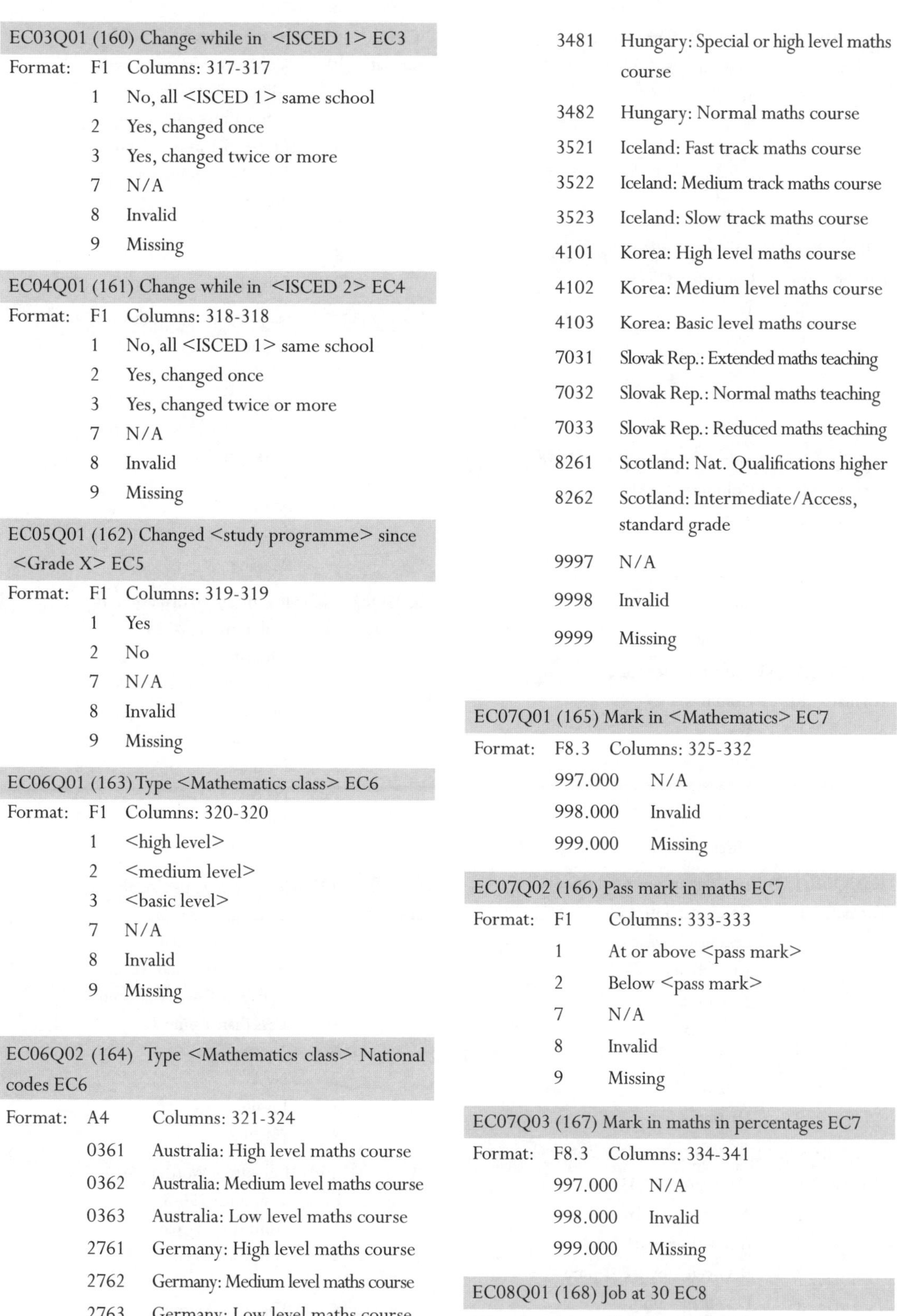

EC03Q01 (160) Change while in <ISCED 1> EC3

Format: F1 Columns: 317-317

1	No, all <ISCED 1> same school
2	Yes, changed once
3	Yes, changed twice or more
7	N/A
8	Invalid
9	Missing

EC04Q01 (161) Change while in <ISCED 2> EC4

Format: F1 Columns: 318-318

1	No, all <ISCED 1> same school
2	Yes, changed once
3	Yes, changed twice or more
7	N/A
8	Invalid
9	Missing

EC05Q01 (162) Changed <study programme> since <Grade X> EC5

Format: F1 Columns: 319-319

1	Yes
2	No
7	N/A
8	Invalid
9	Missing

EC06Q01 (163) Type <Mathematics class> EC6

Format: F1 Columns: 320-320

1	<high level>
2	<medium level>
3	<basic level>
7	N/A
8	Invalid
9	Missing

EC06Q02 (164) Type <Mathematics class> National codes EC6

Format: A4 Columns: 321-324

0361	Australia: High level maths course
0362	Australia: Medium level maths course
0363	Australia: Low level maths course
2761	Germany: High level maths course
2762	Germany: Medium level maths course
2763	Germany: Low level maths course
3001	Greece: Advanced level maths course
3002	Greece: Medium level maths course
3003	Greece: Basic level maths course
3481	Hungary: Special or high level maths course
3482	Hungary: Normal maths course
3521	Iceland: Fast track maths course
3522	Iceland: Medium track maths course
3523	Iceland: Slow track maths course
4101	Korea: High level maths course
4102	Korea: Medium level maths course
4103	Korea: Basic level maths course
7031	Slovak Rep.: Extended maths teaching
7032	Slovak Rep.: Normal maths teaching
7033	Slovak Rep.: Reduced maths teaching
8261	Scotland: Nat. Qualifications higher
8262	Scotland: Intermediate/Access, standard grade
9997	N/A
9998	Invalid
9999	Missing

EC07Q01 (165) Mark in <Mathematics> EC7

Format: F8.3 Columns: 325-332

997.000	N/A
998.000	Invalid
999.000	Missing

EC07Q02 (166) Pass mark in maths EC7

Format: F1 Columns: 333-333

1	At or above <pass mark>
2	Below <pass mark>
7	N/A
8	Invalid
9	Missing

EC07Q03 (167) Mark in maths in percentages EC7

Format: F8.3 Columns: 334-341

997.000	N/A
998.000	Invalid
999.000	Missing

EC08Q01 (168) Job at 30 EC8

Format: A4 Columns: 342-345

9997	N/A
9998	Invalid
9999	Missing

IC01Q01 (169) Available at home IC1a

Format: F1 Columns: 346-346

1	Yes
2	No
7	N/A
8	Invalid
9	Missing

IC01Q02 (170) Available at school IC1b

Format: F1 Columns: 347-347

1	Yes
2	No
7	N/A
8	Invalid
9	Missing

IC01Q03 (171) Available at other places IC1c

Format: F1 Columns: 348-348

1	Yes
2	No
7	N/A
8	Invalid
9	Missing

IC02Q01 (172) Used computer IC2

Format: F1 Columns: 349-349

1	Yes
2	No
7	N/A
8	Invalid
9	Missing

IC03Q01 (173) How long using computers IC3

Format: F1 Columns: 350-350

1	Less than 1 year
2	1 to 3 years
3	3 to 5 years
4	More than 5 years
7	N/A
8	Invalid
9	Missing

IC04Q01 (174) Use often at home IC4a

Format: F1 Columns: 351-351

1	Almost every day
2	A few times each week
3	Between 1 pwk & 1 pmn
4	Less than 1 pmn
5	Never
7	N/A
8	Invalid
9	Missing

IC04Q02 (175) Use often at school IC4b

Format: F1 Columns: 352-352

1	Almost every day
2	A few times each week
3	Between 1 pwk & 1 pmn
4	Less than 1 pmn
5	Never
7	N/A
8	Invalid
9	Missing

IC04Q03 (176) Use often at other places IC4c

Format: F1 Columns: 353-353

1	Almost every day
2	A few times each week
3	Between 1 pwk & 1 pmn
4	Less than 1 pmn
5	Never
7	N/A
8	Invalid
9	Missing

IC05Q01 (177) How often: information IC5a

Format: F1 Columns: 354-354

1	Almost every day
2	A few times each week
3	Between 1 pwk & 1 pmn
4	Less than 1 pmn
5	Never
7	N/A
8	Invalid
9	Missing

IC05Q02 (178) How often games IC5b

Format: F1 Columns: 355-355

1	Almost every day
2	A few times each week
3	Between 1 pwk & 1 pmn
4	Less than 1 pmn
5	Never
7	N/A
8	Invalid
9	Missing

IC05Q03 (179) How often: Word IC5c

Format: F1 Columns: 356-356

1	Almost every day
2	A few times each week
3	Between 1 pwk & 1 pmn
4	Less than 1 pmn
5	Never
7	N/A
8	Invalid
9	Missing

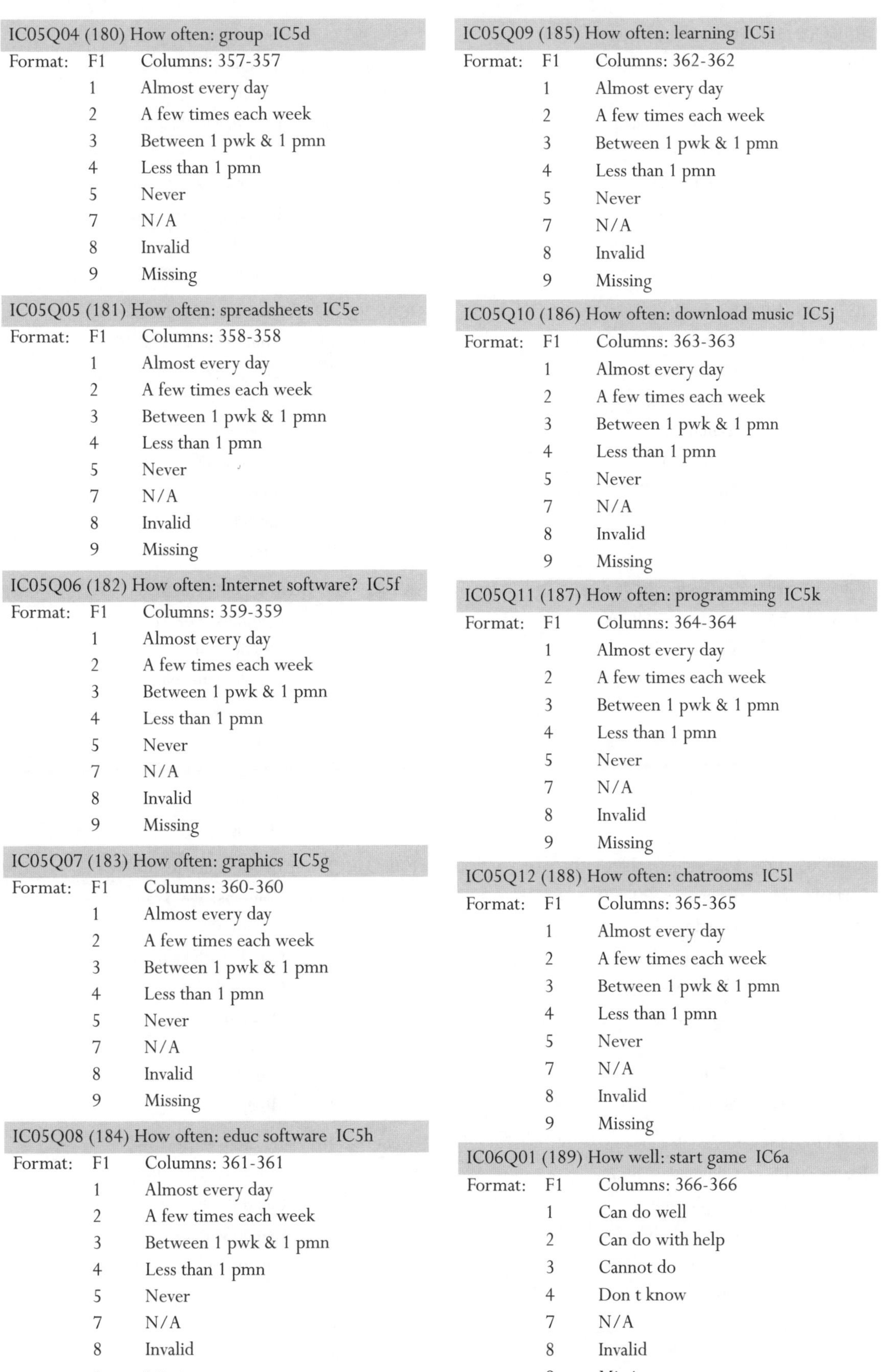

IC05Q04 (180) How often: group IC5d

Format: F1 Columns: 357-357

1 Almost every day
2 A few times each week
3 Between 1 pwk & 1 pmn
4 Less than 1 pmn
5 Never
7 N/A
8 Invalid
9 Missing

IC05Q05 (181) How often: spreadsheets IC5e

Format: F1 Columns: 358-358

1 Almost every day
2 A few times each week
3 Between 1 pwk & 1 pmn
4 Less than 1 pmn
5 Never
7 N/A
8 Invalid
9 Missing

IC05Q06 (182) How often: Internet software? IC5f

Format: F1 Columns: 359-359

1 Almost every day
2 A few times each week
3 Between 1 pwk & 1 pmn
4 Less than 1 pmn
5 Never
7 N/A
8 Invalid
9 Missing

IC05Q07 (183) How often: graphics IC5g

Format: F1 Columns: 360-360

1 Almost every day
2 A few times each week
3 Between 1 pwk & 1 pmn
4 Less than 1 pmn
5 Never
7 N/A
8 Invalid
9 Missing

IC05Q08 (184) How often: educ software IC5h

Format: F1 Columns: 361-361

1 Almost every day
2 A few times each week
3 Between 1 pwk & 1 pmn
4 Less than 1 pmn
5 Never
7 N/A
8 Invalid
9 Missing

IC05Q09 (185) How often: learning IC5i

Format: F1 Columns: 362-362

1 Almost every day
2 A few times each week
3 Between 1 pwk & 1 pmn
4 Less than 1 pmn
5 Never
7 N/A
8 Invalid
9 Missing

IC05Q10 (186) How often: download music IC5j

Format: F1 Columns: 363-363

1 Almost every day
2 A few times each week
3 Between 1 pwk & 1 pmn
4 Less than 1 pmn
5 Never
7 N/A
8 Invalid
9 Missing

IC05Q11 (187) How often: programming IC5k

Format: F1 Columns: 364-364

1 Almost every day
2 A few times each week
3 Between 1 pwk & 1 pmn
4 Less than 1 pmn
5 Never
7 N/A
8 Invalid
9 Missing

IC05Q12 (188) How often: chatrooms IC5l

Format: F1 Columns: 365-365

1 Almost every day
2 A few times each week
3 Between 1 pwk & 1 pmn
4 Less than 1 pmn
5 Never
7 N/A
8 Invalid
9 Missing

IC06Q01 (189) How well: start game IC6a

Format: F1 Columns: 366-366

1 Can do well
2 Can do with help
3 Cannot do
4 Don t know
7 N/A
8 Invalid
9 Missing

IC06Q02 (190) How well: antiviruses IC6b		
Format:	F1	Columns: 367-367
	1	Can do well
	2	Can do with help
	3	Cannot do
	4	Don t know
	7	N/A
	8	Invalid
	9	Missing

IC06Q03 (191) How well: open file IC6c		
Format:	F1	Columns: 368-368
	1	Can do well
	2	Can do with help
	3	Cannot do
	4	Don t know
	7	N/A
	8	Invalid
	9	Missing

IC06Q04 (192) How well: edit IC6d		
Format:	F1	Columns: 369-369
	1	Can do well
	2	Can do with help
	3	Cannot do
	4	Don t know
	7	N/A
	8	Invalid
	9	Missing

IC06Q05 (193) How well: scroll IC6e		
Format:	F1	Columns: 370-370
	1	Can do well
	2	Can do with help
	3	Cannot do
	4	Don t know
	7	N/A
	8	Invalid
	9	Missing

IC06Q06 (194) How well: addresses IC6f		
Format:	F1	Columns: 371-371
	1	Can do well
	2	Can do with help
	3	Cannot do
	4	Don t know
	7	N/A
	8	Invalid
	9	Missing

IC06Q07 (195) How well: copy IC6g		
Format:	F1	Columns: 372-372
	1	Can do well
	2	Can do with help
	3	Cannot do
	4	Don t know
	7	N/A
	8	Invalid
	9	Missing

IC06Q08 (196) How well: save IC6h		
Format:	F1	Columns: 373-373
	1	Can do well
	2	Can do with help
	3	Cannot do
	4	Don t know
	7	N/A
	8	Invalid
	9	Missing

IC06Q09 (197) How well: print IC6i		
Format:	F1	Columns: 374-374
	1	Can do well
	2	Can do with help
	3	Cannot do
	4	Don t know
	7	N/A
	8	Invalid
	9	Missing

IC06Q10 (198) How well: delete IC6j		
Format:	F1	Columns: 375-375
	1	Can do well
	2	Can do with help
	3	Cannot do
	4	Don t know
	7	N/A
	8	Invalid
	9	Missing

IC06Q11 (199) How well: move IC6k		
Format:	F1	Columns: 376-376
	1	Can do well
	2	Can do with help
	3	Cannot do
	4	Don t know
	7	N/A
	8	Invalid
	9	Missing

IC06Q12 (200) How well: Internet IC6l		
Format:	F1	Columns: 377-377
	1	Can do well
	2	Can do with help
	3	Cannot do
	4	Don t know
	7	N/A
	8	Invalid
	9	Missing

IC06Q13 (201) How well: download file IC6m		
Format:	F1	Columns: 378-378
	1	Can do well
	2	Can do with help
	3	Cannot do
	4	Don t know
	7	N/A
	8	Invalid
	9	Missing

IC06Q14 (202) How well: attach IC6n		
Format:	F1	Columns: 379-379
	1	Can do well
	2	Can do with help
	3	Cannot do
	4	Don t know
	7	N/A
	8	Invalid
	9	Missing

IC06Q15 (203) How well: program IC6o		
Format:	F1	Columns: 380-380
	1	Can do well
	2	Can do with help
	3	Cannot do
	4	Don t know
	7	N/A
	8	Invalid
	9	Missing

IC06Q16 (204) How well: spreadsheet plot IC6p		
Format:	F1	Columns: 381-381
	1	Can do well
	2	Can do with help
	3	Cannot do
	4	Don t know
	7	N/A
	8	Invalid
	9	Missing

IC06Q17 (205) How well: PowerPoint IC6q		
Format:	F1	Columns: 382-382
	1	Can do well
	2	Can do with help
	3	Cannot do
	4	Don t know
	7	N/A
	8	Invalid
	9	Missing

IC06Q18 (206) How well: games IC6r		
Format:	F1	Columns: 383-383
	1	Can do well
	2	Can do with help
	3	Cannot do
	4	Don t know
	7	N/A
	8	Invalid
	9	Missing

IC06Q19 (207) How well: download music IC6s		
Format:	F1	Columns: 384-384
	1	Can do well
	2	Can do with help
	3	Cannot do
	4	Don t know
	7	N/A
	8	Invalid
	9	Missing

IC06Q20 (208) How well: multimedia IC6t		
Format:	F1	Columns: 385-385
	1	Can do well
	2	Can do with help
	3	Cannot do
	4	Don t know
	7	N/A
	8	Invalid
	9	Missing

IC06Q21 (209) How well: draw IC6u		
Format:	F1	Columns: 386-386
	1	Can do well
	2	Can do with help
	3	Cannot do
	4	Don t know
	7	N/A
	8	Invalid
	9	Missing

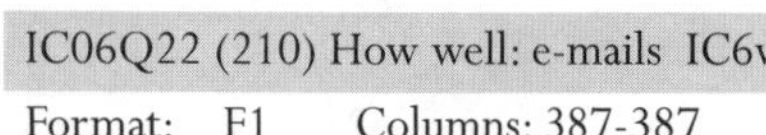

IC06Q22 (210) How well: e-mails IC6v

Format:	F1	Columns: 387-387
	1	Can do well
	2	Can do with help
	3	Cannot do
	4	Don t know
	7	N/A
	8	Invalid
	9	Missing

IC06Q23 (211) How well: web page IC6w

Format:	F1	Columns: 388-388
	1	Can do well
	2	Can do with help
	3	Cannot do
	4	Don t know
	7	N/A
	8	Invalid
	9	Missing

IC07Q01 (212) Feel: important IC7a

Format:	F1	Columns: 389-389
	1	Strongly agree
	2	Agree
	3	Disagree
	4	Strongly disagree
	7	N/A
	8	Invalid
	9	Missing

IC07Q02 (213) Feel: fun IC7b

Format:	F1	Columns: 390-390
	1	Strongly agree
	2	Agree
	3	Disagree
	4	Strongly disagree
	7	N/A
	8	Invalid
	9	Missing

IC07Q03 (214) Feel: interested IC7c

Format:	F1	Columns: 391-391
	1	Strongly agree
	2	Agree
	3	Disagree
	4	Strongly disagree
	7	N/A
	8	Invalid
	9	Missing

IC07Q04 (215) Feel: forget time IC7d

Format:	F1	Columns: 392-392
	1	Strongly agree
	2	Agree
	3	Disagree
	4	Strongly disagree
	7	N/A
	8	Invalid
	9	Missing

IC08Q01 (216) Learn: computer IC8

Format:	F1	Columns: 393-393
	1	My school
	2	My friends
	3	My family
	4	Taught myself
	5	Others
	7	N/A
	8	Invalid
	9	Missing

IC09Q01 (217) Learn: Internet IC9

Format:	F1	Columns: 394-394
	1	Don t know how to use
	2	My school
	3	My friends
	4	My family
	5	Taught myself
	6	Others
	7	N/A
	8	Invalid
	9	Missing

SC07Q01 (218) Instructional weeks in year

Format:	F3	Columns: 395-397
	997	N/A
	998	Invalid
	999	Missing

CLCUSE3A (219) How much effort was invested in the test

Format:	F5	Columns: 398-402
	997	N/A
	998	Invalid
	999	Missing

CLCUSE3B (220) How much effort would has been invested if marks were counted by schools

Format:	F5	Columns: 403-407
	997	N/A
	998	Invalid
	999	Missing

AGE (221) age of student

Format: F5.2 Columns: 408-412

97.00 N/A

98.00 Invalid

99.00 Missing

GRADE (222) Grade compared to modal grade in country

Format: F2 Columns: 413-414

9 Missing

ISCEDL (223) ISCED Level

Format: F1 Columns: 415-415

1 ISCED level 1

2 ISCED level 2

3 ISCED level 3

7 N/A

8 Invalid

9 Missing

ISCEDD (224) ISCED designation

Format: F1 Columns: 416-416

1 A

2 B

3 C

4 M

7 N/A

8 Invalid

9 Missing

ISCEDO (225) ISCED orientation

Format: F1 Columns: 417-417

1 General

2 Pre-vocational

3 Vocational

7 N/A

8 Invalid

9 Missing

PROGN (226) Unique national programme code

Format: A6 Columns: 418-423

Value	Label
036001	AUS: <Year 10 in a general academic program
036002	AUS: <Year 10 in a general program (vocational)
036003	AUS: Year 11 or 12 in a general academic program
036004	AUS: Year 11 or 12 in a VET (vocational) course
040002	AUT: Hauptschule (Lower Secondary school)
040003	AUT: Polytechnische Schule (Vocational)
040004	AUT: Sonderschule (Special school (lower sec.))
040005	AUT: Sonderschul-Oberstufe (Special school (upper sec.))
040006	AUT: AHS-Unterstufe (Gymnasium Lower Secondary)
040007	AUT: AHS-Oberstufe (Gymnasium Upper Secondary)
040010	AUT: Berufsschule (Apprenticeship)
040011	AUT: BMS (Medium vocational school)
040012	AUT: Haushaltungs- und Hauswirtschaftsschulen (Medium voc.)
040014	AUT: BHS (Higher vocational school)
040015	AUT: Anst. Der Kindergarten-/ Sozialpadagogik (Voc. college)
056111	BEL: 1st year A of 1st stage of General Education (Fl.)
056112	BEL: 1st year B of 1st stage of General Education (Fl.)
056113	BEL: 2nd year of 1st stage, prep. voc. sec. education (Fl.)
056114	BEL: 2nd year of 1st stage, prep. reg. sec. education (Fl.)
056115	BEL: 2nd & 3rd stage regular sec. education (Fl.)
056116	BEL: 2nd & 3rd stage technical sec. education (Fl.)
056117	BEL: 2nd & 3rd stage artistic sec. education (Fl.)
056118	BEL: 2nd & 3rd stage vocational sec. ed. (Fl.)
056119	BEL: Part-time vocational sec. ed. for labour market (Fl.)
056120	BEL: Special sec. education (Fl.)
056197	BEL: Missing (Fl.)
056231	BEL: (1st grade of)General Education (Fr.)

056232	BEL: Special needs (Fr.)
056233	BEL: Vocational Education (Fr.)
056234	BEL: Complementary year or programme for 1st degree (Fr.)
056235	BEL: General Education (Fr.)
056236	BEL: Technical or Artistical Education (transition) (Fr.)
056237	BEL: Technical or Artistical Education (qualif.) (Fr.)
056238	BEL: Vocational Education (Fr.)
056239	BEL: Vocational training for labour market (Fr.)
056242	BEL: Special sec. education (form 3 or 4 – voc.) (Fr.)
056244	BEL: Special sec. education form 3 (Germ.)
056245	BEL: Part-time Vocational Education (Germ.)
056246	BEL: Vocational Education (Germ.)
056297	BEL: Missing (Fr.&Germ.)
076001	BRA: Lower sec. education
076002	BRA: Upper sec. education
076097	BRA: Missing
124102	CAN: Grades 7 – 9
124103	CAN: Grades 10 – 12
124197	CAN: Missing
203001	CZE: Basic school
203002	CZE: 6, 8-year gymnasium & 8-year conservatory (lower sec.)
203003	CZE: 6, 8-year gymnasium (upper sec.)
203004	CZE: 4- year gymnasium
203005	CZE: Voc/tech sec. school with maturate
203006	CZE: Conservatory (upper sec.)
203007	CZE: Voc/tech sec. school without maturate
203008	CZE: Special schools
203009	CZE: Practical schools, vocational education predominantly
208001	DNK: Lower sec.
208002	DNK: Continuation school
208004	DNK: Upper sec.
208097	DNK: Missing
246001	FIN: Comprehensive sec. school
250001	FRA: 5ème, 4ème, 3ème (lower sec.)
250002	FRA: SEGPA, CPA (special education)
250003	FRA: 2nde ou 1ère (générale ou techn.) (upper sec. general)
250004	FRA: Enseignement professionnel (upper sec. vocational)
250005	FRA: apprentissage (upper sec. vocational)
276001	DEU: Lower sec. access to upper sec. (compr., special educ.)
276002	DEU: Lower sec. no access to upper sec. (Hauptschule)
276003	DEU: Lower sec. no access to upper sec. (Realschule)
276004	DEU: Lower sec. access to upper sec. (Gymnasium)
276005	DEU: Lower sec. access to upper sec. (comprehensive)
276006	DEU: Lower sec. no access to upper sec. (Koop. Gesamtschule)
276009	DEU: Lower sec. no access to upper sec.
276010	DEU: Lower sec. no access to upper sec.
276011	DEU: Lower sec. no access to upper sec.
276012	DEU: Lower sec. no access to upper sec.
276013	DEU: Lower sec. with access to upper sec. (comprehensive)
276014	DEU: pre-vocational training year
276015	DEU: Vocational school (Berufsschule)
276016	DEU: Vocational school (Berufsfachschule)
276017	DEU: Upper sec. (Gymnasium)
276018	DEU: Upper sec. (comprehensive)
276097	DEU: Missing

300001	GRC: Gymnasio (lower sec. education)
300002	GRC: Eniaio Lykeio (upper sec. education)
300003	GRC: Technical-vocational training inst.): 1st & 2nd cycle
344001	HKG: Lower sec. in G & I Sch.
344002	HKG: Upper sec. in G & I Sch.
344003	HKG: Lower sec. in P & T Sch.
344004	HKG: Upper sec. in P & T Sch.
348001	HUN: Primary school
348002	HUN: Grammar school
348003	HUN: Vocational sec. school
348004	HUN: Vocational school
352001	ISL: Lower sec. school
360002	IDN: Junior sec. School
360003	IDN: Islamic Junior sec. School
360004	IDN: High School
360005	IDN: Islamic High School
360006	IDN: Vocational & Technical School
372001	IRL: Junior Cert
372002	IRL: Transition Year Programme
372003	IRL: Leaving Cert. Applied
372004	IRL: Leaving Cert. General
372005	IRL: Leaving Cert. Vocational
380001	ITA: Lower sec. education
380002	ITA: Technical Institute
380003	ITA: Professional or Art Institute, Art High School
380004	ITA: Scientif., Classical or linguistic High School
380005	ITA: Professional School (only in Bolzano)
392001	JPN: Upper sec. school (General)
392002	JPN: Technical college (1st 3 years)
392003	JPN: Upper sec. school (Vocational)
410001	KOR: Lower sec. Education (Jung-hakgyo)
410002	KOR: Upper sec. Education (Ilban Kodeung-hakgyo)
410003	KOR: Upper sec. Education (Silup Kodeung-hakgyo)
428001	LVA: Basic education
428004	LVA: General sec. education
428097	LVA: Missing
438001	LIE: sec. education, 1st stage
438002	LIE: Preparatory course for vocational education
438003	LIE: School prep. for the university entrance certificate
442001	LUX: Year 7 or 8 or 9
442002	LUX: Year 7 or 8 or 9
442003	LUX: Year 10 or 11, with mostly VET (vocational) subjects
442004	LUX: Year 10-12, in a program leading to an apprenticeship
442005	LUX: Year 10-12 in a program leading to higher education
442006	LUX: Year 10-12 in a program leading to university
446001	MAC: Lower sec. in G & I Sch.
446002	MAC: Upper sec. in G & I Sch.
446003	MAC: Lower sec. in P & T Sch.
446004	MAC: Upper sec. in P & T Sch.
484001	MEX: General Lower sec.
484002	MEX: Technical Lower sec.
484003	MEX: Lower sec. for workers
484004	MEX: General Lower sec. by Television
484005	MEX: Job Training
484006	MEX: General Baccalaureate or Upper sec.(Years prog.)
484007	MEX: General Baccalaureate or Upper sec.(semester prog.)
484008	MEX: General Baccalaureate or Upper sec.(two years prog.)
484009	MEX: Technical Baccalaureate or Upper sec. (semester prog.)
484010	MEX: Professional Technician (semester prog.)
528001	NLD: PRO
528002	NLD: VMBO
528003	NLD: VMBO BB
528004	NLD: VMBO KB
528005	NLD: VMBO GL
528006	NLD: VMBO TL

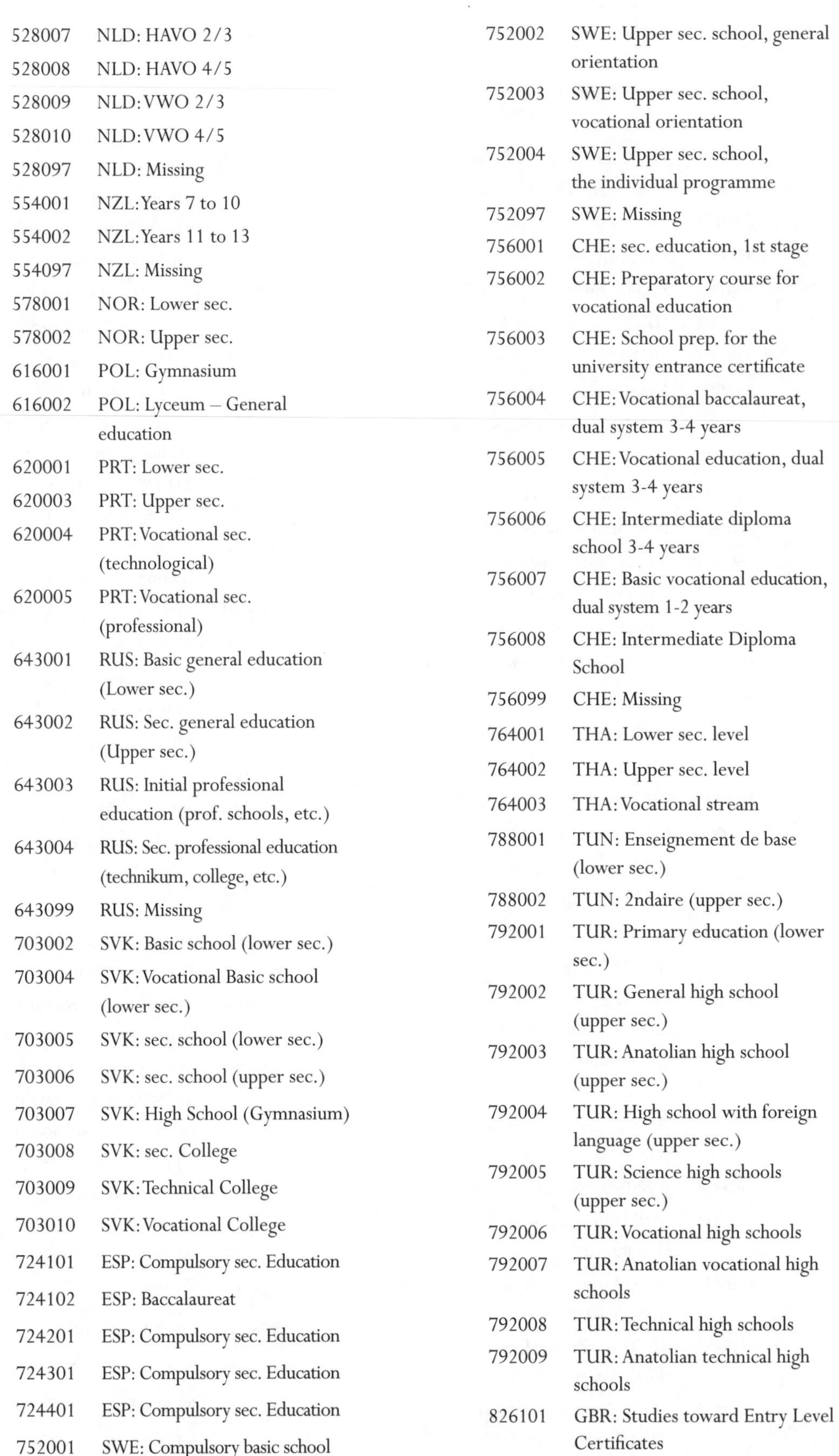

Code	Description
528007	NLD: HAVO 2/3
528008	NLD: HAVO 4/5
528009	NLD: VWO 2/3
528010	NLD: VWO 4/5
528097	NLD: Missing
554001	NZL: Years 7 to 10
554002	NZL: Years 11 to 13
554097	NZL: Missing
578001	NOR: Lower sec.
578002	NOR: Upper sec.
616001	POL: Gymnasium
616002	POL: Lyceum – General education
620001	PRT: Lower sec.
620003	PRT: Upper sec.
620004	PRT: Vocational sec. (technological)
620005	PRT: Vocational sec. (professional)
643001	RUS: Basic general education (Lower sec.)
643002	RUS: Sec. general education (Upper sec.)
643003	RUS: Initial professional education (prof. schools, etc.)
643004	RUS: Sec. professional education (technikum, college, etc.)
643099	RUS: Missing
703002	SVK: Basic school (lower sec.)
703004	SVK: Vocational Basic school (lower sec.)
703005	SVK: sec. school (lower sec.)
703006	SVK: sec. school (upper sec.)
703007	SVK: High School (Gymnasium)
703008	SVK: sec. College
703009	SVK: Technical College
703010	SVK: Vocational College
724101	ESP: Compulsory sec. Education
724102	ESP: Baccalaureat
724201	ESP: Compulsory sec. Education
724301	ESP: Compulsory sec. Education
724401	ESP: Compulsory sec. Education
752001	SWE: Compulsory basic school
752002	SWE: Upper sec. school, general orientation
752003	SWE: Upper sec. school, vocational orientation
752004	SWE: Upper sec. school, the individual programme
752097	SWE: Missing
756001	CHE: sec. education, 1st stage
756002	CHE: Preparatory course for vocational education
756003	CHE: School prep. for the university entrance certificate
756004	CHE: Vocational baccalaureat, dual system 3-4 years
756005	CHE: Vocational education, dual system 3-4 years
756006	CHE: Intermediate diploma school 3-4 years
756007	CHE: Basic vocational education, dual system 1-2 years
756008	CHE: Intermediate Diploma School
756099	CHE: Missing
764001	THA: Lower sec. level
764002	THA: Upper sec. level
764003	THA: Vocational stream
788001	TUN: Enseignement de base (lower sec.)
788002	TUN: 2ndaire (upper sec.)
792001	TUR: Primary education (lower sec.)
792002	TUR: General high school (upper sec.)
792003	TUR: Anatolian high school (upper sec.)
792004	TUR: High school with foreign language (upper sec.)
792005	TUR: Science high schools (upper sec.)
792006	TUR: Vocational high schools
792007	TUR: Anatolian vocational high schools
792008	TUR: Technical high schools
792009	TUR: Anatolian technical high schools
826101	GBR: Studies toward Entry Level Certificates

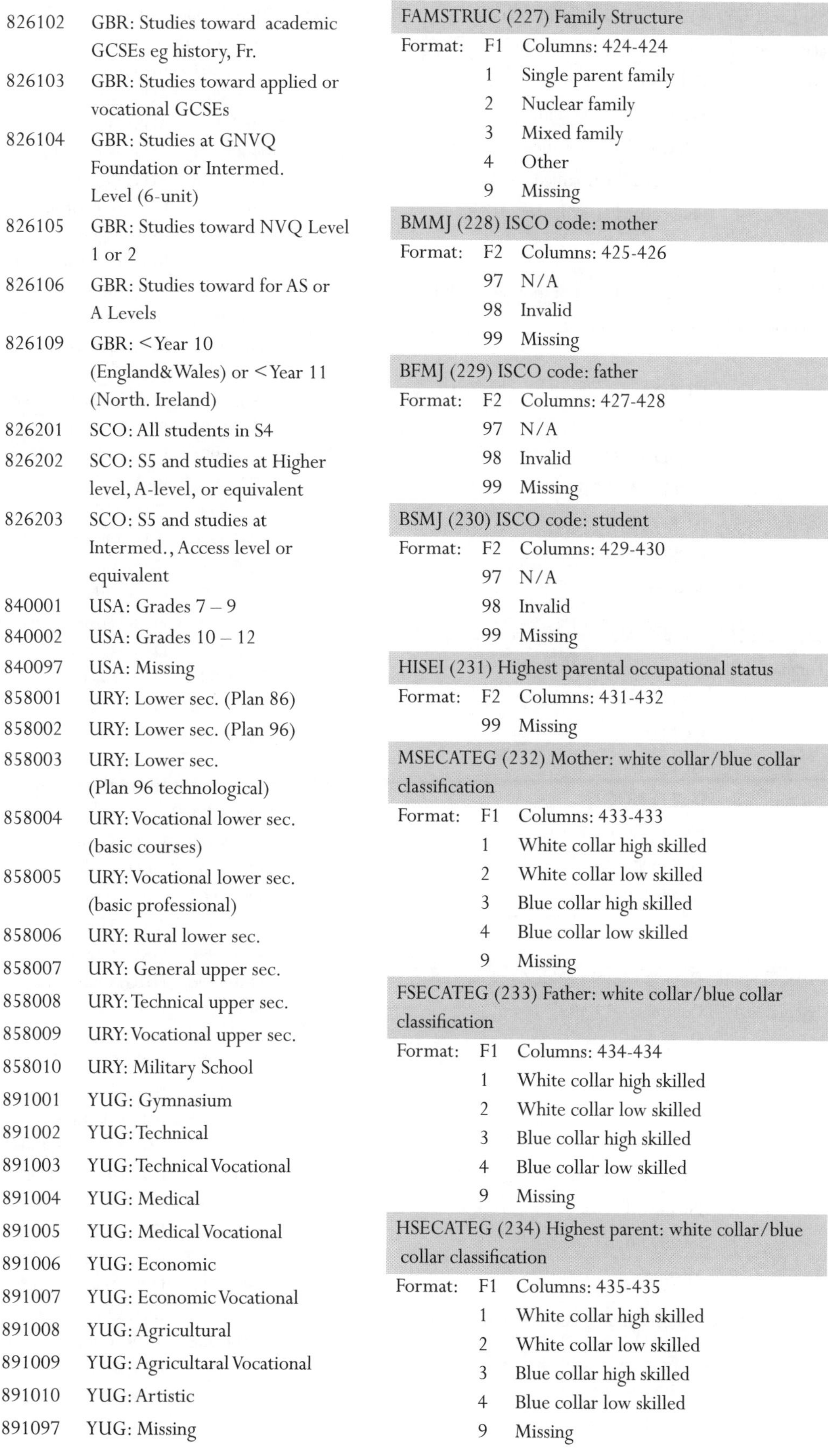

Code	Label
826102	GBR: Studies toward academic GCSEs eg history, Fr.
826103	GBR: Studies toward applied or vocational GCSEs
826104	GBR: Studies at GNVQ Foundation or Intermed. Level (6-unit)
826105	GBR: Studies toward NVQ Level 1 or 2
826106	GBR: Studies toward for AS or A Levels
826109	GBR: <Year 10 (England&Wales) or <Year 11 (North. Ireland)
826201	SCO: All students in S4
826202	SCO: S5 and studies at Higher level, A-level, or equivalent
826203	SCO: S5 and studies at Intermed., Access level or equivalent
840001	USA: Grades 7 – 9
840002	USA: Grades 10 – 12
840097	USA: Missing
858001	URY: Lower sec. (Plan 86)
858002	URY: Lower sec. (Plan 96)
858003	URY: Lower sec. (Plan 96 technological)
858004	URY: Vocational lower sec. (basic courses)
858005	URY: Vocational lower sec. (basic professional)
858006	URY: Rural lower sec.
858007	URY: General upper sec.
858008	URY: Technical upper sec.
858009	URY: Vocational upper sec.
858010	URY: Military School
891001	YUG: Gymnasium
891002	YUG: Technical
891003	YUG: Technical Vocational
891004	YUG: Medical
891005	YUG: Medical Vocational
891006	YUG: Economic
891007	YUG: Economic Vocational
891008	YUG: Agricultural
891009	YUG: Agricultaral Vocational
891010	YUG: Artistic
891097	YUG: Missing

FAMSTRUC (227) Family Structure

Format:	F1	Columns: 424-424
	1	Single parent family
	2	Nuclear family
	3	Mixed family
	4	Other
	9	Missing

BMMJ (228) ISCO code: mother

Format:	F2	Columns: 425-426
	97	N/A
	98	Invalid
	99	Missing

BFMJ (229) ISCO code: father

Format:	F2	Columns: 427-428
	97	N/A
	98	Invalid
	99	Missing

BSMJ (230) ISCO code: student

Format:	F2	Columns: 429-430
	97	N/A
	98	Invalid
	99	Missing

HISEI (231) Highest parental occupational status

Format:	F2	Columns: 431-432
	99	Missing

MSECATEG (232) Mother: white collar/blue collar classification

Format:	F1	Columns: 433-433
	1	White collar high skilled
	2	White collar low skilled
	3	Blue collar high skilled
	4	Blue collar low skilled
	9	Missing

FSECATEG (233) Father: white collar/blue collar classification

Format:	F1	Columns: 434-434
	1	White collar high skilled
	2	White collar low skilled
	3	Blue collar high skilled
	4	Blue collar low skilled
	9	Missing

HSECATEG (234) Highest parent: white collar/blue collar classification

Format:	F1	Columns: 435-435
	1	White collar high skilled
	2	White collar low skilled
	3	Blue collar high skilled
	4	Blue collar low skilled
	9	Missing

SSECATEG (235) Self: white collar/blue collar classification

Format: F1 Columns: 436-436

1 White collar high skilled
2 White collar low skilled
3 Blue collar high skilled
4 Blue collar low skilled
9 Missing

MISCED (236) Educational level of mother (ISCED)

Format: F1 Columns: 437-437

0 None
1 ISCED 1
2 ISCED 2
3 ISCED 3B, C
4 ISCED 3A, ISCED 4
5 ISCED 5B
6 ISCED 5A, 6
9 Missing

FISCED (237) Educational level of father (ISCED)

Format: F1 Columns: 438-438

0 None
1 ISCED 1
2 ISCED 2
3 ISCED 3B, C
4 ISCED 3A, ISCED 4
5 ISCED 5B
6 ISCED 5A, 6
9 Missing

HISCED (238) Highest educational level of parents

Format: F1 Columns: 439-439

0 None
1 ISCED 1
2 ISCED 2
3 ISCED 3B, C
4 ISCED 3A, ISCED 4
5 ISCED 5B
6 ISCED 5A, 6
9 Missing

PARED (239) Highest parental education in years of schooling

Format: F2 Columns: 440-441

99 Missing

ISO_S (240) ISO code country of birth: student

Format: A8 Columns:

03608261 AUS: England
03608262 AUS: Scotland
03609996 AUS: Other
04000391 AUT: Former Yugoslavia
04009996 AUT: Other
05610021 BFL: An African country (not Maghreb)
05610151 BFL: A Maghreb country
05611501 BFL: Another country of the EU
05619996 BFL: Other
05620021 BFR: An African country (not Maghreb)
05620151 BFR: A Maghreb country
05621501 BFR: Another country of the EU
05629996 BFR: Other
07609996 BRA: Other
12419996 CAE: Other
12429996 CAF: Other
12439996 CAN: Other
20309996 CZE: Other
20800391 DNK: Former Yugoslavia
20809996 DNK: Other
24609996 FIN: Other
25009996 FRA: Other
27601501 DEU: Russia, Kazakhstan or another Republic of the Former Soviet Union
27608911 DEU: Montenegro
27608912 DEU: Serbia
27609996 DEU: Other
30001501 GRC: Republics of the Former Soviet Union
30009996 GRC: Other
34409996 HKG: Other
34809996 HUN: Other
35209996 ISL: Other
36009996 IDN: Other
37200701 IRL: Bosnia
37203761 IRL: Palestine
37208261 IRL: Northern Ireland
37208262 IRL: Great Britain
37209996 IRL: Other
38001501 ITA: An European country that is not member of the EU
38009996 ITA: Other
39209996 JPN: Other
41009996 KOR: Other
42809996 LVA: Other
44209996 LUX: Other
44609996 MAC: Other

Code	Label
48409996	MEX: Other
52801501	NLD: Other European country
52809996	NLD: Other
55409996	NZL: Other
57809996	NOR: Other
61609996	POL: Other
62009996	PRT: Other
64301501	RUS: Republics of the Former Soviet Union
64309996	RUS: Other
70301501	SVK: Other European country of Europe
70309996	SVK: Other
72419996	ESC: Other
72429996	ECL: Other
72439996	ECT: Other
72449996	EBS: Other
75209996	SWE: Other
75600391	CHE: Former Yugoslavia
75600392	CHE: Albania or Kosovo
75601551	CHE: Germany or Austria
75601552	CHE: France or Belgium
75607560	CHE: Switzerland
75609996	CHE: Other
76409996	THA: Other
78809996	TUN: Other
79209996	TUR: Other
82619996	GRB: Other
82620301	SCO: China (incl Hong Kong)
82621421	SCO: Middle East
82621501	SCO: Other European country
82628261	SCO: England, Wales, N Ireland
82628262	SCO: Scotland
82629996	SCO: Other
84009996	USA: Other
85809996	URY: Other
89101491	YUG: Former Yugoslavia
89109996	YUG: Other
99990020	Africa
99990080	Albania
99990290	Caribbean
99990320	Argentina
99990360	Australia
99990400	Austria
99990500	Bangladesh
99990560	Belgium
99990600	Bermuda
99990700	Bosnia-Herzegovina
99990760	Brazil
99991000	Bulgaria
99991040	Myanmar (Burma)
99991120	Belarus
99991240	Canada
99991440	Sri Lanka
99991490	Former Yugoslavia
99991510	An East-European country
99991560	China
99991840	Cook Islands
99991910	Croatia
99992030	Czech Republic
99992080	Denmark
99992330	Estonia
99992420	Fiji
99992460	Finland
99992500	France
99992680	Georgia
99992760	Germany
99993000	Greece
99993440	Hong Kong
99993480	Hungary
99993520	Iceland
99993560	India
99993600	Indonesia
99993640	Iran
99993680	Iraq
99993720	Ireland
99993800	Italy
99993880	Jamaica
99993920	Japan
99994000	Jordan
99994100	Korea
99994220	Lebanon
99994280	Latvia
99994340	Libya
99994400	Lithuania
99994420	Luxembourg
99994460	Macau
99994580	Malaysia
99994840	Mexico
99995160	Namibia
99995280	Netherlands
99995540	New Zealand
99995660	Nigeria
99995780	Norway
99995860	Pakistan
99996080	Philippines
99996160	Poland
99996200	Portugal
99996420	Romania
99996430	Russia
99996820	Saudi Arabia
99997030	Slovakia

99997040	Vietnam
99997050	Slovenia
99997100	South Africa
99997160	Zimbabwe
99997240	Spain
99997520	Sweden
99997560	Switzerland
99997640	Thailand
99997760	Tonga
99997880	Tunisia
99997920	Turkey
99998040	Ukraine
99998070	Macedonia
99998180	Egypt
99998260	United Kingdom
99998340	Tanzania
99998400	United States
99998580	Uruguay
99998820	Samoa
99998910	Yugoslavia
99998940	Zambia

ISO_M (241) ISO code country of birth: mother

Format: A8 Columns:

See ISO_ S

ISO_F (242) ISO code country of birth: father

Format: A8 Columns:

See ISO_ S

IMMIG (243) Country of birth

Format: F1 Columns: 466-466

1	Native students
2	First-generation students
3	Non-native students
9	Missing

LANG (244) Foreign language spoken at home

Format: F1 Columns: 467-467

0	Test language or other national language
1	Foreign language
7	N/A
8	Invalid
9	Missing

LANGN (245) Language at home, national

Format: A6 Columns: 468-473

Value	Label
036001	AUS: English
036002	AUS: Indigenous Australian languages
036003	AUS: Italian
036004	AUS: Greek
036005	AUS: Cantonese
036006	AUS: Mandarin
036007	AUS: Arabic
036008	AUS: Vietnamese
036009	AUS: German
036010	AUS: Spanish
036011	AUS: Tagalog (Philippines)
036012	AUS: Other languages
036097	AUS: N/A
036098	AUS: Invalid
036099	AUS: Missing
040001	AUT: German
040002	AUT: Turkish
040003	AUT: Serbo-Croat
040004	AUT: Romanian
040005	AUT: Polish
040006	AUT: Hungarian
040007	AUT: Albanian
040008	AUT: Czech
040009	AUT: Slovak
040010	AUT: Slovenian
040011	AUT: Other languages
040097	AUT: N/A
040098	AUT: Invalid
040099	AUT: Missing
056101	BEL (Fl.): Dutch
056102	BEL (Fl.): French
056103	BEL (Fl.): German
056104	BEL (Fl.): Flemish dialect
056105	BEL (Fl.): English
056106	BEL (Fl.): Other EU languages
056107	BEL (Fl.): Arabic
056108	BEL (Fl.): Turkish
056109	BEL (Fl.): Eastern European languages
056110	BEL (Fl.): Other languages
056197	BEL (Fl.): N/A
056198	BEL (Fl.): Invalid
056199	BEL (Fl.): Missing
056201	BEL (Fr.): French
056202	BEL (Fr.): Dutch
056203	BEL (Fr.): German
056204	BEL (Fr.): Wallon
056205	BEL (Fr.): English
056206	BEL (Fr.): Other EU languages
056207	BEL (Fr.): Arabic
056208	BEL (Fr.): Turkish
056209	BEL (Fr.): Eastern European languages

Code	Label
056210	BEL (Fr.): Other languages
056297	BEL (Fr.): N/A
056298	BEL (Fr.): Invalid
056299	BEL (Fr.): Missing
056301	BEL (German): German
056302	BEL (German): French
056303	BEL (German): Dutch
056304	BEL (German): Wallon
056305	BEL (German): English
056306	BEL (German): Other EU languages
056307	BEL (German): Arabic
056309	BEL (German): Eastern European languages
056398	BEL (German): Invalid
056399	BEL (German): Missing
076001	BRA: Portuguese
076002	BRA: Other national language – indigenous
076003	BRA: Other languages
076097	BRA: N/A
076098	BRA: Invalid
076099	BRA: Missing
124101	CAN: English
124102	CAN: French
124103	CAN: Other languages
124197	CAN: N/A
124198	CAN: Invalid
124199	CAN: Missing
203001	CZE: Czech
203002	CZE: Slovak
203003	CZE: Romani
203004	CZE: Other languages
203097	CZE: N/A
203098	CZE: Invalid
203099	CZE: Missing
208001	DNK: Danish
208002	DNK: Turkish
208003	DNK: Serbo-Croatian
208004	DNK: Punjabi
208005	DNK: Urdu
208006	DNK: Arabic
208007	DNK: Other languages
208097	DNK: N/A
208098	DNK: Invalid
208099	DNK: Missing
246001	FIN: Finnish
246002	FIN: Swedish
246003	FIN: Sami
246004	FIN: Romani
246005	FIN: Russian
246006	FIN: Estonian
246007	FIN: Other language
246097	FIN: N/A
246098	FIN: Invalid
246099	FIN: Missing
250001	FRA: French
250002	FRA: Other national dialects or languages
250003	FRA: Other languages
250097	FRA: N/A
250099	FRA: Missing
276001	DEU: German
276004	DEU: Bosnian
276005	DEU: Greek
276006	DEU: Italian
276007	DEU: Croatian
276008	DEU: Polish
276009	DEU: Russian
276010	DEU: Serbian
276011	DEU: Turkish
276012	DEU: Kurdish
276013	DEU: Other languages
276097	DEU: N/A
276098	DEU: Invalid
276099	DEU: Missing
300001	GRC: Greek
300002	GRC: Albanian
300003	GRC: Languages of the former Soviet Union
300004	GRC: Bulgarian
300005	GRC: Other languages
300097	GRC: N/A
300098	GRC: Invalid
300099	GRC: Missing
344001	HKG: Cantonese
344002	HKG: English
344003	HKG: Other national dialects or languages
344004	HKG: Other languages
344097	HKG: N/A
344098	HKG: Invalid
344099	HKG: Missing
344298	HKI: Invalid
348001	HUN: Hungarian
348002	HUN: Other languages
348097	HUN: N/A
348098	HUN: Invalid
348099	HUN: Missing

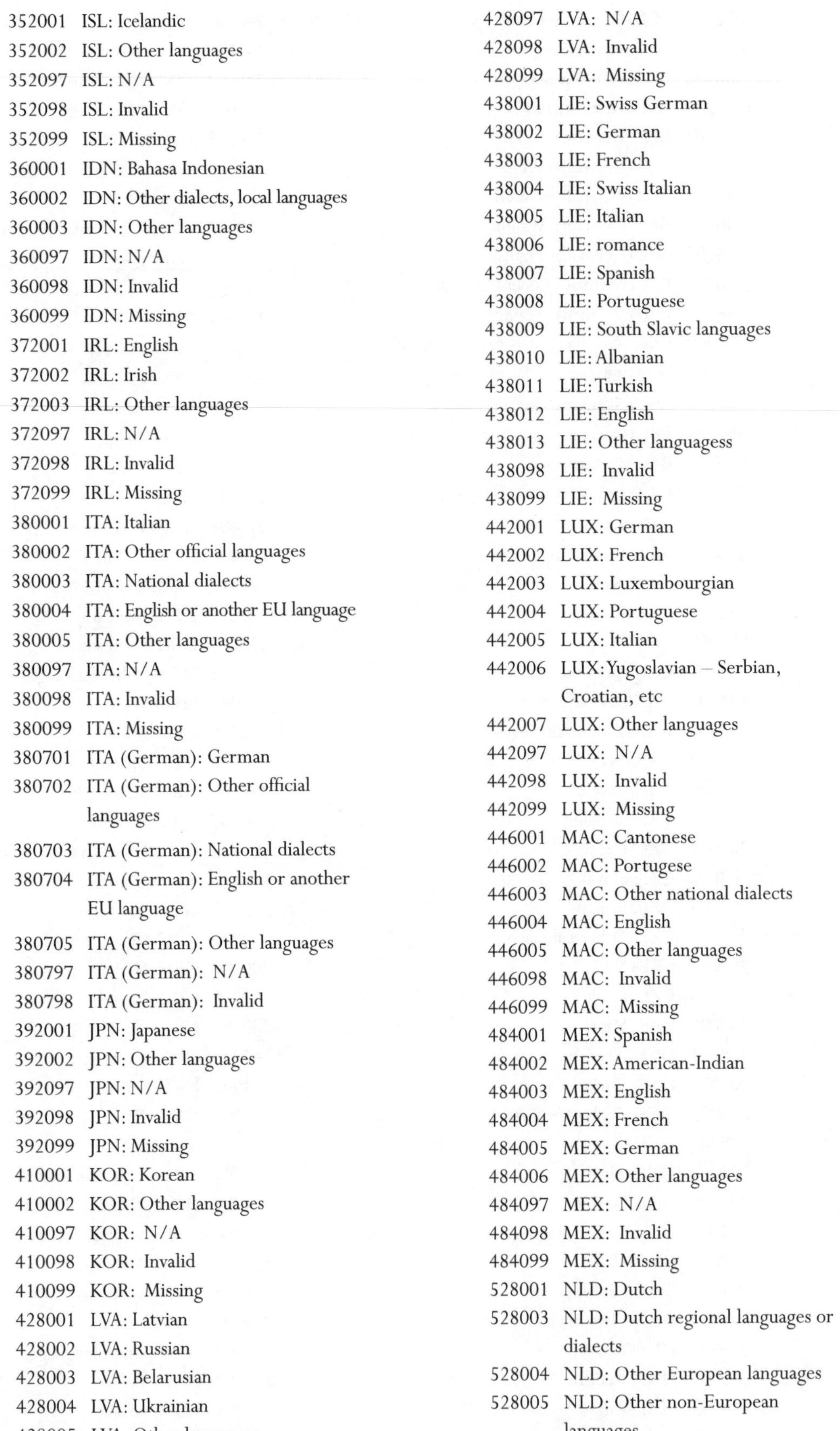

352001 ISL: Icelandic
352002 ISL: Other languages
352097 ISL: N/A
352098 ISL: Invalid
352099 ISL: Missing
360001 IDN: Bahasa Indonesian
360002 IDN: Other dialects, local languages
360003 IDN: Other languages
360097 IDN: N/A
360098 IDN: Invalid
360099 IDN: Missing
372001 IRL: English
372002 IRL: Irish
372003 IRL: Other languages
372097 IRL: N/A
372098 IRL: Invalid
372099 IRL: Missing
380001 ITA: Italian
380002 ITA: Other official languages
380003 ITA: National dialects
380004 ITA: English or another EU language
380005 ITA: Other languages
380097 ITA: N/A
380098 ITA: Invalid
380099 ITA: Missing
380701 ITA (German): German
380702 ITA (German): Other official languages
380703 ITA (German): National dialects
380704 ITA (German): English or another EU language
380705 ITA (German): Other languages
380797 ITA (German): N/A
380798 ITA (German): Invalid
392001 JPN: Japanese
392002 JPN: Other languages
392097 JPN: N/A
392098 JPN: Invalid
392099 JPN: Missing
410001 KOR: Korean
410002 KOR: Other languages
410097 KOR: N/A
410098 KOR: Invalid
410099 KOR: Missing
428001 LVA: Latvian
428002 LVA: Russian
428003 LVA: Belarusian
428004 LVA: Ukrainian
428005 LVA: Other languages
428097 LVA: N/A
428098 LVA: Invalid
428099 LVA: Missing
438001 LIE: Swiss German
438002 LIE: German
438003 LIE: French
438004 LIE: Swiss Italian
438005 LIE: Italian
438006 LIE: romance
438007 LIE: Spanish
438008 LIE: Portuguese
438009 LIE: South Slavic languages
438010 LIE: Albanian
438011 LIE: Turkish
438012 LIE: English
438013 LIE: Other languagess
438098 LIE: Invalid
438099 LIE: Missing
442001 LUX: German
442002 LUX: French
442003 LUX: Luxembourgian
442004 LUX: Portuguese
442005 LUX: Italian
442006 LUX: Yugoslavian – Serbian, Croatian, etc
442007 LUX: Other languages
442097 LUX: N/A
442098 LUX: Invalid
442099 LUX: Missing
446001 MAC: Cantonese
446002 MAC: Portugese
446003 MAC: Other national dialects
446004 MAC: English
446005 MAC: Other languages
446098 MAC: Invalid
446099 MAC: Missing
484001 MEX: Spanish
484002 MEX: American-Indian
484003 MEX: English
484004 MEX: French
484005 MEX: German
484006 MEX: Other languages
484097 MEX: N/A
484098 MEX: Invalid
484099 MEX: Missing
528001 NLD: Dutch
528003 NLD: Dutch regional languages or dialects
528004 NLD: Other European languages
528005 NLD: Other non-European languages

528097 NLD: N/A
528098 NLD: Invalid
528099 NLD: Missing
554001 NZL: English
554002 NZL: Te Reo Maori
554003 NZL: Samoan
554004 NZL: Tongan
554005 NZL: Mandarin
554006 NZL: Cantonese
554007 NZL: Hindi
554008 NZL: Other languages
554097 NZL: N/A
554098 NZL: Invalid
554099 NZL: Missing
578001 NOR: Norwegian
578002 NOR: Sami
578003 NOR: Swedish
578004 NOR: Danish
578005 NOR: Other languages
578097 NOR: N/A
578098 NOR: Invalid
578099 NOR: Missing
616001 POL: Polish
616002 POL: Other languages
616099 POL: Missing
620001 PRT: Portuguese
620002 PRT: Other languages
620097 PRT: N/A
620098 PRT: Invalid
620099 PRT: Missing
643001 RUS: Russian
643002 RUS: Other languages
643097 RUS: N/A
643098 RUS: Invalid
643099 RUS: Missing
703001 SVK: Slovak
703002 SVK: Hungarian
703004 SVK: Czech
703005 SVK: Other Slavonic languages
703006 SVK: Romani
703007 SVK: Other languages
703097 SVK: N/A
703098 SVK: Invalid
703099 SVK: Missing
724001 ESP: Castilian
724002 ESP: Catalonian
724003 ESP: Galician
724004 ESP: Valencian
724005 ESP: Basque
724006 ESP: Other languagess
724097 ESP: N/A
724098 ESP: Invalid
724099 ESP: Missing
752001 SWE: Swedish
752002 SWE: Finnish, Yiddish, Romani, Sami or Tornedalen
752003 SWE: Other languages
752097 SWE: N/A
752098 SWE: Invalid
752099 SWE: Missing
756101 CHE (French): Swiss German
756102 CHE (French): German
756103 CHE (French): French
756104 CHE (French): Swiss Italian
756105 CHE (French): Italian
756106 CHE (French): Romansch
756107 CHE (French): Spanish
756108 CHE (French): Portuguese
756109 CHE (French): South Slavic languages
756110 CHE (French): Albanian
756111 CHE (French): Turkish
756112 CHE (French): English
756113 CHE (French): Other languages
756197 CHE (French): N/A
756198 CHE (French): Invalid
756199 CHE (French): Missing
756201 CHE (German): Swiss German
756202 CHE (German): German
756203 CHE (German): French
756204 CHE (German): Swiss Italian
756205 CHE (German): Italian
756206 CHE (German): romance
756207 CHE (German): Spanish
756208 CHE (German): Portuguese
756209 CHE (German): South Slavic languages
756210 CHE (German): Albanian
756211 CHE (German): Turkish
756212 CHE (German): English
756213 CHE (German): Other languagess
756297 CHE (German): N/A
756298 CHE (German): Invalid
756299 CHE (German): Missing
756301 CHE (Italian): Swiss German
756302 CHE (Italian): German
756303 CHE (Italian): French
756304 CHE (Italian): Swiss Italian
756305 CHE (Italian): Italian
756306 CHE (Italian): romance
756307 CHE (Italian): Spanish
756308 CHE (Italian): Portuguese
756309 CHE (Italian): South Slavic languages
756310 CHE (Italian): Albanian

756311 CHE (Italian): Turkish
756312 CHE (Italian): English
756313 CHE (Italian): Other languages
756397 CHE (Italian): N/A
756398 CHE (Italian): Invalid
756399 CHE (Italian): Missing
764001 THA: Thai central
764002 THA: Other Thai dialects
764003 THA: Other languages
764099 THA: Missing
788001 TUN: Arabic
788002 TUN: Arabic, Tunisian dialect
788003 TUN: French
788004 TUN: Other languages
788097 TUN: N/A
788098 TUN: Invalid
788099 TUN: Missing
792001 TUR: Turkish
792002 TUR: Other national dialects or languages
792003 TUR: English
792004 TUR: French
792005 TUR: German
792006 TUR: Other languages
792097 TUR: N/A
792098 TUR: Invalid
792099 TUR: Missing
826101 GBR (Eng., Wales, NI): English
826102 GBR (Eng., Wales, NI): Irish
826103 GBR (Eng., Wales, NI): Ulster Scots
826104 GBR (Eng., Wales, NI): Welsh
826105 GBR (Eng., Wales, NI): Other languages
826197 GBR (Eng., Wales, NI): N/A
826198 GBR (Eng., Wales, NI): Invalid
826199 GBR (Eng., Wales, NI): Missing
826201 GBR (Scotland): English or Scots
826202 GBR (Scotland): Gaelic
826204 GBR (Scotland): Arabic
826205 GBR (Scotland): Bengali
826206 GBR (Scotland): Cantonese or Mandarin
826207 GBR (Scotland): Gujarati
826208 GBR (Scotland): Hindi
826209 GBR (Scotland): Malay
826210 GBR (Scotland): Punjabi
826211 GBR (Scotland): Urdu
826212 GBR (Scotland): Other European languages
826213 GBR (Scotland): Other non-European languages
826297 GBR (Scotland): N/A
826298 GBR (Scotland): Invalid
826299 GBR (Scotland): Missing
840001 USA: English
840002 USA: Spanish
840003 USA: Other languages
840097 USA: N/A
840098 USA: Invalid
840099 USA: Missing
858001 URY: Spanish
858002 URY: Portuguese
858003 URY: English
858004 URY: Other languages
858097 URY: N/A
858098 URY: Invalid
858099 URY: Missing
891001 YUG: Serbian
891002 YUG: Hungarian
891003 YUG: Albanian
891004 YUG: Romanian
891005 YUG: Slovak
891006 YUG: Other languages
891097 YUG: N/A
891098 YUG: Invalid
891099 YUG: Missing

SISCED (246) Expected educational level of student

Format: F1 Columns: 474-474
0 ISCED 1
1 ISCED 2
2 ISCED 3B, C
3 ISCED 3A, ISCED 4
4 ISCED 5B
5 ISCED 5A, 6
9 Missing

MMINS (247) Minutes of maths per week

Format: F5 Columns: 475-482
997 N/A
998 Invalid
999 Missing

TMINS (248) Total minutes of instructional time p/w

Format: F5 Columns: 483-490
997 N/A
998 Invalid
999 Missing

PCMATH (249) Ratio of maths and total instructional time

Format: F8.3 Columns: 491-496
997.000 N/A
998.000 Invalid
999.000 Missing

RMHMWK (250) Relative time spent on maths homework
Format: F9.4Columns: 497-504
999.0000 Missing

COMPHOME (251) Computer facilities at home (WLE)
Format: F9.4Columns: 505-513
999.0000 Missing

CULTPOSS (252) Cultural possessions of the family (WLE)
Format: F9.4Columns: 514-522
999.0000 Missing

HEDRES (253) Home educational resources (WLE)
Format: F9.4Columns: 523-531
999.0000 Missing

HOMEPOS (254) Index of home possessions (WLE)
Format: F9.4Columns: 532-540
999.0000 Missing

ATSCHL (255) Attitudes towards school (WLE)
Format: F9.4Columns: 541-549
999.0000 Missing

STUREL (256) Student-teacher relations at school (WLE)
Format: F9.4Columns: 550-558
999.0000 Missing

BELONG (257) Sense of belonging to school (WLE)
Format: F9.4Columns: 559-567
999.0000 Missing

INTMAT (258) Interest in mathematics (WLE)
Format: F9.4Columns: 568-576
999.0000 Missing

INSTMOT (259) Instrumental motivation in mathematics (WLE)
Format: F9.4Columns: 577-585
999.0000 Missing

MATHEFF (260) Mathematics self-efficacy (WLE)
Format: F9.4Columns: 586-594
999.0000 Missing

ANXMAT (261) Mathematics anxiety (WLE)
Format: F9.4Columns: 595-603
999.0000 Missing

SCMAT (262) Mathematics self-concept (WLE)
Format: F9.4Columns: 604-612
999.0000 Missing

CSTRAT (263) Control strategies (WLE)
Format: F9.4Columns: 613-621
999.0000 Missing

ELAB (264) Elaboration strategies (WLE)
Format: F9.4Columns: 622-630
999.0000 Missing

MEMOR (265) Memorisation strategies (WLE)
Format: F9.4Columns: 631-639
999.0000 Missing

COMPLRN (266) Competitive learning (WLE)
Format: F9.4Columns: 640-648
999.0000 Missing

COOPLRN (267) Co-operative learning (WLE)
Format: F9.4Columns: 649-657
999.0000 Missing

TEACHSUP (268) Teacher support in maths lessons (WLE)
Format: F9.4Columns: 658-666
999.0000 Missing

DISCLIM (269) Disciplinary climate in maths lessons (WLE)
Format: F9.4Columns: 667-675
999.0000 Missing

INTUSE (270) ICT: Internet/entertainment use (WLE)
Format: F9.4Columns: 676-684
999.0000 Missing

PRGUSE (271) ICT: Programs/software use (WLE)
Format: F9.4Columns: 685-693
999.0000 Missing

ROUTCONF (272) ICT: Confidence in routine tasks (WLE)
Format: F9.4Columns: 694-702
999.0000 Missing

INTCONF (273) ICT: Confidence in internet tasks (WLE)
Format: F9.4Columns: 703-711
999.0000 Missing

HIGHCONF (274) ICT: Confidence in high-level tasks (WLE)
Format: F9.4Columns: 712-720
999.0000 Missing

ATTCOMP (275) ICT: Attitudes towards computers (WLE)
Format: F9.4Columns: 721-729
999.0000 Missing

ESCS (276) Index of Socio-Economic and Cultural Status
Format: F10.5 Columns: 730-739
999.00000 Missing

PV1MATH (277) Plausible value in math
Format: F9.4Columns: 740-748
9997.0000 N/A

PV2MATH (278) Plausible value in math
Format: F9.4Columns: 749-757
9997.0000 N/A

PV3MATH (279) Plausible value in math
Format: F9.4Columns: 758-766
9997.0000 N/A

PV4MATH (280) Plausible value in math
Format: F9.4Columns: 767-775
9997.0000 N/A

PV5MATH (281) Plausible value in math
Format: F9.4Columns: 776-784
9997.0000 N/A

PV1MATH1 (282) Plausible value in math – Space and Shape
Format: F9.4Columns: 785-793
9997.0000 N/A

PV2MATH1 (283) Plausible value in math – Space and Shape
Format: F9.4Columns: 794-802
9997.0000 N/A

PV3MATH1 (284) Plausible value in math – Space and Shape
Format: F9.4Columns: 803-811
9997.0000 N/A

PV4MATH1 (285) Plausible value in math – Space and Shape
Format: F9.4Columns: 812-820
9997.0000 N/A

PV5MATH1 (286) Plausible value in math – Space and Shape
Format: F9.4Columns: 821-829
9997.0000 N/A

PV1MATH2 (287) Plausible value in math – Change and Relationships
Format: F9.4Columns: 830-838
9997.0000 N/A

PV2MATH2 (288) Plausible value in math – Change and Relationships
Format: F9.4Columns: 839-847
9997.0000 N/A

PV3MATH2 (289) Plausible value in math – Change and Relationships
Format: F9.4Columns: 848-856
9997.0000 N/A

PV4MATH2 (290) Plausible value in math – Change and Relationships
Format: F9.4Columns: 857-865
9997.0000 N/A

PV5MATH2 (291) Plausible value in math – Change and Relationships
Format: F9.4Columns: 866-874
9997.0000 N/A

PV1MATH3 (292) Plausible value in math – Uncertainty
Format: F9.4Columns: 875-883
9997.0000 N/A

PV2MATH3 (293) Plausible value in math – Uncertainty
Format: F9.4Columns: 884-892
9997.0000 N/A

PV3MATH3 (294) Plausible value in math – Uncertainty
Format: F9.4Columns: 893-901
9997.0000 N/A

PV4MATH3 (295) Plausible value in math – Uncertainty
Format: F9.4Columns: 902-910
9997.0000 N/A

PV5MATH3 (296) Plausible value in math – Uncertainty
Format: F9.4Columns: 911-919
9997.0000 N/A

PV1MATH4 (297) Plausible value in math – Quantity
Format: F9.4Columns: 920-928
9997.0000 N/A

PV2MATH4 (298) Plausible value in math – Quantity
Format: F9.4Columns: 929-937
9997.0000 N/A

PV3MATH4 (299) Plausible value in math – Quantity
Format: F9.4Columns: 938-946
9997.0000 N/A

PV4MATH4 (300) Plausible value in math – Quantity
Format: F9.4Columns: 947-955
9997.0000 N/A

PV5MATH4 (301) Plausible value in math – Quantity
Format: F9.4Columns: 956-964
9997.0000 N/A

PV1READ (302) Plausible value in reading
Format: F9.4Columns: 965-973
9997.0000 N/A

PV2READ (303) Plausible value in reading
Format: F9.4Columns: 974-982
9997.0000 N/A

PV3READ (304) Plausible value in reading
Format: F9.4Columns: 983-991
9997.0000 N/A

PV4READ (305) Plausible value in reading
Format: F9.4Columns: 992-1000
9997.0000 N/A

PV5READ (306) Plausible value in reading
Format: F9.4Columns: 1001-1009
9997.0000 N/A

PV1SCIE (307) Plausible value in science
Format: F9.4Columns: 1010-1018
9997.0000 N/A

PV2SCIE (308) Plausible value in science
Format: F9.4Columns: 1019-1027
9997.0000 N/A

PV3SCIE (309) Plausible value in science
Format: F9.4Columns: 1028-1036
9997.0000 N/A

PV4SCIE (310) Plausible value in science
Format: F9.4Columns: 1037-1045
9997.0000 N/A

PV5SCIE (311) Plausible value in science
Format: F9.4Columns: 1046-1054
9997.0000 N/A

PV1PROB (312) Plausible value in problem solving
Format: F9.4Columns: 1055-1063
9997.0000 N/A

PV2PROB (313) Plausible value in problem solving
Format: F9.4Columns: 1064-1072
9997.0000 N/A

PV3PROB (314) Plausible value in problem solving
Format: F9.4Columns: 1073-1081
9997.0000 N/A

PV4PROB (315) Plausible value in problem solving
Format: F9.4Columns: 1082-1090
9997.0000 N/A

PV5PROB (316) Plausible value in problem solving
Format: F9.4Columns: 1091-1099
9997.0000 N/A

W_FSTUWT (317) Student final weight
Format: F9.4Columns: 1100-1108
9997.0000 N/A

CNTFAC1 (318) Country weight factor for equal weights (1000)
Format: F8.6Columns: 1109-1116

CNTFAC2 (319) Country weight factor for normalised weights (sample size)
Format: F8.6Columns: 1117-1124

OECD (320) OECD country indicator
Format: F1 Columns: 1125-1125
0 Partner country
1 OECD country

UH (321) One-hour booklet indicator
Format: F1 Columns: 1126-1126
0 Two-hour booklet
1 One-hour booklet

W_FSTR1 (322) BRR replicate
Format: F9.4Columns: 1127-1135
9997.0000 N/A

W_FSTR2 (323) BRR replicate
Format: F9.4Columns: 1136-1144
9997.0000 N/A

W_FSTR3 (324) BRR replicate
Format: F9.4Columns: 1145-1153
9997.0000 N/A

W_FSTR4 (325) BRR replicate
Format: F9.4Columns: 1154-1162
9997.0000 N/A

W_FSTR5 (326) BRR replicate
Format: F9.4Columns: 1163-1171
9997.0000 N/A

W_FSTR6 (327) BRR replicate
Format: F9.4Columns: 1172-1180
9997.0000 N/A

W_FSTR7 (328) BRR replicate
Format: F9.4Columns: 1181-1189
9997.0000 N/A

W_FSTR8 (329) BRR replicate
Format: F9.4Columns: 1190-1198
9997.0000 N/A

W_FSTR9 (330) BRR replicate
Format: F9.4Columns: 1199-1207
9997.0000 N/A

W_FSTR10 (331) BRR replicate
Format: F9.4Columns: 1208-1216
9997.0000 N/A

W_FSTR11 (332) BRR replicate
Format: F9.4Columns: 1217-1225
9997.0000 N/A

W_FSTR12 (333) BRR replicate
Format: F9.4Columns: 1226-1234
9997.0000 N/A

W_FSTR13 (334) BRR replicate
Format: F9.4Columns: 1235-1243
9997.0000 N/A

W_FSTR14 (335) BRR replicate
Format: F9.4Columns: 1244-1252
9997.0000 N/A

W_FSTR15 (336) BRR replicate
Format: F9.4Columns: 1253-1261
9997.0000 N/A

W_FSTR16 (337) BRR replicate
Format: F9.4Columns: 1262-1270
9997.0000 N/A

W_FSTR17 (338) BRR replicate
Format: F9.4Columns: 1271-1279
9997.0000 N/A

W_FSTR18 (339) BRR replicate
Format: F9.4Columns: 1280-1288
9997.0000 N/A

W_FSTR19 (340) BRR replicate
Format: F9.4Columns: 1289-1297
9997.0000 N/A

W_FSTR20 (341) BRR replicate
Format: F9.4Columns: 1298-1306
9997.0000 N/A

W_FSTR21 (342) BRR replicate
Format: F9.4Columns: 1307-1315
9997.0000 N/A

W_FSTR22 (343) BRR replicate
Format: F9.4Columns: 1316-1324
9997.0000 N/A

W_FSTR23 (344) BRR replicate
Format: F9.4Columns: 1325-1333
9997.0000 N/A

W_FSTR24 (345) BRR replicate
Format: F9.4Columns: 1334-1342
9997.0000 N/A

W_FSTR25 (346) BRR replicate
Format: F9.4Columns: 1343-1351
9997.0000 N/A

W_FSTR26 (347) BRR replicate
Format: F9.4Columns: 1352-1360
9997.0000 N/A

W_FSTR27 (348) BRR replicate
Format: F9.4Columns: 1361-1369
9997.0000 N/A

W_FSTR28 (349) BRR replicate
Format: F9.4Columns: 1370-1378
9997.0000 N/A

W_FSTR29 (350) BRR replicate
Format: F9.4Columns: 1379-1387
9997.0000 N/A

W_FSTR30 (351) BRR replicate
Format: F9.4Columns: 1388-1396
9997.0000 N/A

W_FSTR31 (352) BRR replicate
Format: F9.4Columns: 1397-1405
9997.0000 N/A

W_FSTR32 (353) BRR replicate
Format: F9.4Columns: 1406-1414
9997.0000 N/A

W_FSTR33 (354) BRR replicate
Format: F9.4Columns: 1415-1423
9997.0000 N/A

W_FSTR34 (355) BRR replicate
Format: F9.4Columns: 1424-1432
9997.0000 N/A

W_FSTR35 (356) BRR replicate
Format: F9.4Columns: 1433-1441
9997.0000 N/A

W_FSTR36 (357) BRR replicate
Format: F9.4Columns: 1442-1450
9997.0000 N/A

W_FSTR37 (358) BRR replicate
Format: F9.4Columns: 1451-1459
9997.0000 N/A

W_FSTR38 (359) BRR replicate
Format: F9.4Columns: 1460-1468
9997.0000 N/A

W_FSTR39 (360) BRR replicate
Format: F9.4Columns: 1469-1477
9997.0000 N/A

W_FSTR40 (361) BRR replicate
Format: F9.4Columns: 1478-1486
9997.0000 N/A

W_FSTR41 (362) BRR replicate
Format: F9.4Columns: 1487-1495
9997.0000 N/A

W_FSTR42 (363) BRR replicate
Format: F9.4Columns: 1496-1504
9997.0000 N/A

W_FSTR43 (364) BRR replicate
Format: F9.4Columns: 1505-1513
9997.0000 N/A

W_FSTR44 (365) BRR replicate
Format: F9.4Columns: 1514-1522
9997.0000 N/A

W_FSTR45 (366) BRR replicate
Format: F9.4Columns: 1523-1531
9997.0000 N/A

W_FSTR46 (367) BRR replicate
Format: F9.4Columns: 1532-1540
9997.0000 N/A

W_FSTR47 (368) BRR replicate
Format: F9.4Columns: 1541-1549
9997.0000 N/A

W_FSTR48 (369) BRR replicate
Format: F9.4Columns: 1550-1558
9997.0000 N/A

W_FSTR49 (370) BRR replicate
Format: F9.4Columns: 1559-1567
9997.0000 N/A

W_FSTR50 (371) BRR replicate
Format: F9.4Columns: 1568-1576
9997.0000 N/A

W_FSTR51 (372) BRR replicate
Format: F9.4Columns: 1577-1585
9997.0000 N/A

W_FSTR52 (373) BRR replicate
Format: F9.4Columns: 1586-1594
9997.0000 N/A

W_FSTR53 (374) BRR replicate
Format: F9.4Columns: 1595-1603
9997.0000 N/A

W_FSTR54 (375) BRR replicate
Format: F9.4Columns: 1604-1612
9997.0000 N/A

W_FSTR55 (376) BRR replicate
Format: F9.4Columns: 1613-1621
9997.0000 N/A

W_FSTR56 (377) BRR replicate
Format: F9.4Columns: 1622-1630
9997.0000 N/A

W_FSTR57 (378) BRR replicate
Format: F9.4Columns: 1631-1639
9997.0000 N/A

W_FSTR58 (379) BRR replicate
Format: F9.4Columns: 1640-1648
9997.0000 N/A

W_FSTR59 (380) BRR replicate
Format: F9.4Columns: 1649-1657
9997.0000 N/A

W_FSTR60 (381) BRR replicate
Format: F9.4Columns: 1658-1666
9997.0000 N/A

W_FSTR61 (382) BRR replicate
Format: F9.4Columns: 1667-1675
9997.0000 N/A

W_FSTR62 (383) BRR replicate
Format: F9.4Columns: 1676-1684
9997.0000 N/A

W_FSTR63 (384) BRR replicate
Format: F9.4Columns: 1685-1693
9997.0000 N/A

W_FSTR64 (385) BRR replicate
Format: F9.4Columns: 1694-1702
9997.0000 N/A

W_FSTR65 (386) BRR replicate
Format: F9.4Columns: 1703-1711
9997.0000 N/A

W_FSTR66 (387) BRR replicate
Format: F9.4Columns: 1712-1720
9997.0000 N/A

W_FSTR67 (388) BRR replicate
Format: F9.4Columns: 1721-1729
9997.0000 N/A

W_FSTR68 (389) BRR replicate
Format: F9.4Columns: 1730-1738
9997.0000 N/A

W_FSTR69 (390) BRR replicate
Format: F9.4Columns: 1739-1747
9997.0000 N/A

W_FSTR70 (391) BRR replicate
Format: F9.4Columns: 1748-1756
9997.0000 N/A

W_FSTR71 (392) BRR replicate
Format: F9.4Columns: 1757-1765
9997.0000 N/A

W_FSTR72 (393) BRR replicate
Format: F9.4Columns: 1766-1774
9997.0000 N/A

W_FSTR73 (394) BRR replicate
Format: F9.4Columns: 1775-1783
9997.0000 N/A

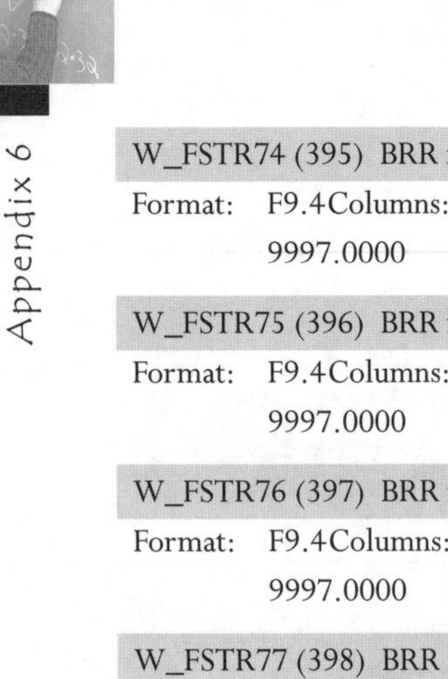

W_FSTR74 (395) BRR replicate

Format: F9.4Columns: 1784-1792

9997.0000 N/A

W_FSTR75 (396) BRR replicate

Format: F9.4Columns: 1793-1801

9997.0000 N/A

W_FSTR76 (397) BRR replicate

Format: F9.4Columns: 1802-1810

9997.0000 N/A

W_FSTR77 (398) BRR replicate

Format: F9.4Columns: 1811-1819

9997.0000 N/A

W_FSTR78 (399) BRR replicate

Format: F9.4Columns: 1820-1828

9997.0000 N/A

W_FSTR79 (400) BRR replicate

Format: F9.4Columns: 1829-1837

9997.0000 N/A

W_FSTR80 (401) BRR replicate

Format: F9.4Columns: 1838-1846

9997.0000 N/A

WVARSTRR (402) Randomised final variance stratum (1-80)

Format: F2 Columns: 1847-1848

UNIT (403) Final variance unit (1,2,3)

Format: F1 Columns: 1849-1849

STRATUM (404) Stratum

Format: A5 Columns: 1851-1855

03601 Australia: ACT
03602 Australia: NSW
03603 Australia: VIC
03604 Australia: QLD
03605 Australia: SA
03606 Australia: WA
03607 Australia: TAS
03608 Australia: NT
04002 Austria: Hauptschule
04003 Austria: Polytechn. Schule
04005 Austria: Gymnasium
04006 Austria: Realgymnasium
04007 Austria: Oberstufenrealgymnasium
04009 Austria: Berufsschule (techn.-gewerbl.)
04010 Austria: Berufsschule (kaufmänn. /Handel/Verkehr)
04012 Austria: BMS (gewerblich-technisch-kunstgewerbl.)
04013 Austria: BMS (kaufmännisch /Handelschulen)
04014 Austria: BMS (wirtschafts- /sozialberufl.)
04015 Austria: BMS (land-/forstwirtschaftl.)
04016 Austria: BHS (techn.-gewerblich)
04017 Austria: BHS (kaufmännisch)
04018 Austria: BHS (wirtschafts-/sozialberufl)
04019 Austria: BHS (land-/forstwirtschaftl.)
04020 Austria: Anstalt der Kindergarten- /Sozialpädagogik
04021 Austria: Moderately small schools
04022 Austria: Very small schools
05601 Belgium (Flemish): Only general education, private
05602 Belgium (Flemish): Only general education, public
05603 Belgium (Flemish): Gen.-techn.-vocat.-arts, private
05604 Belgium (Flemish): Gen.-techn.-vocat.-arts, public
05605 Belgium (Flemish): Techn.,arts, not general, private
05606 Belgium (Flemish): Techn.-vocat.-arts, not gen., public
05607 Belgium (Flemish): Special education – private
05608 Belgium (Flemish): Special education – public
05609 Belgium (Flemish): Part time vocational
05610 Belgium (Flemish): Moderately small schools
05611 Belgium (Flemish): Very small schools
05612 Belgium (French): Organised by community
05613 Belgium (French): Organised by community, spec. ed.
05614 Belgium (French): Official schools subsidised by comm.
05615 Belgium (French): Subsidised special education
05616 Belgium (French): Subsidised confessional
05617 Belgium (French): Subsidised confessional – spec. ed.

05618	Belgium (French): Subsidised non-confessional
05619	Belgium (French): Subsidised non-confessional – spec. ed.
05620	Belgium (German)
07601	Brazil: Central (private)
07602	Brazil: Central (public)
07603	Brazil: North (private)
07604	Brazil: North (public)
07605	Brazil: Northeast (private)
07606	Brazil: Northeast (public)
07607	Brazil: South (private)
07608	Brazil: South (public)
07609	Brazil: Southeast (private)
07610	Brazil: Southeast (public)
07611	Brazil: Small schools
07612	Brazil: Very small schools
12400	Canada
20301	Czech Republic: Stratum 1
20302	Czech Republic: Stratum 2
20303	Czech Republic: Stratum 3
20304	Czech Republic: Stratum 4
20305	Czech Republic: Stratum 5
20306	Czech Republic: Stratum 6
20307	Czech Republic: Stratum 7
20308	Czech Republic: Stratum 8
20309	Czech Republic: Stratum 9
20310	Czech Republic: Stratum 10
20311	Czech Republic: Stratum 11
20312	Czech Republic: Stratum 12
20313	Czech Republic: Stratum 13
20314	Czech Republic: Stratum 14
20315	Czech Republic: Stratum 15
20316	Czech Republic: Stratum 16
20317	Czech Republic: Stratum 17
20318	Czech Republic: Stratum 18
20319	Czech Republic: Stratum 19
20320	Czech Republic: Stratum 20
20321	Czech Republic: Stratum 21
20322	Czech Republic: Stratum 22
20323	Czech Republic: Stratum 23
20324	Czech Republic: Stratum 24
20325	Czech Republic: Stratum 25
20326	Czech Republic: Stratum 26
20327	Czech Republic: Stratum 27
20328	Czech Republic: Stratum 28
20329	Czech Republic: Stratum 29
20330	Czech Republic: Stratum 30
20331	Czech Republic: Stratum 31
20332	Czech Republic: Stratum 32
20333	Czech Republic: Stratum 33
20334	Czech Republic: Stratum 34
20801	Denmark: Large schools
20802	Denmark: Moderately small schools
20803	Denmark: Very Small schools
24601	Finland: Stratum 1
24602	Finland: Stratum 2
24603	Finland: Stratum 3
24604	Finland: Stratum 4
24605	Finland: Stratum 5
24606	Finland: Stratum 6
24607	Finland: Stratum 7
24608	Finland: Stratum 8
24609	Finland: Stratum 9
24610	Finland: Stratum 10
24611	Finland: Stratum 11
24612	Finland: Stratum 12
25001	France: Lycées généraux et technologiques
25002	France: Collèges
25003	France: Lycées professionnels
25004	France: Lycées agricoles
25005	France: Moderately small schools
25006	France: Very small schools
27601	Germany: Stratum 1
27602	Germany: Stratum 2
27603	Germany: Stratum 3
27604	Germany: Stratum 4
27605	Germany: Stratum 5
27606	Germany: Stratum 6
27607	Germany: Stratum 7
27608	Germany: Stratum 8
27609	Germany: Stratum 9
27610	Germany: Stratum 10
27611	Germany: Stratum 11
27612	Germany: Stratum 12
27613	Germany: Stratum 13
27614	Germany: Stratum 14
27615	Germany: Stratum 15
27616	Germany: Stratum 16
27617	Germany: Stratum 17
27618	Germany: Stratum 18
30001	Greece: Stratum 1
30002	Greece: Stratum 2
30003	Greece: Stratum 3
30004	Greece: Stratum 4
30005	Greece: Stratum 5
30006	Greece: Stratum 6

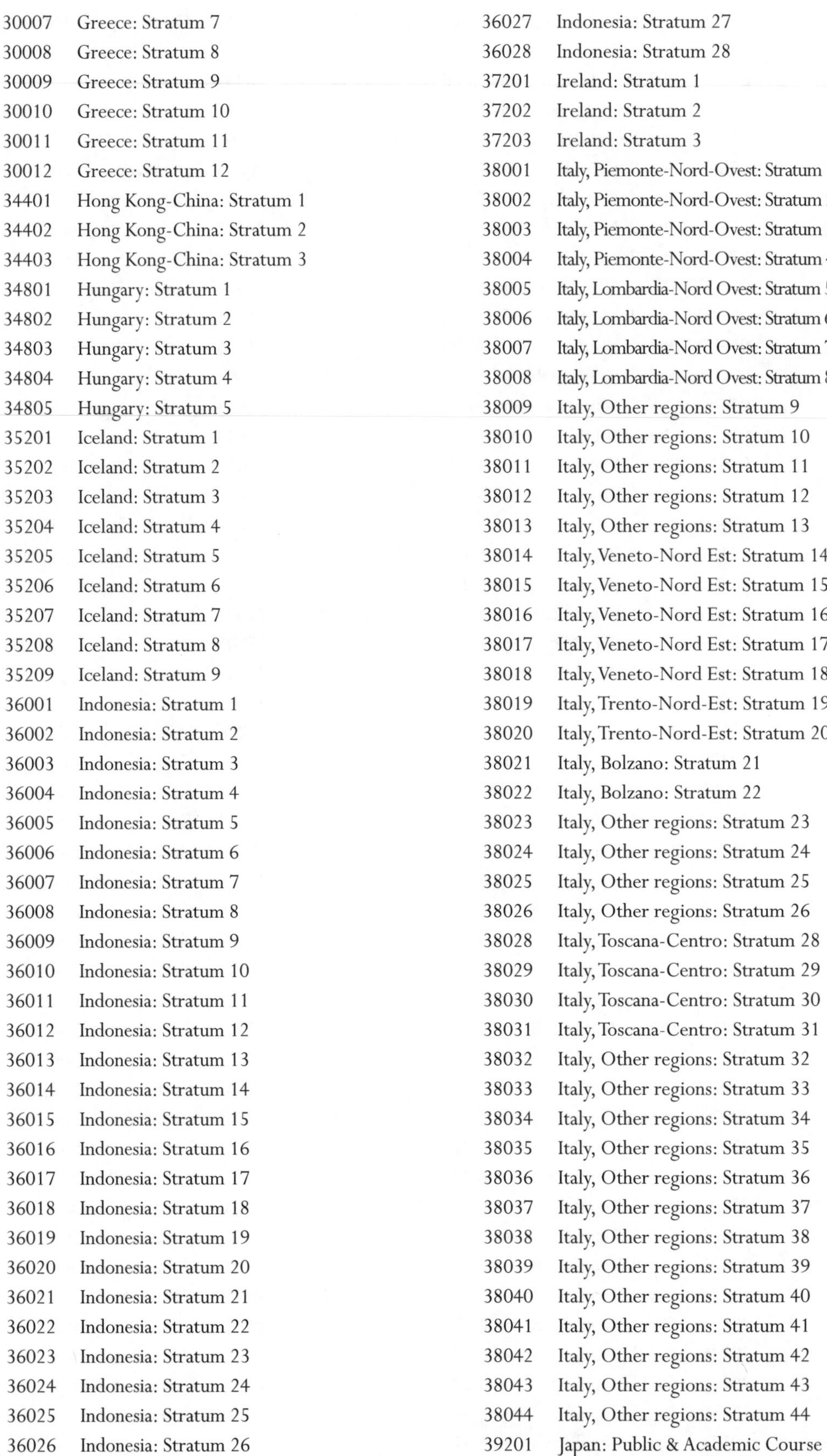

30007	Greece: Stratum 7
30008	Greece: Stratum 8
30009	Greece: Stratum 9
30010	Greece: Stratum 10
30011	Greece: Stratum 11
30012	Greece: Stratum 12
34401	Hong Kong-China: Stratum 1
34402	Hong Kong-China: Stratum 2
34403	Hong Kong-China: Stratum 3
34801	Hungary: Stratum 1
34802	Hungary: Stratum 2
34803	Hungary: Stratum 3
34804	Hungary: Stratum 4
34805	Hungary: Stratum 5
35201	Iceland: Stratum 1
35202	Iceland: Stratum 2
35203	Iceland: Stratum 3
35204	Iceland: Stratum 4
35205	Iceland: Stratum 5
35206	Iceland: Stratum 6
35207	Iceland: Stratum 7
35208	Iceland: Stratum 8
35209	Iceland: Stratum 9
36001	Indonesia: Stratum 1
36002	Indonesia: Stratum 2
36003	Indonesia: Stratum 3
36004	Indonesia: Stratum 4
36005	Indonesia: Stratum 5
36006	Indonesia: Stratum 6
36007	Indonesia: Stratum 7
36008	Indonesia: Stratum 8
36009	Indonesia: Stratum 9
36010	Indonesia: Stratum 10
36011	Indonesia: Stratum 11
36012	Indonesia: Stratum 12
36013	Indonesia: Stratum 13
36014	Indonesia: Stratum 14
36015	Indonesia: Stratum 15
36016	Indonesia: Stratum 16
36017	Indonesia: Stratum 17
36018	Indonesia: Stratum 18
36019	Indonesia: Stratum 19
36020	Indonesia: Stratum 20
36021	Indonesia: Stratum 21
36022	Indonesia: Stratum 22
36023	Indonesia: Stratum 23
36024	Indonesia: Stratum 24
36025	Indonesia: Stratum 25
36026	Indonesia: Stratum 26
36027	Indonesia: Stratum 27
36028	Indonesia: Stratum 28
37201	Ireland: Stratum 1
37202	Ireland: Stratum 2
37203	Ireland: Stratum 3
38001	Italy, Piemonte-Nord-Ovest: Stratum 1
38002	Italy, Piemonte-Nord-Ovest: Stratum 2
38003	Italy, Piemonte-Nord-Ovest: Stratum 3
38004	Italy, Piemonte-Nord-Ovest: Stratum 4
38005	Italy, Lombardia-Nord Ovest: Stratum 5
38006	Italy, Lombardia-Nord Ovest: Stratum 6
38007	Italy, Lombardia-Nord Ovest: Stratum 7
38008	Italy, Lombardia-Nord Ovest: Stratum 8
38009	Italy, Other regions: Stratum 9
38010	Italy, Other regions: Stratum 10
38011	Italy, Other regions: Stratum 11
38012	Italy, Other regions: Stratum 12
38013	Italy, Other regions: Stratum 13
38014	Italy, Veneto-Nord Est: Stratum 14
38015	Italy, Veneto-Nord Est: Stratum 15
38016	Italy, Veneto-Nord Est: Stratum 16
38017	Italy, Veneto-Nord Est: Stratum 17
38018	Italy, Veneto-Nord Est: Stratum 18
38019	Italy, Trento-Nord-Est: Stratum 19
38020	Italy, Trento-Nord-Est: Stratum 20
38021	Italy, Bolzano: Stratum 21
38022	Italy, Bolzano: Stratum 22
38023	Italy, Other regions: Stratum 23
38024	Italy, Other regions: Stratum 24
38025	Italy, Other regions: Stratum 25
38026	Italy, Other regions: Stratum 26
38028	Italy, Toscana-Centro: Stratum 28
38029	Italy, Toscana-Centro: Stratum 29
38030	Italy, Toscana-Centro: Stratum 30
38031	Italy, Toscana-Centro: Stratum 31
38032	Italy, Other regions: Stratum 32
38033	Italy, Other regions: Stratum 33
38034	Italy, Other regions: Stratum 34
38035	Italy, Other regions: Stratum 35
38036	Italy, Other regions: Stratum 36
38037	Italy, Other regions: Stratum 37
38038	Italy, Other regions: Stratum 38
38039	Italy, Other regions: Stratum 39
38040	Italy, Other regions: Stratum 40
38041	Italy, Other regions: Stratum 41
38042	Italy, Other regions: Stratum 42
38043	Italy, Other regions: Stratum 43
38044	Italy, Other regions: Stratum 44
39201	Japan: Public & Academic Course

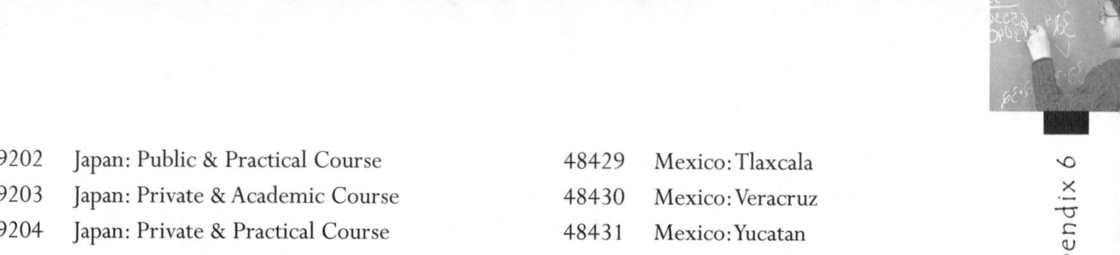

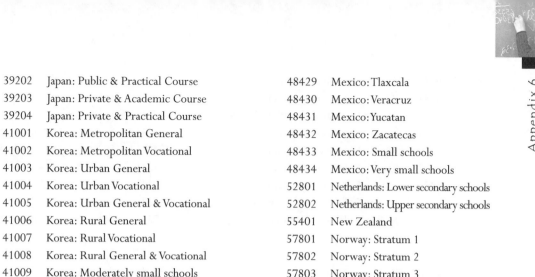

39202 Japan: Public & Practical Course
39203 Japan: Private & Academic Course
39204 Japan: Private & Practical Course
41001 Korea: Metropolitan General
41002 Korea: Metropolitan Vocational
41003 Korea: Urban General
41004 Korea: Urban Vocational
41005 Korea: Urban General & Vocational
41006 Korea: Rural General
41007 Korea: Rural Vocational
41008 Korea: Rural General & Vocational
41009 Korea: Moderately small schools
42801 Latvia: Large schools
42802 Latvia: Moderately small schools
42803 Latvia: Very small schools
43840 Liechtenstein
44201 Luxembourg: Stratum 1
44202 Luxembourg: Stratum 2
44203 Luxembourg: Stratum 3
44601 Macao-China: Stratum 1
44602 Macao-China: Stratum 2
44603 Macao-China: Stratum 3
48401 Mexico: Aguascalientes
48402 Mexico: Baja California
48403 Mexico: Baja California Sur
48404 Mexico: Campeche Coahuila
48405 Mexico: Coahuila
48406 Mexico: Colima
48407 Mexico: Chiapas
48408 Mexico: Chihuahua
48409 Mexico: Distrito Federal
48410 Mexico: Durango
48411 Mexico: Guanajuato
48412 Mexico: Guerrero
48413 Mexico: Hidalgo
48414 Mexico: Jalisco
48415 Mexico: Mexico
48417 Mexico: Morelos
48418 Mexico: Nayarit
48419 Mexico: Nuevo Leon
48420 Mexico: Oaxaca
48421 Mexico: Puebla
48422 Mexico: Queretaro
48423 Mexico: Quintana Roo
48424 Mexico: San Luis Potosi
48425 Mexico: Sinaloa
48426 Mexico: Sonora
48427 Mexico: Tabasco
48428 Mexico: Tamaulipas
48429 Mexico: Tlaxcala
48430 Mexico: Veracruz
48431 Mexico: Yucatan
48432 Mexico: Zacatecas
48433 Mexico: Small schools
48434 Mexico: Very small schools
52801 Netherlands: Lower secondary schools
52802 Netherlands: Upper secondary schools
55401 New Zealand
57801 Norway: Stratum 1
57802 Norway: Stratum 2
57803 Norway: Stratum 3
57804 Norway: Stratum 4
61601 Poland: Gimnazja
61602 Poland: Licea (vss)
62001 Portugal: Açores
62002 Portugal: DREA
62003 Portugal: DREALG
62004 Portugal: DREC
62005 Portugal: DREL
62006 Portugal: DREN
62007 Portugal: Madeira
62008 Portugal: Small schools
62009 Portugal: Very small schools
64303 Russian Federation: Stratum 3
64304 Russian Federation: Stratum 4
64307 Russian Federation: Stratum 7
64308 Russian Federation: Stratum 8
64314 Russian Federation: Stratum 14
64316 Russian Federation: Stratum 16
64318 Russian Federation: Stratum 18
64321 Russian Federation: Stratum 21
64322 Russian Federation: Stratum 22
64323 Russian Federation: Stratum 23
64324 Russian Federation: Stratum 24
64325 Russian Federation: Stratum 25
64326 Russian Federation: Stratum 26
64327 Russian Federation: Stratum 27
64331 Russian Federation: Stratum 31
64332 Russian Federation: Stratum 32
64334 Russian Federation: Stratum 34
64335 Russian Federation: Stratum 35
64336 Russian Federation: Stratum 36
64337 Russian Federation: Stratum 37
64338 Russian Federation: Stratum 38
64342 Russian Federation: Stratum 42
64343 Russian Federation: Stratum 43
64347 Russian Federation: Stratum 47
64348 Russian Federation: Stratum 48

64350	Russian Federation: Stratum 50
64351	Russian Federation: Stratum 51
64352	Russian Federation: Stratum 52
64353	Russian Federation: Stratum 53
64354	Russian Federation: Stratum 54
64355	Russian Federation: Stratum 55
64356	Russian Federation: Stratum 56
64358	Russian Federation: Stratum 58
64359	Russian Federation: Stratum 59
64361	Russian Federation: Stratum 61
64363	Russian Federation: Stratum 63
64364	Russian Federation: Stratum 64
64366	Russian Federation: Stratum 66
64370	Russian Federation: Stratum 70
64371	Russian Federation: Stratum 71
64374	Russian Federation: Stratum 74
64376	Russian Federation: Stratum 76
64377	Russian Federation: Stratum 77
64378	Russian Federation: Stratum 78
64386	Russian Federation: Stratum 86
70301	Slovak Republic: Stratum 1
70302	Slovak Republic: Stratum 2
70303	Slovak Republic: Stratum 3
70304	Slovak Republic: Stratum 4
70305	Slovak Republic: Stratum 5
70306	Slovak Republic: Stratum 6
70307	Slovak Republic: Stratum 7
70308	Slovak Republic: Stratum 8
70309	Slovak Republic: Stratum 9
70310	Slovak Republic: Stratum 10
70311	Slovak Republic: Stratum 11
70312	Slovak Republic: Stratum 12
70313	Slovak Republic: Stratum 13
70314	Slovak Republic: Stratum 14
70315	Slovak Republic: Stratum 15
70316	Slovak Republic: Stratum 16
70317	Slovak Republic: Stratum 17
70318	Slovak Republic: Stratum 18
70319	Slovak Republic: Stratum 19
70320	Slovak Republic: Stratum 20
72401	Spain: Stratum 1
72402	Spain: Stratum 2
72403	Spain: Stratum 3
72404	Spain, Castilia y Leon: Stratum 4
72405	Spain, Castilia y Leon: Stratum 5
72406	Spain, Castilia y Leon: Stratum 6
72407	Spain, Castilia y Leon: Stratum 7
72408	Spain, Catalonia: Stratum 8
72409	Spain, Catalonia: Stratum 9
72410	Spain, Catalonia: Stratum 10
72411	Spain, Basque Country: Stratum 11
72412	Spain, Basque Country: Stratum 12
72413	Spain, Basque Country: Stratum 13
72414	Spain, Basque Country: Stratum 14
72415	Spain, Basque Country: Stratum 15
72416	Spain, Basque Country: Stratum 16
72417	Spain, Basque Country: Stratum 17
72418	Spain, Basque Country: Stratum 18
72419	Spain: Stratum 19
72420	Spain: Stratum 20
72421	Spain: Stratum 21
72422	Spain: Stratum 22
72423	Spain: Stratum 23
72424	Spain: Stratum 24
72425	Spain: Stratum 25
72426	Spain: Stratum 26
72427	Spain: Stratum 27
72428	Spain: Stratum 28
72429	Spain: Stratum 29
72430	Spain: Stratum 30
72431	Spain: Stratum 31
72432	Spain: Stratum 32
72433	Spain: Stratum 33
72434	Spain: Stratum 34
72435	Spain: Stratum 35
72436	Spain: Stratum 36
72437	Spain: Stratum 37
72438	Spain: Stratum 38
72439	Spain: Stratum 39
72440	Spain: Stratum 40
72441	Spain: Stratum 41
72442	Spain: Stratum 42
72443	Spain: Stratum 43
72444	Spain: Stratum 44
72445	Spain: Stratum 45
75201	Sweden: Stratum 1
75202	Sweden: Stratum 2
75203	Sweden: Stratum 3
75204	Sweden: Stratum 4
75205	Sweden: Stratum 5
75206	Sweden: Stratum 6
75207	Sweden: Stratum 7
75208	Sweden: Stratum 8
75209	Sweden: Stratum 9
75601	Switzerland (German): Stratum 1
75602	Switzerland (German): Stratum 2
75603	Switzerland (German): Stratum 3
75604	Switzerland (German): Stratum 4

75605	Switzerland (German): Stratum 5
75606	Switzerland (German): Stratum 6
75607	Switzerland (German): Stratum 7
75608	Switzerland (German): Stratum 8
75609	Switzerland (German): Stratum 9
75610	Switzerland (German): Stratum 10
75611	Switzerland (German): Stratum 11
75612	Switzerland (German): Stratum 12
75613	Switzerland (German): Stratum 13
75614	Switzerland (German): Stratum 14
75615	Switzerland (French): Stratum 15
75616	Switzerland (French): Stratum 16
75617	Switzerland (French): Stratum 17
75618	Switzerland (French): Stratum 18
75619	Switzerland (French): Stratum 19
75620	Switzerland (French): Stratum 20
75621	Switzerland (French): Stratum 21
75623	Switzerland (French): Stratum 23
75624	Switzerland (French): Stratum 24
75625	Switzerland (French): Stratum 25
75626	Switzerland (French): Stratum 26
75628	Switzerland (French): Stratum 28
75629	Switzerland (Italian): Stratum 29
75631	Switzerland (Italian): Stratum 31
75632	Switzerland (Italian): Stratum 32
75634	Switzerland (Italian): Stratum 34
76401	Thailand: Stratum 1
76402	Thailand: Stratum 2
76403	Thailand: Stratum 3
76404	Thailand: Stratum 4
76405	Thailand: Stratum 5
76406	Thailand: Stratum 6
76407	Thailand: Stratum 7
76408	Thailand: Stratum 8
76409	Thailand: Stratum 9
76410	Thailand: Stratum 10
76411	Thailand: Stratum 11
76412	Thailand: Stratum 12
76413	Thailand: Stratum 13
76414	Thailand: Stratum 14
76415	Thailand: Stratum 15
78801	Tunisia: East
78802	Tunisia: West
79201	Turkey: Stratum 1
79202	Turkey: Stratum 2
79203	Turkey: Stratum 3
79204	Turkey: Stratum 4
79205	Turkey: Stratum 5
79206	Turkey: Stratum 6
79207	Turkey: Stratum 7
79208	Turkey: Stratum 8
79209	Turkey: Stratum 9
79210	Turkey: Stratum 10
79211	Turkey: Stratum 11
79212	Turkey: Stratum 12
79213	Turkey: Stratum 13
79214	Turkey: Stratum 14
79215	Turkey: Stratum 15
79216	Turkey: Stratum 16
79217	Turkey: Stratum 17
79218	Turkey: Stratum 18
79219	Turkey: Stratum 19
79220	Turkey: Stratum 20
79221	Turkey: Stratum 21
79222	Turkey: Stratum 22
79223	Turkey: Stratum 23
79224	Turkey: Stratum 24
79225	Turkey: Stratum 25
79226	Turkey: Stratum 26
79227	Turkey: Stratum 27
79228	Turkey: Stratum 28
79229	Turkey: Stratum 29
79230	Turkey: Stratum 30
79231	Turkey: Stratum 31
79232	Turkey: Stratum 32
79233	Turkey: Stratum 33
79234	Turkey: Stratum 34
79235	Turkey: Stratum 35
79236	Turkey: Stratum 36
79237	Turkey: Stratum 37
79238	Turkey: Stratum 38
79239	Turkey: Stratum 39
79240	Turkey: Stratum 40
79241	Turkey: Stratum 41
79242	Turkey: Stratum 42
79243	Turkey: Stratum 43
82601	Scotland: Stratum 1
82602	Scotland: Stratum 2
82603	Scotland: Stratum 3
82604	Scotland: Stratum 4
82605	Scotland: Stratum 5
82611	England
82613	N.Ireland
82614	N.Ireland: Very large schools
82615	Wales
84000	United States
85801	Uruguay: Liceos Publicos (Mdeo/AM)
85802	Uruguay: Liceos Publicos (cap. dptos interior)

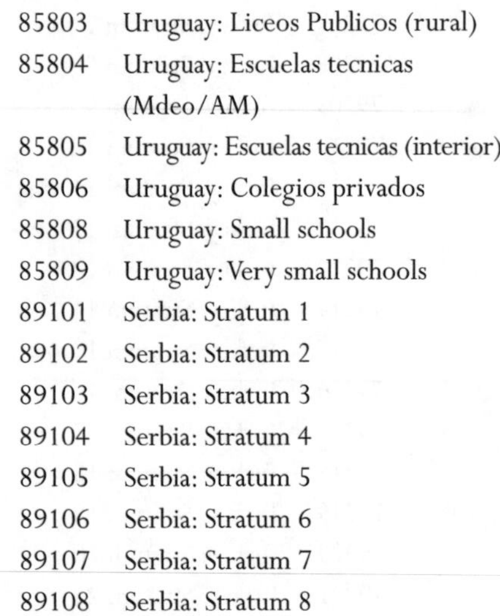

85803	Uruguay: Liceos Publicos (rural)
85804	Uruguay: Escuelas tecnicas (Mdeo/AM)
85805	Uruguay: Escuelas tecnicas (interior)
85806	Uruguay: Colegios privados
85808	Uruguay: Small schools
85809	Uruguay: Very small schools
89101	Serbia: Stratum 1
89102	Serbia: Stratum 2
89103	Serbia: Stratum 3
89104	Serbia: Stratum 4
89105	Serbia: Stratum 5
89106	Serbia: Stratum 6
89107	Serbia: Stratum 7
89108	Serbia: Stratum 8

APPENDIX 7 ▪ SCHOOL QUESTIONNAIRE DATA FILE CODEBOOK

COUNTRY (1) Country ID

Format: A3 Columns: 1-3

See Appendix 6: Student questionnaire data file codebook

CNT (2) Nation code

Format: A3 Columns: 4-6

SUBNATIO (3) Adjudicated sub-region

Format: A4 Columns: 7-10

See Appendix 6: Student questionnaire data file codebook

SCHOOLID (4) School ID

Format: A5 Columns: 11-15

SC01Q01 (5) School location Q1

Format: F1 Columns: 17-17

1 Village (less 3 000)
2 Small town (3 000 to 15 000)
3 Town (15 000 to 100 000)
4 City (100 000 to 1 000 000)
5 Large city (more 1 000 000)
7 N/A
8 Invalid
9 Missing

SC02Q01 (6) Number of boys Q2a

Format: F8 Columns: 18-25

997 N/A
998 Invalid
999 Missing

SC02Q02 (7) Number of girls Q2b

Format: F8 Columns: 26-33

997 N/A
998 Invalid
999 Missing

SC03Q01 (8) Public or private Q3

Format: F1 Columns: 34-34

1 Public
2 Private
7 N/A
8 Invalid
9 Missing

SC04Q01 (9) Funding Government Q4a

Format: F8.3 Columns: 35-42

997 N/A
998 Invalid
999 Missing

SC04Q02 (10) Funding Student fees Q4b

Format: F8.3 Columns: 43-50

997 N/A
998 Invalid
999 Missing

SC04Q03 (11) Funding Benefactors Q4c

Format: F8.3 Columns: 51-58

997 N/A
998 Invalid
999 Missing

SC04Q04 (12) Funding Other Q4d

Format: F8.3 Columns: 59-66

997 N/A
998 Invalid
999 Missing

SC05Q01 (13) Grade 1 Q5a

Format: F1 Columns: 67-67

1 Yes
2 No
7 N/A
8 Invalid
9 Missing

SC05Q02 (14) Grade 2 Q5b

Format: F1 Columns: 68-68

1 Yes
2 No
7 N/A
8 Invalid
9 Missing

SC05Q03 (15) Grade 3 Q5c

Format: F1 Columns: 69-69

1 Yes
2 No
7 N/A
8 Invalid
9 Missing

SC05Q04 (16) Grade 4 Q5d

Format: F1 Columns: 70-70

1 Yes
2 No
7 N/A
8 Invalid
9 Missing

SC05Q05 (17) Grade 5 Q5e

Format: F1 Columns: 71-71

1 Yes
2 No
7 N/A
8 Invalid
9 Missing

SC05Q06 (18) Grade 6 Q5f

Format: F1 Columns: 72-72

1 Yes
2 No
7 N/A
8 Invalid
9 Missing

SC05Q07 (19) Grade 7 Q5g

Format: F1 Columns: 73-73

1 Yes
2 No
7 N/A
8 Invalid
9 Missing

SC05Q08 (20) Grade 8 Q5h

Format: F1 Columns: 74-74

1 Yes
2 No
7 N/A
8 Invalid
9 Missing

SC05Q09 (21) Grade 9 Q5i

Format: F1 Columns: 75-75

1 Yes
2 No
7 N/A
8 Invalid
9 Missing

SC05Q10 (22) Grade 10 Q5j

Format: F1 Columns: 76-76

1 Yes
2 No
7 N/A
8 Invalid
9 Missing

SC05Q11 (23) Grade 11 Q5k

Format: F1 Columns: 77-77

1 Yes
2 No
7 N/A
8 Invalid
9 Missing

SC05Q12 (24) Grade 12 Q5l

Format: F1 Columns: 78-78

1 Yes
2 No
7 N/A
8 Invalid
9 Missing

SC05Q13 (25) Grade 13 Q5m

Format: F1 Columns: 79-79

1 Yes
2 No
7 N/A
8 Invalid
9 Missing

SC05Q14 (26) Ungraded school Q5n

Format: F1 Columns: 80-80

1 Yes
2 No
7 N/A
8 Invalid
9 Missing

SC06Q01 (27) Repeat <grade> at <ISCED2> Q6a

Format: F8.3Columns: 81-88

997 N/A
998 Invalid
999 Missing

SC06Q02 (28) Repeat <grade> at <ISCED3> Q6b

Format: F8.3Columns: 89-96

997 N/A
998 Invalid
999 Missing

SC08Q01 (29) Shortage: maths teacher Q8a

Format: F1 Columns: 97-97

1 Not at all
2 Very little
3 To some extent
4 A lot
7 N/A
8 Invalid
9 Missing

SC08Q02 (30) Shortage: science teacher. Q8b

Format:	F1	Columns: 98-98
	1	Not at all
	2	Very little
	3	To some extent
	4	A lot
	7	N/A
	8	Invalid
	9	Missing

SC08Q03 (31) Shortage: test lang. teacher Q8c

Format:	F1	Columns: 99-99
	1	Not at all
	2	Very little
	3	To some extent
	4	A lot
	7	N/A
	8	Invalid
	9	Missing

SC08Q04 (32) Shortage: other national lang. teacher Q8d

Format:	F1	Columns: 100-100
	1	Not at all
	2	Very little
	3	To some extent
	4	A lot
	7	N/A
	8	Invalid
	9	Missing

SC08Q05 (33) Shortage: foreign lang. teacher Q8e

Format:	F1	Columns: 101-101
	1	Not at all
	2	Very little
	3	To some extent
	4	A lot
	7	N/A
	8	Invalid
	9	Missing

SC08Q06 (34) Shortage: experienced teacher Q8f

Format:	F1	Columns: 102-102
	1	Not at all
	2	Very little
	3	To some extent
	4	A lot
	7	N/A
	8	Invalid
	9	Missing

SC08Q07 (35) Shortage: emergency teacher Q8g

Format:	F1	Columns: 103-103
	1	Not at all
	2	Very little
	3	To some extent
	4	A lot
	7	N/A
	8	Invalid
	9	Missing

SC08Q08 (36) Shortage: support personnel Q8h

Format:	F1	Columns: 104-104
	1	Not at all
	2	Very little
	3	To some extent
	4	A lot
	7	N/A
	8	Invalid
	9	Missing

SC08Q09 (37) Shortage: textbooks Q8i

Format:	F1	Columns: 105-105
	1	Not at all
	2	Very little
	3	To some extent
	4	A lot
	7	N/A
	8	Invalid
	9	Missing

SC08Q10 (38) Shortage: supplies Q8j

Format:	F1	Columns: 106-106
	1	Not at all
	2	Very little
	3	To some extent
	4	A lot
	7	N/A
	8	Invalid
	9	Missing

SC08Q11 (39) Shortage: buildings Q8k

Format:	F1	Columns: 107-107
	1	Not at all
	2	Very little
	3	To some extent
	4	A lot
	7	N/A
	8	Invalid
	9	Missing

SC08Q12 (40) Shortage: heating Q8l

Format:	F1	Columns: 108-108
	1	Not at all
	2	Very little
	3	To some extent
	4	A lot
	7	N/A
	8	Invalid
	9	Missing

SC08Q13 (41) Shortage: classrooms Q8m

Format:	F1	Columns: 109-109
	1	Not at all
	2	Very little
	3	To some extent
	4	A lot
	7	N/A
	8	Invalid
	9	Missing

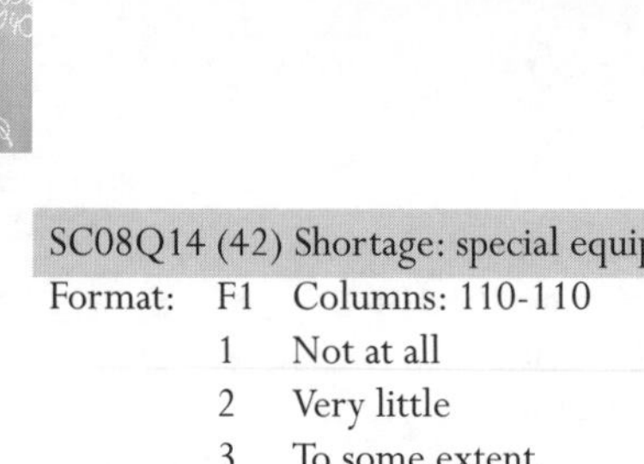

SC08Q14 (42) Shortage: special equipment Q8n

Format: F1 Columns: 110-110

1	Not at all
2	Very little
3	To some extent
4	A lot
7	N/A
8	Invalid
9	Missing

SC08Q15 (43) Shortage: computers Q8o

Format: F1 Columns: 111-111

1	Not at all
2	Very little
3	To some extent
4	A lot
7	N/A
8	Invalid
9	Missing

SC08Q16 (44) Shortage: computer software Q8p

Format: F1 Columns: 112-112

1	Not at all
2	Very little
3	To some extent
4	A lot
7	N/A
8	Invalid
9	Missing

SC08Q17 (45) Shortage: calculators Q8q

Format: F1 Columns: 113-113

1	Not at all
2	Very little
3	To some extent
4	A lot
7	N/A
8	Invalid
9	Missing

SC08Q18 (46) Shortage: library material Q8r

Format: F1 Columns: 114-114

1	Not at all
2	Very little
3	To some extent
4	A lot
7	N/A
8	Invalid
9	Missing

SC08Q19 (47) Shortage: audio-vidio Q8s

Format: F1 Columns: 115-115

1	Not at all
2	Very little
3	To some extent
4	A lot
7	N/A
8	Invalid
9	Missing

SC08Q20 (48) Shortage: lab equipment Q8t

Format: F1 Columns: 116-116

1	Not at all
2	Very little
3	To some extent
4	A lot
7	N/A
8	Invalid
9	Missing

SC09Q01 (49) Computers: altogether Q9a

Format: F8 Columns: 117-124

9997	N/A
9998	Invalid
9999	Missing

SC09Q02 (50) Computers: students Q9b

Format: F8 Columns: 125-132

9997	N/A
9998	Invalid
9999	Missing

SC09Q03 (51) Computers: teachers Q9c

Format: F8 Columns: 133-140

9997	N/A
9998	Invalid
9999	Missing

SC09Q04 (52) Computers: admin Q9d

Format: F8 Columns: 141-148

9997	N/A
9998	Invalid
9999	Missing

SC09Q05 (53) Computers: with Web Q9e

Format: F8 Columns: 149-156

9997	N/A
9998	Invalid
9999	Missing

SC09Q06 (54) Computers: with LAN Q9f

Format: F8 Columns: 157-164

9997	N/A
9998	Invalid
9999	Missing

SC10Q01 (55) Admittance: residence Q10a

Format: F1 Columns: 165-165

1	Prerequisite
2	High priority
3	Considered
4	Not considered
7	N/A
8	Invalid
9	Missing

SC10Q02 (56) Admittance: student record Q10b
Format: F1 Columns: 166-166
1 Prerequisite
2 High priority
3 Considered
4 Not considered
7 N/A
8 Invalid
9 Missing

SC10Q03 (57) Admittance: recommendation Q10c
Format: F1 Columns: 167-167
1 Prerequisite
2 High priority
3 Considered
4 Not considered
7 N/A
8 Invalid
9 Missing

SC10Q04 (58) Admittance: parents' endorsement Q10d
Format: F1 Columns: 168-168
1 Prerequisite
2 High priority
3 Considered
4 Not considered
7 N/A
8 Invalid
9 Missing

SC10Q05 (59) Admittance: special programme Q10e
Format: F1 Columns: 169-169
1 Prerequisite
2 High priority
3 Considered
4 Not considered
7 N/A
8 Invalid
9 Missing

SC10Q06 (60) Admittance: family preference Q10f
Format: F1 Columns: 170-170
1 Prerequisite
2 High priority
3 Considered
4 Not considered
7 N/A
8 Invalid
9 Missing

SC10Q07 (61) <Country Specific> Q10g
Format: F1 Columns: 171-171
1 Prerequisite
2 High priority
3 Considered
4 Not considered
7 N/A
8 Invalid
9 Missing

SC11Q01 (62) Students: enjoy Q11a
Format: F1 Columns: 172-172
1 Strongly agree
2 Agree
3 Disagree
4 Strongly disagree
7 N/A
8 Invalid
9 Missing

SC11Q02 (63) Students: enthusiasm Q11b
Format: F1 Columns: 173-173
1 Strongly agree
2 Agree
3 Disagree
4 Strongly disagree
7 N/A
8 Invalid
9 Missing

SC11Q03 (64) Students: take pride Q11c
Format: F1 Columns: 174-174
1 Strongly agree
2 Agree
3 Disagree
4 Strongly disagree
7 N/A
8 Invalid
9 Missing

SC11Q04 (65) Students: value academic Q11d
Format: F1 Columns: 175-175
1 Strongly agree
2 Agree
3 Disagree
4 Strongly disagree
7 N/A
8 Invalid
9 Missing

SC11Q05 (66) Students: respectful Q11e
Format: F1 Columns: 176-176
1 Strongly agree
2 Agree
3 Disagree
4 Strongly disagree
7 N/A
8 Invalid
9 Missing

SC11Q06 (67) Students: value education Q11f
Format: F1 Columns: 177-177
1 Strongly agree
2 Agree
3 Disagree
4 Strongly disagree
7 N/A
8 Invalid
9 Missing

SC11Q07 (68) Students: learn Q11g

Format: F1 Columns: 178-178

1 Strongly agree
2 Agree
3 Disagree
4 Strongly disagree
7 N/A
8 Invalid
9 Missing

SC12Q01 (69) Standardised test Q12a

Format: F1 Columns: 179-179

1 Never
2 1 to 2 times a year
3 3 to 5 times a year
4 Monthly
5 More once a month
7 N/A
8 Invalid
9 Missing

SC12Q02 (70) Teacher's test Q12b

Format: F1 Columns: 180-180

1 Never
2 1 to 2 times a year
3 3 to 5 times a year
4 Monthly
5 More once a month
7 N/A
8 Invalid
9 Missing

SC12Q03 (71) Teacher's ratings Q12c

Format: F1 Columns: 181-181

1 Never
2 1 to 2 times a year
3 3 to 5 times a year
4 Monthly
5 More once a month
7 N/A
8 Invalid
9 Missing

SC12Q04 (72) Students' portfolios Q12d

Format: F1 Columns: 182-182

1 Never
2 1 to 2 times a year
3 3 to 5 times a year
4 Monthly
5 More once a month
7 N/A
8 Invalid
9 Missing

SC12Q05 (73) Student assignments Q12e

Format: F1 Columns: 183-183

1 Never
2 1 to 2 times a year
3 3 to 5 times a year
4 Monthly
5 More once a month
7 N/A
8 Invalid
9 Missing

SC13Q01 (74) Assessment: inform parents Q13a

Format: F1 Columns: 184-184

1 Yes
2 No
7 N/A
8 Invalid
9 Missing

SC13Q02 (75) Assessment: retention Q13b

Format: F1 Columns: 185-185

1 Yes
2 No
7 N/A
8 Invalid
9 Missing

SC13Q03 (76) Assessment: group students Q13c

Format: F1 Columns: 186-186

1 Yes
2 No
7 N/A
8 Invalid
9 Missing

SC13Q04 (77) Assessment: compare to national Q13d

Format: F1 Columns: 187-187

1 Yes
2 No
7 N/A
8 Invalid
9 Missing

SC13Q05 (78) Assessment: school's progress Q13e

Format: F1 Columns: 188-188

1 Yes
2 No
7 N/A
8 Invalid
9 Missing

SC13Q06 (79) Assessment: teachers' effectiveness Q13f

Format: F1 Columns: 189-189

1 Yes
2 No
7 N/A
8 Invalid
9 Missing

SC13Q07 (80) Assessment: improve curriculum Q13g

Format: F1 Columns: 190-190

1 Yes
2 No
7 N/A
8 Invalid
9 Missing

SC13Q08 (81) Assessment: compare to other schools Q13h

Format: F1 Columns: 191-191

1 Yes
2 No
7 N/A
8 Invalid
9 Missing

SC14Q01 (82) Language percent Q14

Format: F1 Columns: 192-192

1 40% or more
2 more 20% less 40%
3 more 10% less 20%
4 Less than 10%
7 N/A
8 Invalid
9 Missing

SC15Q01 (83) Separate subject Q15a

Format: F1 Columns: 193-193

1 No
2 Yes for one
3 Yes for 2 or more
4 Not Applicable
7 N/A
8 Invalid
9 Missing

SC15Q02 (84) Other parts Q15b

Format: F1 Columns: 194-194

1 No
2 Yes for one
3 Yes for 2 or more
4 Not Applicable
7 N/A
8 Invalid
9 Missing

SC16Q01 (85) Streaming by levels Q16a

Format: F1 Columns: 195-195

1 For all classes
2 For some classes
3 Not for any classes
7 N/A
8 Invalid
9 Missing

SC16Q02 (86) Streaming by content Q16b

Format: F1 Columns: 196-196

1 For all classes
2 For some classes
3 Not for any classes
7 N/A
8 Invalid
9 Missing

SC16Q03 (87) Grouped by ability Q16c

Format: F1 Columns: 197-197

1 For all classes
2 For some classes
3 Not for any classes
7 N/A
8 Invalid
9 Missing

SC16Q04 (88) Not grouped by ability Q16d

Format: F1 Columns: 198-198

1 For all classes
2 For some classes
3 Not for any classes
7 N/A
8 Invalid
9 Missing

SC17Q01 (89) Enrichment mathematics Q17a

Format: F1 Columns: 199-199

1 Yes
2 No
7 N/A
8 Invalid
9 Missing

SC17Q02 (90) Remedial mathematics Q17b

Format: F1 Columns: 200-200

1 Yes
2 No
7 N/A
8 Invalid
9 Missing

SC17Q03 (91) Mathematics competitions Q17c

Format: F1 Columns: 201-201

1 Yes
2 No
7 N/A
8 Invalid
9 Missing

SC17Q04 (92) Mathematics clubs Q17d

Format: F1 Columns: 202-202

1 Yes
2 No
7 N/A
8 Invalid
9 Missing

SC17Q05 (93) Computer clubs Q17e

Format: F1 Columns: 203-203
1 Yes
2 No
7 N/A
8 Invalid
9 Missing

SC18Q11 (94) Full-time teacher in total Q18a1

Format: F8 Columns: 204-211
997 N/A
998 Invalid
999 Missing

SC18Q12 (95) Full-time teacher fully certified Q18b1

Format: F8 Columns: 212-219
997 N/A
998 Invalid
999 Missing

SC18Q13 (96) Full-time teacher ISCED5A in pedagogy Q18c1

Format: F8 Columns: 220-227
997 N/A
998 Invalid
999 Missing

SC18Q21 (97) Part-time teacher in total Q18a2

Format: F8 Columns: 228-235
997 N/A
998 Invalid
999 Missing

SC18Q22 (98) Part-time teacher fully certified Q18b2

Format: F8 Columns: 236-243
997 N/A
998 Invalid
999 Missing

SC18Q23 (99) Part-time teacher ISCED5A in pedagogy Q18c2

Format: F8 Columns: 244-251
997 N/A
998 Invalid
999 Missing

SC19Q11 (100) Full-time maths teacher Q19a1

Format: F8 Columns: 252-259
997 N/A
998 Invalid
999 Missing

SC19Q12 (101) Full-time teacher ISCED5A maths Q19b1

Format: F8 Columns: 260-267
997 N/A
998 Invalid
999 Missing

SC19Q13 (102) Full-time maths teacher ISCED5A no major Q19c1

Format: F8 Columns: 268-275
997 N/A
998 Invalid
999 Missing

SC19Q14 (103) Full-time maths teacher ISCED5A in pedagogy Q19d1

Format: F8 Columns: 276-283
997 N/A
998 Invalid
999 Missing

SC19Q15 (104) Full-time maths teacher ISCED5B Q19e1

Format: F8 Columns: 284-291
997 N/A
998 Invalid
999 Missing

SC19Q21 (105) Part-time maths teacher Q19a2

Format: F8 Columns: 292-299
997 N/A
998 Invalid
999 Missing

SC19Q22 (106) Part-time teacher ISCED5A maths Q19b2

Format: F8 Columns: 300-307
997 N/A
998 Invalid
999 Missing

SC19Q23 (107) Part-time maths teacher ISCED5A no major Q19c2

Format: F8 Columns: 308-315
997 N/A
998 Invalid
999 Missing

SC19Q24 (108) Part-time maths teacher ISCED5A in pedagogy Q19d2

Format: F8 Columns: 316-323
997 N/A
998 Invalid
999 Missing

SC19Q25 (109) Part-time maths teacher ISCED5B Q19e2

Format: F8 Columns: 324-331
997 N/A
998 Invalid
999 Missing

SC20Q01 (110) By students' achievement Q20a

Format: F1 Columns: 332-332

1 Yes
2 No
7 N/A
8 Invalid
9 Missing

SC20Q02 (111) By teacher review Q20b

Format: F1 Columns: 333-333

1 Yes
2 No
7 N/A
8 Invalid
9 Missing

SC20Q03 (112) By principal Q20c

Format: F1 Columns: 334-334

1 Yes
2 No
7 N/A
8 Invalid
9 Missing

SC20Q04 (113) By inspectors Q20d

Format: F1 Columns: 335-335

1 Yes
2 No
7 N/A
8 Invalid
9 Missing

SC21Q01 (114) Innovative teachers Q21a

Format: F1 Columns: 336-336

1 Strongly agree
2 Agree
3 Disagree
4 Strongly disagree
7 N/A
8 Invalid
9 Missing

SC21Q02 (115) Traditional teachers Q21b

Format: F1 Columns: 337-337

1 Strongly agree
2 Agree
3 Disagree
4 Strongly disagree
7 N/A
8 Invalid
9 Missing

SC21Q03 (116) Innovation disagreements Q21c

Format: F1 Columns: 338-338

1 Strongly agree
2 Agree
3 Disagree
4 Strongly disagree
7 N/A
8 Invalid
9 Missing

SC22Q01 (117) Require high achievement Q22a

Format: F1 Columns: 339-339

1 Strongly agree
2 Agree
3 Disagree
4 Strongly disagree
7 N/A
8 Invalid
9 Missing

SC22Q02 (118) Adapt standards Q22b

Format: F1 Columns: 340-340

1 Strongly agree
2 Agree
3 Disagree
4 Strongly disagree
7 N/A
8 Invalid
9 Missing

SC22Q03 (119) Frequent disagreements Q22c

Format: F1 Columns: 341-341

1 Strongly agree
2 Agree
3 Disagree
4 Strongly disagree
7 N/A
8 Invalid
9 Missing

SC23Q01 (120) Goals social development Q23a

Format: F1 Columns: 342-342

1 Strongly agree
2 Agree
3 Disagree
4 Strongly disagree
7 N/A
8 Invalid
9 Missing

SC23Q02 (121) Goals maths skills Q23b

Format: F1 Columns: 343-343

1 Strongly agree
2 Agree
3 Disagree
4 Strongly disagree
7 N/A
8 Invalid
9 Missing

SC23Q03 (122) Goals disagreements Q23c

Format: F1 Columns: 344-344

1 Strongly agree
2 Agree
3 Disagree
4 Strongly disagree
7 N/A
8 Invalid
9 Missing

SC24Q01 (123) High morale Q24a

Format: F1 Columns: 345-345

1 Strongly agree
2 Agree
3 Disagree
4 Strongly disagree
7 N/A
8 Invalid
9 Missing

SC24Q02 (124) Enthusiasm Q24b

Format: F1 Columns: 346-346

1 Strongly agree
2 Agree
3 Disagree
4 Strongly disagree
7 N/A
8 Invalid
9 Missing

SC24Q03 (125) Pride in school Q24c

Format: F1 Columns: 347-347

1 Strongly agree
2 Agree
3 Disagree
4 Strongly disagree
7 N/A
8 Invalid
9 Missing

SC24Q04 (126) Academic Achievement Q24d

Format: F1 Columns: 348-348

1 Strongly agree
2 Agree
3 Disagree
4 Strongly disagree
7 N/A
8 Invalid
9 Missing

SC25Q01 (127) Low expectations Q25a

Format: F1 Columns: 349-349

1 Not at all
2 Very Little
3 To some extent
4 A lot
7 N/A
8 Invalid
9 Missing

SC25Q02 (128) Student absenteeism Q25b

Format: F1 Columns: 350-350

1 Not at all
2 Very Little
3 To some extent
4 A lot
7 N/A
8 Invalid
9 Missing

SC25Q03 (129) Stud-teacher relations Q25c

Format: F1 Columns: 351-351

1 Not at all
2 Very Little
3 To some extent
4 A lot
7 N/A
8 Invalid
9 Missing

SC25Q04 (130) Disruption of classes Q25d

Format: F1 Columns: 352-352

1 Not at all
2 Very Little
3 To some extent
4 A lot
7 N/A
8 Invalid
9 Missing

SC25Q05 (131) Not meeting needs Q25e

Format: F1 Columns: 353-353

1 Not at all
2 Very Little
3 To some extent
4 A lot
7 N/A
8 Invalid
9 Missing

SC25Q06 (132) Teacher absenteeism Q25f

Format: F1 Columns: 354-354

1 Not at all
2 Very Little
3 To some extent
4 A lot
7 N/A
8 Invalid
9 Missing

SC25Q07 (133) Skipping classes Q25g

Format: F1 Columns: 355-355

1 Not at all
2 Very Little
3 To some extent
4 A lot
7 N/A
8 Invalid
9 Missing

SC25Q08 (134) Lack of respect Q25h

Format: F1 Columns: 356-356

1 Not at all
2 Very Little
3 To some extent
4 A lot
7 N/A
8 Invalid
9 Missing

SC25Q09 (135) Resisting change Q25i

Format: F1 Columns: 357-357

1 Not at all
2 Very Little
3 To some extent
4 A lot
7 N/A
8 Invalid
9 Missing

SC25Q10 (136) Use of alcohol Q25j

Format: F1 Columns: 358-358

1 Not at all
2 Very Little
3 To some extent
4 A lot
7 N/A
8 Invalid
9 Missing

SC25Q11 (137) Teacher strictness Q25k

Format: F1 Columns: 359-359

1 Not at all
2 Very Little
3 To some extent
4 A lot
7 N/A
8 Invalid
9 Missing

SC25Q12 (138) Bullying Q25l

Format: F1 Columns: 360-360

1 Not at all
2 Very Little
3 To some extent
4 A lot
7 N/A
8 Invalid
9 Missing

SC25Q13 (139) Lack encouragement Q25m

Format: F1 Columns: 361-361

1 Not at all
2 Very Little
3 To some extent
4 A lot
7 N/A
8 Invalid
9 Missing

SC26Q01 (140) Hiring teachers Q26a

Format: A5 Columns: 362-366

Value Label
77777 N/A
88888 Invalid
99999 Missing

SC26Q02 (141) Firing teachers Q26b

Format: A5 Columns: 367-371

Value Label
77777 N/A
88888 Invalid
99999 Missing

SC26Q03 (142) Teacher salaries Q26c

Format: A5 Columns: 372-376

Value Label
77777 N/A
88888 Invalid
99999 Missing

SC26Q04 (143) Salary increase Q26d

Format: A5 Columns: 377-381

Value Label
77777 N/A
88888 Invalid
99999 Missing

SC26Q05 (144) Budget formulation Q26e

Format: A5 Columns: 382-386

Value Label
77777 N/A
88888 Invalid
99999 Missing

SC26Q06 (145) Budget allocation Q26f

Format: A5 Columns: 387-391

Value Label
77777 N/A
88888 Invalid
99999 Missing

SC26Q07 (146) Disciplinary policies Q26g

Format: A5 Columns: 392-396

Value Label
77777 N/A
88888 Invalid
99999 Missing

SC26Q08 (147) Assessment: policies Q26h

Format: A5 Columns: 397-401

Value Label
77777 N/A
88888 Invalid
99999 Missing

SC26Q09 (148) Student admittance Q26i

Format: A5 Columns: 402-406

Value	Label
77777	N/A
88888	Invalid
99999	Missing

SC26Q10 (149) Textbooks Q26j

Format: A5 Columns: 407-411

Value	Label
77777	N/A
88888	Invalid
99999	Missing

SC26Q11 (150) Course content Q26k

Format: A5 Columns: 412-416

Value	Label
77777	N/A
88888	Invalid
99999	Missing

SC26Q12 (151) Course offer Q26l

Format: A5 Columns: 417-421

Value	Label
77777	N/A
88888	Invalid
99999	Missing

SC27Q01 (152) Decision making: national Q27a

Format: A4 Columns: 422-425

7777 N/A
8888 Invalid
9999 Missing

SC27Q02 (153) Decision making: local Q27b

Format: A4 Columns: 426-429

7777 N/A
8888 Invalid
9999 Missing

SC27Q03 (154) Decision making: employers Q27c

Format: A4 Columns: 430-433

7777 N/A
8888 Invalid
9999 Missing

SC27Q04 (155) Decision making: parents Q27d

Format: A4 Columns: 434-437

7777 N/A
8888 Invalid
9999 Missing

SC27Q05 (156) Decision making: teachers Q27e

Format: A4 Columns: 438-441

7777 N/A
8888 Invalid
9999 Missing

SC27Q06 (157) Decision making: students Q27f

Format: A4 Columns: 442-445

7777 N/A
8888 Invalid
9999 Missing

SC27Q07 (158) Decision making: external Q27g

Format: A4 Columns: 446-449

7777 N/A
8888 Invalid
9999 Missing

SCHLSIZE (159) School size

Format: F8 Columns: 450-457

99997 N/A
99998 Invalid
99999 Missing

PCGIRLS (160) Proportion of girls

Format: F8.3Columns: 458-465

997 N/A
998 Invalid
999 Missing

SCHLTYPE (161) School ownership

Format: F1 Columns: 466-466

1 Private independent
2 Private government-dependent
3 Public
7 N/A
9 Missing

RATCOMP (162) Computer ratio to school size

Format: F8.3Columns: 467-474

97 N/A
98 Invalid
99 Missing

COMPWEB (163) Proportion of computers connected to WEB

Format: F8.3Columns: 475-482

7 N/A
9 Missing

COMPLAN (164) Proportion of computers connected to LAN

Format: F8.3Columns: 483-490

7 N/A
9 Missing

STRATIO (165) Student/teacher ratio

Format: F8.3Columns: 491-498

997 N/A
998 Invalid
999 Missing

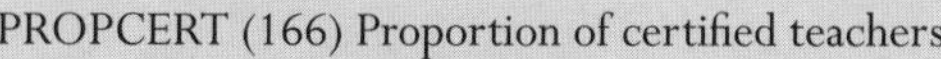

PROPCERT (166) Proportion of certified teachers

Format: F8.3 Columns: 499-506
- 997 N/A
- 998 Invalid
- 999 Missing

PROPQPED (167) Proportion of teachers with ISCED 5A in pedagogy

Format: F8.3 Columns: 507-514
- 997 N/A
- 998 Invalid
- 999 Missing

SMRATIO (168) Maths student/teacher ratio

Format: F8.3 Columns: 515-522
- 997 N/A
- 998 Invalid
- 999 Missing

PROPMATH (169) Proportion of maths teachers

Format: F8.3 Columns: 523-530
- 997 N/A
- 998 Invalid
- 999 Missing

PROPMA5A (170) Proportion of math teachers with a ISCED 5A level in maths

Format: F8.3 Columns: 531-538
- 997 N/A
- 998 Invalid
- 999 Missing

ASSESS (171) Estimated number of assessments per year

Format: F1 Columns: 539-539
- 1 <20
- 2 20-39
- 3 >40
- 7 N/A
- 9 Missing

SELECT (172) School selectivity

Format: F1 Columns: 540-540
- 0 Not considered
- 1 At least one considered
- 2 At least one high priority
- 3 At least one pre-requiste
- 7 N/A
- 9 Missing

ABGROUP (173) Streaming within schools

Format: F1 Columns: 541-541
- 1 Not for any classes
- 2 For some classes
- 3 For all classes
- 7 N/A
- 9 Missing

EXCOURSE (174) School offering extension courses (number of types)

Format: F1 Columns: 542-542
- 9 Missing

MACTIV (175) School offering maths activities (number of types)

Format: F1 Columns: 543-543
- 9 Missing

AUTRES (176) Resource autonomy

Format: F1 Columns: 544-544
- 9 Missing

AUTCURR (177) Curricular autonomy

Format: F1 Columns: 545-545
- 9 Missing

MSTREL (178) Index of poor student-teacher relations (school average)

Format: F5.2 Columns: 546-550
- 7 N/A
- 9 Missing

TCSHORT (179) Shortage of teachers (WLE)

Format: F8.3 Columns: 551-558
- 997 Missing

SCMATBUI (180) Quality of material resources (WLE)

Format: F8.3 Columns: 559-566
- 997 Missing

SCMATEDU (181) Quality of educational resources (WLE)

Format: F8.3 Columns: 567-574
- 997 Missing

STMORALE (182) Student morale (WLE)

Format: F8.3 Columns: 575-582
- 997 Missing

TCMORALE (183) Teacher morale (WLE)

Format: F8.3 Columns: 583-590
- 997 Missing

STUDBEHA (184) Student behaviours (WLE)

Format: F8.3 Columns: 591-598
- 997 Missing

TEACBEHA (185) Teacher behaviours (WLE)

Format: F8.3 Columns: 599-606
- 997 Missing

TCHCONS (186) Mathematics teacher consensus (WLE)

Format: F8.3 Columns: 607-614
- 997 Missing

SCHAUTON (187) School autonomy (WLE)

Format: F8.3 Columns: 615-622
- 997 Missing

TCHPARTI (188) Teacher participation (WLE)

Format: F8.3 Columns: 623-630
997 Missing

SCWEIGHT (189) School weight

Format: F8.5 Columns: 631-638
997 Missing

STRATUM (190) Stratum

Format: A5 Columns: 640-644

See Appendix 6: Student questionnaire data file codebook

APPENDIX 8 ▪ STUDENT COGNITIVE TEST DATA FILE CODEBOOK

COGNITIVE DATA

Country (1) *COUNTRY THREE-DIGIT ISO CODE*

Format A3 Columns 1-3

See Appendix 6: Student questionnaire data file codebook

CNT (2) *COUNTRY ALPHANUMERIC ISO CODE*

Format A3 Columns 4-6

Subnatio (3) *SUB-NATION CODE*

Format A4 Columns 7-10

See Appendix 6: Student questionnaire data file codebook

Schoolid (4) *SCHOOL ID*

Format A5 Columns 11-15

Stidstd (5) *STUDENT ID*

Format A5 Columns 16-20

BOOKID (6) *BOOKLET ID*

Format A2 Columns 22-23

M033Q01 (7) *A VIEW WITH A ROOM Q1* — Multiple Choice

Format A1 Columns 24-24

Code	Label	Booklet	Question
1	No Credit	Booklet 1	Q1
2	No Credit	Booklet 5	Q43
3	No Credit	Booklet 11	Q25
4	Full Credit	Booklet 13	Q10
8	M/R		
9	Missing		
n	N/A		
r	Not reached		

M034Q01T (8) *BRICKS Q1* — Coded Response

Format A1 Columns 25-25

Code	Label	Booklet	Question
0	No Credit	Booklet 1	Q22
1	Full Credit	Booklet 2	Q10
8	Invalid	Booklet 6	Q52
9	Missing	Booklet 12	Q29
n	N/A		
r	Not reached		

M124Q01 (9) *WALKING Q1* — Coded Response

Format A1 Columns 26-26

Code	Label	Booklet	Question
0	No Credit	Booklet 2	Q16
1	No Credit	Booklet 3	Q4
2	Full Credit	Booklet 7	Q37
9	Missing	Booklet 13	Q25
n	N/A		
r	Not reached		

M124Q03T (10) *WALKING Q3*		Coded Response	
Format A1	Columns 27-27		
0	No Credit	Booklet 2	Q17
1	Partial Credit	Booklet 3	Q5
2	Partial Credit	Booklet 7	Q38
3	Full Credit	Booklet 13	Q26
9	Missing		
n	N/A		
r	Not reached		

M144Q01T (11) *CUBE PAINTING Q1*		Coded Response	
Format A1	Columns 28-28		
0	No Credit	Booklet 1	Q33
1	Full Credit	Booklet 3	Q21
9	Missing	Booklet 4	Q9
n	N/A	Booklet 8	Q59
r	Not reached		

M144Q02T (12) *CUBE PAINTING Q2*		Coded Response	
Format A1	Columns 29-29		
0	No Credit	Booklet 1	Q34
1	Full Credit	Booklet 3	Q22
8	Invalid	Booklet 4	Q10
9	Missing	Booklet 8	Q60
n	N/A		
r	Not reached		

M144Q03 (13) *CUBE PAINTING Q3*		Multiple Choice	
Format A1	Columns 30-30		
1	Full Credit	Booklet 1	Q35
2	No Credit	Booklet 3	Q23
3	No Credit	Booklet 4	Q11
4	No Credit	Booklet 8	Q61
8	M/R		
9	Missing		
n	N/A		
r	Not reached		

M144Q04T (14) *CUBE PAINTING Q4*		Coded Response	
Format A1	Columns 31-31		
0	No Credit	Booklet 1	Q36
1	Full Credit	Booklet 3	Q24
8	Invalid	Booklet 4	Q12
9	Missing	Booklet 8	Q62
n	N/A		
r	Not reached		

M145Q01T (15) *CUBES Q1*		Complex Multiple Choice	
Format A1	Columns 32-32		
0	No Credit	Booklet 1	Q13
1	No Credit	Booklet 2	Q1
2	No Credit	Booklet 6	Q43
3	No Credit	Booklet 12	Q20
4	No Credit		
5	No Credit		
6	Full Credit		
8	Invalid		
9	Missing		
n	N/A		
r	Not reached		

M150Q01 (16) *GROWING UP Q1*		Coded Response	
Format A1	Columns 33-33		
0	No Credit	Booklet 2	Q31
1	Full Credit	Booklet 4	Q19
9	Missing	Booklet 5	Q7
n	N/A	Booklet 9	Q47
r	Not reached		

M150Q02T (17) *GROWING UP Q2*		Coded Response	
Format A1	Columns 34-34		
0	No Credit	Booklet 2	Q33
1	Partial Credit	Booklet 4	Q21
2	Full Credit	Booklet 5	Q9
9	Missing	Booklet 9	Q49
r	Not reached		
n	N/A		

M150Q03T (18) *GROWING UP Q3*		Coded Response	
Format A1	Columns 35-35		
0	No Credit	Booklet 2	Q32
1	Full Credit	Booklet 4	Q20
9	Missing	Booklet 5	Q8
n	N/A	Booklet 9	Q48
r	Not reached		

M155Q01 (19) *POPULATION PYRAMIDS Q1*		Coded Response	
Format A1	Columns 36-36		
0	No Credit	Booklet 3	Q29
1	Full Credit	Booklet 5	Q18
9	Missing	Booklet 6	Q5
n	N/A	Booklet 10	Q42
r	Not reached		

M155Q02T (20) *POPULATION PYRAMIDS Q2*		Coded Response	
Format A1	Columns 37-37		
0	No Credit	Booklet 3	Q28
1	Partial Credit	Booklet 5	Q17
2	Full Credit	Booklet 6	Q4
9	Missing	Booklet 10	Q41
n	N/A		
r	Not reached		

M155Q03T (21) *POPULATION PYRAMIDS Q3*		Coded Response	
Format A1	Columns 38-38		
0	No Credit	Booklet 3	Q30
1	Partial Credit	Booklet 5	Q19
2	Full Credit	Booklet 6	Q6
9	Missing	Booklet 10	Q43
n	N/A		
r	Not reached		

M155Q04T (22) *POPULATION PYRAMIDS Q4*		Complex Multiple Choice	
Format A1	Columns 39-39		
0	No Credit	Booklet 3	Q31
1	No Credit	Booklet 5	Q20
2	No Credit	Booklet 6	Q7
3	No Credit	Booklet 10	Q44
4	Full Credit		
8	Invalid		
9	Missing		
n	N/A		
r	Not reached		

M179Q01T (23) *ROBBERIES Q1*		Coded Response	
Format A1	Columns 40-40		
0	No Credit	Booklet 1	Q9
1	Partial Credit	Booklet 5	Q51
	Full Credit	Booklet 11	Q33
9	Missing	Booklet 13	Q18
n	N/A		
r	Not reached		

M192Q01T (24) *CONTAINERS Q1*		Complex Multiple Choice	
Format A1	Columns 41-41		
0	No Credit	Booklet 1	Q20
1	No Credit	Booklet 2	Q8
2	Full Credit	Booklet 6	Q50
3	Full Credit	Booklet 12	Q27
8	Invalid		
9	Missing		
n	N/A		
r	Not reached		

M266Q01T (25) *CARPENTER Q1*		Complex Multiple Choice	
Format A1	Columns 42-42		
0	No Credit	Booklet 4	Q31
1	No Credit	Booklet 6	Q18
2	No Credit	Booklet 7	Q6
3	No Credit	Booklet 11	Q43
4	Full Credit		
8	Invalid		
9	Missing		
n	N/A		
r	Not reached		

M273Q01T (26) *PIPELINES Q1*		Coded Response	
Format A1	Columns 43-43		
0	No Credit	Booklet 4	Q37
1	Full Credit	Booklet 6	Q24
8	Invalid	Booklet 7	Q12
9	Missing	Booklet 11	Q49
n	N/A		
r	Not reached		

M302Q01T (27) *CAR DRIVE Q1*		Coded Response	
Format A1	Columns 44-44		
0	No Credit	Booklet 4	Q26
1	Full Credit	Booklet 6	Q13
9	Missing	Booklet 7	Q1
n	N/A	Booklet 11	Q38
r	Not reached		

M302Q02 (28) *CAR DRIVE Q2*		Coded Response	
Format A1	Columns 45-45		
0	No Credit	Booklet 4	Q27
1	Full Credit	Booklet 6	Q14
9	Missing	Booklet 7	Q2
n	N/A	Booklet 11	Q39
r	Not reached		

M302Q03 (29) *CAR DRIVE Q3*		Coded Response	
Format A1	Columns 46-46		
0	No Credit	Booklet 4	Q28
1	Full Credit	Booklet 6	Q15
9	Missing	Booklet 7	Q3
n	N/A	Booklet 11	Q40
r	Not reached		

M305Q01 (30) *MAP Q1*		Multiple Choice	
Format A1	Columns 47-47		
1	No Credit	Booklet 2	Q13
2	No Credit	Booklet 3	Q1
3	Full Credit	Booklet 7	Q34
4	No Credit	Booklet 13	Q22
8	M/R		
9	Missing		
n	N/A		
r	Not reached		

M402Q01 (31) *INTERNET RELAY CHAT Q1*		Coded Response	
Format A1	Columns 48-48		
0	No Credit	Booklet 1	Q7
1	Full Credit	Booklet 5	Q49
9	Missing	Booklet 11	Q31
n	N/A	Booklet 13	Q16
r	Not reached		

M402Q02 (32) *INTERNET RELAY CHAT Q2*		Coded Response	
Format A1	Columns 49-49		
0	No Credit	Booklet 1	Q8
1	Full Credit	Booklet 5	Q50
9	Missing	Booklet 11	Q32
n	N/A	Booklet 13	Q17
r	Not reached		

M406Q01 (33) *RUNNING TRACKS Q1*		Coded Response	
Format A1	Columns 50-50		
0	No Credit	Booklet 2	Q28
1	Full Credit	Booklet 4	Q16
9	Missing	Booklet 5	Q4
n	N/A	Booklet 9	Q44
r	Not reached		

M406Q02 (34) *RUNNING TRACKS Q2*		Coded Response	
Format A1	Columns 51-51		
0	No Credit	Booklet 2	Q29
1	Full Credit	Booklet 4	Q17
9	Missing	Booklet 5	Q5
n	N/A	Booklet 9	Q45
r	Not reached		

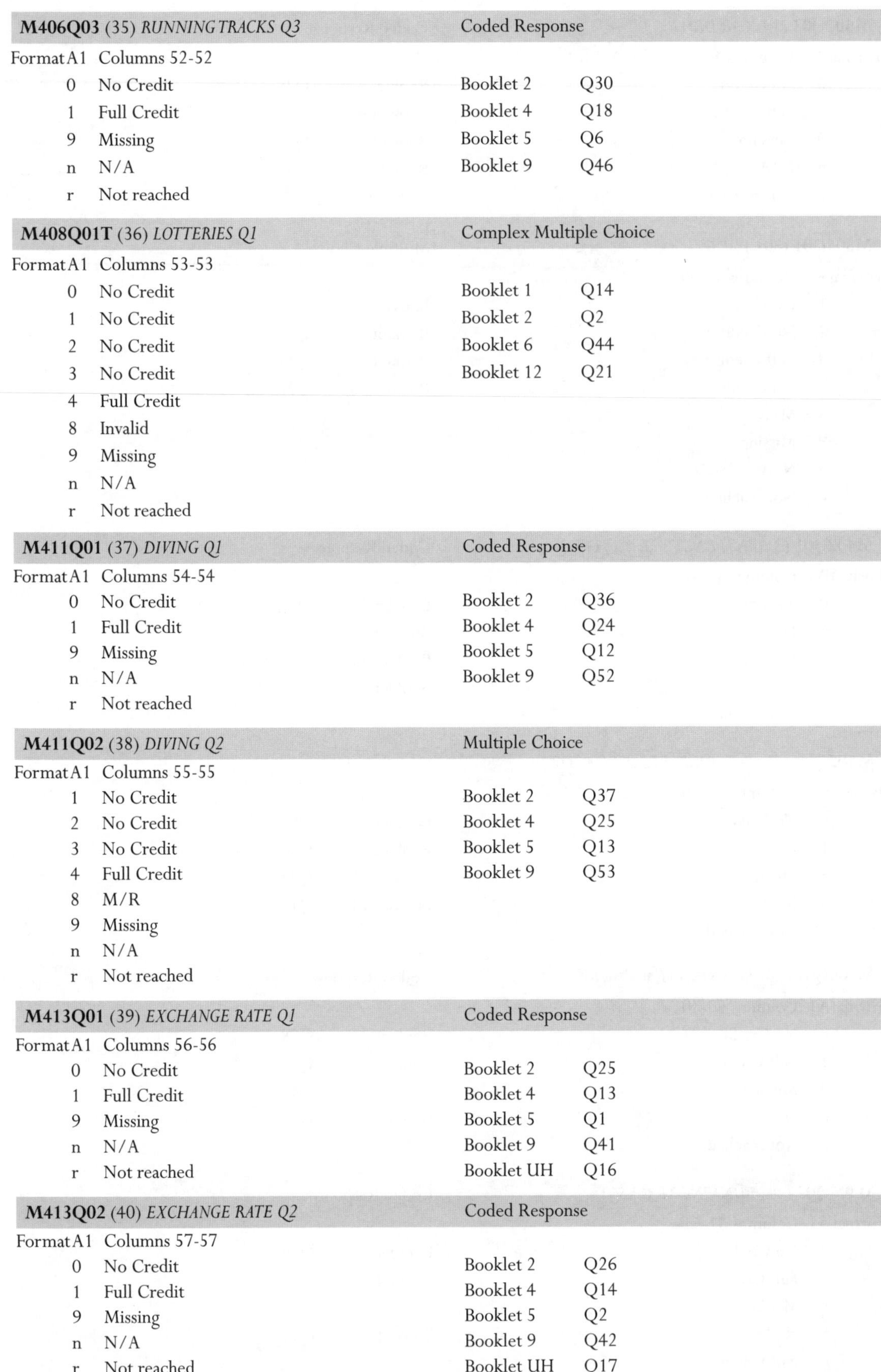

M406Q03 (35) *RUNNING TRACKS Q3*		Coded Response	
Format A1	Columns 52-52		
0	No Credit	Booklet 2	Q30
1	Full Credit	Booklet 4	Q18
9	Missing	Booklet 5	Q6
n	N/A	Booklet 9	Q46
r	Not reached		

M408Q01T (36) *LOTTERIES Q1*		Complex Multiple Choice	
Format A1	Columns 53-53		
0	No Credit	Booklet 1	Q14
1	No Credit	Booklet 2	Q2
2	No Credit	Booklet 6	Q44
3	No Credit	Booklet 12	Q21
4	Full Credit		
8	Invalid		
9	Missing		
n	N/A		
r	Not reached		

M411Q01 (37) *DIVING Q1*		Coded Response	
Format A1	Columns 54-54		
0	No Credit	Booklet 2	Q36
1	Full Credit	Booklet 4	Q24
9	Missing	Booklet 5	Q12
n	N/A	Booklet 9	Q52
r	Not reached		

M411Q02 (38) *DIVING Q2*		Multiple Choice	
Format A1	Columns 55-55		
1	No Credit	Booklet 2	Q37
2	No Credit	Booklet 4	Q25
3	No Credit	Booklet 5	Q13
4	Full Credit	Booklet 9	Q53
8	M/R		
9	Missing		
n	N/A		
r	Not reached		

M413Q01 (39) *EXCHANGE RATE Q1*		Coded Response	
Format A1	Columns 56-56		
0	No Credit	Booklet 2	Q25
1	Full Credit	Booklet 4	Q13
9	Missing	Booklet 5	Q1
n	N/A	Booklet 9	Q41
r	Not reached	Booklet UH	Q16

M413Q02 (40) *EXCHANGE RATE Q2*		Coded Response	
Format A1	Columns 57-57		
0	No Credit	Booklet 2	Q26
1	Full Credit	Booklet 4	Q14
9	Missing	Booklet 5	Q2
n	N/A	Booklet 9	Q42
r	Not reached	Booklet UH	Q17

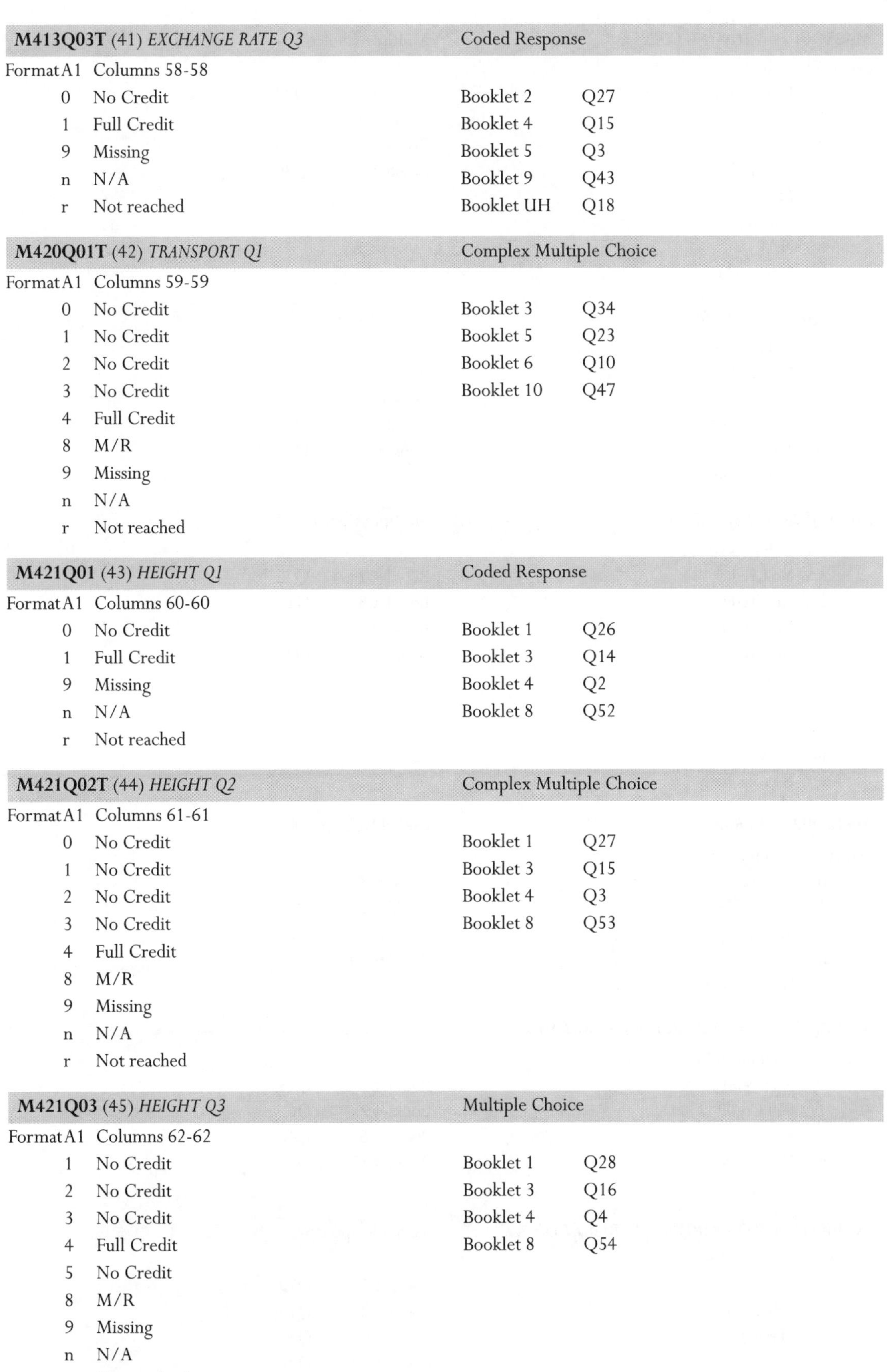

M413Q03T (41) *EXCHANGE RATE Q3*		Coded Response	
Format A1	Columns 58-58		
0	No Credit	Booklet 2	Q27
1	Full Credit	Booklet 4	Q15
9	Missing	Booklet 5	Q3
n	N/A	Booklet 9	Q43
r	Not reached	Booklet UH	Q18

M420Q01T (42) *TRANSPORT Q1*		Complex Multiple Choice	
Format A1	Columns 59-59		
0	No Credit	Booklet 3	Q34
1	No Credit	Booklet 5	Q23
2	No Credit	Booklet 6	Q10
3	No Credit	Booklet 10	Q47
4	Full Credit		
8	M/R		
9	Missing		
n	N/A		
r	Not reached		

M421Q01 (43) *HEIGHT Q1*		Coded Response	
Format A1	Columns 60-60		
0	No Credit	Booklet 1	Q26
1	Full Credit	Booklet 3	Q14
9	Missing	Booklet 4	Q2
n	N/A	Booklet 8	Q52
r	Not reached		

M421Q02T (44) *HEIGHT Q2*		Complex Multiple Choice	
Format A1	Columns 61-61		
0	No Credit	Booklet 1	Q27
1	No Credit	Booklet 3	Q15
2	No Credit	Booklet 4	Q3
3	No Credit	Booklet 8	Q53
4	Full Credit		
8	M/R		
9	Missing		
n	N/A		
r	Not reached		

M421Q03 (45) *HEIGHT Q3*		Multiple Choice	
Format A1	Columns 62-62		
1	No Credit	Booklet 1	Q28
2	No Credit	Booklet 3	Q16
3	No Credit	Booklet 4	Q4
4	Full Credit	Booklet 8	Q54
5	No Credit		
8	M/R		
9	Missing		
n	N/A		
r	Not reached		

M423Q01 (46) *TOSSING COINS Q1*		Multiple Choice	
Format A1	Columns 63-63		
1	Full Credit	Booklet 1	Q23
2	No Credit	Booklet 2	Q11
3	No Credit	Booklet 6	Q53
4	No Credit	Booklet 12	Q30
8	M/R		
9	Missing		
n	N/A		
r	Not reached		

M438Q01 (47) *EXPORTS Q1*		Coded Response	
Format A1	Columns 64-64		
0	No Credit	Booklet 2	Q21
1	Full Credit	Booklet 3	Q9
9	Missing	Booklet 7	Q42
n	N/A	Booklet 13	Q30
r	Not reached		

M438Q02 (48) *EXPORTS Q2*		Multiple Choice	
Format A1	Columns 65-65		
1	No Credit	Booklet 2	Q22
2	No Credit	Booklet 3	Q10
3	No Credit	Booklet 7	Q43
4	No Credit	Booklet 13	Q31
5	Full Credit		
8	M/R		
9	Missing		
n	N/A		
r	Not reached		

M442Q02 (49) *BRAILLE Q2*		Coded Response	
Format A1	Columns 66-66		
0	No Credit	Booklet 3	Q32
1	Full Credit	Booklet 5	Q21
9	Missing	Booklet 6	Q8
n	N/A	Booklet 10	Q45
r	Not reached		

M446Q01 (50) *THERMOMETER CRICKET Q1*		Coded Response	
Format A1	Columns 67-67		
0	No Credit	Booklet 1	Q18
1	Full Credit	Booklet 2	Q6
9	Missing	Booklet 6	Q48
n	N/A	Booklet 12	Q25
r	Not reached		

M446Q02 (51) *THERMOMETER CRICKET Q2*		Coded Response	
Format A1	Columns 68-68		
0	No Credit	Booklet 1	Q19
1	Full Credit	Booklet 2	Q7
9	Missing	Booklet 6	Q49
n	N/A	Booklet 12	Q26
r	Not reached		

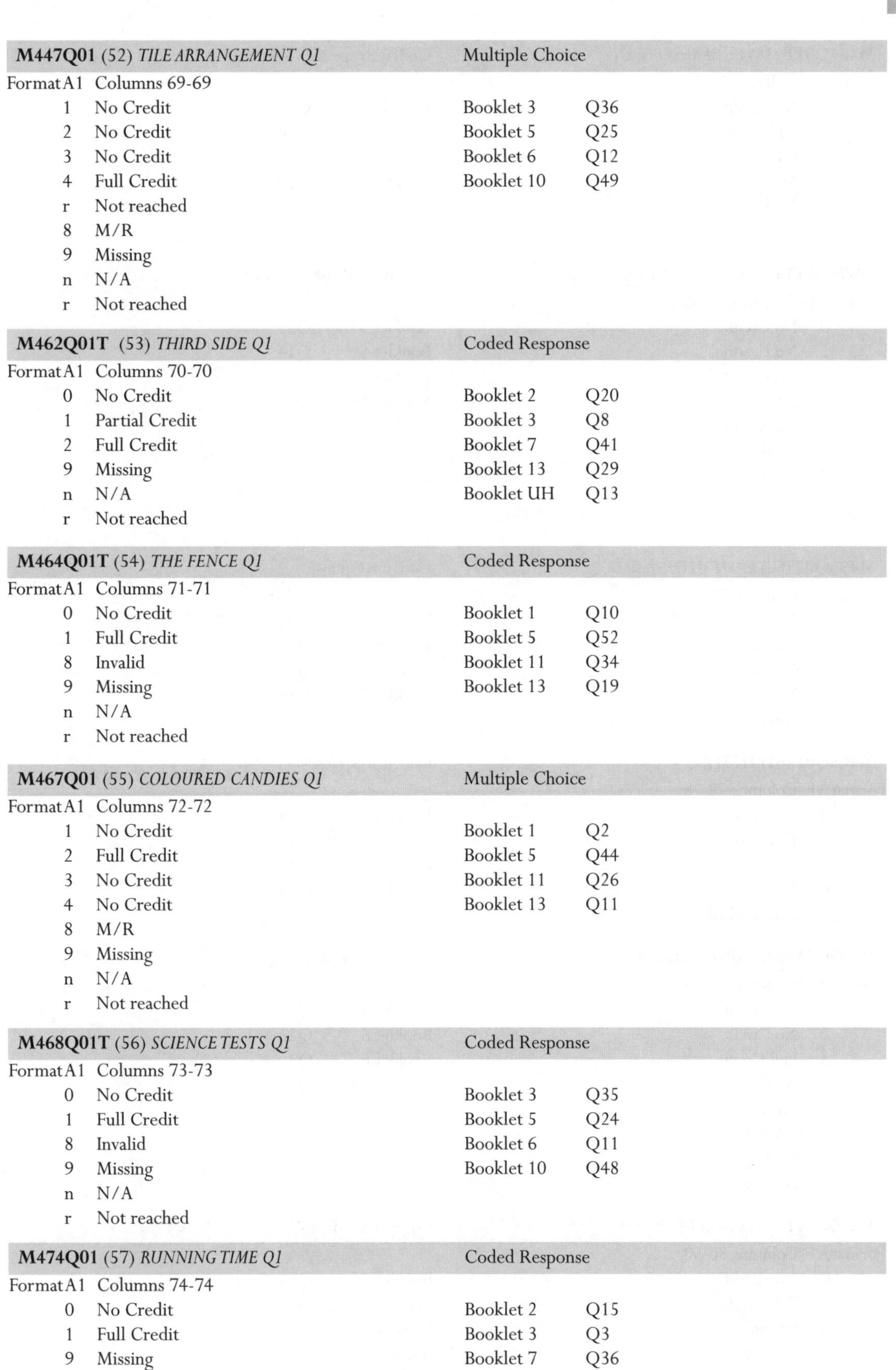

M447Q01 (52) *TILE ARRANGEMENT Q1* — Multiple Choice

Format A1 Columns 69-69

Code	Label	Booklet	Question
1	No Credit	Booklet 3	Q36
2	No Credit	Booklet 5	Q25
3	No Credit	Booklet 6	Q12
4	Full Credit	Booklet 10	Q49
r	Not reached		
8	M/R		
9	Missing		
n	N/A		
r	Not reached		

M462Q01T (53) *THIRD SIDE Q1* — Coded Response

Format A1 Columns 70-70

Code	Label	Booklet	Question
0	No Credit	Booklet 2	Q20
1	Partial Credit	Booklet 3	Q8
2	Full Credit	Booklet 7	Q41
9	Missing	Booklet 13	Q29
n	N/A	Booklet UH	Q13
r	Not reached		

M464Q01T (54) *THE FENCE Q1* — Coded Response

Format A1 Columns 71-71

Code	Label	Booklet	Question
0	No Credit	Booklet 1	Q10
1	Full Credit	Booklet 5	Q52
8	Invalid	Booklet 11	Q34
9	Missing	Booklet 13	Q19
n	N/A		
r	Not reached		

M467Q01 (55) *COLOURED CANDIES Q1* — Multiple Choice

Format A1 Columns 72-72

Code	Label	Booklet	Question
1	No Credit	Booklet 1	Q2
2	Full Credit	Booklet 5	Q44
3	No Credit	Booklet 11	Q26
4	No Credit	Booklet 13	Q11
8	M/R		
9	Missing		
n	N/A		
r	Not reached		

M468Q01T (56) *SCIENCE TESTS Q1* — Coded Response

Format A1 Columns 73-73

Code	Label	Booklet	Question
0	No Credit	Booklet 3	Q35
1	Full Credit	Booklet 5	Q24
8	Invalid	Booklet 6	Q11
9	Missing	Booklet 10	Q48
n	N/A		
r	Not reached		

M474Q01 (57) *RUNNING TIME Q1* — Coded Response

Format A1 Columns 74-74

Code	Label	Booklet	Question
0	No Credit	Booklet 2	Q15
1	Full Credit	Booklet 3	Q3
9	Missing	Booklet 7	Q36
n	N/A	Booklet 13	Q24
r	Not reached		

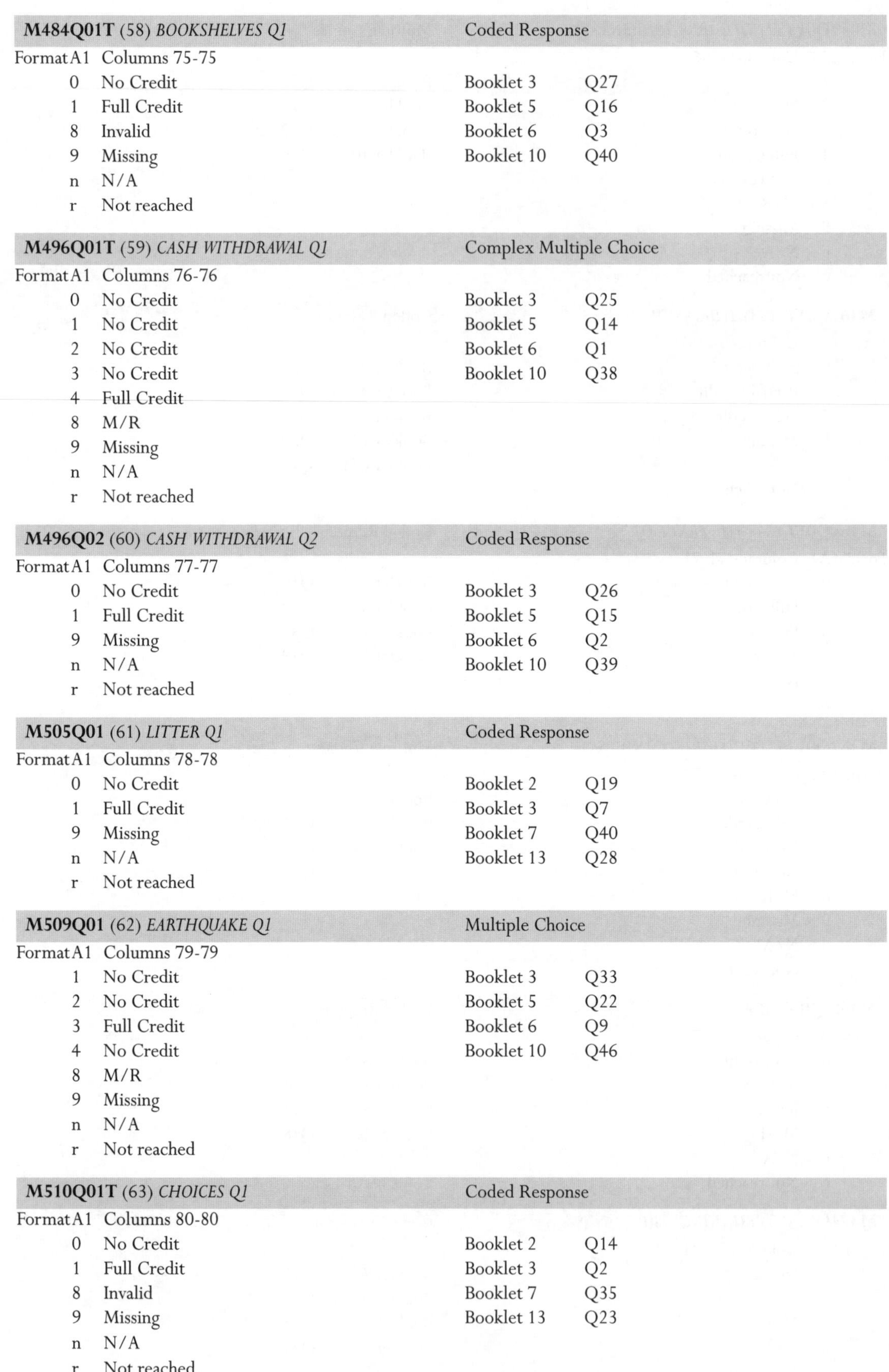

M484Q01T (58) *BOOKSHELVES Q1* — Coded Response

Format A1 Columns 75-75

Code	Label	Booklet	Question
0	No Credit	Booklet 3	Q27
1	Full Credit	Booklet 5	Q16
8	Invalid	Booklet 6	Q3
9	Missing	Booklet 10	Q40
n	N/A		
r	Not reached		

M496Q01T (59) *CASH WITHDRAWAL Q1* — Complex Multiple Choice

Format A1 Columns 76-76

Code	Label	Booklet	Question
0	No Credit	Booklet 3	Q25
1	No Credit	Booklet 5	Q14
2	No Credit	Booklet 6	Q1
3	No Credit	Booklet 10	Q38
4	Full Credit		
8	M/R		
9	Missing		
n	N/A		
r	Not reached		

M496Q02 (60) *CASH WITHDRAWAL Q2* — Coded Response

Format A1 Columns 77-77

Code	Label	Booklet	Question
0	No Credit	Booklet 3	Q26
1	Full Credit	Booklet 5	Q15
9	Missing	Booklet 6	Q2
n	N/A	Booklet 10	Q39
r	Not reached		

M505Q01 (61) *LITTER Q1* — Coded Response

Format A1 Columns 78-78

Code	Label	Booklet	Question
0	No Credit	Booklet 2	Q19
1	Full Credit	Booklet 3	Q7
9	Missing	Booklet 7	Q40
n	N/A	Booklet 13	Q28
r	Not reached		

M509Q01 (62) *EARTHQUAKE Q1* — Multiple Choice

Format A1 Columns 79-79

Code	Label	Booklet	Question
1	No Credit	Booklet 3	Q33
2	No Credit	Booklet 5	Q22
3	Full Credit	Booklet 6	Q9
4	No Credit	Booklet 10	Q46
8	M/R		
9	Missing		
n	N/A		
r	Not reached		

M510Q01T (63) *CHOICES Q1* — Coded Response

Format A1 Columns 80-80

Code	Label	Booklet	Question
0	No Credit	Booklet 2	Q14
1	Full Credit	Booklet 3	Q2
8	Invalid	Booklet 7	Q35
9	Missing	Booklet 13	Q23
n	N/A		
r	Not reached		

M513Q01 (64) *TEST SCORES Q1*		Coded Response	
Format A1	Columns 81-81		
0	No Credit	Booklet 4	Q32
1	Full Credit	Booklet 6	Q19
9	Missing	Booklet 7	Q7
n	N/A	Booklet 11	Q44
r	Not reached		

M520Q01T (65) *SKATEBOARD Q1*		Coded Response	
Format A1	Columns 82-82		
0	No Credit	Booklet 1	Q15
1	Partial Credit	Booklet 2	Q3
2	Full Credit	Booklet 6	Q45
8	Invalid	Booklet 12	Q22
9	Missing		
n	N/A		
r	Not reached		

M520Q02 (66) *SKATEBOARD Q2*		Multiple Choice	
Format A1	Columns 83-83		
1	No Credit	Booklet 1	Q16
2	No Credit	Booklet 2	Q4
3	No Credit	Booklet 6	Q46
4	Full Credit	Booklet 12	Q23
8	M/R		
9	Missing		
n	N/A		
r	Not reached		

M520Q03T (67) *SKATEBOARD Q3*		Coded Response	
Format A1	Columns 84-84		
0	No Credit	Booklet 1	Q17
1	No Credit	Booklet 2	Q5
2	No Credit	Booklet 6	Q47
3	No Credit	Booklet 12	Q24
4	Full Credit		
8	M/R		
9	Missing		
n	N/A		
r	Not reached		

M547Q01T (68) *STAIRCASE Q1*		Coded Response	
Format A1	Columns 85-85		
0	No Credit	Booklet 2	Q23
1	Full Credit	Booklet 3	Q11
8	Invalid	Booklet 7	Q44
9	Missing	Booklet 13	Q32
n	N/A		
r	Not reached		

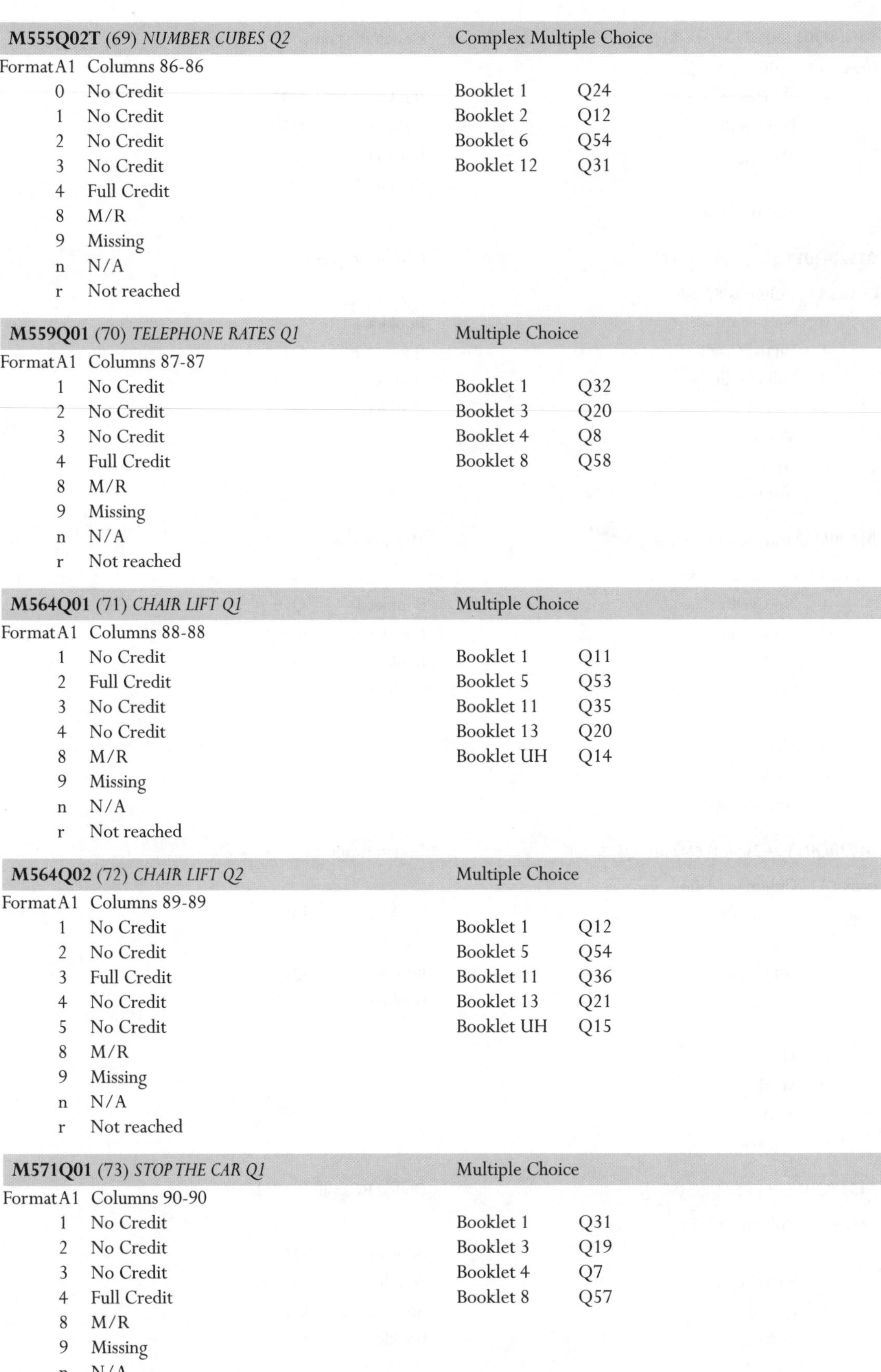

M555Q02T (69) *NUMBER CUBES Q2*		Complex Multiple Choice	
Format A1	Columns 86-86		
0	No Credit	Booklet 1	Q24
1	No Credit	Booklet 2	Q12
2	No Credit	Booklet 6	Q54
3	No Credit	Booklet 12	Q31
4	Full Credit		
8	M/R		
9	Missing		
n	N/A		
r	Not reached		

M559Q01 (70) *TELEPHONE RATES Q1*		Multiple Choice	
Format A1	Columns 87-87		
1	No Credit	Booklet 1	Q32
2	No Credit	Booklet 3	Q20
3	No Credit	Booklet 4	Q8
4	Full Credit	Booklet 8	Q58
8	M/R		
9	Missing		
n	N/A		
r	Not reached		

M564Q01 (71) *CHAIR LIFT Q1*		Multiple Choice	
Format A1	Columns 88-88		
1	No Credit	Booklet 1	Q11
2	Full Credit	Booklet 5	Q53
3	No Credit	Booklet 11	Q35
4	No Credit	Booklet 13	Q20
8	M/R	Booklet UH	Q14
9	Missing		
n	N/A		
r	Not reached		

M564Q02 (72) *CHAIR LIFT Q2*		Multiple Choice	
Format A1	Columns 89-89		
1	No Credit	Booklet 1	Q12
2	No Credit	Booklet 5	Q54
3	Full Credit	Booklet 11	Q36
4	No Credit	Booklet 13	Q21
5	No Credit	Booklet UH	Q15
8	M/R		
9	Missing		
n	N/A		
r	Not reached		

M571Q01 (73) *STOP THE CAR Q1*		Multiple Choice	
Format A1	Columns 90-90		
1	No Credit	Booklet 1	Q31
2	No Credit	Booklet 3	Q19
3	No Credit	Booklet 4	Q7
4	Full Credit	Booklet 8	Q57
8	M/R		
9	Missing		
n	N/A		
r	Not reached		

M598Q01 (74) *MAKING A BOOKLET Q1*		Coded Response	
Format A1	Columns 91-91		
0	No Credit	Booklet 2	Q34
1	Full Credit	Booklet 4	Q22
9	Missing	Booklet 5	Q10
n	N/A	Booklet 9	Q50
r	Not reached		

M603Q01T (75) *NUMBER CHECK Q1*		Complex Multiple Choice	
Format A1	Columns 92-92		
0	No Credit	Booklet 4	Q29
1	No Credit	Booklet 6	Q16
2	No Credit	Booklet 7	Q4
3	Full Credit	Booklet 11	Q41
8	M/R		
9	Missing		
n	N/A		
r	Not reached		

M603Q02T (76) *NUMBER CHECK Q2*		Coded Response	
Format A1	Columns 93-93		
0	No Credit	Booklet 4	Q30
1	Full Credit	Booklet 6	Q17
8	Invalid	Booklet 7	Q5
9	Missing	Booklet 11	Q42
n	N/A		
r	Not reached		

M702Q01 (77) *SUPPORT FOR PRESIDENT Q1*		Coded Response	
Format A1	Columns 94-94		
0	No Credit	Booklet 1	Q21
1	No Credit	Booklet 2	Q9
2	Full Credit	Booklet 6	Q51
9	Missing	Booklet 12	Q28
n	N/A		
r	Not reached		

M704Q01T (78) *THE BEST CAR Q1*		Coded Response	
Format A1	Columns 95-95		
0	No Credit	Booklet 1	Q29
1	Full Credit	Booklet 3	Q17
8	Invalid	Booklet 4	Q5
9	Missing	Booklet 8	Q55
n	N/A		
r	Not reached		

M704Q02T (79) *THE BEST CAR Q2*		Coded Response	
Format A1	Columns 96-96		
0	No Credit	Booklet 1	Q30
1	Full Credit	Booklet 3	Q18
8	Invalid	Booklet 4	Q6
9	Missing	Booklet 8	Q56
n	N/A		
r	Not reached		

M710Q01 (80) *FORECAST OF RAIN Q1*		Multiple Choice	
Format A1	Columns 97-97		
1	No Credit	Booklet 2	Q35
2	No Credit	Booklet 4	Q23
3	No Credit	Booklet 5	Q11
4	Full Credit	Booklet 9	Q51
5	No Credit		
8	M/R		
9	Missing		
n	N/A		
r	Not reached		

M800Q01 (81) *COMPUTER GAME Q1*		Multiple Choice	
Format A1	Columns 98-98		
1	No Credit	Booklet 1	Q25
2	No Credit	Booklet 3	Q13
3	Full Credit	Booklet 4	Q1
4	No Credit	Booklet 8	Q51
8	M/R	Booklet UH	Q12
9	Missing		
n	N/A		
r	Not reached		

M803Q01T (82) *LABELS Q1*		Coded Response	
Format A1	Columns 99-99		
0	No Credit	Booklet 4	Q36
1	Full Credit	Booklet 6	Q23
8	Invalid	Booklet 7	Q11
9	Missing	Booklet 11	Q48
n	N/A		
r	Not reached		

M806Q01T (83) *STEP PATTERN Q1*		Coded Response	
Format A1	Columns 100-100		
0	No Credit	Booklet 2	Q24
1	Full Credit	Booklet 3	Q12
8	Invalid	Booklet 7	Q45
9	Missing	Booklet 13	Q33
n	N/A		
r	Not reached		

M810Q01T (84) *BICYCLES Q1*		Coded Response	
Format A1	Columns 101-101		
0	No Credit	Booklet 1	Q3
1	Full Credit	Booklet 5	Q45
8	Invalid	Booklet 11	Q27
9	Missing	Booklet 13	Q12
n	N/A		
r	Not reached		

M810Q02T (85) *BICYCLES Q2*		Coded Response	
Format A1	Columns 102-102		
0	No Credit	Booklet 1	Q4
1	Full Credit	Booklet 5	Q46
8	Invalid	Booklet 11	Q28
9	Missing	Booklet 13	Q13
n	N/A		
r	Not reached		

M810Q03T (86) *BICYCLES Q3*		Coded Response	
Format A1	Columns 103-103		
0	No Credit	Booklet 1	Q5
1	Partial Credit	Booklet 5	Q47
2	Full Credit	Booklet 11	Q29
9	Missing	Booklet 13	Q14
r	Not reached		
n	N/A		

M828Q01 (87) *CARBON DIOXIDE Q1*		Coded Response	
Format A1	Columns 104-104		
0	No Credit	Booklet 4	Q33
1	Full Credit	Booklet 6	Q20
9	Missing	Booklet 7	Q8
n	N/A	Booklet 11	Q45
r	Not reached		

M828Q02 (88) *CARBON DIOXIDE Q2*		Coded Response	
Format A1	Columns 105-105		
0	No Credit	Booklet 4	Q34
1	Full Credit	Booklet 6	Q21
9	Missing	Booklet 7	Q9
n	N/A	Booklet 11	Q46
r	Not reached		

M828Q03 (89) *CARBON DIOXIDE Q3*		Coded Response	
Format A1	Columns 106-106		
0	No Credit	Booklet 4	Q35
1	Full Credit	Booklet 6	Q22
9	Missing	Booklet 7	Q10
n	N/A	Booklet 11	Q47
r	Not reached		

M833Q01T (90) *SEEING THE TOWER Q1*		Complex Multiple Choice	
Format A1	Columns 107-107		
0	No Credit	Booklet 1	Q6
1	No Credit	Booklet 5	Q48
2	No Credit	Booklet 11	Q30
3	No Credit	Booklet 13	Q15
4	No Credit		
5	Full Credit		
8	M/R		
9	Missing		
n	N/A		

R055Q01 (91) *DRUGGED SPIDERS Q1*		Multiple Choice	
Format A1	Columns 108-108		
1	No Credit	Booklet 2	Q46
2	No Credit	Booklet 8	Q44
3	No Credit	Booklet 10	Q22
4	Full Credit	Booklet 11	Q9
8	M/R	Booklet UH	Q8
9	Missing		
n	N/A		
r	Not reached		

R055Q02 (92) *DRUGGED SPIDERS Q2*		Coded Response	
Format A1	Columns 109-109		
0	No Credit	Booklet 2	Q47
1	Full Credit	Booklet 8	Q45
9	Missing	Booklet 10	Q23
n	N/A	Booklet 11	Q10
r	Not reached	Booklet UH	Q9

R055Q03 (93) *DRUGGED SPIDERS Q3*		Coded Response	
Format A1	Columns 110-110		
0	No Credit	Booklet 2	Q48
1	No Credit	Booklet 8	Q46
2	Full Credit	Booklet 10	Q24
9	Missing	Booklet 11	Q11
n	N/A	Booklet UH	Q10
r	Not reached		

R055Q05 (94) *DRUGGED SPIDERS Q5*		Coded Response	
Format A1	Columns 111-111		
0	No Credit	Booklet 2	Q49
1	Full Credit	Booklet 8	Q47
9	Missing	Booklet 10	Q25
n	N/A	Booklet 11	Q12
r	Not reached	Booklet UH	Q11

R067Q01 (95) *AESOP Q1*		Multiple Choice	
Format A1	Columns 112-112		
1	No Credit	Booklet 1	Q39
2	No Credit	Booklet 7	Q32
3	Full Credit	Booklet 9	Q21
4	No Credit	Booklet 10	Q3
8	M/R		
9	Missing		
n	N/A		
r	Not reached		

R067Q04 (96) *AESOP Q4*		Coded Response	
Format A1	Columns 113-113		
0	No Credit	Booklet 1	Q40
1	Partial Credit	Booklet 7	Q33
2	Full Credit	Booklet 9	Q22
9	Missing	Booklet 10	Q4
n	N/A		
r	Not reached		

R067Q05 (97) *AESOP Q5*		Coded Response	
Format A1	Columns 114-114		
0	No Credit	Booklet 1	Q41
1	Partial Credit	Booklet 7	Q34
2	Full Credit	Booklet 9	Q23
9	Missing	Booklet 10	Q5
n	N/A		
r	Not reached		

R102Q04A (98) *SHIRTS Q4A*		Coded Response	
Format A1	Columns 115-115		
0	No Credit	Booklet 1	Q42
1	Full Credit	Booklet 7	Q35
9	Missing	Booklet 9	Q24
n	N/A	Booklet 10	Q6
r	Not reached		

R102Q05 (99) *SHIRTS Q5*		Coded Response	
Format A1	Columns1 16-116		
0	No Credit	Booklet 1	Q43
1	Full Credit	Booklet 7	Q36
9	Missing	Booklet 9	Q25
n	N/A	Booklet 10	Q7
r	Not reached		

R102Q07 (100) *SHIRTS Q7*		Multiple Choice	
Format A1	Columns 117-117		
1	No Credit	Booklet 1	Q44
2	No Credit	Booklet 7	Q37
3	Full Credit	Booklet 9	Q26
4	No Credit	Booklet 10	Q8
8	M/R		
9	Missing		
n	N/A		
r	Not reached		

R104Q01 (101) *TELEPHONE Q1*		Coded Response	
Format A1	Columns 118-118		
0	No Credit	Booklet 2	Q50
1	Full Credit	Booklet 8	Q48
9	Missing	Booklet 10	Q26
n	N/A	Booklet 11	Q13
r	Not reached		

R104Q02 (102) *TELEPHONE Q2*		Coded Response	
Format A1	Columns 119-119		
0	No Credit	Booklet 2	Q51
1	Full Credit	Booklet 8	Q49
9	Missing	Booklet 10	Q27
n	N/A	Booklet 11	Q14
r	Not reached		

R104Q05 (103) *TELEPHONE Q5*		Coded Response	
Format A1	Columns 120-120		
0	No Credit	Booklet 2	Q52
1	Partial Credit	Booklet 8	Q50
2	Full Credit	Booklet 10	Q28
9	Missing	Booklet 11	Q15
n	N/A		
r	Not reached		

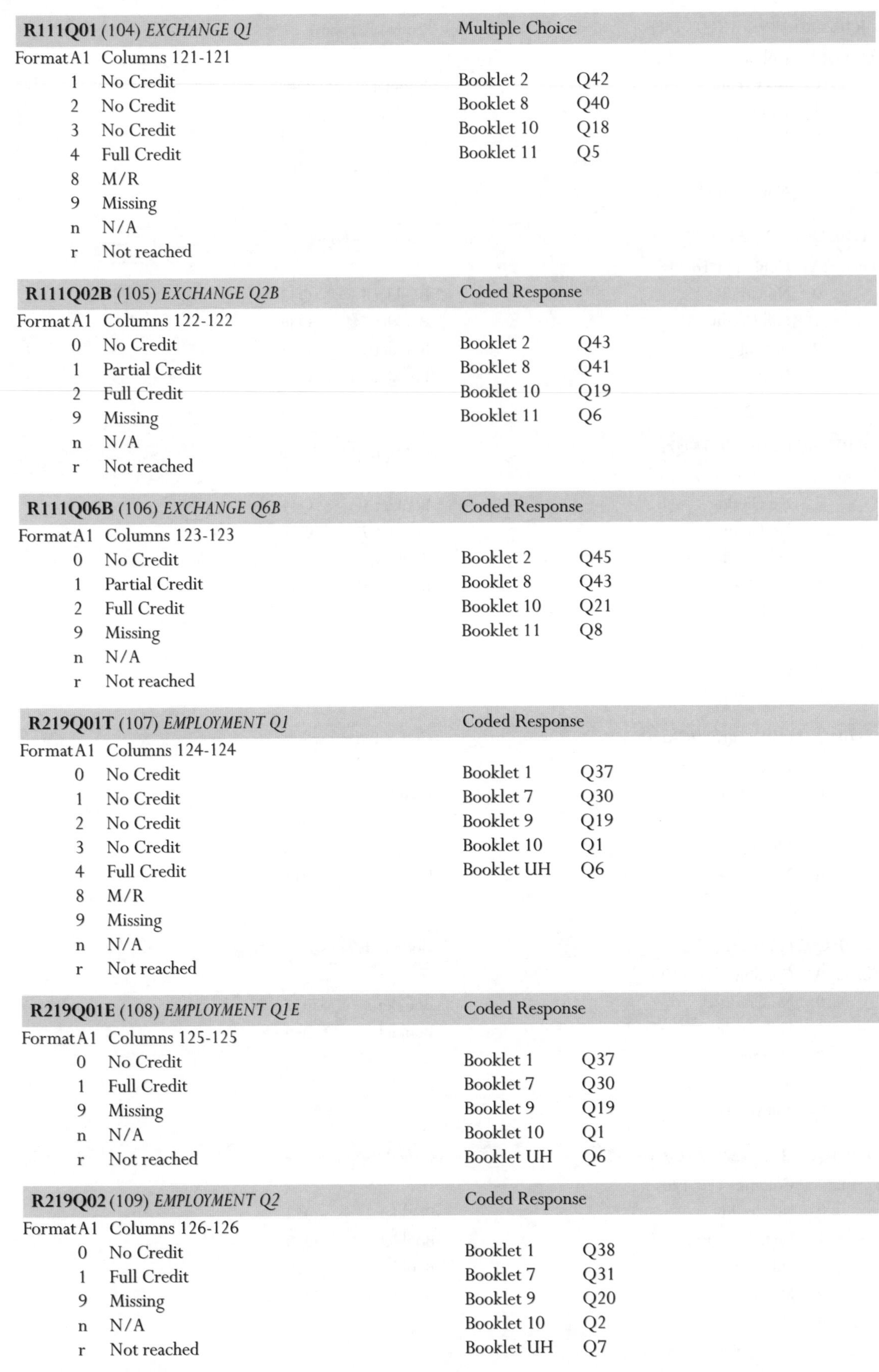

R111Q01 (104) *EXCHANGE Q1*		Multiple Choice	
Format A1	Columns 121-121		
1	No Credit	Booklet 2	Q42
2	No Credit	Booklet 8	Q40
3	No Credit	Booklet 10	Q18
4	Full Credit	Booklet 11	Q5
8	M/R		
9	Missing		
n	N/A		
r	Not reached		

R111Q02B (105) *EXCHANGE Q2B*		Coded Response	
Format A1	Columns 122-122		
0	No Credit	Booklet 2	Q43
1	Partial Credit	Booklet 8	Q41
2	Full Credit	Booklet 10	Q19
9	Missing	Booklet 11	Q6
n	N/A		
r	Not reached		

R111Q06B (106) *EXCHANGE Q6B*		Coded Response	
Format A1	Columns 123-123		
0	No Credit	Booklet 2	Q45
1	Partial Credit	Booklet 8	Q43
2	Full Credit	Booklet 10	Q21
9	Missing	Booklet 11	Q8
n	N/A		
r	Not reached		

R219Q01T (107) *EMPLOYMENT Q1*		Coded Response	
Format A1	Columns 124-124		
0	No Credit	Booklet 1	Q37
1	No Credit	Booklet 7	Q30
2	No Credit	Booklet 9	Q19
3	No Credit	Booklet 10	Q1
4	Full Credit	Booklet UH	Q6
8	M/R		
9	Missing		
n	N/A		
r	Not reached		

R219Q01E (108) *EMPLOYMENT Q1E*		Coded Response	
Format A1	Columns 125-125		
0	No Credit	Booklet 1	Q37
1	Full Credit	Booklet 7	Q30
9	Missing	Booklet 9	Q19
n	N/A	Booklet 10	Q1
r	Not reached	Booklet UH	Q6

R219Q02 (109) *EMPLOYMENT Q2*		Coded Response	
Format A1	Columns 126-126		
0	No Credit	Booklet 1	Q38
1	Full Credit	Booklet 7	Q31
9	Missing	Booklet 9	Q20
n	N/A	Booklet 10	Q2
r	Not reached	Booklet UH	Q7

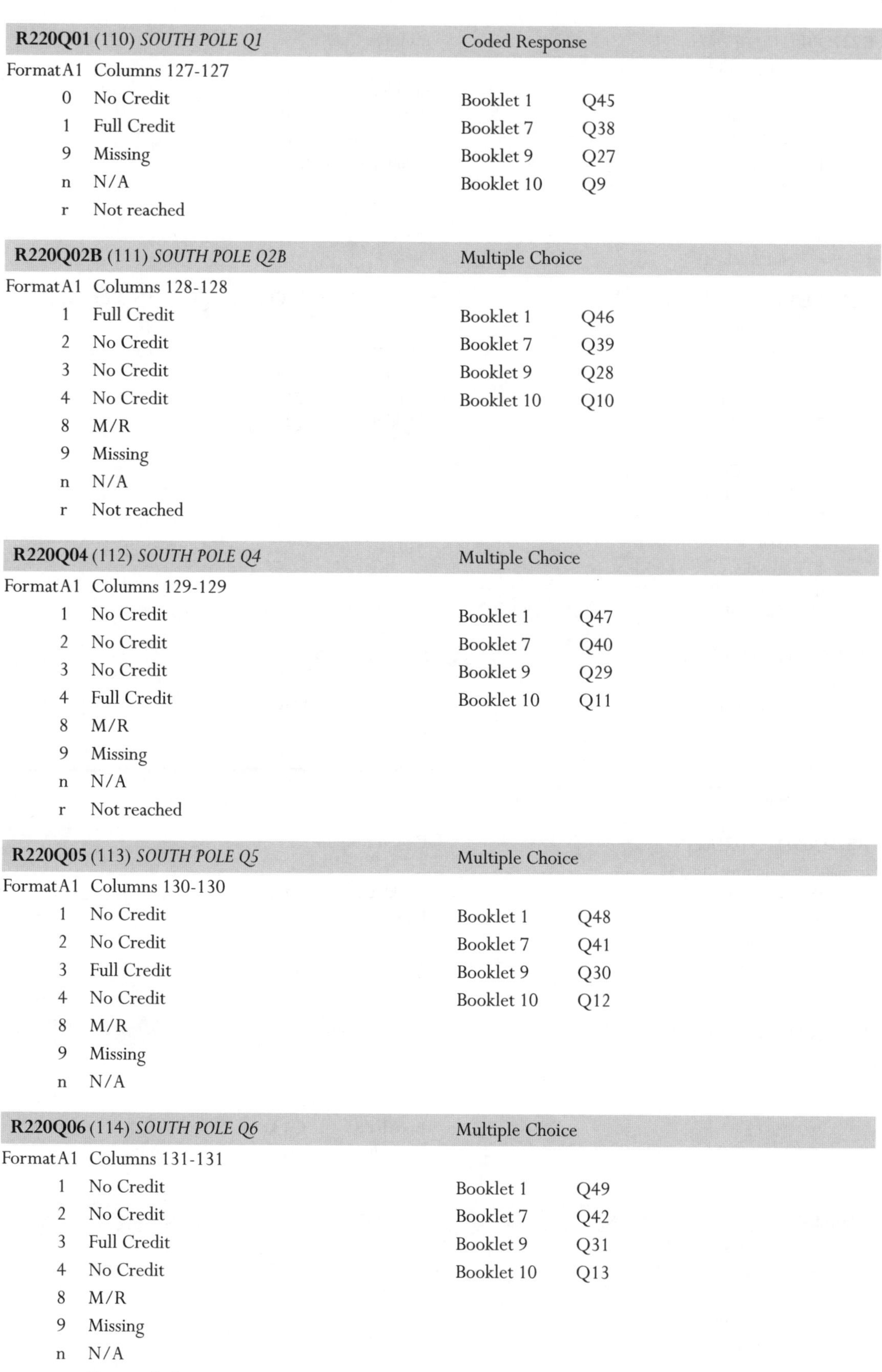

R220Q01 (110) *SOUTH POLE Q1* — Coded Response

Format A1 Columns 127-127

Code	Label	Booklet	Question
0	No Credit	Booklet 1	Q45
1	Full Credit	Booklet 7	Q38
9	Missing	Booklet 9	Q27
n	N/A	Booklet 10	Q9
r	Not reached		

R220Q02B (111) *SOUTH POLE Q2B* — Multiple Choice

Format A1 Columns 128-128

Code	Label	Booklet	Question
1	Full Credit	Booklet 1	Q46
2	No Credit	Booklet 7	Q39
3	No Credit	Booklet 9	Q28
4	No Credit	Booklet 10	Q10
8	M/R		
9	Missing		
n	N/A		
r	Not reached		

R220Q04 (112) *SOUTH POLE Q4* — Multiple Choice

Format A1 Columns 129-129

Code	Label	Booklet	Question
1	No Credit	Booklet 1	Q47
2	No Credit	Booklet 7	Q40
3	No Credit	Booklet 9	Q29
4	Full Credit	Booklet 10	Q11
8	M/R		
9	Missing		
n	N/A		
r	Not reached		

R220Q05 (113) *SOUTH POLE Q5* — Multiple Choice

Format A1 Columns 130-130

Code	Label	Booklet	Question
1	No Credit	Booklet 1	Q48
2	No Credit	Booklet 7	Q41
3	Full Credit	Booklet 9	Q30
4	No Credit	Booklet 10	Q12
8	M/R		
9	Missing		
n	N/A		

R220Q06 (114) *SOUTH POLE Q6* — Multiple Choice

Format A1 Columns 131-131

Code	Label	Booklet	Question
1	No Credit	Booklet 1	Q49
2	No Credit	Booklet 7	Q42
3	Full Credit	Booklet 9	Q31
4	No Credit	Booklet 10	Q13
8	M/R		
9	Missing		
n	N/A		
r	Not reached		

R227Q01 (115) *OPTICIAN Q1*		Multiple Choice	
Format A1	Columns 132-132		
1	No Credit	Booklet 2	Q38
2	Full Credit	Booklet 8	Q36
3	No Credit	Booklet 10	Q14
4	No Credit	Booklet 11	Q1
8	M/R		
9	Missing		
n	N/A		
r	Not reached		

R227Q02T (116) *OPTICIAN Q2*		Complex Multiple Choice	
Format A1	Columns 133-133		
0	No Credit	Booklet 2	Q39
1	No Credit	Booklet 8	Q37
2	No Credit	Booklet 10	Q15
3	No Credit	Booklet 11	Q2
4	No Credit		
5	Partial Credit		
6	Partial Credit		
7	Full Credit		
8	M/R		
9	Missing		
n	N/A		
r	Not reached		

R227Q03 (117) *OPTICIAN Q3*		Coded Response	
Format A1	Columns 134-134		
0	No Credit	Booklet 2	Q40
1	Full Credit	Booklet 8	Q38
9	Missing	Booklet 10	Q16
n	N/A	Booklet 11	Q3
r	Not reached		

R227Q06 (118) *OPTICIAN Q6*		Coded Response	
Format A1	Columns 135-135		
0	No Credit	Booklet 2	Q41
1	Full Credit	Booklet 8	Q39
9	Missing	Booklet 10	Q17
n	N/A	Booklet 11	Q4
r	Not reached		

S114Q03T (119) *GREENHOUSE Q3*		Coded Response	
Format A1	Columns 136-136		
0	No Credit	Booklet 5	Q38
1	Full Credit	Booklet 7	Q25
9	Missing	Booklet 8	Q13
n	N/A	Booklet 12	Q44
r	Not reached		

S114Q04T (120) *GREENHOUSE Q4*		Coded Response	
Format A1	Columns 137-137		
0	No Credit	Booklet 5	Q39
1	Partial Credit	Booklet 7	Q26
2	Full Credit	Booklet 8	Q14
9	Missing	Booklet 12	Q45
n	N/A		
r	Not reached		

S114Q05T (121) *GREENHOUSE Q5*		Coded Response	
Format A1	Columns 138-138		
0	No Credit	Booklet 5	Q40
1	Full Credit	Booklet 7	Q27
9	Missing	Booklet 8	Q15
n	N/A	Booklet 12	Q46
r	Not reached		

S128Q01 (122) *CLONING Q1*		Multiple Choice	
Format A1	Columns 139-139		
1	Full Credit	Booklet 6	Q27
2	No Credit	Booklet 8	Q20
3	No Credit	Booklet 9	Q3
4	No Credit	Booklet 13	Q36
8	M/R		
9	Missing		
n	N/A		
r	Not reached		

S128Q02 (123) *CLONING Q2*		Multiple Choice	
Format A1	Columns 140-140		
1	Full Credit	Booklet 6	Q28
2	No Credit	Booklet 8	Q21
3	No Credit	Booklet 9	Q4
4	No Credit	Booklet 13	Q37
8	M/R		
9	Missing		
n	N/A		
r	Not reached		

S128Q03T (124) *CLONING Q3*		Complex Multiple Choice	
Format A1	Columns 141-141		
0	No Credit	Booklet 6	Q29
1	No Credit	Booklet 8	Q22
2	Full Credit	Booklet 9	Q5
8	M/R	Booklet 13	Q38
9	Missing		
n	N/A		
r	Not reached		

S129Q01 (125) *DAYLIGHT Q1*		Multiple Choice	
Format A1	Columns 142-142		
1	Full Credit	Booklet 6	Q25
2	No Credit	Booklet 8	Q18
3	No Credit	Booklet 9	Q1
4	No Credit	Booklet 13	Q34
8	M/R		
9	Missing		
n	N/A		
r	Not reached		

S129Q02T (126) *DAYLIGHT Q2*		Coded Response	
Format A1	Columns 143-143		
0	No Credit	Booklet 6	Q26
1	Partial Credit	Booklet 8	Q19
2	Full Credit	Booklet 9	Q2
9	Missing	Booklet 13	Q35
n	N/A		
r	Not reached		

S131Q02T (127) *GOOD VIBRATIONS Q2*		Coded Response	
Format A1	Columns 144-144		
0	No Credit	Booklet 6	Q30
1	Full Credit	Booklet 8	Q23
9	Missing	Booklet 9	Q6
n	N/A	Booklet 13	Q39
r	Not reached		

S131Q04T (128) *GOOD VIBRATIONS Q4*		Coded Response	
Format A1	Columns 145-145		
0	No Credit	Booklet 6	Q31
1	Full Credit	Booklet 8	Q24
9	Missing	Booklet 9	Q7
n	N/A	Booklet 13	Q40
r	Not reached		

S133Q01 (129) *RESEARCH Q1*		Multiple Choice	
Format A1	Columns 146-146		
1	No Credit	Booklet 5	Q35
2	No Credit	Booklet 7	Q22
3	Full Credit	Booklet 8	Q10
4	No Credit	Booklet 12	Q41
8	M/R	Booklet UH	Q22
9	Missing		
n	N/A		
r	Not reached		

S133Q03 (130) *RESEARCH Q3*		Multiple Choice	
Format A1	Columns 147-147		
1	Full Credit	Booklet 5	Q36
2	No Credit	Booklet 7	Q23
3	No Credit	Booklet 8	Q11
4	No Credit	Booklet 12	Q42
8	M/R	Booklet UH	Q23
9	Missing		
n	N/A		
r	Not reached		

S133Q04T (131) *RESEARCH Q4*		Complex Multiple Choice	
Format A1	Columns148-148		
0	No Credit	Booklet 5	Q37
1	No Credit	Booklet 7	Q24
2	No Credit	Booklet 8	Q12
3	Full Credit	Booklet 12	Q43
8	M/R	Booklet UH	Q24
9	Missing		
n	N/A		
r	Not reached		

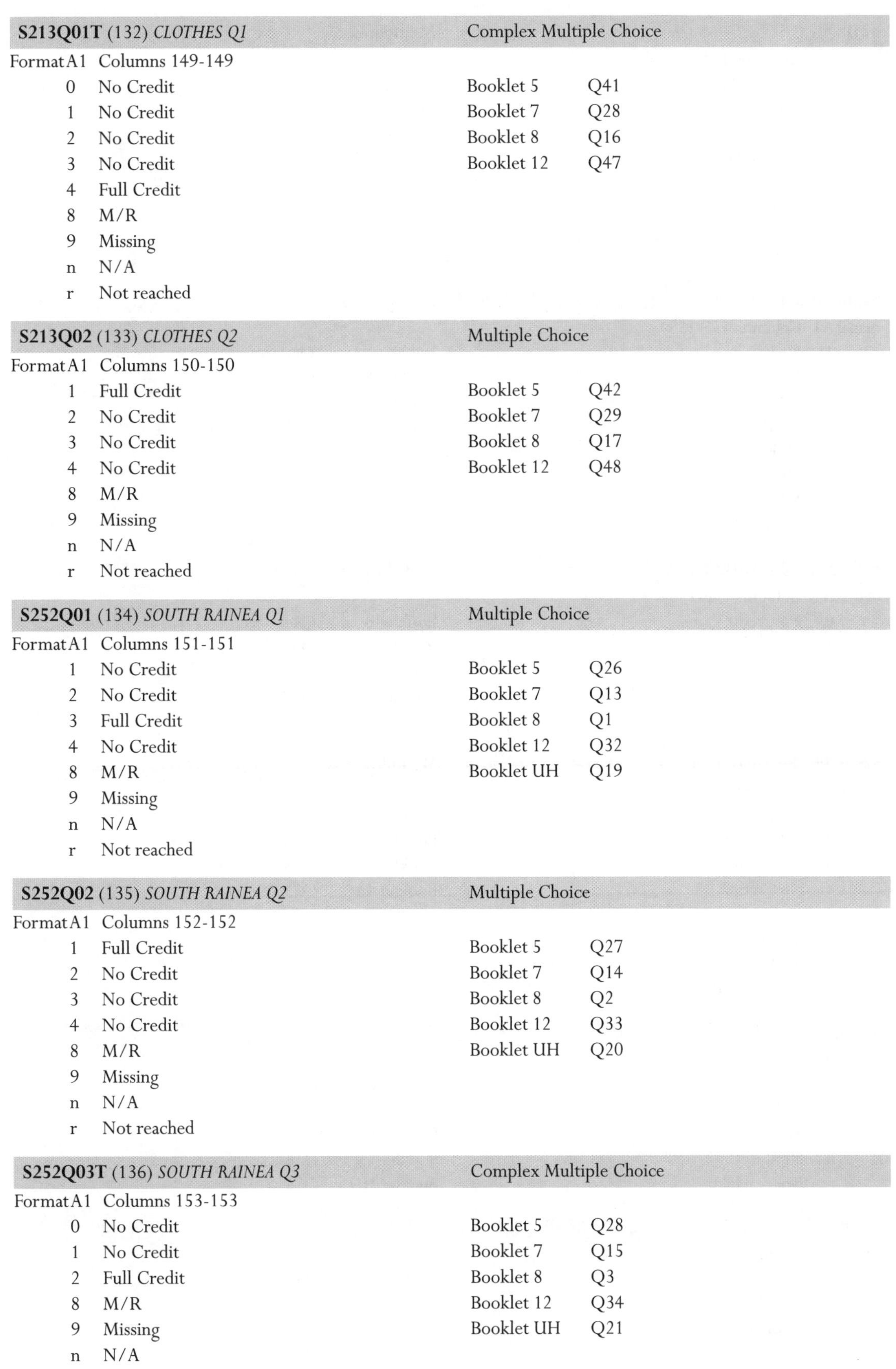

S213Q01T (132) *CLOTHES Q1* — Complex Multiple Choice

Format A1 Columns 149-149

Code	Label	Booklet	Question
0	No Credit	Booklet 5	Q41
1	No Credit	Booklet 7	Q28
2	No Credit	Booklet 8	Q16
3	No Credit	Booklet 12	Q47
4	Full Credit		
8	M/R		
9	Missing		
n	N/A		
r	Not reached		

S213Q02 (133) *CLOTHES Q2* — Multiple Choice

Format A1 Columns 150-150

Code	Label	Booklet	Question
1	Full Credit	Booklet 5	Q42
2	No Credit	Booklet 7	Q29
3	No Credit	Booklet 8	Q17
4	No Credit	Booklet 12	Q48
8	M/R		
9	Missing		
n	N/A		
r	Not reached		

S252Q01 (134) *SOUTH RAINEA Q1* — Multiple Choice

Format A1 Columns 151-151

Code	Label	Booklet	Question
1	No Credit	Booklet 5	Q26
2	No Credit	Booklet 7	Q13
3	Full Credit	Booklet 8	Q1
4	No Credit	Booklet 12	Q32
8	M/R	Booklet UH	Q19
9	Missing		
n	N/A		
r	Not reached		

S252Q02 (135) *SOUTH RAINEA Q2* — Multiple Choice

Format A1 Columns 152-152

Code	Label	Booklet	Question
1	Full Credit	Booklet 5	Q27
2	No Credit	Booklet 7	Q14
3	No Credit	Booklet 8	Q2
4	No Credit	Booklet 12	Q33
8	M/R	Booklet UH	Q20
9	Missing		
n	N/A		
r	Not reached		

S252Q03T (136) *SOUTH RAINEA Q3* — Complex Multiple Choice

Format A1 Columns 153-153

Code	Label	Booklet	Question
0	No Credit	Booklet 5	Q28
1	No Credit	Booklet 7	Q15
2	Full Credit	Booklet 8	Q3
8	M/R	Booklet 12	Q34
9	Missing	Booklet UH	Q21
n	N/A		
r	Not reached		

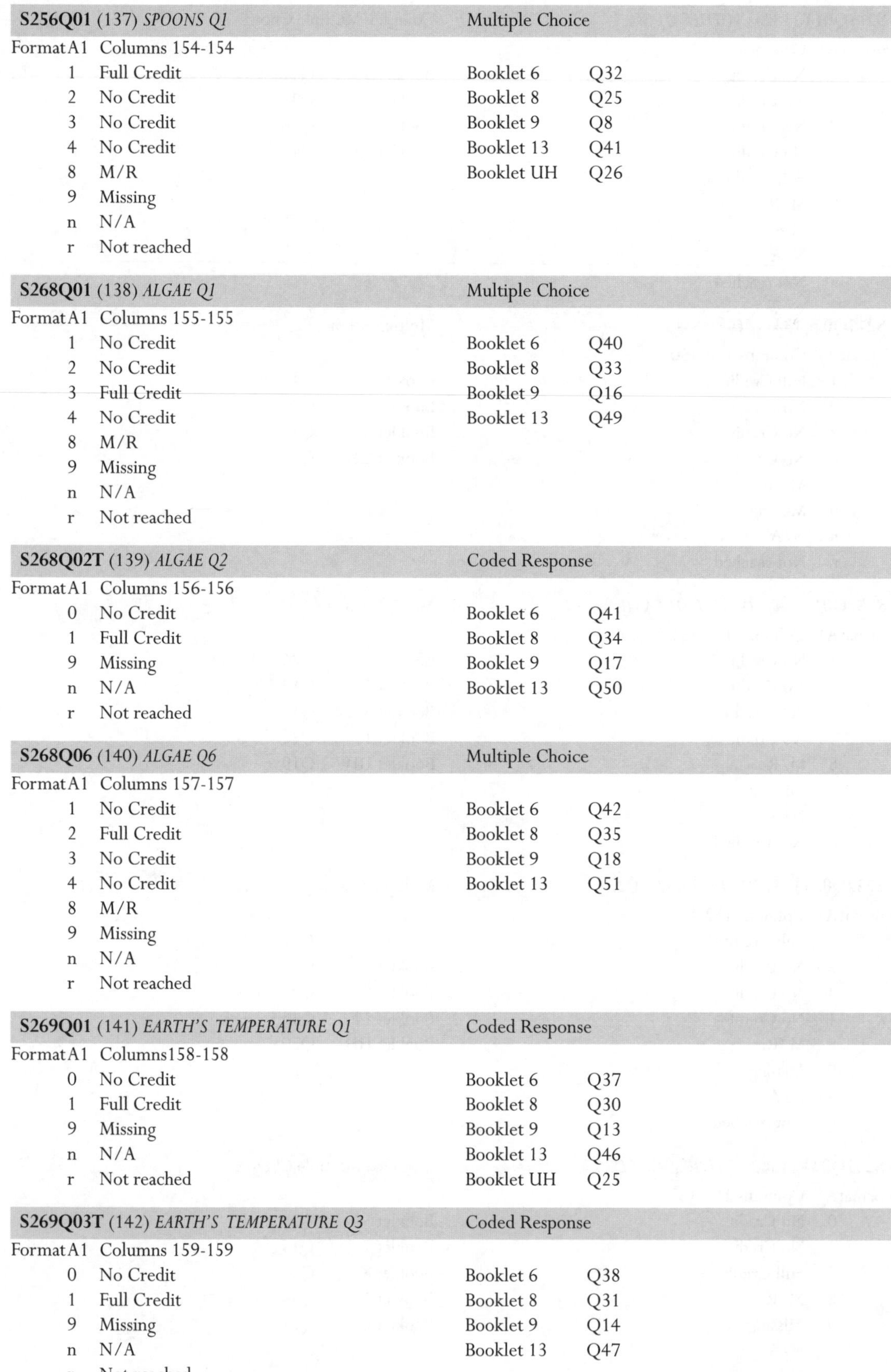

S256Q01 (137) *SPOONS Q1*		Multiple Choice	
Format A1	Columns 154-154		
1	Full Credit	Booklet 6	Q32
2	No Credit	Booklet 8	Q25
3	No Credit	Booklet 9	Q8
4	No Credit	Booklet 13	Q41
8	M/R	Booklet UH	Q26
9	Missing		
n	N/A		
r	Not reached		

S268Q01 (138) *ALGAE Q1*		Multiple Choice	
Format A1	Columns 155-155		
1	No Credit	Booklet 6	Q40
2	No Credit	Booklet 8	Q33
3	Full Credit	Booklet 9	Q16
4	No Credit	Booklet 13	Q49
8	M/R		
9	Missing		
n	N/A		
r	Not reached		

S268Q02T (139) *ALGAE Q2*		Coded Response	
Format A1	Columns 156-156		
0	No Credit	Booklet 6	Q41
1	Full Credit	Booklet 8	Q34
9	Missing	Booklet 9	Q17
n	N/A	Booklet 13	Q50
r	Not reached		

S268Q06 (140) *ALGAE Q6*		Multiple Choice	
Format A1	Columns 157-157		
1	No Credit	Booklet 6	Q42
2	Full Credit	Booklet 8	Q35
3	No Credit	Booklet 9	Q18
4	No Credit	Booklet 13	Q51
8	M/R		
9	Missing		
n	N/A		
r	Not reached		

S269Q01 (141) *EARTH'S TEMPERATURE Q1*		Coded Response	
Format A1	Columns158-158		
0	No Credit	Booklet 6	Q37
1	Full Credit	Booklet 8	Q30
9	Missing	Booklet 9	Q13
n	N/A	Booklet 13	Q46
r	Not reached	Booklet UH	Q25

S269Q03T (142) *EARTH'S TEMPERATURE Q3*		Coded Response	
Format A1	Columns 159-159		
0	No Credit	Booklet 6	Q38
1	Full Credit	Booklet 8	Q31
9	Missing	Booklet 9	Q14
n	N/A	Booklet 13	Q47
r	Not reached		

S269Q04T (143) *EARTH'S TEMPERATURE Q4*		Complex Multiple Choice	
Format A1	Columns 160-160		
0	No Credit	Booklet 6	Q39
1	No Credit	Booklet 8	Q32
2	No Credit	Booklet 9	Q15
3	No Credit	Booklet 13	Q48
4	Full Credit		
8	M/R		
9	Missing		
n	N/A		
r	Not reached		

S304Q01 (144) *WATER Q1*		Coded Response	
Format A1	Columns 161-161		
0	No Credit	Booklet 6	Q33
1	Full Credit	Booklet 8	Q26
9	Missing	Booklet 9	Q9
n	N/A	Booklet 13	Q42
r	Not reached		

S304Q02 (145) *WATER Q2*		Multiple Choice	
Format A1	Columns 162-162		
1	No Credit	Booklet 6	Q34
2	No Credit	Booklet 8	Q27
3	Full Credit	Booklet 9	Q10
4	No Credit	Booklet 13	Q43
8	M/R		
9	Missing		
n	N/A		
r	Not reached		

S304Q03a (146) *WATER Q3A*		Coded Response	
Format A1	Columns 163-163		
0	No Credit	Booklet 6	Q35
1	Full Credit	Booklet 8	Q28
9	Missing	Booklet 9	Q11
n	N/A	Booklet 13	Q44
r	Not reached		

S304Q03b (147) *WATER Q3B*		Coded Response	
Format A1	Columns 164-164		
0	No Credit	Booklet 6	Q36
1	Full Credit	Booklet 8	Q29
9	Missing	Booklet 9	Q12
n	N/A	Booklet 13	Q45
r	Not reached		

S326Q01 (148) *MILK Q1*		Coded Response	
Format A1	Columns 165-165		
0	No Credit	Booklet 5	Q31
1	Full Credit	Booklet 7	Q18
9	Missing	Booklet 8	Q6
n	N/A	Booklet 12	Q37
r	Not reached		

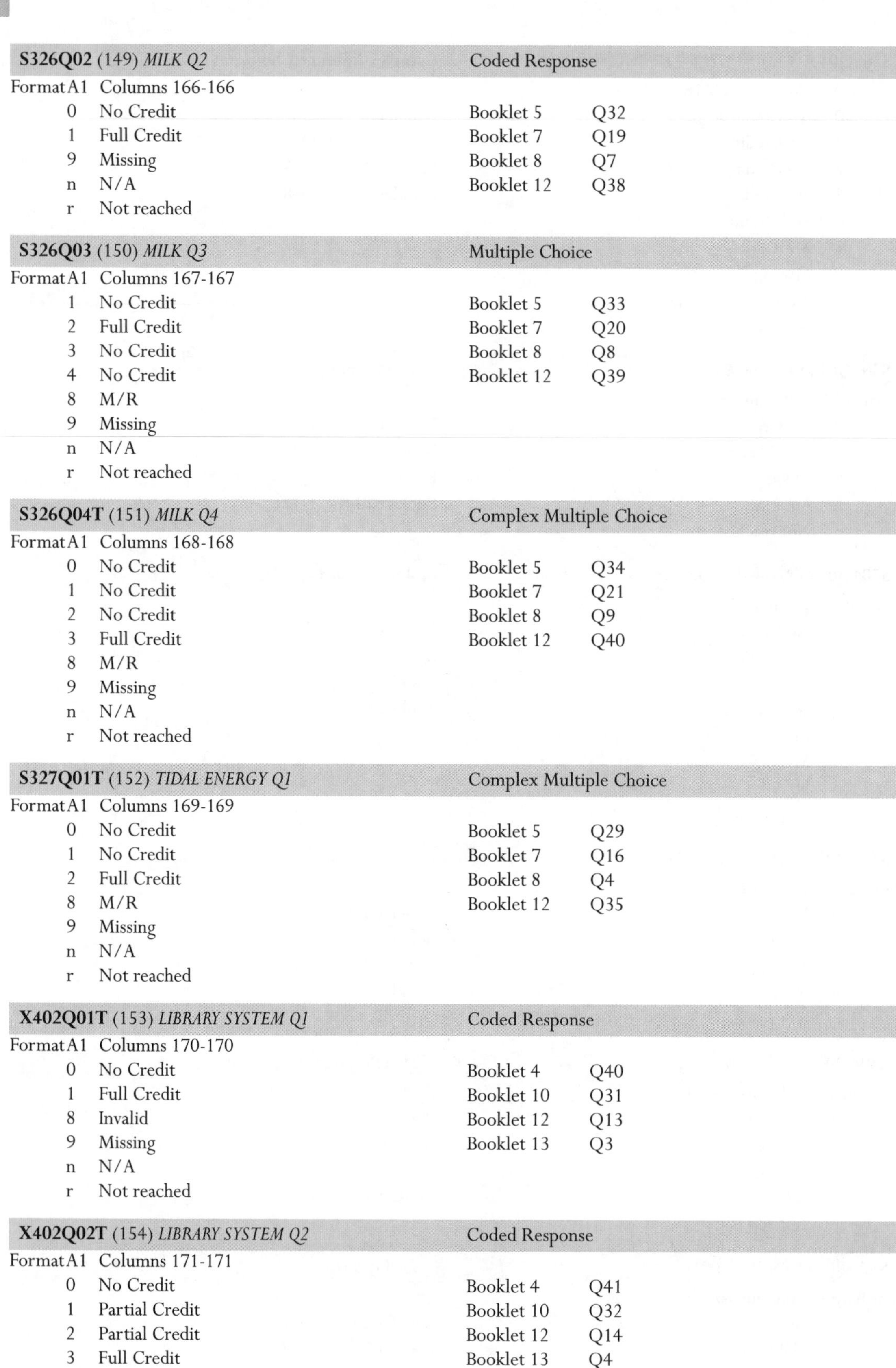

S326Q02 (149) *MILK Q2* — Coded Response

Format A1 Columns 166-166

Code	Label	Booklet	Question
0	No Credit	Booklet 5	Q32
1	Full Credit	Booklet 7	Q19
9	Missing	Booklet 8	Q7
n	N/A	Booklet 12	Q38
r	Not reached		

S326Q03 (150) *MILK Q3* — Multiple Choice

Format A1 Columns 167-167

Code	Label	Booklet	Question
1	No Credit	Booklet 5	Q33
2	Full Credit	Booklet 7	Q20
3	No Credit	Booklet 8	Q8
4	No Credit	Booklet 12	Q39
8	M/R		
9	Missing		
n	N/A		
r	Not reached		

S326Q04T (151) *MILK Q4* — Complex Multiple Choice

Format A1 Columns 168-168

Code	Label	Booklet	Question
0	No Credit	Booklet 5	Q34
1	No Credit	Booklet 7	Q21
2	No Credit	Booklet 8	Q9
3	Full Credit	Booklet 12	Q40
8	M/R		
9	Missing		
n	N/A		
r	Not reached		

S327Q01T (152) *TIDAL ENERGY Q1* — Complex Multiple Choice

Format A1 Columns 169-169

Code	Label	Booklet	Question
0	No Credit	Booklet 5	Q29
1	No Credit	Booklet 7	Q16
2	Full Credit	Booklet 8	Q4
8	M/R	Booklet 12	Q35
9	Missing		
n	N/A		
r	Not reached		

X402Q01T (153) *LIBRARY SYSTEM Q1* — Coded Response

Format A1 Columns 170-170

Code	Label	Booklet	Question
0	No Credit	Booklet 4	Q40
1	Full Credit	Booklet 10	Q31
8	Invalid	Booklet 12	Q13
9	Missing	Booklet 13	Q3
n	N/A		
r	Not reached		

X402Q02T (154) *LIBRARY SYSTEM Q2* — Coded Response

Format A1 Columns 171-171

Code	Label	Booklet	Question
0	No Credit	Booklet 4	Q41
1	Partial Credit	Booklet 10	Q32
2	Partial Credit	Booklet 12	Q14
3	Full Credit	Booklet 13	Q4
9	N/A		
n	Missing		
r	Not reached		

X412Q01 (155) *DESIGN BY NUMBERS Q1*		Multiple Choice	
Format A1	Columns 172-172		
1	No Credit	Booklet 3	Q40
2	Full Credit	Booklet 9	Q35
3	No Credit	Booklet 11	Q19
4	No Credit	Booklet 12	Q4
8	M/R		
9	Missing		
n	N/A		
r	Not reached		

X412Q02 (156) *DESIGN BY NUMBERS Q2*		Multiple Choice	
Format A1	Columns 173-173		
1	No Credit	Booklet 3	Q41
2	No Credit	Booklet 9	Q36
3	No Credit	Booklet 11	Q20
4	Full Credit	Booklet 12	Q5
8	M/R		
9	Missing		
n	N/A		
r	Not reached		

X412Q03 (157) *DESIGN BY NUMBERS Q3*		Coded Response	
Format A1	Columns 174-174		
0	No Credit	Booklet 3	Q42
1	Partial Credit	Booklet 9	Q37
2	Full Credit	Booklet 11	Q21
9	Missing	Booklet 12	Q6
n	N/A		
r	Not reached		

X414Q01 (158) *COURSE DESIGN Q1*		Coded Response	
Format A1	Columns 175-175		
0	No Credit	Booklet 4	Q39
1	Partial Credit	Booklet 10	Q30
2	Full Credit	Booklet 12	Q12
9	Missing	Booklet 13	Q2
n	N/A		
r	Not reached		

X415Q01T (159) *TRANSIT SYSTEM Q1*		Coded Response	
Format A1	Columns 176-176		
0	No Credit	Booklet 4	Q38
1	Partial Credit	Booklet 10	Q29
2	Full Credit	Booklet 12	Q11
9	Missing	Booklet 13	Q1
n	N/A	Booklet UH	Q5
r	Not reached		

X417Q01 (160) *CHILDREN'S CAMP Q1*		Coded Response	
Format A1	Columns 177-177		
0	No Credit	Booklet 3	Q39
1	Partial Credit	Booklet 9	Q34
2	Full Credit		
9	Missing	Booklet 11	Q18
n	N/A	Booklet 12	Q3
r	Not reached		

X423Q01T (161) *FREEZER Q1*		Complex Multiple Choice	
Format A1	Columns 178-178		
0	No Credit	Booklet 3	Q43
1	No Credit	Booklet 9	Q38
2	No Credit	Booklet 11	Q22
3	No Credit	Booklet 12	Q7
4	No Credit		
5	Full Credit		
6	Full Credit		
8	M/R		
9	Missing		
n	N/A		
r	Not reached		

X423Q02T (162) *FREEZER Q2*		Complex Multiple Choice	
Format A1	Columns 179-179		
0	No Credit	Booklet 3	Q44
1	No Credit	Booklet 9	Q39
2	No Credit	Booklet 11	Q23
3	Full Credit	Booklet 12	Q8
8	M/R		
9	Missing		
n	N/A		
r	Not reached		

X430Q01 (163) *ENERGY NEEDS Q1*		Coded Response	
Format A1	Columns 180-180		
0	No Credit	Booklet 3	Q37
1	Full Credit	Booklet 9	Q32
9	Missing	Booklet 11	Q16
n	N/A	Booklet 12	Q1
r	Not reached	Booklet UH	Q3

X430Q02 (164) *ENERGY NEEDS Q2*		Coded Response	
Format A1	Columns 181-181		
0	No Credit	Booklet 3	Q38
1	Partial Credit	Booklet 9	Q33
2	Full Credit	Booklet 11	Q17
9	Missing	Booklet 12	Q2
n	N/A	Booklet UH	Q4
r	Not reached		

X601Q01T (165) *CINEMA OUTING Q1*		Complex Multiple Choice	
Format A1	Columns 182-182		
0	No Credit	Booklet 3	Q45
1	No Credit	Booklet 9	Q40
2	No Credit	Booklet 11	Q24
3	No Credit	Booklet 12	Q9
4	No Credit	Booklet UH	Q1
5	Partial Credit		
6	Full Credit		
8	M/R		
9	Missing		
n	N/A		
r	Not reached		

X601Q02 (166) *CINEMA OUTING Q2*		Multiple Choice	
Format A1	Columns 183-183		
1	No Credit	Booklet 3	Q46
2	No Credit	Booklet 9	Q41
3	Full Credit	Booklet 11	Q25
4	No Credit	Booklet 12	Q10
5	No Credit	Booklet UH	Q2
8	M/R		
9	Missing		
n	N/A		
r	Not reached		

X602Q01 (167) *HOLIDAY Q1*		Coded Response	
Format A1	Columns 184-184		
0	No Credit	Booklet 4	Q42
1	Full Credit	Booklet 10	Q33
9	Missing	Booklet 12	Q15
n	N/A	Booklet 13	Q5
r	Not reached		

X602Q02 (168) *HOLIDAY Q2*		Coded Response	
Format A1	Columns 185-185		
0	No Credit	Booklet 4	Q43
1	Partial Credit		
2	Full Credit	Booklet 10	Q34
9	Missing	Booklet 12	Q16
n	N/A	Booklet 13	Q6
r	Not reached		

X603Q01 (169) *IRRIGATION Q1*		Coded Response	
Format A1	Columns 186-186		
0	No Credit	Booklet 4	Q44
1	Full Credit	Booklet 10	Q35
9	Missing	Booklet 12	Q17
n	N/A	Booklet 13	Q7
r	Not reached		

X603Q02T (170) *IRRIGATION Q2*		Complex Multiple Choice	
Format A1	Columns 187-187		
0	No Credit	Booklet 4	Q45
1	No Credit	Booklet 10	Q36
2	No Credit	Booklet 12	Q18
3	Full Credit	Booklet 13	Q8
8	M/R		
9	Missing		
n	N/A		
r	Not reached		

X603Q03 (171) *IRRIGATION Q3*		Coded Response	
Format A1	Columns 188-188		
0	No Credit	Booklet 4	Q46
1	Full Credit	Booklet 12	Q37
9	Missing	Booklet 10	Q19
n	N/A	Booklet 12	Q9
r	Not reached		

MSCALE (172) *MATH SCALABLE*

Format A1 Columns 189-189

RSCALE (173) *READING SCALABLE*

Format A1 Columns 190-190

SSCALE (174) *SCIENCE SCALABLE*

Format A1 Columns 191-191

PSCALE (175) *PROBLEM SOLVING SCALABLE*

Format A1 Columns 192-192

CLCUSE1 (176) *CALCULATOR USE*

Format A1 Columns 193-193

1	No calculator
2	A simple calculator
3	A scientific calculator
4	A programmable calculator
5	A graphics calculator
8	M/R
9	Missing
n	N/A

CLCUSE3a (177) *EFFORT-REAL: A*

Format F3 Columns 194-196

CLCUSE3b (178) *EFFORT-REAL: B*

Format F3 Columns 197-199

APPENDIX 9 ▪ STUDENT AND SCHOOL QUESTIONNAIRE INDICES

Several of PISA's measures reflect indices that summarise responses from students or school principals to a series of related questions. The questions were selected from larger constructs on the basis of theoretical considerations and previous research. Structural equation modelling was used to confirm the theoretically expected behaviour of the indices and to validate their comparability across countries. For this purpose, a model was estimated separately for each country and, collectively, for all OECD countries.

This section explains the indices derived from the student and school context questionnaires that are used in this report. For a description of other PISA indices and details on the methods see the *PISA 2003 Technical Report* (OECD, forthcoming).

Two types of indices are distinguished:

- Simple indices constructed through the arithmetical transformation or recoding of one or more items: here, item responses are used to calculate meaningful variables; for example, the recoding of ISCO-88 codes into the international socio-economic index of occupational status (ISEI) or the calculation of student/teacher ratio based on information from the school questionnaire.
- Scale indices constructed through the scaling of items. All of these indices are derived via IRT scaling of either dichotomous (Yes/No) or Likert-type items. Unless otherwise indicated, where an index involves multiple questions and student responses, the index was scaled using a weighted maximum likelihood estimate, using a one-parameter item response model (referred to as a WARM estimator; see Warm, 1985) with three stages:
  - The question parameters were estimated from equal-sized sub-samples of students from each OECD country.
  - The estimates were computed for all students and all schools by anchoring the question parameters obtained in the preceding step.
  - The indices were then standardised so that the mean of the index value for the OECD student population was zero and the standard deviation was one (countries being given equal weight in the standardisation process).

It is important to note that negative values in an index do not necessarily imply that students responded negatively to the underlying questions. A negative value merely indicates that a group of students (or all students, collectively, in a single country) or principals responded less positively than all students or principals did on average across OECD countries. Likewise, a positive value on an index indicates that a group of students or principals responded more favourably, or more positively, than students or principals did, on average, in OECD countries.

Terms enclosed in brackets < > in the following descriptions were replaced in the national versions of the student and school questionnaires by the appropriate national equivalent. For example, the term <qualification at ISCED level 5A> was translated in the United States into "Bachelor's Degree,

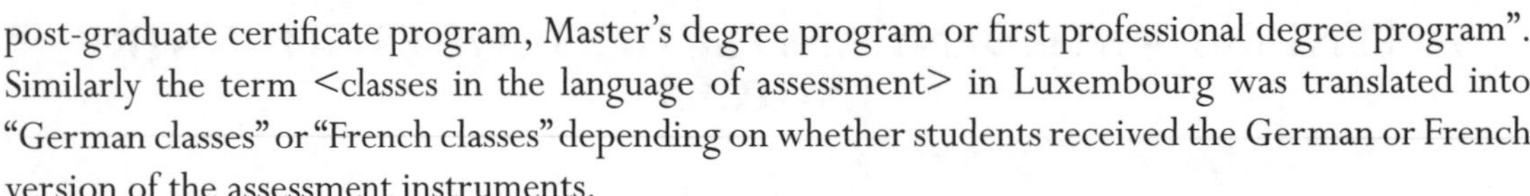

post-graduate certificate program, Master's degree program or first professional degree program". Similarly the term <classes in the language of assessment> in Luxembourg was translated into "German classes" or "French classes" depending on whether students received the German or French version of the assessment instruments.

For the reliabilities of the indices, see the *PISA 2003 Technical Report* (OECD, forthcoming).

STUDENT-LEVEL SIMPLE INDICES

Student background

Age (AGE)

Similar to PISA 2000, the PISA 2003 index of age (**AGE**) is calculated as the difference between year and month of the testing and the year and month of a student's birth (ST02Q02 and ST02Q03).

Study programme (ISCEDL, ISCEDD, ISCEDO and PROGN)

The PISA 2003 indices of study programme are derived from students' responses to the item ST01Q02 asking study programmes available to 15-year-old students in each country. All study programmes are classified by ISCED (OECD 1999). All national programmes are included in a separate index of unique study programme code (PROGN) where the first three digits are the ISO code for a country, the fourth digit the sub-national category and the last two digits the nationally specific programme code.

The following indices are derived from the data on study programmes:

- The PISA 2003 index of programme level (ISCEDL) indicates whether students are on the lower or upper secondary level (ISCED 3 or ISCED 2).
- The PISA 2003 index of programme designation (ISCEDD) indicates the designation of the study programme: (1) = 'A' (general programmes designed to give access to the next programme level); (2) = 'B' (programmes designed to give access to vocational studies at the next programme level); (3) = 'C' (programmes designed to give direct access to the labour market); (4) = "M" (modular programmes that combine any or all of these characteristics).
- The PISA 2003 index of programme orientation (ISCEDO) indicates whether the programme's curricular content is general (1), pre-vocational (2) or vocational (3).

Family structure (FAMSTRUC)

The PISA 2003 index of family structure (FAMSTRUC) is simplified the PISA 2000 index of family structure. Students' responses to the items ST04Q01-ST04Q05 are recoded into the index of family structure with four categories: (1) a single parent family (students reporting to live with only one of the following: mother, female guardian, father, male guardian), (2) a nuclear family (students living with a father and a mother), (3) a mixed family (a father and a guardian, a mother and a guardian, or two guardians) and (4) other responses, except the non-responses which are maintained as missing or not applicable.

Highest occupational status of parents (BMMJ, BFMJ, HISEI, MSECATEG, FSECATEG and HSECATEG)

The occupational data for both the student's mother and student's father were obtained by asking open-ended questions ST07Q01 (from Q7 and Q8) in the student questionnaire for mothers' occupational status and ST09Q01(from Q9 and Q10) in the student questionnaire for fathers' occupational status.

The responses were coded in accordance with the four-digit International Standard Classification of Occupation (ISCO 1988) (ILO, 1990) and then mapped to the international socio-economic index of occupational status (ISEI) (Ganzeboom *et al.*, 1992). Three indices are obtained from these scores.

The PISA 2003 index of mother's occupational status (BMMJ) and the PISA 2003 index of father's occupational status (BFMJ) are derived from recoding ISCO codes into the ISEI. These indices are similar to the PISA 2000 indices of mother's occupation and father's occupation. The PISA 2003 index of the highest occupational level of parents (HISEI) corresponds to the higher ISEI score of either parent or to the only available parent's ISEI score. Higher values on these indices indicate higher level of occupational status.

These indices are also recoded into four occupational categories: (1) white collar high skilled occupation; (2) white collar low skilled occupation; (3) blue collar high skilled occupation; and (4) blue collar low skilled occupation, except the non-responses which are maintained as missing or not applicable. Indices with these categories are provided for mother (MSECATEG), father (FSECATEG) and either one of the parents having higher occupational status (HSECATEG).

Educational level of parents (MISCED, FISCED, HISCED and PARED)

The PISA 2003 indices of parents' educational level are derived from students' responses to the items ST11RQ01 and ST12Q01-ST12Q03 for mothers' educational level and ST13RQ01 and ST14Q01-ST14Q03 for fathers' educational level. The students' responses to these items are coded in accordance with the International Standard Classification of Education (ISCED 1997) (OECD 1999) in order to obtain internationally comparable categories of educational attainment. The format of these items in PISA 2003 is different from the format used in PISA 2000.

Table A9.1 ■ **Levels of parental education converted into years of schooling**

	Did not go to school	Completed ISCED Level 1 (primary education)	Completed ISCED Level 2 (lower secondary education)	Completed ISCED Levels 3B or 3C (upper secondary education providing direct access to the labour market or to ISCED 5B programmes)	Completed ISCED Level 3A (upper secondary education providing access to ISCED 5A and 5B programmes)	Completed ISCED Level 5A (university level tertiary education)	Completed ISCED Level 5B (non-university tertiary education)
OECD countries							
Australia	0.0	6.5	10.0	11.5	12.0	15.0	14.0
Austria	0.0	4.0	8.0	11.0	13.0	17.0	15.0
Belgium	0.0	6.0	8.0	12.0	12.0	16.0	15.0
Canada	0.0	6.0	9.0	12.0	12.0	17.0	15.0
Czech Republic	0.0	5.0	9.0	12.0	13.0	17.0	16.0
Denmark	0.0	6.0	9.5	12.5	12.5	16.5	15.5
Finland	0.0	6.0	9.0	12.0	12.0	15.5	14.5
France	0.0	5.0	9.0	11.0	12.0	15.0	14.0
Germany	0.0	4.0	10.0	12.0	12.5	17.0	15.0
Greece	0.0	6.0	9.0	11.5	12.0	17.0	15.5
Hungary	0.0	4.0	8.0	10.5	12.0	16.5	13.5
Iceland	0.0	7.0	10.0	13.0	14.0	17.0	16.5
Ireland	0.0	6.0	9.0	a	12.0	16.0	14.0
Italy	0.0	5.0	8.0	11.0	13.0	17.0	16.0

a: The category does not apply in the country concerned. Data are therefore missing.

...

Table A9.1 (continued) ■ **Levels of parental education converted into years of schooling**

	Did not go to school	Completed ISCED Level 1 (primary education)	Completed ISCED Level 2 (lower secondary education)	Completed ISCED Levels 3B or 3C (upper secondary education providing direct access to the labour market or to ISCED 5B programmes)	Completed ISCED Level 3A (upper secondary education providing access to ISCED 5A and 5B programmes)	Completed ISCED Level 5A (university level tertiary education)	Completed ISCED Level 5B (non-university tertiary education)
Japan	0.0	6.0	9.0	12.0	12.0	16.0	14.0
Korea	0.0	6.0	9.0	12.0	12.0	16.0	15.0
Luxembourg	0.0	6.0	9.0	12.0	13.0	17.0	17.0
Mexico	0.0	6.0	9.0	12.0	12.0	16.0	14.0
Netherlands	0.0	6.0	10.0	a	12.0	15.0	a
New Zealand	0.0	6.0	10.0	12.0	13.0	16.0	16.0
Norway	0.0	7.0	10.0	13.0	13.0	17.0	15.0
Poland	0.0	a	8.0	11.0	12.0	16.0	15.0
Portugal	0.0	6.0	9.0	12.0	12.0	17.0	15.0
Slovak Republic	0.0	4.0	9.0	12.0	12.5	17.0	15.0
Spain	0.0	6.0	10.0	12.0	12.0	15.0	14.0
Sweden	0.0	6.0	9.0	12.0	12.0	15.5	14.0
Switzerland	0.0	6.0	9.0	12.0	12.5	15.0	14.0
Turkey	0.0	5.0	8.0	11.0	11.0	16.0	14.0
United States	0.0	6.0	9.0	a	12.0	16.0	15.0
United Kingdom	0.0	6.0	9.0	11.0	12.0	16.0	15.0
Partner countries							
Brazil	0.0	4.0	8.0	11.0	11.0	16.0	14.5
Hong Kong-China	0.0	6.0	9.0	11.0	13.0	16.0	14.0
Indonesia	0.0	6.0	9.0	12.0	12.0	16.0	15.0
Latvia	0.0	4.0	9.0	12.0	12.0	16.0	16.0
Liechtenstein	0.0	5.0	9.0	11.0	12.0	15.0	14.0
Macao-China	0.0	6.0	9.0	11.0	13.0	16.0	14.0
Russian Federation	0.0	4.0	9.0	11.5	12.0	15.0	a
Serbia	0.0	4.0	8.0	11.0	12.0	16.0	14.0
Thailand	0.0	6.0	9.0	12.0	12.0	16.0	14.0
Tunisia	0.0	6.0	9.0	12.0	13.0	17.0	16.0
Uruguay	0.0	6.0	9.0	11.0	12.0	16.0	15.0

a: The category does not apply in the country concerned. Data are therefore missing.

Indices are constructed by taking always the highest level for each father or mother and have the following categories: (0) None; (1) ISCED 1 (primary education); (2) ISCED 2 (lower secondary); (3) ISCED Level 3B or 3C (vocational/pre-vocational upper secondary); (4) ISCED 3A (upper secondary) and/or ISCED 4 (non-tertiary post-secondary); (5) ISCED 5B (vocational tertiary); and (6) ISCED 5A, 6 (theoretically oriented tertiary and post-graduate). Indices with these categories are provided for mother (MISCED) and father (FISCED) of the student. The index of the highest educational level of parents (HISCED) corresponds to the higher ISCED level of either parent.

The highest level of educational attainment of parents is also converted into an index of years of schooling (PARED) using the conversion coefficients shown in Table A9.1.

Immigration background (ISO_S, ISO_M, ISO_F and IMMIG)

As in PISA 2000, students reported the country of birth for themselves as well as their mothers and fathers (ST15Q01-ST15Q03). This time, national centres were encouraged to collect more detailed information on countries of birth, for example by including a list of countries where higher frequencies were expected. A variable with ISO codes (where applicable) is added to the international database. Indices with these ISO codes are provided for students (ISO_S) and mothers (ISO_M) and fathers (ISO_F) of the students.

The PISA 2003 index of immigrant background (IMMIG) has the following categories: (1) "native" students (those students born in the country of assessment or who had at least one parent born in the country)[1]; (2) "first generation" students (those born in the country of assessment but whose parent(s) were born in another country; and (3) "non-native" students (those students born outside the country of assessment and whose parents were also born in another country). Students with missing responses for either the student or for both parents, or for all three questions are given missing values.

Language background (LANG and LANGN)

The PISA 2003 index of foreign language spoken at home (LANG) is derived from students' responses to the item ST16Q01 asking if the language spoken at home most of the time was the language of assessment, another official national language, another national dialect or language, or another language. In order to derive this index, responses are grouped into two categories: (1) language spoken at home most of the time is different from the language of assessment, from other official national languages and from other national dialects or languages; and (0) the language spoken at home most of the time is the language of assessment, is another official national language, or other national dialect or language.

Some countries collected more detailed information on language use at home, which is included in the database as the PISA 2003 index of language at home (national) (LANGN) with international language codes.

Learning and instruction

Relative grade (GRADE)

The PISA 2003 index of students' relative grades (GRADE) is derived both from the Student Questionnaire (ST01Q01) and from the Student Tracking Forms.

In order to adjust for between-country variation, the index of relative grade indicates whether students are at the modal grade in a country (value of 0), or whether they are below or above the modal grade (+x grades, –x grades).

Expected educational level (SISCED)

In PISA 2003, for the first time, students were asked about their educational aspirations. Students' responses to the items ST23Q01-ST23Q06 measuring expected educational levels are classified according to ISCED (OECD 1999).

The PISA 2003 index of expected educational level has the following categories: (1) None; (2) ISCED 2 (lower secondary); (3) ISCED Level 3B or 3C (vocational/prevocational upper secondary); (4) ISCED 3A (upper secondary) or ISCED 4 (non-tertiary post-secondary); (5) ISCED 5B (vocational tertiary); and (6) ISCED 5A, 6 (theoretically oriented tertiary and post-graduate).

Expected occupational status (BSMJ and SSECATEG)

As part of the optional questionnaire on educational career, students in 24 countries were asked to write down their expected occupation and a description of this job (EC08Q01). The students' responses are coded to four-digit ISCO codes (ILO, 1990) and then mapped to the international socio-economic index of occupational status (ISEI) (Ganzeboom *et al.*,1992). The PISA 2003 index of expected occupational status (BSMJ) is derived from recoding ISCO codes into ISEI scores. Higher values on this index indicate higher level of expected occupational status.

This index is also recoded into an index with four categories of expected occupational status (SSECATEG): (1) white collar high skilled occupation; (2) white collar low skilled occupation; (3) blue collar high skilled occupation; and (4) blue collar low skilled occupation, except the non-responses which are maintained as missing or not applicable.

Relative time spent on mathematics homework (RMHMWK)

The PISA 2003 index of relative time spent on mathematics homework (RMHMWK) is derived from students' responses to the items ST29Q01 and ST33Q01 measuring time spent for mathematics and overall homework in hours. A value on this index indicates a ratio of time spent on mathematics homework to overall time spent on homework.

Minutes of mathematics instruction (MMINS)

The PISA 2003 index of minutes of mathematics instruction (MMINS) is calculated by multiplying the average length of a class period by the number of class periods receiving mathematics instruction. This index is derived from students' responses to the items ST35Q01 and ST35Q02 measuring average length of a class period and their instructional time in mathematics in class periods. In some countries the amount of instructional time in mathematics varies across the year. This index indicates current instruction minutes in mathematics received by each student.

Minutes of overall school instruction (TMINS)

The PISA 2003 index of minutes of overall school instruction (TMINS) is calculated by multiplying the average length of a class period by the number of class periods receiving instruction in all subjects (including mathematics). This index is derived from students' responses to the item ST35Q03 measuring the average length of a class period and the item below measuring the number of class periods per week.

Relative instructional time on mathematics (PCMATH)

The PISA 2003 index of relative instructional time on mathematics (PCMATH) is calculated by dividing the instructional time in minutes on mathematics by the overall instructional time in minutes.

STUDENT-LEVEL SCALE INDICES

Student background

Computer facilities at home (COMPHOME)

The PISA 2003 index of computer facilities at home (COMPHOME) is derived from students' responses to the three items listed below. These variables are binary and the scale construction is done through IRT scaling. Positive values on this index indicate higher levels of computer facilities at home.

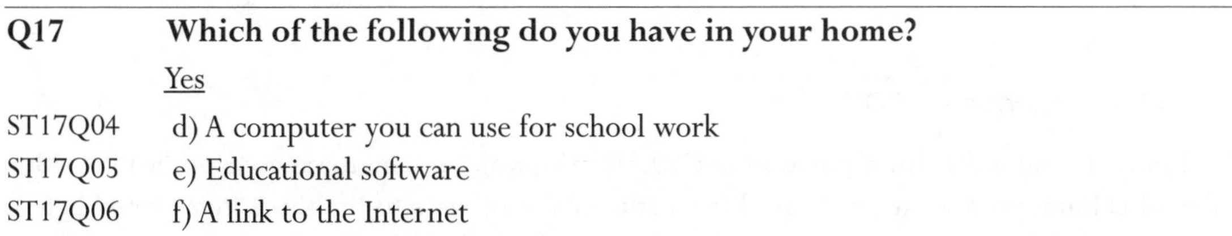

Q17	**Which of the following do you have in your home?**
	Yes
ST17Q04	d) A computer you can use for school work
ST17Q05	e) Educational software
ST17Q06	f) A link to the Internet

Home educational resources (HEDRES)

The PISA 2003 index of home educational resources (HEDRES) is derived from students' responses to the five items listed below. A slightly modified set of items for the PISA 2000 index of home educational resources are used for this PISA 2003 index. These variables are binary and the scale construction is done through IRT scaling. Positive values on this index indicate higher levels of home educational resources.

Q17	**Which of the following do you have in your home?**
	Yes
ST17Q01	a) Desk for study
ST17Q03	c) A quiet place to study
ST17Q07	g) Your own calculator
ST17Q11	k) Books to help with your school work
ST17Q12	l) A dictionary

Home possessions (HOMEPOS)

The PISA 2003 index of home possessions (HOMEPOS) is derived from students' responses to the 14 items listed below. These variables are binary and the scale construction is done through IRT scaling. Positive values on this index indicate higher levels of home possessions.

Q17	**Which of the following do you have in your home?**
	Yes
ST17Q01	a) A desk for study
ST17Q02	b) A room of your own
ST17Q03	c) A quiet place to study
ST17Q04	d) A computer you can use for school work
ST17Q05	e) Educational software
ST17Q06	f) A link to the Internet
ST17Q07	g) Your own calculator
ST17Q08	h) Classic literature (*e.g.* <Shakespeare>)
ST17Q09	i) Books of poetry
ST17Q10	j) Works of art (*e.g.* paintings)
ST17Q11	k) Books to help with your school work
ST17Q12	l) A dictionary
ST17Q13	m) A dishwasher
Q19	**In your home, do you have:**
ST19Q01	More than 100 books (recoded)

Cultural possessions (CULTPOSS)

The PISA 2003 index of cultural possession (CULTPOSS), which retains items used for the PISA 2000 index of cultural possessions, is derived from students' responses to the three items listed below. These variables are binary and the scale construction is done through IRT scaling. Positive values on this index indicate higher levels of cultural possessions.

Q17	**Which of the following do you have in your home?**
	Yes
ST17Q08	h) Classic literature (*e.g.* <Shakespeare>)
ST17Q09	i) Books of poetry
ST17Q10	j) Works of art (*e.g.* paintings)

Economic, social and cultural status (ESCS)

The PISA 2003 index of economic, social and cultural status (ESCS) is derived from three variables related to family background: the index of highest level of parental education in number of years of education according to the ISCED classification (PARED), the index of highest parental occupation status (HISEI) and the index of home possessions (HOMEPOS). Missing values for these three variables are imputed and then transformed to an international metric with OECD averages of 0 and OECD standard deviations of 1. These OECD-standardised variables were used for a principal component analysis in order to obtain ESCS scores applying an OECD population weight giving each OECD country a weight of 1000. The PISA index of economic, social and cultural status (ESCS) is computed for PISA 2003 and also re-computed for the PISA 2000 data, but items and the wording of items are slightly different between PISA 2000 and PISA 2003. Further details concerning ESCS are found in *PISA 2003 Technical Report* (OECD, forthcoming).

School climate

Attitudes towards school (ATSCHL)

The PISA 2003 index of students' attitudes towards school (ATSCHL) is derived from students' responses to four items listed below. A four-point scale with the response categories recoded as "strongly agree" (=0); "agree" (=1); "disagree" (=2); and "strongly disagree" (=3) is used. As items ST24Q03 and ST24Q04 are inverted for IRT scaling, positive values on this index indicate students' positive attitudes toward school.

Q24 ***Thinking about what you have learned in school:***
To what extent do you agree with the following statements?

Strongly agree	*Agree*	*Disagree*	*Strongly disagree*

ST24Q01	a) School has done little to prepare me for adult life when I leave school.
ST24Q02	b) School has been a waste of time.
ST24Q03	c) School helped give me confidence to make decisions. (+)
ST24Q04	d) School has taught me things which could be useful in a job. (+)

(+) *Item inverted for IRT scaling.*

Student-teacher relations (STUREL)

The PISA 2003 index of student-teacher relations (STUREL) is derived from students' responses to the five items presented below. A four-point scale with the response categories recoded as "strongly agree" (=0); "agree" (=1); "disagree" (=2); and "strongly disagree" (=3) is used. All items are inverted for IRT scaling and positive values on this index indicate students' perception of good student-teacher relations at a school.

Q26 ***Thinking about the teachers at your school:***
To what extent do you agree with the following statements?

Strongly agree	*Agree*	*Disagree*	*Strongly disagree*

ST26Q01	a) Students get along well with most teachers. (+)
ST26Q02	b) Most teachers are interested in students' well-being. (+)
ST26Q03	c) Most of my teachers really listen to what I have to say. (+)
ST26Q04	d) If I need extra help, I will receive it from my teachers. (+)
ST26Q05	e) Most of my teachers treat me fairly. (+)

(+) *Item inverted for IRT scaling.*

Sense of belonging (BELONG)

The PISA 2003 index of sense of belonging at school (BELONG) is derived from students' responses to the six items presented below. A four-point scale with the response categories recoded as "strongly agree" (=0); "agree" (=1); "disagree" (=2); and "strongly disagree" (=3) is used. As Items ST27Q02 and ST27Q03 are inverted for IRT scaling, positive values on this index indicate students' positive feelings about school.

Q27 **My school is a place where:**

Strongly agree	*Agree*	*Disagree*	*Strongly disagree*

ST27Q01	a) I feel like an outsider (or left out of things).
ST27Q02	b) I make friends easily. (+)
ST27Q03	c) I feel like I belong. (+)
ST27Q04	d) I feel awkward and out of place.
ST27Q05	e) Other students seem to like me.
ST27Q06	f) I feel lonely.

(+) *Item inverted for IRT scaling.*

Self-related cognitions in mathematics

Interest in and enjoyment of mathematics (INTMAT)

The PISA 2003 index of interest in and enjoyment of mathematics (INTMAT) is derived from students' responses to the four items listed below. A four-point scale with the response categories recoded as "strongly agree" (=0); "agree" (=1); "disagree" (=2); and "strongly disagree" (=3) is used. All items are inverted for IRT scaling and positive values on this index indicate higher levels of interest and enjoyment in mathematics. The PISA 2000 index of interest in mathematics was derived from a different set of items.

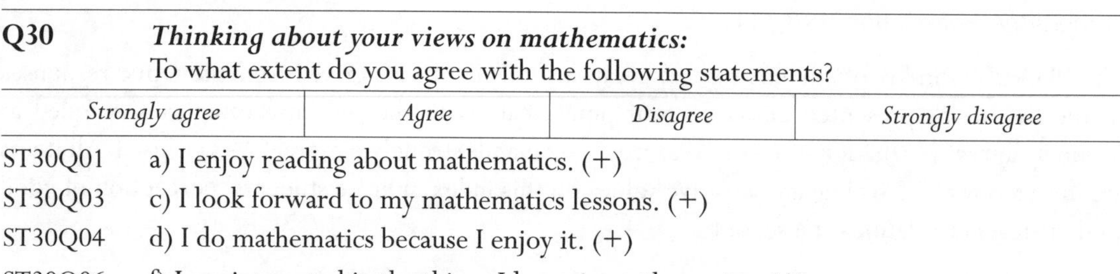

Q30 ***Thinking about your views on mathematics:***
To what extent do you agree with the following statements?

Strongly agree	*Agree*	*Disagree*	*Strongly disagree*

ST30Q01	a) I enjoy reading about mathematics. (+)
ST30Q03	c) I look forward to my mathematics lessons. (+)
ST30Q04	d) I do mathematics because I enjoy it. (+)
ST30Q06	f) I am interested in the things I learn in mathematics. (+)

(+) *Item inverted for IRT scaling.*

Instrumental motivation in mathematics (INSTMOT)

The PISA 2003 index of instrumental motivation in mathematics (INSTMOT) is derived from students' responses to the four items listed below. A four-point scale with the response categories recoded as "strongly agree" (=0), "agree" (=1), "disagree" (=2) and "strongly disagree" (=3) is used. All items are inverted for IRT scaling and positive values on this index indicate higher levels of instrumental motivation to learn mathematics.

Q30 ***Thinking about your views on mathematics:***
To what extent do you agree with the following statements?

Strongly agree	*Agree*	*Disagree*	*Strongly disagree*

ST30Q02	b) Making an effort in mathematics is worth it because it will help me in the work that I want to do later on. (+)
ST30Q05	e) Learning mathematics is worthwhile for me because it will improve my career <prospects, chances>. (+)
ST30Q07	g) Mathematics is an important subject for me because I need it for what I want to study later on. (+)
ST30Q08	h) I will learn many things in mathematics that will help me get a job. (+)

(+) *Item inverted for IRT scaling.*

Mathematics self-efficacy (MATHEFF)

The PISA 2003 index of mathematics self-efficacy (MATHEFF) is derived from students' responses to the eight items measuring the students' confidence with mathematical tasks as listed below. A four-point scale with the response categories recoded as "very confident" (=0), "confident" (=1), "not very confident" (=2) and "not at all confident" (=3) is used. All items are inverted for IRT scaling and positive values on this index indicate higher levels of self-efficacy in mathematics.

Q31 How confident do you feel about having to do the following calculations?

Very confident	*Confident*	*Not very confident*	*Not at all confident*

ST31Q01	a) Using a <train timetable>, how long it would take to get from Zedville to Zedtown (+)
ST31Q02	b) Calculating how much cheaper a TV would be after a 30 percent discount (+)
ST31Q03	c) Calculating how many square metres of tiles you need to cover a floor. (+)
ST31Q04	d) Understanding graphs presented in newspapers. (+)
ST31Q05	e) Solving an equation like $3x + 5 = 17$. (+)
ST31Q06	f) Finding the actual distance between two places on a map with a 1:10,000 scale. (+)
ST31Q07	g) Solving an equation like $2(x+3) = (x + 3)(x - 3)$. (+)
ST31Q08	h) Calculating the petrol consumption rate of a car. (+)

(+) *Item inverted for IRT scaling.*

Mathematics anxiety (ANXMAT)

The PISA 2003 index of mathematics anxiety, which is concerned with feelings of helplessness and emotional stress when dealing with mathematics, is derived from students' responses to the five items presented below. A four-point scale with the response categories recoded as "strongly agree" (=0), "agree" (=1), "disagree" (=2) and "strongly disagree" (=3) is used. All items are inverted for IRT scaling and positive values on this index indicate higher levels of mathematics anxiety.

Q32 ***Thinking about studying mathematics:***
To what extent do you agree with the following statements?

Strongly agree	*Agree*	*Disagree*	*Strongly disagree*

ST32Q01	a) I often worry that it will be difficult for me in mathematics classes. (+)
ST32Q03	c) I get very tense when I have to do mathematics homework. (+)
ST32Q05	e) I get very nervous doing mathematics problems. (+)
ST32Q08	h) I feel helpless when doing a mathematics problem. (+)
ST32Q10	j) I worry that I will get poor <marks> in mathematics. (+)

(+) *Item inverted for IRT scaling.*

Mathematics self-concept (SCMAT)

The PISA 2003 index of mathematics self-concept is derived from students' responses to the five items. A four-point scale with the response categories recoded as "strongly agree" (=0), "agree" (=1), "disagree" (=2) and "strongly disagree" (=3) is used. Items ST32Q04, ST32Q06 and ST32Q07 are inverted for IRT scaling and positive values on this index indicate a positive self-concept in mathematics. The PISA 2000 index of self-concept in mathematics was derived from a different set of items.

Q32 ***Thinking about studying mathematics:***
To what extent do you agree with the following statements?

Strongly agree (1)	*Agree (2)*	*Disagree (3)*	*Strongly disagree (4)*

ST32Q02	b) I am just not good at mathematics.
ST32Q04	d) I get good <marks> in mathematics. (+)
ST32Q06	f) I learn mathematics quickly. (+)
ST32Q07	g) I have always believed that mathematics is one of my best subjects. (+)
ST32Q09	i) In my mathematics class, I understand even the most difficult work. (+)

(+) *Item inverted for IRT scaling.*

Learning strategies and preferences in mathematics

Memorisation/rehearsal learning strategies (MEMOR)

The PISA 2003 index of memorisation/rehearsal learning strategies is derived from students' responses to the four items measuring preference for memorisation/rehearsal as a learning strategy for mathematics as listed below. A four-point scale with the response categories recoded as "strongly agree" (=0), "agree" (=1), "disagree" (=2) and "strongly disagree" (=3) is used. All items are inverted for IRT scaling and positive values on this index indicate preferences for this learning strategy. The PISA 2000 index of memorisation strategies was derived from a different set of items asking not only asking about mathematics, but about learning strategies in general.

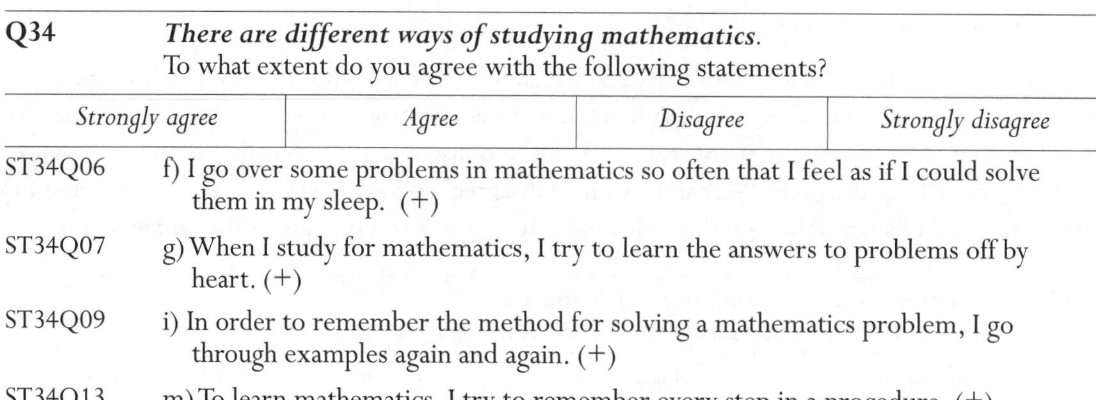

Q34 ***There are different ways of studying mathematics.***
To what extent do you agree with the following statements?

Strongly agree	*Agree*	*Disagree*	*Strongly disagree*

ST34Q06	f) I go over some problems in mathematics so often that I feel as if I could solve them in my sleep. (+)
ST34Q07	g) When I study for mathematics, I try to learn the answers to problems off by heart. (+)
ST34Q09	i) In order to remember the method for solving a mathematics problem, I go through examples again and again. (+)
ST34Q13	m) To learn mathematics, I try to remember every step in a procedure. (+)

(+) *Item inverted for IRT scaling.*

Elaboration learning strategies (ELAB)

The PISA 2003 index of elaboration learning strategies is derived from students' responses to the five items measuring preference for elaboration as a learning strategy as presented below. A four-point scale with the response categories recoded as "strongly agree" (=0), "agree" (=1), "disagree" (=2) and "strongly disagree" (=3) is used. All items are inverted for IRT scaling and positive values on this index indicate preferences for this learning strategy. The PISA 2000 index of elaboration strategies was derived from a different set of items asking about learning strategies in general.

Q34 ***There are different ways of studying mathematics.***
To what extent do you agree with the following statements?

Strongly agree	*Agree*	*Disagree*	*Strongly disagree*

ST34Q02	b) When I am solving mathematics problems, I often think of new ways to get the answer. (+)
ST34Q05	e) I think how the mathematics I have learnt can be used in everyday life. (+)
ST34Q08	h) I try to understand new concepts in mathematics by relating them to things I already know. (+)
ST34Q11	k) When I am solving a mathematics problem, I often think about how the solution might be applied to other interesting questions. (+)
ST34Q14	n) When learning mathematics, I try to relate the work to things I have learnt in other subjects. (+)

(+) *Item inverted for IRT scaling.*

Control learning strategies (CSTRAT)

The PISA 2003 index of control learning strategies (CSTRAT) is derived from students' responses to the five items measuring preference for control as a learning strategy as listed below. A four-point scale with the response categories recoded as "strongly agree" (=0), "agree" (=1), "disagree" (=2) and "strongly disagree" (=3) is used. All of them are inverted for IRT scaling and positive values on this index indicate preferences for this learning strategy. The PISA 2000 index of control strategies was derived from a different set of items asking about learning strategies in general.

Q34	*There are different ways of studying mathematics.* To what extent do you agree with the following statements?		
Strongly agree	*Agree*	*Disagree*	*Strongly disagree*

ST34Q01	a) When I study for a mathematics test, I try to work out what are the most important parts to learn. (+)
ST34Q03	c) When I study mathematics, I make myself check to see if I remember the work I have already done. (+)
ST34Q04	d) When I study mathematics, I try to figure out which concepts I still have not understood properly. (+)
ST34Q10	j) When I cannot understand something in mathematics, I always search for more information to clarify the problem. (+)
ST34Q12	l) When I study mathematics, I start by working out exactly what I need to learn. (+)

(+) *Item inverted for IRT scaling.*

Preference for competitive learning situations (COMPLRN)

The PISA index of preference for competitive learning situation (COMPLRN) is derived from students' responses to the five items measuring preferences for competitive learning situations as listed below. A four-point scale with the response categories recoded as "strongly agree" (=0), "agree" (=1), "disagree" (=2) and "strongly disagree" (=3) is used. All items are inverted for IRT scaling and positive values on this index indicate preferences for competitive learning situations. The PISA 2000 index of competitive learning was derived from a different set of items asking about learning situations in general.

Q37	*Thinking about your <mathematics> classes:* To what extent do you agree with the following statements?		
Strongly agree	*Agree*	*Disagree*	*Strongly disagree*

ST37Q01	a) I would like to be the best in my class in mathematics. (+)
ST37Q03	c) I try very hard in mathematics because I want to do better in the exams than the others. (+)
ST37Q05	e) I make a real effort in mathematics because I want to be one of the best. (+)
ST37Q07	g) In mathematics I always try to do better than the other students in my class. (+)
ST37Q10	j) I do my best work in mathematics when I try to do better than others. (+)

(+) *Item inverted for IRT scaling.*

Preference for co-operative learning situations (COOPLRN)

The PISA index of preference for co-operative learning situation (COOPLRN) is derived from students' responses to the five items measuring preferences for co-operative learning situations as listed below. A four-point scale with the response categories recoded as "strongly agree" (=0), "agree" (=1), "disagree" (=2) and "strongly disagree" (=3) is used. All of them are inverted for IRT scaling and positive values on this index indicate preferences for co-operative learning situations. The PISA 2000 index of co-operative learning was derived from a different set of items asking about learning situations in general.

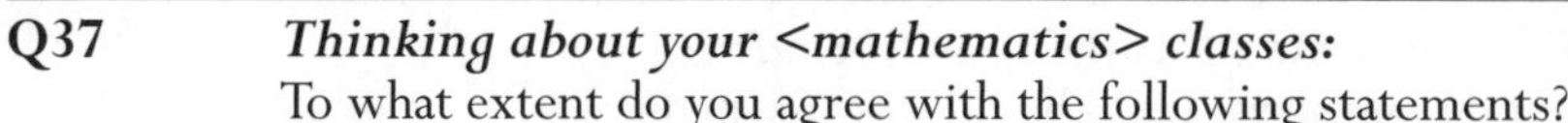

Q37 ***Thinking about your <mathematics> classes:***
To what extent do you agree with the following statements?

Strongly agree	*Agree*	*Disagree*	*Strongly disagree*

ST37Q02	b) In mathematics I enjoy working with other students in groups. (+)
ST37Q04	d) When we work on a project in mathematics, I think that it is a good idea to combine the ideas of all the students in a group. (+)
ST37Q06	f) I do my best work in mathematics when I work with other students. (+)
ST37Q08	h) In mathematics, I enjoy helping others to work well in a group. (+)
ST37Q09	i) In mathematics I learn most when I work with other students in my class. (+)

(+) *Item inverted for IRT scaling.*

Classroom climate

Teacher support (TEACHSUP)

The PISA 2003 index of teacher support in mathematics lessons is derived from students' responses to the five items listed below. These are the slightly modified items used for the PISA 2000 index of teacher support in language lessons. A four-point scale with the response categories recoded as "every lesson" (=0), "most lessons" (=1), "some lessons" (=2) and "never or hardly ever" (=3) is used. All items are inverted and positive values on this index indicate students' perceptions of higher levels of teacher support.

Q38 **How often do these things happen in your <mathematics> lessons?**

Every lesson	*Most lessons*	*Some lessons*	*Never or hardly ever*

ST38Q01	a) The teacher shows an interest in every student's learning. (+)
ST38Q03	c) The teacher gives extra help when students need it. (+)
ST38Q05	e) The teacher helps students with their learning. (+)
ST38Q07	g) The teacher continues teaching until the students understand. (+)
ST38Q10	j) The teacher gives students an opportunity to express opinions. (+)

(+) *Item inverted for IRT scaling.*

Disciplinary climate (DISCLIM)

The PISA 2003 index of disciplinary climate in mathematics lessons is derived from students' responses to the five items listed below. These are the slightly modified items used for the PISA 2000 index of disciplinary climate in language lessons. A four-point scale with the response categories recoded as "every lesson" (=0), "most lessons" (=1), "some lessons" (=2) and "never or hardly ever" (=3) is used. The items are not inverted for IRT scaling and positive values on this index indicate perceptions of a positive disciplinary climate.

Q38 **How often do these things happen in your <mathematics> lessons?**

Every lesson	*Most lessons*	*Some lessons*	*Never or hardly ever*

ST38Q02	b) Students don't listen to what the teacher says.
ST38Q06	f) There is noise and disorder.
ST38Q08	h) The teacher has to wait a long time for students to <quieten down>.
ST38Q09	i) Students cannot work well.
ST38Q11	k) Students don't start working for a long time after the lesson begins.

ICT use, self-confidence and attitudes

Indices in this section will only be available for those countries, which chose to administer the ICT familiarity questionnaire.

ICT Internet/entertainment use (INTUSE)

The PISA 2003 index of ICT internet/entertainment use (INTUSE) is derived from students' responses to the six items measuring the frequency of different types ICT use as listed below. A five-point scale with the response categories recoded as "almost every day" (=0), "a few times each week" (=1), "between once a week and once a month" (=2), "less than once a month" (=3) and "never" (=4) is used. All items are inverted for IRT scaling and positive values on this index indicate high frequencies of ICT internet/entertainment use.

Q5 How often do you use:

Almost every day	*A few times each week*	*Between once a week and once a month*	*Less than once a month*	*Never*

IC05Q01	a) The Internet to look up information about people, things, or ideas? (+)
IC05Q02	b) Games on a computer? (+)
IC05Q04	d) The Internet to collaborate with a group or team? (+)
IC05Q06	f) The Internet to download software? (+)
IC05Q10	j) The Internet to download music? (+)
IC05Q12	l) A computer for electronic communication (*e.g.* e-mail or "chat rooms")? (+)

(+) *Item inverted for IRT scaling.*

ICT program/software use (PRGUSE)

The PISA 2003 index of ICT program/software use (PRGUSE) is derived from students' responses to the six items listed below. A five-point scale with the response categories recoded as "almost every day" (=0), "a few times each week" (=1), "between once a week and once a month" (=2), "less than once a month" (=3) and "never" (=4) is used. All items are inverted for IRT scaling and positive values on this index indicate high frequencies of ICT program/software use.

Q5 How often do you use:

Almost every day	*A few times each week*	*Between once a week and once a month*	*Less than once a month*	*Never*

IC05Q03	c) Word processing (*e.g.* Microsoft® Word® or WordPerfect®)? (+)
IC05Q05	e) Spreadsheets (*e.g.* IBM® Lotus 1-2-3® or Microsoft® Excel®)? (+)
IC05Q07	g) Drawing, painting or graphics programs on a computer? (+)
IC05Q08	h) Educational software such as mathematics programs? (+)
IC05Q09	i) The computer to help you learn school material? (+)
IC05Q11	k) The computer for programming? (+)

(+) *Item inverted for IRT scaling.*

Confidence in ICT routine tasks (ROUTCONF)

The PISA index of confidence in ICT routine tasks (ROUTCONF) is derived from students' responses to the 11 items on self-confidence with ICT tasks. A four-point scale with the response categories recoded as "I can do this very well by myself" (=0), "I can do this with help from someone" (=1), "I know what this means but I cannot do it" (=2) and "I don't know what this means" (=3) is used. All items are inverted for IRT scaling and positive values on this index indicate high self-confidence in ICT routine tasks.

Q6 How well can you do each of these tasks on a computer?

I can do this very well by myself	*I can do this with help from someone*	*I know what this means but I cannot do it*	*I don't know what this means*

IC06Q01 a) Start a computer game. (+)
IC06Q03 c) Open a file. (+)
IC06Q04 d) Create/edit a document. (+)
IC06Q05 e) Scroll a document up and down a screen. (+)
IC06Q07 g) Copy a file from a floppy disk. (+)
IC06Q08 h) Save a computer document or file. (+)
IC06Q09 i) Print a computer document or file. (+)
IC06Q10 j) Delete a computer document or file. (+)
IC06Q11 k) Moves files form one place to another on a computer. (+)
IC06Q18 r) Play computer games. (+)
IC06Q21 u) Draw pictures using a mouse. (+)

(+) *Item inverted for IRT scaling.*

Confidence in ICT Internet tasks (INTCONF)

The PISA 2003 index of confidence in ICT internet tasks is derived from students' responses to the five items listed below. A four-point scale with the response categories recoded as "I can do this very well by myself" (=0), "I can do this with help from someone" (=1), "I know what this means but I cannot do it" (=2), and "I don't know what this means" (=3) is used. All items are inverted for IRT scaling and positive values on this index indicate high self-confidence in ICT internet tasks.

Q6 How well can you do each of these tasks on a computer?

I can do this very well by myself	*I can do this with help from someone*	*I know what this means but I cannot do it*	*I don't know what this means*

IC06Q12 l) Get on to the Internet. (+)
IC06Q13 m) Copy or download files from the Internet. (+)
IC06Q14 n) Attach a file to an e-mail message. (+)
IC06Q19 s) Download music from the Internet. (+)
IC06Q22 v) Write and send e-mails. (+)

(+) *Item inverted for IRT scaling.*

Confidence in ICT high level tasks (HIGHCONF)

The PISA 2003 index of confidence in ICT high level tasks (HIGHCONF) is derived from students' responses to the seven questions listed below. A four-point scale with the response categories recoded as "I can do this very well by myself" (=0), "I can do this with help from someone" (=1), "I know what this means but I cannot do it" (=2), and "I don't know what this means" (=3) is used. All items are inverted for IRT scaling and positive values on this index indicated high self-confidence in ICT high level tasks.

Q6 How well can you do each of these tasks on a computer?

I can do this very well by myself	*I can do this with help from someone*	*I know what this means but I cannot do it*	*I don't know what this means*

IC06Q02	b) Use software to find and get rid of computer viruses. (+)
IC06Q06	f) Use a database to produce a list of addresses. (+)
IC06Q15	o) Create a computer program (*e.g.* in <Logo, Pascal, Basic>). (+)
IC06Q16	p) Use a spreadsheet to plot a graph. (+)
IC06Q17	q) Create a presentation (*e.g.* using <Microsoft® PowerPoint®>). (+)
IC06Q20	t) Create a multi-media presentation (with sound, pictures, video). (+)
IC06Q23	w) Construct a web page. (+)

(+) *Item inverted for IRT scaling.*

Attitudes toward computers (ATTCOMP)

The PISA 2003 index of attitudes toward computers is derived from students' responses to the four items listed below. A four-point scale with the response categories recoded as "strongly agree" (=0), "agree" (=1), "disagree" (=2), and "strongly agree" (=3) is used. All items are inverted for IRT scaling and positive values on the index indicate positive attitudes toward computers. Due to the modifications in the item format and wording, this PISA 2003 index is not entirely comparable to the PISA 2000 index of interest in computers which was using a dichotomous form (Yes/No).

Q7 *Thinking about your experience with computers:*
To what extent do you agree with the following statements?

Strongly agree	*Agree*	*Disagree*	*Strongly agree*

IC07Q01	a) It is very important to me to work with a computer. (+)
IC07Q02	b) To play or work with a computer is really fun. (+)
IC07Q03	c) I use a computer because I am very interested. (+)
IC07Q04	d) I lose track of time when I am working with the computer. (+)

(+) *Item inverted for IRT scaling.*

SCHOOL-LEVEL SIMPLE INDICES

School characteristics

School size (SCHLSIZE)

Similar to PISA 2000, the PISA 2003 index of school size (SCHLSIZE) is derived from summing school principals' responses to the number of girls and boys at a school (SC02Q01 and SC02Q02). Values on this index indicate total enrolment at school.

Proportion of girls enrolled at school (PCGIRLS)

Similar to PISA 2000, the PISA 2003 index of the proportion of girls enrolled at school (PCGIRLS) is derived from school principals' responses regarding the number of girls divided by the total of girls and boys at a school (SC02Q01 and SC02Q02).

School type (SCHLTYPE)

Similar to PISA 2000, the PISA 2003 index of school type (SCHLTYPE) has three categories: (1) public schools controlled and managed by a public education authority or agency, (2) government-dependent private schools controlled by non-government organisation or with a governing board not selected by a government agency which receive more than 50 per cent of their core funding from government agencies and (3) independent private schools controlled by a non-government organisation or with a governing board not selected by a government agency, which receive less than 50 per cent of their core funding from government agencies. This index is derived from school principals' responses to the items (SC03Q01 and SC04Q01 to SC04Q04) classifying schools into either public or private and identifying source of funding.

Indicators of school resources

Availability of computers (RATCOMP, COMPWEB and COMPLAN)

Similar to PISA 2000, the PISA 2003 index of availability of computers (RATCOMP) is derived from school principals' responses to the items measuring the availability of computers. It is calculated by dividing the number of computers at school (SC09Q01) by the number of students at school (SC02Q01 plus SC02Q02).

In addition, the following PISA 2003 indices on computer availability were developed as in PISA 2000:

- The PISA 2003 index of proportion of computers connected to a Local Area Network (COMPWEB) is derived from school principals' responses to the number of computers connected to the Web (SC09Q05) divided by the total number of computers (SC09Q01).
- The PISA 2003 index of proportion of computers connected to LAN (COMPLAN) is derived from school principals' responses to the number of computers connected to a local network (SC09Q06) divided by the total number of computers (SC09Q01).

Quantity of teaching staff at school (STRATIO, PROPCERT and PROPQPED)

As in PISA 2000, school principals are asked to report the number of full-time and part-time teachers at school in PISA 2003. The PISA 2003 indices of quantity of teaching staff at school are derived from questions asking about teachers in general (SC18Q11-SC18Q13 for full time staff and SC18Q21-SC18Q23 for part-time staff).

The PISA 2003 index of student/teacher ratio (STRATIO) is derived from school principals' reports of the school size (sum of SC02Q01 and SC02Q02) divided by the total number of teachers. The number of part-time teachers (SC18Q21) contributes 0.5 and the number of full-time teachers (SC18Q11) 1.0 to the total number of teachers. Values on this index indicate the number of students per teacher.

The PISA 2003 index of proportion of fully certified teachers (PROPCERT) is derived from school principals' reports of the number of fully certified teachers (SC18Q12 plus 0.5 * SC18Q22) divided by the total number of teachers (SC18Q11 plus 0.5 * SC18Q21).

The PISA 2003 index of proportion of teachers who have an ISCED 5A qualification in pedagogy (PROPQPED) is derived from school principals' reports of the number of this kind of teachers (SC18Q13 plus 0.5 * SC18Q23) divided by the total number of teachers (SC18Q11 plus 0.5 * SC18Q21).

Quantity of teaching staff for mathematics at school (SMRATIO, PROPMATH and PROPMA5A)

The PISA 2003 indices of quantity of teaching staff for mathematics at school are derived from questions asking school principals to report the number of full-time and part-time teachers in total and with certain characteristics (SC19Q11-SC19Q15 for full-time staff and SC19Q21-SC19Q25 for part-time staff).

The PISA 2003 index of student/mathematics teacher ratio (SMRATIO) is derived from the school principals' reports of the school size (sum of SC02Q01 and SC02Q02) divided by the total number of mathematics teachers. The number of part-time mathematics teachers (SC19Q21) contributes 0.5 and the number of full-time mathematics teachers (SC19Q11) 1.0 to the total number of teachers.

The PISA 2003 index of proportion of mathematics teachers (PROPMATH) is derived from school principals' reports of the number of mathematics teachers (SC19Q11 plus 0.5 * SC19Q21) divided by the total number of teachers (SC18Q11 plus 0.5 * SC18Q21).

The PISA 2003 index of proportion of mathematics teachers with an ISCED5A qualification and a major in mathematics (PROPMA5A) is derived from school principals' reports of the number of the mathematics teachers with this qualification (SC19Q12 plus 0.5 * SC19Q22) divided by the total number of mathematics teachers (SC19Q11 plus 0.5 * SC19Q21).

Admittance policies and instructional context

School selectivity (SELECT)

The PISA 2003 index of school selectivity (SELECT) is derived from school principals' responses to the items SC10Q02 and SC10Q06. Based on school principals' responses to these two items, schools are categorised into four different categories: (1) schools where none of these factors is considered for student admittance, (2) schools considering at least one of these factors, (3) schools giving high priority to at least one of these factors, and (4) schools where at least one of these factors is a pre-requisite for student admittance. Item SC10Q01 was not included because "residence in a particular area" is not a factor for selecting individual students. These items are similar to those used in PISA 2000, but the wording is slightly different.

Use of assessments (ASSESS)

The PISA 2003 index of use of assessments (ASSESS) is derived from school principals' responses to the items SC12Q01-SC12Q05. All five items are recoded into numerical values, which approximately reflect frequency of assessments per year ("Never"=0, "1-2 times a year"=1.5, "3-5 times a year"=4, "Monthly"=8, and "More than once a month"=12). This index is calculated as the sum of these

recoded items and then divided into three categories: (1) less than 20 times a year, (2) 20-39 times a year, and (3) more than 40 times a year.

Ability grouping (ABGROUP)

The PISA index of ability grouping between classes (ABGROUP) is derived from items SC16Q01 and SC16Q02 measuring the extent to which their school organises instruction differently for student with different abilities. Based on school principals' response to these two items, schools are assigned three categories: (1) schools with no ability grouping between any classes, (2) schools with one of these forms of ability grouping between classes for some classes, and (3) schools with one of these forms of ability grouping for all classes.

School offering mathematics activities (MACTIV)

The PISA 2003 index of mathematics activity index (MACTIV) is derived from five items (SC17Q01-SC17Q05) measuring what activities to promote engagement with mathematics occur at their school. The number of different activities occurring at school is counted.

School offering extension courses (number of types) (EXCOURSE)

The PISA 2003 index of school offering extension courses (EXCOURSE) is derived from two items (SC17Q01 and SC17Q02) which are also used for the index of school offering mathematics activities (MACTIV). This index is computed as the sum of extension course types offered at school: (0) none, (1) either remedial or enrichment, and (2) both.

School management

Resource autonomy (AUTRES)

The PISA 2003 index of resource autonomy (AUTRES) is derived from school principals' responses to the six items (SC26Q01-SC26Q06) measuring who has the main responsibility for different types of decisions regarding the management of the school. This index indicates the number of decisions related to school resources that are a school responsibility.

Curricular autonomy (AUTCURR)

The PISA 2003 index of curricular autonomy (AUTCURR) is derived from school principals' responses to the four items (SC26Q08, SC26Q10-SC26Q12) measuring who has the main responsibility for different types of decisions regarding the management of the school. This index indicates the number of decisions related to curriculum that are a school responsibility.

School climate

Poor student-teacher relations (school average) (MSTREL)

The PISA 2003 index of poor student-teacher relations at school is derived from students' responses to the five items (ST26Q01-ST26Q05) measuring students' perception of various aspects of student-teacher relationships. The four-point scale with the response categories "strongly agree", "agree", "disagree", and "strongly disagree" was recoded into binary variables with "strongly disagree" coded 1 and other valid responses coded 0. These responses were summarised by taking the average item response per student and computing the mean for each school.

SCHOOL-LEVEL SCALE INDICES

School resources

Quality of schools' physical infrastructure (SCMATBUI)

The PISA 2003 index of quality of schools' physical infrastructure (SCMATBUI) is derived from school principals' responses to the three items below measuring the school principal's perceptions of potential factors hindering instruction at school. Similar items were used in PISA 2000, but the question format and item wording have been modified for PISA 2003. A four-point scale with the response categories recoded as "not at all" (=0), "very little" (=1), "to some extent" (=2), and "a lot" (=3) is used. All items are inverted for IRT scaling and positive values on this index indicate positive evaluations of this aspect.

Q8 Is your school's capacity to provide instruction hindered by a shortage or inadequacy of any of the following?

Not at all	*Very little*	*To some extent*	*A lot*

SC08Q11 k) School buildings and grounds (+)

SC08Q12 l) Heating/cooling and lighting systems (+)

SC08Q13 m) Instructional space (*e.g.* classrooms) (+)

(+) *Item inverted for IRT scaling.*

Quality of schools' educational resources (SMATEDU)

The PISA 2003 index of quality of schools' educational resources (SMATEDU) is derived from school principals' responses to the seven items below measuring the school principal's perceptions of potential factors hindering instruction at school. Similar items were used in PISA 2000, but question format and item wording have been modified for PISA 2003. A four-point scale with the response categories recoded as "not at all" (=0), "very little" (=1), "to some extent" (=2), and "a lot" (=3) is used. All items are inverted for IRT scaling and positive values on this index indicate positive evaluations of this aspect.

Q8 Is your school's capacity to provide instruction hindered by a shortage or inadequacy of any of the following?

Not at all	*Very little*	*To some extent*	*A lot*

SC08Q09 i) Instructional materials (*e.g.* textbooks) (+)

SC08Q15 o) Computers for instruction (+)

SC08Q16 p) Computer software for instruction (+)

SC08Q17 q) Calculators for instruction (+)

SC08Q18 r) Library materials (+)

SC08Q19 s) Audio-visual resources (+)

SC08Q20 t) Science laboratory equipment and materials (+)

(+) *Item inverted for IRT scaling.*

Teacher shortage (TCSHORT)

The PISA 2003 index of teacher shortage (TCSHORT) is derived from school principals' responses to the following four items measuring the school principal's perceptions of potential factors hindering instruction at school. Similar items were used in PISA 2000 but question format and item wording have been modified for PISA 2003. Furthermore, for PISA 2003 these items were administered together with the items on the quality of physical environment and educational resources. A four-point scale with the response categories recoded as "not at all" (=0), "very little" (=1), "to some extent" (=2), and "a lot" (=3) is used. The items are not inverted for IRT scaling and positive values on this index indicate school principal's reports of teacher shortage at a school.

Q8 Is your school's capacity to provide instruction hindered by a shortage or inadequacy of any of the following?

Not at all	*Very little*	*To some extent*	*A lot*

SC08Q01 a) Availability of qualified mathematics teachers
SC08Q02 b) Availability of qualified science teachers
SC08Q03 c) Availability of qualified <test language> teachers
SC08Q05 e) Availability of qualified foreign language teachers
SC08Q06 f) Availability of experienced teachers

School climate

School principals' perceptions of teacher morale and commitment (TCMORALE)

The PISA 2003 index of school principals' perceptions of teacher morale and commitment (TCMORALE) is derived from school principals' responses to the following four items measuring the school principal's perceptions of teachers at school. Similar items were used in PISA 2000, but question format has been modified for PISA 2003. The categories "disagree" and "strongly disagree" were collapsed into one category for IRT scaling because of very few responses in the category of "strongly disagree". Response categories of four-point scale items are recoded as "strongly agree" (=0), "agree" (=1), and "disagree/strongly disagree" (=2). All items are inverted for IRT scaling and positive values on this index indicate principals' reports of higher levels of teacher morale and commitment.

Q24 ***Think about the teachers in your school:***
How much do you agree with the following statements?

Strongly agree	*Agree*	*Disagree*	*Strongly disagree*

SC24Q01 a) The morale of teachers in this school is high. (+)
SC24Q02 b) Teachers work with enthusiasm. (+)
SC24Q03 c) Teachers take pride in this school. (+)
SC24Q04 d) Teachers value academic achievement. (+)

(+) *Item inverted for IRT scaling.*

School principals' perceptions of student morale and commitment (STMORALE)

The PISA 2003 index of school principals' perceptions of student morale and commitment (STMORALE) is derived from school principals' responses to the following seven items measuring the school principal's perceptions of students at school. The items are, in part, a parallel to those on

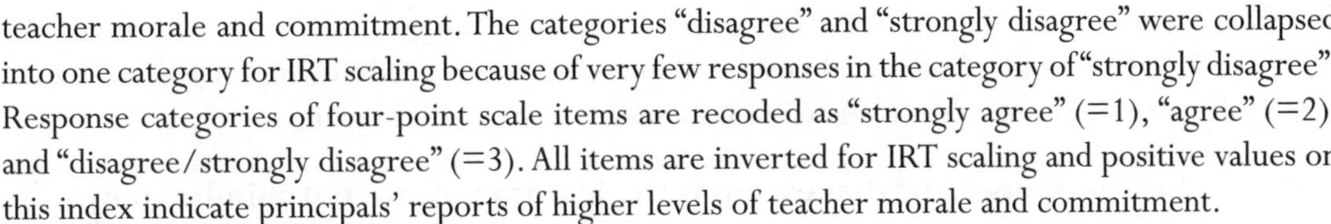

teacher morale and commitment. The categories "disagree" and "strongly disagree" were collapsed into one category for IRT scaling because of very few responses in the category of "strongly disagree". Response categories of four-point scale items are recoded as "strongly agree" (=1), "agree" (=2), and "disagree/strongly disagree" (=3). All items are inverted for IRT scaling and positive values on this index indicate principals' reports of higher levels of teacher morale and commitment.

Q11 ***Think about the students in your school:***
How much do you agree with the following statements?

Strongly agree	*Agree*	*Disagree*	*Strongly disagree*

SC11Q01 a) Students enjoy being in school. (+)
SC11Q02 b) Students work with enthusiasm. (+)
SC11Q03 c) Students take pride in this school. (+)
SC11Q04 d) Students value academic achievement. (+)
SC11Q05 e) Students are cooperative and respectful. (+)
SC11Q06 f) Students value the education they can receive in this school. (+)
SC11Q07 g) Students do their best to learn as much as possible. (+)

(+) *Item inverted for IRT scaling.*

School principals' perceptions of teacher-related factors affecting school climate (TEACBEHA)

The PISA 2003 index of school principals' perceptions of teacher-related factors affecting school climate (TEACBEHA) is derived from school principals' responses to the following seven items measuring the school principal's perceptions of potential factors hindering the learning of students at school. These items were used in PISA 2000, but the question format and the wording of some items have been modified for PISA 2003. A four-point scale with the response categories recoded as "strongly agree" (=0), "agree" (=1), "disagree" (=2), and "strongly disagree" (=3) is used. All items are inverted for IRT scaling and positive values on this index indicate higher level of school principals' perceptions of teacher-related factors hindering students' learning.

Q25 In your school, to what extent is the learning of students hindered by:

Not at all	*Very little*	*To some extent*	*A lot*

ST25Q01 a) Teachers' low expectations of students? (+)
ST25Q03 c) Poor student-teacher relations? (+)
ST25Q05 e) Teachers not meeting individual students' needs? (+)
ST25Q06 f) Teacher absenteeism? (+)
ST25Q09 i) Staff resisting change? (+)
ST25Q11 k) Teachers being too strict with students? (+)
ST25Q13 m) Students not being encouraged to achieve their full potential? (+)

(+) *Item inverted for IRT scaling.*

School principals' perceptions of student-related factors affecting school climate (STUDBEHA)

The PISA 2003 index of school principals' perceptions of student-related factors affecting school climate (STUDBEHA) is derived from school principals' responses to the following six items measuring the school principals' perceptions of potential factors hindering the learning of students at school. These items were used in PISA 2000, but the question format and the wording of some items have been modified for PISA 2003. A four-point scale with the response categories recoded

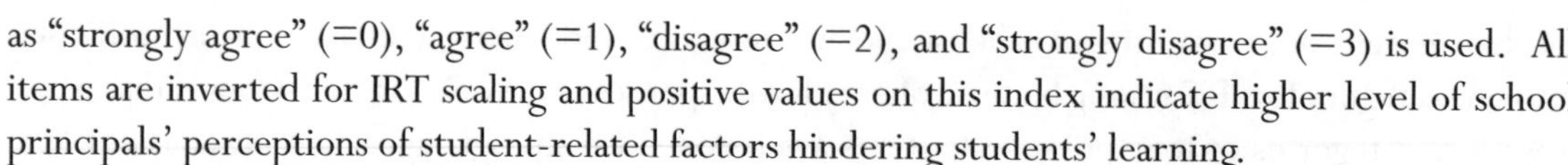

as "strongly agree" (=0), "agree" (=1), "disagree" (=2), and "strongly disagree" (=3) is used. All items are inverted for IRT scaling and positive values on this index indicate higher level of school principals' perceptions of student-related factors hindering students' learning.

Q25 In your school, to what extent is the learning of students hindered by:

	Not at all	Very little	To some extent	A lot
ST25Q02	b) Student absenteeism? (+)			
ST25Q04	d) Disruption of classes by students? (+)			
ST25Q07	g) Students skipping classes? (+)			
ST25Q08	h) Students lacking respect for teachers? (+)			
ST25Q10	j) Student use of alcohol or illegal drugs? (+)			
ST25Q12	l) Students intimidating or bullying other students? (+)			

(+) Item inverted for IRT scaling.

School principals' perceptions of teacher consensus on mathematics teaching (TCHCONS)

The PISA 2003 index of school principals' perceptions of teacher consensus on mathematics teaching (TCHCONS) is derived from school principals' responses to the following three items asking about the school principals' views on having frequent disagreement among teachers regarding innovation, teacher expectations and teaching goals. A four-point scale with the response categories recoded as "strongly agree" (=0), "agree" (=1), "disagree" (=2), and "strongly disagree" (=3) is used. All three items are not inverted for IRT scaling and positive values on this index indicate that higher levels of consensus among teachers are perceived by school principals.

	Strongly agree	Agree	Disagree	Strongly disagree
Q21	**How much do you agree with these statements about innovation in your school?**			
ST21Q03	c) There are frequent disagreements between "innovative" and "traditional" mathematics teachers			
Q22	**How much do you agree with these statements about teachers' expectations in your school?**			
ST22Q03	c) There are frequent disagreements between mathematics teachers who consider each other to be "too demanding" or "too lax".			
Q23	**How much do you agree with these statements about teaching goals in your school?**			
ST23Q03	c) There are frequent disagreements between mathematics teachers who consider each other as "too focused on skill acquisition" or "too focused on the affective development" of the student.			

School management

School autonomy (SCHAUTON)

Similar to PISA 2000, the PISA 2003 index of school autonomy (SCHAUTON) is derived from school principals' responses to the 12 items (SC26Q01-SC26Q12) asking who has the main responsibility for different types of decisions regarding the management of the school. These items were used

in PISA 2000, but the wording has been slightly modified for PISA 2003. As for PISA 2000, the category of "not a main responsibility of the school" (the first column) is recoded to 0 and those with ticks in other columns but not in the first were recoded to 1. The recoded items are scaled using IRT and positive values on this index indicate school principals' perception of higher levels of school autonomy in decision making.

Teacher participation (TCHPARTI)

Similar to PISA 2000, the PISA 2003 index of teacher participation (TCHPARTI) is derived from school principals' responses to the 12 items (SC26Q01-SC26Q12) asking who has the main responsibility for different types of decisions regarding the management of the school. These items were used in PISA 2000, but the wording has been slightly modified for PISA 2003. As for PISA 2000, the category of "teacher" (the last column) indicating that teacher have a main responsibility is recoded to 1 and those with ticks in other columns but not in the last were recoded to 0. The recoded items are scaled using IRT and positive values on this index indicate school principals' perception of higher levels of teacher participation in decision-making.

Final student weight (W_FSTUWT)

In the international data files, the variable W_FSTUWT is the final student weight. The sum of the weights constitutes an estimate of the size of the target population, *i.e.* the number of 15-year-old students in grade 7 or above in that country attending school.

Note

1. Students who were born abroad but had at least one parent born in the country of test are also classified as "native students".

APPENDIX 10 ▪ SCORES ALLOCATED TO THE ITEMS

Item ID	Label	Type	Score 1	Score 2	Score 3
M033Q01	P2000 A View with a Room	Multiple choice	4		
M034Q01T	P2000 Bricks	Closed-constructed response	1		
M124Q01	P2000 Walking	Open-constructed response	2		
M124Q03T	P2000 Walking	Open-constructed response	1	2	3
M144Q01T	P2000 Cube Painting	Closed-constructed response	1		
M144Q02T	P2000 Cube Painting	Closed-constructed response	1		
M144Q03	P2000 Cube Painting	Multiple choice	1		
M144Q04T	P2000 Cube Painting	Closed-constructed response	1		
M145Q01T	P2000 Cubes	Closed-constructed response	6		
M150Q01	P2000 Growing Up	Closed-constructed response	1		
M150Q02T	P2000 Growing Up	Closed-constructed response	1	2	
M150Q03T	P2000 Growing Up	Open-constructed response	1		
M155Q01	P2000 Population Pyramids	Open-constructed response	1		
M155Q02T	P2000 Population Pyramids	Open-constructed response	1	2	
M155Q03T	P2000 Population Pyramids	Open-constructed response	1	2	
M155Q04T	P2000 Population Pyramids	Complex multiple choice	4		
M179Q01T	P2000 Robberies	Open-constructed response	1	2	
M192Q01T	P2000 Containers	Complex multiple choice	2,3		
M266Q01T	P2000 Carpenter	Complex multiple choice	4		
M273Q01T	P2000 Pipelines	Complex multiple choice	1		
M302Q01T	Car Drive	Closed-constructed response	1		
M302Q02	Car Drive	Closed-constructed response	1		
M302Q03	Car Drive	Open-constructed response	1		
M305Q01	Map	Multiple choice	3		
M402Q01	Internet Relay Chat	Short response	1		
M402Q02	Internet Relay Chat	Short response	1		
M406Q01	Running Tracks	Open-constructed response	1		
M406Q02	Running Tracks	Open-constructed response	1		
M406Q03	Running Tracks	Open-constructed response	1		
M408Q01T	Lotteries	Complex multiple choice	4		
M411Q01	Diving	Short response	1		
M411Q02	Diving	Multiple choice	4		
M413Q01	Exchange Rate	Short response	1		
M413Q02	Exchange Rate	Short response	1		
M413Q03T	Exchange Rate	Open-constructed response	1		

Item ID	Label	Type	Score 1	Score 2	Score 3
M420Q01T	Transport	Complex multiple choice	4		
M421Q01	Height	Open-constructed response	1		
M421Q02T	Height	Complex multiple choice	4		
M421Q03	Height	Multiple choice	4		
M423Q01	Tossing Coins	Multiple choice	1		
M438Q01	Exports	Closed-constructed response	1		
M438Q02	Exports	Multiple choice	5		
M442Q02	Braille	Closed-constructed response	1		
M446Q01	Thermometer Cricket	Short response	1		
M446Q02	Thermometer Cricket	Open-constructed response	1		
M447Q01	Tile Arrangement	Multiple choice	4		
M462Q01T	Third Side	Open-constructed response	1	2	
M464Q01T	The Fence	Short response	1		
M467Q01	Coloured Candies	Multiple choice	2		
M468Q01T	Science Tests	Short response	1		
M474Q01	Running Time	Closed-constructed response	1		
M484Q01T	Bookshelves	Short response	1		
M496Q01T	Cash Withdrawal	Complex multiple choice	4		
M496Q02	Cash Withdrawal	Short response	1		
M505Q01	Litter	Open-constructed response	1		
M509Q01	Earthquake	Multiple choice	3		
M510Q01T	Choices	Short response	1		
M513Q01	Test Scores	Open-constructed response	1		
M520Q01T	Skateboard	Short response	1	2	
M520Q02	Skateboard	Multiple choice	4		
M520Q03T	Skateboard	Short response	4		
M547Q01T	Staircase	Short response	1		
M555Q02T	Number Cubes	Complex multiple choice	4		
M559Q01	Telephone Rates	Multiple choice	4		
M564Q01	Chair Lift	Multiple choice	2		
M564Q02	Chair Lift	Multiple choice	3		
M571Q01	Stop the Car	Multiple choice	4		
M598Q01	Making a Booklet	Closed-constructed response	1		
M603Q01T	Number Check	Complex multiple choice	3		
M603Q02T	Number Check	Short response	1		
M702Q01	Support for President	Open-constructed response	2		
M704Q01T	The Best Car	Short response	1		
M704Q02T	The Best Car	Open-constructed response	1		
M710Q01	Forecast of Rain	Multiple choice	4		
M800Q01	Computer Game	Multiple choice	3		
M803Q01T	Labels	Short response	1		

Item ID	Label	Type	Score 1	Score 2	Score 3
M806Q01T	Step Pattern	Short response	1		
M810Q01T	Bicycles	Short response	1		
M810Q02T	Bicycles	Short response	1		
M810Q03T	Bicycles	Open-constructed response	1	2	
M828Q01	Carbon Dioxide	Open-constructed response	1		
M828Q02	Carbon Dioxide	Short response	1		
M828Q03	Carbon Dioxide	Short response	1		
M833Q01T	Seeing the Tower	Complex multiple choice	5		
R055Q01	Drugged Spiders	Multiple choice	4		
R055Q02	Drugged Spiders	Open-constructed response	1		
R055Q03	Drugged Spiders	Open-constructed response	2		
R055Q05	Drugged Spiders	Open-constructed response	1		
R067Q01	Aesop	Multiple choice	3		
R067Q04	Aesop	Open-constructed response	1	2	
R067Q05	Aesop	Open-constructed response	1	2	
R102Q04A	Shirts	Open-constructed response	1		
R102Q05	Shirts	Closed-constructed response	1		
R102Q07	Shirts	Multiple choice	3		
R104Q01	Telephone	Closed-constructed response	1		
R104Q02	Telephone	Closed-constructed response	1		
R104Q05	Telephone	Short response	1	2	
R111Q01	Exchange	Multiple choice	4		
R111Q02B	Exchange	Open-constructed response	1	2	
R111Q06B	Exchange	Open-constructed response	1	2	
R219Q01E	Employment	Short response	1		
R219Q01T	Employment	Closed-constructed response	4		
R219Q02	Employment	Open-constructed response	1		
R220Q01	South Pole	Short response	1		
R220Q02B	South Pole	Multiple choice	1		
R220Q04	South Pole	Multiple choice	4		
R220Q05	South Pole	Multiple choice	3		
R220Q06	South Pole	Multiple choice	3		
R227Q01	Optician	Multiple choice	2		
R227Q02T	Optician	Complex multiple choice	5,6	7	
R227Q03	Optician	Open-constructed response	1		
R227Q06	Optician	Short response	1		
S114Q03T	P2000 Greenhouse	Open-constructed response	1		
S114Q04T	P2000 Greenhouse	Open-constructed response	1	2	
S114Q05T	P2000 Greenhouse	Open-constructed response	1		
S128Q01	P2000 Cloning	Multiple choice	1		
S128Q02	P2000 Cloning	Multiple choice	1		

Item ID	Label	Type	Score 1	Score 2	Score 3
S128Q03T	P2000 Cloning	Complex multiple choice	2		
S129Q01	P2000 Daylight	Multiple choice	1		
S129Q02T	P2000 Daylight	Short response	1	2	
S131Q02T	P2000 Good Vibrations	Open-constructed response	1		
S131Q04T	P2000 Good Vibrations	Open-constructed response	1		
S133Q01	P2000 Research	Multiple choice	3		
S133Q03	P2000 Research	Multiple choice	1		
S133Q04T	P2000 Research	Complex multiple choice	3		
S213Q01T	P2000 Clothes	Complex multiple choice	4		
S213Q02	P2000 Clothes	Multiple choice	1		
S252Q01	P2000 South Rainea	Multiple choice	3		
S252Q02	P2000 South Rainea	Multiple choice	1		
S252Q03T	P2000 South Rainea	Complex multiple choice	2		
S256Q01	P2000 Spoons	Multiple choice	1		
S268Q01	P2000 Algae	Multiple choice	3		
S268Q02T	P2000 Algae	Open-constructed response	1		
S268Q06	P2000 Algae	Multiple choice	2		
S269Q01	P2000 Earth's Temperature	Open-constructed response	1		
S269Q03T	P2000 Earth's Temperature	Open-constructed response	1		
S269Q04T	P2000 Earth's Temperature	Complex multiple choice	4		
S304Q01	Water	Open-constructed response	1		
S304Q02	Water	Multiple choice	3		
S304Q03a	Water	Open-constructed response	1		
S304Q03b	Water	Open-constructed response	1		
S326Q01	Milk	Open-constructed response	1		
S326Q02	Milk	Open-constructed response	1		
S326Q03	Milk	Multiple choice	2		
S326Q04T	Milk	Complex multiple choice	3		
S327Q01T	Tidal Energy	Complex multiple choice	2		
X402Q01T	Library System	Closed-constructed response	1		
X402Q02T	Library System	Open-constructed response	1	2	3
X412Q01	Design by Numbers	Multiple choice	2		
X412Q02	Design by Numbers	Multiple choice	4		
X412Q03	Design by Numbers	Open-constructed response	1	2	
X414Q01	Course Design	Open-constructed response	1	2	
X415Q01T	Transit System	Open-constructed response	1	2	
X417Q01	Children's Camp	Open-constructed response	1	2	
X423Q01T	Freezer	Multiple choice	5,6		
X423Q02T	Freezer	Multiple choice	3		
X430Q01	Energy Needs	Closed-constructed response	1		
X430Q02	Energy Needs	Open-constructed response	1	2	

Item ID	Label	Type	Score 1	Score 2	Score 3
X601Q01T	Cinema Outing	Multiple choice	5	6	
X601Q02	Cinema Outing	Multiple choice	3		
X602Q01	Holiday	Closed-constructed response	1		
X602Q02	Holiday	Open-constructed response	1	2	
X603Q01	Irrigation	Open-constructed response	1		
X603Q02T	Irrigation	Multiple choice	3		
X603Q03	Irrigation	Open-constructed response	1		

REFERENCES

Baumert, J., S. Gruehn, S. Heyn, O. Köller and **K.U. Schnabel** (1997), *Bildungsverläufe und Psychosoziale Entwicklung im Jugendalter (BIJU): Dokumentation - Band 1,* Max-Planck-Institut für Bildungsforschung, Berlin.

Baumert, J., S. Heyn and **O. Köller** (1994), *Das Kieler Lernstrategien-Inventar (KSI),* Institut für die Pädagogik der Naturwissenschaften an der Universität Kiel, Kiel.

Beaton A.E., I.V.S. Mullis, M.O. Martin, E.J. Gonzalez, D.L. Kelly and **T.A. Smith** (1997), *Mathematics Achievement in the Middle School Years: IEA's Third International Mathematics and Science Study (TIMSS),* Boston College, Chestnut Hill.

Beaton, A.E. (1987), *The NAEP 1983-1984 Technical Report,* Educational Testing Service, Princeton.

Beaton, A.E. (1988), *The NAEP 1985-86 Reading Anomaly: A Technical Report,* Educational Testing Service, National Assessment of Educational Progress, Princeton.

Bloom, B.S. (1979), *Caractéristiques individuelles et apprentissage scolaire,* Éditions Labor, Bruxelles.

Bryk, A.S. and **S.W. Raudenbush** (1992), *Hierarchical Linear Models in Social and Behavioral Research: Applications and Data Analysis Methods,* Sage Publications, Beverly Hills.

Cornfield, J. (1951), "A Method for Estimating Comparative Rates from Clinical Data. Applications to Cancer of the Lung, Breast, and Cervix", *Journal of the National Cancer Institute* Vol. 11, Oxford University Press, Oxford, pp. 1269-1275.

Dunn, O.J. (1961), "Multiple Comparisons among Means", *Journal of the American Statistical Association,* Vol. 56, American Statistical Association, Alexandria, pp. 52-64.

Eignor, D., C. Taylor, I. Kirsch and **J. Jamieson** (1998), "Development of a Scale for Assessing the Level of Computer Familiarity of TOEFL Students", *TOEFL Research Report No. 60,* Educational Testing Service, Princeton.

Ganzeboom, H.B.G., P. de Graaf and **D. J. Treiman,** with **J. de Leeuw,** (1992), "A Standard International Socio-economic Index of Occupational Status", *Social Science Research,* Vol. 21(1), Academic Press, New York, pp. 1-56.

Goldstein, H. (1995), *Multilevel Statistical Models,* second edition, Edward Arnold, London.

Goldstein, H. (1997), "Methods in School Effectiveness Research", *School Effectiveness and School Improvement,* 8, Swets & Zeitlinger, Lisse, The Netherlands, pp.369-395.

Gonzalez, E.J. and **A.M. Kennedy** (2003), *PIRLS 2001 User Guide for the International Database,* Boston College, Chestnut Hill.

Guilford, J.P. (1954), *Psychometric Methods,* MacGraw Hill, New York.

Husen, T. (1967), *International Study of Achievement in Mathematics: a Comparison of Twelve Countries,* Almqvist & Wiksells, Uppsala.

Judkins, D.R. (1990), "Fay's Method of Variance Estimation", *Journal of Official Statistics,* Vol. 6, No. 3, Statistics Sweden, Stockholm, pp. 223-239.

Kish, L. and **M.R. Frankel** (1974), "Inference from Complex Sample", Journal of the Royal Statistical Society (B), 36, p. 1-37. Royal Statistical Society, London.

Kish, L. (1987), *Statistical Design for Research,* John Wiley & Sons, New York.

Marsh, H.W., R.J. Shavelson and **B.M. Byrne** (1992), "A Multidimensional, Hierarchical Self-concept", in R. P. Lipka and T. M. Brinthaupt (eds.), *Studying the Self: Self-Perspectives across the Life-Span,* State University of New York Press, Albany.

Monseur, C. and **R.J. Adams** (2002) "Plausible Values: How to Deal with Their Limitations", paper presented at the International Objective Measurement Workshop, New Orleans, 6-7 April.

OECD (Organisation for Economic Co-operation and Development) (1998), *Education at a Glance – OECD Indicators,* OECD, Paris.

OECD (1999a), *Measuring Student Knowledge and Skills – A New Framework for Assessment,* OECD, Paris.

OECD (1999b), *Classifying Educational Programmes – Manual for ISCED-97 Implementation in OECD Countries,* OECD, Paris.

OECD (2001), *Knowledge and Skills for Life – First Results from PISA 2000,* OECD, Paris.

OECD (2002a), *Programme for International Student Assessment – Manual for the PISA 2000 Database,* OECD, Paris.

OECD (2002b), *Sample Tasks from the PISA 2000 Assessment – Reading, Mathematical and Scientific Literacy,* OECD, Paris.

OECD (2002c), *Programme for International Student Assessment – PISA 2000 Technical Report,* OECD, Paris.

OECD (2002d), *Reading for Change: Performance and Engagement across Countries,* OECD, Paris.

OECD (2003a), *Literacy Skills for the World of Tomorrow – Further Results from PISA 2000,* OECD, Paris.

OECD (2003b), *The PISA 2003 Assessment Framework – Mathematics, Reading, Science and Problem Solving Knowledge and Skills,* OECD, Paris.

OECD (2004a), *Learning for Tomorrow's World – First Results from PISA 2003,* OECD, Paris.

OECD (2004b), *Problem Solving for Tomorrow's World – First Measures of Cross-Curricular Competencies from PISA 2003,* OECD, Paris.

OECD (forthcoming), *PISA 2003 Technical Report,* OECD, Paris.

Owens, L. and **J. Barnes** (1992), *Learning Preferences Scales,* Australian Council for Educational Research, Camberwell.

Rust, K. and **S. Krawchuk** (2002), *Replicate Variance Estimation Methods for International Surveys of Student Achievement,* International Conference on Improving Surveys, Copenhagen.

Rust, K.F. and **J.N.K. Rao** (1996), "Variance Estimation for Complex Surveys Using Replication Techniques", *Statistical Methods in Medical Research,* Vol. 5, Hodder Arnold, London, pp. 283-310.

Rust, K.F. (1996), TIMSS 1995 working paper.

Warm, T.A. (1989), "Weighted Likelihood Estimation of Ability in Item Response Theory", *Psychometrika,* Vol. 54(3), Psychometric Society, Williamsburg, Va., etc., pp. 427-450.

Westat (2000), WesVar complex samples 4.0. Westat. Rockville.

Wright, B.D. and **M.H. Stone** (1979), *Best Test Design: Rasch Measurement,* MESA Press, Chicago.

Wu, M. and **R.J. Adams** (2002), "Plausible Values – Why They Are Important", paper presented at the International Objective Measurement Workshop, New Orleans, 6-7 April.

Wu, M.L., R.J. Adams and **M.R. Wilson** (1997), *Conquest: Multi-Aspect Test Software* [computer program], Australian Council for Educational Research, Camberwell.

OECD PUBLICATIONS, 2 rue André-Pascal, PARIS CEDEX 16
PRINTED IN FRANCE
(982005021P) ISBN 92-64-01063-7 – No. 54093 2005